CORPORATE INFORMATION SYSTEMS MANAGEMENT □
Text and Cases

CORPORATE INFORMATION SYSTEMS MANAGEMENT

Text and Cases

James I. Cash, Jr.

F. Warren McFarlan

James L. McKenney

All of
the Graduate School of Business Administration
Harvard University

1983

RICHARD D. IRWIN, INC.
Homewood, Illinois 60430

The text portion of this book was previously published under the title *Corporate Information Systems Management: The Issues Facing Senior Executives* by McFarlan & McKenney.

Case material of the Harvard Graduate School of Business Administration is made possible by the cooperation of business firms who may wish to remain anonymous by having names, quantities, and other identifying details disguised while basic relationships are maintained. Cases are prepared as the basis for class discussion rather than to illustrate either effective or ineffective handling of administrative situations.

ISBN 0-256-02912-1

Library of Congress Catalog Card No. 82-82527

Printed in the United States of America

1 2 3 4 5 6 7 8 9 0 MP 0 9 8 7 6 5 4 3

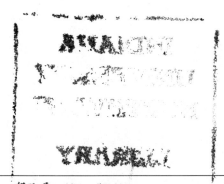

To Clemmie, Karen, and Mary

Preface

This book is aimed at students and managers interested in contemporary information services (IS) management. It is intended to communicate the relevant issues in effectively managing the information services activity. No assumptions are made in the book concerning the prior background of the readers with regard to the details of IS technology. It is, however, assumed that the reader has a basic background of either administrative experience or management training.

Our purpose is to provide perspective and advice for coping with the information explosion. This expansion is best characterized by the doubling of the Library of Congress from 1933 to 1966 and the doubling again from 1967 to 1979; and it is expected to double a third time before 1987. At the same time, the acceleration in the growth of knowledge in science is stimulating a dramatic increase in the number of new products based on new technology. This growth, coupled with the increasing international nature of many businesses, puts an enormous burden on the individual to keep abreast of events. It is a sound scientific conjecture that a human can retain 25 billion characters of information.[1] However, it has proven impossible to retrieve and use everything one knows, let alone keep our knowledge up to date. As Keen and Scott-Morton[2] have suggested, man-machine systems can function to assist the individual in coping with this information overload. We feel the broader issue is to help organizations adapt the new technology to better compete in their industry segments. This book is designed to help present and future managers prepare their organizations to better deal with information services management.

The book is organized around the authors' concept relating to a management audit of the information services activity. We have combined text and cases to convey and illustrate key conceptual frameworks. Chapter 1 begins with an overview of the key questions to resolve in assessing the health of an IS activity. Chapter 2 then presents a series of frameworks which the authors have found useful in analyzing and structuring the problems in this field. The

---

[1] Carl Sagan, *The Dragons in Eden* (New York: Random House, 1977).

[2] Peter F. Keen and Michael S. Scott-Morton, *Decision Support Systems* (Reading, Mass.: Addison-Wesley Publishing, 1978).

subsequent chapters address issues relating to how the activity can best be organized, planned, and controlled.

The material in this book is the outgrowth of a series of research projects conducted by the authors at the Harvard Business School over the past several years. We are indebted to both former Dean Lawrence E. Fouraker and Dean John H. McArthur for making the time available for this work.

We are particularly indebted to the many firms and government organizations which provided us with so much time and insight during the course of our research. All the cases and concepts in this book are based on observation of real practice. Without the aforementioned, it would have been impossible to prepare this manuscript.

We are especially grateful for the many valued suggestions and insights provided us by our colleagues Gregory Parsons, Leslie Porter, Michael Vitale, and Shoshanah Zuboff. In addition we acknowledge the valuable work done by Phillip Pyburn and Kathleen Curley during their time as doctoral students. Lynn Salerno, in her editorial capacity at the *Harvard Business Review*, provided valuable assistance. We would also like to express our appreciation to our office staff, Lillian Braudis, Louise Girard, and Alys Reid, who typed and edited numerous versions of the work.

James I. Cash, Jr.
F. Warren McFarlan
James L. McKenney

Contents

Chapter 1 □ Introduction

THE CHALLENGE OF IS TECHNOLOGY

Over the past 30 years, the rapid evolution and spread of information systems (IS) technology (in this book, IS will include the technologies of computers, telecommunications, and office automation) has created a major new set of managerial changes. Attempting to resolve these challenges has resulted in creation of new departments, massive recruiting of staff, major investments in computer hardware and software, and installation of systems which have profoundly impacted both how the firm operates and how it chooses to compete. The impact of this technology has not been confined to the large corporations but, in its current form, is impacting the very small (i.e., $1 million sales) firms as well. Further, in the large corporations, its impact is now very pervasive, reaching into both the smallest departments of the company and into managerial decision-making processes in a way which could not have been visualized even 10 years ago.

Facing these challenges is complex because many members of senior management received both their education and early work experience in a time prior to the wide-scale introduction of computer technology. Consequently, many feel somewhat uneasy about the subject and lack confidence that they have the appropriate handles to provide managerial oversight. Many IS managers face similar problems, since their firsthand technical experience was with technologies so different from those of the 1980s as to pose unrecognizable problems. Understanding the programming challenges of the rotational delay of the drum of an IBM 650 (a popular machine in the late 1950s) provides no value in dealing with the challenges posed by today's sophisticated computer operating systems. Further, understanding of what makes acceptable management practice in this field has changed dramatically since 1971. Virtually all major, currently accepted conceptual frameworks for thinking about how to manage in this field have been developed since 1971. Consequently, a special burden has been placed on IS management, not just to meet day-to-day operating problems and new technologies, but to assimilate and implement quite different ways of managing the activity. If they are not committed to a process of self-renewal, very quickly they become obsolete.

This book is aimed at two quite different audiences in a firm. The first is the general management which is responsible collectively for providing general guidance for the IS activity. For these readers, this book identifies a set of frameworks for looking at the IS activity in their firm, crystallizes the policies they are responsible for executing, and provides insights on how they can be executed. Also for this group, the attempt is to move from a world view down to an overall perspective of the IS forest and its management challenge.

The second audience is senior IS management. For these readers, we have attempted to develop an integrated view of the totality of IS management for the 1980s. We have tried to identify the key patterns which organize and make sense out of a bewildering cluster of operational detail. The attempt for these senior managers is to move from analysis of bark composition on individual trees to an overall perspective of the IS forest and its management challenge. The book thus tries to integrate the needs of two quite different audiences (who are very operationally interdependent) and provide them with a common set of perspectives and a language system for communicating with each other.

It would be a serious mistake, of course, to consider the problems of IS management as being totally unique and separate from those of general management. While the authors freely admit to having spent most of their professional lives dealing with IS technical and managerial issues, much of their thinking has been shaped by literature dealing with general business. The issue of IS organization, for example, are best thought of as special applications of the work on integration and differentiation first started by the behaviorists Paul Lawrence and Jay Lorsch. Issues of IS planning and strategy are influenced, on the one hand, by the work of Michael Porter and Alfred Chandler in business policy and, on the other hand, by Kirby Warren and Richard Vancil in the area of planning. Notions of budgeting, zero-based budgeting, transfer pricing, profit centers, and so forth, from the general field of management control, are relevant here. The work of Wickham Skinner and Richard Rosenbloom, in the area of factory management and transfer of technology, has shed light on how the computer operations function can be better managed. Many individual aspects of the IS management problems thus are not unique. What is unique is the peculiar confluence of these notions in running an efficient and evolving IS function. In thinking about this, some authors have found it useful to regard IS as a business within a business. Integrating the IS business into the rest of a firm may be conceived of as having special organizational, strategy-formulating challenges.

This book is organized around four concepts of how this kind of business can be better managed.

Strategic Relevance—The strategic relevance to the firm of an efficiently and effectively managed IS activity is not a constant but varies both between firms and over time for an individual firm. It is also of more significance to some operating units and functions of a company than to others. This notion of different strategic relevance is critical in understanding the wide diversity of potential organizational, planning, control, and other practices for managing and integrating this function.

Corporate Culture—"Within a business" is a very important phrase in understanding how the IS business itself should be managed. The values of senior management, approaches to corporate planning, corporate philosophy of control, speed of technological change in the company as a whole are one set of determinants. The other is the dynamics of its external marketplaces. Both have a major influence on what is appropriate management practice in both managing IS internally and integrating it with the rest of the firm. What works in one corporate environment may fail abysmally in another one.

Contingency—IS management in the 1980s is much more influenced by contingent notions than it was in the 1970s. In the 1970s, as IS management systems were being implemented where chaos existed before, simplistic and mechanistic approaches to management control, planning, and so forth were a great improvement over what was there before. As these systems were assimilated into the firm, the initial surge of value from their introduction, has given way to frustration in many cases because of their apparent rigidity. They answered some challenges well and others not at all. Dealing with this problem has required introduction of more complexity and flexibility in the approaches used to adapt them to the changing environment.

Technology Transfer—The diffusion of IS technology can and must be managed. If poorly managed, it will not evolve into a well-functioning support system but more likely a collection of disjointed islands of technology. We draw upon the general work in technology transfer in our thinking but have expanded that experience because of unique aspects of a technology which must deal with information. What makes the introduction and evolution of IS technology so challenging is that in many of its applications, success comes only when people have changed their thinking processes. Hence, we will refer to it as an "intellectual technology." In the field, too frequently, we have a technical success but an administrative failure.

COMPLEXITY OF THE IS MANAGEMENT TASK

There are a number of factors which have made the assimilation of IS technology a particularly challenging task. An understanding of these factors is essential if a sensible IS management strategy is to be developed. The more important of these factors are enumerated below.

1. IS technology, at least in its modern form (with high-speed computers), has had a very short life. Its earliest commercial application occurred in 1952. Thirty years is a very short time for the distilled outline of a new management profession to develop. Fields like marketing, accounting, finance, and production had a thriving body of literature and know-how in place in 1920. An incredible amount of knowledge and changes in thinking have occurred in these fields in this century, but it has been able to be assimilated within an organized field of thought. Evolution, not revolution, has been the challenge in these fields. The challenge in IS has been to develop from a zero base during a period of time where applications grew from being very narrow and specialized to being quite broad and integrated, with budgets and staffs exploding in size. In this environment, not surprisingly, the half-life of administrative knowledge has been quite short. Not a framework or avenue of thinking in this book predates 1973 in a published form, with much of the thinking taking place in the late 1970s and early 1980s. The authors of this book are under no illusion that this will be the last word on the subject but indeed hope to contribute through their further research to better insights.

2. Another source of administrative challenge lies in the fact that the field has undergone sustained and dramatic evolution in its technologies. Over a 10^6 improvement in processing and storage capacity has occurred since 1953, and the rate of change is expected to continue at the same pace at least through the 1980s and early 1990s. As in all technologies, a point of maturity will come, but we are not yet at this point. This technical explosion has continuously cast up new families of profitable applications as well as permitting old ones to be done in different ways. One painful aspect of this has been that yesterday's strategic coup often becomes today's high-overhead, inefficient liability. There is a natural tendency to harvest a particular approach too long. This tendency has been exacerbated by the prevailing accounting practice of writing off software expense as incurred rather than capitalizing it and then amortizing it over a period of years. These practices conceal both the fact that the organization has an asset and that it is becoming an aging asset.

3. The complexities of developing IS systems has forced the creation of specialized departments resulting in a series of strained relationships with the users of their service. This has been an enduring headache from the start of IS, and there is probably not a better example of C. P. Snow's two-culture problem in existence in the 1980s than the relationship between IS and general management. IS has specialized in order to harness the various necessary technical skills to get the job done. The specialists have appropriately developed their own language systems. They speak of *bits, bytes, DOS, CICS,* and so on to communicate among each other. General management,

however, has a quite different language, featuring words such as *sales growth, return on investment,* and *productivity*. While it is clear that some of the newer technologies, such as user-oriented programming languages and microcomputers, will help users, no substantial relief is in sight. A long-term need will exist for continually developing new integrating devices, such as steering committees and user department analysts, to help handle the problem. This problem is not remarkably different from that faced by the accounting profession with its special language. Despite 6,000 years of accounting history, substantial friction and misunderstanding still exist between accounting departments and users of accounting information. It is surprising to the authors that significant numbers of people who enter general management have only a sketchy ability to handle accounting information.

For numerous reasons, education will continue to only partially address these problems. The experience that students have in colleges and high schools in writing one-time, problem-solving programs—while useful and confidence-expanding—develops a very different set of skills than the skills which will be required to generate programs for processing business transactions reliably on a day-in, day-out basis. Unfortunately, this education often does not address the existence of these differences, and it produces graduates who are ill-trained for these tasks but don't know that they are ill-trained, and thus have excessive self-confidence. Another educational issue is that, cognitively, some individuals are better equipped to assimilate IS technology than others. One of our colleagues has colorfully described this as the world being divided into "poets" and "engineers" (roughly equally prevalent in general management).

4. The increased specialization of contemporary technology and the explosion of skills needed to staff it have posed a fourth, major, managerial challenge. As IS technology has evolved, it has created a proliferation of languages, data base management needs, operating systems support staff needs, and so on, all of which have increased significantly the complexity of the IS management job from an internal perspective.

5. A fifth challenge has been a significant shift in the types of applications being automated. Early applications were heavily focused on highly structured problems, such as hard transaction processing, where one could usually be quite precise about the potential stream of benefits. These applications involved automation of a number of clerical functions and operational control functions, such as inventory management, airline seat reservation, and credit extension. In the case of airline seat reservations, it was able to bring a level of structure and decision rules to the activity not previously present.

Increasingly, today's applications are providing new types of decision support information for both management control and strategic planning decisions. Evaluation of the payout of these expenditures on an objective basis either before, during, or after they are expended is almost impossible.

Individuals may have opinions about these values, but quantification turns out to be very elusive. On top of this, the best way to develop these decision support applications is quite different from the conventional wisdom for the transaction-driven systems.[1] The detailed systems study, with its documentation and controls prior to programming, is turning out to be too rigid. For these systems, prototyping or doing it rough-and-dirty is proving to be the best approach. In short, the new types of application are forcing a shift both in the ways to evaluate projects and in the best ways to manage them. This is not an argument for a more permissive approach to system design and evaluation but rather a cry to be tough-minded in a positive way.

In combination, these factors create a very complex and challenging managerial environment. They will form the backdrop in the discussions of specific managerial approaches in the succeeding chapters.

SENIOR MANAGEMENT QUESTIONS

In viewing the health of an organization's IS activity, our research indicated that a series of six critical questions repeatedly emerge in senior management's mind. We will not argue at this stage that these are the questions which *should* be raised, but rather note that they are the questions which *are* raised. Four of these questions are essentially diagnostic in nature, while the remaining two are clearly action oriented.

1. Is my firm being affected *competitively* either by omissions in work being done or by poor execution of this work? Am I missing bets that, if properly executed, would give me a competitive edge? Conversely, maybe I am not doing so well in IS, but I don't have to do well in IS in my industry to be a success. Failure to do well in a competitively important area is a significant problem. Failure to perform well in a nonstrategic area is something that should be dealt with more calmly.

2. Is my development portfolio *effective?* Am I spending the right amount of money, and is it focused at the appropriate applications? This question is one that is often inappropriately raised. An industry survey calculating IS expenditures as a percent of something or other for 15 industry competitors is circulated among the firm's senior managememt. On one dimension or another, it is observed that their firm is distinctly different from the others, which causes great excitement (normally, when their firm's figures are on the high side). After great investigation, two findings often emerge: *(a)* Our company has a different accounting system for IS than our competitors, and therefore the results are not meaningful. *(b)* Our company has a different strategy, geographical location, mix of management strengths and weaknesses than our competitors, and therefore on this dimension also, the results are not meaningful.

[1] Michael Scott-Morton and Peter Keen, *Decision Support Systems,* (Reading, Mass.: Addison-Wesley Publishing, 1980).

In short, raising the question of effectiveness is appropriate in our judgment, but, attempting to identify it simplistically through industry surveys of competitors is not.

3. Is my firm spending *efficiently?* Maybe I have the right expenditure level, but am I getting the productivity out of my hardware and staff resources that I should get? This is a particularly relevant question in the 1980s, a decade which will be dominated both by extreme levels of professional staff shortages and by intensified international competition.

4. Is my firm's IS activity insulated well enough against the *risks* of a major *operational disaster?* There is no general-purpose answer as to what an appropriate level of protection is. Rather, it varies by organization, depending on the current dependence on smoothly operating existing systems.

5. Is the *leadership* of the IS activity appropriate for the role it now plays in our organization, and the special challenges now in front of it? Historically, senior management has used the mechanism of changing IS management as one of its main tools in dealing with frustrating IS performance shortfalls. It seems clear that this high turnover is continuing in the 1980s. One key reason for this is that it represents the quickest and apparently easiest step for senior management to take when they are uneasy about departmental performance. Also, as noted in Chapter 2, the nature of the job and its requisite skills tend to evolve over time, and a set of leadership skills and perspectives for one environment may not be appropriate for another one. Further, in many situations the problem is compounded by lack of suitable metrics and data to assess performance objectively. As will be discussed in subsequent chapters, we believe the development and installation of these metrics is absolutely vital. In their absence a 50 percent improvement in ability to meet service schedules, for example, may be totally overlooked, with the emotional temperature concerning remaining problems simply being raised.

6. Are the IS resources *appropriately placed* in the firm? Organizational issues, such as where the IS resource should report, how development and hardware resources should be distributed within the company, and existence and potential role of an executive steering committee, are examples of topics of intense interest to senior management. They are not only actionable but are similar in breadth to decisions made by general management in other aspects of the firm's operations.

These questions are intuitive from the general management viewpoint and flow naturally from their perspective and experience in dealing with other areas of the firm. We have not found all of them as stated to be easily researchable or answerable in specific situations and have, consequently, neither selected them as the basic framework of the book nor attempted to describe specifically how each can be answered. Rather, we selected a complementary set of questions which not only form the outline of the book, but whose answers will give insight into the earlier questions. The following paragraphs lay out these questions in summary form, and Chapters 3 through

9 deal with them in far greater depth. Together, they form the outline of a "management audit" of the IS activity which can produce a blue book of action items.

Organization (Chapters 3 and 4). The text of Chapters 3 and 4 is most closely aligned to the previous set of questions, covering questions 5 and 6 in more depth. The following main themes are important in this area. First and foremost, What is an appropriate pattern for distributing hardware and software development resources within the corporation? The issues of patterns of distributed resources (including stand-alone mini- and microcomputers) have been well studied, and ways of appropriately thinking about them have been developed. These ways are heavily contingent, being influenced by such items as corporate organization, corporate culture, leadership style of the chief executive officer (CEO), importance of IS to achievement of corporate goals, and current sophistication of IS management. Within any pattern of distributed resources, there is need for appropriate policies administered centrally to ensure that suitable overall direction is being given.

A second complicating issue is to ensure that IS is broadly enough defined and that the coverging and increasingly integrated technologies of computing, telecommunications, and word processing are in fact being adequately integrated. These issues are further complicated when breaking out of the domestic arena and dealing with international coordination. (Chapter 9 is devoted to the issues posed by different national infrastructure—such as staff availability, level of telecommunications sophistication, and specific vendor support, great geographic distance, different spoken languages, transborder data flows, national culture and sensitivity, and so forth.) Finally, issues of organization reporting chains, level of reporting, IS leadership style, and steering committees represent additional topics. In the early 1980s, we believe there are better ways to think about these issues. While common questions and methods of analysis exist, however, in different organization settings very different answers will emerge.

Planning (Chapter 5). The question, "Is my firm competitive and effectively focused on the right questions," we believe is best answered by looking carefully at the IS planning process. The design and evolution of this process had turned out to be much more complicated than anticipated in the early 1970s when some fairly prescriptive ways of dealing with it were identified. Elements creating this complexity can be classified as falling into three general categories. The first is an increased recognition that at any point in time IS plays very different strategic roles in different companies.

This strategic role significantly influences both the structure of the planning process (who should be involved, the level of time and financial resources to be devoted to it, etc.) and its interconnection to the corporate planning process. Firms where new developments are critical to the organization's introduction of new products, and to achievement of major operating efficiencies or speeded up competitive response times, must devote significantly more senior management time to planning than in settings where this is not the case.

The second category of issues relates to both IS and user familiarity with the nuances of the specific technologies being planned. Applications of IS technologies which both IS and user staff have considerable experience with can be planned in more considerable detail with great confidence. The newer technologies to IS and/or the users pose very different planning problems, both as to why planning is being done and how it can best be done. In any individual year a company will be dealing with a mix of older and newer technologies which complicates the planning task tremendously.

The third category of issues relates to the matter of the specific corporate culture. The nature of the corporate planning process, formality versus informality of organizational decision making and planning, geographic and organizational distance of IS management from senior management—all influence how IS planning can best be done. These issues suggest that as important as IS planning is, it must be evolutionary and highly individualistic to fit the specific corporation.

Management Control (Chapter 6). The questions of efficiency and, to a lesser degree, those of effectiveness are best addressed by ensuring that an appropriate IS management control architecture and process are in place. Planning's role is to ensure that long-term direction is hammered out and that steps to acquire the necessary hardware/staff resources to implement it are taken. The role of management control is to ensure that the appropriate short-term resource allocation decisions are made and that acquired resources are being utilized efficiently. The key issues in this field include the following:

1. Establishing an appropriate (for the organization) balance between user and IS responsibility for costs. Establishment of IS as a managed cost center, profit center, investment center, etc. is a critical strategic decision for an organization, as is the election of an appropriate IS transfer pricing policy to go along with it. Again, not only does this policy appropriately change over time, but it varies by type of organization as well.

2. Identification of an appropriate budgeting policy for IS represents a second key cluster of issues. While many components of the IS budget are either fixed or transaction driven, there are others which are discretionary. These discretionary components need to be examined to ensure both that they are still being allocated to essential missions and that an appropriate balance is struck between the needs of many legitimate end users. This balance is necessary in a world where there are not unlimited financial resources for projects and where project benefits in many cases are not

easily quantifiable. Zero-based budgeting has proven to be a useful tool in some IS settings (albeit with some operational difficulties as will be discussed in Chapter 6).

3. Finally, there is need for a regular weekly and monthly performance reporting cycle, not just against goals but against standards where possible. The move of IS operations from a primarily batch to an online activity not only reduces the territory for objective standard setting but has obsolesced many of the older approaches.

Project Management (Chapter 7). The questions of efficiency and effectiveness are also addressed through analysis of the project management process. The past decade has given rise to a proliferation of so-called project management processes and methodologies which have helped to rationalize a formerly very diverse area. The installation of these methodologies, an obvious improvement in the 1980s, has created a new set of opportunities.

The first opportunity ties in the area of implementation risk. The advocates of these methodologies have implied that by utilizing their approach implementation risk will be eliminated. A careful examination of the long list of partial and major project fiascoes in the past four to five years suggests clearly that this is not the case. As will be described in the chapter on project management, our contention is that project risk not only exists, but it can be measured, and a decision can be made regarding its acceptability long before the majority of funds have to be committed to a project development effort. In the same vein, it is possible and appropriate to talk about the aggregate risk profile of the development and maintenance portfolio of projects. Not only does risk information provide a better language between general management, user management, and IS management during the project planning phase (where many options can be considered), but it provides a firmer and more valid context for after-the-fact performance assessment.

The second opportunity is the recognition that different types of projects can best be attacked by quite different kinds of project management methodologies. A single methodology is better than the anarchy and chaos which often precede its introduction. Several years of its use, however, can create a straitjacket environment. The approach will normally fit one kind of project very well and others considerably less well. Different organization structures within a project team, different types of user interfaces, and different planning and control approaches are suitable for different types of projects. In the early 1980s it is clear that the most appropriate project management approach for any project should flow out of the project's innate characteristics.

Operations Management (Chapter 8). Appropriate controls over the IS daily operations ensure both cost efficiency and operational reliability in an important part of the IS activity. The IS operations activity represents a very specialized form of manufacturing environment with some unique problems.

First, operations is in a significant transition from a batch job-shop style to a continuous-process manufacturing or utility style. Not only has this changed the way it can best be organized, but it has dramatically altered the type of controls which are appropriate.

Second, for a number of firms, the IS activity has embedded itself so deeply in the heart of the firm's operations that uneveness in its performance causes immediate operating problems. These firms need significantly greater controls and backup arrangements than firms which have less dependence.

The performance of operations can be measured on a number of dimensions. Cost control, ability to meet batch report deadlines, peak-load response time of no greater than X seconds, and speed of response to complaints or unexpected requests are examples of these dimensions. It is impossible to optimize all of these simultaneously. Each firm needs a clear identification and prioritization of these items before it can come up with a coherent operations strategy. Different firms will have quite different priorities, and hence a search for a universal operations strategy and set of management tools represents a fruitless quest.

Multinational Issues (Chapter 9). International operations pose special problems in dealing with the IS activity. Geographic separation, different cultures, and availability of IS staff skills vary widely from one country to another. When combined with differing cost and availability of telecommunications gear, different vendor support from one country to another, and issues related to transborder data flows, it becomes clear that execution of an international IS strategy is much more complex than when one is operating primarily within the borders of one country.

The IS Business (Chapter 10). The concluding chapter attempts to integrate this discussion by considering the challenge of managing IS technology development and diffusion from the perspective of a business within a business. In that chapter, we emphasize the present marketing posture of the IS business. We characterize the 1950–64 era as one captured by the words *R&D*—"Could it work, and could we learn to make it work?" The 1964–72 era we characterize by start-up production—"Could large projects be managed in a way which would create useful, reliable services in a high period of growth when technology was new and changing?"

The 1972–81 era was one of striving for control and learning to manage a service organization with a newly established technology as applications continued to proliferate. The era of the 1980s will be one characterized by marketing. The challenge is to blend new-product opportunities posed by new technologies with their new customers in a thoughtful manner.

SUMMARY

This chapter has identified, from a managerial viewpoint, the key forces which are shaping the IS environment, senior management's most frequent questions in assessing the activity, and the questions which we think are most useful in diagnosing the situation and taking corrective action. In this final section we would like to leave you with a set of questions which we believe both IS management and general management should ask on a periodic basis (once every six months or so). They are a distillation of the previous analysis and, we believe, a useful managerial shorthand.

1. Do the perspective and skills of my IS management team fit the firm's changing applications, operations, and user environment? There are no absolute, for-all-time answers to these questions but rather only transitional ones.
2. Is the firm organized to identify, evaluate, and assimilate new IS technologies? In this fast-moving field, an insensitive low-quality staff can generate severe problems. Unprofitable, unwitting obsolescence (which is hard to recover from) is terribly easy here. There is no need for a firm to adopt leading-edge technology (indeed, many are ill-equipped to do so), but it is inexcusable not to be aware of what the possibilities are.
3. Are the three main management systems for integrating the IS environment to the firm as a whole in place and architected? These are the planning system, the management control system, and the project management system.
4. Are the security, priority setting, manufacturing procedure, and change control systems in the IS operations function appropriate for the role it now plays in your firm?
5. Are appropriate organization structures and linking mechanisms in place to ensure both appropriate senior management guidance of the IS activity and appropriate user dialogue?

To answer these questions, we have developed a framework based upon our four organizing concepts of strategic relevance, corporate culture, contingent action planning, and technology transfer. In each of the areas of organization, planning, management control, project management, and operations, we will be examining their implications for action. Realistically, today we are moving in a complicated space of people, differing organization strategies, different cultures, and changing technologies. We have taken as our task the identification of a sequence of frameworks which allow better analysis of the problems and issues facing organizations in relation to IS. We rely upon the reader to apply this discussion to his own business situation to formulate a realistic action plan.

Case 1–1 □ Quality Life of New York*

Quality Life of New York was one of the large insurance companies having more than 13,200,000 policyholders, 525,000 new holders in 1977. New life insurance sold by Quality Life in 1977, 105 million above 1976 sales, totaled $4,137,000,000, of which individual insurance contributed $2,919,000,000. Premium income on individual insurance, annuities, and health insurance totaled $531 million, of which $20,832,000 was on policies written in 1977.

DATA PROCESSING AT QUALITY LIFE

Since 1953, electronic computers had played an ever-increasing role in the operation of Quality Life. The nature of the company's business involved the handling of vast amounts of data. The functions which were performed in connection with each policy were divided among sales, underwriting, issuance, billing, collection commission payments, dividend calculations and apportionment, valuation of reserves, claims handling, termination operations (upon maturity, death, lapse, or surrender), and the preparation of general operating reports. Each of these functions included a variety of processing activities which were handled by various types of data processing equipment.

Functions being performed by the data processing department of Quality Life are presented in Exhibit 1. Projects being developed and projects under study are also listed in that exhibit.

ESTABLISHMENT OF THE DATA PROCESSING DEPARTMENT

Machine equipment had been used by various departments in Quality Life for many years. The actuarial department (see Exhibit 2 for a partial organization chart) had used various types of machines since 1916. When the accounting department needed equipment in 1942, the actuarial department was reluctant to share its equipment because of anticipated problems

* This case was prepared from materials collected from a previous case by Dean Glenn Overman of Arizona State University as a basis for class discussion rather than to illustrate either effective or ineffective handling of an administrative situation. The names of company and persons are disguised.

EXHIBIT 1 □ Data Processing at Quality Life of New York in 1977

	Premium notice business*			Debit business†			Group business‡		
Activity	Ordinary	Annuity	Personal health	MDO§	MPI‖	Industrial#	A&H**	Life & DD††	Annuity‡‡
Sales	D	D	D	D		S	S	S	S
Underwriting				S		D			
Issue	P			P		D			
Premium billing	P	P	P	P	S	S	D	D	S
Premium accounting	P	P	P	P	S	S	P	P	S
Dividend calculation	P	P		P			P	P	
Valuation	P	P	P	P	P	P			S
Claims		P		S	S	S	P	D	P
Statistics	P	D	D	D			D	D	D

Legend: P—being performed; D—being developed; S—under study.

* Policies billed by mail (mostly large-sized policies).

† Policies on which premiums were collected at the home of the insured.

‡ Large combination policies covering whole factories or businesses.

§ Monthly debit ordinary insurance (intermediate-sized policies).

‖ Monthly premium industrial insurance (no longer issued).

\# Industrial insurance (small-sized policies).

** Accident and health coverages.

†† Life and accidental death and dismemberment.

‡‡ Retirement income coverages.

EXHIBIT 2 □ Abbreviated Organization Chart*

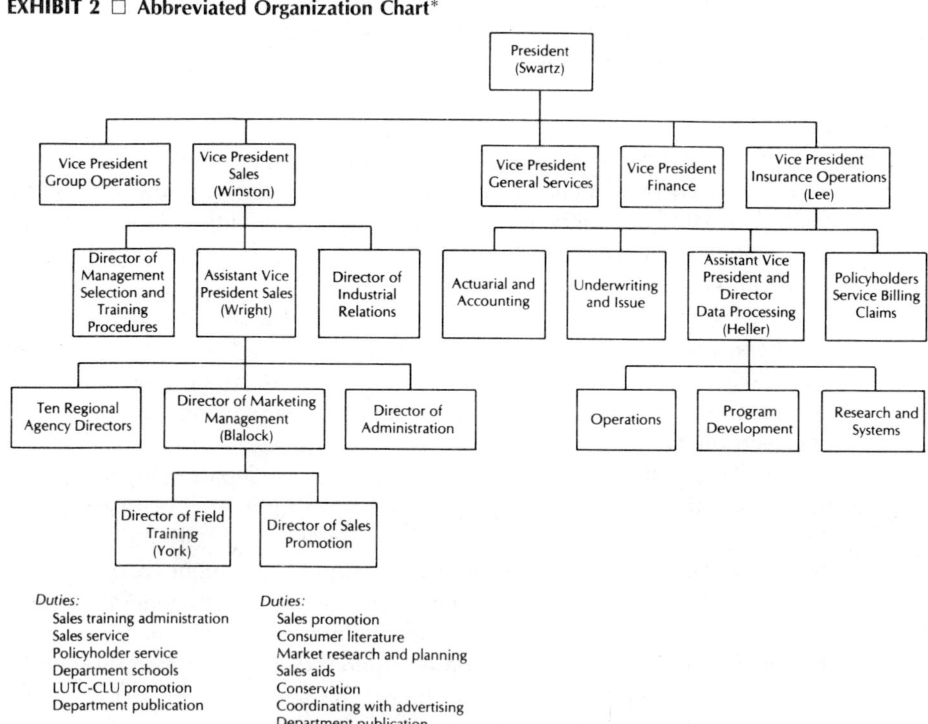

Duties:
Sales training administration
Sales service
Policyholder service
Department schools
LUTC-CLU promotion
Department publication

Duties:
Sales promotion
Consumer literature
Market research and planning
Sales aids
Conservation
Coordinating with advertising
Department publication

* Within the past year, some reorganization had taken place in the management of the company, reducing the number of vice presidents reporting directly to the president and combining formerly independent units. A number of the units so combined fell under the direction of the vice president, insurance operations, a new position in the organization.

in scheduling work from two departments on the same equipment. The accounting department therefore obtained its own equipment. During the next few years, a large number of other functional groups obtained either mechanized or electronic data processing equipment.

By 1958 the large investment in equipment led top management to appoint a committee to study the entire data processing function. An outside consultant was also employed. Based on the recommendations contained in the two reports, President John Swartz issued an order to begin centralizing responsibility for all data processing activities into one department and providing for the gradual merger of the existing equipment of all departments.

Mr. O. D. Heller was appointed assistant vice president and director of data processing to administer the new department. Mr. Heller had previously been manager of the data processing section in the policy department. In this department he had had experience with both major types of data processing equipment used by Quality Life, i.e., mechanized punch-card machines and medium- and large-sized electronic computers. Mr. Heller had been with the company since 1956. His prior training and experience included a degree in business administration and five years' experience in systems and procedures work with a large manufacturer of data processing equipment.

The physical merging of equipment and data processing activities began in 1959 when two departments were brought under the new centralized control. In 1961, the merger of the data processing facilities of the remaining departments was completed, and an active program of new applications development was begun.

In 1976, a new large computer (370/168) and a smaller one (370/158) had been purchased. These machines were intended to replace five medium-sized computers. It was also planned to use the new equipment to service one functional group (monthly debit ordinary) which previously had not been mechanized.

In 1975, a PDP-10 was acquired for the actuarial department for research purposes, although general responsibility for the equipment was retained by the data processing department. This equipment had considerable processing capacity, but the limited input and output equipment made it more adaptable to scientific or problem-type applications than to general business applications. Auxiliary input and output equipment could be purchased, but the irregularly occurring needs of the actuarial department made it difficult to integrate the PDP-10 with the computers being scheduled for regular business applications. So auxiliary equipment was not a part of the present installation. To the best of Mr. Heller's knowledge, no other equipment was present in Quality.

PROBLEMS ARISING FROM THE UNIFICATION

Over the years, the manager of the data processing department was confronted not only with the technical problems inherent in the management of data processing activities but also with the human relations problems which arose from the centralizing of responsibility and equipment outside the functional areas. Managers of these functional areas frequently made requests to the central data processing department for services which were considered by the manager of the DP department to be uneconomical or unsuited for handling by a computer. Under the pressure of work, the manager had frequently rejected such requests and was concerned that these refusals were resulting in a reputation that the department was often uncooperative.

Mr. Heller expressed the problem by saying, "How can we control these excessive and uneconomical requests for work on the new computers so that we can live within our budget and still keep good relations with the management of the functional departments which we serve?"

Reasons for this problem, as viewed by Mr. Heller, were:

1. Widespread publicity in the press about the capabilities of computers without explanations of their limitations, costs, and proper role.
2. Lack of rudimentary understanding by functional managers about business uses of computers.
3. Overenthusiastic reports from earlier advisory committees on results which might be expected.
4. The presentation of vague service requests that had not been thoroughly analyzed before presentation.

ORGANIZATION AND OPERATION OF THE NEW DEPARTMENT

To carry out his responsibilities, Mr. Heller had organized the department into three sections: (1) operations, (2) program development, and (3) research and systems. The operations section was the largest of the three and employed about 250 persons. This section was responsible for routine production. Only work that had previously been approved and programmed by the other two sections was handled by operations.

The program development section consisted of 62 persons, chiefly programmers, who did the coding, debugging, and preparing of programs for new applications. Only programs approved by the research and systems section were handled by the program development section.

Requests for new computer applications or variations of existing applications were received first by the research and systems section. If the request appeared to the staff of the section to have merit and indicated to them that the person making the request had rather thoroughly thought through the need, the research and systems section made an advisability study. During the study process, requests were often modified in line with suggestions from the research and systems section. This study served as a guide to the department manager in making a decision to approve or reject the request. It also served as a basis for the requesting officials to determine if they wished to adopt the new procedure.

An advisability study was sometimes called a feasibility study, but the term *advisability* was considered by personnel in the research and systems section as more accurate, since a request might be feasible but not advisable because of cost, anticipated change in operation, or other reasons. These studies usually included:

1. Statement of the problem.
2. Description of the present system, including schedules, volumes, personnel requirements, and costs.
3. Findings and recommendations, including the suggested approach and equipment, systems and programming development, time and man-

power requirements, estimated computer production time, and costs and suggested conversion schedules.

4. Advantages and limitations of the suggested approach.
5. Net savings or costs.
6. Alternate approaches.

The cost of an advisability study was usually charged to the department making the request. The cost varied greatly according to the nature and complexity of the problem. The written report was often 20 to 25 pages in length.

COSTS OF PROCESSING DATA

The advisability study suggested probable costs of machine time and programming. The actual costs, however, might vary considerably from the estimate, since they were computed at the time of performance. An internal costing group outside the data processing department allocated costs according to a current rate schedule.

Rate schedules for machine usage were difficult to formalize and publish in advance because of fluctuating work volumes and a complex 32-parameter chargeout algorithm. In addition, costs were affected by many factors, such as rate of depreciation, number of shifts being operated, idle machine time, and amount of set up time in relation to running time.

Before any project could be placed on the computer, a program had to be prepared by the program development section. Costs of programming varied greatly according to the nature of the job. A simple program using a "canned" routine might be prepared for as little as $75. Programs for major applications, such as setting up premium billing on the machine, might require the service of six programmers for two years at a cost of approximately $720,000. Program costs generally ranged from $24,000 to $650,000 and were charged to users at actual hours of work times standard rates (these rates included allowances for department overheads and machine test time).

Because of the nature of the machine operation, Mr. Heller was strongly convinced that computers should be devoted to large-volume, continuous-operation types of jobs and that small-volume, infrequent or sporadically occurring jobs could not be economically handled on the large computers because of the setup costs for short runs.

These sporadically occurring jobs also created scheduling problems since it was difficult to schedule the machine usage in advance if there were no way of knowing whether the job might require three minutes or three hours on a specified day. In order to keep costs down, the new computer was being carefully scheduled several weeks in advance.

A REQUEST FROM THE SALES DEPARTMENT

In July of 1978, Mr. W. A. York, CLU, training director for the 5,200 agents of Quality Life, read an article in *National Underwriter* magazine briefly describing a new service being introduced by the sales division of the Mutual Benefit Life Insurance Company, a competitive insurance firm. This service was an online individualized proposal setting forth the insurance program that a prospective customer should be carrying. Pertinent facts were obtained from the customer and were fed into a portable computer terminal which promptly computed a recommended insurance program based on the individual's specific needs.

Insurance programs prepared for the individual prospect were currently in use in the insurance industry. These were of two types. One was a rather simple form which assisted a salesman in comparing a customer's stated insurance needs with his present insurance program and in recommending additional coverage if needed. The form could be completed by the salesman within a few minutes in the presence of the prospect but was based upon the prospect's judgment of his personal insurance needs rather than upon an objective analysis of the facts.

A second type of program planning was done by analysis using a computer program at the home office. These "comprehensive proposals" were based upon facts obtained from the prospect by the salesman and included such items as age, income, number and status of dependents, indebtedness, social security status, retirement plan, insurance now in force, veterans benefits, and total assets. These comprehensive proposals required roughly two hours to prepare. All proposals in the past had been processed in a batch fashion, and the announcement from Mutual Benefit was the first indication to Mr. York that such a comprehensive personalized proposal might be prepared by an electronic computer in the customer's home.

Mr. York had discouraged the use of comprehensive program planning because of the time required either by salesmen or by the home office. He felt that salesmen could more profitably spend their time in contacting prospective policyholders and selling them insurance than in spending time "preparing computer input." In addition, computer processing on a batch basis in the home office was expensive and was generally discouraged. In spite of this discouragement, salesmen regularly requested the service. Roughly 1,000 proposals of this type per month had been prepared by Quality Life during 1977. The average policy value in these cases was $36,680. Of the proposals prepared, one out of every three resulted in a sale, while the average of completed sales without use of the device was one out of every four or five sales presentations. The average annual premium income on the 1,000 prepared proposals was $1,922, of which the agent received approximately 43 percent the first year and 9 percent during each of the following four years, plus additional benefits in succeeding years which totaled approximately 3 percent. Commission rates varied on different types of policies, but the above schedule was representative of typical returns to the salesmen on the premium-notice type of business. This type of business represented 63 percent of the dollar volume of individual life, annuity, and health sales, and 10 percent of the total number of policies annually issued by the company.

Mr. York strongly favored the use of the online program technique if the new machines could do the detail work at a reasonable cost. Among the benefits which he could see from this new plan were:

1. It would help the salesman to establish a customized professional counselor-client relationship with the prospect.
2. The prospect who provided the detailed information would be more likely to make a favorable decision.
3. Repeat sales to present policyholders would be easier.
4. The salesmen would not be required to learn any new sales techniques since the principle was already generally understood.
5. The prospect would receive a valuable service by having an answer to the question: How much insurance is enough for me?

The average number of sales annually per agent in 1977 was 56.4. It was Mr. York's opinion that this average was too low and that some technique, such as the proposed program planning, would help increase this average.

Mr. York attempted to obtain information on how the new plan had worked in the competitor's operation. He learned it was used primarily by one general agent who was a large producer, but he could not obtain other details. The competitor reported that the new technique had given his firm a competitive advantage and stated that the new service was being advertised in the *New Yorker* magazine (see Exhibit 3). This information further strengthened Mr. York's conviction that the plan had genuine merit. Because of the availability of the new and superior computers at Quality Life, he believed it would be possible to provide a more comprehensive sales proposal using a few more variables than that pioneered by the competitor.

Mr. York requested from the data processing department general estimates of cost for the proposal. He was informed that costs could not be quoted as they were dependent upon the nature of the project and the amount of estimated input and output expected. Mr. York at that time was not able to furnish specific items which should be included in the analysis. He had, however, heard that Mutual Benefit Life used 19 variables in preparing each program. He was also unable to estimate precisely the amount of expected usage, because he felt this was dependent upon probable costs and the amount of encouragement given the agents by the home office. He reported that he attempted to determine if the cost might be $5,000 or $500,000, since this would determine whether or not he wished

EXHIBIT 3 □ The Competitors Advertisement

An important breakthrough in life insurance planning —the "*Electronic* Analagraph"—is a new, exclusive Mutual Benefit Life service• The "Analagraph" is a scientific device that lets *you* chart your family protection and retirement needs• A pioneer in its field, the "Analagraph" complements the Mutual Benefit Life man's experience and knowledge to furnish superior life insurance service• Now, through the magic of electronics, a new dimension has been added—the "*Electronic* Analagraph "• Write us for further information.

Benefit is our middle name

MUTUAL BENEFIT LIFE

INSURANCE COMPANY • NEWARK, NEW JERSEY • SINCE 1845

to pursue the matter further. No general estimate could be obtained from the data processing department. He was informed that the project as presented did not appear to be acceptable for running on the new computer.

In explaining his position concerning cost and usage figures, Mr. York stated:

> The home office should provide service to the field agents and to the public. In sales work we can never actually tell whether a specific sales tool will pay out or not. We spend money on a sales brochure, but how can we tell exactly what the return will be? A sales meeting costs money, but we can't measure the direct returns in relation to costs. Indirect sales resulting from the expenditures can't be computed.
>
> Why then must the computer people have definite figures on the usage before accepting a sales idea? I want to be practical about the matter, but I can't be too concerned over internal costs until we've had an opportunity to try out the new procedure to see how it works. Some things must be taken on faith when your judgment tells you it is a good idea. Obviously, acquisition cost of new business can't exceed a reasonable figure, but often we can't definitely evaluate this until we try it.
>
> Sales are the lifeblood of our business, and we must move ahead when we are convinced a new idea is a good one.

DATA PROCESSING DEPARTMENT RESPONSE

When Mr. York made his initial contact, Mr. Heller attempted to determine what would be expected in the form of programming and anticipated output if the new idea were approved. Mr. Heller received the general impression that the project would result in a low-volume, irregularly occurring operation, so he informed Mr. York that he would be unable to set it up on the new computer. When Mr. York pressed for a general estimate of probable costs, Mr. Heller informed him that such an estimate was impossible without extensive study of the proposal, and this study could not be undertaken unless Mr. York could provide more definite information regarding his proposal. Mr. Heller also informed him that the new computer would soon be heavily scheduled with other types of work, in both the first and second shifts, which were clearly adapted to the new equipment.

Mr. York inquired if the job might be set up on one of the old 360/40 computers, because Mutual Benefit Life had used this type of equipment. Mr. Heller replied that a decision had been made to dispose of these machines to help defray the costs of the new computer installation. Mr. Heller explained that if one of the 360/40 computers, valued at $520,000 were retained for Mr. York, the air conditioning, space, and other costs might bring the total costs to $1 million. These costs would, of course, be charged to the sales department. The possibility of keeping a 360/40 for the sole purpose of service to the sales department was not acceptable to Mr. York.

In discussing the case, Mr. Heller analyzed it as being typical of the type of request that had to be refused. His analysis was stated as follows:

> This is a low-volume job and isn't suited for a large-scale computer in an online mode. The only low-volume online jobs which we should consider are the "by-products" request which can be taken off existing information already in our basic file of stored information. This is not such a request.
>
> Furthermore, we have no way of determining how many emergency or "quickie" requests we are likely to receive if the plan were adopted.
>
> This case sounds more like a gimmick than a real computer problem.
>
> We don't even know if the other personnel of the sales department support this request. Only the training director has requested it, and we don't know if the sales vice president and the field agents really want this plan. It is true that Mr. York is a good, old-line salesman who knows how to teach men to sell insurance instead of policies, but we don't have any way of knowing if the rest of the sales department will support this idea if we approve his request. Anyway, I doubt Mr. York has really thought through this request. Any computer installation works on a decreasing scale of costs after the setup has been completed, and he hasn't any information as to whether there might be one case or a thousand cases per week. It sounds like he's acting primarily on a whim based on the report of a sales gimmick at Mutual Benefit.
>
> We have to say "No" to such requests as these because the big computer

can be operated only 24 hours a day and a burst of unexpected volume can kill our online response time for key applications; and, we can't always be bringing in a new computer, for computers are not like punched-card equipment where small components can be added at will. It hasn't sunk in on the managers of the other departments that I can't justify asking for another $1.5 million computer just to be of service on every whim they get. We ought to avoid as many of these requests as possible.

It is true that we may nip in the bud some ideas which would save or make money for the company, but we can't "cost them all out," so we are bound to make some mistakes.

We don't have the staff or the time to make detailed advisability studies of every vague idea that comes in to us, and we can't give general estimates of costs without careful study of what is involved. If we did, this would lead to all sorts of trouble. Costs can vary too greatly depending upon what is included in the request. Unless the person has taken time to sit down for a day or two to crystallize what he expects in the form of output, it is usually just a whim, so we say, "No."

In this business can you afford to be a good fellow? If I said, "Yes" to all service requests, I wouldn't ever get our main job done. Seventy percent (70%) of my staff is tied up in maintenance efforts as it is. Costs would go up. Then top management would think I was doing a poor job. I don't mind being called an S.O.B. by lower management as long as top management feels I am doing a good job. After all, this is a selfish world. If by being "uncooperative" we save the company thousands of dollars, then it would seem irresponsible for us to use less than extreme care in scrutinizing requests. People used to come in on Friday afternoon and say, "Put this on the 360/40. We want the answers on Monday." We stopped that foolishness. Now they usually have to request service in a written memorandum unless we have real confidence in their sincerity and genuine need.

Of course, we often provide a real service to a department which has a problem that is suitable for computers, such as mailing a confirmation notice on the anniversary date of a policy—this was suggested by our public accounting firm. But the volume in that case was 2 million. We did a smaller job for payroll recently, and they wrote us a letter of appreciation for our service.

But we take on only these jobs which we feel are worthwhile projects for the company as a whole. Even though the department requesting the service will be charged for it, it is our responsibility to try to keep things off the computer that have no business being on it.

We've given 40-minute talks in the various departments to inform management about the use and misuse of computers and encouraged key executives to go to customer briefings. If they know anything about computers, they don't come in with foolish requests, making such statements as, "I want it set up so I can get the information I need in one minute," when it takes much longer than that just to set up the machine. I believe that a general knowledge of computers should be a part of the training of all managers. We have a couple of good examples of men who worked for awhile in this department and are now managers in functional departments. Our relations with these departments are excellent.

MANAGEMENT'S CONSIDERATION

In October of 1978, President John Swartz was presented a formal request from Mr. David Winston, vice president in charge of sales. This request contained a proposal that Quality Life adopt a sales technique similar to that of Mutual Benefit Life in a trial region and that the data processing department be directed to provide the necessary service on the new electronic computer.

The request received by Mr. Swartz had been originated by Mr. York and had been approved by Mr. Blalock, director of marketing management, and Mr. Wright, assistant vice president for sales. Mr. Winston reported that he has previously discussed the matter with Mr. Lee, vice president of operations, who had rejected the proposal upon the advice of Mr. Heller.

In attempting to arrive at a decision on the request, Mr. Swartz weighed the following possibilities:

1. If the request were approved, this might set a precedent so that other requests of this nature would be directed to him, rather than to the established data processing department which was technically qualified to make decisions in such matters.
2. The data processing department might use this approved request from top management as leverage to obtain approval for additional computers.
3. Disapproval of the request might be used by the sales department to shift blame to top management in case sales quotas were not reached in the coming year.

Mr. Swartz was aware that regardless of his decision on the present request, some action was needed to prevent similar cases from arising in the future. Mr. Swartz had pointed out frequently to the board of directors that over the past three years continued centralization of equipment and responsibility had reduced costs and improved efficiency in data processing. Executive demands on the new equipment might jeopardize the basic objective of cost reduction, but he was aware that data processing efficiency required that functional departments have service available when their requests could be economically justified.

Chapter 2 □ IS Manageable Trends

INTRODUCTION

In the first chapter, we identified some of the key issues which make the assimilation of IS technology so challenging. We then suggested what the implications of these issues were for management practice. The major headings in this book—Organization, Planning, Management Control, Project Management, and Operations Management—collectively are selected to provide a comprehensive treatment of these issues. Analysis of these areas in a firm's situation, complete with appropriate recommendations, is normally called an IS management audit. Underlying our treatment of each of these headings is a cluster of six themes which reflect both changing insight into management practice and guidance for administrative action.

A discussion of the nature and implications surrounding each theme is presented here, as well as our identification of its future. These themes represent, in our opinion, the most useful ways to think about the forces driving transition in the IS unit in the early 1980s. Candidly, our expectation, as mentioned in Chapter 1, is that, inevitably, additional experience, research, and evolving technology will produce new formulation of these and other themes in subsequent years. These themes form the basis of organizing our discussion within each chapter on an aspect of management.

In outline form these six themes include:

1. IS technology impacts firms in different ways strategically. The thrust of this impact strongly influences the appropriate selection of IS management tools and approaches.
2. The merging of office automation, telecommunications, and data processing technologies. Formerly disparate areas of technologies now requires coordination at least at a policy level and later at a line control level.

3. Organizational learning about IS technology is a dominant fact of life. The type of management approaches appropriate for assimilating a technology change sharply as the organization gains familiarity with it.
4. Environmental forces are shifting the balance of IS services on make-or-buy decisions in the direction of buy, which profoundly impacts the kind and quality of IS support an organization can receive.
5. While the functions of the system life cycle remain, the best approaches to executing them, and the problems of implementation, have changed significantly, with a wide diversity of approaches being appropriate for different systems.
6. Effective IS policy and responsibility involves a continuous reshifting and rebalancing of power between general management, IS management, and user management. Each group has a legitimate and important role to play in ensuring an appropriate level of IS support to the firm.

The following paragraphs define the nature of these themes.

THEME 1—STRATEGIC IMPACT

It has become increasingly clear that good management of IS technology is not of equal significance for all organizations. For some organizations, IS activities represent an area of great strategic importance while for other organizations they play, and appropriately will continue to play, a cost-effective and useful role but one which is distinctly supportive in nature. Organizations of this latter type should expect that a lesser amount of senior management strategic thinking would be devoted to their IS organization. This issue is complicated by the fact that while today the IS function may not have strategic importance to the firm in meeting its goals, the thrust of its applications portfolio may be such as to have great significance for the future.

The opposite, of course, could also be true where IS plays a strategic operational role in the company's day-to-day operations but their future development applications do not seem to offer the same payoff or significance. However, in any case, it is important to understand what role IS is and should be playing.

Exhibit 2–1 summarizes these points by identifying four quite different IS environments.

Strategic. These are companies for whom smooth functioning of the IS activity is critical to their operation on a daily basis and whose applications under development are critical for their future competitive success. Banks and insurance companies are examples of firms which frequently fall into this category. Appropriately managed, not only do these firms require considerable planning, but the organizational distance between IS and senior

EXHIBIT 2-1 □ Categories of Strategic Relevance

Strategic impact of existing operating systems		Low	High
	High	Factory	Strategic
	Low	Support	Turnaround

Strategic impact applications development portfolio

management is very short. In fact, in some firms the head of the IS function, broadly defined, sits on the board of directors.

Turnaround. These are firms that may receive considerable amounts of IS operational support, but where the company is not absolutely dependent on the uninterrupted cost-effective functioning of this support to achieve either short-term or long-term objectives. The impact of the applications under development, however, is absolutely vital for the firm to reach its strategic objectives. A good example of this was a rapidly growing manufacturing firm. The IS technology embedded in its factories and accounting processes, while important, was not absolutely vital to their effectiveness. The rapid growth of the firm's domestic and international installations in the form of items such as number of products, number of sites, and number of staff, however, had severely strained its management control systems and had made its improvement of critical strategic interest to the company. Enhanced IS leadership, new organizational placement of IS, and an increased commitment to planning were all steps taken to resolve the situation. Another firm had systematically stunted the IS development function for a period of years—until existing systems were dangerously obsolete. Retrieving this situation had become a matter of high corporate priority.

Factory. These firms are heavily dependent on cost effective, totally reliable IS operational support for smooth operations. Their applications portfolios, however, are dominated by maintenance work and applications which, while profitable and important in their own right, are not fundamental to the firm's ability to compete. Some manufacturing, airline, and retailing firms fall into this category very nicely. In these organizations, even a one-hour disruption in service from existing systems has severe operational consequences on the performance of the business unit.

Support. These firms, some of which may have very large IS budgets, are neither fundamentally operationally dependent on the smooth functioning of the IS activity nor are their applications portfolios aimed at the critical strategic needs of the company. A recently studied large manufacturing company fit this category perfectly. It spent nearly $30 million per year on IS activities, with more than 500 employees involved. There was no doubt that this sum was being well spent, and the firm was getting a good return on its investment. It was also clear that the firm could operate, albeit unevenly, in the event of major operational difficulties and that the strategic impact of the application portfolio under development was limited. IS was at a significantly lower organizational level than in other settings, and the commitment to planning, particularly at the senior management level, was quite low. Our research has uncovered a surprisingly large number of companies in this category.

In attempting to diagnose where a firm or business unit should be on the dimension of the strategic impact of the applications development portfolio, examination of the business strategy of the corporation as a whole provides useful context. Chapter 5 describes two of the currently widely used frameworks of competitive analysis and suggests how the bridge can be built between their frameworks and the identification of the strategic impact of the IS development portfolio.

THEME 2—MERGING OF TECHNOLOGIES

It is our contention that management of DP or computing can no longer be considered as a useful concept around which to organize a program of management focus. Rather, the technologies of computing, telecommunications, and office automation must be thought of as providing in aggregate a common cluster of policies and management focus. When we refer to the information systems (IS) departments or policies, we will be including all three of these technologies under this umbrella. At present there is a clear trend toward coordination of these technologies in most firms.

There are at least two major reasons why they must be viewed and managed, at least at a policy level, as a totality. The first is the enormous level of physical interconnections which increasingly must take place between the three technologies. Online inquiry systems, electronic mail, and end-user programming terminals are a few examples of the type of applications which require the physical integration of two or more of the technologies. The second major reason is that, today, execution of projects utilizing any one of these technologies poses very similar management problems. Each tends to involve large projects in terms of expenditures, rapidly changing technology, substantial disruptions in many people's work styles, and often the development of complex computer programs. As will be discussed in Chapter 3, the integration of these technologies has been complicated by the fact that 10 years ago not only were they not integrated but they had come from vastly different managerial traditions. These traditions made them independent, and unless actively managed to move together, they will remain apart. In dealing with the three technologies as a totality, we see the need for integration of them, at a minimum at a policy setting level, and, in many settings, a common line management for all three.

THEME 3—ORGANIZATIONAL LEARNING

Throughout the development of IS there has been an ongoing effort to understand the managerial issues associated with implementing and evolving automated systems in an organization. Starting from Whisler and Leavitt's article[1] on the demise of middle management and going on to Dick Nolan's and Cyrus Gibson's stages[2] and Chris Argyris' espoused theory versus theories in actions,[3] there have been a range of concepts on how to deal with the problem of getting individuals to use automated systems appropriately. After field studies over a seven-year period on 28 organizations, we have concluded that the managerial situation can be best framed as one of managing technological diffusion. Successful implementation of a technology requires individuals to learn new ways of performing intellectual tasks. As this learning takes place changes in the information flows as well as in individual roles occur. Often this results in organization changes substantiating the Leavitt and Whisler conjecture and reinforcing Nolan's and Gibson's original four stages.

We consider this process to be closely akin to the problems of organizational change identified by Lewin[4] and described in action form by Ed Schien[5] as an unfreezing, moving, and then refreezing again. They can best be summarized by rephrasing Nolan's and Gibson's original *four stages* (calling them *phases* here) and considering the process ongoing with a new start for each new technology, be it data base, office automation, or CAD/CAM. This approach usefully emphasizes the enduring tension that exists between efficiency and effectiveness in the use of IS. At one time it is necessary to relax and let the organization search for effectiveness while at another it is necessary to test for efficiency to maintain control.

---

[1] Thomas L. Whisler and Harold J. Leavitt, "Management in the 1980s," *Harvard Business Review* (November–December 1958).

[2] Cyrus F. Gibson and Richard L. Nolan, "Managing the Four Stages of EDP Growth," *Harvard Business Review* (January–February 1974).

[3] C. Argyris, "Double Loop Learning in Organizations," *Harvard Business Review,* (September–October 1977), p. 115.

[4] K. Lewin, "Group Decision and Social Change," in *Readings in Social Psychology,* ed. G. E. Swanson, T. M. Newcomb, and E. L. Hartley (New York: Holt, Rinehart & Winston, 1952).

[5] E. Schien, "Management Development as a Process of Influence," *Industrial Management Review* 2 (1961), pp. 59–77.

Phase 1—Technology Identification and Investment. This phase involves identifying a technology of potential interest to the company and funding a pilot project. In this phase, the pilot project may be considered akin to R&D. The key outputs of the project should be seen as expertise on technical problems involved in how to use the technology, plus a first cut at the types of applications where it might be most useful. It is generally inappropriate to demand any hard profit and loss payoff identification either before or after the implementation of this pilot project.

Phase 2—Technological Learning and Adaptation. The objective during this phase is to take the newly identified technology of interest to an organization where a first level of technical expertise has been developed and to encourage user-oriented experimentation with it through a series of pilot projects. The primary purpose of these pilot projects is to develop user-oriented insights as to where the potential profitable applications of this technology might be, and to stimulate user awareness of the existence of the technology. Repeatedly, what the IS department thought were going to be implications of a technology turned out to be quite different in reality. As is true of phase 1, there is a strong effectiveness thrust to phase 2.

Phase 3—Rationalization/Management Control. Phase 3 technologies are those which are reasonably understood by both IS personnel and key user personnel as to their end applications. The basic challenge in this phase is the development of appropriate tools and controls to ensure that it is being utilized efficiently. In the earlier phases, the basic concerns revolve around stimulating awareness and experimentation. In this phase, the primary attention turns to development of controls and appropriate IS hygiene to ensure that the applications are done for a minimum amount of money and can be maintained over a long period of time. Formal standards, cost-benefit studies and user chargeout mechanisms are all appropriate for technologies in this phase as their use is rationalized.

Phase 4—Maturity/Widespread Technology Transfer. Technologies in this phase have essentially passed through the gauntlet of organizational learning, with technological skills, user awareness, and management controls in place. Often the initiating organization will move on to new technologies and spend no energy on transferring the expertise. If not managed, organizational rigidity may slow the process of adaption to the new technology.

The key point in this discussion is that technologies in all four phases exist simultaneously in an organization at any point in time. The art of management in the 1980s is to bring the appropriate perspectives to bear on each technology simultaneously (that is, supporting IS phase 1 research, IS phase

2 aggressive selling to the end user, and intensive IS phase 3 generation of controls). This calls for a subtlety and flexibility from IS management and general management that too often they do not possess or see the need for. A monolithic IS management approach, however, will not do the job. This will be discussed further in Chapters 3 and 5.

THEME 4—MAKE-OR-BUY

A source of great tension and repositioning of IS in the 1980s is the acceleration of the pressures which are pushing firms towards greater reliance on external sourcing of software and computing support as opposed to the internal delivery of these services. Escalating costs of development of large systems, limited staff, availability of proprietary industry data bases, and dramatic increase in the number of potential applications are some of the factors driving this trend.

Make. Key pressures pushing in the direction of the make decision include the following:

The firm has the potential to develop a customized product totally responsive to its very specific needs. This is true not only for initial development but for necessary system enhancements and maintenance throughout its life. Further, one has the psychological comfort gained by having key elements of one's firm under one's supervision (corollary of "not invented here").

The ability to maintain confidentiality about data and type of business practices being implemented. This point is particularly important in situations where IS-type services are at the core of how the firm chooses to compete.

Ability to avoid vulnerability to the fluctuating business fortunes of outside software or data services suppliers.

Increased ease in developing one's systems due to the growth of user-oriented programming language, online debugging aids, and other user-oriented pieces of software.

Ease of adapting made software to rapidly changing business needs without having to coordinate your requirements with other firms.

Buy. Key pressures moving in the direction of the buy decision include the following:

Ability to gain access to specialized skills that either cannot be retained or where there is insufficient need to have them continuously available.

These include skills in end-use application, skills in programming, etc. to construct a system, skills to operate a system, and skills to maintain a system. Both demographic trends (in reduced work force entrants) and increased end-use specialization needs are making this a more important rather than less important item.

Cost: The ability to leverage a portion of the development cost over a number of firms can drive the costs down for everyone and make the in-house development alternative unattractive. This is particularly significant for standard accounting applications and data base systems.

Staff utilization: Scarce in-house resources can be saved for applications that are so company-specific or so confidential that they cannot safely be subcontracted. Saving these resources may involve buying into a set of systems specifications for the common applications which are less than optimal.

Ability to get the job done faster either through bypassing the corporate priority queue or buying access to a piece of totally or partially developed software.

Ability to make a short-term commitment for IS processing support instead of having to make a major facilities investment.

Immediate access to high standards of internal control and security offered by the large, well-run, service organization.

A proliferation in the types of information services that can be bought, and the active marketing of those services. The key categories involved include the following:

- Programmer availability (contract programmers, etc.).
- Proprietary data bases.
- Access to service bureau computer processing.

The change in balance of these pressures in favor of the *buy* alternative has significantly impacted IS management practice, as internally supplied services lose market share. Care must be taken to ensure that adequate management procedures are in place. For example, the management control system must be checked to ensure it is not tilting the balance too much in favor of buy through excess charges. Another example is that as project management for software is being delegated more to the outside, procedures to ensure that these suppliers have suitable project management systems must be developed. Implementation risk on a fixed-price contract becomes strongly related to vendor viability. (A good price is no good if the supplier goes under before completion.) Managing this shift to buy is a dominant concern in planning the necessary IS human resource. A critical factor in implementing new programs to complement existing activities (which must be maintained), this shift is discussed further in Chapter 8 on operations.

THEME 5—SYSTEMS LIFE CYCLE

The activities necessary to be undertaken to provide a specific information service can be characterized classically as the following series of steps:

DESIGN/CONSTRUCT/IMPLEMENT/OPERATE/MAINTAIN

The test of the appropriateness of an IS organization and set of policies is how successful they are in encouraging and controlling each of these steps for multiple systems. While changing technology and improved managerial insights have significantly altered the way each of these steps can be implemented, the functions of each have remained relatively unchanged for a considerable period. However, with an increasing shift to buy (versus make) occurring, some significant changes in many of these steps have to be made, with IS management in many cases becoming more like a broker.

Design. The objectives of the design step are: a definition of the information service desired and the important criteria for selection of the service, identification of the users and the initial tasks to be implemented, and, if relevant, the long-run form of service and support. The first step has traditionally been either a joint IS-user proposal based on the IS plan or a user request. More and more it is being initiated by a user request, often stimulated by the marketing effort of an IS hardware/software/service supplier. The design step is a critical activity which demands careful attention to short- and long-term information service requirements as well as to ensuring the delivery of reliable service. This step was traditionally dominated by the IS technical staff but more and more is being assumed by the user. The shift should be managed carefully.

The substance of the design work normally begins with an analysis to determine the feasibility and potential costs and benefits of the proposed system, which, if favorable, leads to an explicit decision to proceed. This is followed by substantive joint work by the potential user and a systems professional to develop a working approach to a systems design. Depending on the systems scope, these design efforts may cover the range from formal systematic analysis to informal discussions and a flowchart. The end product of this work is both a definition of the desired service and an identification of a means of providing it (including in-house or purchased).

Construction. A highly specialized activity, the structuring of automatic procedures to perform a timely, errorless, information service is a combination of art and logic. Professional judgment is needed in area of:

1. Selection of form and brand equipment and/or service bureau.
2. Selection of programming language, data base system, etc.

3. Documentation of operating procedures and content of software.
4. Identification and implementation of appropriate testing procedures.
5. Review of adequacy or long-term viability of purchased software service.

Very technical in content, this work depends on both good professional and IS management skills. In the past it was very dependent upon good organization linkage to the users. As more services are purchased this phase may be eliminated in entirety, although often a portion exists to adopt the standard system to the specific details of the situation.

Implementation. This activity still involves extensive user-IS coordination as the transition is made from the predominantly technical IS-driven tasks of the construction step to its completed installation and operation in the user environment. Whether the system is bought or made, the implementation is still a joint effort. Establishment and testing of necessary communication links, bringing new skills and an assortment of intrusions into the normal habits of the organization, are critical. A key general management concern is to ensure adequate technical support to a user of a purchased system during implementation.

Operations. In most settings the operation of systems has received the least amount of attention and creates an enormous residue of frustration and ill will. Further, as more users are becoming operators the subtleties of operations are becoming common to all managers. A significant amount of the difficulty, as will be discussed in the chapter on operations management, stems from inadequate attention being paid to clear definition of the critical performance specifications to be met by the new system and from failure to recognize that there are often inherent conflicts between specific service goals. At the front end of operations is the need for specific procedures to test and document services, including a formal acceptance procedure by operations. This clearly separates responsibility for construction of a service from responsibility for its operation. This separation of roles is particularly important when the same department (or even individuals) is responsible for both construction and operation of the system. In addition, operations approval procedures are needed for systems enhancements and maintenance. At the back end of operations is the actual delivery of service and measurements to assess its quality.

Maintenance. Ongoing design, construction, and implementation activities on existing services are labeled maintenance. When action is desired on a steadily growing need, normally caused by an outside change or user desire, it requires some technical support. (The word *maintenance* is a complete misnomer because it implies an element of deferrability which does not exist. It could better be labeled modernization. Much of maintenance stems from real-world changes in tax laws, organization shifts, such as new offices or unit mergers, business changes, such as new-product line creation or elimination, new technology, etc. It can be as simple as changing a number in a data base of depreciation rates or as complex as rewriting the tax portion of the payroll. Effective execution of maintenance faces three serious problems:

1. It is considered by most professionals to be dull and noncreative as it involves working on systems created by someone else.
2. In actuality, for older systems, it is very complex, requiring competent professionals to safely perform necessary changes.
3. Accounting procedures do not recognize that software is an asset or that over time it tends to age, making eventual conversion vastly more complex and in extreme cases putting the entire organization at risk as it struggles to free itself from both obsolete hardware and software.

Newer systems are permitting users to develop their own adaptations by including report writers or editors. Because these complex systems require maintenance, however, a cost comes with the benefit. Managing maintenance continues to be a troublesome problem, but organization, planning, and management control all provide critical context to ensure that these issues are resolved appropriately.

Summary. The description of the systems life cycle helps capture much of the complexity of IS management. At any point in time an organization has hundreds of systems, all in different positions along this life-cycle line. Of necessity, the IS management system in the overwhelming majority of cases must be organized by IS function rather than by specific application system. This inevitably creates significant friction because IS organization forces the handing off from one unit to another of responsibility for an application system as it passes through these steps. The user is often the only link (although changes often take place here) as the system's responsibility is passed from one group of technical specialists to another.

Further complicating the situation is that the execution of this process (and the dividing line between the steps) varies widely from one type of application system to another. For example, a structured transaction-oriented system requires an intensive up-front design effort to get firm specifications which can then be programmed. A decision support system, however, involves more a process of user learning. An appropriate methodology here is often a crude design followed by a simple program. Use of the programs by the user leads to successively different and more comprehensive design as its performance is analyzed and then to a series of new programs. Interactively, one cycles through this sequence a number of times. Such a design process (pragmatically useful) flies in the face of many generally held nostrums about good development practices.

In Chapter 8 we deal with the issues of operations management and the impact of *buy* on the systems life cycle.

THEME 6—POWER BALANCE AMONG THREE CONSTITUENCIES

Much of the richness of IS management problems stems from managing the conflicting pressures of three different and vitally concerned constituencies. There are IS management, user management, and the general management of the organization. The relationship between these groups quite appropriately varies over time as the organization's familiarity with different technologies evolves, as the strategic impact of IS shifts, and as the company's overall IS management skills grow. The next five chapters are largely devoted to identifying the various aspects of managing this relationship.

IS Management. A number of forces drive the creation of an IS department and ensure its existence. It provides a pool of technical skills which can be developed and deployed to meet complex problems facing the firm. Appropriately staffed, an important part of its mission is to scan leading-edge technologies and make sure that the organization is aware of their existence. It represents a critical mass, responsible for conveying knowledge of the existence of this technology, and of how to use it, to appropriate clusters of potential users. By virtue of its central location it can conceive where potential interconnection between the needs of different user groups exists, and it can help to facilitate their connection. In a world of changing and merging technologies, this unit is under continued pressure to modernize if it is to remain relevant. Basically, the raison d'être of the unit is that its specialization permits implementation of otherwise undoable tasks. As the technology has evolved the problem has become more complex because IS staff members themselves have become *users* of the system (through development of operating systems, etc.). Further complicating the situation is the growing availability of user-friendly systems and experienced users who do not feel the need to call on IS for help.

User Management. The specialization of the IS function has taken place at the cost of eroding some of the tasks of the user department while not relieving users of responsibility for ensuring that ultimately the tasks are well done. In the past, requirements of the technology served to disenfranchise users in the designing of services. This was coupled with a complicated chargeout system which further estranged the user from IS. Also complicating matters is the aggressively marketed availability of outside services which go directly to the user.

As the ultimate customer of IS service, the user best understands and has internalized the key operating problems. If the existing service is poor, the user feels the full impact in terms of inability to execute the corporate mission and wants to buy without IS help.

In the early stages of a technology, particularly, the user is a specialist in living with the problem and not a specialist in the technologies which can be brought to solve the problem. Another complication is that the term *user* often implies more precision than actually exists in a real situation. Often the user involves many individuals at different levels scattered across multiple departments. Further, as the user is becoming more sophisticated through experience with the older IS technologies, and as the technologies are becoming more user-friendly, some (not all) of the reasons for having a specialized IS organization have disappeared. Finally, user management, through increased experience with personal computing, is gaining more confidence (unwarranted) in its ability to manage all stages of the project life cycle (the same is true of general management; see below). Thus the balancing point of services between the specialist department and the consumer is appropriately being reappraised continuously.

General Management. The task of general management in this environment is to ensure the appropriate structure and management processes are in place to referee the balance between user and IS to fulfill the overall needs of the organization. Their ability and enthusiasm for playing this role varies widely, both as a function of their comfort with IS and their perception as to its strategic importance to the firm as a whole. Since many have reached their positions with little exposure to IS issues early in their careers or to radically different types of IS issues, this discomfort is often extremely acute. Much of this book is aimed at helping this group to feel more comfortable about their grasp of this activity. As the years pass, however, this group, through their experience with personal computing and encounters earlier in their careers with different (now obsolete) IS technologies, have gained confidence (often misplaced) in their ability to handle the policy issues implicit in IS technology.

In brief, each group's perspective and confidence is evolving. This change, however, while solving some problems is creating new ones.

SUMMARY

In this chapter we have identified six manageable trends that are intimate to all aspects of managing information services in the 1980s. Exhibit 2–2 is our map of the remaining chapters and identifies the emphasis in each chapter in relation to these organizing themes. Chapter 3 considers, in depth, the management issues of merging of the three technologies of OA, DP, and TP. It treats this issue as an organizational learning problem requir-

EXHIBIT 2-2 □ Map of Chapters and Themes

Chapter \ Manageable Trend	Strategic Impact	DP/TP/OA	Organization Learning	Make/Buy	Life Cycle	GM/User/IS
IS Technology Organization Issues **Chapter 3**		●	●			●
Organizational Issues in IS Development **Chapter 4**	●		●	●		●
Information Systems Planning **Chapter 5**	●		●			●
IS Management Control **Chapter 6**	●		●	●		●
A Portfolio Approach to Information Systems Development **Chapter 7**	●				●	●
Operations Management **Chapter 8**	●			●	●	●
Multinational IS Issues **Chapter 9**		●				●
The IS Business **Chapter 10**	●		●	●		●

ing a series of contingent actions in order to effectively manage the diffusion of technology. In Chapter 4, we deal with the organization issues of shifting power and role among GM-User-IS in order to balance innovation and effectively control new IS technologies in environments where IS has different strategic impact. The planning discussion in Chapter 5 focuses upon the strategic relevance of IS and its potential impact on the organization. This includes both corporate culture and the type of contingent actions needed to assimilate the technology. In management control (Chapter 6) the emphasis is on how corporate cultures influence the managerial roles and the nature of how to integrate the services. Chapter 7 on project management focuses on developing a set of contingent actions for IS, users, and general management for different types of projects. Managing the life cycle and the make-or-buy decisions are the prime subjects of both Chapters 8 and 9. In Chapter 8 the discussion is on ensuring an efficient operation. In Chapter 9 we extend the culture concept to include the range of complexities present in international situations. Chapter 10 uses the marketing mix model to synthesize the overall issues to interface the IS activity to the company as a whole.

Case 2–1 □ Automatic Data Processing, Inc.*

Automatic Data Processing (ADP) has succeeded on a large scale where others have not because we are intensively service based." Frank Lautenberg, chairman of the board of ADP was summarizing his views on the success of ADP in the computing service business. "We realized early on that our clients did not care how we provided the service, but that our clients cared immensely that the service met their business needs. Our advantage over our competition has been that we thoroughly understand our market; we've had 32 years in the business of learning what makes the small or medium business tick and how to help the owner of the business. We've seen less successful competitors take a technology-based approach and fail to understand that our customers do not care about the technology, they are busy running their businesses. ADP will develop products which are competitive even if computers reach near-zero hardware costs.

"ADP's mission is to help an ever-increasing number of businesses improve their performance by regularly using ADP's computing services for record-keeping and improved information services. We will offer computing services that can be efficiently and profitably mass-marketed and mass-produced with recurring revenues."

ADP's primary objectives are stated as:

a. *For our clients,* to earn their continuing loyalty and support. Our growth objectives leave little room for losing clients and the clients need us only as long as we serve them accurately, efficiently, and responsively.
b. *For our stockholders,* to increase the value of their investment by continuing our historical growth of *at least* 15 percent per year, every year, in revenues and earnings.
c. *For our employees,* to offer participation in ADP's success in which they play an important role . . . by offering challenges, security, and substantial personal skills development.

THE COMPUTER SERVICES INDUSTRY

The computer services industry includes the three primary business segments of *(a)* processing services which consist of firms supplying the physical computing resources, including software and operating personnel,

* This case was prepared by Assistant Professor Gregory L. Parsons as a basis for class discussion rather than to illustrate either effective or ineffective handling of an administrative situation.

(b) software products which consist of firms supplying software packages, and *(c)* professional services which consist of firms supplying consulting services. The companies competing in the computer services industry may compete in just one segment, such as Informatics in the software products part of the industry, or, like ADP, may overlap into all three segments.

The computer services industry is special in a number of ways. First, the industry has grown more rapidly than the computer industry as a whole, increasing 22 percent in sales in 1978–79 and then 26 percent in 1979–80. This compares to a 14 percent increase in total U.S. electronic data processing (EDP) expenditures in the 1979–80 period. More rapid growth will come as new markets, specifically the small-business markets, are opened. Second, the computer services industry seems not only to survive recession times, but in fact, 60 percent of the participants in the industry claim that the recession has a positive impact on their businesses.[1] Third, the acclaimed shortage of data processing personnel which is a primary constraint in in-house DP departments has proven to be an advantage to the computer services industry. And, finally, the drastic reduction in mergers and acquisitions in the last 10 years in most industries has been just the opposite in computer service, where there has been a tremendous amount of realignment in the industry. In fact, acquisitions and mergers in the computer services industry represented 10 percent of the total merger activity among U.S. companies in 1980. Judging from the current trends in the industry a two-tier industry structure is evolving. (See Exhibit 3 for current industry structure.) At one end will be the multiservice vendors which will offer a broad range of products to a worldwide market. The opposite end of the industry will be composed of smaller companies that will market highly specialized services to specific types of customers.

Presently, there are over 6,000 computer service companies in the United States, producing approximately $14 billion in revenue in 1980. (See Exhibits 1 and 2 for industry growth and size.) This is over 25 percent of the total U.S. EDP expenditures for 1980, which is estimated at $56 billion. In major U.S. companies, purchased computer services compose over 7 percent of the total EDP budget. In smaller companies it represents a larger percentage. By 1985, the services industry is expected to grow to nearly $30 billion. The industry showed pretax profit margins of 9.7 percent in 1978 and 9.1 percent in 1978 and 9.1 percent in 1979 (equaling $298 million in profits for 1979). These profitability measures also exceed the overall computer industry margins by approximately 2 percent.

The computer services industry has an organized leadership in the Association of Data Processing Service Organization, Inc. (ADAPSO). ADAPSO serves as the official voice of the industry in battles attempting to keep various parties out of the computer services arena of competition. Recently,

[1] Input Survey, 1980.

EXHIBIT 1 □ Computer Services Industry Sales ($ billions)

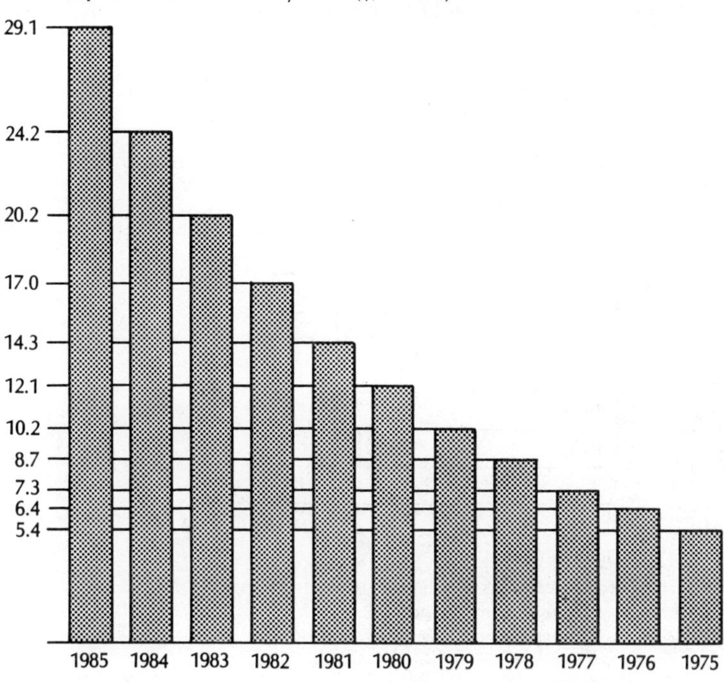

ADAPSO has been involved in a suit with Citibank and is also challenging AT&T's right to compete in this business because of subsidizations from other monopolistic business lines. At this time it is not clear how these legal issues will be resolved, but is definitely not the end of competition from outside the current industry.

The 1980 lineup of the competition will not reflect the future industry. Although ADP is the largest independent company in the business of computer services, it is still very small compared to major U.S. companies which have begun competing or are considering it. For example, GE has the subsidiary GEISCO; Service Bureau Corporation, SBC, has been acquired by Control Data Corporation from IBM; IBM has developed SBS (Satellite Business System); AT&T is embroiled in legal disputes to determine the degree of competitive license ("Baby Bell"); American Express has built a large communications network including Warner Cable T.V. (Warner Am Ex Cable $17 million) and First Data Resources, Inc. ($50 million), a credit card processor; and Citibank figures to be a contender, forecasting $250 million in yearly profits from its Financial and Information Services Group by 1990.[2]

Aside from the competitive pressures within the computer services mar-

[2] *Business Week,* August 1980, p. 54.

EXHIBIT 2

A. 1979 Computer Services Industry Performance (growth)

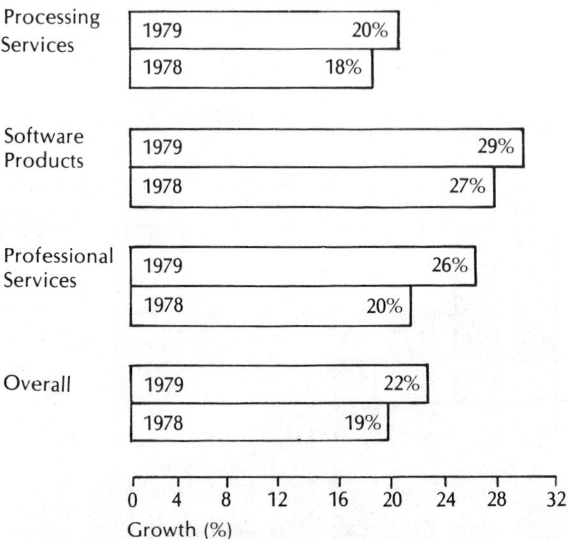

Note: 1979 percentage represents growth from 1976 to 1979. 1978 percentage represents growth from 1977 to 1978.

Source: Input Survey, 1980.

B. Computer Services Industry Performance by Type of Company (revenues—$ billions)

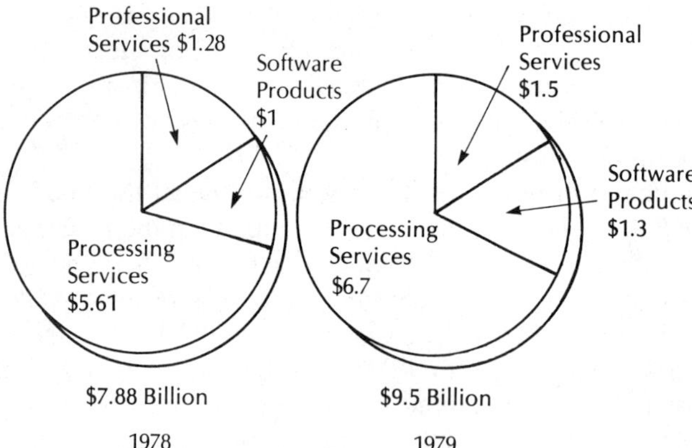

ket, the rapidly changing technology provides another challenge for the industry. One example of this challenge has been the result of the dramatic reduction of hardware costs over the past five years. This has caused many current users of computer services to install their own in-house facilities. Some companies will install computers to replace individual time-sharing or remote batch terminals while others will install complete in-house time-sharing systems of their own. A survey of computer service users shows that 28 percent of those users in certain applications planned to bring these services in-house.[3] The computer service companies which are hardest hit by this trend are those with only time-sharing to offer. In response to this threat a new product has been developed which combines new generation hardware, application software, and traditional support services by the computer service company on user sites. The competitive thrust of this product is to give a client his own computer—he is not sharing resources with other users; response time is dictated only by his own usage. The advantage of the computer services product over a purchased system is the degree of support for hardware and software maintenance, product enhancements, and employees training that are included as part of the product. A fuller description of ADP's version of this product is given below.

COMPANY BACKGROUND

ADP is the world's largest independent company exclusively in the business of computing services. (See Exhibit 3 for competitors and relative sizes.) Founded in 1949 as strictly a payroll processing company named Automatic Payrolls Incorporated, ADP's sales have averaged a 28 percent compound growth rate over its 20-year life as a public corporation. Approximately 20 percent of this growth has resulted from acquisitions; 80 percent

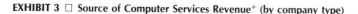

EXHIBIT 3 □ Source of Computer Services Revenue* (by company type)

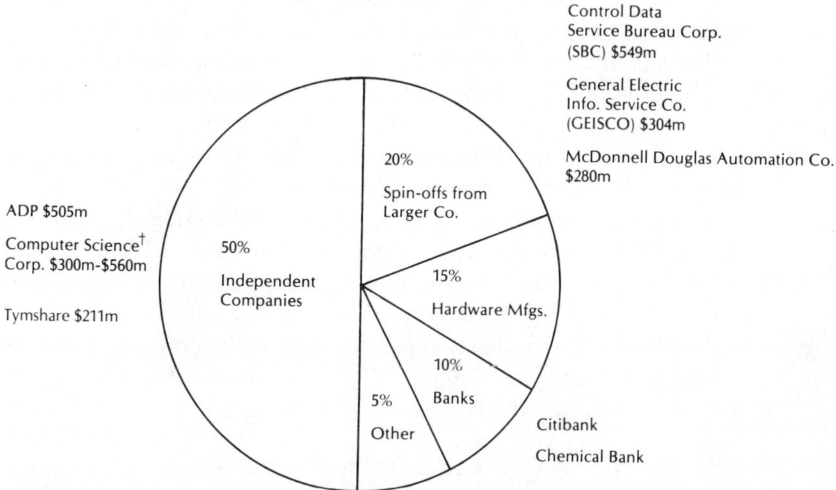

* All dollar amounts indicate 1980 revenues produced for computer service activities only.

† Range indicated because of various timing and sources of CSC's 1980 revenue mix.

[3] Input Survey, 1980.

has been internally generated. Likewise, profitability has paralleled sales growth through a wide variety of general economic considerations. (See Exhibit 4 for prior five years' income statement and Exhibit 5 for prior two years' balance sheets.)

> ADP's profits have never dropped, and are likely to continue increasing at a 15 percent to 20 percent pace . . . Recession can't overcome the nature of ADP's well-managed business.[4]

The success of ADP depends upon good business savvy and attention to the client.

Josh Weston, president of ADP, says, "ADP's success comes from matching client needs (wants) with those capabilities unique to ADP. What we do very well is to isolate a situation where large groups of businesses require a standard service. We look for business opportunity in the presence of a third force (in addition to the customer and ADP), such as the regulatory environment. This third force creates a market for our standardized, high quality products by requiring many individual businesses to do one standard thing, very accurately."

The quality of client service is the banner of ADP and even Josh Weston shares responsibility for a number of customer accounts. To measure the perceived quality of service, a survey is sent out to ADP customers every six months. In 1980, 40,000 of the questionnaires were completed and returned to ADP. The results of the survey are a part of the management evaluation process and are used as guides to improve services. A quote from the 1980 President's Bulletin states, "the Commercial Service Group (described below) attained its highest quality score ever . . . 81, with 31 of the regions showing improvement over the corresponding point last year. . . . This probe was most revealing in that we received excellent scores on the truly tougher parts of our service, our pricing, and our product features."

ADP has gone through a series of stages from its origin in a storefront, one-man operation, in Paterson, New Jersey, to its current status. Although started in 1949, the company did not go public until 1961, coincidentally when the computer processing was first used at ADP. It wasn't until 1963 that a second product was introduced. This was a brokerage processing service for the Wall Street community's transaction processing needs. In 1964 the sales force became professionalized as a separate function, and has continued to remain an important force in the company (see Exhibit 6 for the present organization chart). In 1967 an accounts receivable service was started and this introduced a second line of accounting services as a complementary product to the payroll service product in the small-business market. ADP added a general ledger service in 1970 and an accounts payable service in 1972. In 1975 ADP purchased Cyphernetics, Inc., a time-sharing

[4] *Value Line*, November 1980.

EXHIBIT 4

AUTOMATIC DATA PROCESSING, INC.
Summary of Operations

For the year ended June 30	1980	1979	1978	1977	1976
Revenues	$455,000,000	$369,000,000	$296,000,000	$241,000,000	$195,000,000
Cost of operations	376,000,000	303,000,000	241,000,000	195,000,000	156,000,000
Interest expense	3,000,000	2,000,000	749,000	604,000	513,000
Earnings from continuing operations before income taxes	76,000,000	64,000,000	54,000,000	46,000,000	38,000,000
Provision for income taxes	36,000,000	31,000,000	27,000,000	23,000,000	19,000,000
Earnings from continuing operations	40,000,000	33,000,000	28,000,000	23,000,000	19,000,000
Discontinued operations	(2,000,000)	44,000	22,000	(49,000)	(258,000)
Earnings before extraordinary items	38,000,000	34,000,000	28,000,000	23,000,000	19,000,000
Extraordinary items	2,000,000		155,000		149,000
Net earnings	$ 40,000,000	$ 34,000,000	$ 28,000,000	$ 23,000,000	$ 19,000,000
Earnings per share					
Continuing operations	$2.61	$2.21	$1.83	$1.57	$1.30
Discontinued operations	(.12)	—	—	—	(.02)
Earnings before extraordinary items	2.49	2.21	1.83	1.57	1.28
	.11	—	.01	—	.01
Net earnings	$2.60	$2.21	$1.84	$1.57	$1.29
Average number of common shares outstanding	15,000,000	15,000,000	15,000,000	15,000,000	15,000,000
Cash dividends per share	$67	$55	$43	$28	$21

EXHIBIT 5

AUTOMATIC DATA PROCESSING, INC. AND SUBSIDIARIES
Consolidated Balance Sheets

	June 30, 1980	June 30, 1979
Assets		
Current assets:		
Cash (including certificates of deposit of $28,537,000 and $7,816,000, respectively) (Note 3)*	$ 31,141,000	$ 11,425,000
Marketable securities, principally municipal and governmental securities—at cost, which approximates market value	4,466,000	12,047,000
Accounts receivable, less allowance for doubtful accounts of $3,745,000 and $2,683,000, respectively	72,325,000	56,249,000
Inventories, at the lower of cost (first-in, first-out method) or market	11,876,000	10,814,000
Other current assets	8,362,000	4,947,000
Total current assets	128,170,000	95,482,000
Property, plant, and equipment-at cost (Notes 1B and 1C):*		
Land and buildings	81,260,000	54,871,000
Data processing equipment	139,251,000	122,394,000
Furniture, fixtures and leasehold improvements	30,233,000	24,150,000
Total property, plant, and equipment before depreciation and amortization	250,744,000	201,415,000
Less: Accumulated depreciation and amortization	83,087,000	64,667,000
	167,657,000	136,748,000
Notes receivable and other assets	7,508,000	1,434,000
Excess of cost of investment in subsidiaries over net assets acquired and other intangibles (Note 1D)*	53,364,000	39,153,000
Total assets	$356,699,000	$272,817,000

company headquartered in Ann Arbor, Michigan, and added several products based on time-sharing, a telecommunication network, and a customized programming service, under the divisional name of the Network Services Division.

ADP's products are developed and acquired to meet the needs of a market not a customer. To achieve this objective, products are developed with a large set of parameters to meet a variety of businesses but the basic software is standard to the ADP staff. For example, the payroll product which has evolved over 20 years of development has parameters for *(a)* tax requirements, *(b)* department structure, *(c)* corporate structure, *(d)* employee numbering system, *(e)* job costing including allocation of direct and indirect costs, *(f)* fringe benefit plans, *(g)* voluntary deductions, etc.

ADP will spend over 6 percent of revenue on R&D this year. This includes internal R&D which is the traditional product development, and the annual "carrying costs" of external R&D which represents products

EXHIBIT 5 (*concluded*)

	June 30, 1980	June 30, 1979
Liabilities and Stockholders' Equity		
Current liabilities:		
Accounts payable	$ 25,519,000	$ 17,669,000
Dividends payable	2,944,000	2,425,000
Accrued expenses and other current liabilities	35,975,000	21,431,000
Income taxes (Notes 1E and 6)*	2,794,000	9,713,000
Current maturities on long-term debt (Note 3)*	3,557,000	5,222,000
Total current liabilities	70,789,000	56,460,000
Long-term debt (Note 3)*	53,383,000	22,208,000
Deferred income taxes (Notes 1E and 6)*	20,393,000	16,843,000
Commitments (Note 8)*	—	—
Stockholders' equity (Note 4):*		
Preferred stock (par value $1.00 per share: authorized, 300,000 shares; issued, none)	—	—
Common stock (par value $.10 per share: authorized, 40,000,000 shares; issued, 15,506,648 and 15,297,297 shares, respectively)	1,551,000	1,530,000
Capital in excess of par value	57,593,000	52,437,000
Retained earnings	154,535,000	124,849,000
	213,679,000	178,816,000
Less: Common stock held in treasury-at cost	407,000	468,000
11,611 and 14,905 shares, respectively	1,138,000	1,042,000
Restricted stock plan compensation (Note 4B)*	212,134,000	177,306,000
Total liabilities and stockholders' equity	$356,699,000	$272,817,000

* Notes to consolidated financial statements not included here.

purchased from outside. Arthur Kranseler, corporate vice president of development and acquisitions, says, "ADP will develop very few products in the traditional sense of development from ground zero. Many new ADP service offerings will result from purchases of companies in which an average of 50 percent of the purchase price is a substitute of internal R&D from ADP's standpoint."

ADP currently employs approximately 14,500 people spread throughout the United States, six European countries, and Brazil. Of the 42 senior officials in ADP, 18 of them have less than 5 years with the company and 25 have less than 7 years with the company. However, of the 42 executives, 17 of these officials joined ADP from acquired companies with an average of 5 years tenure at similar positions with those companies.

Geographically and organizationally, ADP is structured by service-type of business segments which are largely run like separate companies. (See Exhibit 6.) The two largest organizational units in ADP, Commercial Services Group and Network Services Division, are detailed below.

EXHIBIT 6 □ ADP Organization

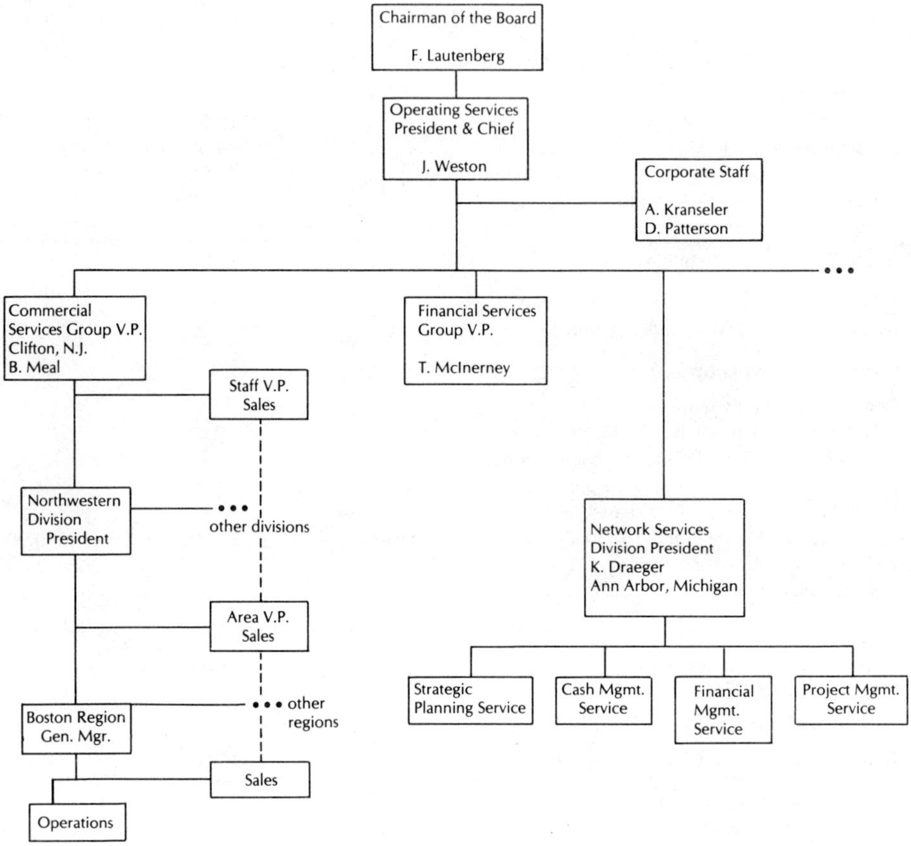

Chairman of the Board
F. Lautenberg

Operating Services
President & Chief
J. Weston

Corporate Staff
A. Kranseler
D. Patterson

Commercial
Services Group V.P.
Clifton, N.J.
B. Meal

Staff V.P.
Sales

Northwestern
Division
President

• • •
other divisions

Area V.P.
Sales

Boston Region
Gen. Mgr.

• • • other
regions

Sales

Operations

Financial Services
Group V.P.
T. McInerney

Network Services
Division President
K. Draeger
Ann Arbor, Michigan

Strategic
Planning Service

Cash Mgmt.
Service

Financial
Mgmt.
Service

Project Mgmt.
Service

• • •

COMMERCIAL SERVICES GROUP (CSG)

The Commercial Services Group (CSG) of ADP is the oldest part of the company, produces over 50 percent of yearly total revenue, and employs 60 percent of the people. The 8,000 ADP employees in CSG average about 24 years of age and are employed as:

3,000 key entry operators
400 programmers and systems analysts
1,300 client relations
700 clerks
500 delivery drivers
700 account executives
550 salespeople

400 computer operators
450 administrative

The center for this group is in Clifton, New Jersey, in the same complex as corporate headquarters. The group is divided into six geographic divisions in the United States with three data centers in Europe, two centers in Canada, and one center in Brazil. The six U.S. divisions contain a total of 36 regional processing centers. The largest of these is the Clifton region which employs over 1,000 people, the next largest region is about one third the size of the Clifton region. Other regions exist in nearly all major U.S. cities; however the size of the operation varies widely. The processing regions are directed by a general manager who operates the region as a profit center. Sales and revenue targets are developed by each region with corporate level review, based upon the previous year's results and market potential. These targets go into the operating budget with a series of known relationships between the sales targets and the expense items such as sales expense, operating expenses, etc. Profit margins between regions of similar size can vary by 10 to 25 percent. Division presidents and regional general managers can receive very significant portions of their compensation by exceeding targeted sales growth, revenue growth, and profit growth.

"It is somewhat easier to budget for the Commercial Services Group than for other businesses," said Dick Patterson, financial corporate vice president. "There are fewer variables in that business and we know from history how to predict many of those variables. If a region's performance starts to slip, it is highly visible to all general managers on our monthly operating reports which are shared with all senior managers. Peer group pride and pressure then becomes a primary motivation item." The average turnover in general managers is about 9 percent a year, which is low for the computing services field.

The CSG client base contains over 70,000 businesses and is growing at approximately 15 percent per year. The average client has a six- to seven-year longevity. This longevity is thought to be better than the industry average. Currently, the U.S. small-business market has approximately 3 million businesses, of which 1 million are seen as potentially ADP clients; thus there is a penetration of less than 10 percent of this market.

Although the largest part of Commercial Services' business has been the small-to-medium-size firm, there is a growing emphasis on marketing to the large company which is called the major-account business. There are 6,800 companies in the United States which have more than 1,000 employees. These firms are considered the target major-account market. Of these 6,800 firms, ADP does some payroll processing for over 1,000 of them. This processing may range from a small executive payroll, or a divisional payroll, to the entire corporate payroll. This market currently provides about 10 percent of the total ADP payroll business. The annual billings for these customers range from $15,000/year to $100,000/year.

This market is expected to grow significantly. To advance in the large-business market a special major-account sales force has been introduced in CSG to develop specialized selling techniques. Using the payroll service as an example, ADP can offer three advantages to major accounts:

1. Price—ADP can process a paycheck for from \$.70 to \$1, including pickup and delivery. The average in-house paycheck costs \$2.50, when all direct and indirect costs are truly included.
2. Standardization—ADP's standardized service can be used to get data standardized in a geographically dispersed organization. A national income tax service uses ADP's payroll service to get standardized data from its hundreds of operating locations for the corporate consolidation statements. This could not be accomplished by using many separate independent payroll services, and it is much more cost effective than attempting to transmit all the data to a central location for in-house processing.
3. Distribution—ADP's comprehensive geographic coverage of the continental United States allows the physical distribution of paychecks from the ADP regional offices to the client's various locations, which standardizes the payday schedule and reduces the distribution costs of mailing. A national restaurant chain uses the payroll service because of this and other reasons.
4. Client queries—ADP will either send the client a tape of the payroll file or down-line load the file to the client's computer to allow the client access to his payroll data.

ADP has developed a tele-data network for its payroll service to major geographically distributed companies. To use this service, the various locations of the client company phone in their payroll data on in-bound WATS lines to the ADP data center; for example, there is currently a tele-data center in St. Louis, Missouri. The consolidated statements will then be produced and the paychecks mailed out to the customer locations. Beginning in November 1981, CSG expects to be able to centrally process reports and print the paychecks at many of the ADP regional processing centers. The paycheck can then be distributed by couriers.

The major-account market is lucrative in terms of revenue per account but also represents certain challenges to commercial services which have primarily been geared toward the smaller less-demanding customer. For the geographically dispersed client, collection, processing, and distribution may require substantial coordination across CSG regions and divisions. This interdivisional negotiation requires a higher level approval of the contract and contract pricing within the ADP organization.

When the agreement has been reached, then the system requirements are handed over to the implementation staff who work out the operating and coordination specifics. The implementation time averages three months.

Even for major accounts the tendency of ADP is definitely to avoid customized software although they will provide special services for larger customers.

ADP in general, and CSG especially, are leveraged by the philosophy and practice of mass production and standardization. In fact, standardization is perceived as being the key ingredient to providing good service. With all standard systems ADP's support staff can be experts and can diagnose and correct problems in minutes. This philosophy is exemplified in the following employer services.

a. A job costing and labor distribution package which provides departmental and job code analysis of productive and nonproductive hours/earnings and distribution of material and overhead to cost centers.

b. An unemployment cost package control which systematizes the handling of unemployment claims by ex-employees, challenges unwarranted claims, and works to reduce the overall unemployment tax rate of the client.

c. A personnel reporting package which provides employee master files and custom-formatted reports, produced as required from an expandable employee data base.

The employer service business (which includes payroll) is currently the largest business at ADP, is the most profitable, and is the business where ADP has clear industry leadership. The strengths of ADP in this business are: reputation, management experience, and extensive distribution channels through its sales force and client service representatives in the regional offices.

Accounting services are also sold through the CSG sales network. These services include:

a. Accounts Payable batch service which provides purchase journals, vendor ledgers and checks, check register, expense distribution reports, cash requirement forecasts, retail reports, markup calculations, open items analysis report, and automatic interface with the general ledger.

b. Accounts Receivable batch service provides customer ledgers, sales analysis, commission reports, aging schedules, transaction journals, and management reports.

c. General Ledger Financial Reporting batch service includes P&L statements, balance sheets, comparative statements, budget statements, working capital and cash flow analysis, and general ledger.

d. Interactive Accounting Services which provides order entry including automatic back ordering and exception reporting, invoicing, sales analysis, inventory control, accounts receivable, purchase orders, bill of materials planning and job costing. This service can be provided by terminals on the client's premises linked to computer in ADP processing centers, or by a computer and terminals at the client's sites with fully supported application software, maintenance, and enhancements. This interactive product is in the early stage of its life cycle. Begun in 1978, it is the most technically sophisticated product of Commercial Services.

These accounting service products produce 12 percent of ADP's revenue and are expected to grow to well over 100 percent in the next five years, with the mix of business going from the current 75 percent batch application revenue (*a, b,* and *c* above) to over 50 percent in interactive (*d* above). The CSG, in line with company policy, does not sell software or hardware. Products are offered as a total service package which includes software maintenance, updates, enhancements, hardware repairs, and client support, all from one source.

CSG has established itself as a price leader in providing its service to its client base. ADP is able to price above some competitors, because client's information needs and, especially, payroll information needs are sensitive and critical at most companies. Customers are willing to pay a premium for the ADP reputation of reliability, product features, and experience of 30 years in the business. As indicated by the title of a recent information systems article ("Remote Computing Services: Cost Doesn't Concern Users"),[5] the market is basically elastic.

For ADP, pricing in the payroll segment of the business is considered the art of determining the "market price" for the payroll service which will meet both the sales growth and profitability targets for the group. However, even at premium prices the average cost of an ADP payroll (averaging under $1) is far less than the in-house produced check (averaging $2.50). The client pays for ADP's services on an as-needed basis, which may be based on:

a. The number of payroll checks needed. For example, a 100-check payroll service will cost about $65 per pay period, a 10,000-check payroll service will cost about $4,000 per pay period.
b. A flat monthly fee for remote interactive accounting services. For example, $1,250/month will include a 64k CPU processor, a 20 meg disk, a printer, a CRT terminal, the broad-based order-entry accounting package, and all the ADP support/maintenance.

A higher-volume service, based on the interactive products may cost $3,500/month at the high end of the line. One may also buy selected accounting services such as the accounts receivable service or general ledger, online through a terminal at the client's location with the processing done at ADP's data centers. The cost for these products is based on usage and would approximate $1,000/month for 500 invoices/month and

[5] *Infosystems,* April 1981, p. 48.

$1,400/month for 5,000 invoices/month. ADP/client service agreements can vary from a handshake for a month-to-month commitment (as in 99 percent of the payroll clients) to a one- or two-year contract for more specialized services.

NETWORK SERVICES DIVISION (NSD)

The Network Services Division began operation in 1975 when ADP purchased Cyphernetics, Inc., of Ann Arbor, Michigan. The division currently provides about 15 percent ($80m) of total ADP revenues and is expected to double that amount to over $160m in the next five years. About 1,100 employees work in NSD, one third of whom are involved in marketing. Many of the key positions in NSD are held by former Cyphernetics employees.

The division's telecommunications network links three processing centers (Ann Arbor, Michigan; Waltham, Massachusetts; and London, England) where the hardware and maintenance personnel are located. The division also has 40 sales offices distributed throughout the United States and Europe.

The NSD product line is completely distinct from the commercial services product line. Although the products may offer a few features similar to commercial services products, they are developed, marketed, distributed, and priced independently, and cater to a different market place.

Currently, the NSD product line and percentage of business is:

- Time-sharing—50 percent of NSD's business. Supported on DEC System-10. Will support 1,200 simultaneous users, on Textronix and other graphic terminals. Will support IBM 2780 and Data 100 batch terminals. FORTRAN, BASIC, and COBOL are offered as conversational languages. FORTRAN and COBOL are offered as batch-mode languages.
- A Database management system and language called IPL (Information Processing Language).
- ADP-On-Site—a data processing communication package comprising the following modules: mainframe computers, an international teleprocessing network, operating system software, application software, data base management systems, technical support and advanced monitoring, and maintenance techniques. This product is placed on the client's premises as a turnkey package within three months of ordering at a minimum of $10,000/month, on a two- to five-year contract with discounts awarded for longer contracts. This product allows distributed data processing at the customer site for local applications or on the large time-sharing computers at network

services processing centers for applications requiring large data bases or special software packages. The On-Site service can act as a central system with just terminals and peripherals distributed to users, or as true distributed processing with the computing power distributed over multiple systems. The use of additional network resources are not part of the $10,000 basic fee.

- The Cash Management Service—a rapidly growing part of the business is marketed to banks of all sizes who subsequently offer this service to their customers. This product is offered as a tool to increase funds management effectiveness by supplying information which allows the financial manager to mobilize cash, control disbursements, and capitalize on investment opportunities. The product includes: deposit reporting, management information reporting, balance reporting, and wire transfers.
- Financial Management Service—a service marketed to the financial manager of the client organization. The product is built around five modules: a financial modeling language, a management control budgeting system, a financial consolidation system, an integrated accounting system, and a fixed assets management system. The philosophy of the product is to supply an easy-to-use set of software tools which are focused on areas where financial managers typically have serious information needs. For example, developing "what if" scenarios to various financial plans. In addition to the off-the-shelf system, the financial management service can be tailored by the Professional Services Group to meet the client's needs for specialized financial information systems.
- Project Management Service—provides tools, including automated PERT/CPM for project management. This product may be used with a terminal at the client's project site.
- Strategic Planning Service—a product comprising automated tools for strategy development and analysis.
- International Trade Service—provides software to handle data processing in the import/export trade.
- Econalyst—provides econometric forecasts, data bases, and models. This product is the result of a joint venture with Townsend Greenspan & Co. Inc., using the econometric model of economist Alan Greenspan. All of these products are used through the Network Services teleprocessing network.

The pricing of the Network Services' products is: (*a*) flat monthly fee for On-Site, including all programs and services. A two-year contract is required and longer terms get a discount. (*b*) A per—transaction price for the cash management service. This scheme is used primarily because of pricing by competitors which necessitates a scheme which relates charges to user-perceived usage. ADP will price slightly below competition on this product. (c) For the other services Network Services charges on the basis of computer-resource-usage (CRU) and connect time. ADP is a price leader for these services. Fees are reevaluated annually and are adjusted to reflect value of service and competitive pressures.

Network Services' target market is large multidivisional companies, companies who are already fairly sophisticated in the use of data processing. Currently, over 200 of the Fortune 500 companies use products from NSD; however, this base is not evenly distributed, with 90 percent of the business coming from 40 percent of the customers. In this customer base 50 percent of the customers are buying straight time-sharing, but for ADP, as well as for the entire industry, the shift is away from time-sharing to value-added products such as software and data bases. NSD's current time-sharing customers are the first candidates for upgrading into these value-added products. The 15 percent/year expected growth in network services will come by intensified selling into the existing market penetration, only adding two to four new cities a year onto the network both through internal growth and acquisitions. Future acquisitions will be made with the objective of strengthening the business by increasing market share or adding a complementary service to fill out a product line. In addition to purchasing new products, NSD has an internal R&D budget of well over 10 percent of sales. This represents the different relative economics between NSD and CSG.

The NSD currently sees its competition coming from many different sources, depending on the product. For the time-sharing product, NSD competes with a wide range of businesses, from local companies serving a geographic region to large companies such as Tymshare and GEISCO which serve the continental United States and parts of Europe. The NSD's cash management service is competing against services offered by National Data Corporation and also Chemical Bank. The financial service is competing against assorted software houses, for example, ADR (Applied Data Research), in-house processing, and micro/minicomputer systems OEMs (original equipment manufacturers). The primary competition for the Econalyst is from Data Resources, Inc. (DRI).

A typical client life cycle with NSD will begin with a call on the financial office of the prospect. These calls will be either a cold call or the result of a consultant referral. Preliminary screening will be done to determine whether the client has needs and characteristics that are particularly suited to NSD's capabilities. For example, a strong need for distributed processing, or on-site project management. If the situation is competitive, a proposal will be put together which emphasizes the value-added nature of the NSD product, shows pricing flexibility (the costs can be backloaded to reduce the front-end expenditure for the customer), and illustrates a modular delivery vehicle which permits the client to pay for only what he currently needs. As the

ADP/client relationship develops, more features are offered to upgrade the service. Network Service will lose a client when: *(a)* they don't really understand the client's business, *(b)* they don't expend the effort to cultivate the relationship, or *(c)* the client goes in-house.

The Network Services Division is quite different from the Commercial Services Group, both in markets, products, and personnel. The geographic and cultural distance between Clifton and Ann Arbor, combined with ADP's corporate philosophy of decentralization, has allowed NSD to continue to operate much like a separate company in terms of product development, organization structure, and pricing. The key to future success in NSD, as an entity, is to maintain a leading edge of technology in the time-sharing and telecommunications areas while focusing in on particular markets to gain leverage out of the products and the sales force. A recent NSD reorganization into product-line business segments emphasizes this strategy.

OTHER BUSINESS

ADP has a number of other businesses organized as service groups and service divisions which are targeted at specific market niches.

- Financial Services Group—contributes 14 percent to ADP's 1980 revenue. This group is composed of *(a) Brokerage Service* which serves the Wall Street brokerage communities' record-keeping needs. *(b) Banking Service* which provides demand deposit accounting services to many banks. *(c) Savings and Loan Service* which provides service to the thrift community.
- Dealer Service—8 percent of 1980 revenues. It provides various accounting and control systems specialized for automobile, trucks, and power equipment dealerships.
- Other miscellaneous services contribute the remaining 20 percent of ADP's business.

THE FUTURE

The growth trend of the computer industry, in general and ADP specifically, is quite strong. ADP predicts that it will reach $1 billion in revenues by 1985. ADP expects to remain strong in its current products and markets and to continue to expand into new products and markets which can complement the ADP organization. (See Exhibit 7.) The basic question does not seem to be one of near-term success. ADP's earnings have never declined and are predicted by financial analysts[6] to increase at a 15 to 20 percent

[6] *Value Line*, November 1980.

EXHIBIT 7 □ ADP Acquisitions (fiscal year 1980)

Companies	Business	Type acquisition	When effective	($ Million) Approximate revenues	Estimated revenues FY 1980	Estimated revenues FY 1981	($ Million) Estimated profit or loss FY 1980
COMTREND	Computerized graphic info for commodities, currencies, and interest rate futures. (Financial Systems Div.)	Purchase—cash $4,000,000 + contingencies	7/15/80	$3.1	$-0-	$3.5–4.0	Loss
Total Systems	Processing services for S&Ls and mortgage banking. (Financial Services)	Purchase—cash $2.5 million	7/1/80	5.5	-0-	6.5	Small loss
Audatex	Cost-estimating service for car damages for insurance companies, auto repair shops, auto dealers. (Cost Estimating Services)	Purchase—cash $15.0 million	4/1/80	4.3	1.0	8.0	(1.3)
Business Systems Research (BSR)	Computerized data bases and accounting systems for customers' house brokers and freight forwarders. (ADP Network Services)	Purchase—cash + contingency	8/1/80	3.5	-0-	4.0	Break even
Philadelphia National Bank	Agreement for ADP to provide data processing support from a Philadelphia data center to support the bank's 80 customer user base. (Financial Services)	Purchased	3/15/80	2.0	0.5	2.4	Loss
Statistical Tabulating	Acquired the payroll and accounting business and customer base. (Commercial Services)	Purchase—cash and notes $3.5 million	3/1/80	7.2	1.5	5.0	Loss
Programmed Tax Systems	Computerized tax preparation services to accountants. (Commercial Services)	130,000 ADP shares "pooling"	1/15/80	3.3	3.3	3.8–4.0	0.3

rate, but there is a question of longer-term success as the entire market for computer-based technology changes in response to technology advances and vendor competition. There is also a question as to whether the current 23 percent growth rate for the service-oriented ADP can be sustained as the company approaches the $1 billion size.

One of the keys to the future for ADP is the management of relations among the various groups and divisions within the company. Historically and currently, there is limited coordination or communication across divisional lines. This separation can be illustrated by the fact that occasionally salesmen from two or three different ADP service divisions could coincidently solicit a prospective client—for example, a bank—and offer ADP's products with different development histories, different host machines, and different support organizations. As the industry for telecommunications and software service becomes more competitive the degree of success of ADP may be dependent upon the potential synergy which could be derived among the ADP service units. For example, there is currently an effort under way to transfer some of CSG's experience in mass marketing and client service to NSD. Also, NSD is attempting to find broader in-house use for its telecommunications expertise.

Other recent responses by ADP to the increased size, complexity, and opportunities of the business have been:

- Development of an enhanced executive training program.
- The hiring or internal development of more professional managers for the field offices.
- The additions (disproportional to the company's growth) of divisional staff. At the corporate level ADP has maintained a "lean" staff.
- Development of a human resources development program.
- Development of a strategic planning cycle.

The most recent market assessment of ADP's performance and opportunities came on May 19, 1981, when a 2-million share common stock issue was successfully accomplished at a post 2–1 split price of $29/share. This was 1/8 off the prior day's closing price. The market price at year's end, June 30, of ADP's stock for the prior five years is given below.[7]

	High	Low	Average
1980	53	32½	42¾
1979	41	28½	34¾
1978	36⅜	23	29⅞
1977	30½	21½	26
1976	35½	27	31¼

[7] Data not adjusted for May 21, 1981, 2-for-1 stock split.

Case 2-2 □ Mark Twain Bancshares, Inc. (1980) (A)*

In early 1980 Tony Guerrerio, the vice president of operations of Mark Twain Bancshares, Inc. and president of Mark Twain Services (a service subsidiary to the bank holding company), faced a difficult decision. Less than one year with the bank, Mr. Guerrerio saw several alternative approaches for serving the bank's data processing needs. Currently, Mark Twain got most of its data processing services from a computer service company. Recent incidents, however, had caused this relationship to be deemed too dangerous to continue.

Mark Twain Bancshares, Inc. (MTB) is a multibank holding company located in St. Louis, Missouri. The organization was started in 1963 as the South County Bank in St. Louis by the current chairman of MTB, Adam Aronson. After the acquisition and start-up of additional community banks in the St. Louis area, the Mark Twain Bancshares Corporation was formed in 1969. Since that time the company grew rapidly through acquisitions and in 1980 totaled 11 banking locations, all in the St. Louis area, controlling nearly one half billion dollars in assets. (See Exhibits 1, 2, and 3 for organization charts and financial results of the past five years.) Five more banks were expected to be added to MTB in the next two years, including two in Kansas City, Missouri.

In 1980, MTB had 500 full-time employees and was the fifth largest banking organization in St. Louis and the fastest growing St. Louis bank in the years 1974–1979. Indeed, MTB ranked sixth in growth rate of all companies in the St. Louis area during this period of time. The target market for MTB has been in the past and continues to be the lower-middle commercial market of entrepreneurs, family-owned businesses, and independent professionals such as doctors and lawyers. MTB has grown in these markets both through acquisition and aggressive marketing to lure customers away from other St. Louis banks. At present the St. Louis market for financial services is static and has been characterized as "stodgy."

The company's goal for the future is one of rapid growth with targets of $1 billion of assets in 1983, $2 billion in 1986, and a total of 26 bank locations

*This case was prepared by Assistant Professor Gregory L. Parsons as the basis for class discussion rather than to illustrate either effective or ineffective handling of an administrative situation.

EXHIBIT 1 □ Organization Chart

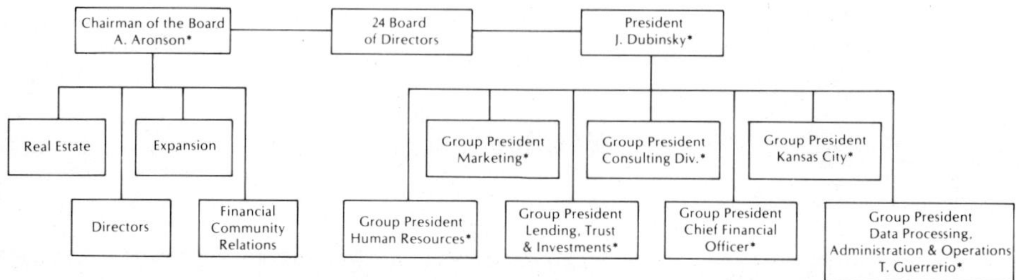

*Members of Executive Committee.

by 1986. It is anticipated that half of this asset growth will be acquired and half will be internally generated. While significant growth of the asset base is planned, profitability is expected to be maintained at the current 20 percent return on equity. To achieve the dual goals of growth and profitability in the St. Louis and surrounding banking market, MTB developed strategies based on marketing and managerial innovation.

An example of the MTB unique approach is its hiring of a large percentage of the new MBAs into the bank's internal management development program. These new hires are quickly moved into areas of significant responsibility, sometimes as bank presidents under senior management guidance. The upshot of this program is that many of the senior officials in the

Exhibit 2 □ Operations, MTBI

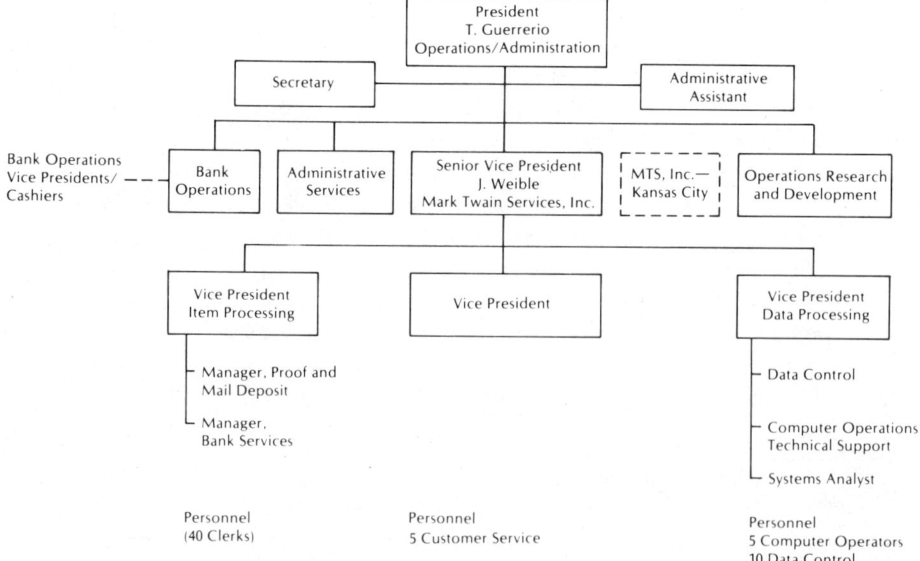

EXHIBIT 3

MARK TWAIN BANCSHARES, INC. (1980) (A)
Selected Financial Data
($000 except per share data)

	Years Ended December 31,			
	1979	1978	1977	1976
Interest income	$ 47,160	$ 32,147	$ 22,583	$ 18,126
Interest expense	26,157	16,679	11,725	9,494
Net interest income	21,003	15,468	10,858	8,632
Provision for loan losses	828	797	740	230
Other income	1,989	1,292	1,278	1,091
Other expenses	13,980	11,282	8,974	7,327
Income before income taxes and securities transactions	8,184	4,681	2,422	2,166
Applicable income taxes	2,584	1,227	194	245
Income before securities transactions	5,600	3,454	2,228	1,921
Net securities gains (losses)	(224)	(35)	190	149
Net income	$ 5,376	$ 3,419	$ 2,418	$ 2,070
Primary earnings per share:				
Income before securities transactions	$2.99	$1.87	$1.22	$1.05
Net income	$2.87	$1.85	$1.32	$1.13
Total average assets	$459,109	$381,663	$313,573	$260,252

MTB banking organization are under 40 years of age. John Dubinsky, president of MTB, has stated that he wants every member of the organization, even down to the clerk level, to have the capabilities to become bank president.

MARK TWAIN SERVICES DATA PROCESSING

Responsibility for both bank operations and data processing is with Tony Guerrerio. He was hired by MTB in 1979 to establish a more effective data processing service for MTB. Mr. Guerrerio, 31, a Harvard MBA of 1977, came to MTB from Salomon Bros. investment firm, with no data processing experience and no formal banking experience. To fulfill this responsibility, a separate subsidiary, Mark Twain Services Inc., had been established; Mr. Guerrerio serves as president. (Exhibit 2 includes the subsidiary organization.) Mark Twain Services has an operating budget of approximately $3 million per year and employs 60 people. The average age of the Mark Twain Services employee is 27 compared to the average age of 31 for the rest of MTB.

In commenting upon a situation which he took over, Mr. Guerrerio noted:

> From very early on, I saw that the data processing resources of the bank were not sufficient to support the business strategy of the corporation. When I joined MTB, the bank was receiving all the data processing service for bank applications such as checking accounts, savings deposits, loans, and saving certificates from Computer Services Inc. (CSI) out of Pittsburgh. MTB had an on-line Bunker-Ramo terminal system which tied directly into the service bureau in Pittsburgh. The teller terminal system hardware was MTB's but all the network software and application software was from the service bureau. At the time (1979) MTB was processing about 50,000 transactions a day through CSI and this represented over 50% of the total volume of that data center in Pittsburgh. We were having severe problems getting an acceptable level of service from the service bureau. MTB member banks were complaining about timeliness of reports and slow on-line response times. Many times reports were a day or more late. I couldn't imagine what would happen as we continued to grow.
>
> The CSI Pittsburgh data center was small; it had poor management, poor operating procedures, and no support from the CSI corporate headquarters. The center had been purchased along with a number of other data centers a few years earlier by CSI during a growth by acquisition phase of CSI. The Pittsburgh center was out of the mainstream of CSI banking development with Honeywell hardware while the rest of the CSI banking division was being standardized on IBM hardware.
>
> The straw that broke the camel's back was a small bank in Nebraska, Westown Bank, with $15 million in assets. This bank was not affiliated with MTB. The Pittsburgh center tried to convert that bank onto their system in their usual fashion ("on the fly") and the whole center blew up. I didn't get reports for a week. I got upset and demanded some answers; that's how I found out about the situation in Nebraska. The regulators almost closed the doors on Westown. At this time I had been on the job 30 days. Since that time CSI has sold the Pittsburgh center.
>
> I began to develop a data processing strategy which would accomplish three objectives: one, it would give us reliable service on a current basis as well as potential to grow with the business, obviously this meant a move away from CSI, Pittsburgh; two, it would give us an opportunity to exploit profitable opportunities in bank operations, this was important since Mark Twain Services is responsible for insuring profitable bank operations for the group as a whole; and, three, it would have to happen very quickly since the bank was moving aggressively in the marketplace, and it didn't appear that the service bureau center could survive it. To begin with, we conceptually split bank data processing into two functions, the item processing function and the account processing function.

ITEM PROCESSING AT MARK TWAIN BANCSHARES

Item processing involves the physical movement of checks, deposit slips, and other similar paper through the banking system. Both the checks written by MTB customers and checks cashed by MTB customers must be collected, the data captured off the checks, and the physical check sorted and either filed at MTB or sent to the bank upon which the check is drawn. The physical piece of paper is still the documentation of a financial transaction.

The economics of item processing are in the midst of change because of Federal Reserve System policies which are changing. Specifically there was legislation in the works wherein the Federal Reserve System would begin charging banks which use its check clearing services a "per item" charge, probably between ½ cent to over 5 cents per check depending on the distance and the routes of the checks. Previously, no per item charge was assigned but MEMBER banks were required to maintain larger RESERVE balances (at zero interest) with the Fed. Now the RESERVE balances will be reduced but banks have to deal with an explicit charge.

Alternatives to using the Fed to clear checks are:

a. Correspondent banks—checks are sent to another bank for clearing. The issues here are the per item costs, the correspondent bank charges, and the speed with which the clearing can be accomplished. The cost and availability factors change, and banks can choose alternative patterns depending upon our customer mix and these factors.

b. Direct courier—if a significant volume is associated with one other bank, then a suitcase of checks may be physically carried to that bank.

c. Clearing houses—are used for most local checks. The member banks form a clearing house association where checks are exchanged by members on a daily basis at no charge.

These checks flowing through the 11 MTB locations can be viewed as a very valuable fast-moving inventory, coming from many locations and traveling to many locations. This situation creates opportunities for creative use of data processing in two ways. One is by reducing the cost of processing the checks. A goal in this area is to process more checks with less people and to clear these checks through the lowest cost routes. A second opportunity is to speed up the check clearing process and thus make more money available to the bank. Because of these opportunities MTB has decided that it would handle its own check processing. Currently MTB has a Honeywell hardware/software package for item capture and makes use of NCR multi-pocket proof machines[1] for transit. However, simultaneous with the decision for a new account processor, MTB was implementing a new item processing system which would greatly improve the effectiveness and efficiency of check processing. The *only interface between the item processing system and the service bureau is a transaction file which is stored on disk at Mark Twain Services* as items are processed. A number of times during the day, this file is dumped through two 9,600 baud lines to the Pittsburgh data center to become part of the customer account systems (discussed below).

[1] The NCR multi-pocket machines sort checks by the specific bank number encoded in magnetic ink at the bottom of the check.

The new hardware and software investment for item processing will be a medium-scale Burroughs computer and Burroughs check processing software. This system will replace both the Honeywell system and the NCR machines and is scheduled to be implemented in May of 1980, at a cost of about $160,000, and is expected to save approximately $15,000/month in check processing costs in addition to increasing the availability of money to the bank. Nearly all of the personnel in the Mark Twain Services organization are involved in the check processing function; this includes one technical person and one contract programmer who will enhance the basic check processing package. The remainder of these people have mainly clerical functions (see Exhibit 2).

ACCOUNT PROCESSING: FRONT AND BACK OFFICE

The second area of bank data processing is account processing. It is an entirely separate set of systems from the item processing system. Account processing includes checking accounts, savings accounts, NOW accounts, saving certificates, commercial loans, and installment loans. The general ledger processing for the bank is also included in this category. Currently all of MTB's account processing is tied to the CSI processing center in Pittsburgh through MTB's Bunker-Ramo terminal system.

Tony Guerrerio then spoke of his work in the account processing area:

> The Monetary Control Act of 1980 will have a substantial influence on all of banking, especially on the operations side. We are expecting a great deal less regulation, specifically in the area of lids on interest rates which can be paid to depositors and also in restriction against inter- and intrastate banking. Currently, Missouri is a unit banking state; that is, banks are prohibited from having more than two facilities within a municipal area. We have 11 locations in the St. Louis area because of the large number of independent municipalities surrounding the city of St. Louis. Our locations form a ring around the city. However, the whole industry is in a state of flux in products, markets, and locations. We on the operations side have to be able to supply products on shorter notice in response to regulations and competition, convert new banks to our systems regardless of physical location, and basically provide a complete product/service line to our customers whose financial service needs are escalating rapidly. Our competition right now is primarily the downtown St. Louis banks; however, our future competition will most certainly be Merrill Lynch, American Express, and even Sears Roebuck as they offer financial services in our target markets.
>
> In the year that I've been with MTB, I've considered the alternative of bringing the account processing function in-house but three issues force me to realize that continuing to buy account processing on the outside is the only real option at this point in time. The first issue is the necessity to make our move very soon. We cannot afford to stay one day longer than necessary on the Pittsburgh system; we are risking a disaster. It simply would take too long to begin building a hardware and software facility from scratch even if we could

purchase software packages. The second issue is that I don't believe that we currently have the management resources and corporate discipline to bite off both check processing and account processing at the same time. The third issue involves the economics of in-house processing. I think that in-house processing is significantly more costly than a service bureau if you can get adequate service on the outside. My feeling is that many banks sincerely wish they didn't have to administer data processing in-house. They're really caught in a crush of user demands, rising costs, and personnel shortages. I personally hope never to be put in a position of competing with Anheuser-Busch, Monsanto, and McAuto (all St. Louis area companies) for "propeller-heads"; that is, data processing professionals who don't know a thing about their own business . . . in this case banking. Maybe this is going beyond the issue of relative economics into my own views of data processing but I'll spend plenty for good bank operations people. However, we have no need or desire for "rocket scientists." My current staff level of two technicians were hired on the mutual goal of being quickly assimilated into the mainstream of bank operations where they could use their talents to make money for the bank.

As a result of these factors we have begun an intensive search for an alternative service bureau for our applications processing. After an initial screening of 12 service bureaus, only three have the abilities to fill our current and future needs.

These three were Western Information Systems Inc. (WIS), Bank Data Corp. (BDC), and Computer Systems Inc. in Cincinnati (CSI). We had a great deal of hesitancy about including CSI on our list again after our negative association with the Pittsburgh operation, but when we investigated it, we found the CSI Cincinnati operation to be totally different. The center had been set up to fit the CSI standards of IBM hardware and had a much larger capacity; they had developed reasonably good services and a good set of operating procedures. Most of all we were impressed with the job the general manager of the Cincinnati operation was doing. He appeared to be a real taskmaster.

The evaluation procedure of the alternatives is being conducted under conditions of mitigated haste. On the one hand we are on a day-to-day basis with the current operations in Pittsburgh; however, we have to make the best choice for the future since, to my mind, we are tying the future of MTB to the service company. The choice is essentially mine as the VP of operations and the president of Mark Twain Services. No other MTB executives are involved in this process.

To assess the three alternatives, I think there are basically three important considerations. First, it is critical to us that the service bureau be able to deliver products and services to MTB on time with a high degree of reliability. The bank and, in turn, my operations are completely exposed in the event of a computer service delay. The second factor is the product/programming flexibility that can be expected by the service bureau. This aspect of the service bureau is critical to our continued success in banking because of the increasingly competitive nature of the banking industry and the aggressive marketing strategy of MTB. MTB wants to be an innovator and requires an innovative data processing service. Cost is the third consideration in the evaluation process, but considering the relative importance of the first two criteria, a premium will be paid if necessary.

Attached in Exhibits 4 through 6 are the data that have been compiled to help with this decision. First we looked at the products each of the companies offered and rated them on a 1 to 4 basis, one being good and 4 being poor; the results are shown in Exhibit 4. The specific product offerings from each of the companies is shown and rated. The key items for MTB are checking (DDA), savings, loans, general ledger, and the customer information file. It was also important that they could accept our POD file. Basically all three companies offered a sufficient range of products at an acceptable level of quality for MTB's needs. But as can be seen from the table they vary from product to product in the quality. Then we contacted other users of each of these companies and tried to assess how MTB fit the current customer base. Next, we identified the hardware and service performance levels of the companies. In Exhibit 5 we

EXHIBIT 4 □ Product Evaluation

	Computer Services (Cincinnati)	Bank Data Corp.	Western Information Systems Inc.
Checking	2	2	1
Savings certificates	1	2	3
Cash reserve	2	1	2
Installment loan	2	1	2
Commercial loan	4 Slightly better than current system	1	2
General ledger	2	1 Generated entries available	3
Customer information File as link of application	Household oriented; history available on deposit accounts only	Household oriented; history available; demographic reports	Individual oriented; history available; demographic report
Proof of deposit (POD)	Available on Burroughs; we support IBM*	Learning experience on IBM	Good
NOW accounts	Current software can handle NOW environment	Running in New York	Will be available 10/80
ATM support	Not currently supporting but can support Diebold	Not currently supporting ATMs	Extensive shared network; can support Diebold, IBM, and Docutal ATMs
Single statement	No	Yes	Scheduled for 10/80
Bulk filing technical requirements	Yes	Yes	Yes
Alpha inquiry	Yes	Yes	Yes
Branch reporting	No—but must develop for Atlanta	Yes	No, and would find it difficult to change
Programming flexibility	Some	A good deal	Virtually none

* CSI would provide software support for a Burroughs remote item processing center. However, if MTB chooses IBM hardware for its item processing work, then MTB will have to support the entire POD application.

EXHIBIT 5 □ Overall Company Posture

	Computer Systems Inc. (Cincinnati)	Bank Data Corp.	Western Information Systems Inc.
Basic business	Service bureau	Service bureau (75% of revenues in government/financial industries)	Wholly owned subsidiary of a $13 billion bank holding company
Revenues FY 1979 (projected FY 1980)	$250 million total company $10 million in bank services business	$38 million ($75 million)	$38 million
"Staying power"	Demonstrated in other computer services areas	Yes?	Yes
Product development staff	20 programmers at year-end 1979 in bank services business	103 systems personnel in Atlanta, Georgia	195 systems personnel in Chicago, Illinois
Depth/banking expertise	Very thin; building	Growing organization, but much banking expertise	Solid
"In a nutshell"	Well established in the computer processing field, feeling its way into a new business	Young, aggressive, dynamic service organization which will become a leader in its field	Large, steady computer processor delivering a good product day in and day out
Length of time	x years: 60 days' termination notice	x years; 90 days' termination notice	3 years; 6 months' termination notice
Price protection	4th year, from time to time; 60 days' notice	4th year, ± Indianapolis CPI	90 days' notice
Costs: Application processing*			
Conversion costs	None	$43,247 + $3,300 per month for 18 months (receive 10% free volume = $40K per year over initial contract term)	$50,000 however, $12,100 have been waived; application conversion training applies to first bank only
Communication costs	$1,643.08 per month for two 9,600 baud lines	$3,358.80 per month	$1,925.56 per month
Other		(Optional) $12,600 (10% of $126,000) to lock in price of licensing software on NCR $X for ARP and POD capability	
Performance guarantees	Yes, but only to the extent that we can get out of the contract if service level does not meet our "specs"	They will guarantee both conversions and subsequent performance with substantial financial penalties	No

*Please refer to following page (Exhibit 6).

tried to evaluate the entire company in several areas such as financial viability and size. Finally, in Exhibit 6, we estimated the costs associated with each of the alternatives on a cumulative basis and also by individual product.

To my knowledge we've covered all the bases and now the only thing left is to make the choice and get started with the conversion.

EXHIBIT 6 □ Monthly Item Charges per Account

	Computer Services Inc. (Cincinnati)	Bank Data Corp.	Western Information Systems, Inc.
DDA (account)	.1365	.36	.208*
SAV (account)	.0780	.13	.0875*
CD (cert.)	.250	.13	.0850*
ISL (loan)	.2145	.27	.1750
CML (loan)	.3375	.33	1.350
Mortgage loan (loan)	N/A	.33	.310
G/L	.1040	.40	.750 (account) .006 (item)

Comparative Pricing (monthly charges by application, 000s)†

	Computer Services Inc. (Cincinnati)	Bank Data Corp.	Western Information Systems, Inc.
DDA	$12.4	$15.1	$ 6.2
CRC	2.0	2.0	—
SAV	3.0	5.2	2.6
ATA	1.4	.8	—
CD	2.6	1.7	0.8
ISL	2.0	2.5	1.4
CML	2.7	2.0	7.0
G/L	2.2	1.5	3.0
Miscellaneous	1.3	1.8	7.1
	$29.6	$32.6	$28.1

*Based upon 28 items per account.
†Based upon July 1979 volumes.

Chapter 3 □ IS Technology Organization Issues

Chapter \ Manageable Trend	Strategic Impact	DP/TP/OA	Organization Learning	Make/Buy	Life Cycle	GM/ User/ IS
IS Technology Organization Issues **Chapter 3**		●	●			●
Organizational Issues in IS Development **Chapter 4**	●		●	●		●
Information Systems Planning **Chapter 5**	●		●			●
IS Management Control **Chapter 6**	●		●	●		●
A Portfolio Approach to Information Systems Development **Chapter 7**	●				●	●
Operations Management **Chapter 8**	●			●	●	●
Multinational IS Issues **Chapter 9**		●				●
The IS Business **Chapter 10**	●		●	●		●

The vice president of services of a large durables manufacturing firm recently faced a dilemma. She had just discovered that her request had been denied for a stand-alone word processor to solve operating problems in her fastest growing sales office. It seemed a trivial request, yet its review created a mess, and she felt the decision set a dangerous precedent. The reason given for the denial was incompatibility with the division's information services network. When she had asked why it was incompatible, an incomprehensible series of technical arguments ensued which appeared to have no relationship to her very real productivity problem. Should she fall in line, fight the decision, or resubmit the request as an operating expense instead of a capital expenditure?

A major manufacturing company over the past four years has reduced the hardware processing capacity and staffing of its corporate data processing center by 60 percent. Dramatic growth, however, has taken place in divisional data centers to such an extent that overall corporate data processing expenditures have risen more than 50 percent during the period.

After careful analysis, senior staff of a major decentralized company recommends an orderly dissolution of the company's $25 million data center and the creation of eight smaller diversified data centers over a 30-month period.

INTRODUCTION

These incidents are not unusual. Repeatedly in the past decade technological change has obsolesced previously valid organization structures for information services in many companies and forced (or will force) major reorganization. There are several key reasons for this.

First, for reasons of both efficiency and effectiveness, in the 1980s information services must include office automation, data and voice communications and data processing, managed in a coordinated and, in many situations, an integrated manner. Development of this coordination is not easy in many organizations because each of these activities in the 1960s and 1970s not only had different technical bases but were marketed to the company quite separately and were usually managed independently. Internally, quite different organization structures and practices for handling them developed. Frequently these old organizations include neither staff levels nor the mix of skills necessary to the new technology. The different managerial histories and decision-making habits associated with each of these technologies in the past has made their current integration exceptionally difficult.

Second, it has become increasingly clear that to ensure success information services technologies new to the organization require quite different managerial approaches than those technologies the organization has had more experience with. These different approaches are often facilitated by reorganization. For example, the problems of implementing new office automation technology projects are quite different from those associated with the more mature technologies of data processing.

Third, where the firm's data and computer hardware resources should be located organizationally requires rethinking. The dramatic hardware performance improvements (of all three technologies) in the past decade *permits* this issue to be addressed quite differently today than in the early 1970s.

These dramatic shifts have been facilitated by the technology shift from the vacuum tube to the very large-scale integrated circuits with their vastly improved cost/performance ratios. These productivity changes are continuing as still smaller, more reliable useful circuits are being developed. Exhibit 3–1 shows the cost trends per individual unit and circuit over the past 20

EXHIBIT 3-1 □ Costs and Performance of Electronics[1]

Technology	1958 Vacuum tube	1966 Transistor	1972 IC	1980 LSI*
\$/unit	\$ 8.00	\$ 0.25	\$ 0.02	\$0.001
\$/logic	160.00	12.00	200.00	.05
Operation time	16×10^{-3}	4×10^{-6}	40×10^{-9}	200×10^{-12}

* Large-scale integrated circuit.

years, trends which will continue for the next decade. The cost reduction and capacity increases caused by these changes have reduced computer hardware cost as a fraction of total IS department cost below 30 percent in most large information services environments. Today, computer cost often does not exceed corporate telecommunications expense and for many firms is significantly less than software development and maintenance charges. Equally significant, this technology has permitted development of stand-alone minicomputer systems or office automation systems which can be tailored to provide specific service for any desired location.

This changed technology has permitted a dramatic shift in both the type of information services being delivered to users and the best organizational structure for delivering them. This structure has evolved and will continue to involve not only the coordination of data processing, teleprocessing, and office automation but also redeployment of both the physical location and organizational placement of the firm's technical and staff resources that provide information services. By technical resources we mean items such as computers, word processors, private telephone exchanges, and intelligent terminals. In staff resources we include all the individuals responsible for either operating these technologies, developing new applications, or maintaining them.

Special Nontechnical Information Services Environmental Factors

Today, several noncomputer technology related issues have propelled the need for reexamination of how information services can be most effectively organized inside the firm. The most important of those issues are the following:

1. An increasing shortage of competent, skilled people in the United States to translate this technology into ongoing systems and processes within organizations. These shortages, severe in 1982, will worsen in the coming decade for the following reasons:

[1] W. D. Frazer, "Potential Technology Implications for Computers and Telecommunications in the 1980's," *IBM Systems Journal* 18, no. 2, pp. 333–36.

   a. The number of individuals reaching their 18th birthday in the 20 years between 1978 and 1998 is estimated to plunge by 27 percent.
   b. The 15 percent decline in Scholastic Aptitude Test scores in the past decade and the reworking and simplification of college freshman curricula.
   c. The shrinking availability of professional information systems curriculum as potential faculty choose industry over university careers. In the spring of 1982 over 100 unfilled openings in information systems existed in major universities.
2. The development of highly reliable, cheap, digital telecommunications systems in the United States and expanding growth in Europe. The economics and reliability of worldwide telecommunications, however, are not consistent with the United States and Canada representing unique environments for the immediate future. In Western Europe, tariffs run an order of magnitude greater than that of U.S. tariffs, often coupled with inordinate installation delays once an order is planned. However, as European countries better coordinate their government-owned system they may develop a more cost-effective environment. In Latin America and other parts of the globe, these problems are further compounded by reliability problems. For example, one South American company was forced to shut down a sophisticated online system supporting multiple branches because of unplanned, unacceptable communication breakdowns (sometimes more than 24 hours in duration). In another situation, the company was able to achieve acceptable reliability only by gaining permission to construct and maintain its own network of microwave towers.
3. Legitimate demand for information services support by users continues to vastly exceed available supply. Supplies of cost-justified applications waiting to be implemented and exceeding available staff resources by three or more years tend to be the norm rather than the exception. This has created widespread user frustration. Further, perceived unsatisfactory support and unhappy interpersonal contacts with the central information services organization continue to persist. This has increased users' natural desire to gain control over this aspect of their work. The new technologies increasingly permit users to gain this control. In addition, users' confidence in their ability to run a computer (through personal experience, such as a home APPLE, for example) is not only growing but is likely to continue to grow (admittedly an often unwarranted self-confidence).
4. A fundamental conceptual shift has occurred in computer-based systems design philosophy. The prevailing practice in the 1960s and early 1970s involved writing computer programs which intermixed data processing instructions and data elements within the computer program structure. In the 1980s world, the management of data elements is

clearly separated from the computer program instructions. The implementation of this shift has placed enormous pressure on information services organizations as they balance investing human resources in new systems developments versus redesign of old systems, while ensuring reliable operation of the old systems until the updated ones can be installed.

The combination of these items with changing hardware economics has meant that organization structures correctly designed in the early 1970s may be seriously flawed for the 1980s and that a major reappraisal is in order. The succeeding sections of this chapter will cover the need for, and challenges in, merging the disparate technologies, the different approaches to assimilating as IS technology (depending on the organization's familiarity with it, and the issues involved in deciding on an approximate centralization/decentralization balance of data and hardware.

MERGING THE ISLANDS OF IS TECHNOLOGY

The problems in speedily integrating the three technologies of data processing, telecommunications, and office automation are largely a result of the very different management practices relating to these technologies (as shown in Exhibit 3–2); the following paragraphs analyze these differences in more depth.

In 1920 an operational style of information services in most corporations—elements of which continue to this day—was in place. The manager and his secretary were supported by three forms of information services, each composed of a different set of technology. For word processing, the typewriter was the main engine for generating legible words for distribution. A file cabinet served as the main storage device for output, and the various organization units were linked by secretaries moving paper from one unit to another. Data processing, if automated at all, was dependent upon card-sorting machines to develop sums and balances, using punched cards as input. The cards served as memory for this system. The telecommunications system involved wires and messages that were manipulated by operator control of electromechanical switches to connect parties. The telecommunication system had no storage capacity.

Also in 1920, as shown in Exhibit 3–3, the designer of each of the three islands had significantly different roles. For word processing the office manager directed the design, heavily influenced by the whim of his or her manager. Although office system studies were emerging, word processing was primarily a means of facilitating secretarial work. The prime means of obtaining new equipment was through purchasing agents and involved selecting typewriters, dictaphones, and file cabinets from a wide variety of medium-sized companies. Standardization was not critical. Data processing

EXHIBIT 3–2 □

Functions of the technology	1920 islands of technology			1965 islands of technology			1980 islands of technology		
	Word processing	Data processing	Communi-cation	Word processing	Data processing	Communi-cation	Word processing	Data processing	Communi-cation
Human-to-machine translation	Shorthand/dictaphone	Form/keypunch	Phone	Shorthand/dictaphone	Form/keypunch	Phone	Shorthand/dictaphone/terminal	Terminal	Phone/terminal
Manipulation of data	Typewriter	Card sort	Switch	Typewriter	Computer	Computer	Computer	Computer	Computer
Memory	File cabinet	Cards	(None)	File cabinet	Computer	(None)	Computer	Computer	Computer
Linkage	Secretary	Operator	Operator	Secretary	Computer	Computer	Computer	Computer	Computer

EXHIBIT 3–3 □

Roles of use	1920 islands of technology			1965 islands of technology			1980 islands of technology		
	Word processing	Data processing	Communi-cation	Word processing	Data processing	Communi-cation	Word processing	Data processing	Communi-cation
Designer	Office manager	Card designer	AT&T	Office system analyst	System analyst	AT&T	System analyst	System analyst	System analyst
Operator	Secretary	Machine operator	AT&T	Secretary	Operator	AT&T	Manager/secretary/editor	Manager/secretary/operator	Manager/secretary/AT&T
Maintainer	Many companies	Single supplier	AT&T	Many companies	Single supplier	AT&T	Many com-panies or single supplier	Multiple suppliers	AT&T/other
User	Manager	Accountant	Manager	Manager	Manager/accountant	Everybody	Everybody	Everybody	Everybody

was the domain of the controller-accountant, and the systems design activity was carried out by either the chief accountant or a card systems manager whose job it was to design the protocols for the flow of information to the processing steps. Both data processing and teleprocessing were sufficiently complex and expensive that they required that managers develop an explicit plan of action.

However, a key difference between data processing and telephones, starting in the 1920s, was that the service of data processing was normally purchased and maintained as a system from one supplier. Thus, from the beginning, a systems relationship existed between buyer and seller. Teleprocessing, however, evolved as a purchased service. As AT&T had made available a network of cheaper inner-city telephones, companies responded by ordering the phones, and the utility developed a monopoly of the phone system. All three islands, therefore, were served in a different manner in 1920; one by many companies, one by a single systems supplier, and one by a public utility.

In 1965 the servicing and management of all three islands was still institutionalized in the 1920s pattern. Word processing had a design content but was still very much influenced by the manager and centered around the secretary. Services, such as typewriters and reproducing systems, were purchased as independent units from a range of competitors offering similar technology. There was little long-term planning, with designs and systems evolving in response to new available technical units. Data processing, however, had emerged as an ever more complex management process. It was dominated by a serious evaluation of major capital investments in computers and software as well as multiyear project management of the design and development of systems support. In addition, extensive training sessions for all employees and users were required to effectively take advantage of the productivity of the new system. At times, even the corporate organization was changed to accommodate the new potential and problems caused by computer technology. For communications, however, in 1965 AT&T completely dominated the provision of communication service and, from a user's perspective, its management was a passive purchase problem. In some organizations managing communications implied placing three-minute hourglasses by phones to reduce length of calls.

Today, however, the management concerns for word processing and teleprocessing have become integrated with those of data processing for three important reasons. First, these areas also now require large capital investments, large projects, large complex implementation, and extensive user training. Further, it has become increasingly possible for significant portions of all three services to be purchased from a single supplier. The managers of these activities, however, have had no significant prior expertise in handling this type of problem. For office automation, a special problem is the move from multiple vendors with small individual dollar purchases to one vendor that will provide integrated support. The size of the purchase decisions and the complexity of the applications are several orders of magnitude larger and more complex than those faced a decade ago. For telecommunications the problem revolves around breaking the psychology of relying on a purchased service decision from a public utility and instead looking at multiple sources for large capital investment decisions. In both cases, this represents a sharp departure from past practices and creates needs for a type of management skill which 15 years ago was added to the data processing function.

The second linkage to data processing is that, increasingly, key sectors of all three components are physically linked together in a network; consequently, the problems of one component cannot be addressed independently of the problems of the other two. For example, in one manufacturing company the same WATS line over a 24-hour period is used to support online data communications, normal voice communication, and, finally, an electronic, mail message switching system.

The situation is complicated by the fact that today, for each of the three islands, a dominant supplier is attempting to market his product position as the natural technological base from which the company can evolve into coordinated automation of the other islands. For example, IBM is attempting to extend its data processing base into products supporting office automation and communications. AT&T is attempting to extend its communications base into products supporting data processing and office automation. Xerox is attempting to expand its office automation effort into communications and data processing.

In our judgment, failure to constructively address these management issues poses great risk to an organization. We believe that over the next few years most organizations will consolidate at least policy control, and perhaps management of the islands, in a single information services unit. The key reasons for this include:

1. Decisions in each area now involve large amounts of money and complex technical/cost evaluations. Similar staff backgrounds are needed to do the appropriate analysis in each case.
2. Great similarity exists in the type of project management skills and staff needed to implement applications of these technologies.
3. Many systems require combining these technologies into integrated networks to handle computing, telecommunications, and office automation in an integrated way.

ORGANIZATIONAL PATTERNS OF MANAGING THE TECHNOLOGIES

Organizationally, there are multiple paths which can be followed in effecting the merger of the three islands of technologies as a firm moves toward a merged information services function. The three most common paths are identified below.

Merging Data Processing and Telecommunications

It is clear why data processing and teleprocessing of data merged under DP leadership some years ago in many organizations. In those organizations early data processing applications had to support multisite situations; thus, the DP staff was forced to become conversant with the technical aspects of data communication. Expertise subsequently was developed to deal with minimizing the changes caused by the Bell telephone company rate structure and to resolve the technical issues of getting terminals to communicate to computers. In the early 1970s the technical issues were formidable because there was a clear dichotomy between voice and data communication. The Bell system was designed for voice, and converting it to data transmission was a challenge requiring significant capital investment to obtain quality digital signals between computer-oriented systems. In the mid-1970s, technical changes in the way information was represented to a telecommunications systems permitted voice and data to be dealt with similarly. On several nontechnical dimensions, however, initially they continued to pose dissimilar management problems: voice (the telephone), a purchased service, was still a carefully regulated utility, while data communications demanded increased sophistication in evaluating capital investments in complex technologies from multiple vendors. However, as the size of data communications has exploded, the economic advantages of merging voice and data communications have become significant. Increasingly, the trend is to merge voice and data communications policy and operations in a single department, typically located within the DP department. For example, a large bank recently installed a system to manage voice and data traffic by controlling switches and line utilization. The system reduced their communication bill 35 percent, with improved service to both the data processing effort and voice communication.

Merging Telecommunications and Office Automation

The new technology of the 1970s facilitated the marriage of word processing and office automation to telecommunications. Designers of word processor equipment could now include in work stations the ability to communicate to other work stations as well as to central storage devices through telecommunications systems. These features permitted word processors in the early 70s to quickly emerge, not as automated typewriters but as the basic building block of an automated office with the potential to link the manager to word storage files, other managers, and to data files. This has been vastly simplified by inclusion in the telecommunications system of storage capacity. Now, two parties do not have to be linked simultaneously. Rather, communication can occur through installation of an office station which retains and assembles messages and responses. For some organizations, acquisition of this capability has been an accidental by-product of acquiring systems to improve word processing. However, this capability has often subsequently equaled or exceeded in importance the productivity gained by introducing word processing. The real impact of these linkages is only beginning to be widely exploited today in relation to their potential. Their development is complicated and slowed when organizational distance exists between telecommunications and office automation.

Merging Data Processing and Office Automation

A less frequent linkage today is that between data processing and word processing. This path has been followed by technologically innovative DP managers through extension of their terminals for data processing into remote sites. These managers learned to move words (as opposed to numeric data) through computers from one site to another. As their experience grew, these innovators found a great demand for systems which could store and forward words to other sites. Often, the remote terminals evolved to become more word than numeric data communicators. As word processing software developed, these DP managers upgraded their terminals to include WP activities. Thus DP assimilated all communications, voice and data, and initiated word processing. This pattern's success has been determined by whether the mature DP organization has been able to develop the sensitivity to nurture the new technologies instead of smothering them with excessive controls.

In summary, at present a wide array of organization patterns are possible as an organization advances toward the totality of information services. We see this heterogeneity as transitional, with the eventual merger of these islands into a central hub occurring in most organizations; certainly for policy making, planning, and control purposes, and in many settings, for line control and execution. The timing of these moves in any organization is situation dependent, involving current corporation structure and leadership style, speed at which the firm has been staying modern in these technologies, individual retirement plans, current development priorities, and so forth.

PHASES OF TECHNOLOGY ASSIMILATION

The merger of these technologies is made more complicated by the fact that quite different approaches are needed to manage a technology as an organization gains experience with it. For example, the current mix of approaches for assimilating a relatively mature DP technology may be quite inappropriate for assimilating brand new office automation or brand new DP technologies. Failure to recognize the need for these different approaches has led to both mismanagement of major projects and missed opportunities in terms of projects which should have been done but weren't (no one knew enough about the technology to see the missed opportunity).

Organizations change much more slowly than technology and must grow to productively assimilate new information services. As Nolan and Gibson demonstrated for data processing, an organization progresses through stages in assimilating technology. Recent work in office automation and data processing have discovered this model to be a special case of the broader problem in the learning cycle of adapting a technology to an organization's needs.[2] These studies show the introduction of new information technologies and must be carefully managed or disaster can occur. Distressingly, there has been surprisingly poor transfer of skills learned in managing DP to office automation. A recent study of 37 firms found that 30 had not built on their DP technology experience when moving into word processing and office automation.[3] Of equal importance, over two thirds had not progressed beyond Nolan and Gibson's stage 2 of automation of tasks and experimentation with respect to word processing and were in a state of arrested development.[4] A longitudinal study, tracing an organization's use of information services technologies in all three components, found four phases of evolution which relate to Nolan and Gibson's original stages and are also consistent with organizational change concepts developed by Schien.[5] These phases are characterized in Exhibit 3–4 as Investment/project initiation, Technology learning and adaptation, Rationalization/management control, and Maturity/widespread technology transfer.

The *first phase* is initiated by a decision to invest in a new (to the organization) information processing technology: it involves one or more complementary project development efforts and initial individual training. These projects are characterized by impreciseness in both their costs and ultimate stream of benefits. The resulting systems when looked at retrospectively often seem quite clumsy. Each step of the project life cycle is characterized by much uncertainty, and considerable learning takes place. The second phase seems to follow unless there is a disaster in phase 1, such as vendor failure or poor user involvement which results in Stagnation Block A.

Stagnation Block A typically generates a two-year lag before new invest-

---

[2] James McKenney, "A Field Study on the Use of Computer-Based Technology to Improve Management Control" (Harvard Business School Working Paper 7–46).

[3] Kathleen Curley, "Word Processing: First Step to the Office of the Future? An Examination of Evolving Technology and Its Use in Organizations" (thesis, June 1981).

[4] Cyrus F. Gibson and Richard L. Nolan, "Managing the Four Stages of EDP Growth," *Harvard Business Review* (January–February 1974).

[5] Edgar Schien, "Management Development as a Process of Influence," *Industrial Management Review* 2 (1961) pp. 59–77.

EXHIBIT 3-4 □ Phases of Technological Use

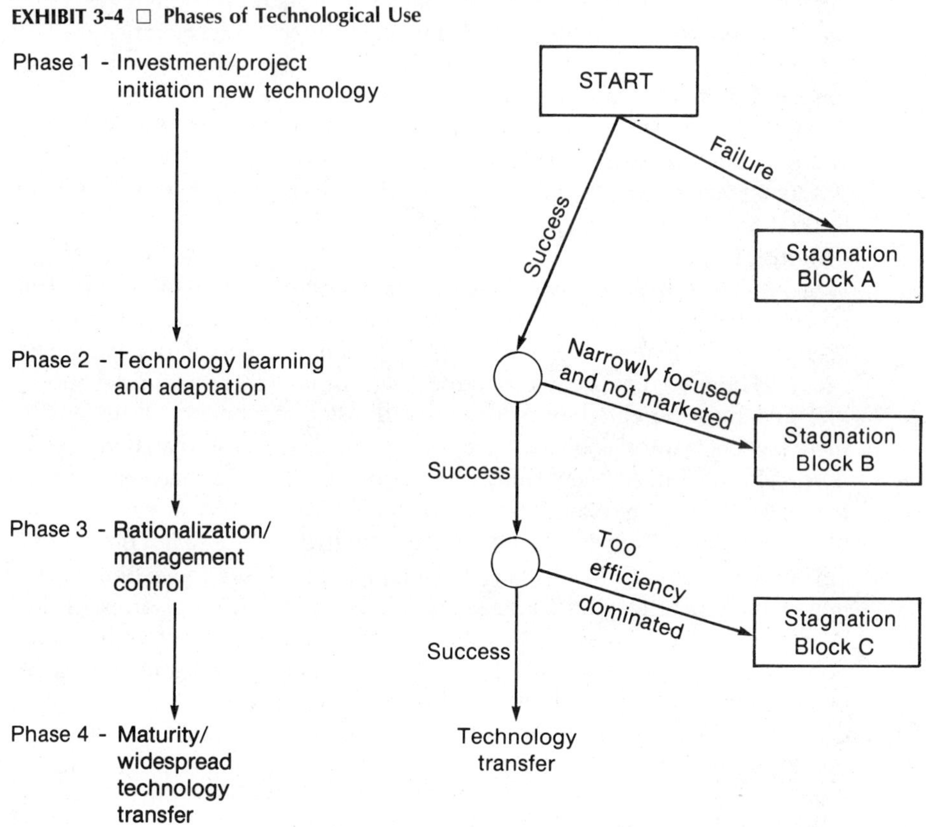

ments in this technology are tried again—normally along with a complete change of personnel. The decision to disinvest normally is a result of there being increased work and little benefit from the system; sources of these problems may be vendor failure, lack of real management attention, incompetent project management, or merely bad choice. Rarely are the problems leading to Stagnation Block A recognized quickly. The complexity and time requirements of implementing new information technology normally hide understanding of the developing failure for 18 to 36 months. The failure typically is not a clear technological disaster but rather an ambiguous situation which is perceived as adding more work to the organization with little perceived benefit. Hence, rejection of the system follows. All projects studied which aborted had significant cost overruns. Each failure created anxieties and prevented development of coordinated momentum. Typically, organizations frozen in this state end up purchasing more services of a familiar technology and become relatively adept at adapting this technology to their use but become vulnerable to obsolescence.

The *second phase* involves learning how to adapt the technology to particular tasks beyond those identified in the initial proposal. Again, as learning takes place, the actual stream of benefits coming from the projects in this phase are often quite different from those anticipated. Again, retrospectively, the resulting systems look clumsy. The project life cycles in this phase, although not characterized by great technical problems, tend to be hard to plan. In none of 37 office automation sites studied was the first utilization of technology implemented as originally planned.[6] In each case, significant learning took place during implementation. If the second phase is managed in an adaptive manner that permits managers to capture, develop, and refine new understanding of how this technology could be more helpful, the organization moves to phase 3. Failure to learn from the first applications, and to effectively disseminate this learning, leads to Stagnation Block B.

A typical Stagnation Block B situation occurred in a large manufacturing company and involved automation of clerical word processing activities which were under the control of a very cost-conscious accounting function. Highly conservative in its approach to technology in data processing, the firm had developed automated accounting systems centrally controlled in a relatively outmoded computer operating system and had yet to enter into data base systems. Having focused on word processing only to do mass mailing in order to save costs, they forfeited additional benefits. After three years of use, mass mailing is the only activity on their system. They are presently reviewing a proposal for microcomputers as executive aids which could be done by their word processors, but the organization is frozen into their use on only mass mailing.

Phase 3 typically involves a change in the organization, continued evolution of the uses of technology to ones not originally considered, and, most important, development of precise controls guiding the design and implementation of systems which use these technologies (to ensure that later applications can be done more cost efficiently than the earlier one). In this phase, the various aspects of the project life cycle are shaken down with the roles of IS and user becoming clearer and the results more predictable.

If, in phase 3, control for efficiency does not excessively dominate and room for broader objectives of effectiveness is left, then the organization moves into a *phase 4,* which involves broad-based communication and implementation of technology to other groups in the organization. Stagnation Block C is reached when excessive controls are developed, which are so onerous as to inhibit the legitimate profitable expansion of the use of technology. An example of Stagnation Block C with respect to data processing is the case of a manufacturing company which entered into large scale centralization with distributed input systems. To justify the expense of

[6] Curley, "Word Processing."

the new operating system, it focused significant attention on gaining all the benefits of a very standardized, highly efficient production shop. In the process of gaining this efficiency, the organization had become so focused on standard procedures and efficiency that it lost its ability and enthusiasm for innovation and change with respect to this technology, and it began to actively discourage users. Further, the rigorous protocols of these standard programs irritated their users and helped set the stage for surreptitious local office automation experimentation (phase 1 in a different technology). Too rigorous an emphasis on control had prevented logical growth. The first incident described at this chapter's beginning was from that company.

Phase 4 can be characterized as a program of technological diffusion. Here, firms take experience gained in one operating division and expand its use throughout the corporation.

Quite naturally, as time passes, new technologies will emerge which offer the opportunity either to move into new applications areas or to restructure old ones (see Exhibit 3–4). Each of the three components of information services is thus confronted over time with a series of waves of new technologies and, at any point in time, must adapt different approaches to managing and assimilating each, as each is in a different phase. For example, in 1981, a manufacturing company studied was in phase 4 in terms of its ability to conceptualize and deal with enhancements to its batch systems over a multiyear period. At the same time, it was in phase 3 in terms of organizing protocols to solidify control over the efficiencies of its online inquiry and data systems whose growth had exploded in the past several years. It had recently made an investment in several word processing systems and was clearly in phase 1 with respect to this technology. Finally, it had just been decided that communications was an important technology to deal with and was at the beginning of phase 1 in terms of considering how to merge data and voice communication.

It requires great subtlety for the IS organization to deal with the quite different control and management problems associated with each phase. One must simultaneously be an innovator, marketer, and controller for different technologies. The phsychological attitudes are so different for these phases that one large consumer products company has found it effective to have two development groups, one for phase 1 and 2 technologies and one for phase 3 and 4 technologies. The controls, aptitudes, and interests of each group are quite different.

As the islands of technology merge, it is critical that the dominant phase 3 approach being used in the technology of one island not be blindly and incorrectly applied to the phase 1 and phase 2 technologies in that island or to the phase 1 and 2 technologies of another island. Depending on the situation, this may be a reason to speed up or slow down a reorganization leading to the merging of the islands.

PATTERNS OF HARDWARE/DATA DISTRIBUTION

As the three islands of technology merge and as structure and procedures emerge to overcome the problem of managing the phases of technology assimilation, a key organizational question that remains is where the data and hardware elements should be located physically. (The issues associated with the location of development staff will be dealt with in the next chapter.) At one extreme is the organization form which has a large centralized hub connected by telecommunications links to remote input/output devices. At the other extreme is a small or nonexistent hub with most or all data and hardware distributed to users. In between these two extremes lies a rich variety of intermediate alternatives.

The early resolution to this organization structure was heavily influenced by technology. The higher cost per computation of hardware in the early 1960s (when the first large investments in computing were instituted) made consolidation of processing power into large data centers very attractive (large machines having a much lower cost per computation than smaller machines). In contrast, the technology of the early 1980s *permits,* but does not demand, cost-effective organizational alternatives. (In the 1980s, technological efficiency of hardware per se is not a prime reason for having a large central data center.)

To retain market share, the vendors of large computers are suggesting (as the comparative difference in efficiency of large computers versus small ones is eroded) that many members of an organization have a critical need to access the same large data files; hence, the ideal structure of an information service is a large central processing unit with massive data files connected by a telecommunications network to a wide array of intelligent devices (often at great distance). While this is certainly true in many situations, unfortunately the problem is more complex as is discussed below. Key factors influencing resolution of the problems include management control, technology, data factors, professional services, and organizational fit. The impact of each of these factors is discussed in the following text, with Exhibit 3–5 presenting a summary.

Pressures toward a Large Central Hub of a Distributed Network

Multiple pressures, both real and perceived, can generate need for a large hub of a distributed network.

Management Control-Related. The ability to attract, develop, maintain, and manage staffs and controls to assure high-quality, cost-effective opera-

EXHIBIT 3-5 □ Summary of Pressures on Balancing the Hub

Pressures	For increasing the hub	For increasing distribution
Management control	More professional operation Flexible backup Efficient use of personnel	User control User responsiveness Simpler control Local reliability improved
Technology-related	Access large-scale capacity Efficient use of capacity	Small is efficient Telecommunications $ reduced
Data-related	Multiple access to common data Assurance of data standards Security control	Easier access Fit with field needs Data only relevant to one branch
Professional services	Specialized staff Reduced vulnerability to turnover Richer career paths	Stability of work force User career paths
Organizational fit	Corporate style—central Corporate style—functional IS centralized from the beginning	Corporate style—decentralized Business need—multinationals

tion of existing systems is a key reason for a strong central unit. The argument is that a more professional, cheaper, and higher quality operation (from the user's perspective) can be put together in a single large unit than through the operation of a series of much smaller units. This administrative skill was what caused the major decentralized company identified at the beginning of the chapter to not eliminate its corporate data center and move to regional centers. In the final analysis, they were unconvinced that eight small data centers could be run as efficiently in aggregate and, even if they could, that it was worth the cost and trauma to make the transition. They felt the corporate data center permitted, through its critical mass, retention of skills for use corporate-wide which could not be attracted or retained if the company had a series of smaller data centers. They decided instead to keep central the operation and maintenance of all three technologies while emphasizing user input to projects in the design and construction phases through development departments in the several divisions.

Further, provision of better backup occurs through the ability to have multiple CPUs in a single site. When hardware failure occurs in one CPU, switching the network from one machine to another can take place by simply pushing a button. Obviously, this does not address the problems of a major environmental disaster which impacts the entire center.

Technology-Related. The ability to provide very large-scale processing capacity for users who need it, but whose need is insufficient to require their own independent processing system, is another strong reason for a large hub. In a day of rapid explosion in the power of cheap computing, it has become easier for users to visualize doing some of their computing on their own personal computer, such as an APPLE or a stand-alone mini. However, at the same time, some users have other problems, such as large linear programming models and petroleum geological reservoir mapping programs that require the largest available computing capacity. The larger the computer capacity available, the more detail they can profitably build into the infrastructure of their computer programs.

Also, in many firms an opportunity is perceived to exist to better manage aggregate computing capacity in the company thus reducing total hardware expenditures. With many machines present in the organization, if each is loaded to 70 percent, the perception is that there are a vast number of wasted CPU cycles that could be eliminated if the processing was consolidated. Although clearly an important issue in the technology economics of the 1960s, the significance of this as a decision element has largely disappeared in the 1980s.

Data-Related. Another pressure for the large central hub is the ability to provide controlled, multiple-user access to common corporate data files on a need-to-know basis. An absolutely essential need from the early days for organizations such as airlines and railroads, with sharp reductions in storage and processing costs, this access has become economically desirable for additional applications in many other settings. Management of data at the hub can also be a very effective way to control access and thus security.

Professional Services. Development of the large staff which accompanies the large IS data center provides an opportunity to attract and keep challenged a specialized technical staff. The ability to work on challenging problems and share expertise with other professionals, not only to attract them to the firms but to keep them focused on key issues, provides a necessary air of excitement. Existence of these skills in the organization permits individual units to undertake complex tasks as needed without incurring undue risks. Furthermore, when the staff has only limited skills, consolidation of such skills in a single unit permits better deployment from a corporate perspective. Further, the large group's resources at a hub permit more comfortable adaptation to inevitable turnover problems. Resignation of one person in a distributed 3-person group is normally more disruptive than 5 persons leaving a group of 100 professionals.

The large unit provides more potential for the technically ambitious individual, who doesn't want to leave the IS field, to find alternative stimuli and avenues of personal development (perceived technical and professional growth has proven to be one of the key elements which can slow down turnover). This is a critical weapon in postponing the so-called burnout problem.

Organizational Fit. In a centralized organization, the above-mentioned set of factors take on particular weight since they lead to congruency between IS structure and overall corporate structure and help eliminate friction. This point is particularly important for organizations where IS hardware was introduced in a centralized fashion and the company as a whole adapted their management practices to its location in this way. Reversal of such a structure can be tumultuous.

Pressures toward a Small Hub and Primary Distributed Environment

Today, important pressures push toward placing significant processing capacity and data in the hands of the users and only limited or nonexistent processing power at the hub of the network.

Management Control-Related. Most important among these pressures is that such a structure better satisfies the user's expectation of control. The ability to handle the majority of transactions locally is consistent with one's desire to maintain a firm grip on their operation. The concept of locally managed data files suggest that the user will be the first person to hear about deviations from planned performance of the unit and hence have an opportunity to analyze and communicate his or her understanding of what has transpired on a planned basis. Further, there now exists a greater number of user managers with long experience in IS activities who have an understanding of systems and their management needs. These individuals are justifiably confident in their ability to manage IS hardware and data.

Also, the user is offered better guarantees of stability in response time by being removed from the hourly fluctuations in demand on the corporate network. The ability to implement a guaranteed response time on certain applications has turned out to be a very important feature from the user's perspective.

This distribution of hardware provides a way to remove or insulate the user from the more volatile elements of the corporate chargeout system. It permits the user to better predict in advance what the costs are likely to be (therefore reducing the danger of having to describe embarrassing negative variances), and not infrequently, it appears to offer the possibility of lower costs.

Distribution of processing power to the user offers a potential for reduction of overall corporate vulnerability to a massive failure in the corporate data center. A network of local minis can keep key aspects for an operation going during a service interruption at the main location. A large forest products company decentralized to local fabricators all raw material and product decisions through installation of a mini system. This reduced the volatility of online demand at the corporate computer center and permitted the service levels to both corporate and distributed users to rise.

A simpler operating environment from the user's perspective is possible in the distributed network both in terms of feeding work into the system and in terms of the construction of the operating system. The red tape of routing work to a data entry department is eliminated, and the procedures can be naturally built right into the ongoing operation of the user department. (Surprisingly, in some cases regaining this control has been viewed with trepidation by the user.) Similarly, with the selection of the right type of software, the problems in interfacing with the basic operating system can be dramatically simplified (to use the jargon of the trade, they are "user friendly").

Technology-Related. The superior efficiency of large central processing units in comparison to that of much smaller units was true in the early days. Today, however, several important changes have occurred in the external environment:

The economics of CPUs and memories in relation to their size have altered, and the common rule that the power of computers rises as the square of the price no longer applies.[7]

The economics of Grosch's law was never claimed to apply to peripheral units and other elements of the network. The CPU and internal memory costs are a much smaller percentage of the total hardware expenditures today then they were in 1970.

The percentage of hardware costs as a part of the total IS budget has dropped dramatically over the past decade as personnel costs, telecommunications costs, and other operating and development costs have become more significant. Efficiency of hardware utilization consequently is not the burning issue it was a decade ago. When these factors are taken in conjunction with the much slower improvement in telecommunications costs (11 percent/year) and the explosion of user needs for online access to data files which can be generated and stored locally, in many cases the economic case for a large hub has totally reversed itself.

As more systems are purchased rather than made, the users are better informed in the procedures of how to select and manage a local system.

Data-Related. Universal access by users to all data files is not a uniformly desired goal. Telecommunications costs and the very occasional

[7] Edward G. Cale, Lee L. Gremillion, James L. McKenney, "Price/Performance Patterns of U.S. Computer Systems *ACM* (April 1979). The statement is commonly referred to as Grosch's law.

needs of access to some data files by users, other than at the site where it is generated, means that in many settings it is uneconomical or undesirable to manage all data in a way in which central access is possible. Further, inability to relate data may be in accordance with corporate strategy. A case in point is the large company mentioned at the beginning of the chapter which recently considered abandoning its corporate computing center. The corporate computing center was a service bureau for its eight major divisions (all development staff resided in the divisions). No common application or data file existed between even two of the divisions in the company (not even payroll). If the company's survival depended on it, it could not identify in under 24 hours what its total relationship as a company was with any individual customer. In senior management's judgment, this lack of data relationships between divisions appropriately reinforced the company's highly decentralized structure. No pressure existed anywhere in the organization for change. The corporate computing center, an organizational anomaly, was conceived simply as a cost-efficient way of permitting each division to develop its network of individual systems.

It is exceedingly easy for technicians to suggest interesting approaches for providing information which has no practical use, and the suggestion may even threaten soundly conceived organization structures.

Professional Services. Moving functions away from the urban environment toward more rural settings offers the opportunity to reduce employee turnover, the bane of metropolitan area IS departments. While the recruiting and training process is very complicated to administer in these settings, once the employees are there, if sensitively managed, the relative lack of headhunters and nearby attractive employers reduces turnover pressures.

When the IS staff is closely linked to the user organization, it becomes easier to plan employee promotions which may take technical personnel out of the IS organization and put them into other user departments. This is critical for a department with low employee turnover, as the former change agents begin to develop middle-age spread and burnout symptoms. Two-way staff transfers between user and IS is a way to deal with this problem and to facilitate closer user IS relations.

Organization Fit. Also important in many settings, the controls implicit in the distributed approach better fit the realities of the corporation's organization structure and general leadership style. This is particularly true for highly decentralized structures (or organizations which wish to evolve in this fashion) and/or organizations which are highly geographically diverse.

Finally, highly distributed facilities fit the needs of many multinational structures. While airlines reservation data, shipping container operations, and certain kinds of banking transactions must flow through a central location, in many settings the overwhelming amount of work is more effectively managed in the local country, with communication to corporate headquarters being either by telex, mailing tapes, transmitting bursts of data over a telecommunications link, or some other way, depending on the organization's management style, size of unit, etc.

Assessing the appropriateness of a particular hardware/data configuration for an organization is very challenging. On one hand, for all but the most decentralized of organizations, there is a strong need for central control over standards and operating procedures. The changes in technology, however, both permit and make desirable in some settings the distribution of the *execution* of significant amounts of the hardware operations and data handling.

SUMMARY

The combination of the trend to merge technologies and the ability to distribute data and hardware must be carefully managed because they are interdependent. Since firms come from different positions, history, culture, and business strategy, they may reach radically different balances. At present, the business strategy and corporate culture heavily dominate the hardware/data distribution issue, while current technology and business strategy dominate the speed of the merging issue. Further, for firms where IS is strategic, such as banking or insurance, there is a strong trend to accelerate the merging of all services into single-office support systems. Support industries can move more slowly. On the other hand, some banks (where IS is clearly strategic) will continue to have centrally supported systems while others will have distributed stand-alone systems providing similar support. A key reason for the difference will lie in the culture of the bank, its geography, and other factors relating to its business practices.

Reexamination of the deployment of hardware/software resources for the information services function is a priority item in the 1980s. Changing technology economics, merging of formerly disparate technologies with different managerial traditions, and the problems of managing each of the phases of IS technology assimilation in different ways have obsolesced many appropriate 1970 organization structure decisions. To ensure that these issues are being appropriately addressed, we believe five steps must be taken.

1. Establishing, as part of the objectives of a permanent corporate group, the development of a program to manage change. This policy group must assess the current program toward merging the technology islands, guide the process of balancing the desires for a strong hub against the advantage of a strongly distributed approach, and ensure that different technologies are being guided in an appropriate way.

2. The policy group must ensure that uniformity in management practice is not pushed too far and that appropriate diversity is accommodated.

Even within a company, it is entirely appropriate that different parts of the organization will have developed, and will continue, different patterns of distributed support for hardware and data. Different phases of development, with respect to specific technologies, geographical distance from potential central service support, etc., are valid reasons for different approaches.

3. The policy group must show particular sensitivity to the needs of the international activities. Without great care, it is inappropriate to enforce common approaches to these problems internationally, either for companies operating primarily in a single country or for the multinational which operates in many countries. Each country has different cost and quality structure of telecommunications, different levels of IS achievement, different reservoirs of technical skills, different culture, etc. These differences are likely to endure for the foreseeable future. What works in the United States often will not work in Thailand.

4. The policy group must ensure that it addresses its issues in a broad strategic fashion. The arguments and reasoning leading to a set of solutions are more complex than simply the current economics of hardware or which persons should have access to certain data files. Corporate organization structure, corporate strategy and direction, availability of human resources, and current operating administrative processes are all additional critical inputs. Both in practice and in writing, the technicians and information theorists have tended to oversimplify a very complex set of problems and options. A critical function of the group is to ensure adequate R&D investment (in phases 1 and 2). A special effort must be taken to ensure appropriate investment occurs in experimental studies, pilot studies, and development of prototypes. Similarly, the group must ensure that proven expertise is being distributed appropriately within the firm to appropriate places that are often unaware of its existence or potential.

5. The policy group must ensure an appropriate balance is struck between long-term and short-term needs. A distributed structure optimally designed for the technology and economics of 1981 may fit the world of 1989 rather poorly. Often it makes sense to postpone feature development or to design a clumsy approach in today's technology which will be quite efficient in the anticipated technologies of the late 1980s. As a practical matter, the group will work on these issues in a continuous, iterative fashion rather than implementing a revolutionary change.

Case 3–1 □ Metropolitan National Bank (A)*

In early March 1980, David Adams was reviewing a comprehensive proposal for a major office automation pilot project that his staff had prepared. Adams, a senior vice president, was in charge of the Information Systems Division of Metropolitan National Bank. He was personally convinced that the new word processing and electronic mail technologies had enormous potential for improving both the productivity and the effectiveness of the bank's operations. In fact, Adams himself had established and funded the four-person Office Automation Group that had produced the proposal he was now considering.

Yet Adams was uncertain about the shape and direction the proposal had taken, and he was deeply concerned that the bank's senior management might not be willing to spend the more than $700,000 that the pilot project potentially called for. As Adams thought about the project, he commented:

> You know, we *have* to get going with office automation, because if we don't I know our users will. It's important for us to keep them from making bad, expensive decisions *now*.
>
> The problem today is that senior management has turned the budget climate around on us. Several months ago things looked great, but now everyone is looking for things to cut and defer. I know the pilot project is really R&D, but I'm afraid my boss is looking for projects that will produce immediate cost savings.

BACKGROUND ON THE INFORMATION SYSTEMS DIVISION

The Metropolitan National Bank was one of the largest commercial banks in the United States. The bank was organized primarily around product/market units, although its "back office," or Operations Group, was a centralized functional unit. The Information Systems Division (ISD) was one of eight divisions within the Operations Group. With over 500 full-time employees, the ISD was basically responsible for the management of all major computer operations and systems development throughout the bank. David Adams had three principal operating units reporting to him (see Exhibit 1 for a simplified organization chart):

* This case was prepared as a basis for class discussion rather than to illustrate either effective or ineffective handling of an administrative situation.

EXHIBIT 1 □ Partial Organization Chart for Information Systems Division in March 1980

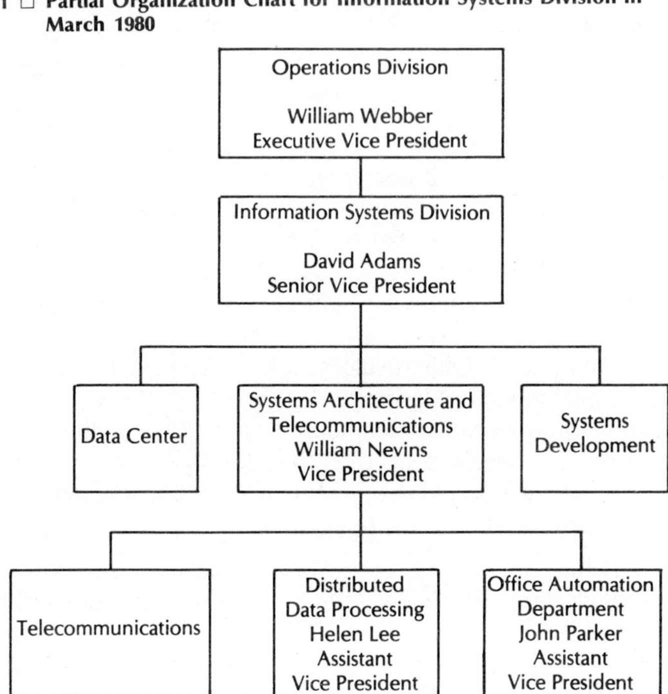

The Data Center, which handled the day-to-day operations of the bank's computers and peripheral hardware.

Systems Development, which was responsible for the design, development, and maintenance of all the basic software application systems.

Systems Architecture and Telecommunications (SAT), which was charged with developing an internal time-sharing and distributed data processing network to cope with a rapidly growing number of minicomputer systems, customer-oriented terminals, and internal information transfer systems.

Adams characterized Metropolitan National as a moderately decentralized organization with respect to data processing. ISD handled almost all of the bank's general-purpose computing and most of the specialized applications as well. In addition, the ISD was responsible for all of the bank's voice and data communication systems, which were managed by the Systems Architecture and Telecommunications group.

David Adams had been hired from outside the bank to head ISD in mid-1978. With over 20 years' experience in DP management in several very large organizations, Adams had inherited a department ripe for a major overhauling. ISD's credibility within the bank had not been strong, and its management team was relatively weak. Consequently, Adams viewed his "personnel management" task as among his most important, and much of his time and energy during his first two years had been devoted to finding and building a strong team of middle managers within ISD. At the same time, he had emphasized to his staff the importance of building positive working relationships with ISD's internal clients throughout the bank.

Adams quickly discovered that one of the bank's major systems problems was the existence of a large number of independent and incompatible automated systems. Historically, ISD had been quite successful at supporting user systems requests, but that support had been largely reactive and applications oriented, so that, as one manager commented, "We have at least *sixteen* different online systems, and most of them can't talk to each other."

At the same time, the bank's marketing divisions were very interested in developing new and more diverse products and services for their customers. By the late 1970s it was becoming increasingly clear that automated systems played a key role in providing the bank with competitive customer services. It was also clear that the various services, often provided by different operating divisions of the bank, must be linked together so that customers could access different systems (i.e., Real Estate Management, Cash Management, and Loan Management) through a single terminal.

Adams had attacked this need for systems integration by rearranging the systems development and management activities within ISD and creating the Systems Architecture and Telecommunications (SAT) group. In mid-1979 he had hired Bill Nevins away from a major paper manufacturer to manage the SAT. Nevins then became responsible for developing an internal data communications network, establishing bankwide data communications standards, and developing a new array of online management support systems.

Within Nevins' SAT group, Helen Lee was responsible for distributed data processing systems. She viewed her role primarily as that of a consultant to users interested in developing specific automated applications. However, Lee was keenly aware of the importance of maintaining a reasonable degree of centralized control over the kinds of applications that were developed. As she put it:

> Users are so short-term oriented; they react to vendor pitches, and they don't realize how often vendors fold up or fail to provide promised software support. So we provide a data base perspective and work toward solutions that meet their needs, in the context of our interest in compatibility, consistency, and long-lasting vendor support. We work *with* users, in a *team* approach to problem solving.

Lee had known for some time that there was extensive user interest in word processing and other office automation technologies, as well as in more traditional distributed data processing applications. In early 1979, she hired Ruth Kowalski and Bob Bernstein to work specifically on office automation projects. Both of them had extensive data processing experience, and in addition, a particular interest in word processing and other office systems technologies.

Ruth Kowalski, who had a bachelor's degree in education, came to Metropolitan National Bank from a small advertising agency, where she had been the entire data processing department. Prior to that she had worked as a marketing representative at IBM for several years. Most of that work had involved installing small business systems in companies with no prior computer experience.

Bob Bernstein had an undergraduate degree in urban transportation planning and had worked for seven years at the local transit authority before joining the bank. For five of those seven years Bernstein held a series of administrative positions within the agency. He had then moved into data processing, where he had successfully managed several office automation projects. Bernstein had extensive experience training secretarial and clerical personnel in the use of automated time-sharing data processing and word processing systems.

Kowalski and Bernstein quickly became involved in several different office automation projects. For example, Kowalski worked with an outside consulting firm on a time-and-motion study of the secretarial tasks within the bank's trust department. She found the study, which had been initiated by the trust department, to be "rather disappointing. It was a document production study that only looked at word processing. And nothing really came of it."

Meanwhile, Bernstein had become involved in the installation of an IBM 3730 word processor that had already been ordered to help the Economic Forecasting Group produce its weekly internal newsletter. The intent of the project was to link the word processor directly to the reprographics equipment that would produce the newsletter.

While these two projects were not the only ones that Kowalski and Bernstein were involved in, they were typical of the kinds of projects that were evolving within the office automation area. As Kowalski later recalled:

> Everyone was chomping at the bit. We tried to get involved whenever we could. Lots of people were asking for help—mostly related to what kind of equipment to buy. But just about everything we did was straight, traditional word processing.

Meanwhile, in February 1979, David Adams had taken another step toward shifting ISD from a reactive to a proactive mode by hiring John Parker as manager of ISD Planning. Parker came to the bank with eight years of MIS planning and project management experience in two large manufacturing organizations, preceded by three years as an IBM marketing representative. Reporting directly to Adams, Parker quickly began developing a formal five-year plan for ISD. During that process Parker became convinced that office automation technology represented a major source of productivity improvement for the bank. More importantly, he began to feel that ISD was not effectively managing the introduction of office technologies:

> I could see that we were really being controlled by one vendor. I knew we could get better equipment for less cost, and I tried to develop a plan that would help us select systems in a more objective manner.
>
> But what I found really frustrating was that I was talking blue sky theory about how we should introduce office automation, while Ruth and Bob were caught up in day-to-day installation problems. I kept inviting them to planning meetings, and they were always too busy to come.

Parker finished the ISD five-year plan in late 1979. He saw the plan as having two broad objectives: to start a regular planning process within ISD, and to open a continuing dialogue with users. Adams was pleased with the document, and he shared Parker's view that it should serve as the basis for ongoing discussions with senior managers throughout the bank. However, Parker suddenly discovered that those senior-level discussions were taking place between Adam and Adams' counterparts in other divisions. There did not seem to be a place for Parker in the ongoing dialogue and he began wondering what role he could play within ISD.

Parker's frustration reached such a peak that he finally confronted Adams and asked for an opportunity to take on line management responsibilities. As a result of that meeting and because of Parker's expressed interest in office automation, Adams and Bill Nevins proposed that Parker head up a new office automation department. Nevins suggested that Parker take on Ruth Kowalski and Bob Bernstein (their present supervisor was in the process of leaving the bank) and report to Helen Lee. Parker balked at reporting to Lee, initially feeling that he should retain his planning responsibilities and treat office automation as an R&D effort under the planning umbrella. After extended discussion and debate, Nevins finally asked Parker to take on the office automation department as a full-time responsibility, reporting directly to him. Nevins also promised Parker that he would be able to hire several additional subordinates as the needs and user demands expanded. Parker accepted the offer, largely because it gave him line responsibilities and a clear mandate to move ahead in an area that he was convinced would have a significant impact on the bank's operations in the next several years.

Nevins and Parker agreed that the office automation department would undertake the following set of tasks:

Assist offices throughout the bank in determining where and how office automation can best be used.

Ensure the selection of systems which are compatible with the bank's overall office automation plan.

Coordinate the development of the user's request through the office automation project life cycle.

Assist the user in selecting the most cost-effective office automation system or equipment.

Monitor the continued cost-effective use of office automation.

Provide technical and software assistance to office automation users.

Provide education in the use of office automation.

During late 1979 and early 1980 the office automation department continued to respond to line managers' requests for general assistance in evaluating and installing word processing equipment. More importantly, however, Parker initiated several new approaches intended to put the group in a more proactive stance.

One of Parker's first actions was to compile a current inventory of word processing applications and equipment already in use within the bank. With little effort Parker and his staff were able to locate 71 existing pieces of equipment. Their compilation (see Exhibit 2) showed 23 separate models of word processing equipment from ten different vendors.

Parker also had his staff work with the bank's Internal Controls Division to define a set of procedures and guidelines that would impose some form of centralized control over the bank's acquisition of additional word processing equipment. (Parker intended eventually to develop an approved vendor list to minimize compatibility problems, to avoid the proliferation of inadequate or unreliable equipment, and to facilitate movement towards a network of WP terminals that could communicate with each other.) Development of the purchasing guidelines was a delicate task, because, as Adams put it, "We don't want to be in the typewriter purchasing business." Eventually the Controls Division and ISD agreed that ISD should become involved any time a potential purchase involved locally programmable equipment. Exhibit 3 contains excerpts from the working document that emerged from this joint effort.

Late in 1979 Parker asked Mary Schneider to join the Office Automation Group. Schneider had been working on employee educational programs within ISD's personnel group. In that capacity she had become closely involved with Bob Bernstein's efforts to train clerical staff in the use of the IBM 3730 equipment. As Schneider recalled:

> I had a background in adult education before I joined the bank in early 1979. Most of what I was doing initially involved writing training manuals for internal use and informing people about outside educational opportunities. Then my boss asked me to help Bob Bernstein train the secretaries in the reception area to use the 3730 terminals. That's when I first got involved with the office automation group. I think John [Parker] asked me to join them because there were several groups I had already worked with whose help they needed. I had a number of relationships that John, Bob, and Ruth didn't have.

EXHIBIT 2 □ Inventory of Metropolitan National Bank Office Automation Equipment

Location	Equipment	Quantity	Number of work stations
Real estate division	Qyx	15	
	IBM MC/ST II	2	
	IBM 6240	1	
Trust department	IBM Memory 50	3	
	IBM 6240	1	3
	IBM MC/ST II	1	
	Qyx—Level IV with Display	1	
Corporate trust	IBM 6240	2	
	IBM MC/ST II	1	
ISD	IBM 3730	1	11
	IBM MC/ST II	1	
	Xerox 850	1	
Purchasing	Qyx—Level I, Level IV	2	
Auditing	A.B. Dick Magna I	1	
Employee activities	A. B. Dick Magna I	1	
MetroCenter	Savin 900 Wordmaster	1	
Administration	Savin 950 Veritext	1	
Urban bank	Savin 950 Veritext	1	
Urban comm.	Wang System 30	1	2
MPD	Wang System 20	1	2
Management recruitment	Xerox 800	1	
	IBM 6/492	1	
International WP	Vydec 1200	1	
	Vydec 1400	1	
	IBM MC/ST I	1	
Government bond	Qyx—Level I	1	
Operations administration	Qyx—Level IV	1	
Branch	Wang System 5A	1	
International operations	Qyx	1	
	DEC WS 212	1	2
	Qyx—Level IV with Display	1	
Risk management	Qyx—Level IV with Display	1	
MNBMG	Qyx—Level IV with Display	1	
Public relations	Qyx—Level IV with Display	1	
MetroLease	Lanier "No Problem"	1	
	Vydec 1146	1	
IOG	Redactron I	4	
	Qyx—Level IV with Display	3	
Investment research	Qyx—Level IV with Display	2	
General administrative	IBM Memory 50	1	
	Xerox 850	1	
	Qyx—Level IV with Display	1	
EDP auditing	IBM Memory 50	1	
Metro marketing	Wang Systems 5—Model II	1	
Corporate banks	Xerox 850	2	
		71	86

EXHIBIT 3 □ Excerpts from Office Automation Purchasing Procedures

Approvals Required

A. A separate Office Automation Authorization Request form (OAAR) must be completed for office automation equipment or service expenses when user units prepare their profit plan for the following year. The form must accompany the profit plan submitted to the Budget Department.

B. All OAARs must be approved by the Head of the Bank or major division and reviewed by the Office Automation Department (OAD) of the Information Systems Division (ISD).

C. All contracts and agreements with vendors of office automation equipment and services must be negotiated by the Office Automation Department of ISD, and final written agreements approved by the Head of ISD and reviewed by the Legal Department.

Contract Negotiations

A. *Requests in profit plan*

Requests for new office automation equipment and services must be prepared on OAAR forms at the time the Banks and major divisions submit their following year's profit plans. Separate requests for office automation expenses must accompany the profit plan and must be approved by the Head of the originating Bank or major division.

The Office Automation Department in ISD will review all requests for technical considerations to ensure that they are consistent with the bank's overall policy regarding rental versus purchase of devices.

No services and/or equipment should be purchased unless an Authorization Request form has been completed and properly approved.

B. *Requests in current year*

An Office Automation Authorization Request (OAAR) must be prepared during the course of the year and approved by the Head of the Bank or Major Division when one of the following situations arises:

1. When the amounts provided in the approved profit plan for the year have been depleted.
2. When office automation expenses will be incurred during the year, and funds were not budgeted for such purpose.

Parker's group met regularly to explore what kinds of approaches they could take to encourage the use of office automation equipment and systems within the bank's operations. Out of these meetings and their individual activities (reading, meeting with vendor sales representatives, visiting other organizations, talking with line managers throughout the bank) the group began to develop the concept of a large-scale pilot project that would enable them and the bank at large to learn first hand the range of office activities that the new technologies could support and enhance.

The group developed several working documents to support their discussions, and to provide them with a means of testing out their ideas with Bill Nevins, David Adams, and line managers outside of ISD. Exhibit 4 contains excerpts from the overview document that defined their rationale for making a major commitment to the new technologies.

EXHIBIT 4 □ Excerpts from Project AIM Preliminary Plan, January 1980

Introduction

This preliminary plan discusses the work required to deliver office automation services to Metropolitan National Bank. The real issue is *productivity*. We are discussing ways of increasing the productivity of people in offices throughout the Bank. But how does office automation increase productivity? By how much? How can it be proven? These are the questions we must answer. It will not be easy, but it *can* be done.

We will deliver office automation services to the Bank in two ways. First, we will provide in-house consulting services to office managers throughout the Bank. These consulting services focus on increasing the productivity of specific offices. Second, we will initiate the AIM Workstation pilot project, which will test the use of multifunction office workstations. This workstation will provide word processing, electronic mail, electronic filing, automated appointment scheduling, and other office functions. This project offers tremendous potential for productivity gains. Another major bank has estimated it will save $25 million per year by installing such a system.

An Office Automation Department has existed for several years, and in 1979, several consulting projects were successfully performed. But we have also witnessed the beginning of an explosion of technological activity in the field of office automation. Demand for office automation services has increased tremendously throughout the Bank. Furthermore, we have embarked upon the development of a bankwide data communication network called MetroLine and future office systems in the Bank will be installed in coordination with the MetroLine plans.

So we recognize the need for a comprehensive office automation plan, and this is the preliminary version. By June 1980 we expect to have a more comprehensive and detailed version of AIM available for review.

I. *Why Office Automation?*

The driving force behind office automation is the need to increase the productivity of the office labor force while decreasing the cost of performing business functions. This need to improve office worker productivity is especially critical at Metropolitan National Bank because most of our employees are office workers.

The Bank's labor costs have grown steadily for the last six years. Figure 1 shows the salary costs of both the official and clerical staff from 1974 through 1979 (1979 4th quarter estimated). The figures shown *do not* include fringe benefit costs.

EXHIBIT 4 *(continued)*

Figure 1 □ Salary Costs at Metropolitan National Bank (base year 1974)

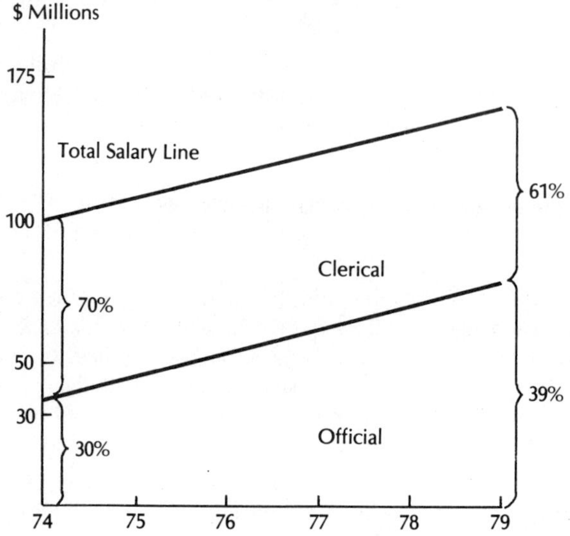

Source: Human Resources Division.

The adjusted annual personnel cost at the Bank increased more than $12 million during this time period. If the inflation costs were included with the salary cost, then this increase would have been even more dramatic. It should be noted that the cost of official staff showed the greatest percentage increase. In 1974, official salaries represented 30 percent of the total labor cost, yet in 1979 official salaries represented 39 percent of the total labor cost.

This increase in labor cost can be compared to the productivity of the labor force over the same period of time. As a rough measure of productivity, Figure 2 compares the year-end total assets of the Bank to the size of the official staff for the year being examined, resulting in an asset/official figure from 1974 through 1979 (June 30th

Figure 2 □ Assets Managed/Official ($ millions)

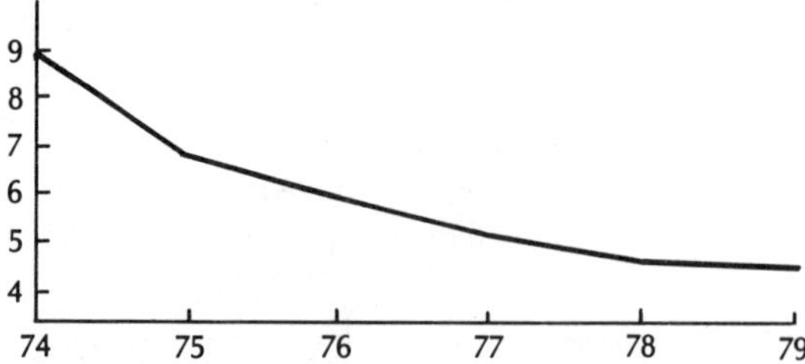

Source: Human Resources Division, and "Metropolitan National Bank Annual Report" for 1974 through 1978.

EXHIBIT 4 *(continued)*

figures used for 1979). The asset amounts were adjusted for inflation, using the Consumer Price Index (base year 1974).

The productivity of the official staff at Metropolitan National Bank, if measured in this fashion, has decreased approximately 17 percent over the time period examined. This decrease has occurred along with an increase in the size of the official staff. If these trends continue, by 1985 the cost of the official staff will have risen by 66 percent, but the ratio of assets to officers will have dropped 45 percent.

Increasing the productivity of the growing official staff is the primary goal of Project AIM.

Until recently, there has been little interest in office automation opportunities. However, due to current cost trends in the industry, and the converging of the computer, data storage, and communications technologies on the office, office automation is now much more attractive, as shown in Figure 3. Communication costs are declining at 11 percent per year, computer logic costs are dropping at 25 percent per year, and computer memory costs are plummeting at a rate of 40 percent per year.

Office automation can potentially increase the productivity of both the official and clerical staff. It will not do this by reducing the number of employees or the cost of these employees. Rather, if office automation is successful, it can reduce the rate of increase of our total labor cost by improving the productivity of the labor force. By increasing the productivity of the labor force at Metropolitan National Bank it will be

Figure 3 □ Technology Cost Trends

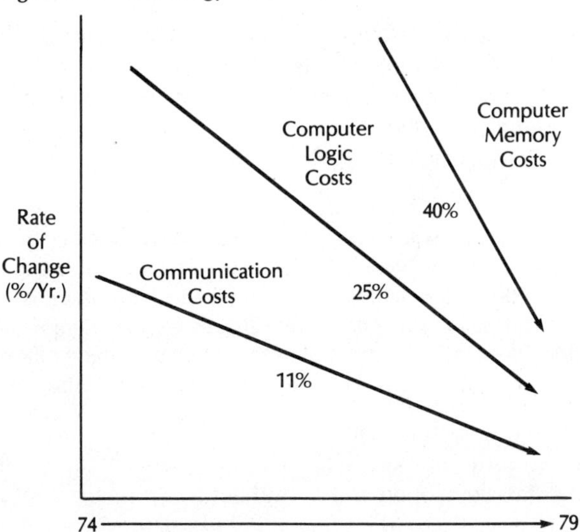

Source: *Datamation,* April 1977.

EXHIBIT 4 ***(concluded)***

Figure 4 □ Salary Costs

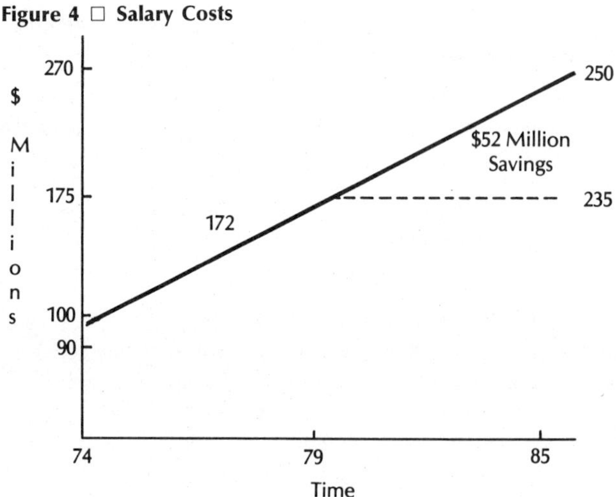

Source: Human Resources Division.

possible to reduce the almost 10 percent annual real salary growth that the Bank has experienced during the last five years.

As Figure 4 shows, if we can reduce the rate of salary growth by 20 percent, the Bank can save $15 million in 1985, and a total of $52 million over the next six years.

The group named the proposed pilot Project AIM (automated information management). Their discussions had led them to a clear realization that what they wanted was an integrated, multifunctional work station that could support a wide range of applications, including not only word processing but data processing, electronic mail, electronic filing, and automated calendar management. As Bob Bernstein put it:

> We don't want to offer just word processing. Word processing by itself is *not* office automation. We're talking about a whole range of office tasks and functions. The 70-plus terminals we have around the bank now cost an average of about $8,100 each. We know we can get far better, more adaptable, multifunctional terminals for about $8,600. Automating these office functions is virgin territory, and that's what is exciting about Project AIM.

Exhibit 5 contains a description of the Project AIM work-station specifications, and a listing of the primary system/vendor performance criteria.

Parker and his staff developed and costed out two possible configurations for Project AIM. Option 1 would involve 35 work stations, with all but six of them remaining within ISD (the other six would be given to David Adams'

EXHIBIT 5 □ AIM Workstation Specifications

The AIM Workstation is an office automation concept which combines the various tools needed by the office staff into one highly integrated module. It will help managers, professionals, and secretaries perform their tasks more productively.

A. Functional description of the AIM Workstation

The AIM workstation will provide both word processing and data processing capability. In addition, it will provide the vital office automation functions of electronic mail, electronic filing, and automated appointment scheduling.

Word processing is the computer-based creation, storage, edit, and printout of text. The AIM Workstation will provide all the standard features available on today's popular WP systems.

Data processing is the input, storage, processing, and output of data via computer programs. The AIM Workstation will provide preprogrammed office functions as well as one or more programming languages, affording office staff or outside programming personnel the ability to create, store, and run programs for processing office data.

Electronic mail involves the automated storing, forwarding, and routing of information. Rudimentary electronic mail systems already exist in the form of cables, TWX, Telex, and facsimile. However, electronic mail is more than just another type of electronic transmission. It involves the creation and editing of information and the storing and forwarding of this information. It provides a value-added electronic in-box. And it permits the multirouting of information.

Electronic filing makes use of computer technology to index for retrieval both internally and externally generated documents. When combined with electronic mail, it provides an extremely powerful information tool for the office.

Automatic appointment scheduling permits meetings to be scheduled for all attendees automatically through AIM Workstations. Queries are made against existing schedules, and confirmations of requests for meeting time are handled by the system, subject to review by the staff members involved. This aspect of the AIM Workstation offers immediate time savings in setting up and attending meetings.

B. Requirements of the system and vendor

1. The AIM Workstations must link to MetroLine. Both data and text will be transmitted throughout the Bank, and MetroLine will be the communication system used.
2. The vendor must be able to show the hardware and software in use today.
3. There must be sufficient built-in security for the system, its programs, and its files.
4. There must be sufficient vendor support to ensure success. This includes training for administrators, programmers, operators, originators, and principals.
5. Minimum reliability by the overall system must be an average time to failure of no less than two months.

EXHIBIT 5 *(concluded)*

6. Minimum availability for the overall system must be no less than 98 percent uptime (9 hours, 48 minutes), from 8 A.M. to 6 P.M.
7. Minimum serviceability for the overall system must be no more than two hours downtime, with either replacements or backups immediately available for terminals.
8. There must be a six-month lease price for the pilot system, with credit accrued toward eventual purchase.
9. There must be a continued lease, purchase, and cancellation option in the pilot contract.
10. Pack-to-pack backup is required.
11. An accounting system must be available on the pilot system to keep track of system performance, usage, and traffic flow.
12. Both full function and limited function terminals should be available. The former will be used for word processing; the latter can be used by principals and other nontypists.
13. A plan must be provided to address future capabilities which are desirable:

    Graphic capability, including charts, diagrams, and plots.

    Photocomposition interface.

    Micrographics interface.

    External message system interface (Telex, TWX, SWIFT, etc.).

    Dictionaries online for spelling, hyphenation, translation.

    FAX interface.

    Voice message storing and forwarding.

    Voice input/output.

boss and several other senior officers in other areas of the bank's Operations Group). Under Option 1, 12 senior ISD managers (including Parker) and each of their secretaries would receive a terminal; the remaining terminals would go to Kowalski, Bernstein, and Schneider, and to two other key managers within ISD.

The second option, and the one preferred by Parker, would bring 74 AIM work stations into the bank. Within ISD the Option 2 configuration would be basically the same as Option 1 (with some additional terminals). Most of the additional terminals would go into the International Operations Division, where ISD was currently deeply involved in a major systems development project. In Parker's view, Option 2 would provide a much stronger test of the concept, since it would involve non-ISD managers and a network of individuals who were in constant communication with each other on matters related to the systems development project. In addition, Dan Rice, head of the International Operations Division, was highly supportive of Project AIM:

> You know, ISD *has* to develop word processing/office automation capabilities, because if they don't, everyone else will. All our departments do is process data; we spend our days answering customer inquiries, and there is no question that automated equipment already exists to help us do it better.
>
> Besides, as people begin to play with the AIM work stations, they'll learn things and think of things they never did before—and that's the kind of benefit you can't write in a proposal.

Parker's staff worked out careful volume and cost projections for both options; their analysis is reproduced in Exhibit 6. For either option the basic plan was for a six-month trial with a detailed post-audit to assess usage frequencies and patterns. The OA (office automation) staff assumed they

EXHIBIT 6 □ Project AIM Word Processing and Electronic Mail (estimated volume specifications)

	Configuration I	Configuration II
Number of work stations	35	74
Number of letter printers	6	12
Number of high-speed line printers	1	1
Number of active users daily	20	25
Number of documents per day per user	5	5
Number of messages per day per user	10	10
Number of characters generated/day/user	15K	15K
Total characters generated per day	300K	400K
Total characters generated per month	6M	8M

All characters other than short messages to be kept *online* for the duration of the pilot study.

Note: Extra processing power and online storage will be required to accommodate people who wish to write small data processing applications for their own use.

	Configuration I (35 work stations)	Configuration II (74 work stations)
1. Cabling and electrical	$ 35,000	$ 50,000
2. Installation by vendor	10,000	20,000
3. Furniture	3,000	6,000
4. Lease cost for six months, for both hardware and software (7/80–12/80)	90,000	160,000
5. Staffing, assuming four people, full-time for six months, at $35K annually, including fringe benefits	70,000	70,000
6. TOTAL SIX/MONTH LIABILITY (total of items 1 through 5)	$208,000	$306,000
7. System purchase price	300,000	550,000
8. Additional cost of purchase (assuming 90% purchase accrual, item 7 less 90% of item 4)	219,000	406,000
9. TOTAL OF ALL COSTS AFTER PURCHASE (item 6 plus item 8)	$427,000	$712,000
Cost per terminal (including staff cost)	$ 12,200	$ 9,600
Cost per terminal (excluding staff cost)	$ 10,200	$ 8,700

would have little trouble getting a vendor to agree to their plans, since they felt there was enormous potential for business beyond Project AIM.

In fact, Parker and his staff had been meeting regularly with vendor sales representatives for several months. By early March they had determined that there were only three vendors that could come close to meeting their Project AIM work-station specifications. Parker encouraged his staff to continue discussions with all three companies; he reported to Adams that he was quite confident they would have no trouble obtaining the kind of equipment they wanted.

The OA group also developed a detailed implementation plan for Project AIM. The major steps and the time schedule are reproduced in Exhibit 7. The schedule called for vendor selection by the end of April, the installation of equipment by the end of June, and a post-implementation review of experience with the system in early 1981.

EXHIBIT 7 □ **Project AIM Workstation Implementation Tasks**

	1980										1981		
Tasks	M	A	M	J	J	A	S	O	N	D	J	F	M
1. Quantifying staffing													
2. Select vendor													
3. Determine information flow													
4. Determine participants													
5. Develop benchmark													
6. Develop training program													
7. Develop data base													
8. Develop productivity measures													
9. Conduct benchmark													
10. Develop user manuals													
11. Develop implementation schedules													
12. Installation													
13. Pilot in operation													
14. Phase in users													
15. Training													
16. Post-implementation review													
	M	A	M	J	J	A	S	O	N	D	J	F	M

DAVID ADAMS' PERSPECTIVE

Parker and his staff were scheduled to make a presentation of their Project AIM proposal to Bill Webber, the executive vice president of the Operations Group, on March 12. David Adams knew Webber would be interested in Adams' views about the project as well. As he looked forward to that session, Adams commented:

> I know the pilot has to be big enough to give electronic mail a fair chance, and it has to have a reasonable mix of users. It's also clear to me that we have to provide AIM with enough money to be comfortable. It just won't work otherwise.
>
> I'm also concerned that we communicate properly with the users about office automation. We don't want to build their expectations too high; I know the pilot *will* have lots of problems. If it creates negative attitudes, it could really get killed.
>
> But the really big question is whether we can sell the expenditure of so much money for R&D at a time when we're all being asked to cut 5 percent to 8 percent of our current budgets. The problem is that there is no way this project can claim any immediate or significant hard dollar savings. Yet, how else can we learn about electronic mail?

Case 3-2 □ Decatur Industries, Inc.*

Gary Templeton, recently appointed director of Management Information Systems (MIS), anxiously awaited a response from his new boss, Ken Bogart—corporate controller, concerning his proposal for achieving better coordination in data processing (DP) activities for the total corporation. Templeton had been with Decatur Industries approximately three years, most of that time was spent as their manager of corporate systems planning. In that role he had been assigned the responsibility for developing an overall plan for information systems—both corporate and divisional—so that data processing resources and activities would be better coordinated in the future. However, work along those lines was severely constrained due to

* This case was prepared as the basis for class discussion rather than to illustrate either effective or ineffective handling of an administrative situation.

excessive demands on his time as a "fire-fighter." Assisting various divisions in the company with the details of their MIS operations, he was left with no time for developing corporatewide plans. Yet, the company had been feeling an especially strong need for such a plan. The controller, in particular, was anxious to get better coordination between DP operations throughout the company and lessen the divergence of various divisional efforts in this area.

For several years he had expected to see some progress in this direction. With no plan in hand after three years, Templeton's former boss was fired and Templeton was put in his place. This management action startled Gary, since, after all, development of the plan was his specific responsibility. Later, though, he realized that the dismissal was consistent with Decatur's basic operating policies—all managers operate highly autonomously, and they alone are ultimately responsible for the performance of their unit. Templeton's promotion had a clear message for him, also—he had to move ahead quickly with the development of DP plans. He recalled all too clearly the words used to announce his promotion to the corporate officers at a corporate staff meeting: "Gentlemen, this is Gary Templeton, the most recent occupant of the position of Director of Management Information Systems."

Within a few months, Templeton had put together a position paper that outlined his thoughts on both structure and management control processes for corporatewide data processing. He identified problems in the current situation and suggested a more centralized approach to MIS development. "In the past," he noted, "the corporate MIS function as a whole has seemed to lack direction and thrust, and the data processing effort at Decatur *in toto* has fallen short of its true potential, while spending more money than necessary to do so." In the future, he proposed that "the corporate data processing organization will have overall responsibility for providing the total spectrum of data processing services required by the divisions. This includes the planning for computer hardware acquisition, operation of the computer centers, and all systems development and related activities."

Bogart had to approve the basic plan before Templeton could proceed. Templeton was anxiously awaiting a response because he foresaw a very busy few months enlisting the support of the division's data processing managers for the new plan.

HISTORY OF DECATUR INDUSTRIES

In 1906 the Owens family of Decatur, Indiana, put together their family savings and established the Decatur Wet Mill in the rolling countryside just outside of their home town. The company thrived in those early years, transforming the corn and wheat of nearby farms into meal that was shipped to bakers and grocers in nearby Indianapolis. As the operations grew in scale, members of the family found themselves spending more and more time in Indianapolis. One of the sons of the family decided to move to the city during the 1920s, and his activities there took the company through its first steps into other lines of business.

First, the company moved into baked goods, using their own grain products. Second, after daughter Cathi married a manager from Eli Lilly, the company opened up its own pharmaceutical operation. Both ventures got off to a good start, and during the next 20 years, the company continued to expand its activities in both food processing and pharmaceuticals.

In 1953, the Owens family was presented with a very attractive offer from a group of well-financed bankers from Chicago, and they decided to sell the business. The company was renamed Decatur Industries, and the new president—Thomas Bruner—took over the company with a commitment to growth through acquisition.

Over the next 20 years, Decatur Industries showed tremendous growth by pursuing a careful acquisition strategy. More than 40 different companies were purchased. From profits of $1,252,000 in 1953, the company's earnings grew to $35,837,000 in 1977, representing an average annual growth rate of roughly 15 percent. Sales increased approximately 19 percent per year over the same period. Exhibit 1 shows sales and profit figures in more detail for the past 10 years, highlighting a very steady and dramatic growth. Without question, the firm's acquisition strategy was largely responsible for this growth pattern, and looking at financial performance measures alone, the strategy proved extremely successful. The excitement of those two decades of growth was so inspiring that it moved a retiring corporate executive to rhyme; Exhibit 2 presents a poem written by this particular founding father of the company, who at the end of 1977 looked back gleefully at the firm's 24-year growth. By the end of that period, Decatur was heavily involved in a wide array of industries completely unrelated to its base in foodstuffs and pharmaceuticals. Industries in which Decatur now competed included heavy machinery, construction materials, and data communications.

Financial statements for Decatur Industries for the 1977 fiscal year appear in Exhibits 3 and 4.

PHILOSOPHY OF DECATUR INDUSTRIES

The company grew by acquiring going concerns in a broad spectrum of industries. Once acquired, though, the new acquisitions were left intact; they became new divisions that were left to operate fairly autonomously. Corporate management selected acquisition candidates in a fashion similar to the way an investor might build a diversified investment portfolio. A

EXHIBIT 1 □ Ten-Year Revenue and Income Growth

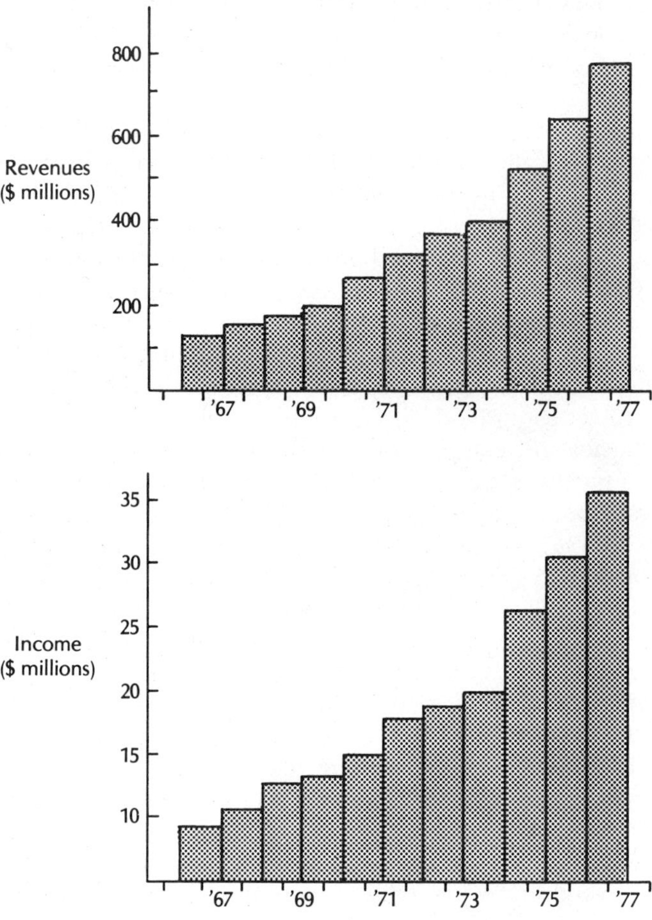

EXHIBIT 2

Ballad of Decatur Industries

'Twas early in the year of fifty-three
When four swashbucklers set forth on a spree;
Established a company for profits to make,
Come hell or highwater, their fortunes at stake.

No money at hand, they signed up for debt,
Hocking their total, all they did bet
That somehow or other they'd favorably cope
With swings of the market to fulfill their hope.

EXHIBIT 2 (*concluded*)

The pressure was on them relentlessly
To keep the cash flowing for solvency.
The goals in those days were clear without doubt;
Take our full swings—but do not strike out!

With our debt to equity at twenty-eight to one,
Some bankers were pale if not downright wan
At the thought of advancing more working lucre
To a fledgling which had a secureless future.

But they did; and we did; to our future we rolled,
Rationalizing capital which in excesses untold
Was tied up in industry by barons of old;
Their monuments full of inventory which couldn't be sold.

We merged; we acquired—*their* common for our *preferred*.
At times we paid cash but stoutly demurred
From issuing our common (to avoid dilution);
'Cause the assets we acquired really begged for solution!

Castrophe avoidance was the first priority;
Maintain operations came secondly,
If energy were left, after meeting these two;
Improvements were in order if confined to a few!

Diversification served us quite well
To dampen the swings of the pell and the mell.
Joint ventures we tried and liked very much;
Developed good deals and patterns for such.

Instructions to divisions were considerate—not rash
Run it your way, but send corporate all cash.
As long as there're profits, you'll have a full say;
But start losing money, you'll lose it our way!

We scratched in our markets for meaningful shares;
And watched competition for treacherous snares.
Our view towards inventory was cautious—not bold;
It's a liability—not an asset—until it is sold!

Then came the day with capital abundant;
Other people's problems looked repulsively redundant.
So, earnings of quality with vigor we sought;
We issued our common for some that we bought.

The torch has been passed to a new generation,
Whose competence commands new heights of veneration.
The journey's been great for me and for mine;
Godspeed and success for thee and for thine!

Robert M. Brown
12/17/74

EXHIBIT 3

DECATUR INDUSTRIES, INC.
Consolidated Balance Sheet
December 31, 1977
(000s omitted)

Assets	
Current assets:	
Cash	$ 17,619
Accounts receivable	124,830
Inventory	143,032
Prepaid expenses	3,575
Other	11,624
Total current assets	300,680
Plant, property and equipment	365,763
Less: Accumulated depreciation	155,694
Net plant investment	210,069
Other assets	63,091
Total assets	$573,840

Liabilities	
Current liabilities:	
Accounts payable	$ 55,574
Accrued expenses	57,757
Income taxes	16,874
Other	5,686
Total current liabilities	135,891
Reserve for divestiture of marginally profitable operations	9,167
Long-term liabilities	136,914
Convertible debentures	22,733
Total liabilities	304,705
Stockholders' Equity:	
Preferred stock	4,608
Common stock	10,401
Capital surplus	54,363
Earned surplus	199,763
Total stockholders' equities	269,135
Total liabilities and stockholders' equity	$573,840

EXHIBIT 4

DECATUR INDUSTRIES, INC.
Consolidated Income Statement
1977
(000s omitted)

Sales	$819,345
Operating costs:	
Cost of sales	628,680
Depreciation	22,165
Selling and administrative expenses	86,097
	736,942
Operating profit	82,403
Other deductions:	
Interest expense	10,863
Other expenses	1,945
	12,808
Income before taxes	69,595
Income taxes	33,758
Net income	$ 35,837

desirable candidate was a well-run company that provided a nice complement to the existing collection of divisions, either (1) by rounding out some divisions' product lines or (2) by introducing an industry into the firm that was characterized by fundamentally different business cycles than were already present in the firm. Companies were bought—and sometimes sold—the way a shrewd investor might buy and sell stocks. This philosophy was brought out quite clearly by the company's formal statement of policy: The goal of the company was:

> To build a strong, highly diversified operating company that will demonstrate consistent growth in earnings per share year after year and constantly build a stronger base for continued growth. Accomplishment of this goal requires continually increasing operating profits and improved profit performance while maintaining satisfactory return on investment.
>
> Of paramount importance in achieving the long-term company goal is the increasingly successful operation of the individual divisions of the company.

COMPANY ORGANIZATION

The company consisted of 16 operating divisions in 1977 that were grouped into five industry categories (referred to as "industry groups"). Divisions were added to the company over the years through acquisition and they were included in an existing industrial group whenever possible. The organization chart in Exhibit 5 illustrates how the divisions were

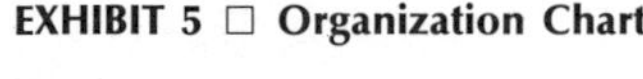

EXHIBIT 5 □ Organization Chart

- Decatur Industries, Inc.
  - Pharmaceuticals Group
    - Bishop Aspirin
    - Kleenist Medical
    - Ozawa-Phillips Laboratories
  - Foodstuffs Group
    - Meat Products
      - Cracker Sausage
      - Vincent Winship Meats
      - W. Virginia Steer
    - Preprocessed Foods
      - Libby Bakeries
      - Bickford Pastries
      - Mme. Zona's Frozen Foods
      - Kolker's Homemade Foods
  - Heavy Machinery Group
    - Commercial Vehicles
    - Hubercraft
    - Buckeye Machinery
    - Olympus Steel
  - Keydisk System
  - Bastille Prefabricated Construction Materials

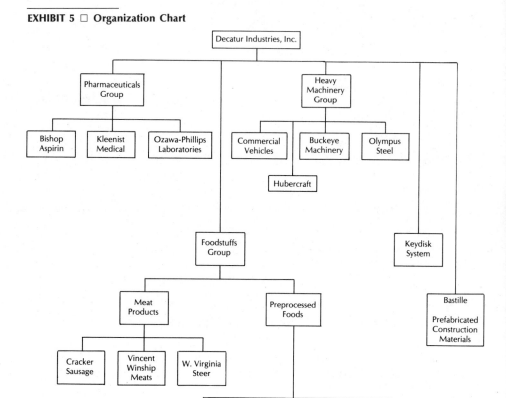

grouped as of mid-1977. The company made specialized products in diverse industries, so dealings across industrial groups were rare. Within each industry group, however, there existed some synergy. The groups were characterized by the kinds of products they manufactured:

a. Pharmaceuticals Group—a group of three (3) divisions that manufactured a wide variety of drugs, medicines, ointments, and medical supplies, some under nationally recognized brand names sold directly to consumers and others aimed at institutions and private-label retailers.
b. Foodstuffs Group—a large group of seven (7) divisions that processed meat products and special types of preprocessed foods. Meat operations sold in local markets, whereas baked goods, frozen foods, and baking mixes were sold regionally.
c. Heavy Machinery Group—four (4) capital-intensive divisions that manufactured a diverse array of specialty heavy-duty equipment for con-

struction, agriculture, and shipbuilding industries. Some vehicles, such as fire engines and amphibious landers were well known, but the majority of products were production equipment and factory material-transfer machines for sale to other manufacturing firms.

d. Keydisk Systems—a young, promising division which manufactures key-to-disk systems, OCR scanners, MICR reader-sorters and other automatic input devices.

e. Construction Materials—a single division that manufactured a flexible set of prefabricated housing materials, and that provided customized prefabricated materials for office buildings and hotels. With sales in all parts of the world, it offered construction supervision services on-site for major projects.

Group-level staff typically consists of the group president, group controller, and no more than four staff assistants. As shown in Exhibit 6, the group controllers report directly to Bogart although they physically reside at the same location as the group president. Corporate headquarters were in Chicago but the industry group presidents and the divisional presidents were located near their operating locations around the country. Decatur operated plants, warehouses, and administrative offices in 27 states and was rapidly expanding its business in Canada, Europe, and Brazil.

EXHIBIT 6 □ Corporate Staff Organization

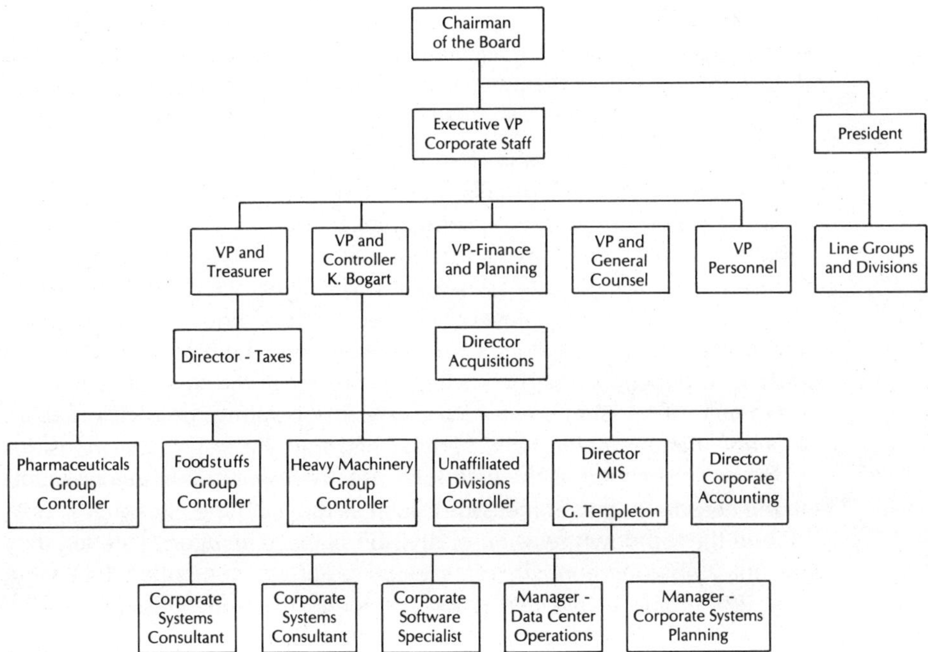

CORPORATE-LEVEL ACTIVITIES

Though the divisions were charged with making their operations profitable as independent businesses, it was corporate headquarters' role both to assist the divisions in their efforts, and to monitor and evaluate their performance. In order to carry out this special role with the divisions, corporate had assembled a talented collection of individuals in a variety of staff positions. While the number of people in staff positions (90) was never large in relation to the number of employees in the whole company (20,400), corporate staff often played a critical role in the activities of company.

According to the corporate policy manual, the corporate staff served as an extension of the president's office to:

i. Support and assist operations management.
ii. Maintain systematic surveillance and administer systems of control.
iii. Evaluate performance and trends continually in operations.
iv. Administer corporate housekeeping functions, including financial, legal, tax, communications, personnel, public, and investor relations.
v. Provide the leadership, planning, and implementation for the company to grow in new areas.

Thus, corporate staff could and often did get involved in the activities of the divisions, but usually only to provide assistance or to review plans, decisions, and actual financial performance. According to the manual:

> Staff personnel at all levels provide expert guidance, in-house consulting, task force assistance, and administration of systems, but make no operating decisions. Staff effectiveness is rooted solely in the powers of persuasion and expertise on the part of staff personnel.

Exhibit 6 is the organization chart of corporate staff officers. Included are the support groups that are usually found at the corporate level at most firms, such as treasurer, controller, personnel, legal counsel, and planning.

In general, most divisions had developed a stable type of working relationship with corporate staff. Some divisions actively sought out the advice and assistance of corporate-level expertise, whereas other divisions tried to maintain the interactions at an absolute minimum. The type of relationship appeared to depend primarily on the personality of the division president. For example, if he (she) were accustomed to operating the division as an independent entrepreneur (who perhaps had sold out to Decatur Industries but who still remained at the helm), he usually resented any involvements with the corporate staff. Some issues, such as the handling of capital allocations and the top-down revision of division plans, when corporate felt they were not ambitious enough, represented points of contention that were thorns in the side of every division president. Over these issues, all the divisions felt some occasional anger and resentment.

BUSINESS PLANNING AND CONTROL

There was a formal commitment to both planning and control in the company. A major effort to make the planning and control procedures more useful and informative to both the divisions and corporate management was currently under way. In the current stage of evolution, the procedures called for a long-term strategic plan and an upcoming-year operating plan (to be prepared on an annual basis). Other procedures generated monthly and quarterly performance reports which tracked divisional activity against plan.

Long-range planning was the responsibility of each operating division. Each division president established objectives for his division based on the business opportunities he anticipated to find over some reasonable planning horizon for his industry. The planning horizon thus varied from division to division, running at least 3 years and in some cases extending as long as 10 years. Long-range plans were reviewed and approved by the presidents of industry groups and by top management at corporate headquarters.

Yearly operating plans were also the responsibility of each operating division, but preparation of these plans usually required the praticipation of a large number of individuals. The operating plan called for very detailed estimates of revenues and costs for the upcoming year. These figures, and the overall profit picture they paint, were to be consistent with the long-term strategic plan (discussed above) that outlined how the division was to develop over the next few years.

Control was made possible through the use of operating reports that tracked performance against operating plan. These reports were compiled by the corporate accounting office which received its data over the telephone from the division controllers. Ten days after the close of every "month,"[1] the phones at headquarters started ringing and staff from division controllers' offices sat perched at the other and ready to report the operating revenues and expenses of the period. Using this information, the corporate staff then prepared the monthly Operating Highlights Report, showing sales and expense data, balance sheets, inventory status, and return on investment (ROI). Also included in this report was a three-month forecast of anticipated revenues and expenses, and compared to the year's operating plan. Every third month, special quarterly reports were also prepared, highlighting changes in debt position and capital expenditures.

Using the mechanisms of formal planning and control reporting, the company attempted to maintain its handle on the diverse activities of its many divisions. Top management saw that these activities deserved greater

[1] A "month" was either 5 weeks or 4 weeks according to the manner in which the fiscal year was subdivided for accounting purposes. For a year of 52 weeks, a quarter consisted of 13 weeks, and each quarter was divided into 3 "months" of durations of 5 weeks, 4 weeks, and 4 weeks.

attention than they had received in the past, and thus they were encouraging the development of more effective procedures. A significant amount of corporate-level staff work was now committed to improving planning and control throughout the company, and their assistance was available to any division upon request.

INFORMATION SYSTEMS

Each division employed, budgeted, and managed data processing in a highly decentralized fashion. There were no data processing personnel at the group level. DP personnel and equipment were reflected directly in each division's budget. This situation had prevailed since computers were introduced into the company (in part due to the manner in which new divisions were added to the company), and now the company faced numerous problems and inefficiencies as a result.

Reflecting on the status of MIS throughout the company, Templeton felt a tremendous need for control:

> The total expenditure within Decatur for data processing in 1975 was approximately $7,168,000 and in 1977 is projected to be $9,102,000, or almost a 27 percent increase in three years. It can be readily demonstrated that, with some notable exceptions, neither the quality nor quantity of the results from these expenditures has increased at a commensurate rate. Decatur cannot afford, in the future, to allocate time, money, and people to developing information systems which do not, in the aggregate, have a significant, positive effect on future performance. The marketplace of today, and in the future, demands that we have information systems which enable us to identify potential business problems earlier (analysis), provide assistance in developing alternate solutions (simulation), and ensure proper execution of the chosen solution (control). In an ever-increasing tempo of change in both the marketplace and the sphere of computer technology, Decatur must *plan ahead.*
>
> It is difficult, if not impossible, for the MIS effort across Decatur to achieve the positive impact it could and should have. This is due to the fact that, with the present organizational structure (data processing personnel and equipment reflected directly in each division's budget), a divisional manager has no incentive to accept a change which, while it might not be the most advantageous alternative for his division, would be the best one for the corporation. Because of this, resource sharing, both personnel (development) and equipment (operations), becomes very difficult to arrange and virtually impossible to administer properly. This, in turn, hinders economies—such as joint development projects for applications with multidivisional utilization and lower computer costs from equipment sharing—from being realized. Additionally, there are further losses in the form of opportunity costs.
>
> In an effort to improve this situation, in mid-1972 the corporate MIS staff had two new positions authorized; manager–corporate systems planning and

EXHIBIT 7 □ Decatur Data Processing Installations

Group	Division	Division headquarters location	Primary equipment	DP personnel* SYS	PRG	OPN	Total group 1977 DP budget† ($ millions)	Percent of group sales revenue
Bastille	PCM	Passaic, N.J.	IBM 370/138	8	14	12	.94	.9 %
Keydisk systems	KS	St. Louis, Ill.	DEC 1099	4	12	5	1.20	3.4
Foodstuffs	CS	Peoria, Ill.	Burroughs 1830	4	8	4		
	VWM	Skokie, Ill.	DEC/PDT 150	10	22	0		
	WVS	Lewisburg, W.V.	HP 3000/9	3	9	3		
	LB	Chicago, Ill.	IBM 370/158‡	6	14	28		
	BP	Bickford, Ind.	Datapoint 5500	4	18	0		
	ZFF	Boston, Md.	Eclipse/300	2	6	2		
	KHF	Madison, Wis.	Burroughs 1870	5	10	5	2.87	.8
Heavy machinery	CV	Detroit, Wis.	Univac 1100/80	12	25	9		
	BM	Deablo, N. Mex.	Dec 2040	4	12	6		
	OS	Pittsburgh, Pa.	DEC 11/45	4	8	4		
	Huber	San Diego, Calif.	DEC 11/34	1	3	3	1.78	.9
Pharmaceuticals	BA	Providence, R.I.	Honeywell 6/43	3	6	3		
	KM	Medfield, Md.	Honeywell 6/36	1	3	1		
	OPL	Corvallis, Oreg.	NCR 8590	9	18	24	2.31	1.88

* SYS includes Jr. and Sr. systems analysts; PRG includes all levels of programmers except trainees (there were currently six different programming languages used in Decatur); OPN includes technical systems and operations personnel but does not include data entry.

† Average major DP budget items for total corporation are:

Hardware	45%
Personnel	52
Leased/purchased software	1
Supplies and other	2

Percent average budget increases 1977 over 1976:

In hardware	50%
In software	24
In personnel	12

‡ Shared system: CS, VWM, BP, and Corporate all use this system. The operations staff reports to a corporate employee, but are paid by Foodstuffs Group. Each division maintains its own systems and programming staff.

corporate software specialist. The intent of this staffing was to provide for (1) closer assistance and guidance for the divisional MIS efforts and (2) a more efficacious companywide data processing effort through better coordination and planning. While some of those objectives have been achieved (notably in the assistance and guidance areas) their efficaciousness has been blunted through the use of the manager–corporate systems planning in a consultant function. By using the person responsible for planning in the areas of consulting and assistance, several opportunities in individual divisions were capitalized on, but at the expense of an overall, coordinated corporate MIS development plan. Consequently, while there were a few bright spots, the corporate MIS function as a whole has seemed to lack direction and thrust, and the data processing effort at Decatur *in toto* has fallen short of its true potential, while spending more money than necessary to do so. There are a number of reasons, chief among them:

1. Development efforts are fragmented—divisions are reinventing very similar wheels.
2. Small divisional staffs are characterized as:
   a. Spending too great a percentage of time on maintenance efforts or minor enhancements.
   b. Lacking in personnel with strong and varied background experience in analyzing business problems and devising comprehensive, integrated, effective systems solutions.
   c. Therefore, not accomplishing as much as is needed in the development of major systems which can have significant, positive impact on business.
3. The cost-per-calculation of many, small, underutilized computers is greater than is the case on larger, more-fully-utilized computers.

In 1975, when several divisions of the Foodstuffs Group simultaneously needed to upgrade their computing capability the company established a centralized facility with capacity to handle all their needs. The center was established when corporate staff recognized several divisions had very similar DP needs which could be met more cost effectively by sharing a single facility. The center was located on the premises of Libby Bakeries, and its users were other food divisions located nearby (Libby Bakeries, Vincent Winship Meats, Bickford Pastries) and Decatur corporate staff. Initially the center was run under the jurisdiction of its "home" division although each division employed its own systems and programming personnel, and operations team for use of the system during scheduled production hours. Administrative squabbles between divisions occurred with such frequency corporate was called in (1976)—as resident arbiter—to manage operations of the center and named the facility—Corporate Data Center. Each division, however, retained its own systems and programming team. At this point the corporate MIS staff was increased to the six positions shown in Exhibit 6 with the manager–data center operations reporting to Templeton, while the operations staff were listed as Foodstuffs Group employees. Costs for the operations staff and center were charged back to the users, and currently neither operations nor the chargeout system were issues of management contention.

PROPOSED RESTRUCTURING

Templeton believed that the problems facing DP in the company would best be met by reorganization. Following the pattern set by the Foodstuffs Group data center, the company should establish regional data centers to perform all DP operations, consolidating the disjointed and costly activity of the separate divisions. Each industry group should then form a control board that would oversee and set priorities for MIS development work at the data centers. Through this arrangement, each DP project would report in matrix fashion to both the regional data center and the group control board.

Templeton, a 45-year-old ex-Coast Guard officer who had amassed 20 years of data processing experience (six with the Coast Guard, five with a large computer manufacturer as a salesman, three as an independent consultant, three with a public accounting firm, and the last three with Decatur) wrote up these suggestions in the MIS plan now awaiting Bogart's review. He argued as follows:

> For a number of years, many multidivisional corporations, such as Decatur, have allowed their subsidiaries to manage their own EDP activities. Recently, however, there has been a trend toward consolidation of all divisional EDP activities into a corporatewide function. Such consolidation may result in lower costs, less duplication of systems and development efforts and improved corporate control. Against this must be weighed possible disadvantages such as reduced autonomy for the divisions, disruption of services during conversion and greater performance demands placed on EDP personnel due to increased complexity of multiaccess systems. It is important that top management be involved at the feasibility plan stage, long before the consolidated function becomes a fact.
>
> Based on observations at Decatur over the last few years, the following is suggested as a strategy for consolidation to be examined, tested, and developed in a feasibility study.
>
> Establishment of a separate organization with corporatewide responsibilities for administrative and operating control over all systems development and computer operations.
>
> Consolidation of the present computer operations centers into regional data centers, supplemented as required by outside vendor time-sharing and/or remote batch processing services.
>
> A combining of all computer operations at these regional centers.
>
> A combining of the divisional business system development groups at the regional data centers.
>
> A reduction in the number of computer mainframe manufacturers represented to a single vendor within three years.

A standardization of the approach to computer systems development, maintenance, and operations through the corporation.

(Exhibit 8 contains details of the MIS Objectives and Reorganization which support the consolidation effort.)

While expression of these ideas is a result of my experience in general business and data processing over the past 15 years, the ideas themselves are neither unique nor unproven. Many companies of Decatur's size, structure, and philosophy have successfully implemented similar plans.

While, at this point, it is evident that the course of action proposed above poses many difficult decisions, and, if proven feasible, will require a good deal of effort over what could easily be a two- to three-year period, it should also be evident that this analysis and the facing of the questions it will pose is overdue. Halfway measures and personal efforts, however well intentioned and well performed, over the past few years have demonstrably not had the impact desired or possible. Now is the time to fully examine the alternatives, and, on a rational and well-informed basis, make a decision and proceed to implement it.

Due to the import of this subject, I would obviously like to discuss it thoroughly with you at your earliest convenience.

G. L. Templeton

EXHIBIT 8 □ Proposed Restructuring of MIS

I. *Statement of Objective for MIS*

The charter of the MIS effort in Decatur Industries should be:

1. To act as a consultant to corporate, group, and divisional management on the adequacy of existing systems, both automated and manual, and the feasibility of new systems, for acquiring, controlling, and disseminating information required to manage the business.
2. To develop both short- and long-range plans which provide for the identification, development, and implementation of the most cost-effective solutions to information and control problems at plant, divisional, group, or corporate levels.
3. To assure that these plans, once approved, are implemented in the most cost-effective manner from systems definition and development to the acquisition and utilization of data processing equipment.
4. To audit the ongoing information systems to assure that they continue to be the most cost-effective solution in a changing environment.

The current corporate MIS department staffing and organizational relationship with divisional systems staffs and management is compatible with the above charter. Unfortunately, the efficacy of the corporate MIS effort in fulfilling the four

EXHIBIT 8 *(continued)*

elements of the charter has not, to varying degrees, been what it could and should be.

The more this area is studied, the more inescapable is the conclusion that even with a larger staff to do more planning and auditing, and still maintain the proper levels of consulting and assistance, it would still be almost impossible to achieve corporatewide effective and efficient data processing given the current organization structure.

II. *Reorganization*

In order to obtain as many of the benefits of consolidation as possible, while minimizing the potential disadvantages, the organization depicted in the accompanying chart, and the functions covered below are suggested for the strategy to be utilized in the feasibility study.

A. Corporate Services and Regional/Group Data Centers

The *corporate data processing* organization will have over-all responsibility for providing the total spectrum of data processing services required by the company and its divisions. This includes the planning for commuter hardware acquisition and the operation of the computer centers, and all systems development and related activities. Control and budgeting of the total expenditure for data processing is a major assignment, as is the promotion of corporatewide use of common software and systems. The regional systems and computing centers would report directly to this level. Specific responsibilities of this level are:

Information systems consulting—responsible for advising corporate, group, and divisional management on the adequacy of the existing systems, both automated and manual, and the feasibility of new systems, for acquiring, controlling, and disseminating information required to manage the business.

Equipment planning and acquisition—responsible for the long-range planning of computer requirements for the entire corporation, and negotiating purchase/rental/lease agreements with computer vendors or leasing companies.

Purchasing evaluation and audit—responsible for evaluating the performance of regional/group systems and computing centers, and for evaluating the adequacy of existing systems in terms of user satisfaction, corporate requirements, production costs, etc., and making appropriate recommendations for improvement or replacement.

Corporate systems development—responsible for studying the feasibility of developing systems to be used throughout the corporation, the review of existing divisional group systems to determine their transferability to other divisions/groups, the review of divisional/group systems development projects to avoid duplication of effort, and the development of systems for use in the corporate office.

EXHIBIT 8 *(continued)*

Proposed Consolidated Decatur Industries Management Information Systems Organization

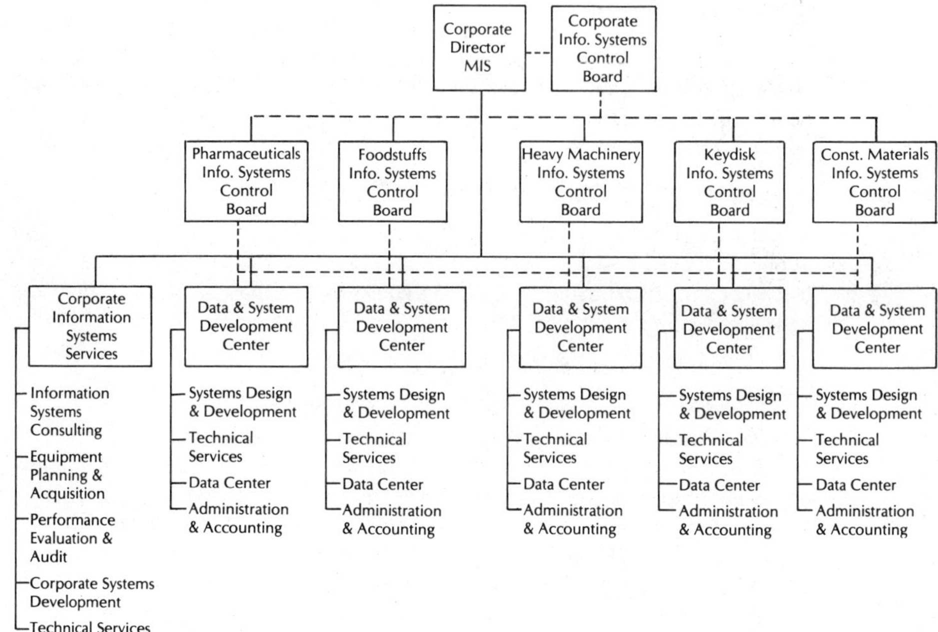

Technical services—responsible for coordinating technical services throughout the corporation in terms of software use and development, technical standards, the evaluatio and planning of hardware usage, communications, and for evaluating new software and communications developments and their impact on the operation of regional systems and computing centers.

The primary responsibilities of the *regional/group centers* would include the actual operation of the computers, the detailed design and programming of systems. The divisional sites, including both those with and without terminals, would report to this level. Functions of the areas within the regional/group center would be:

Detail systems design and development—responsible for the detail development of data processing systems in various functional areas, the coordination and short-range planning of these systems, and for providing application programming support.

Technical services—responsible for the evaluation and planning of hardware and operating systems software usage, for systems programming support, for maintaining the systems software at the regional/group center,

EXHIBIT 8 *(continued)*

and for providing teleprocessing and communication hardware and software support.

Data center—responsible for the regular operation of production programs, the testing of programs being developed, the control of input data and output reports, the control and operation of computer file libraries, short-range planning and scheduling of the computer installation, and the control and operation of data communications equipment.

Administration and accounting—responsible for the development and training of regional personnel, the operation of a mechanized project control system, the retention of regional budget and accounting records, the preparation of budget comparisons, and the enforcement of corporate standards and procedures.

B. Information Systems Control Board

In order to assure that the consolidated information systems function, (1) remains as responsive as possible to the legitimate systems development needs of division/group business operations, and (2) provides a consistently high quality of service in daily operations, it is necessary that a structure of committees or boards be established on a formal basis for the purpose of placing direct control of the use of computers and the development of information systems with corporate, group, and division management, and with the major users of data processing systems. Key objectives of establishing this structure would be to clearly and formally define and carry out the responsibilities of management for the assessment of the overall performance of the systems functions, and to aid the users of data processing by providing a well-defined medium to make their requirements known, and to obtain the satisfaction of these requirements.

The *corporate information systems control board* would ensure sound planning and control of the development of management information systems throughout Decatur. The board would be charged with taking all possible steps to ensure utilization of data processing equipment and personnel in a manner that would improve the quality and timeliness of information reporting at a cost commensurate with improvement in operating results; and, by the extension of information to the various levels of management who can best utilize it, to maximize their performance and profitability and competitive position in the marketplace.

Membership of the board would consist of the chairman of the board, corporate president, group presidents, the corporate vice president/controller, vice president/finance and planning, and the corporate director of management information systems. Meetings of this board would initially be at least quarterly, but could become less frequent once the group computer boards are well established and all regional/group computing centers are fully operational.

EXHIBIT 8 ***(concluded)***

The board would establish corporate computer policies and procedures, assess and approve the group/divisional plans, review and assess overall effectiveness of services provided by the regional/group systems and computing centers to the various divisions of the group.

Membership of the boards would consist of the group president, plus division presidents, the corporate director of MIS, and the head of the regional/group computer center. Meetings of the group information systems control board should be held monthly, or more often if warranted by the number of projects.

Through the use of both regional centers and control boards, Decatur would attain a higher degree of control over its data processing activities than had existed previously. A reorganization of the MIS function along these lines would eliminate many of the inefficiencies of current operations, and would open the door to innovative applications that would enable the divisions to compete more effectively in their respective markets.

Chapter 4 □ Organization Issues in IS Development

Manageable Trend / Chapter	Strategic Impact	DP/TP/OA	Organization Learning	Make/Buy	Life Cycle	GM/ User/ IS
IS Technology Organization Issues **Chapter 3**		●	●			●
Organizational Issues in IS Development **Chapter 4**	●		●	●		●
Information Systems Planning **Chapter 5**	●		●			●
IS Management Control **Chapter 6**	●		●	●		●
A Portfolio Approach to Information Systems Development **Chapter 7**	●				●	●
Operations Management **Chapter 8**	●			●	●	●
Multinational IS Issues **Chapter 9**		●				●
The IS Business **Chapter 10**	●		●	●		●

In the preceding chapter, we noted that information services operations in the future will be characterized by a central hub with some data files linked via telecommunications to a variety of remote devices which may or may not have extensive data files and processing power. The balance between work done at the hub and at distributed locations will vary widely from one organization to another. Evolution of this network will require the integration, at least at a policy level, of the formerly separate technologies of computers, telecommunications, and word processors. The rapid evolution in these technologies during their integration means the organization will simultaneously manage a blend of technologies, some which they have familiarity with (such as batch data processing) and others which they have limited experience with (such as electronic mail). The management structures needed for guiding new technologies to the organization are quite different from those for the older technologies. In dealing with these technologies, the corporation must encourage innovation, by both IS and user, in the newer ones while focusing on control and efficiency in the more mature ones.

Policies for guiding the deployment of information services development staff and activity in the 1980s must deal with two sets of tension. The first is the balance between *innovation* and *control*. This follows from our discussion of the phases of technology assimilation in the previous chapter. The emphasis in phase 1 and phase 2 technologies is on discovery of how to operate technologies and their implications for use in the company, while the emphasis in phase 3 and phase 4 technologies is on turning these findings into efficient reality. The relative emphasis a firm should place on aggressive phase 1 and 2 innovation will vary widely, depending on a broad assessment of the potential strategic impact of IS technology on the firm, corporate willingness to take risk, and so on. If there is a perception that this technology could be of great impact in helping the firm reach its strategic objectives, significantly greater emphasis must be given to these investments than if it is seen to be merely helpful.

The second tension is that between *IS dominance* and *user dominance* in the retention of development skills and in the active selection of priorities. The user often has a predilection to drive toward short-term need fulfillment (at the expense of long-term IS hygiene and orderly development). IS on the other hand can become preoccupied with the mastery of technology and an orderly development plan at the risk of slow response to legitimate user needs. Effectively balancing the roles of these two groups is a complex task, which must be dealt with in the context of the potential strategic role of IS technology, in the context of the corporate culture, and in a contingent manner.

Exhibit 4–1 illustrates some consequences of either excessive IS or excessive user domination in environments. It shows clearly that very different application portfolios and operating problems will emerge in each setting. Throughout this chapter a strong focus will be on the need for experimentation because of the repeated inability of organizations to foresee the real implications of their launching into a new technology. The following four incidents are typical of this problem.

1. A Short-Term User-Need Situation—Strategically Important. The present number one priority at a large machine-tool manufacturer engineering department is computer-aided design (CAD). Early success has led to a major expansion of the effort. They are modifying the digital information design output to enable them to control directly computer-driven machine tools. This work has deliberately been done independently of their bill of materials/cost system which is in a data base format and maintained by the IS unit. Short of staff to immediately integrate the new system in their data base structure, it was a user decision to go ahead, despite major future system integration problems. The work was done over the objection of IS management, but user management (engineering) has received full support

EXHIBIT 4-1 □ Possible implications of excess dominance

IS dominates control of systems life cycle

Too much emphasis on data base hygiene.

No recent new supplier or new distinct services (too busy with maintenance).

New systems always must fit data structure of existing system.

All requests for service require system study with benefit identification.

Standardization dominates—few exceptions.

IS designs/constructs everything.

Benefits of user control over development discussed but never implemented.

Study always shows construction costs less than outside purchase.

Head count of distributed minis and development staff growing surreptitiously.

IS specializing in technical frontiers, not user-oriented markets.

IS spending 80 percent on maintenance, 20 percent on development.

IS thinks they are in control of all.

Users express unhappiness.

Portfolio of development opportunities firmly under IS control.

No strong user group exists.

General management not involved but concerned.

User dominates control of systems life cycle

Too much emphasis on problem focus.

IS says out of control.

Explosive growth in number of new systems and supporting staff.

Multiple suppliers delivering services. Frequent change in supplier of specific service.

Lack of standardization and control over data hygiene and system.

Hard evidence of benefits nonexistent.

Soft evidence of benefits not organized.

Few measurements/objectives for new systems.

Technical advice of IS not sought or, if received, considered irrelevant.

User buying design/construction/maintenance services and even operations from outside

User building networks to own unique needs (not corporate need).

While some users are growing rapidly in experience and use other users feel nothing is relevant because they do not understand.

No coordinated effort for technology transfer or learning from experience between users.

Growth in duplication of technical staffs.

Communications costs are rising dramatically through redundancy.

from senior management because of the project's potential major impact on shortening the product development life cycle.

The engineers are enthusiastically working on the CAD project to make it work; the IS team is lukewarm. Early results appear to have justified the decision.

2. *User Control to Achieve Automation.* At a division of a large consumer products manufacturer, a substantial investment in office automation was undertaken with modest, up-front, cost/benefit justification. Managers and administrative support personnel were encouraged by IS to "use" the systems with only modest direction and some introductory training on a Wang word processor which was made available to them. In four months time, three product managers had developed independent networks to support sales force activities; two had automated portions of their word processing, with substantial savings; two others did little but encourage their

administrative support staff to "try it out." The users gained confidence and were pursuing new programs with enthusiasm.

The challenge to the IS management now, after only six months, is to develop and evolve an efficient program with these seven different "experienced" users. The IS manager currently estimates it will take roughly two years to achieve this efficient integration. However, both he and divisional management feel, retrospectively, that it would have been impossible to implement office automation (OA) with a standard IS-dominated systems study and that the expense of the after-the-fact rationalization is an acceptable price for these benefits. This word processing program was in sharp contrast to the strong central control IS was exerting over its mature data processing technologies.

3 *Step-by-Step Innovation of a New Technology.* A third example is the experience of a large grocery chain which acquired a system of point-of-sales terminals. These terminals were initially purchased by the retail division (with the support of the IS manager) to assist store managers in controlling inventory. They were to be used exclusively within individual stores to accumulate daily sales totals of individual items. These totals would permit individual stores to trigger reorders in case lots at a given point in time. Once installed, however, these isolated systems evolved quickly into links to central headquarters. These links were established to supply data to new computer programs which provided a better measurement of advertising effectiveness and the ability to manage warehouse stock levels on a chainwide level.

Implementation of this nonplanned linkage involved significant extra expense because the communication protocols in the selected terminals were incompatible with those in the computer at headquarters. However, the possibility and benefits of the resulting system would have been difficult to define in advance as this eventual use was not considered important when the initial point-of-sale terminals were being installed. Further, in management's opinion, even if the organization had considered it, the ultimate costs of the resulting system would have been seen as prohibitive in relation to benefits (in retrospect, *incorrectly* prohibitive).

4. *User Innovation as a Source of Productivity.* A final example concerns the separate introductions by a large bank of an electronic mail system and a word processor system strictly to facilitate preparation of bank loan paperwork. However, the two systems soon evolved to link the loan managers (who were initially not planned for as customers of either system) to a series of analytical programs. This evolution developed as a result of conversations between a loan officer and a consultant. They discovered that the word processor loan system included a powerful analytical tool which could be used for analyzing loan performance. Because of the bank's electronic mail system, the analysis could be easily accessed by loan personnel (both at headquarters and in branches). After three months of use, the bank was

faced with a series of internal tensions as the costs of both the electronic mail and the word processing systems unexpectedly rose. Further, there was no formal means to review "experiments" or evaluate this unexpected use of the systems by participants not initially involved. Eventually, a senior management review committee supported the project, and it was permitted to continue, with substantial enhancements made to the word processing software.

These examples are typical of emerging new services which support professionals and managers in doing work. They form the underpinning of our conviction that it is impossible to foresee in advance the full range of consequences of introducing IS technology. Excessive control and focus for quick results in the early stages can deflect important learning. Neither IS nor users have had outstanding records in predicting all the consequences of new technology in terms of its impact on the organization. Consequently, a necessary general management role is to help facilitate this assimilation.

This chapter is divided into three main sections. The first focuses on the pressures that are on users to gain control not only over development but, when possible, to have the resulting product run on stand-alone mini or micro systems operating in their departments. The second section identifies the advantages which come from a strong IS development coordination effort and the potential pitfalls of uncontrolled proliferation of user-developed systems. The third section identifies the core policies which must be respectively implemented by IS management, user management, and general management in order to ensure a good result. In our judgment, the general management role is critical in facilitating technological change and organizational adaptation.

PRESSURES TOWARD USER DOMINANCE

The intense pressures which are encouraging stronger control by users over their development resources and the acquisition of independent IS resources can be clustered into four main categories.

Pent-Up User Demand

The backlog of development work in front of an information services department is frequently very large in relation to its staff resources (three- to five-year backlogs tend to be the norm). The sources of these staffing crunches are multiple, and the problems are not easily solved. First, existing systems require sustained maintenance to deal with changing regulatory and other business requirements. As more systems are automated the maintenance needs continue to rise, forcing either increases in development staff or postponing of new work. This problem is intensified by the shift in systems design philosophy (in the early 1970s) from one which incorporated data into programs to one which clearly separates data base management from processing procedures. Effecting this one-time conversion of data systems is expensive in terms of staff resources.

Further, the most challenging high-status jobs tend to be with computer vendors and software houses. This puts great pressure on the in-company IS department because its most talented staff is tempted to move into more challenging (and often more financially remunerative) assignments. Frequently, it is easier for the IS development unit to get the budget allocations than find the staff resources to use them.

There are strong reasons for users to develop their own expertise. Systems people linked to the user organization make it easier to plan employee promotions which move IS personnel to other functional jobs enhancing user/IS coordination. Combining IS experience with user responsibilities creates a knowledgeable IS user. Some care must be taken on local development, however, as user groups often have a tendency to buy or develop systems tailored to their very specific situation, and this may lead to long-term maintenance problems. In an environment characterized by local development, often there is also poor technology transfer between similar users and nonachievement of leverage, issues of low importance to the local unit. A large forest products company, organized geographically, combined a regional-system-minded regional manager with an aggressive growth-oriented IS manager who was promoted to be in charge of all administrative support. In three years, their budget for IS was double that of a comparable region but only one application was exported. Subsequent review of this unit's work indicated that nearly half of their developments had focused on problems of potential general interest to the company.

Finally, the protocols of interfacing into a network and of meeting corporate control standards can be very time-consuming and complex. A stand-alone system purchased by a user which is independent of the network can simplify the job and permit less-skilled staff resources to be utilized. It may require no major changes, particularly, if it is a system familiar to one or more employees from prior experience.

These items, in aggregate, for reasons beyond IS management control, make IS *appear* to be unresponsive to users' demands. These perceived shortcomings of IS management by users (on the dimensions of responsiveness and excessive focus on detail) make user-developed systems and stand-alone minis an attractive nonconfrontational way of getting work done. Using either their own staffs or outside software houses, users significantly speed up the process of obtaining "needed" service.

The IS Market Is Growing in Services and in a Competitive Fashion

Thousands of stand-alone computer systems are available for specific applications ranging from simple accounts payable systems to complete office automation products. Their existence makes them beguilingly easy solutions to short-term problems. Marketed by hardware or software vendors to end-user managers, the emphasis is on functional features, with technical and software problems being soft-pedaled. This is particularly true of most standard word processing systems. Most systems are marketed with no mention of their computer foundation. A stand-alone solution is seen as particularly attractive because faster and more consistent online response times are given than from distributed systems. The stand-alone provides easy access to online systems; it also permits the user to avoid the problems associated with being only one of multiple users of a system who, in aggregate, over the hours of the day and the weeks, provide a highly volatile (in terms of volume) stream of transactions. Additionally, the system appears simple operationally, needing only an operator to run it when developed. Air conditioning, physical maintenance, and power availability are not seen as issues.

Frequently the local solution *appears* to be more cost effective than work done or purchased by the control IS development group. Not only is there no cumbersome project proposal to be proposed and defended in front of IS technicians who have their own special agendas but often a simple up-front price is quoted. Developed under user control, the project is perceived to be both simple and relatively red-tape free.

User Control

The notion of regaining control over a part of their operations, particularly if IS technology is a critical part of their units' operations, is very important to users (often reversing a trend which began 20 years ago in a very different technology). Control in this context has at least three different dimensions.

The first is the ability to exert direct control over systems development priorities. By using either their own staffs or self-selected software houses, users often believe they can get a system up and running in less time than it would take to navigate the priority-selling process in the corporate IS department, let alone get staff assigned to projects. This control ensures that the systems will be closer and more responsive to user needs. Mistakes made by a local group are often more easily accepted than those made by a remote group and rarely discussed; successes are often topics of conversation.

The second dimension of desired control is that users see themselves gaining control over the maintenance priorities. This is done either themselves or by contracting with suppliers that are dependent upon the users for income. Quite often the promotional message is that the maintenance can be performed by a clerk following a manual. A rare occurence!

The third dimension which is of importance for stand-alone computer systems is that users see themselves as gaining control over day-to-day operations. Insulated from the vicissitudes of the corporate computer scheduling, users believe they will be able to exert firmer control over the pace of their departments' operations. This is particularly important to small marginal users of heavily utilized data centers with volatile loads. Today, these points are intensified in many users' minds because of previous experiences with service degradation in large computer systems at month-end, or with jobs not run because of corporate priorities. Additionally, as a result of home computers, managers are becoming more confident in their ability to successfully manage a computer project. Clever computer-vendor marketing has helped to increase their confidence. However, often this experience, is of insufficient depth, and the user has more confidence than is warranted.

FIT TO ORGANIZATION

As the company becomes more decentralized in structure and geographically diverse, a distributed development function becomes a much better fit and avoids heavy marketing and coordination expenses. In conglomerates, for example, only a few have tried to centralize development, with most leaving it with the original units. Another advantage of distributed development is that if you have any intention of spinning off a unit, the less integrated its IS activities are with the rest of the company, the easier it is to implement the divesture.

USER LEARNING

As suggested in the four examples at the beginning of the chapter, it is very hard to predict the full ramifications of the introduction of a new technology. Firsthand, enthusiastic experimentation by the user can unlock creativity and stimulate new approaches to troublesome problems. Systems developed by an IS unit have to overcome more resistance in adoption. This is a special case (in the IS field) of broader work done in the fields of organization development and control where this factor has been identified as one of the principal forces in favor of organizing in multiple profit centers, as opposed to functionally. As noted in Chapter 3, this is increasingly evident in office automation and new professional support such as CAD.

Summary

In aggregate, these items represent a powerful set of arguments in favor of a strong user role in systems development and suggest when that role might be the dominant one. They further suggest that a summary statement capturing the flavor of the pressures driving users toward stand-alone, mini-based systems and local systems development or purchase of software, mini, and locally developed systems is: *short-term user driven.* The stand-alone, mini, and local development offer users solutions today to their problem under their *control* in a perceived enjoyable fashion. While, clearly, benefits associated with phase 1 and 2 learning can be achieved, as noted below often these are gained with not much regard for information hygiene.

PRESSURES TOWARD IS CONTROL OVER DEVELOPMENT

There are heavy internal pressures to consolidate or keep consolidated the development resource in one or more large clusters. The principal pressures are the following:

Staff Professionalism

A large support staff provides an opportunity to attract, and keep challenged, specialized technical individuals. The central unit also provides useful support for a small division or function which does not have its own data processing staff, but needs occasional access to data processing skills.

Further, as the average age of many IS development staffs continues to rise (graying of IS) these opportunities become a critical element in trying to increase productivity. The importance of this is intensified by the fact that salary levels, individual interests, and perceived interpersonal communication problems make lateral movement out of the department for some individuals an unfeasible option.

It is also easier to develop and enforce better standards of IS management practice in a large group. Documentation procedures, project management skills, and disciplined maintenance approaches are examples of critical development-department infrastructure items. In 1971, a large financial service organization faced with a deteriorating relationship between its central development department and key users was forced to split the development department into a number of smaller units and distributed these units around the company, thereby changing both reporting responsibility and office location. The quality of IS professionalism, although initially successful in stimulating new ideas and better relationships with users (many development people came to identify better with users than with technical development issues), had dropped so low by 1977, through neglect, that several major project fiascoes occurred which required assistance from an outside service organization. Today, significant parts of the development function have been recentralized, with much tighter controls installed over management practices in the remaining distributed development groups.

This is particularly important in relating to user-designed or user-selected computer-based systems. Lacking practical systems design experience and purchased software standards, the user often ignores normal data control procedures, documentation standards, and conventional costing practices. Consequently, purchasing from several suppliers, or incrementally from one, results in a clumsy system design which is hard to maintain. For example, one large financial organization discovered that all those involved in the design and purchase of software of three of their stand-alone computer systems used to process data on a daily basis had left the company, no formal documentation or operating instructions had been prepared, and all source programs had been lost. All that remained were disk files with object programs on them. The system ran, but why it ran no one knew, and even if the company's survival depended on it, changes were very difficult and time-consuming to execute.

Feasibility Study Concerns

An important problem is that a user-driven feasibility study may contain some major technical mistakes, resulting in the computer system being inadequate to handle the growing processing requirements. Because of inexperienced staff, such a feasibility study tends to underestimate both the complexity of the software needed to do the job and the growth in the number of transactions to be handled by the system. (The risk rises if there were limited technical inputs to the feasibility study or if the real business needs were not well understood.)

Often users organize a feasibility study to focus on a specific service and fail to recognize that a successful first application leads to the generation of an unexpected second application, then a third, and so forth. Each application appears to require only a modest incremental purchase price and therefore may not receive a comprehensive full-cost review. The result may be that the hardware configuration or software approach selected is unable to handle the necessary work. Unless great care was taken in the initial hardware selection and system design process to allow for growth, expansion can result in both major business disruptions and very expensive software modifications.

User-driven feasibility studies are more susceptible to acquiring an unstable vendor. In this rapidly growing industry sector, it is unlikely that all the current vendors will remain viable over the next five years. The same trends to hit the pocket calculator and the digital watch industry in the late 1970s will hit this industry sector as it reaches a point of maturity. This is critical because many of these systems insinuate themselves into the heart of a department's operations. Because these are software-intensive investments, failure of a vendor will mean both expensive disruption in service provided by the department and intensive crisis-spending efforts to convert the software to another machine. These concerns apply not just to hardware suppliers but also the packages and services provided by software suppliers. A single experience with a product from a failed software vendor provides painful learning.

Corporate Data Base System

Development of corporate data base strategy includes collection of files at a central location for reference by multiple users. The availability of staff in a central unit provides a focal point for both conceptualizing and developing systems which can serve multiple users. If such needs exist, a central department can best develop and distribute such systems to users (or manage the development process in a company where development of these systems is farmed out to local development units). The need for this varies widely with the nature of the corporation's activities. A conglomerate often has less need for this data than does a functionally organized, one-product company.

Inevitably, the first concern raised in discussing stand-alone islands of automation is that the company is losing the opportunity to manage and control its data flows. It is visualized that data of significance to many people beyond those in the originating unit will be locked up in a nonstandardized format, in inaccessible locations. Without denying the potential validity of this (there is substantial truth here), several mitigating factors exist which demand that this objection be carefully examined in any specific situation.

One factor is the issue of timing. In many cases, the argument of the erosion of data as a corporate resource is raised against a stand-alone system. It is alleged that in order to preserve flexibility for future data base design this stand-alone computer should not be acquired. Frequently, however, it turns out that this flexibility is not needed for three or more years in the future. In this context, a well-designed system may be an equally good (if not better) point of departure in evolving toward these long-term systems as would be jumping directly from the present set of manual procedures. This possibility must be pragmatically assessed.

Another mitigating factor, often overlooked, is that on planned frequent intervals data can be abstracted, if necessary, from a locally managed system and sent directly to a central computer. This is further supported by the fact that ordinarily not all information in a stand-alone file is relevant to other users (indeed, often only a small percentage is).

On the other hand, uniquely designed data handling systems can prove expensive to maintain and link. A clear need exists to identify in operational terms the data requirements of the central files and, if relevent, to suggest guidelines for what data can be stored locally. This problem is exemplified by the typical word and data processing systems which generate voluminous records in electronic format. Unless well designed these files may be bulky, lock up key data from potential users, and pose potential security problems. For example, a mail-order house recently discovered that each customer representative was using over 200 disks per day and storing them in boxes by date of order receipt, making aggregate customer information impossible to obtain in a timely manner. A new procedure reduced the number of disks to five.

The organization of and access to electronic files may require central storage to maintain the availability of data and ensure appropriate security. It is often easier to maintain good security when all files are in a single location than when scattered around a number of locations.

Initiative Center for New Ideas

A central unit helps identify new technologies of potential value to the company and communicate their existence to prospective users *(Phase 1 learning).* It can also function as a research unit and take financial and implementation responsibility for leading-edge projects legitimately too adventuresome for an individual user but which offer significant potential for organizational learning. Several organizations use this group to initiate and to manage corporately mandated productivity improvement programs. In these settings, senior management has viewed the user departments as being relatively weak, needing productivity improvements but incapable of implementing them. They consequently selected a change agent for initiating these changes, running roughshod if necessary over the users.

A problem related to this view, however, is that the central development group may push to "make" decisions, when instead they should "buy." Its high level of professionalism can generate an excessively critical attitude toward any purchase as being too general and incorporating inappropriate features. Recently the IS staff of a large government agency, following a reduction of staff, ended up with very well-trained individuals who had suffered the early stages of all of IBM's new standard systems. A request for a new data retrieval system for the entire agency met with their insistence that it be resolved with an expensive in-house development project. This project soaked up all available systems expertise and forced user management into buying, without help, several outside services to meet immediate operational needs. Subsequently, when the development group started to test the retrieval system, they discovered that unmanaged proliferation of new services made key data files inaccessible, perhaps an unnecessary problem had they used an outside data software package. Procedures are needed to ensure that the true economics of make-or-buy are considered by central groups.

Fit to Corporate Structure and Strategy

Centralized IS's development role is clearest in organizations where there is centrally directed planning and operational control. A large manufacturer of farm equipment which has a tradition of central functional control from corporate headquarters had successfully implemented a program where all software for factories and distribution units worldwide was developed by their corporate systems group. Now as these groups are growing in size the company's structure is becoming more decentralized. Consequently the cost of running effective central systems development is escalating, and they are having to implement a marketing function to educate users and decentralize some functions. It is becoming increasingly common for centralized development groups to have an explicitly defined and staffed internal marketing activity.

Cost Analysis

A significant edge that a centralized IS group has, through their practical experience in other system efforts, is the ability to produce a realistic software development estimate (subject to all the problems discussed in Chapter 7) which takes into account the interests of the company as a whole. Software development estimates turned out to be a real problem in user feasibility studies. There are two contributing factors to this. The first is that in most cases a new system turns out to be more software intensive than hardware intensive. Typically, software costs run from 75 percent to 85 percent of the total costs for a customized system. Since the user often has had little or no experience in estimating software development costs, an order of magnitude mistake in a feasibility study (particularly if it is an individually developed system and not a "turnkey" package) is not unknown.

The second factor is the lack of experience with true costs of service because of complicated chargeout systems. Many corporate chargeout systems present calculations in terms of utilization of computer resource units that are completely unintelligible to the user. The result is that each month or quarter an unintelligible and unpredictable bill arrives. In management control environments where the user is held responsible for variance from budget, this causes intense frustrations. A locally developed system, particularly if it is for a mini, is perceived as a solution to this.

Further, many chargeout systems are designed on a full-cost basis. Consequently, the charges from the corporate center often seem high to the user. Since, particularly in the short run, there are significant fixed cost elements to a corporate information systems center, what appears a cost reduction opportunity to the user may be a cost increase for the company. Policies for ensuring that appropriate cost analyses are prepared must be established.

Summary

A phrase capturing the spirit of these problems would be *long-term information hygiene.* The problems, in many respects, are not immediately evident at the time of system installation but tend to grow in importance with the passage of time. Policies to manage the trade-offs between the obvious short-term benefits and long-term risks are delicate to administer but are necessary. Further, what were long-term problems may be short term as we learn to buy new cheaper software and throw away expensive-to-maintain code.

IS–USER RESPONSIBILITIES

The tension over control can be managed by establishing clear core policies as to what make up the user domain, what make up the IS domain, and what is senior management's role. Senior management must play a significant role in ensuring both that these policies are developed and that they evolve appropriately over time. Both IS and the users must understand the implications of these roles and the possible conflicts.

IS Responsibilities

To manage the long-term information hygiene needs of an organization the following central core of IS responsibilities emerge as the irreducible minimum:

1. Development of procedures to ensure that for potential information services projects of any size a comparison is made of internal development versus purchase. If the projects are implemented outside the firm or by the user this must include establishment of the appropriate professional standards for project control and documentation. These standards need to be flexible, since user-developed systems for micros pose demands quite different from systems to be run on large mainframe computers. Further, a process for forcing adherence to the selected standards must be defined.
2. Maintenance of an inventory of installed or planned-to-be-installed information services.
3. Development and maintenance of a set of standards which establish:
   a. Mandatory telecommunication standards.
   b. Standard languages for classes of acquired equipment.
   c. Documentation procedures for different types of systems.
   d. Corporate data dictionary with clear definitions for when elements must be included. Identification of file maintenance standards and procedure.
   e. Examination procedure for systems developed as independent islands to ensure that they do not conflict with corporate needs and that any necessary interfaces are constructed.
4. Identification and provision of appropriate IS development-staff career paths throughout the organization. These include sideways transfers within and between IS units, upward movements within IS, and appropriate outward movement to other functional units. (More difficult in distributed units, it is still doable.)
5. Establishment of appropriate internal marketing efforts for IS support activities. These should exert pressure to speed up, and coach, the units which are lagging, while slowing down the units which are exceeding technological prudence.
6. Preparation of a detailed checklist of questions to be answered in any hardware/software acquisition to ensure that relevant technical and managerial issues are raised. These questions should concern:

   a. How the proposed system meets corporate communication standards (item 3).
   b. For word processing systems, questions on upward growth potential and built-in communication and data processing capability.
   c. For data processing systems, availability of languages which support systems growth potential, available word processing features, etc.
   d. For communication systems, the types of data transfer capabilities, list of available services, storage capacity, etc.

7. Identification of preferred systems suppliers and the conditions for entertaining exceptions to the list of standards to be met by vendors before a business relationship is established. For example, size, number of systems in place, and financial structure should be clearly spelled out.
8. Establishment of education programs for potential users, to communicate both the potential and the pitfalls of new technology and to define the users' roles in ensuring its successful introduction in their departments.
9. An ongoing review of which systems are not feasible to manage and which should be redesigned.

These comments apply with particular force to the design of systems which embed themselves operationally in the company. Decision support systems do not pose nearly the same problems.

These functions, of course, can be significantly expanded with much tighter and more formal controls if the situation warrants it. In this regard, a diagnostic framework presented in 1980 in the *Harvard Business Review*[1] is particularly useful in assessing both the current position of an organization and where it should move.

User Responsibilities

To assist in the orderly implementation of new IS services and grow in an understanding of their use, cost, and impact on the organization, the following responsibilities should be fulfilled by the user of IS service.

1. Maintain a financial control system of all user IS-type activities. Increasingly, in the more experienced organizations a user-understandable IS chargeout system has been installed.
2. Make an appraisal of the user-people investment for each new project, in both the short term and the long term, to ensure a satisfactory service.
3. Develop a comprehensive user support plan for projects that will support vital aspects of the business or that will grow in use. This includes

[1] Jack R. Buchanan and Richard G. Linowes, "Understanding Distributed Processing," *Harvard Business Review,* July–August 1980, pp. 143–53.

inputs to networks' architecture, data base policies, filing policies for word processors, and user training programs at both the staff and managerial levels.

4. Manage the IS/user interface consistently with its strategic relevance, as an integral aspect of the business. The mix of central site, prepackaged programs, outside contracts, and all new services expenditure should be approved by the user.
5. Perform periodic audits on the appropriateness of system reliability standards, communications services, and security requirement documentation.

These represent the very minimum sets of policies that the users should develop and manage. Depending on the firm's geography, corporate management style, stage of IS development, and mix of technology phases of development, expanded levels of user involvement may be appropriate, including acquisition of their own staff. As these items evolve over time, the appropriateness of certain policies will also evolve.

General Support and Policy Overview

Distinct from the issues involved in the distribution of IS services are a cluster of broad policy and direction activities which require *senior management perspective*. In the past, these activities were built into the structure of a central IS organization. Now, because of the need to link IS to business planning, they are not infrequently separated. A major oil company recently reorganized to produce a 300-person systems and operations department reporting directly to the head of administrative services. This department does the implementation and operational IS work of the company on a month-to-month, year-to-year basis. At the same time, an 8- to 10-person IS policy group reports directly to the head of corporate planning, which works on overall policy and long-range strategy formulation. A major conglomerate which has all its development hardware distributed to key users has at the same time a three- to four-person group at headquarters level. Key functions of this corporate policy group should include the following:

1. Ensuring that there is an appropriate balance between IS and user inputs across the different technologies and that one side is not dominating the other inappropriately; initiating appropriate personnel and organizational moves if the situation is out of balance. Executive steering committees, for example, are a common response to a user imbalance.
2. Through its broad overview and perspective on the total role of information systems in the company, ensuring that a comprehensive IS corporate strategy is developed. In particular, in an environment where the resources are widely distributed it is critical that a comprehensive overview of technology, corporate use thereof, and linkage to overall corporate goals be put together. The relative amount of resources to be

devoted to this will appropriately vary widely from organization to organization as the perceived contribution to corporate strategy, among other things, changes. (This will be discussed in more depth in Chapter 5.)

3. Auditing the inventory of hardware/software resources to assure that the corporate view is provided in the establishment of purchasing relationships and contracts. In certain settings the corporate group will be the appropriate place to initiate standard vendor policies.
4. Ensuring development and evolution of appropriate sets of standards for both development and operations activities and ensuring that those standards are being applied appropriately. In this regard, the corporate policy group plays a combined role of consultant on the one hand and auditor (particularly if there is a weak or nonexistent IS auditing function) on the other hand. The implementation of this role requires staff that is both technically competent and interpersonally sensitive.
5. Acting as the facilitating authority in managing the transfer of technology from one unit to another. This will occur through recognizing common systems needs between units and the stimulation of joint projects. Actual transfer will require a combination of sustained visits to the different operating units, organizing of periodic corporate MIS conferences, development of a corporate information systems newsletter, and other means.
6. Acting as an initiative center to identify and encourage appropriate forms of technical experimentation. A limited program of research is a very appropriate part of the IS function and an important role of the corporate policy group is to ensure that that does not get swept away in the press of urgent operational issues. Further, the corporate function is in a position to encourage patterns of experimentation that smaller units might feel pose undue risk if they were the sole beneficiary.
7. Assuming responsibility for the development of an appropriate planning and control system to link IS firmly and appropriately to the company's goals. Planning, system appraisal, chargeout, and project management processes should be monitored and, if necessary, encouraged to develop by the policy group. In this context, the group should work closely with the corporate steering committee.

These roles suggest the group needs to be staffed heavily with individuals who in aggregate represent both broad technical backgrounds and extensive practical IS administrative experience. Except in very limited numbers, it is not a very good entry-level department for new staff members.

SUMMARY

The last two chapters have focused on the key issues surrounding organization of the information systems activity for the 1980s. It can be seen that there has been a significant revolution in what is regarded as good managerial practice in this field. Conventional wisdom has changed considerably and seems likely to continue its evolution. Consequently, many IS organization structures effectively put together in the 1970s are inappropriate for the 1980s. A significant contributing component of this change has been the development of new hardware and software technologies. These technologies not only permit quite different types of services to be delivered but also offer the potential for quite different ways of delivering these services.

The subject of determining the appropriate pattern of distribution of IS resources within the organization is both complex and multifaceted. We suggest that the general manager should develop a program to encourage innovation and to maintain overall control to manage the distribution of services. The final resolution of these organization and planning issues is inextricably tied to non-IS-oriented aspects of the corporate environment. Current leadership style at the top of the organization and that person's view of the future provide one important thrust for redirection. A vision of tighter central control sets a different context for these decisions than one which emphasizes the autonomy of operating units. Closely associated and linked to this is the broad corporate organization structure and culture and the trends which are occurring there.

The realities of geographical spread of the business units have a heavy impact on the art of the possible. The large corporate headquarters of an insurance company poses different constraints than the multiple international plants and markets of an automobile manufacturer.

On a less global scale are the realities of quality and location (organizationally and physically) of current IS resources. Equally important is how responsive and competent these resources are seen to be by current users. The unit which is perceived (no matter how unfairly or inaccurately) as unresponsive has different organization challenges than the well-regarded unit. Similarly, the current and perceived appropriate strategic role of IS on dimensions of applications portfolio and operations has important organizational implications. The support unit, for example, must be placed to deal with its perceived lack of relevance to corporate strategy. In dealing with all of these forces one is trying to find an appropriate balance between innovation and control, and the input of the IS specialist versus the user.

Not only do appropriate answers to these questions vary between companies, but different answers and structures are often appropriate for individual units in an organization. In short, there is a right series of questions to ask, and an identifiable but a very complex series of forces which, appropriately analyzed, determine for each organizational unit what the direction of the right answer is (for now).

Case 4–1 □ Air Products and Chemicals, Inc. MIS Evaluation of End-User Systems*

In January of 1981, Peter Mather, director of Management Information Systems (MIS) at Air Products and Chemicals, faced a decision regarding the selection of an online data base inquiry package. The inquiry package would be used by various operating groups within the company as a decision support tool. The Industrial Gas Division (IGD) had found a package on its own and was pushing hard to have Mather's organization choose this package. They emphasized the point by indicating that they wanted to use it even if Mather decided to adopt something different for the rest of the company.

THE COMPANY

Air Products and Chemicals, Inc., based in Allentown, Pennsylvania, had 1980 sales of $1.6 billion ($1.4 billion after intersegment eliminations) with net earnings of $115.5 million. Over the last four years, sales had been growing at 15 percent annually, net income at 17 percent. The company employed approximately 16,000 people and had over 150 plants in the United States and 11 other countries. As shown in Exhibit 1, Air Products was organized into three operating groups and one relatively autonomous subsidiary.

The Industrial Gas Group produced, distributed, and sold a variety of industrial, medical, and specialty gases around the world. In 1980, IGG sales were $733.5 million. IGD was the domestic arm of IGG, contributing a significant percentage of IGG total sales.

The Process Systems Group (PSG) manufactured and sold cryogenic equipment, and provided energy conservation systems for coal solids and liquids fuel processing systems and metallurgical industry products and services. PSG sales were $271.9 million in 1980.

The Chemicals Group manufactured and sold chemical intermediates, polymers, plastics, and catalysts. These products were used in a broad range of applications such as urethane foams, crop protection products, adhesives, coatings, textiles, and molded plastics. Sales for 1980 were $535.2 million for the Chemicals Group.

* This case was prepared by Alexander E. Nedzel under the direction of Associate Professor James I. Cash. It is intended to serve as the basis for class discussion rather than to illustrate either effective or ineffective handling of an administrative situation.

EXHIBIT 1 □ Corporate Organization*

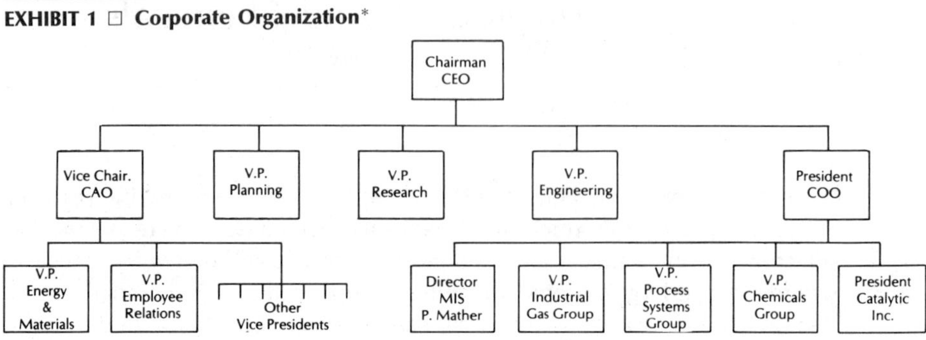

* Depicts reporting relationships only.

The Catalytic, Inc., subsidiary engaged in engineering design, procurement and construction of plants for the chemical, petrochemical, fiber, plastics, food, drug, and metallurgical industries. It also performed construction management and plant maintenance services. Because it dealt regularly with the competition of the other operating groups, Catalytic was managed at arm's length by Air Products. Catalytic's 1980 sales, net of direct contract costs, were $35.8 million.

The company operated in a generally centralized fashion with corporate offices and the three product groups all headquartered in one facility. A central management committee, which meets weekly, oversaw the budgeting process and approved all major pricing and capital expenditure decisions. Once the budget was approved, the product group vice presidents were given latitude in making operating decisions.

THE MANAGEMENT INFORMATION SERVICES ORGANIZATION

Senior management at Air Products had long recognized the importance of an efficient, well-coordinated data processing effort. Because of this, data processing planning, development, operations, and support activities were concentrated in the corporate MIS organization. Peter Mather, the director of MIS, reported directly to the president. In 1980, data processing costs for Air Products were $22.9 million. Corporate MIS accounted for two thirds of this amount. The remaining costs were accounted for primarily by parallel departments within the Catalytic subsidiary and Air Products Europe, headquartered in England. The data processing group in Europe was referred to as MIG (Management Information Group).

The service demands placed upon corporate MIS by the operating groups and corporate staff had been steadily increasing. Volume for existing data processing applications was growing as Air Products expanded, but, more important, users were constantly recognizing new ways in which the collection, storage, and analysis of data could help them in their drive for growth and efficiency. The MIS budget was growing at over 25 percent annually, as Exhibit 2 shows. Mather realized that severe organizational problems would result if faster growth were attempted, and yet a sizable backlog of proposed applications was ever present.

Management Information Services was organized with eight corporate MIS departments (Exhibit 3) reporting to Mather directly and the two remote DP organizations reporting to him on a functional basis. The administrative services department handled such items as internal MIS standards, accounting, user training, and data security. The long-range planning position was not yet filled; Mather and his managers presently performed that function.

The facilities department was responsible for operating the corporate computer installation, including an interactive terminal network, managing Data Entry, and Technical Support. The computer complex included an Amdahl 470/V8 dedicated primarily to batch jobs and an IBM 370/3033U dedicated primarily to online applications. The systems were coupled, had 12 Meg internal memories, and operated under MVS/SE operating systems. Peripheral devices (shared between systems) included 16 tape drives (6250 BPI), 28.6 gigabytes of disk storage, laser, and impact printers. The complex supported 300 terminals, including CRTs, RJE stations, and graphics terminals. Approximately two thirds of these terminals were located at or near the Allentown facility; the remainder were dispersed across the United States. Technical Support was responsible for maintaining the operating systems and other basic software packages used by corporate MIS.

The business systems, the engineering & scientific systems, and the management sciences departments composed the corporate MIS organization's user applications development arm. These departments would make use of the basic systems and support offered by the facilities department to develop and maintain specific application programs and packages for corporate staff and operating group users.

In the spring of 1979 MIS selected CICS[1] and IDMS[2] as their standard software tools for their online systems. In order to manage the transition to shared data base management systems (DBMS) and avoid application-oriented uses of DBMS, the data resources management department was formed. Bob Bruno, formerly the business systems department manager, was selected to head the new department. The data resources department was responsible for the design and organization of the various computerized

---

[1] CICS is an acronym for customer information control system, an IBM product which supports online communications.

[2] IDMS is an acronym for integrated data management system, a data base management package marketed by Cullinane Corporation.

EXHIBIT 2 □ Air Products and Chemicals, Inc. Corporate MIS Facts (historical budget—FY 1977–1981, $000)

	Actual				Budget	Compound
	FY 77	FY 78	FY 79	FY 80	FY 81	growth %
Personnel	4,229.2	4,711.3	6,076.3	9,390.0	10,824.7	26.5
Equipment	1,170.9	1,918.6	2,202.5	2,381.9	4,585.5	40.7
Supplies/misc/occup	1,502.6	1,450.7	1,838.2	2,832.0	2,779.7	16.6
Total	6,902.7	8,080.6	10,117.0	14,603.9	18,189.9	27.4
Percent increase		17.1%	25.2%	44.4%	24.6%	
Employees (year end)						
Exempt	131	133	164	238	247	17.2
Contract	—	—	15	9	0	—
Nonexempt	90	91	97	118	118	7.0
Total	221	224	276	365	365	13.4
Percent increase		1.4%	23.2%	32.2%	(0.0%)	

Allocation of 1981 budget to services

System development service	47.4%
System support service	16.6
Production service	36.0
	100.0%

EXHIBIT 3 □ Corporate MIS Organization

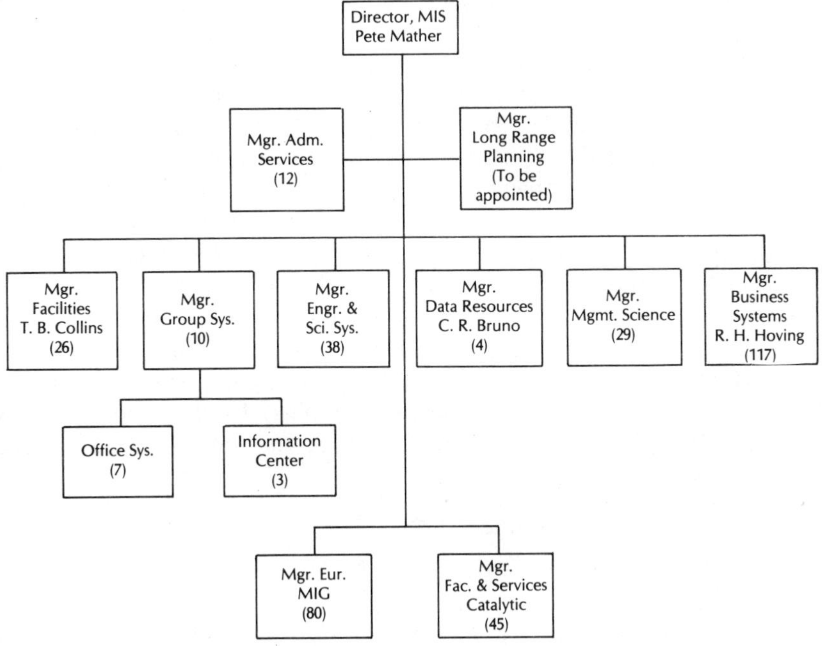

Numbers in parentheses indicate staffing levels.

data bases at Air Products, promoting consolidation and standardization wherever feasible. This department chose IDMS as the foundation for their ultimate goal of moving to integrated corporate data bases.

The group systems department was the link between the users and the three applications-development departments. There were managers in the group systems department responsible for the Gas Group, the Process Systems Group, the Chemicals Group, and corporate staff groups, respectively. Each of these managers was responsible for addressing the client's information processing problems by enlisting the services of the appropriate departments within corporate MIS. The Group Systems managers interfaced primarily at the senior management level, promoting the ability of corporate MIS to understand the client's needs and respond to them in a timely fashion. Their activities were heavily oriented toward planning and budgeting for MIS services within their respective groups. A recent addition to Group Systems was the Information Center, modeled after IBM Canada's approach to offering internal time-sharing services. Mather considered the "Info Center" the appropriate location for support of an end-user programming system.

As the user applications backlog of corporate MIS expanded, so too did the importance of the Group Systems function. Group Systems managers served to give the MIS organization a better understanding of the scope and relative importance of the various user needs. Additionally, they could help the client groups understand why MIS could not be highly responsive to each and every item in the applications backlog.

Peter Mather, the MIS director, joined Air Products in 1967. His first assignment led to the creation of Group Systems, which he initially managed. Later he managed the MIS group of Air Products Europe, served as assistant director of MIS (managing Group Systems, Scientific and Engineering, Office Automation and Business Systems). His appointment to director of MIS had taken place just a few months earlier, in October of 1980. Before joining Air Products, Mather started his career with a British public accounting firm. After five years, he joined the Berman Leasing Company in 1962 as manager of internal audit, was subsequently promoted to regional controller and then to assistant corporate controller. By the time he left Berman, Mather had complete responsibility for that firm's data processing operations.

ONLINE SYSTEMS AT AIR PRODUCTS

In 1980, the user applications run by corporate MIS still operated primarily in a batch mode (development work on some online applications was nearing completion, however). There was increasing user pressure to support more online time-shared applications wherein a user could run applications interactively from a terminal. In such a mode of operation, a user could obtain significant productivity benefits by receiving program results and data instantly instead of having to wait for a job to run and for report listings to be delivered. Faced with a significant backlog and committed to holding the growth of applications and technology to a manageable level, corporate MIS was not always as responsive as the users would have liked to requests for the development of online applications.

The Industrial Gas Division (IGD), a progressive computer user at Air Products, felt a particularly strong need for online systems. In 1979, because they did not perceive corporate MIS to be responsive enough to their needs, IGD asked Eric Osmundson, one of their "applied research and development" engineers (later given the title information systems manager by IGD management) to liaise with MIS in the development of their systems applications. It was part of his job to solicit bids from outside vendors if it did not appear that corporate MIS was prepared to respond adequately to an IGD need.

IGD solicited outside bids for a tank control system and a material control system (MCS) two years after MIS began working on the project. Subsequently, corporate MIS implemented both systems. The material control system was developed using an existing time-sharing system but a language new to MIS. This experimental approach was adopted to address IGD's requirement for an online interactive system. The tank control system was developed using the CICS/IDMS systems. IGD was dissatisfied with the operating cost and response time of the MCS. They decided not to wait for MIS to revise the initial version of the system. Instead, after their controller had completed a financial study of the problem, IGD purchased software and its own minicomputer system to meet its material control needs. (Subsequently a revised version of MIS's original MCS was successfully implemented elsewhere in the company.)

The potential proliferation of applications not under the control of corporate MIS concerned Mather. Even if the operation of a system such as the IGD material control system were to be decentralized, system procurement, development, administration, and ongoing support by corporate MIS would make more efficient use of staff expertise and would facilitate corporate hardware, software, and data standardization. Corporate MIS had the necessary functional authority to stop the IGD procurement, but Mather knew that such action would not serve to enhance the working relationship between IGD and corporate MIS, which was of major concern to him. As Mather and managers in the group systems department had pointed out to the previous MIS director, the only solution to the problem would be to improve MIS's credibility with users by an increase in responsiveness on the part of corporate MIS to requests for online applications.

THE NEED FOR ONLINE DATA BASE INQUIRY

IGD, through its MIS applications, maintained numerous disk and tape files pertaining to its sales and operations. If they had the ability to inspect and generate reports using the data in these files, and on an ad hoc and unstructured basis (at the time they were receiving only periodic, predefined reports), IGD managers could make better operating decisions. Some of the managers had heard that program products which facilitated online ad hoc data base inquiry existed and were available on the market.

Early in 1980, the IGD systems manager completed an evaluation of an inquiry product called FOCUS, marketed by Information Builders Incorporated (IBI). When he informed corporate MIS of his desire to try FOCUS, he was told that corporate MIS would be willing to participate in a presentation and an operational test of the package. By June, with the support of corporate MIS in contract negotiations, IGD had contracted with an independent time-sharing vendor to perform trials.

The IGD staff were very satisfied with the results of the tests, and they wished to go ahead with regular use of FOCUS. The IGD systems manager communicated his belief that FOCUS was the preferred inquiry package, and that corporate MIS should install it on their system. He also indicated that IGD would want to use FOCUS even if corporate MIS chose another package for corporatewide use.

Corporate MIS, as well, was impressed with FOCUS. It would provide a far easier way for users to access and analyze the various computerized data bases at Air Products than was presently possible, and potentially could have a significant impact on end-user productivity. The language of FOCUS, while not self-explanatory to the laymen, did not require experienced systems analysts once the definitions and layouts of all the data base files were established. With FOCUS, a manager (possibly with the help of a relatively junior staff member) could conceive and run an ad hoc data query/analysis in half an hour that would have taken days to implement and run using the software languages presently supported by corporate MIS. In addition to improved information timeliness, these time savings also meant cost savings.

If it were to cost less for a manager to perform an ad hoc analysis the manager might be encouraged to do more analysis. Increased data analysis would lead the manager to more thoroughly examined decisions as well as a better understanding of operations. On the data processing side, the increased requirement for data access and analysis would provide further justification for the costs of data collection and data base maintenance. Additionally it would help reduce the applications backlog, which would aid enhancing MIS's credibility.

Because of these benefits, Mather was certain that an online data base inquiry language would see extensive use at Air Products. He and his managers wanted to ensure that a standard, single package was adopted by all users and that the package selected would be the best available for Air Products' purposes. Mather also believed it to be crucial that corporate MIS be able to participate in influencing how the inquiry language would be used:

> We have an implicit ability to control and forecast our batch system usage fairly well. This is because we schedule the design, implementation, and execution of every application. When our scheduled applications point to a shortfall in computing capacity at some time in the future, we can budget a capacity increase in plenty of time.
>
> With time-shared applications such as ad hoc data base inquiry, job execution takes place solely at the discretion of the user. With a good "user friendly" inquiry language, users would design and implement their applications as well. We would therefore receive little advance indication of how heavy the future time-shared system usage would be, thus impacting service levels and greatly complicating our capacity planning and budgeting process.

Shortly after his appointment in 1980, Mather had to secure management approval for an additional large mainframe computer. This had resulted from an 80 percent per annum growth in resource utilization resulting from online systems usage—as opposed to the historical growth rate of 30 percent per annum for batch. Mather had to request more funds from top management than either his strategic plan or budget had called for. He did not want it to happen again. Bob Bruno, the data resources manager, expressed an additional concern:

> We were impressed with what we saw at the FOCUS demonstration, but we saw more than just a decision support package capable of accessing and analyzing data files. FOCUS, as well as many packages like it, has complete data base management capabilities, including data base definition, creation, and modification. At a time when we are trying to coordinate and consolidate the various data bases at Air Products, we do not want users to create their own ad hoc data bases at a whim. We must encourage users to continue interfacing with corporate MIS and its applications development departments to create and maintain their data. In this way, my department can continue in its efforts to manage and integrate the proliferation of data within the company, and more important, to make this resource available on an organized secure basis.

IDENTIFYING THE ALTERNATIVES

As convinced as the IGD systems manager was concerning FOCUS, Mather and his managers knew they had the functional responsibility to consider all appropriate, available products. After a careful, objective evaluation, corporate MIS would decide which package was most appropriate for use at Air Products. Mather put Bob Bruno, the Data Resources manager, in charge of the identification and evaluation of alternative packages.

Bob Bruno teamed up with a member of the group systems department covering IGD to identify candidate data base inquiry packages. By consulting publications such as *Datapro* and periodicals such as *Computerworld,* and by talking with some consultants that corporate MIS had dealt with in the past, they drew up an initial list of 25 candidate packages. Based on broad criteria such as compatibility with Air Products' computer hardware and operating systems, and general functional features, all but eight candidates were screened out.

Bob Bruno invited the eight vendors to visit Air Products and give sales presentations. In addition to people from corporate MIS, and IGD, corporate Employee Relations and Energy & Materials representatives were invited. (These organizations had also been vocal in pushing for an online inquiry language.) From the information gained at these presentations, it was possible to eliminate four more candidates, leaving QUICKDRAW, FOCUS, QUESTION, and RAMIS II.[3]

In mid-September, Mather and Bruno put together a committee of 12

[3] Packages listed in the text and exhibits are disguised, with the exception of FOCUS and RAMIS II.

people to perform a formal, in-depth evaluation of the candidate systems. The committee included eight people from corporate MIS—two from Group Systems, two from Data Resources (Bob Bruno was one), two from Business Systems, one from Management Science, and one from Technical Support. The other four participants were the IGD systems manager and an IGD analyst that had been working with FOCUS, a representative from Employee Relations, and a representative from Energy & Materials. Bob Bruno chaired the committee.

DEFINING THE EVALUATION CRITERIA

In order to select a system, the committee had to define appropriate evaluation criteria. The first step was to gain an understanding of who the users would be, the types of queries and reports they would require, the data files to be accessed, the type and extent of file updating to be done and the relative requirements for batch and interactive inquiry. Following is the description of potential usage determined by the committee:

> It is anticipated that query language software will be used widely throughout the company. Primary users are expected to be end users that wish to access existing data which is available as a result of previously developed information systems or data collection.
>
> Generally it will be preferable to transfer, or download, this data from existing files on a scheduled daily, weekly, or monthly basis into the special form of data base file which the query software is able to process rapidly and efficiently. These "derived" data base files would be held available specifically for purposes of end-user query; they would rarely be updated, since updating would take place in the source file as part of the existing information system. Generally the derived data base would be replaced in total with each scheduled load.
>
> Queries would most often be on an interactive basis, with response in the form of screens or short reports and graphs being produced while the user waits. However, it is also anticipated that a significant number of queries which involve greater volumes of data would be submitted at a terminal to be run in a batch mode with output being returned to the user at a later time (perhaps an hour or up to a day later).
>
> While primary usage would be against derived data base files, it is also anticipated that end users will develop reports from existing files which have not been converted to derived data bases. The existing files could be production IDMS data base files, or other production files. This type of query request would generally be executed in a batch mode, although the request would be structured and submitted by the user in an interactive session.
>
> Another important type of usage for this software is in the development of small volume, stand-alone information systems. System developers who would otherwise develop such systems using the more complex languages of COBOL or FORTRAN will have an opportunity to achieve a major productivity advan-

tage in employing this much simpler software in appropriate cases. It is anticipated that this type of usage would be applicable primarily to corporate MIS, although it could also be applicable to end users for very small volume systems where data would never be shared with other users or systems.

The committee attempted to weight the frequency of each of the types of usage described above, as illustrated in Exhibit 4.

EXHIBIT 4 □ Query Language User Profile

	Weights	
1. Query		
Interactive	60	
Batch	40	
Ad hoc		25
Macro		75
2. Interactive query		
Package data base	90	
Production IDMS DB	5	
OS tapes	0	
OS others	5	
Combinations	X	
3. Batch query		
Package data base	65	
Production IDMS DB	15	
OS tapes	15	
OS others	5	
Combinations	X	
4. Source of own data base files		
Derived	60	
Live production	10	
User private	15	
Working	15	
5. Load	Interactive	Batch
Derived	0	100
Live production	X	X
User private	90	10
Working	75	25
6. Update		
Derived	20	80
Live production	50	50
User private	100	0
Working	100	0
7. Add-On		
Derived	0	100
Live production	X	X
User private	X	X
Working	X	X

The committee then identified nine major evaluation categories, each to be handled in detail by a subcommittee.

File definition and loading
File updating
Query and reporting capabilities
File interface capabilities
Environmental flexibility
Performance
Security
Vendor
Cost

Exhibit 5 contains a brief description of each category.

EVALUATING THE ALTERNATIVES

To handle a category, a subcommittee would break it down into as many separately weighted subcategories as was felt appropriate.[4] To obtain the necessary data, subcommittees conducted in-depth reviews of documentation, held frequent discussions with vendor technical and marketing representatives, and interviewed various established users of the products being evaluated. Each subcategory would be given a numeric rating. These subcategory ratings would then be weighted and combined, resulting in an overall numeric rating for the category. As an example of this, Exhibit 6 illustrates the work of the File Updating evaluation subcommittee.

As category evaluations were completed, the full committee assigned weights to the categories in order to arrive at an overall numeric rating for each inquiry package. After completing and weighting the first three categories, it became obvious to the committee that QUICKDRAW and QUESTION could be eliminated, leaving FOCUS and RAMIS II as the final candidates. Exhibit 7 summarizes the reasons for the elimination.

By January of 1981, the committee had completed its evaluation of all nine categories. Bob Bruno did not want the committee's entire decision to be dictated by a simple numeric comparison. Accordingly without weighting the final categories, he presented to Mather a draft version of the committee's final report. The report included the commentary in Appendix A.

Conflict developed in the committees—MIS was looking to RAMIS II for efficiency and perceived vendor strength. The Employee Relations and

[4] The weights assigned within a category were independent of the weights shown in Exhibit 4.

EXHIBIT 5 □ Major Categories of Evaluation*

1. *File definition and loading.* With regard to internal and external files, examine the ease of use for both corporate MIS and end users. Also determine the ease of building and updating the data dictionary, content of the dictionary, field and report attributes, and query facilities.

2. *File updating.* Research the ability to add, delete, and modify all types of data base records. Evaluate the syntax employed, ease of use, and appropriateness for low or high volumes of update. Review the adequacy of audit facilities, backup, and recovery.

3. *Query and reporting capabilities.* Examine the simplicity, naturalness, ease of learning, and using for batch/interactive and internal/external file queries. Determine the macro capabilities, conversational facilities, and full-screen edit features. Identify the host language interfaces, user exits, interfaces to statistics, graphics, financial modeling, and other software. Review all of the reporting, sorting, formatting, and computational features identified by the evaluation committee.

4. *File interface capabilities.* Evaluate the extent to which external files can be processed. Examine the OS access methods supported, ease of use, capability to combine file types in a query, and usefulness of the IDMS interface.

5. *Environmental flexibility.* Investigate the ability of each package to run in the various operating environments that corporate MIS is contemplating. The research will take into consideration any cost of conversion, as well as the functions that should be suppressed to maintain likeness across environments.

6. *Performance.* With regard to query, update, and loading, evaluate the different file structures and indexes available. Identify the use of data compression, journaling, and recovery facilities. Examine the suitability of the data structures for both small and large files.

7. *Security.* Identify the various levels of security available for files, records, and fields. Evaluate the ease of administration, effectiveness, and compatibility with existing data security conventions.

8. *Vendor.* Identify the vendor's capability to support their product both overseas and locally. Examine the support policy and overall satisfaction of the existing user community.

9. *Cost.* Determine costs of initial acquisition and annual maintenance support.

* Each category was assigned to a subcommittee for detailed investigation.

Energy & Materials representatives were somewhat indifferent, feeling that either product would be a major improvement in capability for their departments. IGD was strongly disposed toward FOCUS for greater functional capabilities in graphics and statistical analysis. IGD felt MIS was more concerned with efficiency than capability. Without a consensus, Mather was faced with having to make the decision.

EXHIBIT 6 □ Example of Output of Subcommittees

FILE UPDATING

	WT	FOCUS		RAMIS II		QUESTION		QUICKDRAW	
Individual updates	20	10	200	10	[4]200	10	200	10	[4]200
Generic updates	20	8	160	9	180	10	200	6	[4]120
Syntax	10	10	100	10	100	9	90	9	90
Volume dependencies	5	0	[2] 0	0	[2] 0	0	[2] 0	0	[2] 0
Audit facilities	5	0	[1] 0	0	[1] 0	0	[1] 0	0	[1] 0
Backup and recovery	20	2	[3] 40	10	200	0	0	2	40
Restart	20	10	200	0	0	0	0	0	0
	100		700		680		490		450

SUPERSCRIPTS
[1] = The feature being evaluated does not exist.
[2] = The assumption has been made that updates consisting of large volume would be deferred to batch-overnight processing.
[3] = The feature being evaluated is a user option, not a function that happens automatically.
[4] = Feature could be used directly against production files.

EXHIBIT 7 □ Packages Eliminated during Second Review (reduction from four vendors to two)

QUICKDRAW

a. Limitations exist with the creation of work fields.
b. Does not meet the requirement to produce reports "by" and "across."
c. Graphics facilities are limited.
d. General report output capabilities are weak.
e. File definition is much more difficult and not user-friendly. (This results from its having to rely on the vendor's data dictionary).

QUESTION

a. Does not meet the requirements to produce reports "by" and "across."
b. Graphics facilities are limited.
c. Capability to process external files directly does not exist.
d. File definition syntax is difficult.
e. Use of macro facility is limited.

Category	Weight*	FOCUS	RAMIS II	QUESTION	QUICKDRAW
1. File definition and loading	7	980	920	881	805
2. File update	5	700	680	490	450
3. Query and reporting capabilities	10	985	1,000	770	795
Weighted total		20,210	19,840	16,317	15,385
4. File interface capabilities		948	610		
5. Environmental flexibility		450	1,000		
6. Performance		1,890	2,250		
7. Security		1,000	995		
8. Vendor		874	1,000		
9. Cost		more	less (see Appendix A)		

* Entries here reflect relatives emphasis for this evaluation (i.e., query and reporting is two times as important as file update).

CHOOSING A SYSTEM

Mather was beginning to get some pressure for a decision, yet he hoped to get a consensus. At least, he wanted to identify the remaining prerequisites for making a decision, at a meeting to which he called Bob Bruno (data resources manager), Joe Schulter (group systems manager for IGD), Tom Collins (facilities manager), and Rick Gobrecht, (technical support manager). With respect to his choice of attendees, Mather said:

> I included Joe in order to factor IGD's needs into our decision. Tom's department had to provide system service in support of whatever product we

> chose, and Rick had a good handle on just how our choice would impact the overall technical performance of our computing facility.

At the meeting, Mather began by stating that the decision to be made had to be in the best interest of the corporation at large but as consistent as possible with IGD needs. He then asked each of the attendees what their individual choices would be based on the facts generated by the evaluation. Joe Schulter indicated that he favored FOCUS. His main reason was that FOCUS had an interface to IDMS data base files. The RAMIS II vendor had promised an interface in short order, but did not then have one in production. Joe reminded the committee that IDMS was to be the standard medium for all Air Products' centralized data bases.

Bob Bruno did not want to express a strong perference, but Mather sensed a leaning toward RAMIS II, due mainly to Bob's belief that Mathematica was the more solid and reliable vendor.

Rick Gobrecht thought Mathematica had a superior field support operation (especially in Europe), and also thought the superior computing efficiency of RAMIS II was important. He hence favored RAMIS II.

Tom Collins favored FOCUS because it was a more complete package and would not require in-house development effort on Air Products' part to provide a statistical capability. His department would have to implement an interface to the SAS statistics package if RAMIS II were selected. As Collins pointed out "We have a lot of other things to do with our staff; besides hardware costs are declining and the difference in FOCUS's computing efficiency could be more than compensated for by the impact on professional productivity."

It was clear to Mather that there was no overwhelming consensus. Each person stated his preference based on perceived risk of the system not preferred. For example, Joe's recommendation for FOCUS was primarily based on the risk he perceived that RAMIS II might not provide an IDMS interface. Mather found all the concerns to be valid. Given the benefits associated with trading off CPU cycles for professional productivity, he was indifferent between the two packages. Therefore, only one variable seemed to involve both significant negative consequences and a significant probability of those negative consequences happening. That concern was the issue of vendor support for the Management Information Group (MIG) in Europe.

To get more data on the subject, Bob Bruno agreed to contact the business systems department of MIG to get their feelings about the choice. Within a week, their response arrived via telex. To Bob's surprise, MIG was not concerned about the technical support issue. They had been running other products on their system with a similar support situation and had not run into difficulty getting service. MIG did not have the SAS statistics package either, which meant that they would have to purchase SAS to get statistics support if RAMIS II were selected. Finally, they were anxious for the chosen system to have an IDMS interface just as soon as possible. As he gave Mather the input from England, Bob Bruno commented:

> In evaluating our inquiry language alternatives, we've gone to a lot of effort. I'm sure we are all wondering if we couldn't have made the purchase decision last summer after a much more casual evaluation process. I believe that the evaluation process used in acquiring a decision support package depends largely on what our objectives are.
>
> The evaluation process we have gone through has provided several benefits. First, the characteristics of our choice and our use of it will be very well defined in our minds. We are likely to engage in very little aimless use and experimentation. Second, we will be able to monitor the implementation process very carefully since we have identified all the potential red flags and the contingent remedies. Finally, although through this process we have minimized the probability of error in selection, if it turns out that our acquisition was in some way a mistake, we will be in a position to know exactly why, and what in detail to look for the next time around.
>
> In deciding how much effort to invest in a review such as this, we must clearly have some idea of how important to us the benefits are. Obviously their importance varies with the nature of the object being acquired, its cost, and its impact on the operation of the company as a whole.

With the arrival of the response from Europe, Mather felt that there was no further data he could get in the short term that would in any way have a bearing on his decision.

In addition to considering the relative merits of the two systems. Mather had to consider the effect his decision would have on relations with IGD. His gaze shifted momentarily from the desk to the view from his office of the expansive grounds surrounding the Air Products corporate headquarters complex. He wondered as well what impact, if any, the decision and the events leading up to it would have on the future of corporate MIS within Air Products and Chemicals. Was the evaluation process adequate? Was he appropriately concerned with the impact on capacity planning? Was it too early in the hardware and software technology evolution to assume a direct trade-off between CPU cycles and personnel productivity?

APPENDIX A □ EVALUATION COMMENTARY

General

Two products are clearly superior to the others evaluated and substantially meet the requirements set forth by the study group. These are:

FOCUS, from Information Builders, Inc. (IBI), of New York City.

RAMIS II, from Mathematica, Inc., of Princeton, New Jersey.

Although these two products are close in terms of overall evaluation, there are some important differences which need to be considered in arriving at a decision. A summary of the evaluation and a discussion of major points of difference are presented below.

Capabilities and Base of Use

Included in this category are capabilities associated with file load, file definition, file update, query and reporting, and security. Strong emphasis was placed on user friendliness of the features as well as on the features themselves.

Despite literally hundreds of differences between the products the two are considered virtually equal in terms of user friendliness. They are also considered equal in terms of capability with the following exceptions:

FOCUS offers a statistics module, RAMIS II does not.

FOCUS graphics are somewhat superior to RAMIS II.

To provide an equal statistics and graphics capability with RAMIS II it would be necessary to develop an interface to SAS (APCI's existing software package for statistics and graphics). In order to provide such an interface with a degree of user friendliness equal to that currently within FOCUS, an investment of about two man-weeks of corporate MIS effort would be required.

SAS would provide a more powerful statistics and graphics capability for the few users who would require that; but a more important advantage of utilizing SAS could be found in the avoidance of a proliferation of redundant software.

File Interfaces

This category deals with the capability of the software to allow users to access various types of existing files.

The major difference in this category is the following:

FOCUS has an interface to IDMS files; RAMIS II does not.

The lack of an IDMS interface is considered a major shortcoming of RAMIS II since it is anticipated that a majority of production systems will be built around the IDMS data base over the course of the next few years.

Mathematica was approached on this matter early in the study and they stated a willingness to contract to provide such an interface within six to nine months. There is a definite uncertainty in this approach and, if undertaken, would have to be supported by strong contractual assurances.

However, alleviating the concern to some extent is the fact that Mathematica has developed interfaces to other data base management systems—IMS, ADABAS, and TOTAL. This offers some assurance that they have an appreciation for the magnitude of the development effort. They also cite a growing demand for an IDMS interface.

The fact that FOCUS has had such an interface for over a year and has it operational in at least one installation is a strong plus in its favor.

One additional difference between the products on the matter of file interfaces is:

> RAMIS II permits accessing of a more than one external file at a time; FOCUS does not.

This is a point of lesser significance, but one which provides the RAMIS II user with additional desired capability.

Performance

The category addresses the question of computer resources used in performing the functions of the software.

Based on an analysis of file structures, storage techniques, as well as methods of loading, updating, and backup and recovery, it is estimated that RAMIS II will perform about 25 percent more efficiently than FOCUS. This analysis was supported by discussion with a user who had performed a benchmark comparison of the two products.

A 25 percent performance advantage for RAMIS II would translate into a savings of about $30,000 per year in corporate MIS, based on anticipated usage over the next several years.

Vendor

This category includes an analysis of the stability of the vendor's organization, and a judgment as to the quality of support and the extent of enhancement of the product that we could expect.

Company Size. Mathematica is a larger company, with annual sales of about $25 million compared to about $2.5 million for IBI. FOCUS is the only product of IBI, whereas Mathematica offers products and services in addition to RAMIS II. Both are profitable companies showing good growth and both are considered financially viable.

User Base. Mathematica has been marketing RAMIS II since 1975 and has about 350–400 users. IBI has marketed FOCUS since 1977 and has about 100 users. The user base for both products is growing steadily. The larger user base that RAMIS II has is considered an advantage in that it provides greater leverage for users in dealing with the vendor. It also provides a larger pool of users with whom to consult and exchange information.

Overseas Support. Mathematica offers support from nine locations, including an office in London to support its 12 U.K. users. IBI supports all U.S. users from its New York City office. IBI has one user in the U.K. At present this user is supported by the TYMSHARE service bureau; however, IBI expects to establish a European corporate presence during 1981.

Mathematica's ability to support the product, particularly in the U.K., is considered an important advantage.

DOS Availability. RAMIS II is available under DOS and FOCUS is not. It is anticipated that Catalytic will offer a time-sharing service under DOS, and has expressed an interest in acquiring software of this type. RAMIS II would have an advantage here in allowing greater software uniformity throughout the company and also in allowing Catalytic to take advantage of second and third site discounts.

Product Uniformity. Both products operate under TSO[5] and CMS.[6] Our interest currently is for the TSO versions, although it is possible that we would at some future time be interested in using the CMS version and perhaps in operating with both versions concurrently in the same computer installation.

Mathematica's policy on issuing new releases is to do so across the board for all operating systems at the same time. IBI has, in the past, issued CMS releases six to nine months prior to TSO releases, although we have been told that they do not plan to continue this practice.

A former user of FOCUS expressed dissatisfaction with an apparent preference given by IBI to the CMS users and attributed this to a too-close association between IBI and TYMSHARE, an influential major user.

Costs

Purchase prices for the two products are in the range of $80,000 for installation in Trexlertown and New Malden. Price differential is in the order of 10 percent and is not considered significant when considering only two installations.

However if a third installation at Catalytic is considered, there would be a price differential of about $50,000 in favor of RAMIS II. This is due to the fact that FOCUS does not offer a DOS version, and it is anticipated that Catalytic will install a DOS system. Additional cost would be incurred as a result of installing FOCUS at Trexlertown and New Malden, and RAMIS II at Catalytic.

---

[5] TSO is an acronym for timesharing system option.

[6] CMS is an acronym for conversational monitor system.

Case 4–2 □ McGraw-Hill Book Company—Microcomputer Resource Center*

In just eight days, February 19, 1981, John Diesem was to celebrate one year as director of business systems development for the McGraw-Hill Book Company. He remembered well his first day on the job because even then he had recognized the inevitability of the proposal which he had just completed. During a break in that first orientation session, John had wandered down to the McGraw-Hill bookstore in the building lobby. There he had come face to face with a display of Apple microcomputers; and his reaction had been immediate, "My God, I'll bet every one of my users has been down here thinking—'There are lots of things I could do on these Apple computers, and I wouldn't have to deal with our corporate computer people!'"

The 6-inch layer of orientation reading which had covered his desk that first day was now gone, but the realization that microcomputer proliferation would need to be controlled was an even more pressing reality. The proposal which he had recently sent for review and, hopefully, approval addressed this control issue. His recommendations keyed on the establishment of a microprocessor resource center (MRC) as a means of controlling microcomputer use by providing convenient access, assistance, and education for potential users. Sitting behind his stylish, chrome-and-glass desk, John was trying to anticipate what the reaction would be to his proposal.

COMPANY BACKGROUND

Headquartered in New York City, McGraw-Hill was engaged in the worldwide business of providing informational products and services for business and industry, the professions, education, government, and the general public. Between 1976 and 1980, operating revenue increased at a rate of 14 percent compounded annually, from $589 million to just over $1 billion. During the same period, net income grew at an annually compounded rate of 21 percent, from $40 million to $86 million; and, return on average equity increased significantly from 15.7 percent to 20.9 percent.

McGraw-Hill comprised seven, largely autonomous operating units. (See

* This case was prepared by H. Christopher Peterson, research assistant, under the direction of Associate Professor James I. Cash, as a basis for class discussion rather than to illustrate either effective or ineffective handling of an administrative situation.

Exhibit 1 for an organizational chart.) The Books and Education Services segment consisted of two operating units: McGraw-Hill Book Company (domestic) and McGraw-Hill International Book Company. The two companies offered thousands of product items and, in 1980, contributed the largest portion of corporate revenues ($355 million, 35.5 percent) and the second largest portion of operating profits ($49 million. 26.1 percent). McGraw-Hill Book Company produced a wide range of books, audiovisuals, learning systems, and materials for the entire population. Its educational publishing programs included basic, remedial, and specialized instructional materials, tests, and evaluation systems for elementary and secondary schools; texts and outlines covering the major part of college curricula; and courses, books, and audiovisuals for continuing education and training in government and industry. It published professional programs in engineering, architecture, law, business medicine, and nursing, while it also served the interests of the general reader with works of fiction, biography, history, politics, and general reference. Marketing efforts included direct sales through advertising and mail; several sales forces calling on outlets in professional, educational, and consumer markets; book clubs; and a variety of special sales programs. The International Book Company conducted the most widespread international book operations of any U.S. book publisher. It had sales representatives in more than 50 cities around the world.

The McGraw-Hill Publications Company gathered, processed, and disseminated useful information for the business, industrial, and professional communities. This company produced almost three dozen magazines and 29 newsletters, plus newswires, seminars, conferences, directories, catalogs, and audiovisual materials. *Business Week* was perhaps the best known of the Publications Company's general audience products. Other publications were industry specific, such as *Chemical Engineering,* which focused on the

EXHIBIT 1 □ Abbreviated McGraw-Hill Organization Chart

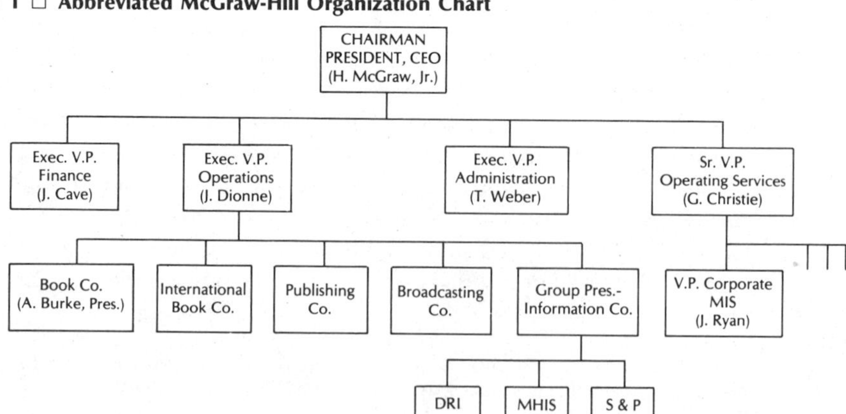

chemical process industries. In 1980, Publications contributed 29.5 percent ($295 million) of corporate revenues and 30.3 percent of operating profits (the largest percentage of any operating company).

Of the remaining four operating companies, one managed television stations while the other three were information companies reporting to a group president. The McGraw-Hill Broadcasting Company, Inc., owned and operated four television stations, which represented 5.4 percent of corporate revenue and 12.1 percent of profits. The largest of the three information companies was McGraw-Hill Information Systems (MHIS), which provided essential business information to a variety of industries and contributed 17.5 percent and 20.4 percent of corporate revenues and profits, respectively. MHIS included the F. W. Dodge Division (construction), Sweet's Division (building products), Datapro Research Corporation (computer and office systems), and Multi-List/McGraw-Hill (real estate). The second information company was Standard & Poor's Corporation, whose products and services consisted of debt-rating services, stock reports, stock and bond guides, the Blue List and Blue List bond ticker system, Trendline, and S&P Compustat Services, Inc. S&P brought in 7.3 percent of corporate revenue and 7.9 percent of profit. The newest company to be added to the McGraw-Hill portfolio was Data Resources, Inc. (DRI), a leading economic information service company, which contributed 4.8 percent of corporate sales and 3.2 percent of 1980 profits.

Each of the seven operating companies was headed by a president who could operate in an autonomous fashion in most circumstances. There did exist corporate guidelines for legal, financial, accounting, personnel, and other matters to which they had to adhere. Since the early 1970s, a formal strategic planning system had existed at McGraw-Hill and included broad performance goals (such as yearly eps growth) set by the corporation. Each company president formulated objectives for his divisions based on the corporate goals and his knowledge of the specific situation faced by each one in the coming year. Company plans were reviewed individually by the corporate staff. In general, there appeared to be an effective balance between corporate control and operating company autonomy. Growth in revenue and profitability was a key McGraw-Hill goal for the 1980s. Strategically, the firm planned to utilize fully evolving computer technology to compete more effectively in the many information markets which it served.

EDP HISTORY AND PRESENT ENVIRONMENT

McGraw-Hill entered the computer age in the 1950s with the installation of an IBM 650, first in New York, then at the Highstown, N.J., distribution center. Organizationally, the computer resource was highly centralized, and priorities were set by the MIS head. As the years progressed, contention between the centralized MIS group and the users grew to the point where many of the users began end runs outside the company to meet their data processing needs. Ultimately, this led to decentralization of analysis and programming with separate systems development groups reporting to each company president. The results of this attempt to decentralize were less than desirable.

As a result of a special biannual management conference called by Harold McGraw in February 1978, Mr. McGraw asked Gus Christie, senior vice president for operating services, to investigate the overall MIS organization at McGraw-Hill. The firm's public accountants, Arthur Young & Co., were brought in as consultants, while an executive task force was formed internally to study the situation. In March 1979, Jim Ryan (a 14-year veteran of systems development activities at Singer) was brought on board to become vice president of MIS, reporting to Gus Christie. A joint planning conference was convened with representatives of end-user departments, applications systems development, data center staff, and corporate staff. This committee drew up and prioritized a list of significant MIS problems.

In July 1979, a major reorganization of MIS took place to facilitate implementation of a new information systems strategy and computer communication architecture. The systems and programming functions, previously decentralized, were centralized at Highstown; telecommunications operations were brought into MIS for the first time; and new functions were added, e.g., systems assurance. Each operating company was to maintain responsibility for identifying its computer application needs and priorities, while corporate MIS was to handle all detailed and technical development work. A phased systems development methodology was established which divided the authority and responsibility accordingly (see Exhibit 2). In each operating company a director of business systems development was appointed to oversee the development steps of initial survey, requirements definition, and functional external design (John Diesem held this position for the Book Company).

The reorganization had attempted to balance centralization and decentralization rather than adhere to one extreme or the other. The operating presidents had control of use, but corporate MIS dealt with the technical issues. As of 1981 this new structure had partially facilitated major improvements to McGraw-Hill's information systems. An entirely new computer architecture had been put in place with new hardware, a new operating system, and data base technology; documentation of applications had become mandatory; and standardization efforts were proceeding on schedule. With the new architecture completed, the next major phase of change would involve the replacement of the aging primary application systems.

In 1981, corporate MIS had 400 employees and an annual budget of $24 million, which was split between hardware (40 percent) and personnel (60 percent). McGraw-Hill operated two data centers, one at Highstown and the other in Denver. Highstown hardware included IBM 3033, 3032, and

EXHIBIT 2 □ Data Processing Standards

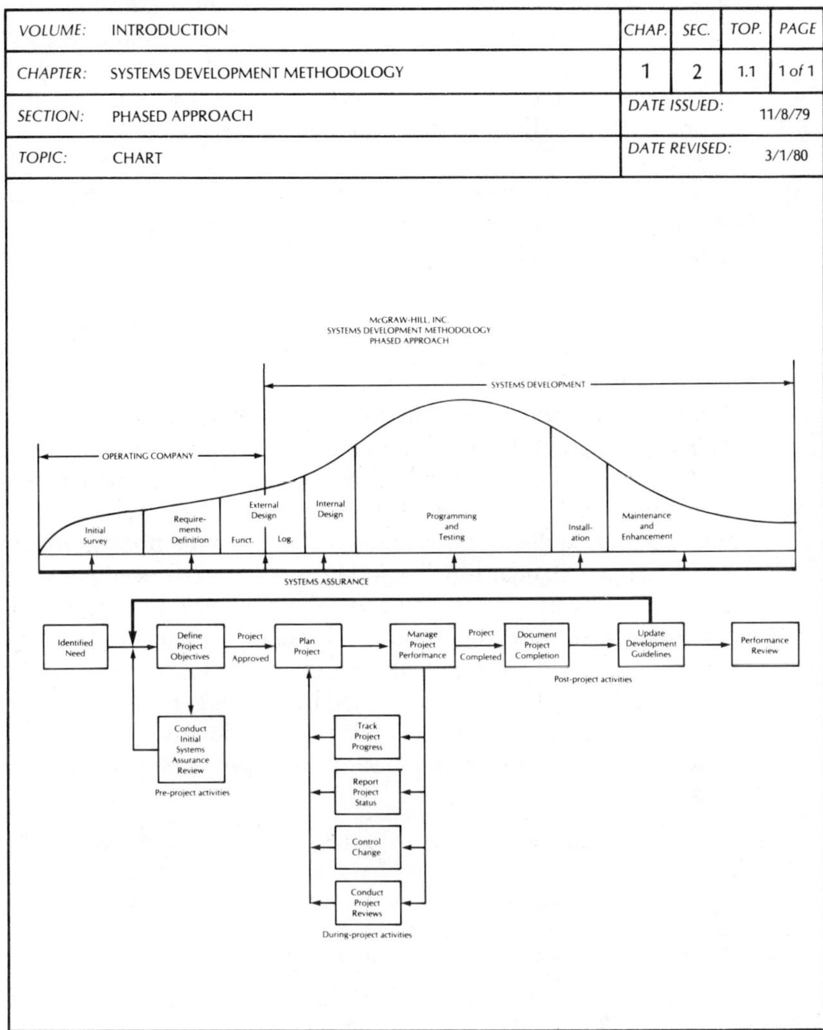

VOLUME:	INTRODUCTION	CHAP.	SEC.	TOP.	PAGE
CHAPTER:	SYSTEMS DEVELOPMENT METHODOLOGY	1	2	1.1	1 of 1
SECTION:	PHASED APPROACH	DATE ISSUED: 11/8/79			
TOPIC:	CHART	DATE REVISED: 3/1/80			

158/3, plus two Honeywell 6600s, while the Denver facility contained two IBM 158/3s. Predominant software consisted of MVS 3.8, CICS 1.4, IDMS/DB-DC, WILBUR, and FOCUS.

THE EMERGING USE OF MICROS AT BOOK

The McGraw-Hill Book Company was one of the largest and most diverse book companies in the country, with most of its divisions being one of the top three competitors in a particular market segment. Between 60 and 70 different strategy centers made up the Book Company. These centers were organized under three group vice presidents, and were supported by company staff in the areas of marketing, finance, and planning. (See Exhibit 3 for an organization chart of Book.) Al Burke who had 21 years of experience with McGraw-Hill was company president. Each division faced a different business climate, but in many segments of the educational book business, where McGraw-Hill dominated, the market had become extremely tight because of declining enrollments and government funding cuts. In some segments, profits had suffered over the past several years as a result; and, not surprisingly, improving margins through increased productivity was one of Burke's major goals.

The emergence of the microcomputer as a business tool at Book had been affected by both the economic environment and the past history of corporate MIS. Rick Van Dalen, Controller of the College Division and chairman of the Controllers Committee within Book, was among the first to bring in a microcomputer. Although Rick had no formal background in computer technology, he had attempted to computerize some element of every job in which he served since joining McGraw-Hill in 1971. In 1979, Rick had purchased an Apple microcomputer to program the Book Company's Common Financial Standards (CFS) and generate reports needed by the College Division. CFS was a common financial model used to project and track the performance of individual books. The data used in the program encompassed anticipated costs, potential revenues, and projected publishing dates (see Exhibit 4). Although programmed by McGraw-Hill staff, CFS was run on TYMSHARE, a remote computing service company.

Rick's justification for purchasing the Apple rested on need and economics:

> We had some special marketing reports which we wanted to use. The centralized systems group was not going to adjust the basic reports just because I needed them. In a way, you can not blame them because 50 to 60 percent of

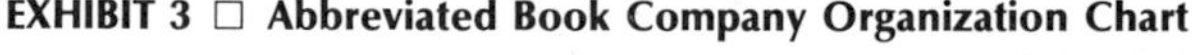

EXHIBIT 3 □ Abbreviated Book Company Organization Chart

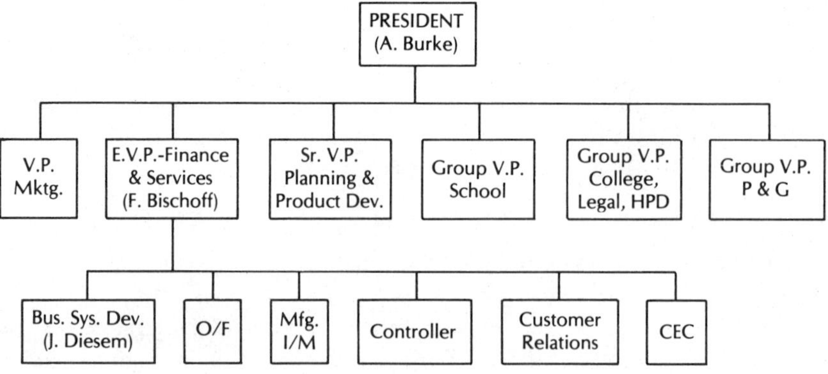

EXHIBIT 4

McGRAW-HILL BOOK COMPANY
PRO FORMA FINANCIAL ANALYSIS
SUMMARY STATEMENT

TITLE: | EDITOR:
PROJECT: 81/05/29 | SPONSOR: 22
PUB. DATE: January ,1982 PROPOSAL | DISCIPLINE: 56

Year	Dollars Net Sales	Units Requirements Domestic	Foreign	Comps
1981				
1982	611,250	9,700	2,000	200
1983	488,520	7,200	1,000	
1984	427,362	5,875	550	
1985	404,685	5,150	300	
1986	391,440	4,575	150	
1987				
1988				
1989				
1990				
1991				
TOTAL	2,323,257	32,500	4,000	200

Units Requirements Domestic Market	1st Year	Total
Div. Sales Force:		
P & G:	3,200	7,500
Direct Marketing:	2, 500	5,000
Book Club:	4,000	20,000
Other:		
	9,700	32,500

Consolidated P&L	Total	% NS
NET SALES	2,323,257	100.0
Manufacturing	261,909	11.4
Royalty	185,269	8.0
GROSS MARGIN	1,857,490	79.8
Plant Cost	160,929	7.3
Prov. for Res.	118,486	5.1
Other Inc.-Reg.	50,000	2.4
Other Inc.-Fgn.	56,299	2.6
TOTAL INCOME	1,684,374	72.3
Sales Expense	646,680	27.7
Promotion		0.0
Comps	1,535	0.1
Editorial	2,087	0.1
EDP		0.0
General Expenses	127,779	5.5
Service Expenses	429,802	18.5
NOT	76,490	20.4

Financial Measures & Guidelines	
Profitability Index	2.55
NPV of Project	$159,524
PV of Investment	$103,107
IRR	26.2
Break-Even	$1,893.334
Author Advances	$0
First Year Royalties	$60,717
Total Royalties	$202.862
Advance Earn Out	0.0y
List Price	$74.93
Net Price	$57.41
Unit Mfg Cost	$6.51
First Printing	$10,000
Initial Inventory	$70,899

GUIDELINES FOR 16.0% NOT		%FCT
List Price	$72.18	96.3
Units Sold	31,182	95.9
Unit Mfg.	$6.94	106.5
Royalty Rate	8.5%	106.2
Plant	$170,830	106.2

EXHIBIT 4 *(concluded)*

PROJECT NAME:		
TITLE:		
SPONSOR, DISCIPLINE:	22	56
PUBLICATION DATE:	1	82
DISCOUNT SYMBOL: HB		
PRINTINGS:	10000	3000
UNIT COST:	7.090	8.970
METHOD-ROYALTY:		

	STEP 1	STEP 2	STEP 3	STEP 4
STEP-ROYALTY:	99,999			
SF-ROYALTY:	10.00			
TBC-ROYALTY:	5.00			
DM-ROYALTY:	5.00			
BC-ROYALTY:	5.00			

	1980	1981	1982	1983	1984	1985	1986	1987	1988	1989	1990
PRICE:	75.00										
SALES FORCE:											
P & G Sales:		3,200	1,900	1,200	800	400					
DIRECT MARKETING:		2,500	1,300	675	350	125					
BOOK CLUB:		4,000	4,000	4,000	4,000	4,000					
OTHER SALES:											
INTERNATIONAL SALES:		2,000	1,000	550	300	150					
COMPLIMENTARY SALES:		200									
PLANT:	77,000	77,000									
ADVANCES:											
PROMOTION:											
EDITORIAL:	1,000	1,000									
EDP:											
INCOME-OTHER:		25,000	25,000								
ROYALTIES-OTHER:											
ASSETS-OTHER:											

the divisions were able to use those reports. They can not go back and create new reports for other divisions; it does not make economic sense. With us being unhappy with the centralized group and not wanting to spend the money on time-sharing, we decided to go out and get our own Apple and start doing our reports. We figured we could tailor those reports to fill our needs. They were not reports that we really wanted to share with anybody else in the company because a lot of them were modeling and "what if" situations. We did not feel they were for publication, but for divisional management use only.

> We spoke to a lot of people about the purchase. Basically, at McGraw-Hill, if you can financially justify a purchase of any type of equipment, you can buy it. We did not want to take anything away from the central systems group. Instead, we attacked time-sharing. We had the CFS program, which is a profit and loss statement and balance sheet on each individual product, running on time-sharing at a cost of $30,000 a year. We argued that an Apple could be purchased for $6,000, the software could be converted from time-sharing for $3,000, and the payback would be approximately three months. We went ahead with the purchase and made the conversion.
>
> Unfortunately, six months after we got the Apple up and running, corporate decided to change the Common Financial Standards significantly. We were forced to abandon the original Apple programs and return to time-sharing. We will soon be converting CFS to the Apple again, but this time the application will be designed for the whole company.
>
> Presently operating on the Apple is an application which we call a "sub-ed" estimating system. A production supervisor will go to the Apple and put in the specifications for a new book, and the computer will do all of the calculations and tell us that it is going to cost X number of dollars to develop the project from manuscript development through total plate preparation. The second phase of this report, which is just up, estimates the manufacturing costs of paper, printing, and binding. We even have inflation factors built in. Soon we will have a program to estimate prices from our costs, and we hope to track incentive contracts on the Apple as well. A sales forecasting model is in operation, while plans for a program on sales territorial analysis is in the works.
>
> The important thing is that the Apple is not for information to be shared or compiled at the company level. It is just for the data which the division needs and wants. As long as you can justify it from that standpoint, I think more people should be using microcomputers.

Rich Peterson, director of research and development for the Gregg Division (School Group), was also an early user of microcomputers. Rich, who had been with McGraw-Hill four years, had formerly worked in various areas of education and had done his graduate work in educational psychology with a minor in computer science. He originally got his Apple to aid in the data crunching so necessary to his position. In addition to using common microcomputer software, such as Visicalc and Desktop Plan, Rich wrote a number of statistical programs in Pascal. One of the most interesting applications pioneered in Rich's area involved listing the division's books about microcomputers on the Apple Bulletin Board System (ABBS). Any Apple user, anywhere in the country, could dial up the ABBS listing and ask for basic information on McGraw-Hill book offerings. The user was then referred to a regional sales representative who would complete the sale verbally in a separate transaction.

Barry Richman (senior editor, Professional and Reference Books, P&G Group) had a 15-year editorial career, dealing with technical subjects, prior to coming to McGraw-Hill three years ago. When Barry originally saw the

Gregg ABBS application, he was immediately impressed with its strategic implications for McGraw-Hill:

> When Mark Haas [who developed Gregg's ABBS application] invited me to try out the system, it was at the end of a very trying day for me. But Mark is one of the "invisible network" of people at McGraw-Hill interested in computers, and I decided it would be worth some of my time to see what he had. After getting on the system and working through the responses, it struck me that there needed to be some way for the person phoning to order the book directly through the system and not through the extra step of contacting a regional sales office. At the moment of the call, we knew something very important about the person on the other end of that line—that person was seated at a computer terminal and that made him a bona fide prospect for the product we were selling. We spend uncountable dollars in other direct response areas, and much of what we do is speak to people who don't have the slightest interest in what we're selling. Our philosophy is to group related materials in some fashion in hopes of recouping our promotion costs. At that point, I realized that Mark had come up with a new marketing channel. The idea of an "electronic bookshelf" was born.
>
> The concept had some very appealing elements for management. I could offer an application which would cost no more $5,000 to test. Since I had already seen a preliminary version work, I could promise immediate results. Setting up a legitimate test would be relatively easy, and the cost of failure was low because the Apple could be used for office productivity purposes if the marketing application proved unsuccessful.
>
> I immediately brought the idea to the attention of the marketing vice president for Book [Exhibit 5], and set up a demonstration on the Gregg Apple for him and several other people who would be interested. From the moment people saw it, their question was not "Will people phone in?" but rather "What will we do if more than one person calls at the same time?" There were a lot of marketing questions that had to be answered, but a phased marketing test in which we dedicated an Apple to selling books around the clock could supply the answers. The application will soon be operating, and who knows what we might be able to sell if we are successful. Magazine subscriptions and book clubs are obvious things to consider.
>
> I would have never had the energy to go through central data processing to develop this application; it would have taken at least 18 months. Ultimately, this application could justify being put on a time-sharing network, and I do not think doing this with DRI or TYMSHARE would conflict with anything corporate MIS is doing. Of course, a very desirable interface with Book Company systems would be the ability to transfer orders from whatever system we develop directly to the central order fulfillment system.

A 20-year McGraw-Hill employee with no background in computer technology, Henry Shaw (the director of marketing services for the P&G Group) had recently requested his first microcomputer for use in a potential budgeting application:

> In my various jobs with McGraw-Hill, I have been working with the systems people and have had the same continuing problems with our mailing list

EXHIBIT 5

interoffice memorandum

To	James Bowman	From	Barry Richman
Company	Book	Company	Book
Dept. or Pub.	Exec.	Dept. or Pub.	P&RB
Floor or Branch	26	Floor and Ext. or Branch	26/4780
Subject	Marketing with an electronic bulletin board	Date	November 5, 1980

Jim:

Mark Haas, Gregg Division, has done something very exciting with the Division's Apple that I think you ought to know about.

He has hooked it into a national "bulletin board" and put a small catalog of McGraw-Hill books on it. Virtually anyone with a microcomputer (or any other kind of terminal) can call the bulletin board on the telephone and find Mark's book catalog.

That person then calls Mark's number. The Apple answers the telephone (!) and gives the caller a choice of the kinds of books for which it will produce information. When the choice is made the Apple displays the titles and offers a more complete description of the book. And so on.

So far Mark has been running this as an experiment, simply offering information. But he has a log of calls received (they've come from all over the country) and has exchanged messages with callers via the system.

The real potential of this, of course, is to take orders, perhaps using VISA or Mastercharge, or simply forwarding the orders to Highstown. It seems to me that this could be an entirely new sales channel for technical books, especially computer books, from all the publishing divisions.

I am sure Mark would be happy to give you a demonstration and discuss the system.

Barry

cc. Al Wieboldt

operation. In the period since 1974, I have been going through the frustrations of not being able to get what we wanted out of the big computer. What really triggered this was a particular problem in the Professional and Reference Books Division which uses direct mail primarily and has a different problem in budgeting than any other division in the company. Other divisions have promotional seasons and finite promotion campaigns. At P&RB, their mailing process is continuous. They will send out a test mailing on a new book, say to 20,000 architects when the potential market may be 300,000. They will see if the book is going to sell, and if it does, they will go back and mail 50,000 more. They then will go back again and again. There is no way of predicting the budget. Since, at any given time, things are being processed to be mailed, printed to be mailed, in the mail, and in the customers' hands for evaluation, nobody in the division could say exactly what the commitment of expenses was.

We kept trying to work out a system where we could input what the projected cost would be and then, as the costs were incurred, deduct them from the estimate. We could have a variance between the actual cost and the budgeted cost as well as follow those items which had not been expensed as yet. The first time we went up to the central systems group, it was going to cost $10,000 to do; the next time we went back it was $19,000; and, the next time it was $40,000. I will not tell you what we said to that. When I was looking around for alternatives, someone recommended an independent consultant who suggested we could get a TRS-80 for $2,000 and he could program it to fit our application. I got involved with the microcomputer at that point, but everybody said "No" to the TRS-80. They pushed the Apple. As it turns out, whomever you talk to is dedicated to the proposition that whatever they own is the only system that works.

Ed Monagle had worked in various areas of accounting services since joining McGraw-Hill in 1973. As controller of Professional and Reference Books, Ed had strong thoughts about the manner in which a microcomputer could eventually fit into his financial operation:

I have come to recognize in this position that there are so many things that we do manually. I have a staff here of six people, and we do financial reporting and all the support work for the budgets and the operating statements. We put ourselves in a position where we are constantly taking information, massaging it, and updating it. We spend a lot of time just taking that same information and manipulating it to come up with new reports on different time frames. I can give you a primary example.

When we go to do a budget for a given book, the editor has to get sales estimates from marketing and cost estimates from production. Also, an estimate of the publication date must be made. We put all these things together through CFS and make a no or no-go decision. At any one point in time, you may have 200 or 300 books in progress, and they are spread through different editorial programs. When you want to do the total budget and publishing plan by product line, there is no data base that collects the individual information. Publishing dates and other factors are constantly changing, and we are in the

> process of continuously redoing our publishing plans. We need some way of constructing the information so that it is easily up-dated.
>
> What we want to do in the near future with an Apple is input all the product line information and get back the projections for a given point in time. I could turn to editor X and say, "Here are your 50 books. This is the way the projection looks right now. I want you to update this with realistic publication dates." The editor goes down the line, puts the changes into the system, and reruns the publishing plan. For all the systems within the company, this kind of application does not exist. We presently do it manually.

Barry, Henry, and Ed were all part of the Professional and General Publishing Group headed by group vice president Bob Biewen. Bob had only worked for McGraw-Hill one year, but he brought with him extensive general management experience and an exposure to computer operations in several other companies. He had his own position on microcomputers:

> The acquisition of information is an important priority, and I found myself and other people either operating on incredibly imperfect information or wasting man-hours on manually constructing data over and over again. My concurrence with Henry and Ed on the microcomputer requests was based on my asking for things, which I had been used to getting, and then waiting until someone put them together by hand. My frustration grew from the fact that we could not get applications in a timely fashion if we had to go to Highstown and stand in line, and my personal feeling that these applications did not belong on the mainframe anyway.

THE MRC PROPOSAL

The evidence was clear that the interest in microcomputers had been steadily growing at Book. In the fall of 1980, no less than six divisions had included some type of microcomputer proposal in their 1981 budget, but the first hard proposals emanated from Bob Biewen's group. Ed Monagle had packaged his request for an Apple with Henry Shaw's and forwarded a memo to Al Burke, Book Company president (see Exhibit 6). Before beginning his 21-year career at McGraw-Hill, Al had taught college English and operated a reading clinic. When he received the Monagle/Shaw requests in January 1981, Al decided that the time had arrived to address the issue of control over microcomputer proliferation:

> We had a lot of different divisions each making requests to us for the purchase of microcomputers. I became concerned that we were putting a lot of money into them, and I was fearful that they would be underutilized if we allowed them to proliferate. We did not want to lose the control, not so much in the sense of management, as in the sense of benefiting and sharing the experience with them. I was also afraid we would have a number of divisions reinventing the wheel, that everybody would be trying to do similar things on

EXHIBIT 6

interoffice memorandum

To	Al Burke	From	Ed Monagle
Company		Company	
Dept. or Pub.		Dept. or Pub.	
Floor or Branch		Floor and Ext. or Branch	
Subject	Apple II purchase	Date	January 15, 1981

Attached are two orders which require your signature to purchase two Apple II computers from the bookstore to be used in the direct mail unit on the 35th floor and within the P&G financial unit on the 26th floor.

The primary applications within the direct mail unit will be (1) to maintain an expense control system by project that is currently handled manually by each product manager within P&RB; (2) to experiment with in-house typesetting for catalogs and Book Club bulletins aimed at reducing type costs by 20–30 percent, and (3) for word processing functions.

The primary applications within the financial unit will be (1) to mechanize a number of the management information reports currently being done manually; (2) to enable us to develop a data base that contains the publishing plan for each editor within the P&G Group (the data base will include plant and sales estimates); (3) to provide us with a modeling capability that can be incorporated into the budget process; and (4) for word processing functions.

EM/1pl
Attch.

cc: R. Biewen
J. Dill
H. Shaw
D. Horton
T. Hicks

the micros with each one going about it on their own. I asked Fred Bischoff [Executive vice president for Finance & Services] that we ought to do about approving so many requests. Wasn't there a better way to handle this than giving each division its own micro? Fred then handed it to John Diesem to develop a viable alternative to rubber-stamping each request.

Given the present educational marketing environment of declining enrollment and funding cuts, we are looking hard to improve our margins and to establish better productivity. Time-sharing helped us do this previously with regard to preparation of budgets, publishing plans, reeditions, and reiterations of these. Micros offer us a new opportunity to decentralize these functions internally and still maintain or increase some of that productivity.

As I asked for a policy on control, I felt that a number of the managers were going to be unhappy. We are reasonably decentralized with regard to each manager having his own corporation to operate, even though the financial controls are fairly tight. We were going to have a lot of disappointed managers if they did not get their own micros. A typical comment might be "Gee, it is not such a big expense; how come you are not going to give me mine?" The people asking for microcomputers are generally the better, more innovative managers, who are on top of their jobs.

The microcomputer issue per se is a lower priority item. It does not affect the immediate fate of the company, but it has become a higher priority issue because of the proliferation of requests and the real need for micros. We have had the old problem of centralized computing not developing applications in a timely and effective manner. The decentralized use of micros could give our divisions the potential to handle some of their own applications, with only themselves to blame if specific problems recur.

I am very comfortable with the time investment which we are making in learning about microcomputers, because we are using them, not only for internal purposes, but for making new computer-based products for the marketplace. These new products place demands on our editors and managers to develop a computer literacy. We have an opportunity to have our people gain a knowledge, about micros, which will be beneficial both for the implementation of operational changes within the company and for the better understanding of the products sold to our customers.

I developed my own knowledge of computers because our business is being so affected by them. Our book business is misnamed; we not only produce books but any medium that will serve our markets. As Book executives, we must know a lot more than we currently do about computers, microcomputers, programming, and information technology in general. In addition, we understand that competitors are considering the acquisition of companies in this field. We better have more than a superficial knowledge of the related computer industry if we are to stay ahead competitively.

Under control procedures for normal capital expenditures, a division would include a desired item in its capital budget. Once the company president had approved the budget, a group vice president could sign-off on the actual expenditure of funds. If an item had not been budgeted for the year but was subsequently needed, a proposal justifying the new request could be submitted. The company president would have to review and decide on the proposal. Any budgeted or unbudgeted expenditure over $50,000 dictated some type of corporate involvement. MIS equipment and services were already outside this policy when Al Burke asked for a means of controlling microcomputers. Any MIS expenditure, regardless of cost, had to have special approval. In the case of Book Company, this meant that all such proposals required John Diesem's endorsement.

Fred Bischoff, John's immediate boss, joined McGraw-Hill in 1965 and had served in a number of financial/administrative positions within the corporation. Fred had a clear sense of how he would measure the success of any control proposal recommended by John:

> The level of success will depend upon the degree of sharing which develops among users, the amount of satisfaction which each individual user has, and the impact, primarily on productivity, of the applications which are implemented. In the final analysis, if a year from now microcomputers are housed exclusively in closed or central facilities, the MRC concept will not have been successful.

This was the environment in which John was to establish control over microcomputer proliferation. John's experience in the data processing field included positions from programming manager to director of data processing. Immediately before coming to McGraw-Hill, John had worked for Arthur Andersen & Company, where he helped clients develop data processing systems and controls. In his position as director of business systems development, John had responsibility for directing the initial phases of the systems development methodology, serving as chief DP officer in Book with a dotted-line relationship to data processing operations in divisions, helping to solve information problems within the divisions, and assisting in planning and product development when electronic-based products were being considered. John's philosophy of control over micros was based on three crucial points:

> First, we must have adequate data standards which dictate the same names for items having the same definitions, the same syntactical and logical meanings, etc. We have not done it yet, but we are working on this. Second, we must have control over the common financially oriented applications because they are very sensitive in our operation. I am referring to such applications as budgeting and the Common Financial Standards. We must all use the same formulas, and consistency of reporting is essential. Third, we need to have some control over those programs which do not have financial impact but are so common that it doesn't make sense to let five people go off to write them separately. Whatever the user can justify after meeting these three levels of control is fine with me. We can not keep them from doing anything beyond this, and I do not think that we should try.
>
> What I am really trying to control is not the proliferation of *hardware* but

> rather the proliferation of *software*. When I first began playing with a microcomputer at home, I decided to experiment with a simple cash flow model. I began programming it in BASIC, and when I was about done someone said, "Don't you know about Visicalc?" So I threw out my BASIC program and tried Visicalc, which was much easier. About the time I understood Visicalc, someone else had drawn my attention to Desktop Plan which was even easier for my application. I really want to spare our people from going through this same trial-and-error process time and time again. The ideal situation would be to establish a professional sharing environment in which the users could continually talk to one another about the applications they have in operation.

John finally settled on the concept of "Microprocessor Resource Centers" as the primary means of control through education. The proposal (Exhibit 7) called for the establishment of two Microprocessor Resource Centers. Each MRC would be equipped with an Apple II Plus computer with appropriate support hardware and software. John's staff would be responsible for providing the initial training to users interested in the system. Scheduling the use of the MRC would involve the users signing up for a given time or series of times. All the user needed to invest in the training was the purchase of a $40 pack of blank diskettes for use on the system. After the initial training, the users would presumably use the MRC to test the feasibility of the application in which they were interested. If the application proved successful, the users then had adequate justification for proposing the purchase of their own system. If the application was unsuccessful, the user would have lost little except the time spent learning the system.

In John's mind the MRC proposal had the advantage of blending the element of control with a service component for the user. The centers offered the user a low risk way of embarking on a microcomputer system. Control was, in essence, established through a central learning facility which offered a common system of both hardware and software from the very start. Appropriate training and support could always be available to the users through the center, and ongoing monitoring of users, to ensure adherence to standards and the best use of software, could likewise be accomplished from John's point of view. The only significant disadvantage seemed to be the requirement that users initially share the MRC until their utilization required an individual system. In the near future, John planned to establish a Book Company users' committee which would identify those potential applications justifying a common, single software development process.

REACTIONS TO THE MRC

The potential users were the first to react to the MRC proposal. Since the microcomputer requests from his two subordinates had precipitated the control issue, Bob Biewen naturally had some mixed feelings:

EXHIBIT 7 □ Proposal to Establish Two Microprocessor Resource Centers for the Book Company

A. PROPOSAL

1. Business Systems Development (BSD) proposes to establish two Microprocessor Resource Centers (MRC), in New York and in Highstown. These centers will consist of Apple II Plus computers with appropriate disk and printer capability and will have standard systems and applications software available for use. The initial hardware and software configuration for each center is listed in Appendix I.

2. These centers will provide assistance to potential Book Company users of microprocessors in the following areas:
   - Introduction to computers and their use.
   - Start-up procedures.
   - Utilities/backup.
   - Administrative procedures, for access control, utilization logging, and scheduling.
   - Standard systems software.
   - Existing applications software.
   - Demonstrations.
   - Training.
   - Sharing of files, report layouts, etc.
   - Identification of the commonality of certain applications and the scheduling of common software development.

3. The centers will provide computer time to new users, with the following objectives:
   - Provide computer time on a shared, scheduled basis, with administrative procedures provided by the MRC.
   - Provide ongoing support in training, optimization techniques, and interfaces with software and hardware vendors, Corporate MIS, and Book Company administrative systems.
   - Enforce data definition and security controls.
   - Ensure the commonality issue between users is addressed.

4. Provide assistance to users in proposing individual systems based *(a)* on a solid utilization base at the MRC, *(b)* properly trained users, and *(c)* familiarity with existing systems and applications software.

5. Provide ongoing support after the user has an individual system, by providing backup facilities, software and hardware releases and updates, vendor interface, and the coordination of common systems development.

EXHIBIT 7 *(continued)*

B. ENVIRONMENT

The Book Company data processing environment has three parts:

1. Large-scale administrative systems, in which there are well-established common needs, large data bases, large input volumes, interactive requirements, and a direct relationship to day-to-day business operations.
2. Increasing use of time-sharing, either with McGraw-Hill Inc. resources, such as DRI, or with external vendors, such as Tymshare. The characteristics of this time-sharing are:

   - A high degree of common data between users.
   - A high degree of software commonality.
   - The use of proprietary data and/or software.
   - Generally a great deal of input, but with the requirement that the input be user-friendly.

3. A pent-up demand for a small, highly interactive, "scratch pad" capability, in such areas as financial modeling, marketing research, and sales and marketing reporting. The characteristics of this demand are the following:

   - Little common data between users.
   - Varying degrees of software commonality.
   - Relatively little data input, but with a high degree of data change.
   - A similar need to be user-friendly.

C. APPROACH

The intermediate- to long-term approach to satisfying the environment, as described above, is three parts:

1. In the area of large-scale systems, no change to our existing approach to the development of these systems.

2. In the area of time-sharing, there should be the ongoing control of each application, with a view toward the possible use of in-house resources, as they develop, and the consolidation of applications between users. In addition, BSD should take steps to ensure that the time-sharing applications are coordinated with the Book Company data administration function to ensure that data definitions and security are addressed.

3. In the area of small, highly interactive, "scratch pad" requirements, the local processing permitted by microprocessors is an appropriate way to satisfy this requirement. However, in order to control the proliferation of these computers, three steps are necessary:

EXHIBIT 7 *(concluded)*

a. In a fashion similar to that required by time-sharing, BSD should ensure that data definitions and access/security requirements are met.

b. By means of a Book Company user committee, applications which display a high degree of commonality between users should be identified and scheduled for common, single software development.

c. With these two controls in place, users should be able to acquire and make appropriate use of microprocessors within the following framework:
- Initial training on the MCR.
- The introduction to common systems.
- The introduction to existing systems and applications software.
- The development of an appropriate utilization base to call for a separate configuration.

D. BENEFITS

1. *Advantages*
   - Control over hardware and software proliferation.
   - Appropriate training and support to users before the acquisition of specific hardware.
   - Identification of common systems.
   - Ongoing monitoring of users to ensure adherence to standards and the appropriate use of systems/applications software.

2. *Disadvantages*
   - Users will initially share the MRC until their utilization requires an individual system.

E. COST SUMMARY (See Appendix I.)

1. Stage I (MRC site in NY)—February 1981	$5,162
2. Stage II (MRC site in HT)—April 1981	3,024
3. Stage III (upgrade to communicate)—July 1981	700
Total 1981	$8,886
4. Stage IV (sophisticated business software (1 site only)—January 1982	$1,545

Not included in costs:
- Development costs for common systems.
- Paper, ribbons, telephone charges.
- Tymshare, or DRI, costs to test.

I see the MRC as a step toward handling my personal concerns about the proliferation of micros without control and with potentially unproductive uses; but, I do not like, at least initially, its being under John Diesem's control—control, I fear, with a capital "C." I worry that John and other DP professionals have a vested interest in keeping their magic to themselves. John is very good about helping people, and his job is the key one in making the MRC work. It is a dangerous key; he can make it *not* work. To this point, I have seen the hand waving, "I will take care of it." However, I will be the first to come to Al Burke or the executive committee if the hand waving continues and the MRC is not getting micros into the hands of the users. I will measure the MRC by checking with the people who I know want to get involved to see if they are indeed getting their systems up and running. If I get the sense that they are running into roadblocks, that would be the important information for me to know, and I would proceed from there.

As to the future of the MRC, my guess is that if a computer ends up in, say, Ed Monagle's area, other people in that vicinity will probably start on that piece of hardware rather than go to the Microprocessor Resource Center. I do not think that will be the only pattern. Some people who might be next door will see something happening and ask how the system began. The Microprocessor Resource Center will be mentioned, and they might go to the MRC or they might skip that step.

Of the two originators of the microcomputer requests, Ed Monagle had the more positive impression of the MRC:

The logic behind the MRC makes a lot of sense, because I do not know how to use an Apple and my people do not know either. Educating yourself is not that difficult, but you do have to go through a learning period. John's rationale simply centers on the fact that we have people who want systems and who must now wait until they get applications to a point where they are worth the $6,000 or $12,000 investment. My people will use the MRC.

On the other hand, Henry Shaw had a very different view of the MRC, which stemmed in part from his own personal reaction to computers:

Last summer, I took a course in operations research and used the computer for the first time. My reaction when I got the thing to finally answer me was, "It's magic!" The individuals who deal with the computer regularly are very jaded. The problem with these data processing people is that they are so sophisticated that they expect everybody else to have the same sophistication. Deep down, I feel that most people are like me. The computer is a magic box, and while we all talk a big game we are still delighted when it works and does what it is supposed to do.

I realize that one of the problems is needing a lot of time to sit down and just get used to the computer. Will the MRC offer that time in an easily accessible manner? I understand that you will have to schedule its use. You have to carve out the time which is very hard for me to do. I wish I had my own cheap little Apple here on my desk where I could dedicate some lunch hours or some time before work to experiment with it. Going to another location, which is under lock and key, is just enough of an inhibition to be discouraging.

I can only partially buy John's point about preventing the proliferation of software instead of hardware. You can have an Apple with all its proliferable equipment for $6,000. Programs cost in the neighborhood of $100. If we all make a $100 mistake, it would not represent a large sum in dollar terms. In contrast, if we all get $6,000 computers, it means a major outlay of money. John states his point very convincingly, but it does not ring true when I think about it further.

The thing which frustrates me most about the MRC proposal is that it seems not entirely fair. I keep hearing about Apples being all over the place and about people buying them. Why do they get them and we do not? I made my proposal the legal way. Will this force managers to hide requests in categories for "office equipment"?

Barry Richman's reaction to the MRC was heavily favorable:

It is an ideal managerial solution. The user could not have a lower risk way of experimenting with the microcomputer. He can test an application and get an instant reaction. On the other hand, the control mechanism is built right into the Center's use. Even with the psychological barriers which many people have about using the computer, I think that the MRC will be overloaded fast. Just a couple of us who are interested could keep it busy ourselves. John will need more hands than he presently has. He can not handle it himself even though his personality will be critical to the idea's success.

Migration of microcomputers away from the MRC to the user will not be easy. Islands of microcomputer users will spring up, but the barriers to use are significant for many people. Some potential users will be afraid even after a neighbor has been successful, and it will be difficult for successful users to have the time to share their knowledge with others. In some cases, I am concerned that the microcomputer will be purchased only for its "prestige" value and not be put to any productive purpose. Nonetheless, from my viewpoint, the MRC is an essential concept in solving our computing problems.

Also, I see no incompatibility between a good central DP operation and the widespread use of microcomputers. If you ran a study of user requests to central DP for applications development projects, I do not believe that you would find the number declining in an environment where microcomputer use was heavily on the rise. Each type of facility has its own place in the corporation's information systems.

Rich Peterson had the most negative response to the MRC proposal:

The resource center concept is just plain silly. It does not coincide with our corporate culture. My people will come to me when they want to know anything about microcomputers, and besides the top-down approach does not work in this company. *No* meaningful activities go on outside of the operating divisions. We have the dollars right here to spend, and corporate gives us nothing but the "OK" to go ahead. As long as I am not interfering with the current corporate direction, any justifiable request is approved. The only way I

> will use the MRC is if corporate mandates that I must use it to get microcomputer proposals accepted.

From the central DP side of the corporation, Jim Ryan (vice president of corporate MIS) had his own reaction to the microcomputer issue in general:

> The microcomputer is here, and we must accept the fact that it is cheap and fast. It has become a new business tool destined to increase personal productivity. To all that, I say, "Great, go to it." I am concerned that micros may be developed for applications where they are inappropriate. If we start seeing them in large data base applications or in networks, then I would probably want our central facility to handle these uses. We are more cost effective in these areas. Microcomputers are not a high priority issue for us at corporate MIS.

Holding a similar position to John's but in a different McGraw-Hill company, Kemp Anderson (vice president of Business Systems Development for the Publishing Company) did not think the same type of demand for microcomputers existed in the Pub environment:

> I am aware and involved in all acquisitions of microcomputers in this organization. We have 10, maybe 12, of these systems, but we don't have the kinds of activities which micros can address effectively. We are introducing a number of end-user programming systems, such as FOCUS, which will serve our needs as currently projected. The MRC concept might be appropriate for Book, but we do not have requirements for a similar approach.

The first round of responses were in and mixed, but John still awaited the reactions of Fred Bischoff and Al Burke. Whatever their decision, it was clear that some action was necessary. If the MRC proposal was approved, John wondered what direction the implementation should take, given the information which he already had about the users' needs and opinions. If the MRC proposal was rejected, he mulled over in his mind what the alternatives might be.

APPENDIX I □ PROPOSED MRC CONFIGURATION

Stage I—NY site (February 1981)

Tentative configuration

Apple II +, 48K	$1,160
Disk w/Controller	516
Disk w/o Controller	396
Sanyo 12'' Monitor	240
Serial Interface Card	168
Decwriter II	1,700*
Modem	200*
Visicalc	N/A†
Desktop Plan	N/A
CCA Data Management	N/A
10 Boxes Diskettes	200
Desk	200
Subtotal	$4,780
Tax	382
One-time costs	$5,162

* Decwriter/MODEM available within Book Company, but only for 6–9 months.

† Software already owned by BSD.

Stage II—HT site (April 1981)

Tentative configuration	Same
One-time costs	$3,024*

* Decwriter/MODEM available at Highstown.

Stage III

Additions

D.C. Hayes Micromodem	$ 280
Apple PLOT software	70
Each site	$ 350

Stage IV (January 1982)

Additions

CP/M 280 Microsoft	$ 350
CBS Data Base System	400
WORD-Star	
Word processing software	445
Data-Star data entry software	350
Total	$1,545

Case 4–3 □ The Marrett Corporation Systems Planning Committee*

In early April 1980, Mike Ross was reflecting on the development of the Marrett Systems Planning Committee (SPC). Ross, manager of Information Services (IS) for Marrett had been instrumental in getting the SPC established in 1979, and now he was wondering whether the group was developing rapidly enough. As of April 1980, the SPC had not yet formally adopted a planning and project approval system. However, the group was actively reviewing projects, and individual SPC members were playing an increasingly active role in developing and monitoring systems projects in their own departments. Although Ross was generally pleased with the SPC's positive acceptance in most parts of Marrett, he recalled with some frustration a comment made by the SPC's marketing representative, Pat Wheler at the time the committee had been formed. Wheler had been openly skeptical:

> I don't see why we need a *group* to manage Information Services. I don't have a committee telling *me* how to run my department!

In spite of Wheler's initial skepticism, Ross knew that the SPC was significantly different from an earlier group that he had worked with, the Systems Development Steering Committee (SDSC). The SDSC had almost universally been recognized as a hotbed of organizational politics and as highly ineffective. Now, as he reviewed the agenda for the upcoming SPC monthly meeting, Ross wondered what he should be doing to keep the positive momentum going, and to build the SPC into an effective, efficient planning body.

BACKGROUND ON THE MARRETT CORPORATION AND THE INFORMATION SERVICES FUNCTION

The Marrett Corporation was a well-known manufacturer of small gasoline and diesel engines. Marrett engines were used in a variety of commercial and consumer products, including electrical power generators, pumps, lawnmowers, snowblowers, snowmobiles, and so on. With corporate headquarters in downtown Boston and operating facilities in several nearby towns, Marrett was a wholly owned subsidiary of the New England

* This case was prepared as a basis for class discussion rather than to illustrate either effective or ineffective handling of an administrative situation.

Power Products Company (NEPPCO). Other major NEPPCO subsidiaries included Manchester Marine (marine diesel engines), Marshfield Motors (small electrical motors used in power tools and appliances) and Soft Power, Inc. (a new division, focusing on solar energy units). Together, this family of companies had generated operating profits of $37 million in 1979, and total sales of $683 million.

NEPPCO itself was a division of Universal Motors, Inc. (UMI), a multinational manufacturing conglomerate. UMI had acquired NEPPCO's predecessor company, the Boston Engine Corporation, in 1974. Boston Engine had been organized along major product lines, with several product-market divisions (consumer, industrial, marine, private label, etc.). In that organization, the corporate IS function had been handled by two departments. One group, Corporate Systems Support, had concentrated on corporate systems and common policies and procedures in areas such as documentation standards, IS and hardware planning, and system guidelines. The applications group, which provided systems development and data processing services to the various user divisions had been known as Divisional Information Services (DIS).

Mike Ross had been manager of DIS. Ross called that DIS had faced many of the user relationship problems that seem inevitable when a centralized IS department attempts to meet user demands in a decentralized, divisional organization:

> We actually took on a marketing orientation. I sent my staff to marketing seminars, and trained them to play down their technical role. We focused on user needs, and generated a terrific backlog of projects.

As a part of his efforts to build positive working relationships with the operating divisions, Ross had established a user committee known as the Systems Development Steering Committee, or SDSC. However, Ross had not had any real influence on who the SDSC members were; each user division had appointed its own representatives. Ross recalled that the assignment had not been considered highly desirable; the SDSC's efforts were often viewed with some suspicion, especially from divisions that were doing their own data processing. The SDSC had been intended as an opportunity for members to get together regularly to share applications problems and inform each other of systems development progress. However, the monthly meetings had involved more open conflict than discussion, and the Board had clearly become political. As one executive who had been a member of the SDSC recalled:

> The old SDSC had the wrong kinds of people. Most of them didn't care at all about DP, and those who did generally got anything they wanted. The SDSC had 11 members; we were lucky if 7 showed up for a meeting, and 3 of those would never say a word. More often than not, those who did were in never-never land.

In March 1979, Boston Engine was substantially reorganized, and its name was changed to New England Power Products Company. The old product divisions were realigned and transformed into independent operating companies. Each new company inherited one or more of the Boston Engine product divisions. For example, Marrett became a gasoline and diesel engine company, combining operations from the old consumer and private label divisions. The two Boston Engine data processing departments (CSS and DIS) disappeared and were essentially combined to form the information services department within the new Marrett Corporation. Mike Ross was named director of Information Services for Marrett, reporting to William F. Perry, newly appointed senior vice president of finance and administration. A simplified organization chart for the new Marrett Corporation appears in Exhibit 1.

The new organizational structure had several implications for Mike Ross

EXHIBIT 1 □ Partial Organization Chart for Marrett Corporation* (as of March 1979)

- President Thomas Clarke
  - Director of Corporate Planning Calvin Wyatt
  - The Harrison Forge Company†
    - Director of Purchasing Robert Douglass
  - V.P. of Engineering
    - Technical Assistant Stephen Walker
  - Senior V.P. of Finance and Administration William F. Perry
    - Treasurer Anthony Bloom
    - Controller Donald Jordan
      - Manager of Business Systems Frank Peters
    - V.P. of Industrial Relations
      - Director of Employee Relations Mark Dunbar
    - Director of Information Services Michael Ross
  - V.P. of Manufacturing
    - Director of Production and Inventory Control John Sommerfield
  - V.P. of Marketing
    - Director of Marketing Services Patrick Wheler

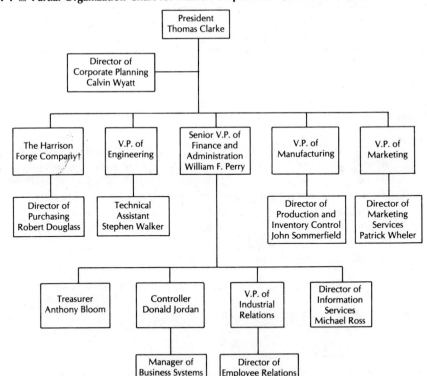

* Names and titles are shown for all individuals mentioned in the case.

† The Harrison Forge Company, technically an independent subsidiary, had been acquired some years earlier to manufacture engine blocks and other castings. Over time, the company had gradually taken over all of Marrett's purchasing functions.

and the information services department. In the first place, the department moved up a level in status, since Perry was the only senior vice president within the new organization structure. Ross viewed this factor as a significant plus, even though Perry had never before been responsible for data processing (he did have extensive familiarity with the function, however; he had been corporate controller in the old Boston Engine organization).

A more important consequence of the reorganization was a significant change in the way Information Services worked with user departments. In Mike Ross's words:

> We no longer need marketing-oriented gimmicks to gain user acceptance. Now we're a functional department just like marketing, manufacturing, the controller, and so on. This is a major shift in department identity. Now we think of ourselves as staff support for selling engines—we're a key part of the company. Where DIS would work on meeting *user*-defined needs, now we go in and do the needs analysis, challenge the user's interest in acquiring a computer, and so on. In fact, what we do is a *business*-systems analysis.
>
> I really believe this reorganization has knocked out a lot of the user games-playing. Now it's clear that *we* do the data processing, and not the users.
>
> One of the first things Bill Perry did was to stress that our task is to be *proactive,* rather than *reactive*. He wants us to *lead* the other functions in how to use IS effectively.

FORMATION OF THE SPC

Several months after the March 1979 corporate reorganization, Perry and Ross began talking about establishing a new DP planning/steering committee. As a long-time DP user, Perry recalled how frustrating it had been to see the DP department set project priorities. Data processing had always reported to a financial person, and Perry believed that over 80 percent of the applications efforts had been financially oriented. Yet he knew there were many other kinds of needs going unmet all over the organization. Perry saw the SPC as a mini board of directors:

> Their charter is not to run the day-to-day IS operations—that's Mike's job. Instead, I want the SPC to do IS planning for the whole organization. Beyond that, I want them to review the IS resource and help determine its optimum staffing level. The IS resource has to be used by *all* the functional areas in the company if it is to be fully effective.

Perry set out to make the SPC a mirror image of the company, with all major functional areas represented. He and Ross jointly determined the departments they wanted represented; they agreed that, whenever possible, each member should be a manager who reported directly to the vice president in his or her functional area. In addition, however, they hoped to get managers whom they felt would be supportive of Information Services efforts and compatible with each other. Perry met personally with each functional vice president to discuss the SPC's role in information systems planning, and to explore what manager from that area would become a member of the SPC. Although the VPs selected their own representatives, Perry made certain that his and Ross's preferences were known. In a few instances Perry actually vetoed a VP's initial selection because he and Ross felt that individual would be a negative influence on the committee. The official memorandum announcing the SPC, describing its purpose and functions, and specifying membership conditions, is reproduced in part in Exhibit 2.

The selection of an SPC chairman was a particularly difficult decision. Perry was clear from the beginning that Ross should not chair the SPC. For some time Perry considered establishing a rotating chairmanship, but finally rejected that as too impermanent. Ross estimated that the chairman might have to commit as much as 25 percent to 30 percent of his time to the SPC, especially during the first year, and it was difficult to find someone with that kind of time availability. Furthermore, Perry knew that they needed to find someone with a personal style that would fit the task—a dedicated, even-tempered approach, but willing to talk up the committee and its charter.

After some discussion the two men agreed that Frank Peters would be an excellent choice. Peters, 35 years old, had joined the old Boston Engine company in 1975 after six years with one of the Big 8 accounting firms. A CPA by background, Peters had become a computer audit specialist, and Perry (as controller) had hired him as manager of Systems Control to create a new internal computer-based systems planning and design group with an emphasis on audit requirements.

Following the March 1979 reorganization, most of Peters' department had been transferred to the Universal Motors corporate staff and relocated to New York. However, Perry had asked Peters to remain on his staff in Boston and appointed him director of business systems, where Peters had continued to work on several internal audit projects. In this position Peters was not a direct user of IS resources, and thus he had the added advantage of not bringing vested interests or biases to the SPC. In addition, Peters had been a member of the SDSC and shared Perry's and Ross's desire not to repeat that experience.

Peters commented to the casewriter:

> The SDSC was far too involved in operating details. The group spent too much time trying to tell Mike how to do his job. It was overly concerned with individual project deadlines. I started out making it clear that the SPC would not be like that.

The other eight SPC members who were finally selected were as follows (office location is listed in parentheses following job title).

EXHIBIT 2 □ Memorandum Announcing the Systems Planning Committee

Our CEO, Tom Clarke, has reviewed and endorsed the proposal to form a Systems Planning Committee.

The key elements that this group will deal with are:

The IS resource is similar to the capital funds of the company, i.e., it must be planned and prioritized in tune with Marrett business needs.

That there is a definite need, as well as benefit to be obtained, from the short- and long-range planning of the IS resource.

There is a Marrett payoff through the exchange of functional needs, airing of problems, and that we have the proper business influence "in touch" with the large dollar expenditures ($3,000,000) invested in IS.

And finally, that IS cannot be a successful influence without the cooperation and direction of such a group.

Objectives

The SPC group will serve as the interface between the IS development function and the operational business segments of The Marrett Corporation. Its primary objectives are to plan and prioritize the disposition of the IS resources in line with The Marrett Corporation business plan, to resolve resource conflicts in the master plan, and monitor activities to ensure proper interaction between functional departments.

Duties

Participate in the annual planning process of the IS function.

Prioritize the IS resource to follow the business plan.

Monitor the progress of development projects with regard to changing business dynamics.

Assist in the development of IS policies.

Review and endorse major IS proposals.

Serve as an education and information channel for all staff personnel with the member's functional area.

Tony Bloom, 35, treasurer (Boston). Joined Marrett in 1975. Served on Boston Engine's corporate staff prior to the reorganization, and had been a member of the SDSC.

Bob Douglass, 43, director of purchasing (Boston). There were few computerized applications within Douglass's area, but Ross considered him basically supportive of the SPC's mission.

Mark Dunbar, 40, director of employee relations (Brockton). With Marrett nine years, Dunbar had been with the old Boston Engine marine division. Dunbar had been project manager for a computerized employee information system several years earlier.

EXHIBIT 2 *(concluded)*

Membership

All members must hold a position that reports directly to a Marrett Corporation officer. He should maintain a departmental position which can fairly represent departmental needs while also being able to recognize and support needs that cross functional departmental lines.

Past systems experience is not a requirement. Emphasis is on an individual's ability to function as a team member, understanding of The Marrett Corporation's business needs, and an appreciation of the IS role in supporting the business functions.

Members are to be appointed by their respective functional officer. Membership is to be considered on a permanent, rather than rotating basis. Members are only replaced at the direction of the corporate executive committee. Members are expected to devote 10 percent of their position time to this responsibility.

Logistics

The SPC will meet monthly with attendance expected to be of high priority. Meetings will take approximately six to eight hours a session, with additional preparation time on the part of each member.

There will also be an annual three-day planning session that members will be expected to participate in. This session will complement the annual one- to five-year business planning development function of Marrett.

There is some urgency in getting this project started and I would appreciate your early identification of your permanent representative. In the initial stages we will invite and expect active participation from several members of the old Systems Development Steering Committee to help in the transition.

W. F. Perry

Don Jordan, 52, controller (Boston). Had been with Marrett for over 20 years. Ross rated Jordan a solid supporter of the SPC, even though Jordan was not generally a strong advocate of computerized systems. As Ross put it, "Don is the *conscience* of the SPC; he makes us justify everything we do."

Jack Sommerfield, 36, manager of production and inventory control (Saugus). He had formerly been with the consumer engine division. Ross considered Sommerfield a "mover and shaker" in terms of accomplishing major system changes within manufacturing.

Stephen Walker, 60, technical assistant to the vice president of engineering (Brockton). Had been with Marrett about 10 years, and had worked in the Marrett Research Center prior to the reorganization.

Pat Wheler, 40, director of marketing services (Saugus). Had been with the industrial division prior to the reorganization. Ross knew Wheler was skeptical about the SPC and suspected Wheler did not really want to serve on the committee.

Calvin Wyatt, 42, director of corporate planning (Boston). Had joined Marrett in late 1978. Wyatt reported directly to Marrett's president, and was quite occupied with developing the planning process within the company.

Bill Perry's congratulatory memorandum to these eight men is reproduced in Exhibit 3.

SUMMER AND FALL 1979 SPC ACTIVITIES

Ross and Peters worked closely together to plan the SPC's initial meeting, to develop their concept of what the group's duties and responsibilities

EXHIBIT 3 □ Memorandum to Newly Appointed SPC Members

Congratulations on your appointment to The Marrett Corporation's Systems Planning Committee (SPC). You have been appointed to this committee by the officer from your functional area because of your ability to fairly represent the needs of your function while also being able to recognize and support the needs of other functions. This trait is essential to the success of the SPC whose primary objectives are to:

Plan and prioritize the disposition of the IS resources.

Resolve resource conflicts.

Monitor plan activities and ensure proper functional interaction.

It is anticipated that the SPC will make a valuable contribution to the overall development and success of The Marrett Corporation. To ensure the SPC's contribution is most meaningful will require your personal effort and contribution.

The first meeting of the SPC has been set for July 25, 1979, at the Park Plaza Hotel in downtown Boston. Mike Ross and Frank Peters are preparing an agenda which will be sent to you shortly.

Also, please mark your calendar for August 20th–22d, 1979. A three-day SPC planning session is being set up for those days and your participation is essential.

W. F. Perry

would be, and to define a set of operating procedures. The two men knew from the beginning that molding the group into an effective unit would not be a simple task. Among other problems, they knew that past experiences with the SDSC were affecting many people's expectations about the SPC. Just as important, most of the members had not worked together before, and several came from parts of the company that had little or no experience with data processing. Peters commented:

> Initially, there were probably three or four subgroups that knew each other fairly well—but between subgroups there was almost no prior interaction. For example, Jack Sommerfield, who's now at Saugus, transferred there from Providence after the reorganization. Pat Wheler has always been at Saugus, but that was part of the old industrial division. Steve Walker's out at Brockton, but that has always been a separate facility.

These concerns led Peters to develop a plan for the first meeting that focused on helping the SPC members get to know each other and the new committee's basic tasks and responsibilities. The meeting, which took place in late July 1979, was kicked off by Bill Perry, who discussed his view of the SPC and why he felt it was an important effort. Peters then asked each member of the group to describe his own department—its size, organization, specific tasks, and so on. Finally, Mike Ross talked about his view of individual member responsibilities and gave a brief status report on current systems projects. Peters closed the meeting by describing plans for a three-day off-site planning session at which the SPC would establish IS project priorities for 1980 in accordance with Marrett's 1980 business plans, which had already been developed.

Bill Perry was mildly discouraged by the tone of the first meeting:

> I was very concerned. I didn't see very much commitment on the part of the members; they really seemed unresponsive. Mike and Frank did almost all the talking, and I wasn't sure how the rest of them were reacting.

Perry thought that perhaps his presence had been inhibiting, and he decided not to attend future meetings. Instead, he monitored the group's efforts by reading the monthly meeting minutes and talking individually with both Peters and Ross.

Peters and Ross were much more optimistic following the first meeting. They recognized that there was an air of cautiousness among the group, but felt that was to be expected. As Peters later recalled, "Mike said he expected the meeting to be a '6,' but he gave it an '8'."

The three-day planning session that Peters announced at the first SPC meeting was originally scheduled for late August. However, scheduling difficulties made the original dates impractical and the meeting was eventually rescheduled for October. The delay was a welcome one, however, as the SPC representatives generally found that their individual preparation for the planning meeting took longer than any of them had expected. Each representative was charged with compiling a list (with brief descriptions) of current and desired systems projects for his functional area.

The SPC had a special meeting in August to review a specific project that involved replacing a computer at the Brockton plant. Peters held the meeting in Brockton, to give the group an on-site exposure to the Brockton facility. In addition to reviewing the conversion project, the group also discussed procedures for developing their project priority lists. Peters provided the group with a set of guidelines outlining the types of projects to include and the information needed on each project. He also handed out a guide for the SPC representatives to follow as they interviewed other managers in their own areas.

Peters set a firm deadline of September 21 for all project proposals (and departmental priority rankings) to be submitted to him. That date would give him enough time to review the plans, clarify any questions, and distribute all the plans to all the members well in advance of the mid-October meeting.

Peters then suggested that the SPC meet for a half day in mid-September to review everyone's progress on the information-gathering process. However, the group balked at this idea, and concluded they did not want to meet. Instead, they asked Peters to send out sample project descriptions as models, and indicated they would call him individually if they had any questions or problems. Peters chose not to push the issue, and acceded to the group sentiment.

Shortly after the August meeting Peters prepared a formal list of operating procedures for the SPC (reproduced in Exhibit 4) and distributed it along with the meeting minutes. About this same time Ross made a formal presentation about the SPC to all the members of the information services department. He wanted to be certain that no one felt threatened or usurped by the SPC, and that everyone within IS understood fully the role that the SPC was intended to play.

Perry, Peters, and Ross all believed it was important for the SPC planning process to be tied as closely as possible to the Marrett corporate plans. By fall 1979 the 1980 business plans were well defined by functional area. (The company planning cycle involved Executive Committee agreement on overall strategies by early June each year. These strategies were then converted into functional area business activity plans during the summer. By the end of each summer the corporate plans were reduced to annual budgets. Thus, by early fall each function had a clear definition of its targets and major activities for the coming year.)

Bill Perry commented on this planning process:

> I view the IS projects as *means* to the ends defined by our business strategy. The IS plans are based on the functional areas' definitions of what they need to accomplish their *business* goals. What's really powerful about this process is that the SPC may get several projects from different functional areas, all aimed at one general business strategy.

EXHIBIT 4 □ Operating Procedures

1. The overriding concept of the SPC is that the Committee is a planning, prioritizing, and monitoring group. It is not a group for checking the status of the IS function.
2. Each SPC member is a permanent member of the Committee. His membership is not for a specified and limited period.
3. Each SPC member is expected to attend each meeting.
4. The SPC will meet on a regular basis. These regular meetings will be held once a month on the *third Wednesday* of each month.
5. The monthly meetings will generally be full-day sessions. Depending upon the agenda, however, the meeting may be only one half day or may be longer than one day.
6. Special meetings may be called by the Chairman if a situation arises which cannot be properly handled as part of a regularly scheduled monthly meeting.
7. SPC meetings generally will be held off-site of company locations to avoid interruption by secretaries, bosses, telephones, and other demands.
8. An agenda for each meeting will be mailed and will be received by members at least one week prior to the meeting date. SPC members are expected to contribute their input to the agenda.
9. A regular meeting location will be established so that the quality of meeting accommodations will be consistent.
10. Minutes of the meetings will be prepared and will be in the mail during the first Monday following the regular meeting date.
11. A three (3) day annual SPC planning meeting will be held to develop a recommended IS plan for the following three (3) years.
12. The SPC-developed annual IS plan will be submitted to the Executive Committee for review and approval.
13. Monthly written reports from each member are required to be sent to the Chairman. The reports should provide a status for projects in the functional area that the member represents.
14. The SPC will, after appropriate review and discussion, take a position on IS policy items. When a written recommendation is issued, majority and minority viewpoints will be included. Such written reports will be given to W. F. Perry for review and decision making by the Executive Committee.
15. All projects for IS will be submitted to IS only after the approval of the appropriate SPC representative.
16. Projects or activities of the SPC generally will not be accomplished through the use of subcommittees. However, IS resources will be available for detail fact gathering when the SPC has a need.

When Peters had collected all of the departmental systems plans he compiled them in a binder for distribution to all the SPC representatives. He also compiled and distributed all the functional area strategies—the first time, to his knowledge, that managers at this level of the company had seen each others' strategic plans. The SPC planning book—a solid four inches of functional business strategies and 53 detailed systems proposals—included a first-cut consolidated priority ranking that Peters prepared on his own. The book was sent out to everyone in mid-October.

THE OFF-SITE PLANNING MEETING

The planning meeting was held at a resort hotel in southern New Hampshire. The session began with cocktails and dinner on a Wednesday evening. Peters had asked the Marrett president to come to the dinner and give a kick-off speech, but the president canceled out at the last minute (due to a sudden change in the scheduling of negotiations for an annual supply contract with one of Marrett's largest customers). Bill Perry gave the after-dinner speech instead. He reviewed the company's year-to-date financial performance (at a level of detail not normally shared with managers at this level), and he stressed the importance of the SPC's task in helping to improve operating results.

On Thursday each SPC member, in turn, described his functional area's business strategy and summarized the key IS projects and needs within the area. This project review took all day, including a final hour after dinner. When the group finally broke up at 9 P.M. everyone was tired, but satisfied that they had a basic understanding of current and projected information services efforts throughout the company.

On Friday morning one of Ross's subordinates described in detail the information services department's resources, covering both personnel and hardware. He also reviewed the projects currently being worked on. Following this session, each SPC member individually ranked all 53 projects. Then Ross and Peters split the group into two teams of five managers each (including themselves) and asked each team to produce a single ranking. (The two men had previously determined the composition of the two teams, based on their assessments of personalities, experiences from the old SDSC, and their desire to avoid hostile clashes between dominant or outspoken individuals.) The two teams spent several hours working independently to resolve individual differences in priority rankings. Then, at 3 P.M. on Friday afternoon, they presented their consolidated rankings to each other.

They discovered that the two independent rankings were relatively close, although there were several significant differences. What was most interesting, however, was the discovery that the two teams had developed slightly different approaches for establishing the rankings. In particular, one group had designed a two-stage process that began by first assigning each project request to one of three categories:

A—necessary or required work; critical to the business.
B—highly desirable.
C—good ideas, but backburner in terms of urgency.

"A" projects were those that related directly to corporate strategy for 1980, or that were related to government regulations (and were thus not postponable), or those that promised an immediate high dollar return.

The second team found this approach helpful, and the total group quickly began discussing projects in terms of this category system. The group worked from 3 to 5 P.M. Friday afternoon attempting to resolve the conflicts between the two teams' independent rankings. However, even though the two lists were very close, they were unable to reach final agreement. Finally, at 5 P.M., Peters suggested they quit for the day and come back Saturday morning to resolve the remaining differences.

Bill Perry joined the group again on Saturday morning and sat in on their final session. He was generally pleased with what he saw, although he recognized that some SPC members were individually disappointed by how their own projects came out on the priority lists.

> This process clearly had to be done, and the group did a good job. Most importantly, they were allocating IS manpower resources to specific projects, and that forced them to push the lower priority projects out to future years. I know that made some of them unhappy; several people are pushing for expanding the IS resource. The thing I want now is for them to commit *user* manpower resources as well as IS resources.

The SPC members themselves seemed very satisfied with the planning session. One member called it a "three-day shirt-sleeve session with lots of sharing and participation—a good experience."

SPC ACTIVITIES IN 1980

As a follow-up to the planning meeting, Peters and Ross made a formal presentation to the Marrett Executive Committee (the president and all the functional vice presidents) in late January 1980. The other SPC members attended the presentation but did not participate, except to respond to questions from Executive Committee members. When the president recognized how many IS projects were *not* going to get worked on during 1980 he offered to increase the IS budget. Ross turned down the offer, however, commenting, "I don't want more money yet—I'm having trouble spending what we have now."

Later, Ross commented to the casewriter:

> I don't want Information Services to be doing projects that don't have a business impact. Perry clearly wants us to spend our budget where it will have a significant effect. We're already growing as fast as we can, and I don't want to make promises I can't fulfill.

The SPC met on its regular monthly schedule through the winter and early spring of 1980. As planned, the meetings were normally held in a hotel a few blocks away from Marrett's headquarters in downtown Boston. During this time period the group's attention was generally focused on reviewing progress on the major ongoing systems projects. However, Peters also tried to include one or two procedural issues on each agenda. Ross had adopted a formal project management system designed by a software consulting firm, and both he and Peters felt it was important for the SPC's project approval procedures to be consistent with the development phases of the project management system. However, Peters was moving very slowly in introducing formal procedures and documentation requirements to the SPC. He was reluctant to overload the members with paperwork, and he believed it was important for the group to participate actively in designing their own approval and monitoring procedures.

Several other more controversial issues were raised at various SPC meetings during this time period. On one occasion Peters brought up the chargeout system. There was a history of strong feeling about charging back IS costs to the users, much of it dating back to the old SDSC relationships (users had frequently complained that costs were too high). When Peters brought the subject up, Ross said, "If it's a factual problem we'll deal with it, but if it's an emotional issue, let's not involve everyone else." Peters suggested that a more comprehensive discussion of chargeout might be an appropriate agenda item for a future meeting, but several members said no, and the subject was dropped.

On another occasion Peters expressed some concern about attendance. Two members (Pat Wheler and Calvin Wyatt) had missed several meetings, and Peters was afraid their absences would affect the group's unity and credibility. However, the group seemed reluctant to discuss the subject, and in fact Peters sensed that those who *were* attending regularly felt indirectly and unjustly accused of lack of commitment. While Peters recognized the validity of this response, he remained frustrated about the problem. However, he did drop the subject at that point, concluding that a formal meeting was not the place to discuss it.

Peters and Ross also tried to include some form of "education" in each monthly meeting, though they were careful not to call it that. The SPC members were busy, pragmatic, results-oriented managers, and they seemed unwilling to commit to regular "educational" programs. There was just too much to do, too many immediate problems to solve and decisions to make. However, Peters and Ross got around this resistance by scheduling some kind of "informational" presentation for each SPC meeting. In April, for example, two managers (one from IS, one from the treasurer's department) were scheduled to report on a new cash management system. Though the report was basically a progress review, Peters and Ross knew that it would also provide useful general background on both cash management techniques and systems development work to the SPC members.

MEMBER VIEWS OF THE SPC

In April 1980, the casewriter spoke individually with several members of the SPC, asking for their assessment of the group's efforts and its impact on their departmental operations.

Tony Bloom, treasurer, was generally very positive about the way the SPC was functioning. Bloom had been a member of the SDSC and was keenly aware of how differently the SPC was working out.

> This is a solid group of people. The members are higher in the organization than the old SDSC people. More important, these people are really on top of their own operations—and they don't want to look bad in front of each other. Each guy has his boss's ear, but they all wear an SPC hat.
>
> Given who we are, I think we make good business decisions. Nothing is sacred; people are willing to challenge each other and we're getting better each meeting. You have to remember that we didn't know each other well when the SPC began. I know there was a lot of feeling that the treasurer sat up in a white tower and didn't know other people's needs. Now, I can go to our meetings and hear other people's needs as well as tell them what I want.
>
> Basically, we're doing what we set out to do. Our purpose is effective resource utilization, and I think we're doing that pretty well.

Don Jordan, the controller, was also positive about the need for the SPC. However, he was more ambivalent about how well the planning process was working out.

> I am pleased that our IS priorities are no longer being set by IS itself. The SPC is basically a good group trying to do the right thing for the company. But I'm not 100 percent confident of the judgments the group is making. The trouble is that we get a lot of "motherhood" projects that no one can argue against. And there's a lot of backscratching, too. You know, I'll support your project if you'll support mine.
>
> The trouble is, we don't always have good information on the project ideas. It's rarely a black/white situation. All the projects are *good* at some level. What worries me is when the needs outstrip the IS resources. I don't want to see IS turning down good projects. We ran out of resources very quickly this year, and a lot of important efforts are getting pushed into 1981.
>
> As an SPC member I do have one problem: I get all hell from my subordinates when I can't get a project approved. What is going to happen when I submit them again next fall and they get turned down again? Will my people react negatively and get discouraged? We had several high-payback projects

> that got low priorities. It's a lot different than it was under the old organization, when we could get anything we wanted, as long as we paid for it. Maybe we should just allocate some part of the IS resource toward direct cash-saving projects.
>
> What really gets me is poorly thought-out proposals. Like last fall, we had one for "a better marketing information system"—that was the extent of the project definition. I ranked it 54th out of the 53 proposals we reviewed—but the group approved it.
>
> But, on balance, the SPC is the best solution for handling very touchy decisions. I can't think of a better way to do it, short of an all-knowing, benevolent dictator.

Jack Sommerfield, the manufacturing representative, was overseeing the largest current systems development project, a consolidated order entry and inventory control system. There were several other, smaller manufacturing systems projects in process as well. Sommerfield estimated that monitoring these efforts and attending SPC meetings was taking close to 25 percent of his time. Sommerfield stressed that the new manufacturing control system was *not* an IS project.

> It's a *manufacturing* project, not a systems project. If it's seen as an IS project I guarantee it will fail. We're not just allocating and measuring system people's time, but our *own* as well. In fact, we have actually hired three people who are doing nothing but manufacturing-control systems. In manufacturing, the attitude is "screw systems, let's build engines." Of course, we see this new system as a competitive tool that will help us improve customer service and deliveries.
>
> What's unfortunate about the SPC is when key areas like marketing aren't involved like they should be. The SPC concept is right, but what matters is getting the right people involved. You have to have people who are willing to come to the meetings and spend time outside the meetings on systems projects. I know it's a lot of time to spend, but there are all kinds of personal benefits too. I never would spend any time on things like cash management systems or payroll systems if it weren't for the SPC. There's an important business payoff to that kind of learning, too. For example, the new manufacturing control system has all kinds of implications for Don Jordan, even though he doesn't yet realize what's in it for him.
>
> One concern I have is whether top management really understands the role and cost of information systems within Marrett. The SPC *needs* top management support, but I'm not sure they know what we've committed to. After Peters and Ross presented our plan to the Executive Committee in January, the president just accepted it. But I think there were too many vague things in that plan for them to take it as is. Will they support us when push comes to shove and we need more funding? I'm not sure they will.

The casewriter also attempted to talk with Pat Wheler, but was unable to schedule a meeting with him. Wheler reported that he was overwhelmed with work; his boss, the vice president of marketing, had left the company in early 1980 and had not yet been replaced. Wheler was temporarily reporting directly to the president, and the entire marketing department was in a state of high uncertainty. Wheler also mentioned that at the time he had been asked to join the SPC he was already serving on "all kinds of committees—and that's not my style."

APRIL MEETING OF THE SPC

The April 1980 meeting of the SPC was held on Wednesday, April 23, at a hotel located just two blocks from Marrett's corporate headquarters in downtown Boston. Frank Peters opened the meeting by commenting that both Pat Wheler and Calvin Wyatt were absent and would miss the meeting because of other commitments. Peters also noted that Stephen Walker and Bob Douglass were not yet present, but were expected momentarily. Mark Dunbar expressed his personal concern that these kinds of absences and latenesses were reducing the SPC's effectiveness. Ten minutes of general discussion followed, and Dunbar's concern was clearly shared by everyone else present (Walker and Douglass arrived just as this discussion was ending). Peters indicated that he would discuss the group's concern privately with both Wheler and Wyatt.

The first item on the agenda was a report by Mike Ross on actual first-quarter manpower allocations versus plan. Most major projects were on schedule, though several were consuming more resources than planned. Ross stressed the importance of timely submission of detailed new project plans (those scheduled in October 1979) in order to stay on the 1980 timetable. But, basically, the core of the 1980 plan was being followed rather closely.

Tony Bloom and several of his subordinates then presented a detailed technical description of the new cash management system now in use. The system was the first major online system installed at Marrett, and it was now complete, operational, and largely successful (though still in shakedown period). Bloom mentioned that a post-implementation audit was planned but not yet under way.

Following a brief break for coffee, Frank Peters spent about 15 minutes describing his ideas for project submission procedures and project status-reporting guidelines. (A rough outline of Peters' proposals is included in Exhibit 5.) Peters distributed draft copies of a Service Request Form and a Progress Report Form, and asked for reactions. Discussion was relatively brief, as the SPC members had not seen the forms prior to the meeting. Peters concluded his presentation by commenting:

> Please look these over and give me some feedback within two weeks. Then we can adjust the forms. We can try using them for a while to see if they're workable. If not, we'll revise them. They're only tools.

EXHIBIT 5 □ Project Submission Procedures Proposed at April 23 Meeting

How is a project submitted?

Functional Area

A. An individual has an idea (need) which involves using the IS resource.
B. The individual takes his idea (need) to his manager.
C. The manager agrees the idea (need) is realistic and is worth pursuing.
D. The need is documented by the project initiator and his manager, using a service request.
E. The service request is forwarded from the manager to the appropriate SPC representative.

SPC Representative

A. The SPC representative reviews the service request and evaluates its merit in relation to other projects, asks questions, becomes familiar with the need.
B. The SPC representative may reject the project at this time and return it to the requesting manager.
C. The SPC representative may concur the project has merit. He will then sign the service request and forward it to IS for "sizing."

Information Services

A. IS receives service requests from SPC representatives (no one else) and assigns the request a project number.
B. IS performs a technical evaluation of the Service request and sizes the project.
C. Is the request a minor project?
D. If yes, return copy of service request to SPC representative and begin work on project.
E. If no, then it must be a major project. Return a copy of the service request along with sizing and estimating data to the SPC representative. Do not begin any work on this service request unless the project is a government requirement or required for the continuation of the business per SPC representative.

Jack Sommerfield mentioned that he hoped both the projected and actual cost and man-hour data on the two forms would include user funding and personnel commitments as well as those coming from Information Services. Following a brief discussion it was decided to include user costs on several "test" projects to determine what kind of impact the data would have.

The remaining 90 minutes of the meeting were devoted to a review of the Consolidated Order Entry Project being managed by Jack Sommerfield, and to several new project requests. The SPC approved Tony Bloom's request to do a Requirements Definition for an online credit management system, but rejected two enhancements to Bloom's existing cash management system. Don Jordan told Bloom that he could provide the needed information from existing independent reports. Bloom agreed to review the reports, but indicated he would resubmit his requests if he felt the reports were insufficient.

EXHIBIT 5 *(concluded)*

SPC Representative

A. Receives "sized" major project service from IS and asks himself the question:

Can project be held for submission at the annual SPC planning meeting?

B. If yes:

Hold project for submission at annual SPC planning session.

C. If no:

Contact SPC chairman to put project submission on agenda for next monthly SPC meeting.

D. Present project at SPC meeting, utilizing the completed service request, cost estimates, and other pertinent information which will aid SPC in determining "worthiness" of project.

Systems Planning Committee

A. Is project being submitted as part of the SPC's annual planning?
B. If yes, review project, prioritize against other projects, and either approve or reject project.
C. If approved, approval is to expand resources for the Systems Requirements phase only.
D. If no, then it must be a project submitted in a monthly meeting. Review project, evaluate its worthiness, determine if it should be added to SPC plan or rejected.
E. If added to SPC plan, determine its priority, and adjust (modify) plan.
F. If a project submitted to SPC (either in annual planning or monthly meetings) is rejected, the SPC member takes this decision back to the appropriate manager with an explanation. The project is then either "dead" or it is revised or restructured for future submission to the SPC.

Don Jordan then presented a request to modify a minor payroll system. The SPC approved a study of the project, although several members questioned the project's ROI and pointed out that the study had been all but rejected during the October 1979 planning session. The study was approved this time, however, because Jordan argued that the issue was not ROI but data accuracy. He maintained that a new system was essential for government reporting purposes.

Following discussion of several other minor support and conversion projects, the meeting was adjourned for lunch at 1 P.M.

MIKE ROSS'S CONCERNS

Following the meeting, Mike Ross spoke briefly with the casewriter regarding his feelings about the development of the Systems Planning Committee. Ross was generally pleased with the role being played by the committee; however, he did express several concerns:

> I guess the thing I really wonder about is whether the time and effort being put into this group is worth it, as far as the company is concerned. Have we saved ourselves a lot of problems? It's awfully hard to measure costs not incurred!
>
> As far as the future is concerned, my major question is, where do we go from here? I think the SPC is developing a good working pattern, but I'm not sure about what direction it should take from now on. How can we best build on the foundation we've got now?

Chapter 5 □ Information Systems Planning: A Contingent Focus

Chapter \ Manageable Trend	Strategic Impact	DP/TP/OA	Organization Learning	Make/Buy	Life Cycle	GM/ User/ IS
IS Technology Organization Issues **Chapter 3**		●	●			●
Organizational Issues in IS Development **Chapter 4**	●		●	●		●
Information Systems Planning **Chapter 5**	●		●			●
IS Management Control **Chapter 6**	●		●	●		●
A Portfolio Approach to Information Systems Development **Chapter 7**	●				●	●
Operations Management **Chapter 8**	●			●	●	●
Multinational IS Issues **Chapter 9**		●				●
The IS Business **Chapter 10**	●		●	●		●

A major manufacturing company eliminates its five-person DP planning staff, reassigning three to other jobs in the IS organization, and letting two go. In commenting on this, the vice president-finance stated, "We just didn't seem to be getting a payoff from this. After three years of trying, we thought we could find a better place to spend our money."

The executive vice president-operation of a large financial institution, in speaking of a recently completed business systems planning effort, stated that this effort has been the key to conceptualizing a new and important direction concerning both the amount of IS expenditures and where they should be directed during the next five years. "We would be lost without it," he noted.

The head of IS planning of a major financial services organization, in discussing his recent disillusionment with planning, noted, "When I started IS planning two years ago, I was very enthusiastic about its potential for invigorating the company. It worked for a while, but now the effort seems to have gone flat."

These comments seem typical of a number of organizations where an IS planning effort is launched with great hopes and apparent early results but subsequently runs into difficulty. This chapter explores key managerial issues surrounding this as they have unfolded in the past 10 years and provides guidelines for assuring success.

As information systems applications have grown in both size and complexity over the past two decades, the job of conceptualizing a strategy for assimilating these resources into the firm's operations has grown steadily more important. A key vehicle for developing this strategy has been a sensitively architected planning process. Such a planning process, to be effective, must deal simultaneously with the realities of the firm's organizational culture, corporate planning culture, stage of IS development, and criticalness of IS activities in relation to the company's achieving corporate goals.

Repeated studies have suggested that a clear correlation exists between effectively perceived IS activities in an organization and a focused, articulated, and appropriate planning process.[1] Since good metrics do not exist for measuring the overall effectiveness of an IS activity, however, the evidence absolutely linking effectiveness of the IS activity with planning processes is more diffuse and fragmentary.

This chapter is organized around four broad clusters of topics:

1. Identification of the external and internal pressures on the firm that generate the need for an articulated IS planning process.
2. Identification of the practical restraining pressures which limit the value to be derived from the planning process.
3. IS planning and corporate strategy.
4. Discussion of important corporate environmental factors which influence both the ultimate effectiveness of IS planning and identification of the key levers to be managed in tailoring the planning process.

PRESSURES TO PLAN—GENERAL CONSIDERATION

There are a variety of critical pressures which force one to plan ahead in the information systems field. The more important include:

Rapid Changes in Technology. Hardware/software technical and cost characteristics have and will continue to evolve rapidly, thereby offering substantially different and profitable approaches to applications develop-

[1] Philip Pyburn, "Information Systems Planning—a Contingency Perspective," (Harvard Business School thesis, 1981).

ment. On the one hand, this requires continued meetings of the IS staff and management groups to ensure that they have properly identified shifts significant to the company and developed plans to manage them. On the other hand, it is equally important that potential users, such as office managers or analytical staffs (often quite different from the traditional users of data processing systems), be made aware of the implications of these changes (as well as potential problems). In this way they can be stimulated to identify appropriate profitable new applications in their areas of responsibility that would not necessarily occur to the IS staff.

As the technology changes, planning becomes increasingly important to ensure that the organization does not unwittingly fall into a proliferation of incompatible systems. It is also important because the lead times for acquiring and updating equipment is often long. Once acquired, integration of new equipment into a company's existing technical configuration and network of administrative procedures frequently forces extended implementation schedules up to four years.

A recently studied regional bank has a three-year installation program to manage its transition from 140 online terminals to over 1,400 terminals on completion of its online teller network. Preparation of a detailed plan was absolutely critical in developing senior management's confidence in the integrity of the installation program and ensuring that sound operations would continue during the implementation.

Personnel Scarcity. The scarcity of trained, perceptive analysts and programmers, coupled with the long training cycles needed to make them fully effective, is a major factor restraining IS development. As discussed in Chapters 3 and 4, these do not appear to be cyclical problems but rather long-term difficulties which will endure throughout the 1980s. Not only will increasing amounts of software have to be sourced from outside the firm, but tough internal resource allocation decisions must be made. In 1981, not only is the computer services industry booming but an increasing number of U.S. firms are looking overseas for English-speaking technical personnel to meet existing shortages at attractive U.S. salaries.

Scarcity of Other Corporate Resources. Another critical factor inducing planning is the limited availability of financial and managerial resources. IS is only one of many strategic investment opportunities for a company and cash invested in it is often obtained at the expense of other areas. This is intensified by the overwhelming financial accounting practice in U.S. companies to charge IS expenditures directly against current year's earnings. Hence, review of both the effectiveness and efficiency of these expenditures is a matter of great interest and is a critical limiting factor for new projects, particularly in companies under profit or cost pressures.

Scarcity of IS middle management personnel, particularly on the development side, is also a significant constraint. Companies' inability to train sufficient project leaders and supervisors has significantly restrained IS development. This has forced either significant reductions in many applications portfolios or the undertaking of unduly high-risk projects with inadequate human resources.

Trend to Data Base Design and Integrated Systems. An increasing and significant percentage of the applications portfolio involves the design of data bases to support a variety of different applications. A long-term view of the evolution of applications is critical in order to appropriately select both the contents of the data bases and the protocols for updating them to adequately support the family of application systems using them.

Validation of Corporate Plan. In many organizations, new marketing programs, new product design, and introduction and implementation of organizational strategies depend on the development of IS support programs. It is critical that these points of dependency be understood and that, if the corporate strategy is infeasible due to IS limitations, this message be highlighted and resolution of the problem be forced when alternatives are still available. In organizations where the IS products are integral to elements of the corporate strategy, this linkage is more important than for those organizations where IS plays an important but distinctly support function. For example, a large paper company recently had to abandon major new billing discount promotions, a key part of their marketing strategy, because they were unable to translate the very complex ideas into the existing computer programs with their present level of staff skills. Coordination with IS in planning sessions would have both identified the problem and permitted more satisfactory solutions to be identified.

PRESSURES TO PLAN—SITUATIONAL CONSIDERATIONS

It is important to note that, at different points in the evolution of an IS technology, the balance between these pressures shifts and substantially different purposes are being served by planning. Reflecting upon the advent and growth of business data processing, data bases, distributed systems, telecommunications, and other new technologies, one can identify four different phases of technology assimilation, each of which poses a quite different planning challenge.

Phase 1—Technology Identification and Investment Phase. The basic focus of planning in the initial phase of a new technology is both technically oriented and human resource acquisition oriented. Key planning problems include identification of an appropriate technology for study, site preparation, development of staff skills, and managing development of the first pilot applications using this technology.

In this phase, short-term technical problem resolution issues are so critical and experience so limited that long-term strategic thinking about the implications of the technology is limited. This is not bad, since those involved usually do not yet have a strong enough background in the technology and its implications for the company to think long term. As the organization gains experience, selection of appropriate applications for this technology become more equal to technical issues and one evolves to the second phase.

Phase 2—Technological Learning and Adaptation Phase. The basic thrust of planning in this phase is focused on developing potential user consciousness of the new technology's existence and communicating a sense of the type of problems it can help solve, sequencing projects, and providing coordination. Initiation of a series of user-supported pilot projects is key to success. As a secondary output, the planning process focuses on numbers of staff and skills to be hired, equipment to be acquired, and generation of appropriate financial data supporting those projects. The written plan (if any) of consensus direction which comes out of this process is not an accurate indicator for predicting the pace of future events because individuals engaged in a learning process do not yet have the insights to be both concise and accurate concerning what their real desires are in relation to this technology and how practical these desires are. It is important to note that, since technology will evolve for the foreseeable future, there will usually be a phase 2 flavor to part of a company's IS development portfolio. Our observations of successful practice at this phase suggest clearly that:

1. The portion of a planning process focusing on introducing new technology is best developed by getting started with a pilot test to generate both IS and user learning rather than by years of advance introspection and design.
2. The critical success factors here involve attracting the interest of some potential users on their terms and stimulating their understanding on adaptation of the technology. Success here leads to later requests for service.
3. Planning during this phase (and phase 1 as well) involves a program of planned technological innovations, encouraging users to build upon past experience and organization receptivity to change.

Planning for phase 2 technologies has a heavy strategic focus to it. However, as is true in companies which are in a rapid growth phase in new industry sectors, precision of such planning suffers from both user and developer lack of familiarity with the technology and its implications. Hence, it does not have the same predictive value as planning for technology at a later phase. What the technical developer thinks are the implications of the new technology often turns out to be quite different after the users have experimented.

Phase 3—Rationalization/Management Control. Effective planning for technologies at this phase has a strong efficiency focus on rationalizing the broad range of experimental operations. Where technological learning and adaptation planning has a long-range (if not terribly accurate) flavor to it, planning in phase 3 is dominated by short-term, one- to two-year efficiency and organization considerations. These include getting troubled development applications straightened away and completed, upgrading staff to acceptable knowledge levels, reorganizing to develop and implement further projects, and efficiently utilizing this new technology. During this phase, planning's objective is to draw appropriate limits concerning the types of applications which make sense with this technology and to ensure they are implemented cost efficiently. In terms of the Anthony framework, during this phase, effective planning has much more of a management control and operational control flavor to it and less of a strategic planning thrust to it.[2]

Phase 4—Maturity/Widespread Technology Transfer. The final phase is one of managed evolution by transferring the technology to a wider spectrum of systems applications within the organization. In this phase, with organizational learning essentially complete and a technology base installed with appropriate controls in place, it is appropriate to look more seriously into the future and plot longer-term trends. Unfortunately, if one is not careful this can become too rigid an extrapolation of trends based on the business and technology as we now understand it. Unexpected quirks in the business and evolution of technology often invalidate what has been done during phase 4 planning.

Given the current dynamic state of IS technology, there is a need for all four phases of planning to be going on in a typical organization. The planning for business batch data processing for most companies in 1982, for example, is phase 4, while word processing and office automation is phase 2. This suggests that uniform orderliness and consistency in the protocols of the planning process are not necessarily appropriate because of organizational variances in familiarity with particular technologies. Not only does the planning process style have to evolve for a particular family of technologies over time, but a consistent, uniform process for the aggregate portfolio of applications for an organizational unit is unlikely to be appropriate. This is so because it is dealing with a cluster of different technologies, each of which is at a different phase of assimilation within the organization. For example, one manufacturing company studied was phase 4 in terms of its

[2] Robert Anthony, *Planning, and Control Systems: A Framework for Analysis* (Harvard Business School, Division of Research, 1965).

ability to conceptualize and deal with enhancements to its batch systems over a multiyear period. At the same time, it was phase 3 in terms of organizing protocols and training a broad group of individuals to solidify control over the efficiencies of its online inquiry and data input systems whose growth had exploded in the past several years. Finally, it had made an investment in several word processing systems and was beginning to examine several different methods of office automation, and was clearly in phase 1 with respect to this technology. In summary, planned clutter (as opposed to consistency) in the approach to IS planning for an organizational unit is a desirable rather than an undesirable feature. Similarly, the approach to IS planning for different organizational units within a company should vary, since each often has quite different familiarity with specific technologies.

LIMITATION IN PLANNING BENEFITS

As new products appear, as the competitive environment shifts, as the laws change, as corporate strategies change, and as mergers and spinoffs take place, the priorities a company assigns to its various applications appropriately evolve as well. Some previously considered low-priority or new (not even conceived of) applications may become critically important, while others previously vital will diminish in significance. This volatility places a real premium on building a fexible framework to permit change to be managed in an orderly and consistent fashion to match evolving business requirements.

In a similar vein, every information systems planning process must make some very specific assumptions about the nature and role of technological evolution. If this evolution occurs at a different rate from the one forecasted (as is often the case), then major segments of the plan may have to be reworked in terms of both scope and thrust of work.

For example, if the present speed of access to a 100-million character file were suddenly increased in the coming year by an order of magnitude beyond current expectations, with no change in cost, most organizations' plans would require careful reexamination, not just concerning the priority of applications but, more important, their very structure.

Some individuals have used this as a reason not to plan but rather to be creatively opportunistic on a year-to-year basis. We have found the balance of evidence supporting this viewpoint unconvincing.

PLANNING AS A RESOURCE DRAIN

Every person, or part of a person, assigned to planning diverts resources away from systems and program development. The extent to which financial resources should be devoted to planning is still very much a question. Not only will the style of planning evolve over time, as parts of the organization pass through different phases with different technologies, but the amount of commitment to planning will also appropriately shift. This suggests that there is incompatibility between the notions of stability in an IS planning process and its role of stimulating a creative view of the future. If not carefully managed, IS planning tends to evolve into a mind-numbing process of routinely changing the numbers as opposed to stimulating a sensitive focus on the company's real problems.

FIT TO CORPORATE CULTURE

An important aspect of IS planning is to implement it in a way which ensures congruence with the realities of the corporate culture. Organizations, for example, which have a very formal corporate planning process, whose relevance is actively supported by senior management, have a presold internal user-management climate which supports formal approaches to IS planning. In middle management's eyes, planning is a legitimate activity, and devoting time to it is appropriate. Other organizations, however, have quite different cultures and approaches to corporate planning. These factors significantly alter both the form and the degree of commitment that can be won from users in an IS planning process and consequently shape the most desirable way to approach the planning task. This is discussed further later in the chapter.

STRATEGIC IMPACT OF IS ACTIVITIES

For some organizations, IS activities represent an area of great strategic importance, while for other organizations they play, and appropriately will continue to play, a cost-effective and useful role but one which is distinctly supportive in nature. It is inappropriate for organizations of this latter type to expect that the same amount of senior management strategic thinking be devoted to the IS organization as for organizations of the former type. This issue is complicated by the fact that while today the IS function may not have strategic importance, the thrust of its applications portfolio may be such as to have great significance for the future and, thus, planning is very important. The opposite, of course, could also be true where IS plays a strategic operational role in the company's operations, but their future applications do not seem to offer the same payoff or significance. Here a less intensive focus on strategic planning is in order with clearly different people involved than in the previous case.

The above points (which were discussed first in Chapter 2) are illustrated below by the identification of four quite different IS environments. (Also see Exhibit 5–1.)

EXHIBIT 5-1 □ Information Systems Strategic Grid

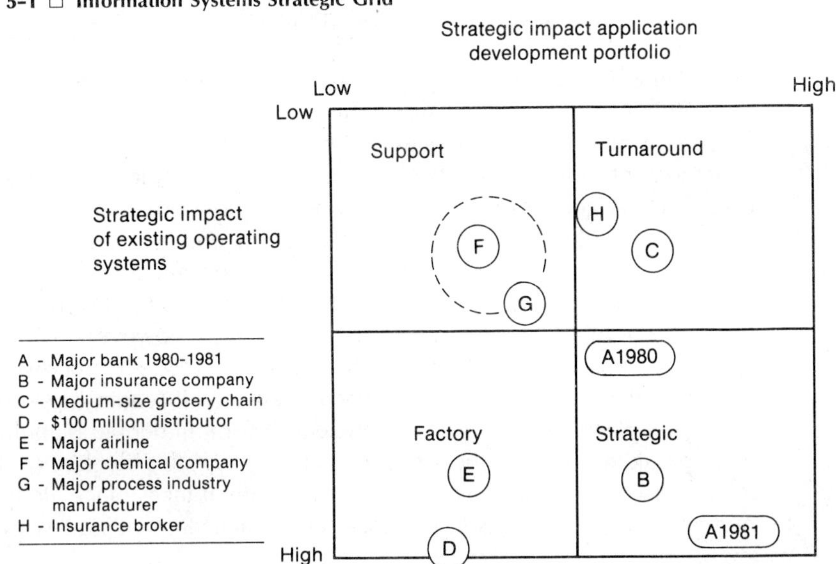

Strategic. These are companies which are critically dependent on the smooth functioning of the IS activity. Appropriately managed, these firms not only require considerable IS planning but IS planning needs to be closely integrated with corporate planning in a two-way dialogue. Not only does IS need the guidance of corporate goals but the achievement of these goals can be severely impacted by IS performance and capabilities or lack thereof. The impact of IS on the firm's performance is such that significant general management guidance in IS planning is appropriate.

Recent comments by the CEO of a large financial institution to his senior staff captured this perspective as he noted: "Most of our customer services and much of our office support for those services involve some kind of systematic information processing. Without the computer hardware and software supporting these processing efforts, we would undoubtedly drown in a sea of paper—unless we were first eliminated from the market because our costs were so high and our services so inefficient that we had no customers to generate the paper. Either way, it is abundantly clear that information systems are critical to our survival and our success."

"In our businesses, the critical resources which ultimately determine our marketing and our operating performance are *people* and *systems*."

Turnaround. In a similar way to companies in the strategic box, these firms also need a substantial IS planning effort, which is linked to corporate planning in a two-way dialogue. Corporate long-term performance can be severely impacted by shortfalls in IS performance and capabilities. Again, the impact of IS on the firm's future is such that significant general management guidance in IS planning is appropriate.

These are firms which may receive considerable amounts of IS operational support, but where the company is not absolutely dependent on the uninterrupted cost-effective functioning of this support to achieve either short-term or long-term objectives. The impact of the applications under development, however, is absolutely vital for the firm to reach its strategic objectives. A good example of this was a rapidly growing manufacturing firm. IS technology embedded in its factories and accounting processes, while important, was not absolutely vital to their effectiveness. The rapid growth of the firm's domestic and international installations in number of products, number of sites, number of staff, etc., however, had severely strained its management control systems and had made its improvement of critical strategic interest to the company. Enhanced IS leadership, new organizational placement of IS, and an increased commitment to planning were all steps taken to resolve the situation. Companies in this block not only have an increased need for IS planning but frequently it takes place along with a number of other changes to enhance senior management's overview of IS.

Factory. Strategic goal setting for IS and linkage to long-term corporate strategy is not nearly as critical in this environment. IS planning can take place with appropriate guidance as to where the corporation is going; only limited feedback on IS constraints needs to go in the other direction. Senior management involvement in IS planning appropriately is much less. Detailed year-to-year operational planning and capacity planning is absolutely critical.

Support. Again, strategic goal setting for IS and linkage to long-term corporate strategy is not nearly as critical as for the turnaround and strategic environments. IS constraints are not a critical input to corporate success. Overachievement or underachievement of IS departmental performance will not cause critical problems. Senior management involvement in the IS planning process can be much less here than in the first two situations.

Example of Use of Grid

Not only should the planning approach differ for each of the environments discussed above, but the situation is further complicated when a mismatch exists between where an organization is in the grid and where senior management believes it should be. In general, more planning is needed when a firm is trying to deal with a mismatch.

The following example illustrates the complexity of this problem in terms of a situation recently faced by a large financial institution. The institution's senior management was very comfortable with the company's IS performance although it came up only infrequently on their agenda. Its IS management team, however, was deeply concerned that they lacked the necessary conception of what the firm's goals were and what its products would be four to five years hence. They wanted to ensure that they could provide the necessary support for the achievement of these goals.

The institution is a large international one with a very sophisticated, but closely held, corporate planning activity. Appropriately in a world of potential major shifts in what financial institutions can and should do, there was great concern at the top about the confidentiality of this information, and only a handful of four or five individuals knew the full scope of this direction. Neither the IS manager nor his boss were among this handful. Consequently, they were substantially in the dark about future direction of the organization and could only crudely assess it in terms of trying to guess why some projects were unfunded while others were funded.

The company had a full-time IS planning manager who had three assistants and who reported to the IS manager. For the last two years, the IS planners had worked closely with both middle-management users and the DP technologists to come up with strategies and applications portfolios which were commonly seen by both sides to be relevant to their needs. Because there was little direct linkage of either a formal or informal nature between the IS planning activity and the corporate planning department (repeatedly, corporate planning had communicated "don't call us, we'll call you"), the IS staff had two overriding concerns:

1. The plans and strategies developed for IS might be technically sound and meet the needs of user management, but could be unproductive or indeed counterproductive in terms of its ability to support the institution's corporate thrust.
2. The corporate plans as developed by the four or five at the top in the know but also isolated from IS could unwittingly place onerous or unworkable pressures on IS in terms of future support requests.

At this stage, senior management perceived IS as a factory, believed it was staffed appropriately, was being managed appropriately, and had no concerns about its planning process. IS saw itself as strategic but couldn't sell the concept to anyone. This frustration was recently resolved when an outside review of the institution's overall strategy convinced senior management that they had misunderstood the role of IS and that IS should be treated as strategic. Unfortunately, in the process of evolution, IS management, who were perceived as being satisfactory to run a factory, were quickly perceived as being inadequate for this newly defined challenge and were personally unable to survive the transition.

IS planning on the surface had looked good when one read the written plan. However, in fact, it had failed to come to grips with the realities of the corporate environment and had left an organization for which IS activities are of significant strategic importance in a state of potential unpreparedness and risk. This was fatal where, on multiple dimensions, IS activities were belatedly perceived as being critical to the organization's achievement of its product and productivity goals.

This IS criticality segmentation is useful, not just for talking about corporate IS planning for the company as a whole but for thinking about individual business units and functions as well. IS technology's impact often varies widely by unit and function and the planning process must be adapted to deal with these differences. While making the planning's execution more complex, it also makes it more useful.

Exhibit 5-2 contains a questionnaire used by one firm to analyze the strategic thrust of the development portfolio for each of its organizational units. These questions are designed to uncover whether on balance the development work being done is *critical* to the firm's future competitive posture or whether it is useful *but* not at the core of what has to be done to be competitively successful. Similarly, Exhibit 5-3 contains a questionnaire used by the firm to analyze how critical the existing systems are to an organization unit in achieving its basic operating objectives. Both exhibits are used by the firm as rough diagnostic tools.

EXHIBIT 5-2 □ Information Systems Planning—a Contingent Focus *(portfolio analysis)*

	Percent of development budget	Strategic weight*
1. Projects involved in researching impact of new technologies or anticipated new areas of applications where generation of expertise, insight, and knowledge is the main benefit.	0–5%	−1
	5–15%	−2
	Over 15%	−3
2. Projects involved in cost displacement or cost-avoidance productivity improvement.	Over 70%	−3
	40–70%	−2
	Under 40%	−1
3. Do estimated aggregate improvements of these projects exceed 10 percent of firm's after-tax profits of 1 percent of sales?	Yes	−2
	No	−0
4. Projects focused at routine maintenance to meet evolving business needs (processing new union-contract payroll data) or meeting new regulatory or legal requirements.	Over 70%	−1
	40–70%	−2
	Under 40%	−3
5. Projects focused on existing system enhancements which do not have identifiable hard benefits.	Under 10%	−3
	10–40%	−2
	Over 40%	−1

	Percent of development budget	Strategic weight*
6. Projects whose primary benefit is providing new decision support information to top three levels of management. No tangible identifiable benefits.	0–5%	−0
	5–15%	−2
	Over 15%	−4
7. Projects whose primary benefit is to offer new decision support information to middle management or clerical staff.	0–5%	−0
	5–15%	−1
	Over 15%	−2
8. Projects which allow the firm to develop and offer new products or services for sale or enable additional significant new features to be added to existing product line.	Over 20%	−4
	10–20%	−3
	5–10%	−2
	Under 5%	−1
9. Projects which enable development of new administrative control and planning processes. No tangible benefit.	Over 20%	−4
	10–20%	−3
	5–10%	−2
	0–5%	−1
10. Projects which offer significant tangible benefits through improved operational efficiencies (reduce inventory, but direct reduction in operating costs, improved credit collection, etc.).	Over 20%	−4
	10–20%	−3
	5–10%	−2
	0–5%	−1
11. Do tangible benefits amount to 10 percent of after-tax profit or 1 percent of gross sales?	Yes	−2
	No	−1
12. Projects which appear to offer new ways for the company to compete (fast delivery, higher quality, broader array of support services).	Over 20%	−4
	10–20%	−3
	5–10%	−2
	Under 5%	−1
13. Do these projects offer ability to generate benefits in excess of 10 percent of after-tax earnings or 1 percent of gross sales?	Yes	−2
	No	0
14. Size of development budget percent of value added.	Over 4%	−3
	3–4%	−2
	2–3%	−1
	2%	−0

*Larger numbers mean more strategic.

Exhibit 5–4 suggests that not only does a firm's placement in this matrix influence how IS planning should be done but has numerous other implications in terms of the role of the executive steering committee, organizational placement of IS, type of IS management control system appropriate, etc. Further, since different organizational units within a company may be at

EXHIBIT 5-3 □ Information Systems Planning—a Contingent Focus *(Operational dependence questionnaire)**

1. *Impact of a one-hour shutdown—main center*
   - Major operational disruption in customer service, plant shutdown, groups of staff totally idle.
   - Inconvenient but core business activities continue unimpaired.
   - Essentially negligible.
2. *Impact of total shutdown—main center—two to three weeks*
   - Almost fatal—no ready source of backup.
   - Major external visibility, major revenue shortfall or additional costs.
   - Expensive—core processes can be preserved at some cost, and at reduced quality levels.
   - Minimal—fully acceptable tested backup procedures exist, incremental costs manageable, transition costs acceptable.
3. *Costs of IS as percent total corporate costs*
   - Over 10%.
   - 2%–10%.
   - Under 2%.
4. *Operating systems*
   - Operating system software totally customized and maintained internally.
   - Major reliance vendor-supplied software but significant internal enhancements.
   - Almost total reliance on standard vendor packages.
5. *Labor*
   - Data center work force organized—history of strikes.
   - Nonunionized work force, either inexperienced and/or low morale.
   - High morale—unorganized work force.

quite different points on the grid, the planning organization and control approach suitable for one unit may be quite inappropriate for another. Finally, an organization and control approach suitable at one point in time may be quite unsuitable at another point in time.

IS MANAGEMENT CLIMATE

In an environment of great management turmoil, turnover, and reassessment, it is unlikely that the same intensity and commitment of effort to planning IS can be productively unleashed as can be in an environment where there is more stability in the structure and where individuals have a stronger emotional attachment to the organization.

In aggregate, while these factors limit the payoff from planning and make its effective execution more complex, they do not eliminate its need. Rather, they both define the multidimensional complexity of the task and place

6. *Quality control—criticalness*
   Processing errors—major external exposure.
   Processing errors—modest external exposure.
   Processing errors—irritating—modest consequence.
7. *Number of operationally critical online systems or batch systems*
   10 or more.
   3–5.
   0–2.
8. *Dispersion of critical systems*
   Critical systems—one location.
   Critical systems—two to three installations.
   Critical systems—run by multiple departments. Geographic dispersion of processing.
9. *Ease of recovery after failure—six hours*
   Three to four days—heavy workload. Critical system.
   12–24 hours critical systems.
   Negligible—almost instantaneous.
10. *Recovery after quality control failure*
    Time-consuming, expensive, many interrelated systems.
    Some disruption and expense.
    Relatively quick—damage well contained.
11. *Feasibility coping manually 80–20 percent basis (i.e., handling 20% of the transactions which have 80% of the value)*
    Impossible.
    Somewhat possible.
    Relatively easy.

*First answer to each question indicates great operational vulnerability; last answer to each question indicates low operational vulnerability.

bounds on the reasonableness of expectations, which appropriately vary from setting to setting.

IS PLANNING AND CORPORATE STRATEGY

In thinking about the role IS should play in a firm, it is important to understand the nature of the overall competitive position of the firm or business unit and how it competes. This position and the competitive weapons primarily used significantly influence whether IS is strategic to a unit, how investments in IS technology should be thought about, and how IS planning should be executed. For illustrative purposes, two of the most widely used current frameworks for competitive analysis will be discussed here in terms of their implications for IS strategy. These are Michael Porter's

EXHIBIT 5-4 □ Examples of Different Managerial Strategies for Companies in Support and Strategic Boxes (assuming they are appropriately located)

Support		Activity		Strategic
Middle-level management membership. Existence of committee less critical.	⟵	Steering committee	⟶	Active senior management involvement. Committee key.
Less urgent. Mistakes in resource allocation not fatal.	⟵	Planning	⟶	Critical. Must link to corporate strategy. Careful attention to resource allocation vital.
Avoid high-risk projects because of constrained benefits. A poor place for corporate strategic gambles.	⟵	Risk profile—project portfolio	⟶	Some high-risk/high-potential benefit projects appropriate if possibility exists to gain strategic advantage.
Can be managed in a looser way. Operational headaches less severe.	⟵	IS capacity management	⟶	Critical to manage. Must leave slack.
Can be lower.	⟵	IS management reporting level	⟶	Should be very high.
A conservative posture one to two years behind state-of-art appropriate.	⟵	Technical innovation	⟶	Critical to stay current and fund R&D. Competitor can gain advantage.
Lower priority—less heated debate.	⟵	User involvement and control over system	⟶	Very high priority. Often emotional.
Managed cost center IS viable. Chargeout less critical and less emotional.	⟵	Chargeout system	⟶	Critical they be sensitively designed.
System modernization and development expenses postponable in time of crisis.	⟵	Expense control	⟶	Effectiveness key. Must keep applications up to date. Other places to save money.
More time to resolve it.	⟵	Uneven performance of IS management	⟶	Serious and immediately actionable.

views as communicated in his book, *Competitive Strategy: Techniques for Analyzing Industries and Competitors*[3], and the Boston Consulting Group's widely discussed framework.

[3] New York: Free Press, 1980.

Generic Strategies

Porter suggests that there are three generic strategies a firm can adopt. These are noted below together with a brief discussion of their impact on IS as a component of corporate strategy.

Strategy #1. *Be the low-cost producer.* (Appropriate for a standardized product.) Significant profit increases and explosion of market share come from being able to drive operating costs significantly below those of competition. IS offers strategic value in this environment if, for example, it can:

1. Permit major reduction in production and clerical staff. (This will hit labor costs, lowering cost/unit.)
2. Permit better utilization of manufacturing facilities by better scheduling, etc. (There will be less fixed asset expense attached to each unit of production.)
3. Allow significant reduction in inventory, accounts receivable, etc. (That is, reduce interest costs and facilities costs.)
4. Provide better utilization of materials and lower overall costs by reduction of wastage. (Better utilization of lower-grade materials is possible in settings where quality degradation is not an issue.)

If the nature of the firm's manufacturing and distribution technologies do not permit these types of savings, IS is unlikely to be of strategic interest as far as the firm's long-term competitive posture is concerned.

Strategy #2. *Produce a unique differentiated product.* This differentiation can occur along a number of dimensions such as quality, special design features, availability, special services that offer end-consumer value. For example, IS offers strategic value to this corporate environment if:

1. IS is a significant component of the product and its costs, and hence is an important differentiable feature. (Banks, brokerage houses, credit card operations all vie to compete with IS-based service differentiation.)
2. IS can significantly impact the lead time for product development, customization, and delivery. In many industries computer-aided design/computer-aided manufacturing (CAD/CAM) provides this advantage today.
3. IS can permit customization of a product to the customer's specific needs in a way not possible before. (CAD/CAM in specialized textile made-to-order operations such as men's suits.)
4. IS can give a visibly higher and unique level of customer service and need satisfaction which can be built into the end price. (Special-order enquiry status for key items.)

If IS cannot produce perceived differentiable features for firms and business units competing in this way, it is unlikely to be of strategic interest as far as the firm's ability to achieve long-term competitive position is concerned.

Strategy #3. *Ability to identify and fill the needs of specialized markets.* These markets could either be special geographic regions or a cluster of very specialized end-user needs. IS offers strategic value for these firms if:

1. IS permits better identification of special customer need niches and various unevennesses in the market's needs, that is, the ability to analyze company or industry sales data bases to spot unusual trends. (Greeting card companies describe each card in a number of dimensions and can spot, for example, that three-line verses and primarily red cards with contemporary designs, are taking off in the Upper Plain states, and thus take appropriate action.)
2. Their outputs are IS-intensive products, or products whose end features can be modified by IS customization to local needs.

Summary. These paragraphs are to suggest that the generic competitive strategy selected by a firm significantly influences the kinds of things that one looks for from IS if it is to be "strategic" as opposed to "support" for the firm. Different competitive strategies bring very different perspectives to bear on assessing and developing IS strategies. It is critical that these perspectives be taken into account in the IS planning process.

Review-of-Operations Strategy

Another useful cut at assessing the strategic impact of IS is to adopt the Boston Consulting Group's framework of looking at a company's operations over the past decade. Exhibit 5–5 contains their time-honored matrix of dividing firms along the dimensions of market growth and position in the market.

The following paragraphs suggest the differing criteria a unit in each box should bring to assessing its IS strategy.

Stars

1. These firms should accept greater implementation and benefit risk to gain or maintain a meaningful competitive position.
2. Excessive return-on-investment (ROI) focus can get the organization into serious problems. Projects with potentially major intangible benefits in terms of preserving market image, etc. can get deferred through lack of specificity.

EXHIBIT 5-5 □ Position in Market

		Low	High
Market growth	High	?	Stars
	Low	Dogs	Cash cows

Source: Adapted from Barry Hedley, "Strategy and the Business Portfolio," *Long-Range Planning,* February 1977, p. 10.

3. Effectiveness is more important than efficiency in viewing new investment opportunities.
4. Unit should receive #1 priority for applications which support its attainment of market share goals. This includes quality of effort and time to implement.
5. While short-term projects are suitable, this is an appropriate place to make long-term strategic investments.

Cash Cows

1. It is important to invest in intangible products if necessary to *maintain* competitive position. These projects are as critical as those in the star units. Projects which are not aimed at maintaining market share need to be justified on the ROI basis.
2. The risk profile of the applications portfolio should be quite low unless a project is aimed at protecting a vital aspect of competitive exposure.
3. ROI is an important focus as the unit attempts to wring extra profits and efficiency out of its operation.

Dogs

1. Investment in this area must be scanned very carefully. Unless they promise to turn the operation and/or industry around, they should not be made without careful ROI focus.
2. Investments here in an environment of limited resources must take a lower priority than those in other units with a bright future.
3. Care should be taken in designing software which links this department with the rest of the company. In the future this unit is a candidate either to be abandoned or spun off.
4. High-risk projects should be avoided here unless major opportunity exists to turn the competitive structure around.
5. Focus of projects should be short term.

Summary

The notions implicit in these two frameworks are introduced here to suggest the following:

1. The competitive position of a business unit and its generic business strategy profoundly influence how one should think about potential IS investments and the contribution from existing IS systems. Key inputs to the strategic/turnaround/factory/support categorizations flow from analysis of these items.
2. Since different business units in a firm often have quite different competitive positions and quite different generic competitive strategies, a common approach to viewing IS's contribution and role is unlikely to be appropriate in these settings.
3. Since competitive position and generic strategy change over time, a constant approach over time to IS strategy formulation may be quite inappropriate.

CORPORATE ENVIRONMENT FACTORS INFLUENCING PLANNING

Recently completed research has identified four clusters of corporate environmental factors which influence how IS planning must be structured to improve the likelihood of success.[4]

1. The perceived importance and status of the systems manager. Proper alignment of status of the IS manager to the role IS plays or should play in the overall operation and strategy formulating process of the company is very important. In environments where IS is in a "strategic" or "turnaround" role, a low status IS manager (reporting level and/or in compensation) makes it hard to get the necessary inputs and credibility from general management in the planning process. If the corporate communication culture at the top is heavily informal, this is apt to be fatal, as IS is outside the key communication loop. If the corporate culture is more formal, development and management of appropriate committees and other formal processes can significantly alleviate the situation. For companies where IS is and should be in the "support" role, lower status of the IS director is appropriate and less effort needs to be made to assure alignment of IS and corporate strategy. Further, a lower level of investment (dollars and type of staff) in IS planning is appropriate for these situations. This is illustrated by the recent comments of a director of strategic planning for a large process-manufacturing company. "We relate to IS by giving them insight on what the corporate goals are and

[4] Pyburn, "Information Systems Planning."

what the elements and forms are of a good planning system. Because of their role in the company, we do not solicit feedback from them as to what the art of the possible is. The nature of their operation is such that they can provide no useful input to the selection of corporate strategy."

2. *Physical proximity of systems group and general management team.* For organizations where many important decisions are made informally in ad hoc sessions, and where IS is playing a "strategic" or "turnaround" role, it is important to keep key IS management staff physically close to the senior line manager. Regardless of the systems manager's status, it is difficult for him to be an active member of the team in this type of organization if he is geographically distant. In the words of one manager in such a company, when a problem surfaces, those people who are around and easily accessible are those who solve it, and "we don't wait to round up the missing bodies." When the prevailing management culture is more formal, physical proximity becomes less important. In these situations, the formal written communications and the scheduled formal meetings largely substitute for the informal give-and-take. In informal organizations, where IS is "strategic" or "turnaround," even if the systems groups must be located many miles from headquarters for other reasons, it is critical that the IS managers, and preferably a small staff, be at corporate headquarters. For "support" and "factory" organizations in informal organizations, location at corporate headquarters is much less critical.

3. *Corporate culture and management "style."* In organizations where the basic management culture is characterized by the words *low key* and *informal,* and where an informal personal relationship exists between the systems manager and senior management, then formal IS planning procedures do not appear to be a critical determinant of perceived systems effectiveness. Development of this relationship is assisted (as mentioned above) by the geographic proximity and IS manager status. As an organization becomes more formal, IS planning discipline becomes more significant as a countervailing force, even for systems environments which are not highly complex.

4. *Organizational size and complexity.* As organizations increase in both size and complexity, and as applications of information systems technology grows larger and more complex, more formal planning processes are needed to ensure the kind of broad-based dialogue essential to the development of an integrated "vision of IS." Of course, this phenomenon is not unrelated to the previous dimension concerning management culture and style as greater size and complexity often leads to more formal practices in general. In environments where the business unit size is small and relatively simple, formal planning approaches become less critical irrespective of the other factors. Similarly, for business units where the systems environment is not terribly complex, IS planning can safely take place in a more informal

fashion. However, as the portfolio of work increases in size and in integration across user areas, more discipline and formality in the planning process become necessary.

In aggregate, these corporate culture items highlight another dimension as to why selection of a planning approach is so complex and why recommendations on how to do IS planning "in general" almost always turn out to be too inflexible and prescriptive for a specific situation. (Even within a company, these issues may force considerable heterogeneity of practice between organization units.)

CORPORATE ENVIRONMENTAL FACTORS— AN EXAMPLE

The following example shows how these issues have shaped the planning process in a billion-dollar manufacturing organization. Key aspects of the corporate environment include:

1. The company had both a medium-sized corporate IS facility and stand-alone IS facilities of some significant size in each of its six major U.S. divisions. These divisional IS facilities report straight line to the divisions and dotted line to the corporate IS function. The corporate IS group is part of a cluster of corporate staff activities in an organization where traditionally some considerable power has been located at corporate level.

2. The vice president of corporate IS also had the corporate planning activity reporting to him. In addition, he had a long personal and professional relationship with both the chairman and chief executive officer which had extended over a period of many years in a company which could be described as having an informal management culture. He was initially given responsibility for IS because the number of operational and development problems had reached crisis proportions. While under normal circumstances, the criticality of IS might be termed "support," these difficulties pushed the firm into the "turnaround" category.

3. The closeness of relationships between the division general managers and their IS managers varies widely. The size of the application portfolios in relation to the overall size of the division also varied considerably, with IS activities playing a more significant role in some settings than in others.

IS planning begins at the divisional level within the bounds of some rather loose corporate guidelines concerning technological direction. At the divisional level, planning culminates in the preparation of a divisional IS plan. The planning processes and dialogues vary widely from division to division in terms of line manager involvement in developing the plans. In some settings, the line managers are intimately involved in the process of developing the plan, with the division general manager investing considerable time in the final review and modification to the plan. In other divisions, however, the relationship is not so close, and IS plans were developed almost entirely by the IS organization with very limited review by the general management. The relationship of IS activities to the strategic functioning of the various units varies widely.

Critical to the IS planning process is an annual three-day meeting of the corporate IS director and his key staff where the divisional IS managers present their plans. The corporate IS director plays a major role in these sessions in critiquing and modifying plans to better fit corporate objectives. His understanding of the corporate plan, the thinking of the divisional general managers (in his capacity as head of corporate planning), and his firsthand knowledge concerning what is on the chairman's and president's minds enables him to immediately spot shortfalls in IS plans. This is particularly true for those divisions where there are weak IS line management relationships. As a result, plans evolve which fit the real business needs of the organization, and the IS activity is well regarded. A set of planning processes, which in other settings might have led to disaster, has worked out well because of the special qualities of the IS director and development of a communication approach between him and general management which is appropriate for this firm's culture.

SUMMARY

There continues to be evidence that there is a clear link between effective planning and effectively perceived IS activity for many organization settings. Quite apart from the generation of new ideas, and so on, a major role of the IS planning process is stimulation of discussion and exchange of insights between the specialists and the users. Effectively managed, it is an important element in cooling the temperature of potential conflict.

For example, a major financial institution that we studied attempted at least four different approaches to IS planning over a six-year period. Each was started with great fanfare, with different staffs and organizations, and each limped to a halt. However, it was only when the firm abandoned efforts to plan that deep and ultimately irreconcilable differences arose between IS and the user organization. Communication of viewpoints and exchange of problems and potential opportunities (key to developing shared understanding) is as important as the selection of specific projects.

In this context our conclusions are:

1. Organizations where the IS activity is integral to corporate strategy implementation have a special need to build links between IS and the corporate strategy formulation process. As indicated earlier, the process of accomplishing this is complex, requiring resolution along multiple dimensions. Key aspects of this dialogue are:

a. Testing elements of corporate strategy to ensure that they are doable within IS resource constraints. On some occasions, the resources needed are obtainable, but in other settings, resources are unavailable, and painful readjustments must be made.

b. Transfer of planning and strategy formulating skills to the IS function.

c. Ensuring long-term availability of appropriate IS resources.

In other "support" and "factory" settings, this linkage is less critical. Appropriately, over time the need for this linkage may change as the strategic mission of IS evolves.

2. As organizations grow in size, complexity of systems, and formality, IS planning must be directly assigned to someone to avoid resulting lack of focus and the risk of significant pieces dropping between cracks. This job, however, is a subtle and complex one. The task is to ensure that planning occurs in an appropriate form. A strong set of enabling and communication skills is critical if the individual is to relate to the multiple individuals and units impacted by this technology and cope with their differing familiarity with it. Ensuring involvement of IS staff and users for both inputs and conclusions occurrence is key. The great danger is that frequently planners evolve the task with more of a *doing* orientation than an enabling one and begin to interpose, inappropriately, their sets of priorities and understanding. To overcome this problem, many organizations have defined this job more as a transitional one than a career one.

3. Planned clutter in the planning approach is appropriate to deal with the fact that the company is in different phases with respect to different technologies and the technologies have different strategic payout to different organization units at different points in time. While it is superficially attractive and orderly to conceive planning all technologies for all business units to the same level of detail and time horizon, in reality this is an inappropriate goal.

4. IS planning must be tailored to the realities of the corporate style of doing business. Importance and status of the IS managers, geographic placement of IS in relation to general management, corporate culture and management style, and organizational size and complexity all influence how IS planning can be best done.

5. The planning process must be considerably broader in the range of technologies it covers than just data processing. It must deal with the technologies of electronic communications, data processing, office automation, stand-alone minis, and so forth, both separately and in an integrated fashion.

Case 5-1 □ Corning Glass Works, Inc.—Information Systems Planning*

INTRODUCTION

Joe Malorzo, corporate manager of information systems planning for Corning Glass Works (CGW), looked out on the gray February landscape in Corning, New York (corporate headquarters), as he commented on the company's EDP planning process:

> You know, we've all come a long way in the past three years. When Dave Luther assigned me to the new full-time planning job in 1977, I couldn't understand why we even needed planning.
>
> Prior to that change, of course, I had managed the systems development effort in the corporate data center for a number of years. In that position I *knew* we were working tremendously hard to satisfy the company's needs as we saw them. My entire career had been concerned with systems activities, and at the time I thought I understood what was required.
>
> It never occurred to me that we might actually be working very efficiently on the wrong problems. In retrospect, though, I think I've learned more about systems *management,* and management in general, in the past 3 years than I did in the prior 12 with the company.
>
> For a number of historical reasons, relationships between corporate and divisional EDP groups had been deteriorating for some time prior to 1977. The situation was so bad three years ago that the major objective of the 1978 planning cycle was simply to get divisional and corporate EDP managers talking to each other. I think we all began to see that we had common objectives and many similar problems, which was a real breakthrough. With a year of such experience under our belts, the plans submitted by the divisions and the corporate data center improved enormously in 1979. Presentations made at the annual planning session in July 1979 really began to address the critical issues such as manufacturing cost control and internationalization of our business. I was really pleased with the improvement.
>
> Not surprisingly, the plans submitted by the line divisions, staff groups, and the corporate data center in 1978 were pretty sparse and incomplete. The entire package barely filled one large looseleaf binder. In 1979, however, the plans were much more complete, reflecting, I think, a new understanding of the role of planning. That package filled two large binders with some left out. My objective for 1980 is to maintain the completeness of the plans, but reduce the paper by being more concise and specific. I hope all of the plans will fit in

* This case was prepared as the basis for class discussion rather than to illustrate either effective or ineffective handling of an administrative situation.

one binder this year. It is imperative that we keep the paper pushing to a minimum, if only because I don't have a staff to process it.

This year we've made some changes that should finally make the plans useful for making some management decisions. Specifically, we've asked that each group concentrate on four areas as they go through the 1980 process: (1) the overall accuracy of the plans and the resource requirements expected, (2) a detailed link between the business objectives of the divisions and the systems plan, (3) an evaluation of performance on last year's plan, and (4) a management summary that can be used to communicate direction to senior divisional corporate managers. If we can get at these issues along with what we did last year, then we should be able to develop a real no-B.S. plan for information systems companywide.

Commenting on the recent change in command (Exhibit 1) for the Information Services Division, Malorzo continued:

Of course, the assignment of a new Information Services Division director, John Parker, may well have an impact on the planning process. With Dave Luther (current vice president–personnel and Parker's predecessor) the planning process was primarily a communications tool. His real concern was to provide a common forum for discussion between the divisions' EDP groups

EXHIBIT 1 □ Organization Chart as of January 1980

CHAIRMAN OF THE BOARD
A. Houghton, Jr.

President
T.C. MacAvoy

Vice Chairman
J. R. Houghton

Financial V.P.
V.C. Campbell

Treasurer

Controller

V.P. & Gen. Mgr.-Europe

V.P. General Counsel & Sec.

V.P. & Director-Corp. Comm. Div.

V.P. & Director-Government Affairs

V.P. & Gen. Mgr.-Latin America/Asia/Pac.

Sr. V.P.-Staffs
F.E. Behm

V.P. of Personnel
David Luther

V.P. & Director-Industrial Relations

V.P. & Director-Mfg. & Eng. Div.

V.P. & Director-Mfg. Services Div.

Director-Purchasing

Director-Inf. Systems Div.
John Parker

Mgr. Information Systems Plan.
Joe Molatzo

Manager Administrative Services

Manager of Communications

Manager of Corp. Data Center (CDC)
Jerry Oakes

Mgr. European Information Services

International D.P. Managers

V.P. & Director-Gen. Emp. Rel.
W.I. McMahon

Exec. V.P. & Gen. Mgr.-Electrical Prod. Div.

V.P. & Gen. Mgr. Corning Electronics

V.P. & Gen. Mgr.-Corning Science & Medical Products

V.P. & Gen. Mgr.-Consumer Prod. Div.

V.P. & Gen. Mgr.-Technical Prod. Div.

V.P. & Mgr.-Manufacturing

V.P. & Gen. Mgr. Ceramic Products Div.

Vice Chairman & Director-Tech. Staffs Div.

V.P. & Director-Research & Dev.

Manager-Aircraft Oper.

President-Steuben Glass

and between the corporate group and the divisional group. The content of the plans, and the data that supported them, were a secondary concern.

John, on the other hand, is more of a production, output-oriented kind of guy than Dave was. I think he views the quality of the plans themselves as critical to managing this resource for the entire corporation. I don't know what this will mean for the planning process as it is now prescribed.

COMPANY BACKGROUND

In 1980, although Corning Glass Works had been in operation for almost 130 years, it was still very much a family-owned and -operated company. Amory Houghton, Jr., the great-great-grandson of the founder, had become president in 1961 at age 35, and in 1964 was appointed chairman of the board. His brother James had been named vice chairman in 1971, assuming responsibility for the company's international operations and many of its corporate staff groups. The Houghton family still owned more than 10 percent of the stock which was listed on the New York Stock Exchange. This long history of family involvement, together with the location of the company headquarters in Corning, a small town in upstate New York, created a corporate environment that was personal and informal. Many of the managers were social friends during nonworking hours, and the company itself played a major role in local civic affairs.

Since its establishment in 1851, the company had built a strong reputation as a manufacturer and marketer of specialty glasses with properties adapted to specific end uses. CGW's stated corporate objective was "to pursue excellence in glass worldwide, making this family of materials, its related products, and its corollary technologies the most unusual and useful in our civilization." This strategy, built around a material and its applications, led Corning to become, in 1908, one of the country's first companies to establish a research laboratory. From this time onward technology-based research was at the center of the company's operation. Over the decades, CGW's determination to become the leader in glass technology, and its willingness to back this objective with a heavy investment in research and development, resulted in the company's entry into an unusually wide diversity of businesses. This pattern of growth was far from a conscious strategy of product line diversification, but rather it was a natural result of a management philosophy which saw application-oriented research as the company's driving force.

Through expansion of existing businesses and diversification into new products, Corning's sales in 1979 exceeded $1.4 billion on total assets of the same amount. Net income after tax in that year was almost $125 million. Worldwide, the company had 30,200 employees, and operated 90 plants in 20 countries. Exhibit 2 highlights CGW's financial figures.

Exhibit 2 □ Corning Glass Works and Subsidiary Companies—Financial Highlights ($000, except per share amount)

	1979	1978
Net sales	$1,421,598	$1,251,728
Income from operations	114,350	120,574
Net income	$ 124,943	$ 104,363
Dividends paid	$ 34,371	$ 30,690
Per share of common stock		
Net income	$7.05	$5.89
Dividends paid	$1.94	$1.73
Income from operations to sales	8.0%	9.6%
Net income to sales	8.8%	8.3%
Net income to total stockholders' equity	15.9%	14.8%
Additions to plant and equipment	$ 137,860	$ 103,232
Depreciation and amortization	$ 62,449	$ 57,428
Number of employees (year-end)	30,200	29,500

CORNING'S BUSINESSES

Mainly through the type of research effort described, Corning had developed over 300 different glasses which it converted into over 60,000 products. These products were consolidated into six major business groupings, each of which was managed by one of CGW's product divisions in the United States.

Electrical Products. Corning got into the television bulb business after gaining experience in manufacturing radar tubes in World War II. By continually developing the product through research and development efforts, particularly on the color picture tube, Corning became one of the two major suppliers to the television manufacturers in the United States. By subsequently starting up bulb manufacturing facilities in France, Brazil, Mexico, and Taiwan, Corning was able to capitalize on the international purchases of major customers such as Phillips, RCA, and Sylvania. The business and its associated technologies were mature by 1980, and were not subject to the rapid changes incurred in the 1950s and 1960s.

Electronics Products. These are largely resistors and capacitors for electronic equipment manufacturers such as the original equipment manufacturers of computer, communications, home entertainment, and military equipment. Most of the products were mature commodities, but the associated technology was changing rapidly and product development had to keep up with customer needs.

Consumer Products. Pyrex bakeware, Corning Ware, Centura and Corelle tableware, and flat-top glass-ceramic cooking surfaces were the major products of this division. There were two broad groups of customers: the mass home market and commercial food operations. Types of retail outlets used to reach the former varied by country, as did the distribution to the retailer. For example, in Argentina distributors sold to independent retailers, while in the United Kingdom a direct sales force fought for shelf space in mass merchandisers' and national chains. A few global competitors existed, such as the popular Noritake line, but most were local or regional.

Ceramics Products. The division manufactures high-performance ceramic and glass-ceramic materials for use in diverse industrial processes involving very high temperatures and/or corrosive environments. In general, the products of the Ceramics Division are marketed to a relatively small number of customers directly.

Medical/Scientific Products. In 1980, two formerly independent divisions were joined to form the Medical/Scientific Division. The medical products included instruments such as blood gas analyzers and white cell analyzers, and the reagents required to calibrate them, which were mainly used to determine body chemistry. In addition, the company had a line of single-test diagnostic reagent materials and kits used, for example, to test patients' blood for thyroid-related disorders. A direct sales force demonstrated products to potential customers in labs and hospitals.

Scientific products, on the other hand, consisted of two major businesses: scientific glassware and the chemical systems. The former was special lab glassware usually manufactured from Pyrex glass. It was an old, mature product line with competition based mainly on price and delivery. End users were small and widely dispersed, and as a result Corning generally sold through local distributors. The second major business was chemical systems, and these consisted of process systems custom-designed for specific applications.

Technical Products. Two very different businesses were included under this grouping. First there were ophthalmic products, which were principally eyeglass blanks produced to a variety of thickness, curvature, and periphery specifications, and made from either fixed or photochromic glass. The second part of Technical Products was known as technical materials, a highly varied business which basically involved the special application of various Corning products and technologies to a variety of industrial situations. These products were manufactured in all 22 domestic plants, and were marketed through every conceivable distribution channel.

INTERNATIONAL BUSINESS SHIFT

As mentioned earlier, CGW began as a small, relatively local, U.S. company which developed overseas branches with relatively modest direct management involvement. The company was almost exclusively manufacturing and technology oriented, and relied heavily on individuals with recognized competence in various technical and nontechnical fields. Communication was mainly oral, which was reinforced because of location and frequent cross-functional rotation of personnel so that managers knew each other personally. In the single, resource-rich economy of this early growth stage, CGW systems tended to emphasize short-term results, tracking manufacturing as the prime measure of business activity. They were often informally built in response to local needs and were thus relatively inflexible when new demands were imposed.

Because of its significant growth during the late 1960s and early 1970s, acquisition of majority interest in offshore subsidiaries, and increasing environmental complexity with respect to economies, resource limitations, products, distances between locations, varying social, political, and cultural customs, etc., CGW made some major changes. First there was a shift in emphasis from manufacturing to marketing. Next, CGW identified the need to integrate business management on a global basis. This would facilitate:

Developing fact-based data for decision making and priority setting.

Focusing on marketplaces in addition to manufacturing concerns.

Monitoring and reacting more quickly to social, political, and other environmental factors.

Developing more-structured reporting processes to offset the effect of geography.

A major consulting firm was hired to help specify necessary changes and to identify appropriate administrative and organizational infrastructure required to support them. As these changes were being implemented during 1975–76, it became apparent that the corporation's information processing capability would not support the new direction and emphasis. This exposure of a lack of standards, uniformity of information and processes, and communication capabilities caused attention to be focused on the corporate data processing staff.

HISTORY OF CORPORATE INFORMATION SYSTEMS

EDP usage at CGW began in July 1958 when an IBM RAMAC was installed. During 1962 the RAMAC was replaced by an RCA 301. Later acquisitions included an IBM 1401G in mid-1964, IBM 360/30, and a third RCA 301 in 1966. In 1968 two RCA Spectra 70/45s replaced all older equipment. In the early 1970s a flood damaged much of CGW's corporate headquarters (Houghton Park) and accelerated a planned move to a single large IBM mainframe in the 370 series.

As in many other large organizations, EDP usage at CGW began in the financial area. Systems were developed for corporate financial reporting, and a centralized data center was established with computer hardware and a large development staff. Currently, the Corning Data Center (CDC) operates an IBM 3033, maintains a centralized development staff of 50 programmers and analysts, and supports administrative staff on a budget of approximately $6 million dollars (one quarter of corporatewide EDP costs). One division general manager noted:

> The tradition of centrally managing technology is strong in this company. Research and manufacturing developments are the key to our success and they are very closely controlled and managed from the top. I guess it just seemed natural to manage this new technology (EDP) the same way. As recently as 1977, the director of Corporate Information Resources (CIR)[1] reported to the controller, which clearly influenced the emphasis of the group. In general, CIR supported the financial and other corporate staff functions more effectively than they did the line divisions. Of course, CIR was responsible for developing and operating systems for the entire company, but most of their real effort was directed at developing corporatewide, financially oriented systems. To a large extent, this is still their focus.

Most corporate staff functions (controller, treasurer, etc.) relied exclusively on the corporate data center for systems development and operations. Their needs were usually represented by a single liaison person who reported within the staff function.

In the 1970–77 period, most divisions established their own EDP departments, reporting directly to divisional management. In the case of larger, more prosperous divisions, these EDP groups created virtually independent data centers, complete with hardware and development personnel. In other cases, the divisional EDP department relied heavily on the corporate data center for development and operational support, though all divisions maintained some development and operational capability. In the largest division, Consumer Products, for example, 19 people were committed to systems development activity, while an additional 30 maintained an operation that included five Digital Equipment Corporation PDP 11 computers (Models 11/34-11/70), two IV Phase computers, two Data General Nova computers, a Digital Equipment Corporation IP300A, and an IBM 370/145.

The level of EDP experience and expense varied substantially from division to division. In the line divisions, for example, 1979 expenditures and staffing were:

[1] Corporate Information Resources (CIR) was the name given the corporate data processing group before a 1979 reorganization and current title—Information Services Division (ISD).

Division	Staff	Expenditures
Ceramic Products	24 people	$ 992,000
Consumer Products	49 people	2,248,000
Electrical Products	22 people	806,000
Electronics Products	35 people	2,012,000
Medical Products	18 people	813,000
Science Products	31 people	1,478,000
Technical Products	24 people	1,531,000

Some line divisions were thus moderately sized information systems operations in their own right, while others were smaller and more dependent on CIR.

Management experience in the divisional EDP groups also varied to some extent, with some managers having extensive non-EDP backgrounds and others having only EDP experience. Reflected in part by variations in expenditure and management selection, some divisions viewed EDP as a relatively low-priority activity while others saw it as essential to overall success. One general manager noted that "EDP is like the mail service or the plumbing; I only notice it when it fails." Another disagreed, suggesting that: ". . . we run on information in this division. Managing it is something we consider frequently." The quality and frequency of communication between EDP and general management thus varied substantially from division to division.

To some extent, however, all of the divisions depended on CIR for support, either for applications system development activity, or for providing EDP operations support on the IBM 3033. The continued CIR focus, primarily on staff functions, created an intolerable situation. According to Malorzo:

> It's not surprising that the communication between CIR and the divisions was poor. Because we didn't have much access to needs and business direction beyond the controller's area, it was difficult to develop comprehensive insight into the real needs of the company. As a department, we just weren't privy to the important decisions affecting the divisions. On the other hand, we controlled the largest pool of resources necessary to address many of their concerns. Without effective management direction, however, we were continually pulled from pillar to post, servicing whichever squeaky wheel was most troublesome. Naturally this created a serious credibility problem for us, and to some extent for the divisional EDP departments as well.
>
> The general perception by divisional management was that computers were a big overhead item that really didn't support many important business objectives. Senior management didn't really know what to expect, so they brought in a veritable parade of consultants to do audits, build systems, and generally be a nuisance.

In early 1977 Dave Luther, who had moved through 14 positions in 16 years with the company, was promoted again; this time from his position as director of financial control and analysis to manager of the corporate information resource department under the controller. At this point in his career, Luther had never previously managed a data processing facility. However, he had been a very participative member of a project team which focused on information systems during the internationalization of CGW. As Luther assumed responsibility for CIR, the corporate data center output was growing at a rate of 40 percent per year, and the CIR budget had been incremented by $1.6 million after several years of an average growth of $300,000 per year.

In 1977 after much discussion of perceived deficiencies in CIR information processing capabilities, "information" was determined to be a key strategic resource. In a presentation by the vice president of finance to a senior management committee it was mentioned that "proper management of this resource is mandatory for a multinational corporation that is to prevail in a worldwide marketplace." In this same meeting approval was granted for CIR to report directly to the vice president of finance.

Near the end of 1977 Luther was given responsibility for corporate planning in addition to CIR. In this new, dual-function role, Luther continued reporting to the vice president of finance, Van Campbell. He was thus at the same organizational level as the controller, reporting to the same boss.

For nearly two years Luther carried this joint planning and CIR responsibility, but in 1979 he shed his planning role when CIR was renamed the Information Services Division (ISD) and established as a division under the senior vice president–corporate staffs (Exhibit 1). The senior vice president, Forrest Behm, was a very highly regarded member of the senior management team, and he was recognized as a major force at CGW. The move was thus generally seen as strengthening the position of information systems vis-à-vis top management.

As a result of this reorganization, the director of the division had direct responsibility for the Corning data center (referred to as CDC), the information systems planning staff (Joe Malorzo and a technology assessment specialist), the corporate office services function, and the corporate telecommunications function. The Corning data center continued to maintain both operations and development functions, reporting to the CDC manager, Jerry Oakes. Additionally, the director had "dotted line" responsibility for the divisional EDP managers.

This dotted-line responsibility is best exemplified by the project approval process, which covered all efforts that required more than two man-years of CDC time or projects which required any additional computer hardware. For such projects, a formal appropriation request (AR) was submitted through divisional channels for approval. Before sign-off by the division general manager, however, it was standard practice to have the ISD director's signature on the AR. In most cases, moreover, large projects that would be accomplished totally within the division were also approved by the ISD director. As a practical matter, the director thus got a look at most projects costing over $100,000 and all projects requiring new computer hardware, regardless of where development took place.

Between 1977 and 1979 a flurry of activity was undertaken to improve the performance of CIR/ISD. Beyond Luther's regular contacts with members of the management committee, a number of specific organizational changes were implemented. At the corporate level a planning department, a data base function, and a technical support group were established to provide direction on critical corporationwide activities. With the realignment to divisional status, responsibility for EDP, telecommunications, and office services was consolidated under ISD. A major hiring and campus recruiting program was undertaken, and a serious personnel review and skills inventory program was started.

Additionally, a number of programs were undertaken to improve the operating performance of Information Systems companywide, including:

1. The initiation of the project proposal and review process discussed above.
2. The implementation of a worldwide planning process that included all line divisions, corporate staff functions, CIR/ISD, and the corporate data center.
3. The publication of systems development standards.
4. The completion of a worldwide cost study and the implementation of a standard cost chargeout system for CDC.
5. The establishment of an EDP audit function (which reports to the Internal Auditing Group) and initiation of security and effectiveness reviews.

With the mechanisms for an ISD turnaround in place by early 1980, the management committee named Luther vice president–personnel, and replaced him with John Parker.

Of this change in command, Joe Malorzo noted:

> Dave and John are very different characters, by training, background, and personality. Which is not to say that one is "better" than the other; but they are different.
>
> Dave's recent background includes the director of salary administration and international personnel, the director of financial analysis and control, and director of corporate planning. While Dave has certainly had his share of plant experience (as a plant controller and production superintendent), in general I think he is viewed as something of a staff person. As a result of his positions he has had regular contact with Mr. Houghton and Tom MacAvoy (the president) for some time. His credibility at the top is good.
>
> Dave's real strengths seem to lie in his "people" skills; his ability to

communicate and build a consensus. He's very much a "word person," and he was always careful to couch everything he said about Information Systems Planning in positive terms. It was never "us" and "them," but rather "we."

John, on the other hand, is very task and product oriented. He was most recently the controller of Corning, Ltd., a wholly owned subsidiary in the United Kingdom, where EDP reported to him. Before that he was production superintendent at the Big Flats plant, where he installed a real-time shop floor reporting system in a labor-intensive, complex environment. Unlike Dave, who didn't have a strong technical background when he started, John is technically knowledgeable.

I guess if I had to summarize the difference between the two men, I'd say that Dave was very "process" oriented, often at the expense of the division's output, while John wants to "get the job done" in the most direct way possible, sometimes glossing over the process of getting there. Of course, neither is at this extreme, but the comparison does help to paint a picture of their differences.

THE ISD PLANNING PROCESS

When asked to describe the planning process he had initiated and nurtured through two iterations, Malorzo continued:

The general philosophy behind our planning was best described by Peter Drucker, who defined planning as the process of making present risk-taking decisions systematically and with the best possible knowledge of their futurity. I think the phrase *risk-taking decisions* is key since most people are reluctant to establish plans without detailed facts. The person doing the planning, however, will often have to make decisions with very few facts about the future and must rely upon history, professional insight, and the best available data regarding future requirements and potential impacts. Nevertheless, long-range planning is a must if we are really interested in moving out of a reactive mode into a more proactive, controlled mode regarding resource allocation, priorities, and organizational effectiveness.

The procedure we've established for the EDP strategic planning process is primarily concerned with deciding on objectives, the strategies selected to carry out objectives, and the resources required to complete the plan. The planning process thus includes all EDP resources and activities for Information Systems, Office Services, Office Systems, and Telecommunications. The Scientific and Process Control development areas have been excluded.

The EDP manager/coordinator/liaison of each CGW operating and staff division or function, and the wholly owned subsidiaries in Europe and South America are required to submit plans. In the line divisions and wholly owned foreign subsidiaries, the planning is performed by the divisional EDP managers, who all maintain some independent level of development and operations capability. In each of the staff divisions or functions, there is an information systems coordinator/liaison who is responsible for planning, though they depend entirely on the CDC for support. None of the groups, staff or line, have anyone other than the EDP manager committed to planning on even a part-time basis.

As can be seen in Appendixes A, B, C, and D, the annual information systems planning cycle begins in December, when planning process instructions and forms are distributed to each division. These instructions focus exclusively on completing the forms in a consistent fashion, providing only nominal guidance on how the planning data should be gathered. On the issue of setting a strong corporate direction in the planning process, Malorzo noted:

> We provide little in the way of formal top-down guidance in the planning process for several reasons. First, the "technology assessment" function, which defines where we should be technically in coming years, is an ongoing responsibility of Carl Ballard, who works for me. Carl works day to day with the divisional people to come to agreement on our technological direction, so they are well aware of technical "boundaries" to their planning before we start. Additionally, the business constraints and objectives of each division are developed individually by the divisions as part of their annual planning. It's foolish for us to publish this kind of direction, when they can get it from the "horse's mouth." Of course, one of my major roles is interpreting the corporate plan and direction, but I do this informally rather than as part of the planning instructions.

By mid-February each division is supposed to have assessed the current EDP situation (presumably using the previous plan as a touchstone) and developed a list of premises and issues for division (and optional ISD) review. By mid-April objectives and strategies consistent with the major issues are presented to divisional management, and based upon approval, a "plan" of programs and projects is submitted to ISD by June 1.

The December planning process instructions do not, however, prescribe how the information necessary for systems planning is to be gathered. To the degree that the systems manager is apprised, by his division's management, of the business objectives, strategies, and plans of the division, then these are usually reflected in the systems planning. If, on the other hand, the line managers are not forthcoming with this business planning information, then the systems manager must develop premises, issues, etc., using his own experience and judgment.

In Appendix E, the various forms to be completed by the divisional systems managers are listed. *Organizational Information* and *Systems Profiles* detail the current state of the hardware, people, and applications systems and project changes in these areas over the coming three years. *Assessments* of the current information systems effort describe the business objectives of the division and rank applications systems relative to support of these objectives. The *Strategic Plan* details the premises, issues, and objectives used in the planning process, and describes a set of projects that are consistent with them. The *Resource Plan* details the financial, personnel, and computer resources necessary to achieve the plan, while the *Executive Summary* reduces the entire plan to a 3–5 page overview.

In some divisions the systems manager completes most of the forms himself, using his experience and judgment to do the assessments and develop the plans. The package is then presented to the division general management for approval. In one line division, this review lasted less than one hour.

In other cases, however, the general managers are more intimately involved in the detailed planning activity. In the Consumer Products Division, for example, an executive steering committee reviews the systems managers' assessments and strategic plan periodically. While the systems manager generates the plan himself, in this division the management review is much more thorough.

Not surprisingly, therefore, there is a wide range of quality in the linkage between business plans and systems plans. Where the line managers have clearly specified *how* they are going to achieve their business strategies, *and* the systems manager is aware of these plans, then the systems plan is usually directly linked to business needs. Where such specification of plans is not available, or where the systems manager is not aware of them, then the systems manager must develop his plan with little outside guidance.

Interestingly, the *corporate* strategic planning process specifies only the broad development of strategy by business unit. The units are not required to formally "get under" these strategies to determine in more detail how they will be achieved. Some divisions continue beyond the corporate planning requirement, however, and involve line managers in the long-range planning necessary to implement strategies.

In any case, the divisional (and, in summary, the corporate) systems plans reflect the business plans of the organization only to the extent that line managers and systems managers discuss these issues anyway. The formal corporate ISD planning process merely documents the extent of this discussion.

After the divisional plans are submitted to ISD, a three-day planning conference is held in mid-July for systems managers/coordinators. Each participant presents important pieces of their plan, and a set of corporatewide issues, objectives, and strategies are developed. This conference is held off-site, and provides a unique opportunity for the entire EDP management group of CGW to meet in an informal setting. Based upon the results of this meeting, major objectives are consolidated into a corporatewide program for information systems. A budget for ISD is then developed at the corporate level to support these objectives, and a summary plan and budget is presented to the Corporate Management Committee (CMC) in September. This committee consists of the chairman, the vice chairman, the president, the senior vice president–staffs, and the vice president–finance. Budgets for each division are developed (by the division EDP manager) in approximately the same time frame, though they are included in the divisions' individual requests to the CMC.

This annual meeting with the CMC is typically scheduled for 80 minutes, and thus covers only major ISD thrusts, large capital requirements, or other important issues such as significant reorganization. While this meeting is the only formal review of the information systems plan for the corporation, Dave Luther had traditionally used his informal discussions with senior management (especially in his role in corporate planning) to broach ongoing concerns. Due to the brief time allotted to ISD in the annual review meeting, it was in these informal discussions that most substantive issues were resolved.

On his relationship with senior management, Luther noted:

> I think it is important to "presell" the significant points in the annual CMC presentation before that meeting. Fortunately, I had good opportunities to deal with the individual members of the CMC (especially in corporate planning), so that the major ISD issues were worked out in advance. If the planning is going to continue to work, then I think John (Parker) will have to develop a similar kind of forum.

Malorzo concurred, noting:

> A lot of the real work in the planning area goes on behind the scenes with informal meetings and discussions. My role, beyond managing the formal planning apparatus, is to do the kind of selling of the corporate ISD strategy to the divisions that Dave talks about with the CMC. To do this, I spend most of my time in literally hundreds of meetings with systems folks throughout the company. It is here that we discuss issues like the kind of technology we expect to use in coming years, or the way we should be organized.
>
> For example, when we decided that all of CGW's telecommunications would be SNA compatible (IBM's standard), we made this constraint known in the monthly meeting of all EDP managers (Computer Utilization Committee—CUC) rather than wait for the annual planning cycle. My role between annual planning sessions, it seems to me, is to sell the corporate position and provide guidance as the issues arise. Dave (Luther) really encouraged this kind of informal process, so that I now spend most of my effort planting seeds and selling direction. The real risk of this approach, of course, is that the formal mechanism will become little more than a rubber stamp.
>
> Overall, though, I think the process works fairly well, but there is still a significant range in the quality of plans submitted. Some divisions have really tied their activity to the critical success factors in the division, while others seem content to address only those issues that come to their attention. To some extent I guess this is a result of the relationship the EDP manager has with his line managers. In those cases where the EDP folks are considered part of the team, the plan seems to reflect the real needs of the division and the corporation. Where they are viewed as second string, this is not so true.
>
> In general, though, the planning process is taken pretty seriously by most of the EDP managers. They typically spend several man-weeks developing their

plans, discussing them with their line managers, and completing the forms. In general, it is the systems managers who individually "do" the planning, though of course they sometimes get help from others in the division.

At least in terms of budgeting *corporate* resources for division projects, we look very carefully at the divisions' plans. If it wasn't in the plan, it usually won't get into the budget. And if it's not in the budget, it's not going to get done (by the CDC). In the more effective divisions this sort of link between planning and budgeting is also true for internal activity, though in some cases the linkage is pretty loose.

I'm sure a major contributing factor to receptivity of this process is the corporate culture of formal planning and control systems. Planning is an accepted business practice in CGW, and I tried to design the DP forms to look as similar as possible to our regular business planning forms.

In fact, the whole process mirrors the corporate planning style to a large extent by focusing on the operational implications of broad objectives. For the most part, business planning at CGW entails the divisions' telling corporate how they will achieve overall corporate goals (e.g., X percent ROI). It is very much a bottoms-up process, with the corporate plan being an aggregation of the divisions' plans. We've pretty much followed that annual bottoms-up philosophy for systems planning as well.

The plans presented at the 1978 conference were really an exercise in understanding the process and developing a common language. In 1979, however, we really began to get some important issues raised that helped us all understand where we needed to head. The opportunity for 1980 and 1981 is to really get "inside the heads" of the line managers: to identify those opportunity areas that haven't even occurred to them yet. The marketing areas, for example, might be fruitful ground if we understood their needs better. I suspect there are lots of opportunities we haven't begun to address yet. In my opinion, the planning process will have "succeeded" if it provides a forum for this kind of line manager/EDP dialogue.

Additional information regarding the planning forms, submission requirements, etc. are shown in Appendix E.

APPENDIX A □ INFORMATION SERVICES PLANNING PROCESS

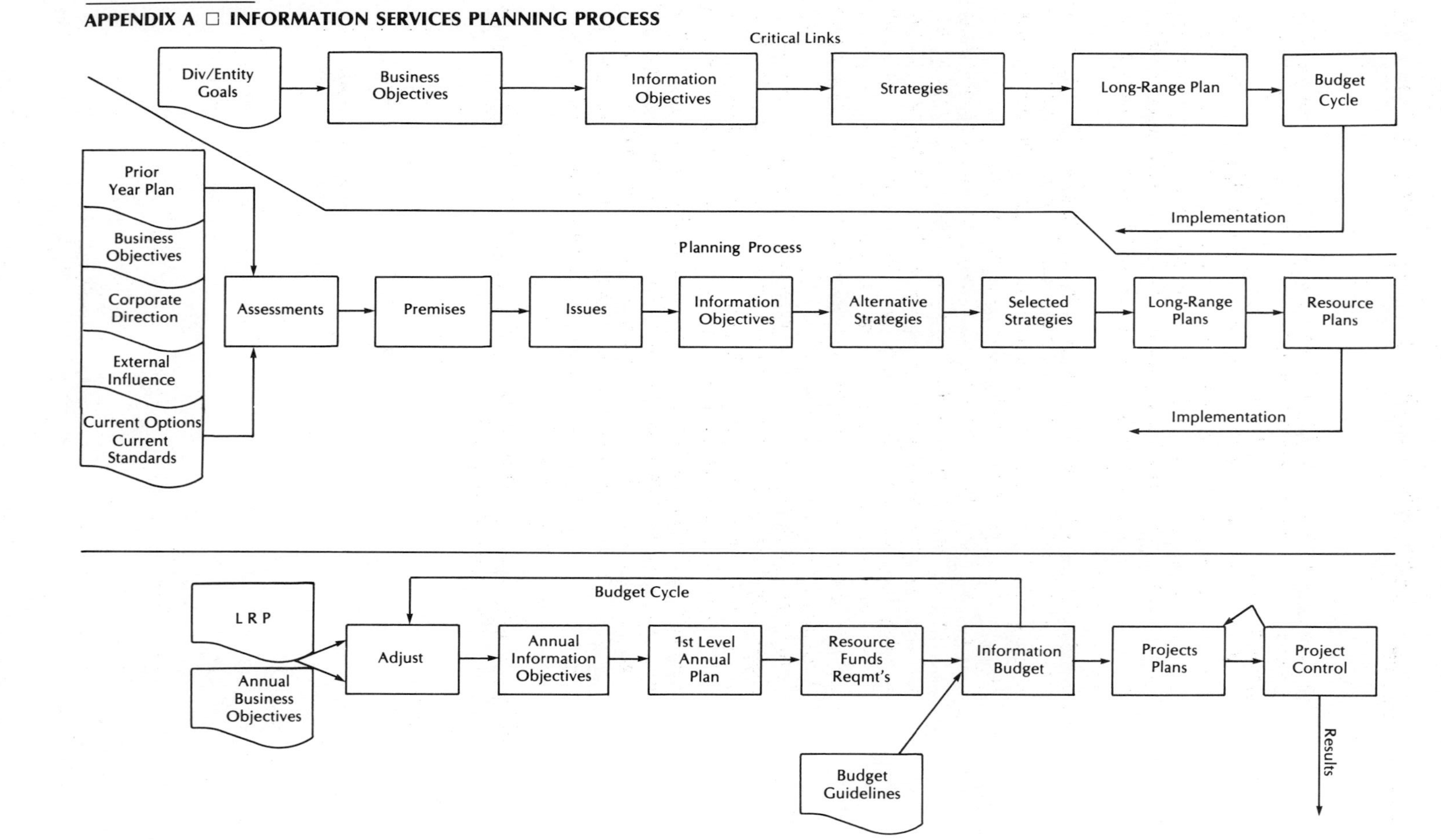

APPENDIX B □ FLOW AND RELATIONSHIPS OF PLANNING PROCESS (Effective January 18, 1980)

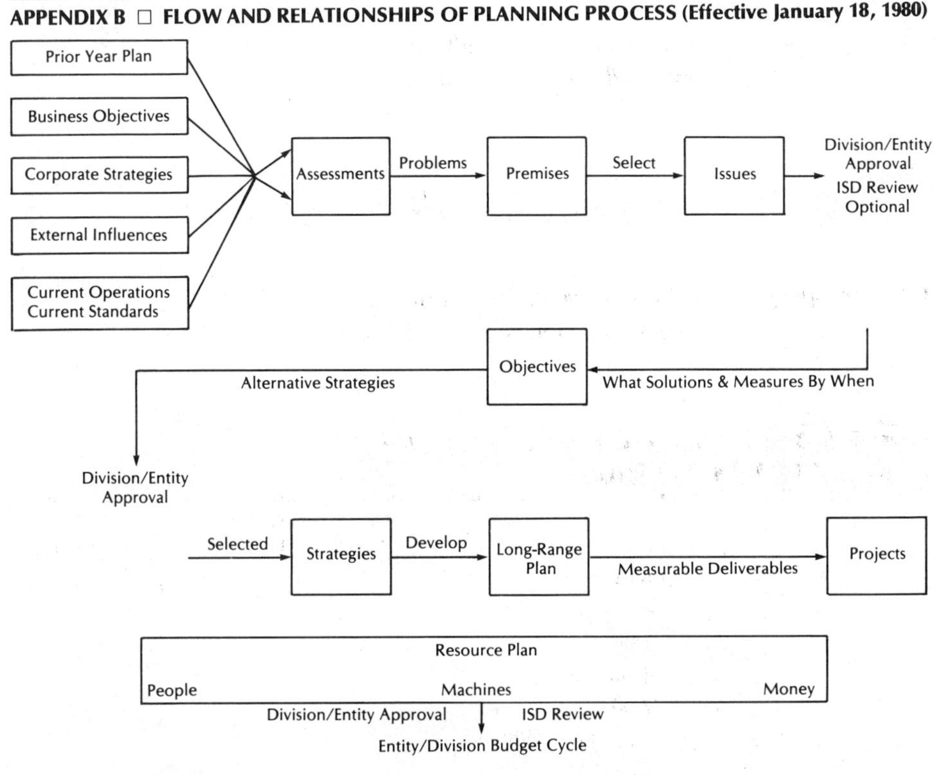

APPENDIX C □ INFORMATION SYSTEMS PLAN— DEFINITIONS

I. *Assessments* — What organizations and businesses do we support?
What are the business objectives?
What have we accomplished?
What are we doing now?
How well are we doing it?

II. *Premises* — Where are the problems?
What are the trends and assumptions?

III. *Issues* — Which problems will we address?

IV. *Objectives* — What solutions by when?
What measures of success?

APPENDIX D *(concluded)*

V.	*Strategies*	What are the alternatives? How will we approach it?
VI.	*Long-range plan*	What planned deliverables by when?
VII.	*Resource plan*	How will we affect resources? People, machines, money?

APPENDIX D □ INFORMATION SERVICES PLAN—PLANNING PROCESS SCHEDULE

	Task	Division/entity target	Submit to ISD
1.	Refine planning process		January 15
2.	Distribute updated planning instruction book		January 31
3.	1979 financial information (Schedule VI-D)		March 15
4.	1979 and through June 1980 staff movement (Schedule I-3)		March 15
5.	Assessments		June 1
6.	Premises		Not required
	Issues		June 1
7.	Objectives		June 1
8.	Long-range plans		June 1
9.	Resource plans		June 1
10.	Executive summary		June 1
11.	Resource allocation requests		June 1
	Planning conference		Mid-June
	ISD and senior management plan reviews		TBA

APPENDIX E □ CGW INFORMATION SYSTEMS PLANNING FORMS

The division systems managers are required to complete the following forms as part of the information system planning process:

Organizational information
- Organization chart
- Staff summary
- Staff movement

Profiles
- Application systems
- Computer
- Telecommunications

Resource plan
- Financial and staff plan
- Data center usage
- Hardware and software
- Telecommunications

Assessments
- Prior-year plan
- Business objectives
- Functional support
- Systems effectiveness
- Service responsiveness
- Staff

Strategic plan
- Premises
- Issues
- Objectives
- Long-range plans

Executive summary
- Resource allocation request

Chapter 6 □ IS Management Control

Chapter \ Manageable Trend	Strategic Impact	DP/TP/OA	Organization Learning	Make/Buy	Life Cycle	GM/ User/ IS
IS Technology Organization Issues **Chapter 3**		●	●			●
Organizational Issues in IS Development **Chapter 4**	●		●	●		●
Information Systems Planning **Chapter 5**	●		●			●
IS Management Control **Chapter 6**	●		●	●		●
A Portfolio Approach to Information Systems Development **Chapter 7**	●				●	●
Operations Management **Chapter 8**	●			●	●	●
Multinational IS Issues **Chapter 9**		●				●
The IS Business **Chapter 10**	●		●	●		●

INTRODUCTION

The IS management control system is a critical network which integrates the information services activities with the rest of the firm's operations. Whereas the project management system *guides* the life cycle of individual projects (which often last more than a year) and the planning process takes a multiyear view in assimilating technologies and systems to match the company's evolving needs and strategies, the IS management control system focuses primarily on guiding the entirety of the information services department on a year-to-year basis. The management control system builds on the output of the planning process to develop a portfolio of projects, hardware/software enhancements and additions, facilities plans, and staffing levels for the year. It then monitors their progress, raising red flags for action when appropriate. The broad objectives an effective IS management control system must meet include the following:

1. Facilitate appropriate communication between the user and deliverer of IS services and provide motivational incentives for them to work together on a day-to-day, month-to-month basis. The management control system must encourage users and IS to act in the best interests of the organization as a whole. It must motivate users to use IS resources appropriately and help them balance investments in this area against those in other areas.
2. Encourage the effective utilization of the IS department's resources, and ensure that users are educated on the potential of existing and evolving technology. In so doing, it must guide the transfer of technology consistent with strategic needs.
3. It must provide the means for efficient management of IS resources and give necessary information for investment decisions. This requires development of both standards of performance measures and the means to evaluate performance against those measures to ensure productivity is being achieved. It should help facilitate make-or-buy decisions.

Early IS management control systems tended to be very cost focused, relying heavily, for example, upon ROI evaluations of capital investments. These proved workable in situations where the technology was installed on a cost displacement justification basis. However, in firms where the computer was a competitive wedge (CAD/CAM, or industrial robotics today) or the technology was pervasively influencing the industry structure of operations, such as in banking and financial services, focus on cost analysis and displacement alone was not an appropriate metric, and development of additional management control techniques has been necessary. For example, a large metropolitan bank several years ago instituted an expensive, complex chargeout system to improve user awareness of costs. Poorly thought out in broad context, the system generated a surge in demand for "cheap" minicomputers, triggered an overall decline in quality of central IS support, and ultimately created market image and sales difficulties for the bank as a whole. Recently, the system was abandoned.

Four special inputs now appear to be critical to the specific structuring of an appropriate IS management control system for an organization. These are:

1. The control system must be adapted to a very different software and operations technology in the 1980s then was present in the 1970s. An important part of this adaptation is development of appropriate sensitivity to the mix of phases of IS technologies in the company. The more mature technologies must be managed and controlled in a tighter, more efficient way than ones in an early start-up phase which need protective treatment appropriate to a research development activity.
2. Specific aspects of the corporate environment influence the appropriate IS Management Control System. Key issues here include IS sophistica-

tion of users, geographic dispersion of the organization, stability of the management team, the firm's overall size and structure, nature of relationship between line and staff departments, etc. These items influence what is workable.

3. The general architecture of the organization's overall corporate management control system and the philosophy underlying it.
4. The perceived strategic significance of IS both in relation to the thrust of its applications portfolio and the role played by currently automated systems.

IS TECHNOLOGY EVOLUTION AND MANAGEMENT CONTROL

Software Issues. The management control problem posed by software development has become more complex because an increasing percentage of DP software support is for maintenance while most OA is bought. This has meant that necessary operational changes to keep the business running have become intermixed with a stream of small, long-term, service-improving capital investments. These two streams are not easily decomposable in many organizations; consequently inadequate controls on operating expense maintenance have developed in many organizations. These controls are often inappropriately applied to stimulate or choke off systems enhancements that are really capital investments.

A second software issue is posed by outside software sourcing. As the percentage of development money devoted to outside software acquisition grows, management control systems designed for an environment where all sourcing was done internally may be inappropriate for environments now dominated by software and make/buy alternatives.

Operations Issues. For IS operations, management control is complex because of the difficulty in measuring and allocating costs in a way which will encourage appropriate behavior in a situation where short-term costs are relatively fixed, and there is considerable volatility in the mix of uses of the IS resource. The operations cost control problem has been further complicated by the cost behavior of IS technology over time. Technical change has created a world where the replacement for a previous computer generally has 4 to 10 times more capacity than the existing one while costing somewhat less than the original one's purchase price. This has created an interesting control issue.

Should the cost per unit of IS processing be lower in the early years (to reflect the lower load factor) so that it can be held flat over the life of the gear, while permitting full (but not excessive) recovery of costs? Conversely, as utilization grows over the years, should the cost per unit of IS processing to the user decline?

An example of coping with this is provided by a large insurance company which replaced an IBM 370/158 several years ago with an Amdahl V5, gaining four times the computing capacity at 15 percent less cost. Because the machine, after conversion, was loaded to barely 30 percent capacity, the managers were faced with the choice of spreading all the present costs on to their current users or forecasting future costs (assuming future volume activity) and setting a three-year average which would recover costs at the period's end. The first approach would have covered expenses from the start but, through its higher prices, would inhibit the initiation of useful work that was economically justified long term. Consequently, they chose the three-year average cost as the price basis to encourage use and to pass on the immediate productivity improvement to their current users. The unabsorbed costs were directly closed to corporate overhead.

The selection of a particular financial structure varies with the firm's experience with technology. Many organizations' current control architecture gives complete management to the user for office automation, while giving the same authority to IS for communications. This leaves traditional DP as the focus for negotiation. As we have noted, however, these are so interrelated as to make this former control architecture highly suspect. A critical contemporary problem is to ensure that these controls evolve forward to meet this new technical environment. For example, a large industrial organization was given free OA support to stimulate users while simultaneously charging for its traditional data base time-sharing decision support system. Very quickly they discovered that users started creating their own data bases on the micro OA equipment which both limited their OA experimentation and underutilized the time-sharing, thereby undercutting the firm's objectives. Our discussion of control structure, while recognizing these issues, does not attempt to definitely resolve it.

Corporate Culture Forces on the Control System

The User Growth in Influence. A major stimulant to growth is IS usage has been the emergence of a group of experienced IS users familiar with how to solve problems with IS technology. After 20 years, it is clear that effective applications by users generate additional ideas for use on their part. This is desirable and healthy, provided a control system exists to encourage appropriate appraisal of the new use in terms of its potential costs and benefits to the organization. The absence of such a control system may result in explosive growth (often unprofitable and poorly managed) with new capacity required every one or two years or, alternatively, little growth with frustrated users obtaining necessary services surreptitiously (and more expensively).

Both events cause confidence in the IS department and its management control system to erode. The problem is further complicated by the fact that many of the new generation of user demands pose more difficulty in benefit articulation than in costs of provision. Repeatedly, we uncover situations where the control system has caused the hard cost of implementation numbers of an application to attain undue weight against the soft, but often very strategic, management benefits.

The preceding discussion suggests a paradoxical aspect of controlling information services; namely that, while the area is technologically complex, most of the critical success factors for its effective and efficient use are *highly* human dependent and, thus stated, pose very familiar management control challenges from a corporate perspective. A complicating element is, since both technology and user sophistication are continually changing, the types of applications to be done are changing. Many individuals are sufficiently set in their ways (reinforced by a control approach) that they find change difficult to implement and attempt to resist it. A by-product is that often the user perceptions of the change agent department (IS) are unnecessarily poor. For example, all sorts of spurious effects are attributed by the users to the introduction of a change to new computer systems, word processors, etc. In addition to technology and user learning, hidden forces of change also exist in external items, such as new tax laws, and in internal strategic items such as adding customers or products, moving offices, and modifying the organization. Recognition and appropriate implementation of these changes can be facilitated by a well-designed management control system.

The Geographic and Organizational Structure Influences. Other important control aspects relate to the organization's geographic dispersion and size. As the number of business sites grow and staff levels increase, often substantial changes are needed in organization structure, corporate management control, and IS management control. Informal personnel supervision and control which fits the more limited setting will fall apart in the larger and more dispersed ones. Similarly, the nature of relationships between line and staff departments within the company, in general, influences what relationship between the IS department and its users can be reasonably expected to evolve and thus the type of IS management control which is appropriate.

The organization structure of the firm plays an important role in the IS management control architecture. Firms which have a strong functional organization with central services function maintained as unallocated cost centers often find it appropriate to keep IS as an unallocated cost center. On the other hand, firms which are heavily decentralized into profit or investment centers, or which have a tradition of charging out for corporate services, are quickly propelled down the path of charging for corporate IS activities and often will move as far as setting it up as a profit or investment center. Over time, it becomes increasingly difficult to manage with good results an IS organization where the control architecture is sharply different from that present in the rest of the firm.

Corporate Planning and Control Process

In concept, the process of an appropriate IS planning and management control system should be similar to the corporate planning and control system. Ideally, in both cases there should be a multiyear plan linked appropriately to the overall business strategy which is also linked to a budget process that allows the responsible managers to negotiate an operating budget. As such, IS planning/budgeting should be compatible with overall business planning/budgeting. However, if business planning primarily includes an annual budget with periodic follow-up of performance during the year, a very difficult environment exists for IS management control. This is because the project life-cycle implementation of any sizable change can easily take two or more years from beginning to end, including as much as a year to formulate, select, and refine the appropriate design approach.

Thus, an IS organization often must maintain at least a three-year view of its activities to ensure the resources are available to meet these demands. In many cases, this extends the IS planning horizon beyond the organization's planning horizon. To be useful, these IS project plans must systematically and precisely identify alternative steps for providing necessary service. For example, to upgrade reservation service in a large hotel chain, the IS department, in concert with key hotel managers, had to project the type of service the hotels would need four years out. This was necessary in order to select the correct terminals and provide an orderly transition from the present situation to the new one over a 30-month period. A key bottleneck in this massive, one-time, 600-terminal installation was the total lack of a corporate planning and control approach which extended more than a year into the future.

This combination of short corporate horizons, long IS time horizons, and technical innovation generates conflict within the firm concerning management control that can only be resolved by repeated judgments over time. These conflicts pose two major clusters of managerial issues:

First, how congruent/similar should the management control architecture and process of information services be to that present in other parts of the organization? Where differences do exist, how can this dissonance be best managed, and should they be allowed to exist long term? Secondly, how can the tension between sound control and timely innovation be best balanced? Control typically depends on measuring costs against budgets, actual achievements versus promised, and evaluation of investments against returns. Innovation involves risk taking, gaining trial experience with emerging technologies, relying on faith, and at times moving forward despite a lack of clear objectives. A portfolio excessively balanced in either direction poses grave risks. (As will be discussed in Chapter 7, different companies will appropriately balance their portfolios quite differently.)

Strategic Impact of IS on the Congruence of IS Business Controls

An important input on how closely the IS control system should be matched to the business planning/control process is the strategic importance of IS for the next three years. If very strategic for the firm to achieve its goals, then development of a close linkage between corporate planning and control and IS planning and control is important, and differences between the two will cause great difficulty. Additionally, investment decisions and key product development innovations must be subject to periodic top management review.

The control system for these strategic environments must encourage value-based innovations even in the face of the reality that perhaps as few as one out of three will produce payoff. Often, in this situation the key control challenge is to encourage the generation, evaluation, and management of multiple and unplanned sources of suggestions for new services. Several now defunct brokerage houses and soon-to-be merged banks were unable to do this.

If IS is not strategically core to the business but is more a factory or support-type effort, congruency of links to the rest of the business planning and control activities are not as critical. IS can more appropriately develop an independent planning/control process to deal with its need to manage a changing user demand with an evolving technology.

A factory environment, for example, must emphasize efficiency controls, while a turnaround should focus upon effective utilization of new technology.

Summary

The theme of the above discussion is that to achieve appropriate results, the specific approach to IS management control must vary widely by organization because of its specific context, and also over time, as the context evolves on one or more of the dimensions discussed above. The rest of the chapter describes the key factors, beyond these contextual items, which influence selection of different forms of control architecture (financial), control process (financial), nonfinancial controls, and audit.

Our treatment of IS management control divides it into three parts. Each part is briefly defined here and discussed in depth later in the chapter.

1. Control Architecture. Should the IS function be set up as a cost center (unallocated), cost center (allocated), profit center, or an investment center or residual income center? Further, if costs are allocated from the IS function to the users, should the transfer price be market based, cost based, cost plus, split level, or negotiated? Each of these alternatives generates quite different behavior and motivation and are fundamental decisions which once made are not lightly changed. Finally, what nonfinancial measurements should be designed to facilitate effective use of IS.

2. Control Process (Financial and Nonfinancial). What form of developing action plans is most appropriate? Typically, this is represented by the annual budget and drives both operations and project development. Particular attention will be given here to the issues surrounding zero-based budgeting. What form of periodic reporting instruments and exception reporting tools (against budget targets) during the year are appropriate? As opposed to architectural issues, these are changed much more frequently.

3. Audit Function. Issues here include ensuring that an IS audit function exists, that it is focused on appropriate problems, and that it has suitable staff.

CONTROL ARCHITECTURE

Unallocated Cost Center

Establishment of the information services department as an *unallocated cost center* is a widely used approach and has many advantages associated with it. As an essentially free resource to the users, it stimulates a number of user requests and creates a climate which is conducive to encouraging user experimentation. This is particularly good for technologies which are in phase 1 or 2 of their assimilation into the firm. The lack of red tape makes it easier for the IS department to sell its services. All the controversy and acrimony over the IS chargeout process is avoided since no chargeout system exists. Further, very low expenditures need to be made on development and operations of IS accounting procedures. In aggregate, these factors make this a good alternative for situations where a small IS budget is present. Innovation is critical in settings where financial resource allocation is not a high-tension activity.

A large western bank has been introducing electronic mail and word processing for two years as an unallocated cost center. Their intent is to build a network and establish standard procedures. They see the value in the short run of encouraging a growing network as outweighing the cost savings from a standard systems development.

On the other hand, significant problems exist when IS is treated as an unallocated cost center. With no financial pressure being placed on the user,

IS can quickly be perceived as a free resource where each user should be sure to get their piece of the action. This can rapidly generate a series of irresponsible user requests for service which may be difficult to turn down. Further, in a situation where staff or financial resources are short, the absence of this chargeout framework increases the possibility of excessive politicization around IS resource allocation decisions. The unallocated cost center insulates the IS department from competitive pressures and external measures of performance, permitting the hiding of operational inefficiencies. Further, this approach fits the management control structure of some firms poorly (i.e., firms which have a strong tradition of charging out corporate staff services to users). Finally, this approach poses particular problems for organizations where IS charges are perceived to be both large and strategic. In combination, these pressures explain why, although many firms start with an unallocated cost center approach, they often evolve forward to another approach, at least for their more mature technologies and more mature users.

One approach widely followed is to keep IS as an unallocated cost center but inform users through memos of what their development and operations charges would have been if a chargeout system was in place. Without raising the friction associated with chargeout procedures (described below), this approach stimulates awareness by users that they are not using a free resource of the corporation, and gives them a feel for the general magnitude of their charges. The approach is often adopted as a way station when a firm is moving IS from an unallocated cost center to some other organizational form. Unfortunately, however, a memo about a charge does not have the same bite as the actual assignment of the charge.

Allocated Cost Center and Chargeout

The approach of establishing the information services department as an *allocated cost center* has the immediate virtue of helping to stimulate honesty in user requests from a corporate perspective. This approach fits rather well the later phases of technology assimilation where the usefulness of the technology has been widely communicated within the firm. While it opens up a debate as to what cost is, it avoids controversy about whether an internal service department should be perceived as a profit-making entity. This approach particularly fits environments which have a strong tradition of corporate services charges.

Inevitably, however, the allocated cost center introduces a series of complexities and frictions, since such a system necessarily has arbitrary elements in it. The following paragraphs suggest some of the practical problems which come from allocating IS department costs to users (irrespective of whether in a cost center or some other approach). The first problem is that the IS charges will be compared to IS charges prepared both by other companies in the same industry and by outside service organizations. This opens the possibility of generating clearly misleading and invidious conclusions. The words *misleading* and *invidious* are related because the prices prepared by other organizations often have one or more of the following characteristics:

1. The service being priced out is being treated as a by-product rather than as a joint costing problem.
2. IS is being treated under a different management control architectural scheme from that present in the company which is making the evaluation. Thus the comparison of costs is highly misleading.
3. An independent IS services firm or an in-house operation selling services to outside customers may deliberately produce an artificially low price as a way of buying market share, over a short-term horizon. Thus, their prices may be perceived as fair market when, in fact, they are nothing of the sort.

Consequently, since the prices produced by other companies are not the result of an efficient market, there is substantial possibility that comparing them to our prices may produce misleading data for management decisions.

Another issue of concern is that unless carefully managed, the chargeout system tends to discourage phase 1 and phase 2 research projects. These activities must be carefully segregated and managed in a different way than projects utilizing the more mature technologies. It is unnecessary in our view that 100 percent of IS costs be charged to the users. Segregating as much as 15 percent to 25 percent as a separately managed R&D function to be included in corporate overhead is a sound strategy. This is particularly important in the technology of the 1980s to ensure that artificial and inappropriate incentives are not stimulating inappropriately the installation of mini/microcomputers. Repeatedly, minicomputer systems have looked good to the user when their estimated costs were compared with the full cost charges of a central IS installation. From the corporate perspective, however, when an incremental analysis of costs is done, a quite different picture may emerge.

On a more technical note today, in the majority of companies which are charging out IS costs, two major concepts underlie the chargeout process. The first concept is that the chargeout system for IS operations costs is based on a very complex formula (based on use of computer technology by an application) which spreads the costs in a supposedly equitable fashion to the ultimate users. Featuring terms such as EXCPU's, the concept is that each user should bear computer costs in relation to his pro-rata use of the underlying resource. The second concept is that the chargeout system ensures that *all* costs of the activity are passed out to consumers of the service. Not infrequently, this involves zeroing out all IS costs each month and certainly by year end.

Rigorous application of these concepts have led to a number of unsatisfactory consequences from the user's perspective. Most important, the charges are absolutely *unintelligible* and *unpredictable* to the end user. Clothed in technical jargon and highly impacted by whether it has been a heavy or light month in the IS department, there is no way for the user to predict or control them short of disengaging from the IS activity (hence the explosion of stand-alone minis).

Not infrequently the charges are highly *unstable*. The same application, processing the same amount of data, run at the same time of the week or month will cost very different amounts depending on what else happens to be scheduled in the IS department during the month. In addition, if all unallocated costs are closed to the users at the end of the year, they may be hit with an entirely unwelcome and unanticipated surprise, generating considerable hostility.

Further, the charges tend to be *artificially high* in relation to incremental costs. As mentioned earlier, this can cause considerable friction with the users and encourage examination of alternatives which optimize short-term cost behavior at the expense of the long-term strategic interests of the firm.

Additionally, in both operations and development, this approach makes no attempt to segregate IS efficiency variances out and hold IS uniquely responsible for them. Rather, all efficiency variances are directly assigned to the ultimate users, creating additional friction and allegations of IS irresponsibility and mismangement. Finally, administration of a chargeout system of this type not infrequently turns out to be very expensive.

The combination of these factors have generated chargeout systems which do not satisfactorily meet the needs of many organizations. We believe this is a direct result of the technical and accounting foundations of the system. We believe that, for most situations, technology and accounting are the wrong disciplines to bring to the problem and that the task can be better approached as a problem in applied social psychology. What type of behavior do you want to trigger on the part of the IS organization and the users? What incentives can be provided to them to assure that, as they move to meet their individual goals, they are simultaneously moving more or less in a goal-congruent fashion with the overall interests of the corporation?[1] The design of such a system is a very complex task requiring trade-offs along multiple dimensions. As needs of the corporation change, the structures of the chargeout system will also appropriately change. Critical issues to be dealt with include:

1. Should the system be designed to encourage use of IS services (or components thereof) or should it set high hurdles for potential investments? The answer for phase 1 and phase 2 technology projects will be different from that for phase 3 and phase 4 technology projects.

[1] Robert N. Anthony and James S. Reece, *Accounting: Text and Cases*, 6th ed. (Richard D. Irwin, 1979), pp. 778–79.

2. Should the system encourage IS to adopt an efficiency or an effectiveness focus? The answer here may evolve over time.
3. Should the system provide a tilt in favor of use of IS department resources or encourage outside IS service sourcing decisions?
4. What steps must be taken to ensure that the system is congruent with the general control architecture in the organization, or if not congruent, ensuring that this deviation is acceptable?

While the answers to these questions will dictate different solutions for different settings, some generalizations spring out—which fit most settings and represent the next step in the evolution of a chargeout system. First of all, for an IS chargeout system to be effective in this environment, it is critical that it be understandable by the users. The corollary of understandability is that the system be simple. Repeatedly, evidence suggests that a chargeout system for IS operations which is a gross distortion of the underlying electronics but which the user can understand is vastly preferable to a technically accurate system which no one can understand (even taking into account the games some programmers will play to reduce costs). Partial motivation and goal congruence is better than none. In this context, systems which are based on an agreed-upon standard cost/unit are better than those which allocate all costs to whoever happened to use the system. Even better (and the clear trend today) is to design these standards not in IS resource units but in items which are user-understandable transactions (e.g., so much per paycheck, so much per order line, so much per inquiry).

A second desirable characteristic is that the IS operations chargeout system should be *perceived* as being fair and reasonable on all sides. In an absolute technical sense, it doesn't have to be fair. It is enough that all involved believe that it is a fair and reasonable system. In this vein the IS operations chargeout system should produce replicable results. A job processing the same amount of transactions at 10 A.M. on Tuesday morning should cost the same thing week after week. When it doesn't, an air of skepticism sets in which undermines the system's credibility.

A third desirable characteristic of an IS operations chargeout system is that it should separate IS efficiency-related issues from user utilization of the system. IS should be held responsible for its inefficiencies. Clearly, closing at month- or year-end any over- or under-absorbed cost variances to the user usually accomplishes no useful purpose (other than raising emotional temperatures). After appropriate analysis of the causes for the variance it is appropriate to close it directly to corporate overhead.

The issues involved in charging for IS maintenance and systems development are fundamentally different from those of IS operations and must be decoupled and dealt with separately. For development and maintenance expenditures of any size a professional contract must be prepared between IS and the users in advance of major work (as though it were a relationship with an outside software company). Elements of a good contract include:

1. Estimates of the job costs are prepared by IS, and IS is held responsible for all costs in excess of this.
2. Procedures are established for re-estimating and, if necessary, killing the job if changes in job scope occur.
3. If a job is bid on a time and materials basis (very frequent in the software industry), a clear understanding must be developed in advance with the user as to what represents such a change in scope that the contract should be reviewed.

In this context, of course, for many systems, such as data base systems, the most challenging (sometimes impossible) task is to identify the definable user (or group thereof) to write the contract with. Further, if the contract is written with one group of users and others subsequently join, are they charged at incremental cost, full cost, or full cost plus (because they have none of the development risks and are buying into a sure thing)? There are neither easy nor general-purpose answers to these questions.

The following paragraphs describe how a recently studied company approached the tasks. This company provides computer services to 14 user groups, many of which have very similar needs. Operations expenses were spread in the following ways:

1. Every time a piece of data was inputted or extracted on a CRT, a standard charge was levied on the user, irrespective of the type of processing system involved. This was understandable by the user.
2. Since all costs from the modems out (terminal, line, modem) could be directly associated with a user in a completely understandable fashion, these charges were passed directly to the end user.
3. All report and other paper costs were charged to the user on a standard cost/ton basis, irrespective of the complexity of the system which generated them.
4. All over- or under-recovered variances were analyzed for indications of IS efficiency and then closed directly to a corporate overhead account bypassing the users.

With respect to maintenance and development cost, the following procedures were used:

1. Items budgeted for less than 40 hours were charged directly to the users at a standard rate/hour times number of hours spent.
2. Projects budgeted to take more than 40 hours were estimated by the IS organization. If the estimate was acceptable to the user, work would be done. Any variances, in relation to budget, were debited or credited to the IS organization, with the user being billed only budget.
3. A process of job re-estimating was created to handle potential changes in job specification, with the users being given the option of accepting the new costs, using the old specifications, or aborting the job.

4. Research and development projects were budgeted separately by the IS organization. IS was accountable to corporate for the costs of these jobs and the users were not charged for them.

The combination of these items over a several year period did a remarkable job of defusing the tensions in user/IS relationships, enabling them to work together more easily.

Profit Center

A third, frequently discussed and used method of management control is the establishment of the IS department as a profit center. Advocates of this approach note that this puts the inside service on the same footing as an outside one and brings the pressures of the marketplace to bear on it. Consequently, it puts pressures on the IS function to hold costs down by stressing efficiency and to market itself more aggressively inside the company. This structure hastens the emergence of the IS marketing function which, if well managed, will improve user relationships. Further, excess IS capacity tends to be promptly dealt with by IS management, with their being willing to run more risks on the user service side. It also encourages sales of services by the IS department to outside firms. This later, however, has often turned out to be a mixed blessing. Often priced as incremental sales (rather than on a full-cost basis), not only are these sales unprofitable, but many IS departments, excited by the volatile *hard* outside dollars as opposed to the captive *soft* inside ones, begin to give preferential treatment to these outside customers, with a resulting erosion of treatment to inside users.

Establishing IS as a profit center, however, has other problems. First, a significant amount of concern often is raised inside the firm whether it is appropriate for an inside *service* department to establish itself as a profit center, particularly when it does not sell any products outside the company. "Profits come from outside sales, not service department practices" is the dominant complaint. The problem is further complicated by the fact that because of geography, shared data files, and privacy and security reasons, many users do not have a legitimate alternative of going outside. Therefore, the argument that the profit center is subject to normal market forces is widely perceived by many users to be a spurious one.

Setting up the IS activity as a profit center, at least in the short run, leads to higher user costs because a profit figure is added on to the user costs. Not only can this create user hostility, but in many settings, it prevents the user from having legitimate full-cost data from the corporation for external pricing decisions. In summary, the combination of these issues must be addressed before an organization precipitously moves to the installation of a profit center approach. A deceptively intriguing approach on the surface, underneath it has many pitfalls.

Investment Center

Many of the issues involved in establishing the IS activity as an investment center, or residual income center (a profit center where a carrying charge for net assets employed is subtracted from the profit figure for both budget and actual performance), are similar to those involved in the establishment of IS as a profit center. The critical reason for moving in this direction (as opposed to a profit center), of course, is to make the IS department fully responsible for the assets employed and force them to make appropriate trade-offs of investment versus additional profits. In a nonstrategic support role this may work well. This must be managed very sensitively because it produces strong IS motivations to delay capacity expansion and run close to the margin on service. It must also be monitored very closely because it is easy to make a good short-term residual income through serious erosion in service levels. Another problem is that almost no one worries about software as an asset for these purposes but focuses only on hardware. This can result in serious misunderstanding about the real assets of the company and the amount of maintenance necessary to service them.

In general, if IS is to be held responsible for the profit/net asset trade-off, it is better to do it on a residual income than on a ROI basis. This is because residual income has every unit of a company thinking in the same way about the attractiveness of new investment. When return on investment is used, one result is that high ROI units are reluctant to make investments which would be to the overall benefit of the firm. Similarly, low ROI units are willing to make some marginal investments, which would improve their ROI but are not in the best interest of the company.

An additional advantage of IS being a stand-alone investment or residual income center is that it can be perceived as being fully organizationally neutral, instead of being the captive of a particular business unit. Several years ago a multibank holding company found it attractive for this reason to spin the IS activity out of the lead bank and put it as a stand-alone unit (measured on residual income) in the holding company. Over the years, the quality of the relationships of the other member banks with the IS department improved markedly as a result of this move which has allowed the department to be perceived as independent.

Transfer Pricing. When an IS activity is set up as a profit, investment, or residual income center, establishment of the IS transfer price becomes a critical issue. There are at least four different conceptual ways of approaching it, each with specific strengths and weaknesses (the issues involved are very similar in nature to those found in transfer pricing situations in general).

For the purpose of this discussion, we will assume that IS operations is being priced in end user transaction terms (i.e. so much per paycheck, so much per invoice line, etc.), while for IS development and maintenance a fixed price contract is being written. Obviously, as described in our earlier discussion on chargeout issues, there are many other ways to approach these items. We believe, however, these assumptions are useful in order to introduce the different cluster of issues described in these paragraphs. These include:

Cost-Based Price. Assuming a full-cost method is used, this method has the advantage of producing the lowest cost from the user's perspective and is thus most likely to produce minimal user complaints. In this setting, establishing IS as a profit center is largely similar to making it a cost center since profits can only be earned on internal sales by generating positive efficiency variances (obviously sales outside the company can be priced to generate a profit). This approach does not permit one to sidestep the previously mentioned issue as to what constitutes cost and how it should be determined (joint versus by-product, etc.)

A variant of this approach is a cost-plus basis. On the positive side, this makes IS generate profits and at the same time provides an understandable number for users to deal with. On the negative side, the users raise both the narrow issue of capriciousness in how the "plus" was selected and the broader issue of the general inappropriateness of an internal service department earning profits.

Market-Based Price. A key alternative, this method is used in many companies, particularly as the availability of outside services has grown. Its implementation however, poses several problems similar to creating profit centers. The first is the near impossibility in many settings of finding comparable products and services to establish the market. Unique data bases or process control systems are examples of items where it is impossible to find them. Even so-called standardized services such as payroll and accounting turn out to have so many special ramifications and alternative designs as to make identification of a market price very elusive. Also, suppliers of IS services treat some IS products as a by-product. Still other organizations calculate prices for in-house use; they make no attempt at rigor but only attempt to achieve ballpark figures. To use these figures as market price surrogates is to invite difficulty.

Split-Level. This approach is designed to satisfy simultaneously the motivational needs of the IS department and the key users. As long as a single transfer price is used, it is impossible to come up with a price which will simultaneously allow IS to feel that it is earning a fair profit and the users to be given prices which will permit them to manage aggregate costs on behalf of the company's overall interests. The pain can be spread around but in the end it is reallocation of a finite amount of pain as opposed to its elimination. Split-level transfer pricing in IS works as follows:

1. The users are charged items either at direct or full cost, depending on the company's overall management control philosophy.
2. The IS department is allocated revenue on a standard cost of services delivered, plus a standard fixed markup (or at a market price if a good one happens to exist). Improvements in actual profits vis-à-vis plan come either from selling more services than planned or from gaining unanticipated cost efficiencies.
3. The difference between the revenue of the IS department and the cost figure charged to the user is posted to an overhead expense account, which on a monthly basis is closed to corporate overhead.

This method at least in theory allows both the IS department and users to be simultaneously motivated to behave in the best overall corporate interest. Users are given appropriate economic trade-offs to consider, while IS is provided incentives both to operate efficiently and sell extra services. This has worked satisfactorily in a number of settings and has dramatically changed the tenor and quality of relationships where the accounting system now permits them to work together instead of against each other. Its Achilles heel is that careful attention must be paid to the establishment of the cost target to ensure that the IS group is being asked to stretch enough and is not building in excess slack into its budget. Also, its implementation involves some additional accounting work.

Negotiated. This is quite difficult to execute in the IS business environment because the two parties often bring quite different strengths to the negotiating table. For example, systems which interface directly with other systems or which share proprietary data bases must be run by the central IS department, hence the negotiating positions of the two parties cannot be considered equal.

Summary

In aggregate, there are a wide variety of potential IS control architectures. No one represents a perfect general-purpose solution. The challenge is to pick the one which fits well enough the company's general management control culture, present user/IS relationships, and current state of IS sophistication. The typical firm has approached these issues in an evolutionary fashion rather than being able to get it "right" the first time.

CONTROL PROCESS (FINANCIAL AND NONFINANCIAL)

The foundation of the IS management control process is the budgeting system. Put together under a very complex set of trade-offs and interlocked with the corporate budgeting process, its first objective is to provide a mechanism for appropriately allocating scarce financial resources. While the planning effort sets the broad framework for the IS activity, the budgeting process ensures that fine-tuning in relation to staffing, hardware, and resource levels takes place. A second important objective of budgeting is to set a dialogue in motion to ensure that organizational consensus is reached on the specific goals and possible short-term achievements of the IS activity. This is particularly important in organizations where the planning process is not well formed. Finally, the budget establishes a framework around which an early warning system for negative deviations can be built. Without a budget, it is difficult to spot deviations in a deteriorating cost situation in time to take appropriate corrective action.

The budget system must involve senior management, IS management, and user groups. Its key outputs include the establishing of planned service levels and costs of central operations, the amount of internal development and maintenance support to be implemented, and the amount and form of external services to be acquired. The planned central IS department service levels and their associated costs must flow from review of existing services and the approved application development portfolio as well as user desires for new services and the degree of available purchased service. In addition, these planned service levels must take into account long-term systems maintenance needs. This ensures that appropriate controls are in place on purchased services (software and hardware, such as minis), as opposed to being focused only on the activities of the central IS department.

The dialogue between users and the IS department on their forecast of needs/usage for the budget year helps generate an understanding of the IS department's goals and constraints which iteratively leads to a better IS plan as well as to clarification of what the user intends to provide. To ensure this happens, for example, a leading chemical company asks both the user and the IS department to develop two budgets, one for the same amount of dollars and head count as last year and one for 10 percent more dollars and 2 percent more head count. Typically, the IS department's proposals involve an expansion of central services while the users involve an expansion of distributed services. To ensure communication, the main description of key items are all in user terms, such as the number of personnel records and types of pension planning support, with all the jargon relating to technical support issues being confined to appendixes. Both groups are asked in this process to rank services of critical importance as well as identify those that are of lower priority or which are likely to be superseded. A senior management group then spends one day reviewing a joint presentation which "scopes" the budget in terms of probable levels of expenditure and develops a tentative ranking of priority. This meeting allows senior management to provide overall direction to guide the final budget negotiations between the two groups. The priorities coming out of these discussions are then consolidated by the IS manager for final approval. This modified, zero-based budgeting approach is judged to have provided good results in this setting.

The budget must establish benchmark dates for project progress, clarify type and timing of technical changeovers, and identify needed levels and mixes of personnel as well as fix spending levels. A further mission is identifying key milestones and completion dates and tying them to the budget to ensure that periodic review and early detection of variance from plan can take place. Budgeting the key staff head count and levels is a particularly important management decision. A major cause for project overruns and delays in many situations is lack of talent available in a timely manner to support multiple projects. Shortage of personnel must be dealt with realistically in fitting projects together. This, of course, needs to be done not just in the budget process but periodically through the year as well.

An important benefit of involving both users and suppliers in the budget is the joint educational process. On the one hand, it helps the IS department to truly understand the particular needs of each business and to assess their real needs for IS support vis-à-vis other programs. On the other hand, it helps the users develop an awareness of what is possible with available technology and to better define their potential needs. For example, in one financial institution the budget process is used heavily as a stimulus for innovation. During budget preparation, both user and IS take many trips to other installations and receive debriefing from their hardware/software suppliers to generate thinking on potential new banking services. Over a several-year period this has significantly improved the relationship between the two groups.

Zero-Based Budgeting

One of the dangers of the budgeting process is that it can become too routinized and incorporate successive layers of fat in the discretionary costs. An effective tool for separating out this fat in many organizations has been zero-based budgeting. Although called zero-based budgeting (ZBB), in practice most firms don't do real zero-based budgeting because building a department's budget up from scratch would be prohibitively expensive. Rather, each staff (as opposed to line) department begins by taking a 15 to 20 percent reduction in budget from the previous year and then identifies the services it can deliver for this amount of money which would best support the organization. This is called the base increment. The staff department then identifies in descending priority a series of discretionary increments of services, each with a price tag attached to it. (If it gets more money, here is how it will be spent, and here are the benefits.) This base increment and the associated sequence of prioritized discretionary increments then ascend through the various levels in the organization. At each level they are reviewed for appropriateness and blended with increments from other departments. Finally, at the very top of the organization, the overall list of priorities are reviewed, and a line is drawn through the sheet of prioritized discretionary increments. Items above the line are funded and those below the line are not funded. All departments do not have equally favorable outcomes in this process. A department whose mission is perceived to be vital in the coming year might have its budget increased by 51 percent, while two other departments whose mission is decreasing in perceived significance might have their budgets decreased.

At its heart, therefore, ZBB is a reallocation process for expenditures on the margin, not an aggregate budget reduction tool. Under ZBB it is perfectly appropriate for discretionary expenditures to rise in aggregate. This process has turned out to be very appropriate for the discretionary level IS staff departments such as technical support, development, and planning. It is not so appropriate for manufacturing departments whose staffing is driven by the physical volume of work passing through it, such as computer operations, data entry, or maintenance.

Zero-based budgeting is attractive to IS organizations (particularly when it is also being done elsewhere in the firm) in the first place because it forces careful examination of all expenditures and should identify redundant or obsolete services. All too often in companies realistic budgeting starts with last year's budget and attempts are then made to add extra items to it. Unfortunately, however, staffing and expenditure levels which made sense at one point in time may have been obsolesced by later developments. Zero-based budgeting is an important discipline for ensuring that the layers of fat are exposed and peeled away.

Often ZBB's most important benefit is that it is a sharp change from the past. People are forced to budget in a very different way, with the positive by-product being that old ways of thinking are challenged and creativity is stimulated.

The theory behind ZBB is conceptually clean and sound. However, resolving the many problems of practical administration has been the key to whether it has been successful in specific situations. As the subsequent paragraphs will discuss, these problems are real and failure to resolve them has turned ZBB into a very expensive game in some organizations.

First, effective ZBB is heavily dependent on good top-down communication within the corporation during planning. This is because ZBB is fundamentally a bottoms-up process. If a clear understanding of corporate mission and department goals is not communicated to the department head who prepares the initial ZBB materials, the formation of the base package and discretionary increments may be so flawed as to prevent effective review and action on priorities of the package increments when it reaches senior level.

Further, since the priorities of different increments are reviewed in the organization chain of command, it is not until very late in the review process that a general management input is provided to the reviewers. By that time, often, so much detail is present that it is hard for management to gain the perspective needed to spot trends and meaningfully influence overall direction. Additionally, because the ranking process works up the organization hierarchy, there is a substantial possibility of gamesmanship in the establishment of priorities.

It is important to recognize that the ZBB process takes place independently of the personnel system. Consequently, a series of adjustments between different programs of activities may be suggested which turn out to be undoable from a personnel staffing viewpoint. People are not infinitely retrainable, and simultaneous layoffs and hirings often have their hidden pitfalls, if indeed they are possible.

Critical to successful ZBB is the establishment of integrity in the base increment. In reality, the process of reviewing the priority of the discretionary increments is often so time-consuming that inadequate attention is paid to the base increment's contents. Consequently, it becomes an attractive hiding place for a department's pet projects which cannot stand the light of day.

Zero-based budgeting in its full-blown form is very time-consuming and expensive. During a company turnaround year it is very useful and can produce a significant series of benefits by finding layers of fat and stimulating creative ideas as to how they should be dealt with. Often, however, the same payoff is not present in immediately subsequent years and a number of firms have moved to doing it only every three to four years (or conversely only a few departments each year). Finally, ZBB with its one-year departmental focus runs directly contrary to the thrust of multiyear programs (which cut across a number of departments) and therefore poses dangers through bringing a nonintegrated short-term focus to the overall IS function. Related to this is the problem of how to develop a satisfactory approach for projects and service relationships between departments, where the service being offered is relatively low priority to the generating department but very high priority to the receiving department.

In combination, these factors have tended to make ZBB a more useful ad hoc tool for the technical services and development groups than to the IS operations groups. The red tape and complexity associated with it makes it more attractive to utilize on an every-three-to-four-year basis than annually. To get payoff from it, however, requires that careful attention be paid to multiple administrative dimensions. Unassailable in logic, in reality it can be very frail.

Periodic Reporting

Effective monitoring of the department's financial performance requires a variety of tools, most of which are common to other settings. These normally include a series of reports which highlight actual performance versus plan on a monthly basis with variances. Often this includes the generation of exception reports. Design and operation of these systems is rather routine. Relatively routine, obvious issues present in them include the following. Are budget targets readjusted during the year through a forecasting mechanism? If so, is the key performance target actual versus budget, or actual versus forecast? Are budgets modified for seasonal factors or are they prepared on a basis of one-twelfth of the annual expense each month?

The IS financial reporting task is complicated by the fact that an IS organization requires a matrix cost reporting system as it grows in size. One side of the matrix is represented by the IS department structure and the need to track costs and variances by IS organizational unit; the other side of the matrix involves keeping track of costs and variances by programs or projects. An issue that will not be discussed in this book, other than its identification, is whether budget numbers and actual results should be reported in nominal dollars or in inflation-adjusted dollars. Obviously, today this is an issue of major importance for corporate management control systems in general.

Nonfinancial Reporting Process

At least in an operational sense, the nonfinancial controls are of more importance than financial ones in assuring management that the day-to-day and month-to-month aspects of the IS function remain on target. Critical items here include preparation of regular six-month surveys of user attitudes toward the adequacy of the type of IS support with which they are being provided. Not only do such surveys identify problems, but they provide a benchmark against which progress can be measured over time. Their distribution to the users for filling out also clearly communicates to them that IS is concerned about user perception of service. Clearly, the problems surfacing in such a survey need to be acted on promptly if the survey is to be an effective control.

Another important set of controls are those relating to staff. Reports which monitor personnel turnover trends over time provide a critical early insight into the problems of this notoriously unstable group. These data allow timely action to be taken on items such as sensitivity of leadership, adequacy of salary levels, and working climate conditions. In the same vein, development of formal training plans and periodic measurement of progress toward their implementation is an important management tool in both ensuring a professionally relevant group and maintaining morale.

In relation to IS operations, reports and other procedures for generating absolute measures of operational service levels are very important. These include data on items such as trends in network uptime, ability to meet schedules on batch jobs, average transaction response time by type of system, number of mis-sends and other operational errors, and a customer complaint log. Critical to the effectiveness of these systems is not just that they be set up but that they be maintained and adhered to on a constant basis. It is easy to allow quality control errors to creep in and show better performance than is actually present. Those issues are discussed further in Chapter 8, with a particular emphasis on the fact that all dimensions of service cannot be simultaneously optimized. Additionally, reliable records concerning installed equipment and its location is important infrastructure data. Lack of sound fact-based registers of equipment opens the possibility of excess equipment, and inadequate and excessive payments of bills.

In relation to systems development the reports on development projects (in terms of elapsed time and work-months expended vis-à-vis budget) are a critical early warning system in assessing overall performance. The type of data needed and appropriately available varies widely by company. The company's maturity in dealing with IS technology, the relative strategic role of IS development and operations, and the corporation's general approach to managerial control also influence both the form and detail with which these issues are approached.

IS AUDIT FUNCTION[2]

This department provides a vital check and balance on the IS activity as it moves to meet cost and service goals. Located as a part of the office of the general auditor, the elements of its basic missions are threefold. The first is to ensure that appropriate standards for the IS development and operations functions have been developed and installed consistent with the control architecture. With both technology and the organization's familiarity with it changing, development of these standards is not a one-time job but requires continuous effort.

The second mission is to ensure that these standards are being adhered to by the various operating units. This includes both regular progress reviews and the conduct of surprise audits. These audits should reduce exposure to fraud and loss. Ensuring adherence to these standards should help reduce operations errors and omissions and increase user confidence and satisfaction. These audits also act as a prod towards improving operating efficiency.

The third mission is to be actively involved in both the systems' design and maintenance functions to ensure that systems are designed to be easily auditable and that maintenance changes do not create unintended problems. This clearly compromises the supposedly independent mission of the auditor, but is a necessary accommodation to the real world. Such involve-

[2] This is an introductory discussion to emphasize the role and importance of auditing. For a fuller treatment see B. Allen, "Embezzler's Guide to the Computer," *Harvard Business Review* (July–August 1975).

ment helps ensure the smooth running of the final system. Successful execution of all three missions help to reduce the amount of outside assistance needed by the firm.

These apparently straightforward tasks, however, have turned out to be very hard to implement in the real world. The three main causes of this IS auditing difficulty are the following. The first and most important block is the difficulty in recruiting necessary staff skills. Operating at the intersection of two disciplines (IS and auditing), good practice demands thorough mastery of both. In fact, because IS auditing frequently turns out to be a dead-end career path, staff members who can be retained often are sufficiently deficient in both disciplines to be ineligible as practitioners in either. Better salaries and visibly attractive career paths are essential precondition steps to reverse this situation.

Second, the art of IS auditing continually lags behind the challenges posed by new technologies. Today, understanding methodologies for controlling batch systems for computers is not very relevant for a world dominated by complex operating systems, networks, and online technologies. Managing catch-up for these lags poses a key IS auditing challenge for the foreseeable future.

Third, there has been an unevenness of senior management support for IS auditing due in part to the lack of formally defined requirements from an outside authority. Support for a strong IS auditing function tends to be very episodic, with periods of strong interest following either a conspicuous internal or conspicuous external failure. (This interest, however, tends to erode rapidly as time passes and the calamity is over.)

The IS auditing function at this time has a poorly defined role in most organizations. It is typically part of the internal auditing organization and often does not report to senior management. This is a function that deserves serious consideration by senior management.

SUMMARY

Many of these issues are clearly similar to the general issues of management control which face an organization. Several dimensions, however, do make it especially interesting. The first is posed by the rapid changes in the underlying technology and the long time span required for users to adapt to new technologies. The phase 1 and phase 2 technologies require a commitment to R&D and user learning which is in direct conflict with the chargeout techniques appropriate for the phase 3 and phase 4 technologies. It is very easy for an organization to become too uniform in its control system and try to standardize, in order to use systems "efficiently", and as a by-product stamp out appropriate innovation. In most organizations today, different divisions (which are at separate stages of learning and using varying mixes of technologies) require quite different control approaches. Further, as organizational learning occurs, different types of control approaches become appropriate. Thus quite apart from any breakthroughs in the general cluster of IS control notions, their practice in an organization undergoes a continual process of evolution. In most organizations there is continuing change in what constitutes good IS control practice.

As IS technologies bury themselves deeper into the fabric of an organization's operation the penalties of uneven performance of their technology may come to have very severe consequences for the organization as a whole. As a company (department or system) evolves from turnaround to factory to support very different control philosophies become appropriate.

When these comments are added to the issues, discussed at the beginning of the chapter concerning the changing corporate environment and evolving corporate planning and control processes (in a world shifting from make to buy in software), the full complexity of the IS management control problem is apparent. Different organizations must adopt quite different control approaches, which must evolve over time to deal with their changing corporate environment, changing strategic role of IS technologies, and changing IS technologies.

Case 6–1 □ Lane Bryant Data Management*

Prior to 1972, major data processing organizations existed in both the Retail and Mail Order divisions of Lane Bryant, Inc. Beginning in 1972 and extending through 1974, a major reorganization of these activities resulted in the centralization of data processing within the Data Management Center (DMC) located in Indianapolis, Indiana. This process required both a substantial amount of facilities and software conversion plus a detailed study of the organizational issues facing DMC. This later study was completed in 1972 and the establishment of a permanent organization structure for DMC was essentially complete in early 1974.

1973 was a transition year for DMC. The major technological problems associated with the reorganization had been resolved. Most of the systems serving the Mail Order Division (MOD) had been converted and the phase-out of the last "local" computer was in May 1974. Conversion of those systems serving the Retail Division (RET) was also nearing completion.

The highest priority issue facing the DMC was the need to reorient its organization structure and operating procedures to deal with this more orderly world. Among the action recommendations presented to management by a systems consultant at this point were:

1. The preparation of a set of project administration and control procedures for continuing systems development.
2. The establishment of a mechanism for identifying, recording, reporting, and controlling DMC costs.

These two recommendations were closely related. The capability for project control would have to be founded, in large part, on the prior capability of the organization to quantify and express project-related costs in sufficient detail.

DMC—ORGANIZATION AND OPERATION

The functions of computer system design, computer programming and testing, computer standards and documentation, and computer operation were all centralized within DMC. One exception to this overall principle involved the location of certain systems analysts (in New York) for both the Retail and Mail Order divisions. The responsibility for systems development

* This case was prepared by Associate Professor Richard L. Nolan and Assistant Professor Gerard G. Johnson as a basis for class discussion rather than to illustrate either effective or ineffective handling of an administrative situation.

was designed to be split among operating and data processing personnel. A typical development project would be managed by division personnel and staffed largely with DMC personnel.

Personnel within DMC were organized into three groups—Administrative, Operations, and Development (Systems & Programming). Exhibit 1 illustrates the responsibility accounting structure adopted in 1975.

The Administrative section consisted of the management and staff of DMC. This section designed and maintained DMC policies and procedures and generally coordinated the activities of the other sections. It was also responsible for the design of the DMC accounting and control system, for quality assurance, manpower management, documentation and liaison with operating divisions.

The Operations section was composed of two units—Central Operations and Terminal Operations. DMC personnel operated all company telecommunications facilities (located principally in New York and Indianapolis) and Terminal Operations was organized into three units according to (1) location and (2) the type of equipment operated. The principal terminal equipment within DMC was Mohawk Data 2400 Series. These units were used to transmit and receive data from both the New York (Retail) and Indianapolis (Mail Order) locations. A Singer 10 Series was used exclusively on behalf of the Retail Division to accept store-generated cash register data (point of sale).

The Central Operations section was responsible for the overall operation of two IBM 370/145 type systems together with associated I/O equipment. This section was, in turn, divided into a processing unit and a control unit (program library, scheduling, etc.). In addition to these units, there was an Operations Software Support Unit (operating system maintenance and documentation) and an Operations Technical Resources Unit (vendor liaison, equipment forecasting and planning, technical planning, etc.).

The majority of systems development personnel were located at DMC in Indianapolis. There were, however, two smaller groups of systems analysts located at the company's New York headquarters. Programmers and analysts were organized into separate groups which served the needs of the company's two major operating divisions—Mail Order and Retail. This structure was adopted, in part, to offset the effects of physical centralization to enable DP personnel to understand more thoroughly the user requirements. Within the two major groupings (MOD/RET), analysts and programmers were organized into teams with explicit project responsibility. New York systems personnel were involved primarily in liaison and conceptual design activities.

DMC operated basically a batch processing system. A few applications—such as the Mail Order Division's order entry system—operated in real time but this was the exception rather than the rule. Most operations were planned to occur according to a fixed schedule although I/O problems

EXHIBIT 1

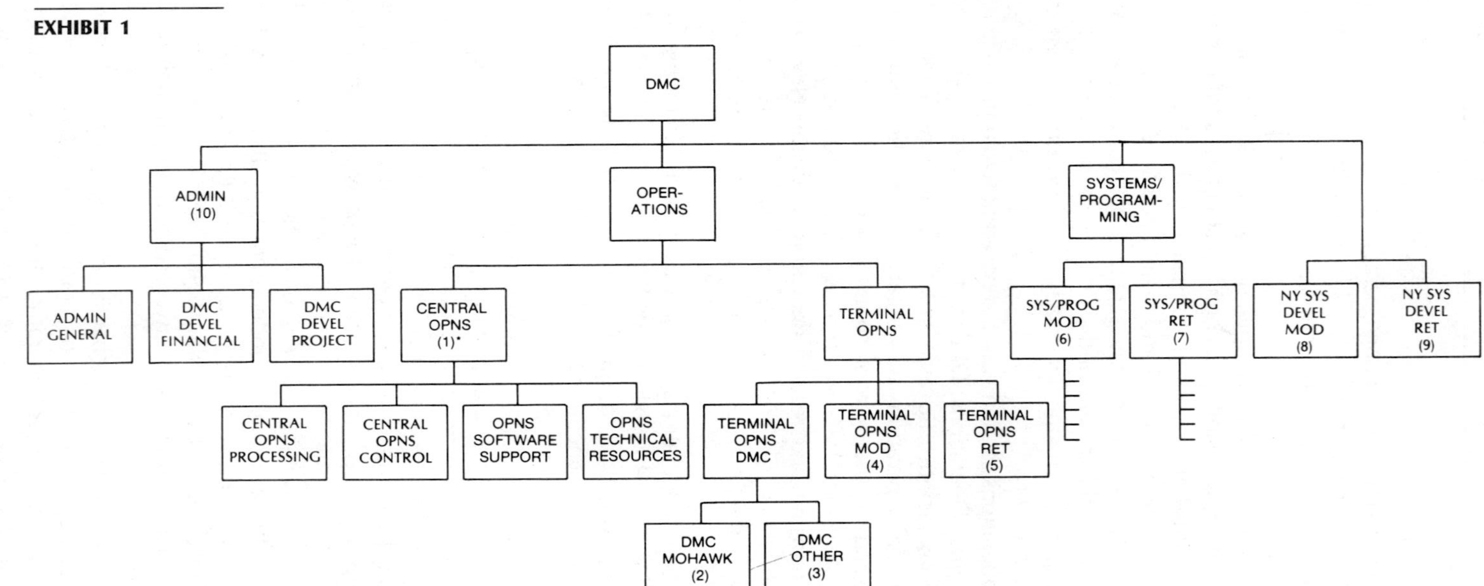

* Numbers are reference numbers for the responsibility centers that correspond to the other exhibits.

frequently required short-term schedule changes. DMC looked at overall computer usage in terms of three general categories:

1. Operations—scheduled use on behalf of operating division applications.
2. Development—use on behalf of DMC personnel engaged in developing new applications or revisions.
3. DMC internal—use by DMC personnel for strictly internal requirements (e.g., job accounting and chargeback system operation).

DMC COST ACCOUNTING—GENERAL

DMC had designed and was operating a system which was used for identifying DMC expenditures by class and object. These expenditures, in turn, were aggregated and distributed to user divisions by application.[1] The general approach used to accomplish this distribution is illustrated in Exhibit 2.

In its simplest form, the financial subsystem first recorded and identified all the financial transactions encountered in the operation of DMC. These individual transactions were grouped and summarized by expense center within the division. (Exhibit 1 also served as a basis for identifying these expense centers.)

Costs were collected by detailed expense center (e.g., Central Operations

EXHIBIT 2

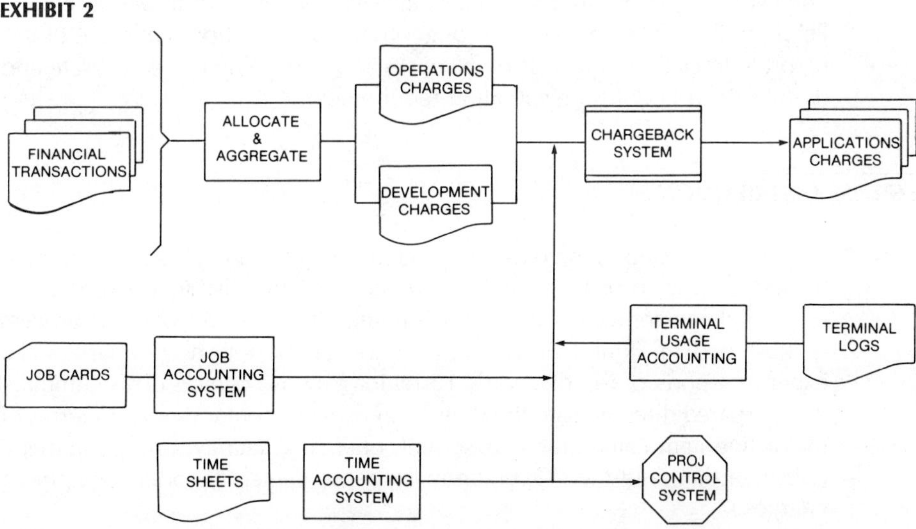

[1] As used here, "application" refers to a subsystem, including input/output (I/O), operated on behalf of a user division function.

Processing, Central Operations Control, and Operations Software Support) and then distributed to functional categories—Operations or Development. Operational inputs were collected from three main sources—job cards, time sheets, and terminal logs—and used to distribute functional costs to individual applications. These, then, were summarized by division.

EXPENSE CENTER ACCOUNTING

The basic control unit within DMC was the expense center. Individual, detailed expense accounts were maintained for each administrative unit of DMC. Exhibit 3 is an example of one such statement prepared for the Mail Order Division unit of the Systems/Programming Section. Equally detailed reports were also available, for example, for each project team within this expense center. All such expenses, with the exception of the "rent" item were direct expenses of the expense center. The rent item represented an allocation of overall DMC occupancy (rent) costs. Expense center reports were also summarized into groupings according to function. For example, the Systems/Programming Section summary appears as Exhibit 4 and the overall summary as Exhibit 5.

As the formats of Exhibits 3, 4, and 5 suggests, DMC had adopted a budgetary control approach to managing expense center operations. Budgets were negotiated and established the last two months of the fiscal year and incorporated into the data base used by the expense report generated. The expense center input ran to 27 pages for the one-month period ending February 28, 1975. Managers throughout the organization made use of this report to track their forecasts of expenses and to develop more accurate and useful forecasts of future spending requirements.

EXPENSE DISTRIBUTION

The second step in the process of determining the amounts to be charged to operating divisions was the distribution of administrative expenses to functional categories. For the period ending 28 February 1975, this process is illustrated in Exhibit 6. The top section of the report summarizes the expense reports of the division's 10 major expense centers. This summary was prepared directly from the individual expense center reports in terms of major line item categories—personnel, operating, facility, and equipment. (Observe that only the "Operations" expense centers reported equipment charges.)

The expenses of the administration (Admin.) expense center were then distributed to the other nine expense centers, based on the ratio of personnel

EXHIBIT 3

LB-FCS REPORTING PERIOD FOR L.B. FINANCIAL CONTROL SYSTEM
9FC020-1 FEB(4-WKS) ENDING 02 28 75 GENERAL OPERATING EXPENSE RPT DATE 03/13/75

DIVISION: DMC EXPENSE CENTER: SYS/PROG-SUMMARY

ACCOUNT NO. MJ-MINOR	DESCRIPTION........		CURRENT ACTUAL	CURRENT BUDGET	CURRENT VARIANCE	CURRENT PERCENT	SEASON-TO-DATE ACTUAL	SEASON-TO-DATE BUDGET	SEASON-TO-DATE VARIANCE	SEASON-TO-DATE PERCENT
10-PAYROLL										
10 1010	PAYROLL-REGULAR		34 39,306	34 39,632	326-		39,306	39,632	326-	
10 1020	PAYROLL-OVERTIME		54	25	29+		54	25	29+	
10	PAYROLL	TOTAL	39,360	39,657	297-	.7-	39,360	39,657	297-	.7-
12-BENEFITS										
12 1500	EMPLOYEE BENEFITS		5,965	4,756	1,209+	25.4+	5,965	4,756	1,209+	25.4+
12	BENEFITS	TOTAL	5,965	4,756	1.209+	25.4+	5,956	4,756	1,209+	25.4+
15-OPERATING EXPENSES										
15 2003	TRAVEL		2,760	1,848	912+	49.3+	2,760	1,848	912+	49.3+
15 2004	OUTSIDE SERVICE		38		38+		38		38+	
15 2005	TRAVEL-EDUCATION			650	650-	100.0-		650	650-	100.0-
15 2012	DUES & SUBSCRIPTIONS			65	65-			65	65-	
15 2013	EDUCATION		242	656	414-	63.1-	242	656	414-	63.1-
15	OPERATING EXPENSES	TOTAL	3,040	3,219	179-	5.5-	3,040	3,219	179-	5.5-
17-FACILITY										
17 2510	DMC RENT		1,518	1,528	10-		1,518	1,528	10-	
17	FACILITY	TOTAL	1,518	1,528	10-	.6-	1,518	1,528	10-	.6-
TOTAL SYS.PROG/SUMMARY			49,883	49,160	723+	1.4+	49,883	49,160	723+	1.4+

EXHIBIT 4

LB-FCS REPORTING PERIOD FOR L.B. FINANCIAL CONTROL SYSTEM
9FC020-2 FEB(4-WKS) ENDING 02 28 75 DETAIL OPERATING EXPENSE RPT DATE 03/13/75

DIVISION: DMC . EXPENSE CENTER: SYS/PROG-MOD

ACCOUNT NO. MJ-MINOR	DESCRIPTION..........			CURRENT ACTUAL		CURRENT BUDGET	CURRENT VARIANCE	CURRENT PERCENT	SEASON-TO-DATE ACTUAL	SEASON-TO-DATE BUDGET	SEASON-TO-DATE VARIANCE	SEASON-TO-DATE PERCENT
10-PAYROLL												
10 1010	PAYROLL-REGULAR		16	19,344	16	19,377	33-		19,344	19,377	33-	
10	PAYROLL	TOTAL		19,344		19,377	33-	.1-	19,344	19,377	33-	.1-
12-BENEFITS												
12 1500	EMPLOYEE BENEFITS			2,956		2,325	631+	27.1+	2,956	2,325	631+	27.1+
12	BENEFITS	TOTAL		2,956		2,325	631+	27.1	2,956	2,325	631+	27.1+
15-OPERATING EXPENSES												
15 2003	TRAVEL		5	599	3	693	94-		599	693	94-	
15 2005	TRAVEL-EDUCATION				2	218	218-			218	218-	
15 2012	DUES & SUBSCRIPTIONS					50	50-			50	50-	
15	OPERATING EXPENSES	TOTAL		599		961	362-	37.6-	599	961	362-	37.6-
17-FACILITY												
17 2510	DMC RENT			640		644	4-					
17	FACILITY	TOTAL		640		644	4-	.6-	640	644	4-	.6-
TOTAL SYS/PROG-MOD				23,539		23,307	232+	.9+	23,539	23,307	232+	.9+

EXHIBIT 5

LB-FCS REPORTING PERIOD FOR L.B. FINANCIAL CONTROL SYSTEM
9FC020-1 FEB(4-WKS) ENDING 02 28 75 GENERAL OPERATING EXPENSE RPT DATE 03/13/75

DIVISION: DMC EXPENSE CENTER:SUMMARY(INDPLS AND NY SYS DEV)

ACCOUNT NO. MJ-MINOR	DESCRIPTION........		CURRENT ACTUAL	CURRENT BUDGET	CURRENT VARIANCE	CURRENT PERCENT	SEASON-TO-DATE ACTUAL	SEASON-TO-DATE BUDGET	SEASON-TO-DATE VARIANCE	SEASON-TO-DATE PERCENT
10-PAYROLL										
10 1010	PAYROLL-REGULAR		97 102,946	98 100,640	2,306+		102,946	100,640	2,306+	
10 1020	PAYROLL-OVERTIME		367	1,058	691-	65.3	367	1,058	691-	65.3
10 1030	PAYROLL-NIGHT BONUS		761	1,060	299-		761	1,060	299-	
10 1050	PAYROLL ADJUSTMENT FOR 4-5-4		8,014-		8,014-	100.0+	8,014-		8,014-	100.0+
10	PAYROLL	TOTAL	96,060	102,758	6,698-	6.5-	96,060	102,758	6,698-	6.5-
12-BENEFITS										
12 1500	EMPLOYEE BENEFITS		15,782	12,248	3,534+	28.8+	15,782	12,248	3,534+	28.8+
12	BENEFITS	TOTAL	15,782	12,248	3,534+	28.8+	15,782	12,248	3,534+	28.8+
15-OPERATING EXPENSES										
15 2002	PROPERTY TAX		2,154	2,154			2,154	2,154		
15 2003	TRAVEL		4,345	4,369	24-		4,345	4,369	24-	
15 2004	OUTSIDE SERVICE		891	894	3-		891	894	3-	
15 2005	TRAVEL-EDUCATION			975	975-	100.0-		975	975-	100.0-
15 2006	RECRUITMENT/RELOCATION		3,330	5,350	2,020-	37.7-	3,330	5,350	2,020	37.7-
15 2008	ENTERTAINMENT		161	262	101-		161	262	101-	
15 2010	SUPPLIES		2,359	1,720	639+	37.1+	2,359	1,720	639+	37.1+
15 2011	LETTER POSTAGE		10	20	10-		10	20	10-	
15 2012	DUES & SUBSCRIPTIONS		34	355	321-	90.4-	34	355	321-	90.4-
15 2013	EDUCATION		610	3,151	2,541-	80.6-	610	3,151	2,541-	80.6-
15 2014	SMALL OFFICE FIXTURES		80	475	395-	83.1-	80	475	395-	83.1-
15 2016	OFFICE EQUIPMENT RENTAL		801	800	1+		801	800	1+	
15 2018	TELEPHONE		2,868	1,750	1,118+	63.8+	2,868	1,750	1,118+	63.8+
15 2020	FREIGHT			75	75-			75	75-	
15 2024	DEPRECIATION		1,496	1,431	65+		1,496	1,431	65+	
15 2026	INSURANCE		372	440	68-		372	440	68-	
15 2028	ACCOUNTING-PAYROLL		600	600			600	600		
15	OPERATING EXPENSES	TOTAL	20,111	24,821	4,710-	18.9-	20,111	24,821	4,710-	18.9-
17-FACILITY										
17 2510	DMC RENT		6,805	6,850	45-		6,805	6,850	45-	
17 2520	COMPUTER ROOM ELECTRIC		1,308	1,075	233+		1,308	1,075	233+	
17 2530	FACILITY REPAIRS & SUPPLIES		481	175	306+	174.8+	481	175	306+	174.8+
17	FACILITY	TOTAL	8,594	8,100	494+	6.0+	8,594	8,100	494+	6.0+
20-COMPUTER EXPENSES										
20 3000	COMPUTER EQUIPMENT		86,654	85,448	1,206+		86,654	85,448	1,206+	
20 3100	UNIT RECORD EQUIPMENT		8,414	9,022	608-	6.7-	8,414	9,022	608-	6.7-
20 3200	SOFTWARE		739	1,251	512-	40.9-	739	1,251	512-	40.9-
20 3300	COMMUNICATION LINES		4,350	4,229	121+		4,350	4,229	121+	
20 3500	TAPE/DISK STORAGE		2,419	2,748	329-	11.9-	2,419	2,748	329-	11.9-
20	COMPUTER EXPENSES	TOTAL	102,576	102,698	122-	.1-	102,576	102,698	122-	.1-
TOTAL DMC			243,123	250,625	7,502-	2.9-	243,123	250,625	7,502-	2.9-

EXHIBIT 6 □ Expense Distribution Report ***(Period of February 1975)***

		OPERATIONS				
			TERMINALS			
	TOTAL	CENTRAL OPERATIONS	DMC-MOHAWK	DMC-OTHER	MOD	RETAIL
PERSONNEL EXPENSES						
PAYROLL	104,074	24,461	2,493	831	9,017	8,288
BENEFITS	15,782	3,685	375	125	1,355	1,246
4-5-4 PAYROLL ADJ.	8,014–					
TOTAL PERSONNEL	111,842	28,146	2,868	956	10,372	9,534
TOTAL OPERATING	20,111	4,277	-0-	-0-	520	-0-
TOTAL FACILITY	8,594	4,243	277	277	-0-	-0-
TOTAL EQUIPMENT	102,576	58,898	2,449	3,536	24,785	12,908
TOTAL EXPENSES	243,123	95,564	5,594	4,769	35,677	22,442
*EXPENSE ALLOCATION		4,759	485	162	1,754	1,612
CHARGEBACK EXPENSES	243,123	100,323	6,079	4,931	37,431	24,054
			(C)	(D)	(E)	(F)
USED COMPUTER (75%)**	75,242			2,465—BURROUGHS 2,466—SINGER 4,931		
LESS MISC. INCOME ON USED COMPUTER TIME:	-0-	-0-				
NET USED COMPUTER COST		75,242	(A) (75%)			
NET UNUSED COMPUTER COST		25,081	(B) (25%)			
NET DMC EXPENSES	243,123					

*ALLOCATION RATE = .19455 (17,725 ÷ 104,074 − 12,966)
**1,904 ÷ (28 DAYS × 144 × .630 MULTIPROGRAMMING FACTOR)
1,904 ÷ 2,540 = 75 percent

costs to total personnel costs (excluding Admin.). These expenses were then totaled to produce the item "Chargeback Expenses."

One additional operation was then performed. All Central Operations expenses were presumed to be "computer expenses." These were therefore divided into net *USED* and *UNUSED* computer costs. This operation attempted to assign (more accurately) costs based on operating division usage of actual computer time and it treated *UNUSED* computer costs more or less as an overhead item.

CHARGEBACK

The chargeback system consisted of four subsidiary information systems (see Exhibit 7):

1. Financial accounting (financial reporting system)
2. Job accounting (equipment utilization reporting system)

	DEVELOPMENT				ADMIN.
	SYSTEM/PROGRAMMING		NY SYSTEM DEVELOPMENT		*
TOTAL OPERATIONS	MOD	RETAIL	MOD	RETAIL	
45,090	19,344	13,974	6,862	5,838	12,966
6,786	2,956	2,101	1,032	,954	1,953
					8,014–
51,876	22,300	16,075	7,894	6,792	6,905
4,797	599	2,441	158	3,813	8,303
4,797	640	640	-0-	-0-	2,517
102,576	-0-	-0-	-0-	-0-	-0-
164,046	23,539	19,156	8,052	10,605	17,725
8,772	3,763	2,719	1,335	1,136	17,725–
172,818	27,302	21,875	9,387	11,741	-0-
	(G)	(H)	(I)	(J)	

3. Time accounting (personnel time reporting system)
4. Terminal usage accounting

JOB ACCOUNTING SYSTEM

The job accounting system was based upon a built-in software package which observed and recorded detailed data for each job run on the main system. Job control cards (see Exhibit 8 for an illustration) are used to record various pieces of information and to initiate the job accounting process for each run. The job name (e.g., "AR"), purpose (production, test & compile, rerun, etc.), division name, project number, and various other items are entered on the job control card.

The job accounting software automatically observed, recorded, and stored several additional pieces of information—elapsed CPU time, wall time, amount of memory used, devices used, and number of times, etc. This information was stored on a disk, reviewed for accuracy, and used as a basis

EXHIBIT 7 □ Division Chargeback Summary Report

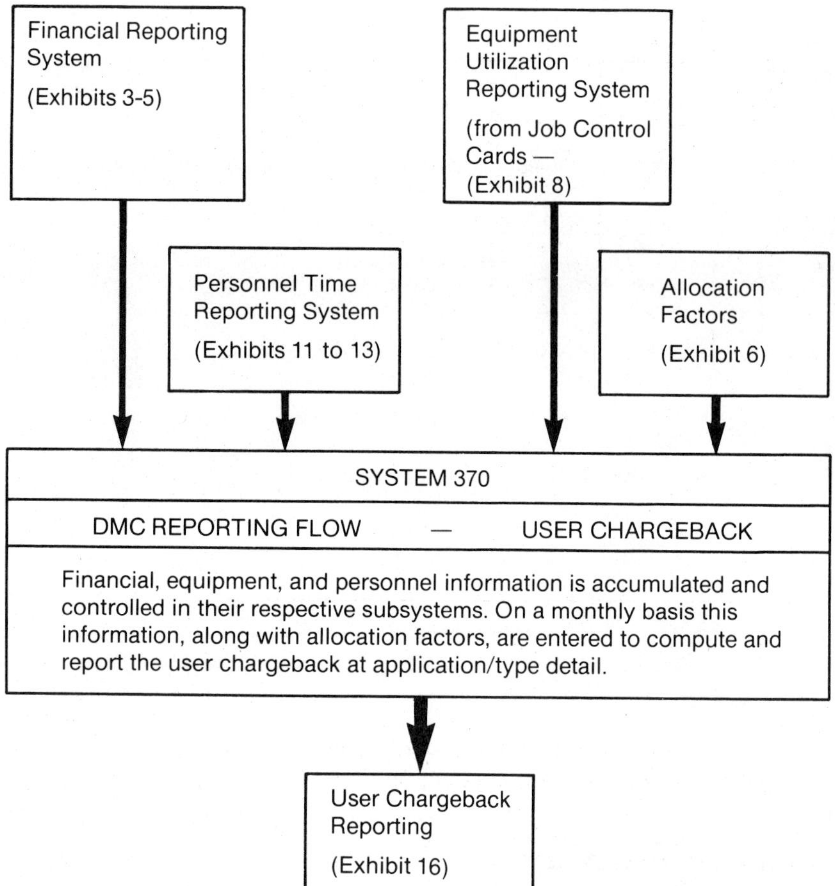

for generating the statistics required to distribute Central Operations costs among applications.

TIME ACCOUNTING SYSTEM

The time accounting system generated a detailed record of the activities of all "development" personnel during the period. Standing behind the time accounting system was an evolving concept of project control and a project coding system. All development activities were coded at the source by

EXHIBIT 8 □ Job Control Card

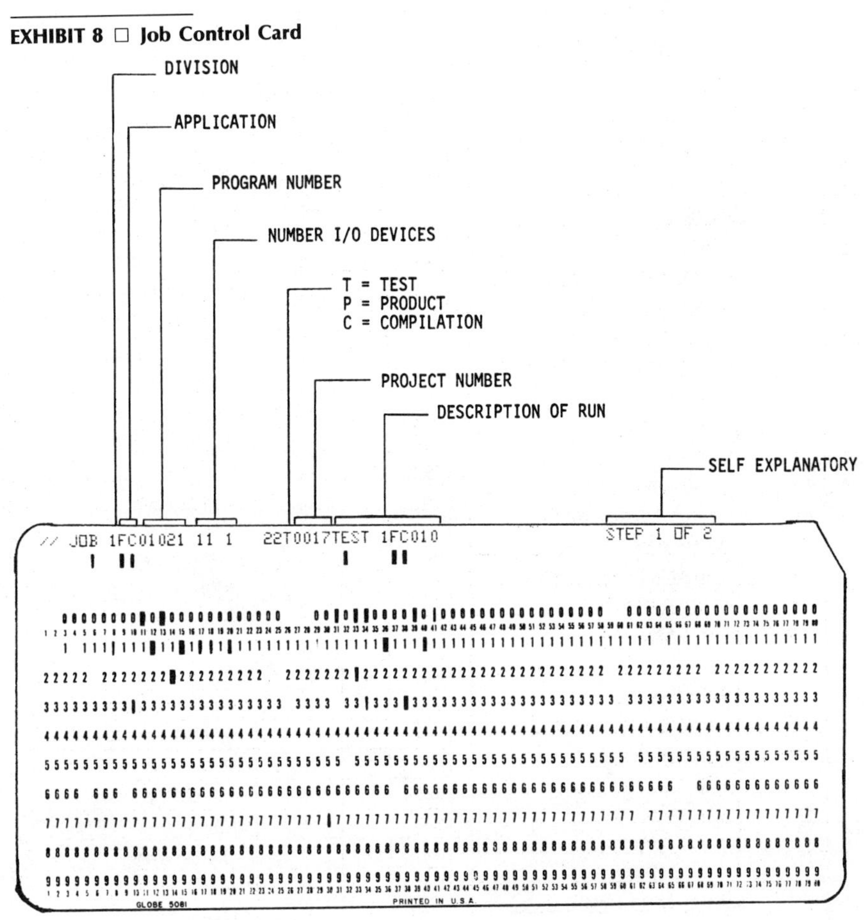

project number (see Exhibit 9 for a partial history of projects codes). Ongoing software maintenance activities were also supposed to be identified with a specific project number. In many cases, the project code exactly matched an application. In other cases, project codes were used for activities which could not be associated with an identifiable application. Generally, however, each project number was keyed to a specific project (e.g., Project 0052 with the Retail Division's nationwide Accounts Receivable application). The first digit of the project number was used to identify the source of the activity (6 = overhead, 9 = emergency, 7 = user request, 3 = operating procedures, etc.).

In addition to the project number, DMC management was beginning to require each analyst and programmer to indicate from a standard project profile code which phase of the overall project is involved (see Exhibit 10).

EXHIBIT 9

CURRENT PROJECTS

PROJECT NUMBER	DIV.	APPLICATION CODE	PROJECT NAME
6000	*	ZZ	GENERAL ADMINISTRATION (NON-PROJECT i.e., TEAM LEADER MEETINGS, ETC.)
6001	*	ZZ	EDUCATION
6002	*	ZZ	VACATION
6003	*	ZZ	ILLNESS
6004	*	ZZ	PERSONAL TIME (OFF PREMISE)
6005	*	ZZ	HOLIDAY
7000	*	ZZ	USER REQUEST ADMINISTRATION
9999	*	ZZ	EMERGENCY MAINTENANCE ADMINISTRATION
9999	*	**	EMERGENCY MAINTENANCE
0002	1	MR	MARKET RESEARCH
0012	2	ST	STARS
0015	9	CB	DMC CHARGEBACK SYSTEM
0017	*	FC	FINANCIAL CONTROL SYSTEM
0019	2	*	YEAR END REPORTING
0022	1	MB	STAPLE REPLENISHMENT (MINIMAX)
0025	1	**	MOD 3330 CONVERSION
0026	1	SA	SELECTIVE ADDRESSING
0028	1	OE	ORDER CONTROL
0029	1	RM	MERCHANDISE/ORDER RETURNS
0031	1	MR	STATISTICAL ANALYSIS
0032	2	CR	RETAIL P.O.S.
0033	*	RA	PROFIT CONTRIBUTION
0034	9	TR	DMC TIME REPORTING
0035	9	VS	OS/VS1 CONVERSION
0036	2	MR	MANAGERS REPORT PHASE II
3002	2	**	OPERATIONS CLEANUP * GENERAL PROGRAM CHANGES
0037	9	SC	PRE-SCHEDULER
0038	2	AN	ACCOUNT NUMBERING MICROFICHE
0040	2	MS	MERCHANDISE REPORTING SYSTEM
0041	9	ZZ	TECH RESOURCES ONGOING SUPPORT
0042	9	ZZ	TRP PHYSICAL PLAN - DMC
0043	9	ZZ	TRP F.E.P. PHASES I, II, III
0044	9	ZZ	TRP SOURCE PROGRAM PACKAGE
0045	9	ZZ	TRP BURROUGHS BANKING SYSTEM
0046	9	ZZ	TRP CHICAGO DATA COLLECTION
0047	9	ZZ	TRP N.Y. KEY DISK
0048	1	IC	END SEASON PROFILING
0049	1	MB	MEDIA ANALYSIS ENHANCEMENTS
0050	9	ZZ	TRP RESEARCH
0051	2	CR	NATIONWIDE P.O.S.
0052	2	AR	NATIONWIDE A/R
0053	1	CF	CUSTOMER DATA BASE
0054	1	PE	PERSONNEL EVALUATION
0055	1	VS	PURCHASE ORDER MGMT.
0056	1	ZZ	M.O.D. L.R.S.P.
0057	2	ZZ	RETAIL L.R.S.P.
0058	1	IM	INVENTORY MANAGEMENT
3003	*	**	PRE-PROJECT INVESTIGATION
3004	*	**	MINI-TEST FILES
0059	1	IM	GATHER FILE STATISTICS
0060	1	RM	MERCHANDISE/ORDER RETURNS-MEDIA
0061	9	PJ	PROJECT REPORTING
0062	2	MR	MANAGER'S REPORT PHASE III
0063	8	PY	CORPORATE PAYROLL
0064	2	MS	MERCHANDISE CLASS REPORTING
0065	1	AP	APPROVAL SYSTEM
0066	2	**	PROFIT & LOSS ENHANCEMENTS

* ENTER THE DIVISION CODE REPRESENTING THE AREA YOU WORK IN - 1 = MAIL ORDER, 2 = RETAIL

** ENTER THE APPLICATION CODE OF THE SYSTEM YOU ARE WORKINGON

NOTE: ALL USER REQUESTS HAVE A PROJECT NUMBER IN THE 7000 SERIES. FOR EXAMPLE, USER REQUEST #334 IS PROJECT NUMBER 7334. BE SURE TO ENTER THE PROPER APPLICATION CODE.

This information, although not required as an input to the chargeback system, was destined to be a major input to an evolving formal project control system.

Exhibit 11 illustrates the format used for input to the time accounting system. Personnel were instructed to enter actual hours worked on project-related activities, not standard or forecast hours. An individual could, for example, record 28 hours one week and 61 hours the following week (all

EXHIBIT 10 □ Task List

TASK NUMBER	SUB TASK NO.	TASK DESCRIPTION
10		PRELIMINARY STUDY
11		DEFINE STUDY OBJECTIVES
12		DATA GATHERING AND ANALYSIS
13		SPECIFY USER REQUIREMENTS
14		EVALUATE MAJOR SYSTEM DESIGN
15		APPROVE ACTIVITY COMPLETION & FURTHER DEVELOPMENT
20		SYSTEM DESIGN
21		PRESENT SYSTEM DESCRIPTION
22		FUNCTIONAL SPECIFICATIONS
23		OPERATIONAL REQUIREMENTS
24		CLERICAL FUNCTIONS
25		TECHNICAL DESIGN
26		PROJECT PLAN
27		APPROVE ACTIVITY COMPLETION & FURTHER DEVELOPMENT
30		PROGRAM DESIGN
31		ORDER HARDWARE AND FORMS
32		COMPONENT DESIGN
33		RECORD DOCUMENTATION
34		PROGRAM SPECIFICATIONS
35		PROJECT PLAN
36		APPROVE ACTIVITY COMPLETION
40		PROGRAMMING
41		PROGRAM DESIGN AND CODING
42		PROGRAM UNIT TEST
43		PROGRAM DOCUMENTATION
44		INTEGRATED TEST PREPARATION
45		INTEGRATED TEST
46		APPROVE ACTIVITY COMPLETION
50		PRE-INSTALLATION
51		PREPARE USER MANUAL
52		PREPARE OPERATIONS DOCUMENTATION
53		DATA COLLECTION
54		INSTALLATION PLANNING
55		APPROVE ACTIVITY COMPLETION

EXHIBIT 11

DAILY TIME SHEET

TEAM # ____ (1)   MAN # ____ (2)   DATE __/__/__ (3)

PROJECT NUMBER	DIV.	APPLICATION	PROGRAM NUMBER	CAUSE*	TASK NUMBER	SUB TASK NO.	TIME SPENT HRS.	TIME SPENT MIN.	START TIME	STOP TIME
9	13	14	16	21	22	24	25	27		

*EMERGENCY MAINTENANCE ONLY

U - USER
O - OPERATIONS
P - PROGRAM
H - HARDWARE

R - REMOTE OPERATIONS
S - SOFTWARE
D - DOCUMENTATION
E - EMERGENCY ENHANCEMENTS

X - OTHER (TO BE DEFINED)

programmers and analysts were on salary). The object of this procedure was to develop more accurate and realistic time forecasts for project activities. Exhibit 12 shows the Time Report by Person; Exhibit 13 shows the Time Report by Project.

The time accounting system provided the basic statistics used to distribute development costs among applications. As might be expected, certain applications exhibited relatively higher development expenses than operations expenses. Others exhibited the reverse. The time accounting system also served as the basis for personnel and project reporting.

TERMINAL USAGE ACCOUNTING SYSTEM

The terminal usage accounting system represented a straightforward and simple device for apportioning the cost of shared terminal systems (principally the Mohawk Data 2400 Series). I/O data was logged (Exhibit 14) with the same basic criteria as the job accounting system (division, application, program number, and time). In this way, the cost of the terminals could be assigned to the two major operating divisions. For example, in the period ending 28 February 1975, the Mail Order Division accounted for 38 percent of the total used time. No breakdown of used/unused time was kept.

REPORTING

Three major reports were available to operating division management:

1. Expense Distribution Report (see Exhibit 6).
2. Division Chargeback Summary Report (see Exhibit 16).
3. Report of Charges (Exhibit 15).

Both operating divisions treat EDP charges in approximately the same way. The total charge made to the division for EDP services was treated as division overhead and allocated to individual profit centers as such.

The final step in the process is illustrated by Exhibit 16. (The letters (A), (B), (C), etc., are keys to corresponding columns on Exhibit 6.) The Divisional Chargeback Report summarizes the results of the actual chargeback process of overall costs charged to each division. Five categories of cost were summarized to each division:

1. Central Operations—the sum of USED and UNUSED computer.
2. Terminal Operations—Mohawk.
3. Terminal Operations—Other.
4. Systems/Programming.
5. New York Systems.

EXHIBIT 12 □ Time Report by Person

```
REPORT NO.  9TR020-R1      DIVISION  DMC INTERNAL      L. B.  DATA MANAGEMENT CENTER          ATD AVAILABLE HOURS  640
DATE-TIME   05/23/75-1051                         T I M E   R E P O R T   B Y   P E R S O N               WEEK ENDING 05/22/75
```

TEAM MAN #	NAME	PROJECT	APPLICATION	PROG	CAUSE TASK	SUB	WTD	MTD	ATD
21	BRINEY	0017 FINANCIAL CTL SYSTEM	FC FINANCIAL CTL SYSTEM	1			.00	12.00	12.00
		0017 FINANCIAL CTL SYSTEM	FC FINANCIAL CTL SYSTEM	1	62 USER TRAINING		.00	3.00	27.00
		0017 FINANCIAL CTL SYSTEM	FC FINANCIAL CTL SYSTEM	1	64 USER SYSTEM TESTING		16.00	16.00	69.45
					TOTAL FOR APPLICATION FC	*	16.00	31.00	207.15
					TOTAL FOR PROJECT 0017	**	16.00	31.00	208.15
		6000 GENERAL ADM	ZZ	9			30.00	101.00	430.45
					TOTAL FOR APPLICATION ZZ	*	30.00	101.00	430.45
					TOTAL FOR PROJECT 6000	**	30.00	101.00	440.45
					TOTAL FOR PERSON 21	***	45.00	132.00	715.45
22	MEYER	0015 DMC CHARGEBACK SYS	CB DMC CHARGEBACK SYS	9			.00	3.00	55.00
					TOTAL FOR APPLICATION CB	*	.00	3.00	55.00
					TOTAL FOR PROJECT 0015	**	.00	3.00	55.00
		0017 FINANCIAL CTL SYSTEM	FC FINANCIAL CTL SYSTEM	1			.00	12.00	36.00
		0017 FINANCIAL CTL SYSTEM	FC FINANCIAL CTL SYSTEM	1	64 USER SYSTEM TESTING		11.30	31.30	81.15
		0017 FINANCIAL CTL SYSTEM	FC FINANCIAL CONTROL	9			5.30	33.00	161.15
					TOTAL FOR APPLICATION FC	*	17.00	76.30	346.15
					TOTAL FOR PROJECT 0017	**	17.00	76.30	346.15
		0033 PROFIT CONTRIBUTION	RA PROFIT CONTRIBUTION	2			2.30	2.30	16.15
					TOTAL FOR APPLICATION RA	*	2.30	2.30	31.00
					TOTAL FOR PROJECT 0033	**	2.30	2.30	31.00
		6000 GENERAL ADM	ZZ	9			21.30	41.00	274.15
					TOTAL FOR APPLICATION ZZ	*	21.30	41.00	274.15
					TOTAL FOR PROJECT 6000	**	21.30	41.00	274.15
					TOTAL FOR PERSON 22	***	41.00	123.00	721.45

EXHIBIT 13 □ Time Report by Project

REPORT NO. 9TR020-R1 DIVISION MAIL ORDER L. B. DATA MANAGEMENT CENTER
DATE-TIME 05/23/75-1051 T I M E R E P O R T B Y P R O J E C T WEEK ENDING 05/22/75

PROJECT	TEAM MAN #	NAME	APPLICATION	PROG	CAUSE TASK	SUB	WTD	MTD	ATD
0017 FINANCIAL CTL SYSTEM	D3	JACK	FC FINANCIAL CTL SYSTEM				2.00	2.00	3.00
	21	BRINEY	FC FINANCIAL CTL SYSTEM				.00	12.00	12.00
	22	MEYER	FC FINANCIAL CTL SYSTEM				.00	12.00	36.00
	D3	JACK	FC FINANCIAL CTL SYSTEM	GL071	30 PROGRAM DESIGN		.00	2.30	2.30
					**** MAJOR TASK **** 30		.00	2.30	36.00
	21	BRINEY	FC FINANCIAL CTL SYSTEM		62 USER TRAINING		.00	3.00	27.00
	21	BRINEY	FC FINANCIAL CTL SYSTEM		64 USER SYSTEM TESTING		16.00	16.00	69.45
	22	MEYER	FC FINANCIAL CTL SYSTEM		64 USER SYSTEM TESTING		11.30	31.30	81.15
					**** MAJOR TASK **** 60		27.30	50.30	178.00
					TOTAL FOR APPLICATION FC	*	29.30	79.00	392.15
					TOTAL FOR PROJECT 0017	**	29.30	79.00	393.15

EXHBIT 14

DATE ______/______/______ MOHAWK LOG FOR SYSTEM ______________ PAGE ______

ITEM #	REPORT NAME	# OF RECORDS	T	R	S	TRANS		TAPE SERIAL #	REEL # -OF-	OPR	TRANS ERRORS	PRINTED				REFERENCE	REMARKS	SCRATCH
												START		COMPL.				
						START	COMPL.					DATE	TIME	DATE	TIME			
1.																		
2.																		
3.																		
4.																		
5.																		
6.																		
7.																		
8.																		
9.																		
10.																		
11.																		
12.																		
13.																		
14.																		
15.																		
16.																		
17.																		

EXHIBIT 15 □ Report of Charges

LB-DMC 9CB000.1

L. B. - DATA MANAGEMENT CENTER

REPORT OF CHARGES

Report Date 03/15/75

Division : Mail Order

Period : 2/01/75 thru 2/28/75

Application	OPERATIONS: CENTRAL WALL HOURS	C.P.U. HOURS	C.P.U. PCNT	C.P.U. COST	TERMINAL: MOHAWK HOURS	MOHAWK PCNT	MOHAWK COST	OTHER HOURS	OTHER PCNT	OTHER COST	DEVELOPMENT: SYS/PROG HOURS	SYS/PROG COST	N.Y.SYSTEMS HOURS	N.Y.SYSTEMS COST	TOTAL COST
AC-ACCOUNTS PAYABLE															
PRODUCTION	5.59	.86	.3	222	4.60	1.2	74								296
PROBLEM MAINT.	.03										1.00	10			10
USER REQUEST 7415	.02														
APPLICATION TOTAL	5.64	.86	.2	222	4.60	1.2	74				1.00	10			306
AP-APPROVAL															
PRODUCTION	24.33	3.70	1.2	930	1.05	.3	17								947
PROBLEM MAINT.											23.50	238			238
USER REQUEST 7422											3.00	30			30
USER REQUEST 7441	.74	.09		23							10.08	103			126
DEVELOPMENT 00	.29	.04		11											11
OTHER CHARGES	.09														
APPLICATION TOTAL	25.45	3.83	1.2	964	1.05	.2	17				36.58	371			1,352
AR-ACCTS RECEIVABLE															
PRODUCTION	133.61	47.44	15.8	11,894	13.55	3.6	219								12,113
USER RERUN	4.88	2.13	.7	534											534
PROBLEM MAINT	.10										15.00	151			151
USER REQUEST 7406											3.00	30			30
USER REQUEST 7439	.11	.01		3											3
USER REQUEST 7443											1.00	10			10
DEVELOPMENT 000	.25	.02		6											6
OTHER CHARGES	.55														
APPLICATION TOTAL	139.50	49.60	16.5	12,437	13.55	3.6	210				19.00	191			12,847
BO-BACKORDER															
PRODUCTION	23.46	3.92	1.3	980	2.67	.7	43								1,023
PROBLEM MAINT	1.31	.09		24							25.00	252			276
USER REQUEST 7414	.16	.01		3							.50	5			8
USER REQUEST 7418											1.50	16			16
USER REQUEST 7457	2.50	.20	.1	55							38.02	386			441
DEVELOPMENT 0024	.77	.03		8							55.50	564			572
DEVELOPMENT 0029	1.29	.15		40											40
SCHED.MAINT. 3002											3.50	35			35
OTHER CHARGES	.48	.02		6											6
APPLICATION TOTAL	29.97	4.42	1.4	1,116	2.67	.7	43				124.02	1,258			2,417
CF-CUSTOMER FILE															
PRODUCTION	14.87	5.92	2.0	1,486	.23	.1	4								1,490
PROBLEM MAINT.											4.75	49			49
USER REQUEST 7427											2.50	25			25

EXHIBIT 16 □ Divisional Chargeback Report (period of February 1975)

	MOD		Retail		Total
OPERATIONS					
USED COMPUTER (A)	$ 57,537	(76.5%)	$17,705	(23.5%)	$ 75,242
UNUSED COMPUTER (B)	15,049	(60%)	10,032	(40%)	25,081
TERMINALS					
DMC–MOHAWK (C)	2,284	(38%)	3,795	(62%)	6,079
DMC–OTHER (D)			4,931	(100%)	4,931
MOD TERMINAL (E)	37,431	(100%)			37,431
RETAIL TERMINAL (F)			24,054	(100%)	24,054
TOTAL OPERATIONS	112,301		60,517		172,818
DEVELOPMENT					
SYSTEMS/PROGRAMMING	27,302	(G)	21,875	(H)	49,177
N.Y. SYSTEMS DEVELOPMENT	9,387	(I)	11,741	(J)	21,128
TOTAL CHARGEBACK	$148,990	(61.3%)	$94,133	(38.7%)	$243,123

The amounts in each category were apportioned to one or the other of the two major operating divisions. This was accomplished as follows:

1. Central Operations
   a. USED Computer—on the basis of relative proportion of total recorded CPU hours. For example: During the one-month period ending 2/28/75, 300.21 CPU hours were recorded as "operating hours." Of this amount, MOD accounted for 229.83 hours, or 76.5 percent.
   b. UNUSED Computer—This amount determined on Exhibit 6 to amount to $25,081, was apportioned 60/40 to the two divisions—Mail Order and Retail. This apportionment was negotiated between the two divisions.
2. Terminal Operations—Mohawk. This total amount ($6,079) was apportioned by chargeback on the basis of a relative amount of time used by each system. In this case, MOD accounted for 141.28 of a total of 375.95 recorded hours. Unused terminals time was not determined or used in the calculation.
3. Terminal Operations—Others. In this case, the units are used exclusively by one or another of the divisions.
4. Systems/Programming. This amount for each division was taken directly from summary expense center reports.
5. New York Systems. Same as above.

FUTURE REQUIREMENTS

The approach taken thus far has allowed the DMC to categorize EDP dollars by the various user functional areas. It has also allowed the operating management of the DMC to control expenses at the level at which action can be applied.

One major enhancement required will be the ability to accumulate the chargeback information into *project*-oriented levels. Another enhancement would be to relate EDP cost more closely to the "end product" of the user operating management, such as reports and terminal usage. Still another requirement will be to automate and integrate any remaining manual steps in the chargeback process, such as administrative allocation (Exhibit 6), and terminal time keeping (Exhibit 14).

Assignment:

1. What actions does this chargeout system motivate users to take? For example, consider the impact on the MOD manager responsible for the Accounts Receivable System if "Unused Computer Time" increased because of the implementation of VS?
2. How can the user employ the DMC chargeout system in exercising control over his use of data processing resources?
3. What recommendations would you make to Lane Bryant about their chargeout system?

Case 6–2 □ BARCO*

In March 1979, Mr. Anthony Larkin was considering a major revision in the way BARCO's costs were spread among its 13 customer-stockholders. It had been an area of considerable friction during the past ten years since the company was founded. Now Mr. Larkin was wondering whether the proposed revision might both eliminate the enormous amounts of time that he was spending refereeing conflicts and facilitate a climate of cooperation as opposed to conflict among the customer-stockholders.

BARCO is a nonprofit stand-alone service bureau which provides computing support to 13 small insurance companies. Located in a midwestern state, BARCO was founded in 1968 to permit these companies access to technology which would be prohibitively expensive for any one of them to develop and utilize on its own. BARCO was owned by these 13 insurance

* This case was prepared as the basis for class discussion rather than to illustrate either effective or ineffective handling of an administrative situation.

companies, and all costs of its operation were billed out to each company at the end of the year.

As shown in Exhibit 1, there was a significant difference in size among the companies. At the beginning of 1979, BARCO had 40 employees, had a 370/135 with 512K, and supported one or more terminals in each of the insurance companies. Its budget for 1979 was a little less than $1.5 million. The major components of its costs included $756,000 in personnel expenses, $300,000 of hardware and communication expenses (this included all terminals and time expenses) $200,00 of purchased office supplies and outside services, and roughly $100,000 for office rental. Over the 10 years, BARCO's products had grown to where it offered the following major services:

1. Online data entry and editing of all premium and loss data for all companies.
2. Monthly production of a wide variety of premium-related reports, including, for example, installment/expiration lists, agents accounts, and unearned premium reports.
3. Production monthly of many claims-related reports, including monthly loss listing, accepted payment transactions, loss by line, by state, year-to-end, etc.
4. Monthly production of a combined premium–loss report showing a composite picture of all businesses for each line of insurance.

EXHIBIT 1 □ 1978 COST ANALYSIS

Comparison of Direct Written Premium
to BARCO Cost and Relative Ranking

Company	Direct written premium 1978 ($ millions)		BARCO total cost compared to written premium		Number of screens
A	$ 7.13	(4)	.44	(2)	46,420
B	3.59	(9)	.46	(3)	24,321
C	6.22	(7)	.59	(9)	55,667
D	6.72	(6)	.54	(6)	48,226
Exeter	33.93	(2)	1.05	(13)	355,815
Aden	41.29	(1)	.49	(5)	287,949
E	2.60	(12)	.60	(10)	23,344
F	6.99	(5)	.47	(4)	46,747
G	7.81	(3)	.57	(8)	66,095
H	6.07	(8)	.56	(7)	49,067
I	3.37	(10)	.64	(11)	33,636
J	2.15	(13)	.78	(12)	20,987
K	3.14	(11)	.37	(1)	15,224
	$131.01	Total	.65	Average	1,073,659

( ) = Relative ranking: Column 1—High to Low (premium)
Column 2—Low to High (cost)

5. Production of a variety of monthly, quarterly, semiannual, and annual statistical reports for various state agencies.
6. Quarterly preparation of agents' experience reports for all agents of all companies.
7. Annual reports to city and town governments to meet a variety of regulatory requirements.
8. Ongoing maintenance of files containing agency information and dividend device information.
9. A variety of specific requests. Although these requests are handled on an ad hoc basis, the production of special reports is considered to be a part of the basic service.
10. Homeowner policy rating and writing. Different companies utilized different mixes of the reports and systems.

From the beginning, BARCO was confronted with a variety of difficult operating problems. Those which extended beyond the normal problems of starting and running a data processing activity included the following:

1. The vast difference in stockholder size meant that there were significant differences in needs. The large companies needed much more comprehensive software features than were required by the small companies.
2. The insurance company stockholders all had different lines of business and styles of management. Consequently, on this dimension, they also had different reporting requirements. Therefore, nearly every system was overengineered for the needs of any individual user to be responsive to the needs of all users.
3. A philosophical difference existed as to whether services to the large companies should be billed as a by-product of the basic systems developed for the small companies, or alternatively, whether services to the small companies should be billed as a by-product of the systems developed for the large companies. Both company groups had strong views on this issue.

Despite these problems, BARCO's growth had been reasonably rapid. In 1978, a series of heated meetings between stockholders had once again raised to the surface the question of how costs should be split, with all parties feeling that they were being unfairly prevailed upon. As a consequence, the issue had become one of high priority for Mr. Larkin to resolve.

Mr. Larkin began by examining the current method for charging costs to the users. The following paragraphs describe the key features of this charge-out system.

1. Standard billing rates had been created to charge back both operating and project development costs to members. Operating costs are charged back to members at a $300 rate per CPU hour for jobs run for a single company. For common systems:

   a. Online entry time is divided among the members, based on the percentage of the total transaction volume submitted over the billing period.
   b. For batch processing systems, the number of master file records for each company as a percentage of the total is used as a basis for allocating the time for a given common system to each member.
2. A minimum charge exists to recognize the cost of certain fixed resources which are required, whether or not they are used directly. These costs are $1,000/month. As a practical matter in 1979, everyone was operating above this point.
3. Project development costs are shared among participants, based on a specific formula. Under this basis, project participants share equally the first 20 percent of the charges, with the remainder allocated on the appropriately agreed-upon basis for the system.
4. A member may discontinue participation in a project at completion of the Preliminary Systems Design Phase. After this checkpoint, the remaining members share the costs of the installation phase, based on the predetermined allocation formula adjusted to reflect the reduced participation in the project.
5. If nonparticipants desire to use a system after its completion, each successive one must pay a price equal to twice what their original share would have been had they joined the project initially. These funds are then distributed to the original project members, based on their dollar participation in the project.
6. Variances between standard and actual costs are allocated back to members, based on standard dollars charged to them during the year. Variances are developed and allocated separately for Operating costs and Project Development costs. Actual variances for 11 months are used to project December's variance. This allows BARCO to project the annual variance for inclusion in the December billing. Any difference between the projected and actual variance for the last month is adjusted on the January bill. This allows members to close their books without delay. This January adjustment has been historically very small.

In order to begin to deal with this problem, Mr. Larkin commissioned an outside study to be done on recommended modifications to the chargeout system. This report, which took three months to prepare, is contained in summary form as Appendix A. In evaluating this proposal, Mr. Larkin noted the following issues as posing important perspectives in reaching for a solution:

1. All parties must be educated that the problem is intrinsically incapable of a clean, definitive solution which will make everyone 100 percent happy. The problem is how to spread the pain in the most equitable way, and it is critical that the members understand and be sympathetic

to this problem. If it were an internal company transfer pricing system, where cost could be left in the data center to be picked up in corporate overhead, then this would not be true. (In this context, the joint costing alternative seems appropriate and Mr. Larkin was confident he could sell it.)

2. A particularly difficult problem arises from the fact that overall, it is cheaper for BARCO to have a single software package for each application as opposed to one for the larger companies and one for the smaller companies. Consequently, the systems will always be overdesigned for the smaller companies, that is, standard cost per transaction will be obviously onerous to them as opposed to a charge which comes from a system designed only for the small companies' needs.
3. It is impossible to get responsible outside market price data in this situation because of the product's uniqueness. It is also impossible to generate any meaningful rules of thumb as to how data processing costs should vary over time for these size companies.
4. We are dealing with an operation whose short-term costs behavior makes it a largely fixed-cost operation. When viewed in the perspective of a three- to five-year horizon, however, most of the costs become variable.

Finally, Mr. Larkin noted that even if the system produced radically different costs than were currently being produced, and if it appeared to equitably and comprehensively address the problems, he was anxious to put it in front of the stockholders as a starting point for their discussion.

APPENDIX A

This memorandum is a second cut at a conceptual framework for the design of a cost allocation system for BARCO following our meeting last week with four of your stockholders. Key assumptions we agreed on at this meeting included the following:

1. All stockholders should be considered as partners in a *joint* venture and, as such, should bear costs which cannot be directly isolated as being caused by them, roughly in relation to the percent of the total service they receive from BARCO. Very specifically, this is a joint costing problem rather than a by-product costing one. (If it was a by-product one, it would be a very exciting debate as to who should be treated as the by-product.)
2. There is wide variance in the size of the partners and hence the complexity of their data processing needs. Since systems have to be designed for the most sophisticated partner, they are inevitably overdesigned for the small user. Charging the small partner a propor-

tionate share of the computing resource they use is in fact already an overcharge because the underlying system utilizes more computing resource than if it had been designed only to meet their relatively simple needs.

3. Cost allocation systems can be very burdensome and procedures must be designed which pose as little administrative burden as possible (although you may not believe my ideas achieve this goal).
4. Your stockholders are in very different types of businesses, consequently their needs for certain kinds of data processing services legitimately vary widely. Thus, for example, a simple 1 percent charge on premium income is excessively simplistic for this particular environment.
5. While it would be desirable for your stockholders to be reasonably well-educated consumers of data processing service and the underlying economics thereof, in reality this is not true. Consequently, a major purpose of this cost-allocation design process is to help facilitate this.
6. Measuring the internal efficiency of your operation is not an appropriate item to worry about in the design of this cost-allocation system. Designing the control mechanisms to accomplish that represents an entirely different project.

The subject of cost allocation can be effectively broken into three parts. These parts are systems maintenance, systems development, and computer operations. Each of these subjects is dealt with below.

I. Systems Maintenance. In our last conversation, we noted this subject can be broken into five pieces, each of which should be handled separately.

1. Maintenance either initiated by BARCO or by a stockholder which clearly helps all stockholders. This expense should be allocated to the stockholders on a basis corresponding to their share of the previous year's total computer operations bill (see Item III). Thus, if 3 percent of computer operation is billed to a stockholder during a year, he should absorb 3 percent of this category of maintenance expense the following year. Each month, this maintenance expense should be spread to the stockholders by the following procedures:
   a. All systems analysts and programmers should be assigned to one of five labor pools (the lowest pool will be junior programmers and the highest, senior analysts). I understand your current system has already permitted categorization of your employees into five pools.
   b. The total hours of this type of maintenance done during the month should be multiplied by a standard charge/labor hour for each pool[1]

[1] This standard charge/hour includes an average labor charge/hour plus increments to cover both overhead and computer test time. Each year this charge should be reassessed for the following year.

and the resulting numbers added to come to the total cost for this type of maintenance.

c. This maintenance should then be allocated to each stockholder on a proportionate basis to their share of the previous year's computer operations expense.

2. Requests by a stockholder of no benefit to other stockholders where the estimated work is less than one man-week. This expense should be charged directly to the requesting stockholder at actual hours times the appropriate *standard* rates (the same rates as in the preceding item).
3. Requests by a stockholder of no benefit to other stockholders where the estimated work is more than one man-week. This expense should be charged directly to the requesting stockholder at *estimated* hours times the appropriate standard rate (the same rate as item 1). This is designed to put the onus of cost misestimates on BARCO rather than the customer. For large charges this may encourage a two- or three-stage project approval process which is okay.
4. Requests by a subgroup of stockholders where the estimated work is less than one man-week, which will benefit only them as a group, as opposed to all stockholders. These costs should be allocated to the subgroup of these stockholders on a basis corresponding to their percentage of the subgroup's percentage of the previous year's computer operations. The appropriate members of the subgroup will be identified by BARCO. The total amount of the expense to be so allocated will be actual hours times the appropriate standard rates.
5. Requests by a subgroup of stockholders where the estimated work is more than one man-week. These costs should be allocated to the subgroup of these stockholders on a basis corresponding to their percentage of the total overall subgroup's percentage of the previous year's computer operations. The total amount of the expense to be so allocated will be estimated hours times the appropriate standard rates. BARCO will identify the appropriate members of this group. At either BARCO's initiative or that of any stockholder, the equity of this allocation may be raised for examination because of a disproportionate emphasis on one or more users. I would expect this to be unusual for maintenance. The mechanism to resolve this dispute is to refer it to a five-person committee made up of representatives of two smaller stockholders, the two larger companies, and BARCO. No committee decision would be effective unless four out of the five agreed.

Implementation of this implies:

1. Establishment of records to categorize maintenance work between these five labor categories. My understanding is that these records are already in place and therefore this poses no problem.
2. Development of five standard cost-per-hour figures for development work. I understand the data for doing this is readily available.

3. At the end of the year, these procedures will result in a modest amount of maintenance expense being either over- or under-absorbed by the stockholders. If historic experience is to be relied upon, this will not be a large amount and it will be appropriate to handle it by expedient procedures such as allocating it to the stockholders on a basis corresponding to their percentage of BARCO's total operations bill for the previous year.

The most difficult aspect to manage will be the interface between the end of systems installation work and the beginning of maintenance. Systems which have been prematurely rushed into production without enough testing often require considerably more work in the first several months than more thoroughly tested systems. This work is appropriately classified as systems development. I suggest that a formal sign-off procedure be instituted for each system within two weeks or so of installation, where the users formally sign off that it is not operational and additional work will be maintenance. If these operating problems are present, BARCO will prepare a list of additional changes that when made will be deemed to make the system operational. These will be discussed and agreed upon by the users.

II. Systems Development. This subject is particularly complex because the majority of your systems are designed to serve all or most of your stockholders. Unfortunately, the needs of the two large stockholders operations are very different from those of the others; consequently, the costs of the resulting systems are much higher because of the special features required to service these two stockholders. The recommendations in this section are based on your observation that for a typical $100,000 effort (systems, programming, and computer time for testing) roughly $70,000 is for common needs of the 13 stockholders and $30,000 for the unique needs of the two large stockholders. My recommendations are as follows:

1. Systems designed for a single stockholder should be charged to him at estimated cost. This estimated cost should be derived by multiplying anticipated man-days of effort for each labor category times the standard charge per man-day (the same one as in item I–1) for the category and adding the resulting figures for jobs of more than one man-week. For jobs of less than one man-week, the stockholder should be charged actual man-days of effort for each labor category times the standard charge per man-day for the category.
2. Systems designed to meet the needs of all stockholders should be handled in the following way:
   a. Only the estimated cost should be charged to the stockholders. The difference between actual and estimated costs should be absorbed by BARCO. The estimated cost will be derived by estimating the number of hours of work for each of the five labor categories and multiplying it by the standard labor charge for the category.

b. BARCO will review the system and suggest a methodology for spreading the costs to the various stockholders. The underlying principles guiding this recommendation will include evaluation of:

(1) The extent to which this work benefits all stockholders.

(2) The extent to which the work has special features in it which are there for the purposes of only one or two stockholders.

(3) The extent to which the total operating time of the system is going to be impacted by the needs of only one or two stockholders.

The suggested breakdown of estimated charges will be reviewed by a five-person committee made up of representatives from the two large shareholders, two smaller shareholders, and BARCO. This committee would come to a decision, before work would commence, as to how development work should be charged to each of the stockholders.

Recognizing that most systems are considerably larger because of the special needs of the two large shareholders, a typical solution might be as follows: 15 percent of the cost estimate should be charged outright to each of the large shareholders, i.e., for a $100,000 project Aden would be charged $15,000 and Exeter $15,000. The remaining 70 percent would then be charged to all stockholders in a manner similar to that described in Part III. I would emphasize that this is only illustrative. The key is to agree on the cost spread before the costs are incurred.

This system should force BARCO and the stockholders to be more rigorous in preparing systems development proposals and evaluating their benefits and costs. While it will be initially painful, I see it as a critical step in moving the stockholder/BARCO relationships to a still more professional basis.

III. Charge for Computer Operations. I am uncomfortable about the present proposal of using 1 percent of premium volume as a minimum charge to the stockholders. This discomfort stems from a wide variety in the mix of businesses your stockholders operate in, and their differing data intensity. Items which appear to impact this computational complexity include:

1. Widely different emphases on product lines between Automobiles, Home Owners, Special Peril, and Fire. Each of these lines requires quite different amounts of computing support.
2. Significant differences in average premium for the same line of business. These differences lead to widely varying data intensity needed to support each line.
3. The more states a line is sold in, the more complex becomes the application, etc.

These factors make me believe it would be appropriate that for some stockholders their computer operations expenses should be dramatically lower than 1 percent, while for others they should dramatically exceed 1 percent. This observation is perfectly consistent with the wide dispersal of data processing expenditures as a percentage of sales in other industries, such as manufacturing. Therefore, the thrust of this recommendation is to find a fair way to spread actual costs among the different users in proportion to their utilization. To do this, the following methodology is proposed:

a. All expenses from the modems out should be charged directly to the stockholder in question. This includes modem, telephone line charge, and terminals. These are direct costs caused by the stockholder and can be most fairly attributed to him. I am sympathetic, however, with the argument against the geographically distant stockholder and would be willing to consider lumping these charges in with the CPU charges as described in the paragraphs below. My feeling, however, is that doing it that way makes the charges more obscure and does not identify real cost behavior with the ultimate stockholder. For obvious reasons, you have chosen not to service accounts in Hawaii.

b. The actual 1980 computer operation expense from the modem in should be handled as follows:

i. There are four basic items which appear to drive the costs of the computing operations for BARCO. They are:

Total number of screens requested.

Total number of premium screens requested.

Total number of claims screens requested.

The percentage of premium coverages.

For each of these items, a total projected activity level for the item for 1980 should be calculated.

ii. The total costs of the computing activity for 1980 should be budgeted in total and then spread as follows to each of the items:

Total screens—15 percent.

Total premium screens—33 percent

Total claims screens—27 percent

Premium coverage—25 percent

These charges come from your analysis of last year's results. These costs should be divided by the projected activity level to come to a cost/item.

iii. Each month, the stockholder would be billed by multiplying his activity volume for each category by the standard cost/item identified in Point (ii). At the end of the year, any overcharge or undercharge of computer operations expense would be assigned to the stockholders based on their percent of allocation of the total year's computer operations billed to date. This system is biased in favor of Aden and Exeter since without them the software would be simpler and hence the cost/item lower. While significant, this bias is consistent with current practice and therefore probably pragmatically acceptable. Attempts to correct it would not only be expensive but also highly controversial.

iv. A final point which I believe should be investigated is the development of a fifth category. This category would represent the number of pages of reports sent to a stockholder and he would be billed a standard charge for each page. This will help control the volume of paper requested by the stockholders. Your current weighing equipment should make it easy to handle this by simply keeping track each month of the number of pounds of material charged to each stockholder.

Dues for the Club

A final set of issues was raised at our last meeting concerning the desirability of all stockholders having a fixed dues payment to become a "member of the Club." Recognizing that it would be inappropriate for this to be a fixed amount for each stockholder because of the wide range in size, the idea of 1/4 percent charge on premium volume was suggested. This 1/4 percent would be deducted from the total BARCO bill and would result in lower per-hour charges for system and programming charges for handling premium service, etc. My reactions to this are as follows:

1. Per your study, this approach will not sharply change the charges to any users. Consequently, while from a cost accounting viewpoint it leaves something to be desired, it will not seriously distort the results.
2. If it helps build the feeling of partnership and jointness in the BARCO operation, then I think it is a desirable feature and we should incorporate it.

Chapter 7 □ A Portfolio Approach to IS Development

Manageable Trend / Chapter	Strategic Impact	DP/TP/OA	Organization Learning	Make/Buy	Life Cycle	GM/ User/ IS
IS Technology Organization Issues **Chapter 3**		●	●			●
Organizational Issues in IS Development **Chapter 4**	●		●	●		●
Information Systems Planning **Chapter 5**	●		●			●
IS Management Control **Chapter 6**	●		●	●		●
A Portfolio Approach to Information Systems Development **Chapter 7**	●				●	●
Operations Management **Chapter 8**	●			●	●	●
Multinational IS Issues **Chapter 9**		●				●
The IS Business **Chapter 10**	●		●	●		●

A major industrial products company discovers one and a half months before the installation date for a computer system that a $15 million effort to convert from one manufacturer to another is in trouble, and installation must be delayed a year. Eighteen months later, the changeover has still not taken place.

A large consumer products company budgets $250,000 for a new computer-based personnel information system to be ready in nine months. Two years later, $2.5 million has been spent, and an estimated $3.6 million more is needed to complete the job. The company has to stop the project.

A sizable financial institution slips $1.5 million over budget and 12 months behind on the development of programs for a new financial systems package, vital for the day-to-day functioning of one of its major operating groups. Once the system is finally installed, average transaction response times are much longer than expected.

A Midwest mail-order house found nine months after it had installed a state-of-the-art office automation system for $900,000 that 50 percent of the terminals were unused and 90 percent of the work was simple word processing. Further, the communications system was incompatible with the main data processing, and system support was unobtainable. They returned the system.

Stories from the stage 1 and stage 2 days of the late 1960s and early 1970s?[1] No! All these events took place in 1980 in Fortune 500 companies. (We could have selected equally dramatic examples from overseas.) Although it is almost too embarrassing to admit, the day of the big disaster on a major information systems project has not passed. Given business's more than 20 years of IS experience, the question is, Why?

An analysis of these cases and firsthand acquaintance with a number of IS projects in the past 10 years suggest three serious deficiencies in practice that involve both general management and IS management. The first two are the failure to assess the individual project risk and the failure to consider the aggregate risk of the portfolio of projects. The third is the lack of recognition that different projects require different managerial approaches.

These aspects of the IS project management and development process are so important that we have chosen to deal with them in a separate chapter. Chapter 8 discusses project management further in terms of how different corporate cultures and perceived strategic relevance of the technology influences how control over different pieces of the project management life cycle should be balanced between IS and the user. Since many projects have multiyear life cycles, these project management issues have to be dealt with separately from those of the management control system with its calendar-year focus as discussed in Chapter 6.

ELEMENTS OF PROJECT RISK

The typical project feasibility study covers exhaustively such topics as financial benefits, qualitative benefits, implementation costs, target milestones and completion dates, and necessary staffing levels. In precise, crisp terms the developers of these estimates provide voluminous supporting documentation. Only rarely, however, do they deal frankly with the risk of slippage in time, cost overrun, technical shortfall, or outright failure. Rather, they deny the existence of such possibilities by ignoring them. They assume the appropriate human skills, controls, and so on that will ensure success.

[1] Richard L. Nolan and Cyrus F. Gibson, "Managing the Four Stages of EDP Growth," *Harvard Business Review*, (January–February 1974), p. 76.

Consequences of Risk. By risk we are suggesting exposure to such consequences as:

1. Failure to obtain all, or even any, or the anticipated benefits.
2. Costs of implementation that is much greater than expected.
3. Time for implementation that is much greater than expected.
4. Technical performance of resulting systems that turns out to be significantly below estimate.
5. Incompatibility of the system with the selected hardware and software.

These kinds of risk in practical situations, of course, are not independent of each other; rather, they are closely related. In discussing risk, we are assuming that the manager has brought appropriate methods and approaches to bear on the project (mismanagement is obviously another element of risk). Risk, in definition here, is what remains after application of proper tools.

In our discussion, we are also not implying a correlation between *risk* and *bad*. These words represent entirely different concepts, and the link between the two normally is that higher-risk projects must yield higher benefits to compensate for the increased downside exposure.

Dimensions Influencing Inherent Risk. At least three important dimensions influence the risk inherent in a project:

1. Project Size. The larger it is in dollar expense, staffing levels, elapsed time, and number of departments affected by the project, the greater the risk. Multimillion-dollar projects obviously carry more risk than $50,000 projects and also, in general, affect the company more if the risk is realized. A related concern is the size of the project relative to the normal size of a systems development group's projects. The implicit risk is usually lower on a $1 million project of a department whose average undertaking costs $2 million to $3 million than on a $250,000 project of a department that has never ventured a project costing more than $50,000.

2. Experience with the Technology. Because of the greater likelihood of unexpected technical problems, project risk increases as the familiarity of the project team and IS organization with the hardware, operating systems, data base handler, and project application language decreases. Phase 1 and phase 2 technology projects are intrinsically more risky for a company than phase 3 and phase 4 technology projects. A project that has a slight risk for a leading-edge, large systems development group may have a very high risk for a smaller, less technically advanced group. Yet the latter group can reduce risk through purchase of outside skills for an undertaking involving technology that is in general commercial use.

3. Project Structure. In some projects, the very nature of the task defines completely, from the moment of conceptualization, the outputs. We classify such schemes as highly structured. They carry much less risk than those whose outputs are more subject to the manager's judgment and hence are vulnerable to change. The outputs of highly structured projects are fixed and not subject to change during the life of the project.

An insurance company automating preparation of its agents' rate book is an example of such a highly structured project. At the project's beginning, planners reached total agreement on the product lines to be included, the layout of each page, and the process of generating each number. Throughout the life of the project, there was no need to alter these decisions. Consequently the team organized to reach a stable, fixed output rather than to cope with a potentially mobile target.

Quite the opposite was true in the personnel information project we mentioned at the beginning of the chapter, which was a low-structure project. In that situation, the users could not reach a consensus on what the outputs should be, and these decisions shifted almost weekly, crippling progress.

PROJECT CATEGORIES AND DEGREE OF RISK

Exhibit 7–1, by combining the various dimensions of risk, identifies eight distinct project categories, each carrying a different degree of risk. Even at this gross intuitive level, such a classification is useful to separate projects for quite different types of management review. IS organizations have used it successfully to distinguish the relative risk for their own understanding and as a basis for communicating these notions of risk to users and senior corporate executives.

A legitimate concern is how to ensure that different people viewing the same project will come to the same rough assessment of its risks. While the best way to assess this is still uncertain, several companies have made significant progress in addressing the problem.

ASSESSING RISK IN INDIVIDUAL PROJECTS

Exhibit 7–2 presents, *in part,* a method one large company developed for measuring risk: a list of 42 questions about a project, which the project manager answers both prior to senior management's approval of the proposal and several times during its implementation.

This company developed the questions after carefully analyzing its experience with successful and unsuccessful projects. We include some of them as an example of how to bridge concepts and practice. No analytic framework lies behind these questions, and they may not be appropriate for

EXHIBIT 7-1 □ Effect of Degree of Structure, Company-Relative Technology, and Size on Project Risk

	High structure	Low structure
Low company-relative technology	Large size—low risk	Large size—low risk (very susceptible to mismanagement)
	Small size—very low risk	Small size—very low risk (very susceptible to mismanagement)
High company-relative technology	Large size—medium risk	Large size—very high risk
	Small size—medium-low risk	Small size—high risk

all companies; however, they represent a good starting point, and several other large companies have used them.

Both the project leader and the key user answer these questions. Differences in the answers are then reconciled. (Obviously, the questionnaire provides data that are no better than the quality of thinking that goes into the answers.)

These questions not only highlight the risks but also suggest alternative ways of conceiving of and managing the project. If the initial aggregate risk score seems high, analysis of the answers may suggest ways of lessening the risk through reduced scope, lower-level technology, multiple phases, and so on. Thus managers should not consider risk as a static descriptor; rather, its presence should encourage better approaches to project management. Numbers 5 and 6 under the section on structure are particularly good examples of questions that could trigger changes.

The higher the score, the higher must be the level of approval. Only the executive committee in this company approves very risky projects. Such an

EXHIBIT 7–2 □ Risk Assessment Questionnaire (sample from a total of 42 questions)

		Weight
Size risk assessment		
1. Total development man-hours for system*		**5**
100 to 3,000	Low—1	
3,000 to 15,000	Medium—2	
15,000 to 30,000	Medium—3	
More than 30,000	High—4	
2. What is estimated project implementation time?		**4**
12 months or less	Low—1	
13 months to 24 months	Medium—2	
More than 24 months	High—3	
3. Number of departments (other than IS) involved with system		**4**
One	Low—1	
Two	Medium—2	
Three or more	High—3	

		Weight
Structure risk assessment		
1. If replacement system is proposed, what percentage of existing functions are replaced on a one-to-one basis?		**5**
0% to 25%	High—3	
25% to 50%	Medium—2	
50% to 100%	Low—1	
2. What is severity of procedural changes in user department caused by proposed system?		**5**
Low—1		
Medium—2		
High—3		
3. Does user organization have to change structurally to meet requirements of new system?		**5**
No	—0	
Minimal	Low—1	
Somewhat	Medium—2	
Major	High—3	

Structure risk assessment		*Weight*
4. What is general attitude of user?		**5**
Poor—anti data-processing solution	High—3	
Fair—sometimes reluctance	Medium—2	
Good—understands value of DP solution	—0	
5. How committed is upper-level user management to system?		**5**
Somewhat reluctant, or unknown	High—3	
Adequate	Medium—2	
Extremely enthusiastic	Low—1	
6. Has a joint data processing/user team been established?		**5**
No	High—3	
Part-time user representative appointed	Low—1	
Full-time user representative appointed	—0	

Technology risk assessment		*Weight*
1. Which of the hardware is new to the company?†		**5**
None	—0	
CPU	High—3	
Peripheral and/or additional storage	High—3	
Terminals	High—3	
Mini or micro	High—3	
2. Is the system software (nonoperating system) new to IS project team?†		**5**
No	—0	
Programming language	High—3	
Data base	High—3	
Data communications	High—3	
Other—specify	High—3	
3. How knowledgeable is user in area of IS?		**5**
First exposure	High—3	
Previous exposure but limited knowledge	Medium—2	
High degree of capability	Low—1	

EXHIBIT 7-2 ***(concluded)***

Technology risk assessment		Weight
4. How knowledgeable is user representative in proposed application area?		**5**
Limited	High—3	
Understands concept but no experience	Medium—2	
Has been involved in prior implementation efforts	Low—1	
5. How knowledgeable is IS team in proposed application area?		**5**
Limited	High—3	
Understands concept but no experience	Medium—2	
Has been involved in prior implementation efforts	Low—1	

Note: Since the questions vary in importance, the company assigned weights to them subjectively. The numerical answer to the questions is multiplied by the question weight to calculate the question's contribution to the project's risk. The numbers are then added together to produce a risk score number for the project. Projects with risk scores within 10 points of each other are indistinguishable, but those separated by 100 points or more are very different to even the casual observer.

* Time to develop includes systems design, programming, testing, and installation.

† This question is scored by multiplying the sum of the numbers attached to the positive response by the weight.

Source: This questionnaire is adapted from the Dallas Tire case, no. 9-180-006 (Boston, Mass.: Harvard Business School Case Services, 1980).

approach ensures that top managers are aware of significant hazards and are making appropriate risk/strategic-benefit trade-offs. Managers should ask questions such as the following:

1. Are the benefits great enough to offset the risks?
2. Can the affected parts of the organization survive if the project fails?
3. Have the planners considered appropriate alternatives?

On a periodic basis, these questions are answered again during the undertaking to reveal any major changes. If all is going well, the risk continuously declines during implementation as the size of the remaining task dwindles and familiarity with the technology grows.

Answers to the questions provide a common understanding among senior, IS, and user managers as to a project's relative risk. Often the fiascoes occur when senior managers believe a project has low risk and IS managers know it has high risk. In such cases, IS managers may not admit their assessment because they fear that the senior executives will not tolerate this kind of uncertainty in data processing and will cancel a project of potential benefit to the organization.

PORTFOLIO RISK PROFILE

In addition to determining relative risk for single projects, a company should develop an aggregate risk profile of the portfolio of systems and programming projects. While there is no such thing as a correct risk profile in the abstract, there are appropriate risk profiles for different types of companies and strategies. For example, in an industry where IS is strategic (such as banking and insurance), managers should be concerned when there are no high-risk projects. In such a case, the company may be leaving a product or service gap for competition to step into. On the other hand, a portfolio loaded with high-risk projects suggests that the company may be vulnerable to operational disruptions when projects are not completed as planned.

Conversely in support companies heavy investment in high-risk projects may not be appropriate. However, often even those companies should have some technologically exciting ventures to ensure familiarity with leading-edge technology and to maintain staff morale and interest. This thinking suggests that the aggregate risk profiles of the portfolios of two companies could legitimately differ. Exhibit 7–3 shows in more detail the issues that

EXHIBIT 7-3 □ Factors that Influence Risk Profile of Project Portfolio

	Portfolio low-risk focus	Portfolio high-risk focus
Stability of IS development group	Low	High
Perceived quality of IS development group by insiders	Low	High
IS critical to delivery of current corporate services	No	Yes
IS important decision support aid	No	Yes
Experienced IS systems development group	No	Yes
Major IS fiascoes in last two years	Yes	No
New IS management team	Yes	No
IS perceived critical to delivery of future corporate services	No	Yes
IS perceived critical to future decision support aids	No	Yes
Company perceived as backward in use of IS	No	Yes

influence IS toward or away from high-risk efforts (the risk profile should include projects that will come from outside software houses as well as those of the internal systems development group). In short, the aggregate impact of IS on corporate strategy is an important determinant of the appropriate amount of risk to undertake.

In summary, it is both possible and useful to talk about project risk during the feasibility study stage. The discussion of risk can be helpful both for those working on the individual project and for the department as a whole. Not only can this systematic analysis reduce the number of failures, but equally important, its power as a communication link helps IS managers and senior executives reach agreement on the risks to be taken in line with corporate goals.

CONTINGENCY APPROACH TO PROJECT MANAGEMENT (BY PROJECT TYPE)

Now the organization faces the difficult problem of project operations. Much of the literature and conventional wisdom about project management suggest that there is a single right way of doing it. A similar theme holds that managers should apply uniformly to all such ventures an appropriate cluster of tools, project management methods, and organizational linkages.

While there may indeed be a general-purpose set of tools, the contribution each device can make to planning and controlling the project varies widely according to the project's characteristics. Further, the means of involving the user—through steering committees, representation on the team, or as leader (not DP or IS professional)—should also vary by project type. In short, there is no universally correct way to run all projects.

Management Tools. The general methods (tools) for managing projects are of four principal types:

1. *External integration* tools include organizational and other communication devices that link the project team's work to the users at both the managerial and the lower levels.
2. *Internal integration* devices ensure that the team operates as an integrated unit.
3. *Formal planning* tools help to structure the sequence of tasks in advance and to estimate the time, money, and technical resources the team will need to execute them.
4. *Formal control* mechanisms help managers evaluate progress and spot potential discrepancies so that corrective action can be taken.

Exhibit 7–4 gives examples of the tools in each category commonly used by companies. The next paragraphs suggest how the degree of structure and the company-relative technology influence the selection of items from the four categories.

EXHIBIT 7-4 □ Tools of Project Management

External integration tools	Internal integration tools
Selection of user as project manager	Selection of experienced DP professional to lead team
Creation of user steering committee	Selection of manager to lead team
Frequent and in-depth meetings of this committee	Frequent team meetings
User-managed change control process	Regular preparation and distribution of minutes within team on key design evolution decision
Frequent and detailed distribution of project team minutes to key users	
Selection of users as team members	Regular technical status reviews
Formal user specification approval process	Managed low turnover of team members
Progress reports prepared for corporate steering committee	Selection of high percentage of team members with significant previous work relationships
Users responsible for education and installation of system	Participation of team members in goal setting and deadline establishment
Users manage decision on key action dates	Outside technical assistance
Formal planning tools	Formal control tools
PERT, critical path, etc. networking	Periodic formal status reports versus plan
Milestone phases selection	Change control disciplines
Systems specification standards	Regular milestone presentation meetings
Feasibility study specifications	Deviations from plan
Project approval processes	
Project postaudit procedures	

High Structure–Low Technology

Projects that are highly structured and that present familiar technical problems are not only the lower-risk projects but are also the easiest to manage (see Exhibit 7–1). They are also the least common. High structure implies that the outputs are very well defined by the nature of the task, and the possibility of the users changing their minds as to what these outputs should be is essentially nonexistent. Consequently, the leaders do not have to develop extensive administrative processes in order to get a diverse group of users both to agree to a design structure and to keep to that structure. Such external integration devices as inclusion of analysts in user departments, heavy representation of users on the design team, formal approval of the design team by users, and formal approval by users of design specifications are cumbersome and unnecessary for this type of undertaking. Other integrating devices, such as training users in how to operate the system, remain important.

The system's concept and design stage, however, are stable. At the same time, since the technology involved is familiar to the company, the project can proceed with a high percentage of persons having only average technical backgrounds and experience. The leader does not need strong IS skills. This type of project readily gives opportunity to the department's junior managers, who can gain experience that may lead to more ambitious tasks in the future.

Project life-cycle planning concepts, with their focus on defining tasks and budgeting resources against them, force the team to develop a thorough and detailed plan (exposing areas of soft thinking in the process). Such projects are likely to meet the resulting milestone dates and keep within the target budget. Moreover, the usual control techniques for measuring progress against dates and budgets provide very reliable data for spotting discrepancies and building a desirable tension into the design team to work harder to avoid slippage.

An example of this type of highly structured project is the agent's rate book project mentioned earlier. A portfolio of which 90 percent comprises this type of project will produce little excitement for senior and user managers. It also requires a much more limited set of skills for the IS organization than might be needed for companies whose portfolios have a quite different mixture of projects.

High Structure–High Technology

These projects, vastly more complex than the first kind, involve some significant modifications from the practice outlined in project management handbooks. A good example of this type is the conversion of systems from one computer manufacturer to another with no enhancements (which is of course, easier said than done). Another example of this kind of project is the conversion of a set of manual procedures onto a minicomputer with the objective only of doing the same functions more quickly.

The normal mechanisms for liaison with users are not crucial here (though they are in the next type of project), because the outputs are so well defined by the nature of the undertaking that both the development of specifications and the need to deal with systems changes from users are sharply lower. Liaison with users is nevertheless important for two reasons: (1) To ensure coordination on any changes in input-output or other manual procedure changes necessary for project success and (2) to deal with any systems restructuring that must follow from shortcomings in the project's technology.

It is not uncommon in this kind of project to discover during implementation that the technology is inadequate, forcing a long postponement while new technology is chosen or vital features pruned in order to make the task fit the available technology. In one such situation, a major industrial products company had to convert some computerized order-entry procedures to a manual basis so that the rest of an integrated materials management system could be shifted to already-purchased, new hardware.

Such technological shortcomings were also the main difficulty in the financial institution described at the start of this chapter. In such a case, where system performance is much poorer than expected, user involvement is important both to prevent demoralization and to help implement either an alternative approach (less ambitious in design) or a mutual agreement to end the project.

The skills that lead to success in this type of project, however, are the same as for effective administration of projects involving any kind of technical complexity. The leader needs this experience (preferably, but not necessarily, in an IS environment) as well as administrative experience, unless the project is not very large. The leader must also be effective in relating to technicians. From talking to the project team at various times, the ideal manager will anticipate difficulties before the technicians understand that they have a problem. In dealing with larger projects in this category, the manager's ability to establish and maintain teamwork through meetings, a record of all key design decisions, and subproject conferences is vital.

Project life-cycle planning methods, such as PERT (program evaluation and review technique) and critical path, identify tasks and suitable completion dates. Their predictive value is much more limited here, however, than in the preceding category. The team will not understand key elements of the technology in advance, and seemingly minor bugs in such projects have a curious way of becoming major financial drains.

In one company, roughly once an hour an online banking system generated garbage across the CRT screen. Although simply hitting a release key erased this screen of zeroes and x's, four months and more than $200,000 went into eliminating the so-called ghost screen. The solution lay in uncovering a complex interaction of hardware features, operating system functions, and application traffic patterns. Correction of the problem ultimately required the vendor to redesign several chips. Formal control mechanisms have limits in monitoring the progress of such projects.

In summary, technical leadership and internal integration are the keys in this type of project, and external integration plays a distinctly secondary role. Formal planning and control tools give more subjective than concrete projections, and the great danger is that neither IS managers nor high-level executives will recognize this. They may believe they have precise planning and close control when, in fact, they have neither.

Low Structure–Low Technology

When these projects are intelligently managed, they have low risk. Over and over, however, such projects fail because of inadequate direction. In this respect they differ from the first type of project, where more ordinary managerial skills could ensure success. The key to operating this kind of project lies in an effective effort to involve the users.

Developing substantial user support for *only one* of the thousands of design options and keeping the users committed to that design are critical. Essential aspects of this process include the following:

1. A user either as project leader or as the number 2 person on the team.
2. A user steering committee to evaluate the design.
3. An effort to break the project into a sequence of very small and discrete subprojects.
4. Formal user review and approval on all key project specifications.
5. Distribution of minutes of all key design meetings to users.
6. Strong efforts to keep at least chief subproject time schedules. Low managerial and staff turnover in the user areas are vital (since a consensus on approach with the predecessor of a user manager is of dubious value).

The personnel information debacle we mentioned at the start of this chapter is an example of what can happen when this process does not take place. Soon after work started, the director of human resources decided that his senior staff's participation in the design was a waste of their time, and he made sure none of them was involved.

Instead of immediately killing the undertaking, the IS manager attempted to continue work under the leadership of one of his technically oriented staff who had little experience dealing with the human resources department. Bombarded by pressures from the human resources staff that he did not understand, the project manager allowed the systems design to expand to include more and more detail of doubtful merit until the system collapsed. The changing design made much of the programming obsolete. Tough, pragmatic leadership from users in the design stages would have made all the difference in the outcome.

The importance of user leadership increases once the design is final. Almost inevitably, at that stage users will produce some version of "I have been thinking . . ." Unless the desired changes are of critical strategic significance to the user (a judgment best made by a responsible, user-oriented project manager), the requests must be diverted and postponed until they can be considered in some formal change control process.

Unless the process is rigorously controlled (a problem intensified by the near impossibility of distinguishing between the economies of a proposed alternative and those implicit in the original design), users will make change after change, and the project will evolve rapidly to a state of permanent deferral, with completion always six months in the future.

If the project is well integrated with the user departments, the formal planning tools will be very useful in structuring tasks and helping to remove any remaining uncertainty. The target completion dates will be firm as long as the systems target remains fixed. Similarly, the formal control devices afford clear insight into progress to date, flagging both advances and slippages. If integration with user departments is weak, use of these tools will produce an entirely unwarranted feeling of confidence. By definition, the problems of technology management are usually less difficult in this type of project than in the high technology ventures, and a staff with a normal mixture of technical backgrounds should be adequate.

In fact, in almost every respect, management of this type of project differs from the previous two. The key to success is close, aggressive management of external integration supplemented by formal planning and control tools. Leadership must flow from the user rather than from the technical side.

Low Structure–High Technology

Because these projects are complex and carry high risk, their leaders need technical experience and knowledge of, and ability to communicate with, users. The same intensive effort toward external integration described in the previous class of projects is necessary here. Total commitment on the part of users to a particular set of design specifications is critical, and again they must agree to *one* out of the many thousands of options.

Unfortunately, however, an option desirable from the user's perspective may turn out to be infeasible in the selected hardware–software system. In the last several years, such situations have occurred particularly with stand-alone minicomputer systems designs, and they commonly lead either to significant restructuring of the project or elimination of it altogether. Consequently, users should be well represented at both the policy and the operations levels.

At the same time, technical considerations make strong technical leadership and internal project integration vital. This kind of effort requires the most experienced project leaders, and they will need wholehearted support from the users. In approving such a project, managers must face the question whether it can or should be divided into a series of much smaller problems or use less innovative technology.

While formal planning and control tools can be useful here, at the early stages they contribute little to reducing overall uncertainty and to highlighting all problems. The planning tools do allow the manager to structure the sequence of tasks. Unfortunately, in this type of project new tasks crop up with monotonous regularity, and tasks that appear simple and small suddenly become complex and protracted. Time, cost, and resulting technical performance turn out to be almost impossible to predict simultaneously. In the Apollo moon project, for example, technical performance achievement was key, and cost and time simply fell out. In the private sector, all too often this is an unacceptable outcome.

RELATIVE CONTRIBUTION OF MANAGEMENT TOOLS

Exhibit 7–5 shows the relative contribution that each of the four groups of project management tools makes to ensure maximum possibility of project success, given a project's inherent risk. It reveals that managers need quite different styles and approaches to manage the different types of projects effectively. Although the framework could be made more complex by including more dimensions, that would only confirm this primary conclusion.

EXHIBIT 7–5 □ Relative Contribution of Tools to Ensuring Project Success

Project type	Project description	External integration	Internal integration	Formal planning	Formal control
I	High structure, low technology; large	Low	Medium	High	High
II	High structure, low technology; small	Low	Low	Medium	High
III	High structure, high technology; large	Low	High	Medium	Medium
IV	High structure, high technology; small	Low	High	Low	Low
V	Low structure, low technology; large	High	Medium	High	High
VI	Low structure, low technology; small	High	Low	Medium	High
VII	Low structure, high technology; large	High	High	Low+	Low+
VIII	Low structure, high technology; small	High	High	Low	Low

SUMMARY

The usual corporate handbook on project management, with its unidimensional approach, fails to deal with the realities of the task facing today's managers, particularly those dealing with information services. The right approach flows from the project rather than the other way around.

The need to deal with the corporate culture within which both IS and project management operate further complicates the problems. Use of formal project planning and control tools is much more likely to produce successful results in a highly formal environment than in one where the prevailing culture is more personal and informal. Similarly, the selection and effective use of integrating mechanisms is very much a function of the corporate culture.

Thus the type of company culture further complicates our suggestions as to how different types of projects should be managed. (Too many former IS managers have made the fatal assumption that they were in an ideal position to reform corporate culture from their position!)

The past decade has brought new challenges to IS project management, and experience has indicated better ways to think about the management process. Our conclusions, then, are threefold:

1. We will continue to experience major disappointments as we push into new fields. Today, however, the dimensions of risk can be identified in advance and a decision made whether to proceed. If we proceed, we will sometimes fail.
2. The work of the systems development department in aggregate may be thought of as a portfolio. Other authors have discussed what the appropriate components of that portfolio should be at a particular point in time. The aggregate risk profile of that portfolio, however, is a critical (though often overlooked) strategic decision.
3. Project management in the IS field is complex and multidimensional. Different types of projects require different clusters of management tools if they are to succeed.

Case 7-1 □ Studsel Automotive Company*

In January 1977 Bob Chairling, Coordinator of Profit Improvement Projects at Studsel Automotive Company (SAC), was reflecting on the past few years' efforts in the Marketing Project. This project was originally conceived in 1974. Its objective was to reduce SAC's administrative costs by an estimated $4 million, as well as to improve the company's marketing information system. Mr. Chairling felt a critical review of the efforts in this large project would be good preparation for the organization, administration, and eventual implementation of the Production Project, which was now in the throes of initial development.

COMPANY BACKGROUND

In 1975 SAC ranked in the top 100 in sales, assets, and profits in *Fortune* magazine's list of the 500 largest U.S. industrial corporations. Considered a blue-chip stock on Wall Street, SAC had achieved its position through innovation in the technical and marketing areas, coupled with conservatism in the finance and personnel areas.

During the 1970s management began complementing the company's abilities to innovate on the technical nature of the business by strengthening their approach to the finance and personnel areas. The Marketing Project was part of this effort and took place under control of the accounting department of the company which will now be briefly described.

ACCOUNTING DEPARTMENT

Accounting was traditionally under the supervision of the comptroller (see Exhibit 1 for organization chart). The accounting department's work touched upon some aspects of practically every company operation, and its 4,350 employees were found throughout the United States and foreign countries. Three assistant comptrollers aided the comptroller in managing the 13 subdivisions of the department. Three of the 13 subdivisions had a major responsibility in the Marketing Accounting Project and were described as follows:

* This case was prepared as the basis for class discussion rather than to illustrate either effective or ineffective handling of an administrative situation.

EXHIBIT 1 □ Accounting Department

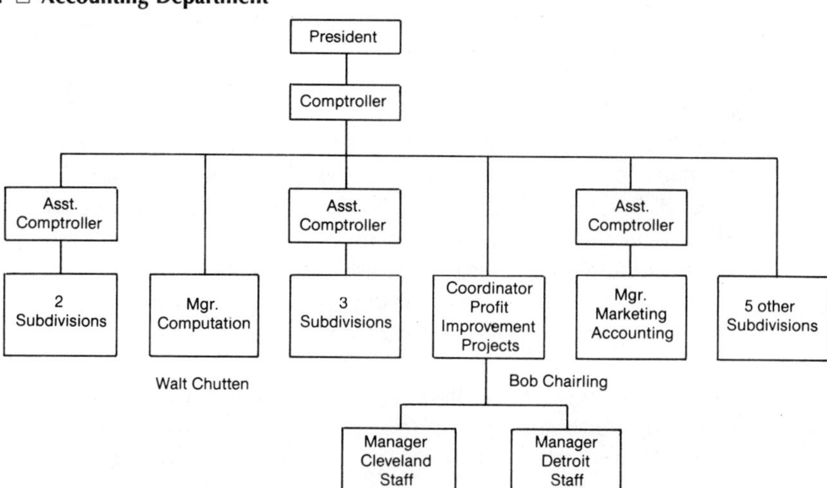

1. Profit Improvement Projects

This department, numbering 60 persons, was organized in the spring of 1974. Overall responsibility for the area rests with Bob Chairling. He reports both directly to the comptroller on all matters and to the functional executive(s) in whose area a particular project is being undertaken.

The department develops tools to improve the effectiveness of the corporate and divisional activities. In carrying out this task, the department defines the business problem, gathers the relevant facts, develops a method of handling the problem, and implements the change.

The department is staffed to handle such activities as management information studies, systems audits, work simplification studies, development of procedures manuals, systems design for computer applications, equipment evaluations, business machine applications, and forms design and control.

The studies undertaken vary from intradepartment activities to problems involving various departments within a functional division or departments in various divisions.

2. Computation Center

The Computation Center, with Walt Chutten as manager, comprises approximately 240 employees organized into major divisions; namely, Data Control, Programming, and Operations. The basic objective of the Center is to provide facilities for using large-scale computers for any profitable applications.

The Data Control Division maintains and verifies both input and output. It also monitors jobs for compliance with critical time schedules of the users and the Center.

The Programming Division offers complete services for placing a new application on the computer. These services include assisting the user in defining his problem and finding a way to solve it, designing a computer solution to the problem, conducting an economic study to explore the profitability of the solution, developing and testing the necessary programs, and maintaining the final programs in an up-to-date condition.

The Operations Division provides a complete computational service to all segments of the company through the use of the computer. It operates three shifts a day. Short-run jobs are scheduled for normal working hours so that the "turnaround time" for users is not unduly extended. Long-running jobs are generally computed on the second and third shifts for delivery the following morning.

An Administrative Division is also maintained for purposes of handling problems of department budgets, machine rentals, and intradepartmental operating records and efficiency studies.

3. Marketing Accounting

This is, numerically, the largest of the accounting departments and is responsible to the comptroller for performance of some 2,000 employees in SAC's marketing territories.

The department's personnel maintain controls over the salable products. This involved tracking the transport, storage, delivery, billing, and, finally, the collection and banking of all monies received.

OVERHAULING THE MARKETING ACCOUNTING SYSTEM

In February 1974, a consulting firm, together with Mr. Chairling's project team, presented a threefold proposal to completely overhaul the marketing accounting system at SAC. The present system utilized the efforts of 2,000 of the accounting department's 4,350 personnel, and made only slight use of data processing equipment. The proposal named the Marketing Project called for a great leap forward from manual accounting operations carried out in 49 district offices to a highly mechanized accounting operation located in Detroit, with district offices eventually supplying inputs through data transmission at their respective offices throughout the United States. The Marketing Project would cover the collecting, processing, and preparing of financial information and related statistics bearing on SAC's marketing activity.

The Marketing Project was broken down into three concurrent parts:

1. Carry out cost reduction in the field offices (i.e., cost reduction short of going to a computer).
2. Improve management information and service to marketing management.
3. Design and install a computer system for various marketing accounting activities.

Although the program was divided into three projects, the projects were very closely interrelated. The consulting firm prepared a schedule that called for completion in three and a half years. Cost reductions in the field were to be completed within 17 months; near-term management information improvements by the end of 9 months; and installation of the computer-based system which was to yield the maximum savings and information improvements was to be completed in 42 months in January of 1978.

The potential net savings from the project was $4 million—$2 million reduction in costs from the field with another $2 million coming from the implementation of the computer system. Management felt that the intangible benefits—better information, more responsiveness reporting and increased decision-making capacity should prove to be significant in the long run.

COST REDUCTION IN THE FIELD

The first parts of the Marketing Project called for streamlining of 7 regional and 49 district accounting offices. The improvement in the rather homogeneous offices included: work elimination, major methods changes, work simplification, and work standardization.

The first estimates showed a potential reduction of 200 jobs, leading to a $2 million annual savings. By January of 1975 some 450 office procedural changes were made with the reduction of 300 personnel, leading to a net savings of $3 million. For the most part, managers of all districts felt that their accounting efforts were as effective as before. In addition, the higher levels of corporate management were well pleased by the apparent success of their effort.

IMPROVEMENT OF MANAGEMENT INFORMATION

The second part of the Marketing Project called for a determination of marketing information requirements in the areas of planning, control, and decision making. By May of 1975 the study had been broken down into five areas: automotive products, industrial products, spare parts, financial reporting, and operations. The major goals of these studies were to improve planning and control of operations and fill in major information gaps in the key areas of sales activities. These new management information systems were scheduled for January of 1977. By October 1975 the studies were nearly completed and planned programming for partial implementation was advanced one year to January 1976. These projects, including the computer implementation, were all completed by the new target date. In January of 1977 Mr. Chairling mentioned that this phase of the Marketing Project was "on line" and functioning well. Managers in the areas affected by the information systems improvements said they were pleased with the results.

DESIGNING AND INSTALLING THE COMPUTER SYSTEM

The third part of the Marketing Project which was to produce $2 million in benefits began in 1974. The objectives of the computer project were:

1. Reduce the costs of operating field and home office marketing accounting and related accounting systems.
2. Improve the quality and timeliness of management information generated from marketing accounting and related activities.
3. Ease the administrative burden on field management.

The overall plan for the computer project was divided into four phases; (1) prepoint zero, (2) specifications development, (3) systems and programming, and (4) conversion. Specific plans for accomplishment during each of these phases were discussed in management meetings during the latter part of 1974.

1. *Prepoint zero:* This was the start-up period during which staffing for the next phase was to be completed and personnel were to be oriented and trained.
2. *Specifications development:* During this phase applications were to be examined in depth, the scope of the system determined, and the approach for conversion selected. Overall computer/communication requirements were to be defined, and systems specifications submitted to manufacturers. Computer and communications manufacturers' proposals were to be evaluated and equipment orders placed.
3. *Systems and programming:* During this period the detailed system was to be designed and programmed.
4. *Conversion:* The conversion phase included installing equipment, parallel operations, and the total conversion from existing manual systems to the automated computer/communications system.

As of March 1975, SAC management felt the first two phases of the computer project had been completed.

Shortly after the specifications development phase began in September 1974, a change in the scope of this phase had been brought about the realization that the Computation Center would need additional computer capacity by the end of 1975. Until that time, there had been an understanding that the project and the Computation Center would develop their respective computer specification needs simultaneously, integrate them, and submit them to manufacturers. It was expected that proposals would be reviewed jointly, and that manufacturers would have the option of proposing one or more systems to meet the needs of both groups.

When the Computation Center began investigating equipment for its own immediate needs, however, it was decided that, because of the new and larger computer equipment available, a single system would best meet the requirements of both groups. The equipment selection and operation responsibility for both units was then assigned to the Computer Center.

Representatives of the Computer Center met with the manager of the project. On several occasions, they listened to a review of the contemplated Marketing System, and had been given preliminary systems flowcharts and expected volumes. As a result, Mr. Chairling was satisfied that the Center had sufficient information to order a new computer system that would include basic equipment necessary to support the Marketing Project.

Mr. Chutten, manager of the Computation Center, informed Mr. Chairling that it was his intention to upgrade his existing equipment. This equipment consisted of two third-generation IBM System 360/Model 65s, two newer IBM System 370/Model 155s, and several less powerful older machines including an IBM 1130, and IBM 360/Model 20, and an IBM 7070. All these machines had been purchased and all but the 370/155s were fully depreciated. They still had a depreciable life of three years and a book value of $455,000 each. The Center proposed to replace all the equipment in a phased process as follows:

Step 1: Install one powerful IBM System 370/Model 168 on June 1, 1975. Disconnect the IBM 1130, the 360/Model 20, the 7070, and both 360/Model 65s. Use same standard operating system as that on the 370/155s, namely OS/MFT.[1]

Step 2: Upgrade the operating system on the 370/168 to the advanced VS1[2] environment by November 1, 1975. Install a data base package also, probably IBM's IMS.[3]

Step 3: Install second 370/168 on January 1, 1976. Use the VS1 operating

[1] OS/MFT (Operating System/Multiprogramming with a Fixed number of Tasks)—IBM-supplied programs which schedule and control the computer hardware and the concurrent execution of multiple application programs and support systems by dividing memory into a fixed number of task (program) areas.

[2] VS1 (Virtual Systems)—Sophisticated IBM-supplied programs which schedule and control the computer hardware and the concurrent execution of multiple application programs and support systems similar to OS/MFT (above) except that memory assignment and management is made assuming virtual (logical) locations far in excess of the physical locations. For example, VS1 might assign programs and data to any of 4 million logical locations where in reality there are only 1 million physical memory locations.

[3] IMS (Information Management System)—A set of programs supplied by IBM for the storing, retrieving, and transmittal of data.

system and the data base package on this one also. Disconnect the two IBM 370/Model 155s and sell to used computer dealer.

Based on this hardware and operating system plan, the Center recommended that Chairling's group design their system to operate under a virtual operating system environment like VS1 and with assumed access to a data base management package like IMS.

After the initial study in early 1974 Mr. Chairling's group made further and more detailed cost analysis of the project. A summary of this detailed economic study is as follows. The gross annual savings would be between $3.4 million and $3.9 million. Annual operating costs would range from $1.2 million to $1.4 million, resulting in a net annual savings of $2.2 million to $2.5 million. The investment required in developing the system was estimated at $2.5 million to $3.0 million. Exhibit 2 shows a more detailed breakdown of the summary statistics.

Approximately 90 percent of the gross annual savings would result from personnel displacement. The remainder would be from displacement of accounting machines and computer equipment in the accounting and payroll Departments. It was estimated that a total of 275 employees would be displaced by this system, 172 from field offices and 103 from home office departments. The personnel savings resulting from the implementation of this system would begin to accrue during the second quarter of 1977, and maximum gross savings would begin during the first quarter of 1978.

Annual recurring operating costs consist of the cost for computer and communications equipment, program maintenance, an input-output control unit (24 people), miscellaneous equipment and supplies, and personnel required to prepare input to the system which includes 45 people to input information using key-to-tape devices in field locations.

The total costs for developing the system were estimated at approximately $3.0 million. More than 85 percent of this amount was for salaries of systems and programming personnel. During the development period the Marketing Project staff was expected to reach 41 persons, including 4 supervisors, 20 analysts, and 17 programmers, all under the control of the Marketing Project leader. During conversion the staff would grow to 52 people and consist of 4 supervisors, 17 analysts, 18 programmers, and 13 field analysts who would assist in implementing the manual part of the computer system in the field.

RANKING OF PROJECTS

During phase two (specifications development phase) the computer project staff examined each of the applications in Appendix A. This review indicated that all were technically possible and economically desirable. The staff made a preliminary ranking of projects at this time. This ranking was based primarily on economics, but included other management considera-

EXHIBIT 2 □ Summary Analysis of Activities

		Estimate of costs and savings ($ 000)				
Priority	Activities	Development costs	Annual gross savings	Annual operating costs	Annual net savings	Percent of total gross saving
I	Accounts receivable	$ 600	$ 700	$ 420	$ 280	21
I	Dealer accounting	470	880	530	330	26
I	Expense analysis	180	170	20	150	5
I	Sales operations	30	130	70	60	4
I	Marketing statistics and analysis	460	460	20	440	14
I	Stock control	150	310	20	290	8
I	Product tax accounting	200	190	20	170	6
I	Nonmarketing functions	120	20	20	—	—
	Subtotal	$2,210	$2,860	$1,140	$1,720	84
II	Payroll					
II	Payroll department and casual payroll	$ 320	$ 400	$ 40	$ 360	10
II	Production and manufacturing	—	—	20	(20)	
III	Accounts payable, purchasing	160	170	20	150	5
IV	Company owned dealership accounting	60	40	20	20	1
	Subtotal	$ 540	$ 610	$ 100	$ 510	100
	Range (total program)	$2,500–$3,000	$3,400–$3,800	$1,200–$1,300	$2,200–$2,500	

tions such as support for management information and field projects, manpower dislocation impact, technical sequencing, development manpower utilization, and conversion risk. Mr. Chairling's staff grouped the projects into four priorities for conversion. At this time the staff decided that fixed asset accounting should be deferred until a later time, as it was closely related to other corporate accounting applications that were not considered a part of this effort. In addition, fixed asset accounting promised potential savings that were relatively small in relation to other systems within this project; was independent of the other systems and could be implemented at any time.

During the detailed feasibility and updated project planning study completed in early 1975 a decision was made to start first-phase computer implementation in January 1977. In so doing some of the projects were deferred for subsequent implementation. First to go was dealer accounting system. The experiment in field-office streamlining had resulted in improvements in manual accounting procedures. The field information processing was now simpler. Therefore, the previous savings potential of electronic data processing was largely negated and moving to computer processing could no longer be justified.

Second, the payroll activity was deferred. Most of the payroll already was on the IBM System 360/Model 20 computer with the exception of casual payroll. The casual payroll was handled manually, but wasn't large enough to justify a computer application. However, the payroll that was on the 360/20 still offered a savings potential because of the inefficiency of present programming and equipment. Although this savings potential remained, two factors caused the reduction in priority. First, it was felt that in light of the schedule requirements and resource limitations time could be better spent in moving manual operations to the computer as opposed to converting the inefficient 360/20 application to a more efficient program. Second the payroll activity could be pulled back without interfering with any of the other programs.

Accounts payable was shelved also because of the limited number of personnel available to design and implement the program. In addition, this program could be backed off without affecting the completion of others.

Although programming activity actually was started on sales operations and nonmarketing activities SAC backed off these two projects by early 1976. These projects utilized SAC equipment. Although it was the original intention to get all work off the 360/20 equipment it subsequently became apparent that this equipment would still be used for some time in the future. In addition, neither of these two areas had demonstrated large savings potential, and both could be pulled out without affecting the designed solutions of remaining projects.

By June 1976 it became necessary to back off some of the programming activities because the second phase of the overall project (improvement of management information systems), which previously had been pushed ahead a full year, cut into available programming time for the remaining activities. At the same time the pilot or data testing was advanced from November to September, making an additional squeeze on available time. It became necessary at this time for SAC's management to look at all the remaining projects to determine which could be pulled out to reduce the remaining workload so completion could still be achieved by January 1, 1977. Because accounts receivable was proving to be rather complex in the systems and programming dimension and because the remaining projects still would not be materially affected by backing this project out, it was decided to lower the accounts receivable priority.

Further reflection showed that the economics of the accounts receivable activity were dependent upon the conversion of the data communication network which was not scheduled for early implementation. As the data communications capability came on line the accounts receivable activities could then be programmed. Thus the lowering of the accounts receivable priority would allow some breathing room in the conversion process without seriously affecting the overall economic benefits of the project.

ORGANIZATION FOR COMPUTER PROGRAMMING

During March of 1975 SAC management had also decided on the separate organization of systems and programming responsibilities; systems under the Marketing Project leadership, and programming under the direction of the Computer Center. This was an organization change from the previous decision to have the analysts and programming under the control of the Marketing Project leader. Previously the reasons for unified control were:

1. It clearly fixed "cradle-to-grave" responsibility for this large, long, and important program.
2. It provided for the most effective planning, coordination, and control over the many complex and highly interrelated program projects.
3. It facilitated communications with the marketing department, which had a vital interest in—and indirect responsibility for—the project's success.

The change was supported by a recommendation from outside consultants who evaluated the above reasons for centralization and compared them with reasons for Computation Center programming responsibility reproduced below.

1. A professional programming group, such as the Computation Center had, would produce more effective, efficient machine programs than a less-qualified or less highly specialized programming group.
2. Consolidating marketing accounting programming requirements with

other programming work of the Computation Center could lead to more efficient manpower utilization, that is, fewer programmers required and/or faster completion of the work to be done.
3. Since the Computation Center already has a unit in being, it could more easily and more effectively carry out the programming staff expansion required.
4. Since many of the programmers will likely be transferred to the Computation Center on completion of the marketing accounting project, it is desirable to recruit them initially into the organization where they will end up.

Furthermore, looking beyond just the Marketing Accounting Project, they argued that this project should be assigned to the Computation Center to demonstrate (1) that the Center is to do not just program maintenance and ongoing jobs, but large-scale, discrete projects as well, and (2) that the Center is to undertake administrative as well as engineering applications.

Because of the broader purpose of the Center—namely, on a centralized basis to provide (within reason) the programming for all applications, large as well as small, administrative as well as engineering—they recommended that Marketing Project programming be done by Computation Center personnel.

For this project and other large-scale, discrete projects the following programming organization and relationships were set forth.

The Computation Center was to be responsible for:

1. Hiring, firing, and compensating all programming personnel and performing the other personnel management activities.
2. Training programming personnel in the programming techniques and operating procedures adopted by the Center.
3. Providing effective, responsive service to "customer" projects, which in the case of large-scale, discrete projects should mean making full-time assignment of programming staff to the project team.

The manager of the large-scale, discrete project (e.g., Marketing Accounting) was to be responsible for:

1. Carefully planning project requirements and informing the Computation Center of significant changes in project programming needs to permit the Center to effectively rebalance its workload and manpower.
2. Monitoring program progress and consulting with the Center if assigned programming manpower is not meeting reasonable standards of technical performance.
3. Maintaining liaison with operating management and achieving projects objectives in terms of cost, timetables and benefits.

In the consultant's judgment this approach was sound and recognized the different contributions from, and the responsibilities of, the technical and administrative unit (the Computation Center) and the customer project team. However, since this was SAC's initial experience with this approach, and in light of the importance of the Marketing Project, SAC was encouraged to establish careful controls over the joint effort to ensure that this approach was operating effectively.

CONTROL OVER ANALYSTS AND PROGRAMMING TIME

In the system analysis area, each computer activity was broken down into five phases for explicit definition and control purposes. These phases were:

1. Integrated system design.
2. Program requirements through flowcharts.
3. Preparation of test data.
4. Preparation of procedures manual.
5. Publication of manuals and documentation of efforts.

A lead analyst was in charge of one or more particular system activities. He supervised the activities of one, two, or three other analysts. As activities were further broken down into the five phases, time was allocated to schedule the accomplishment of each project phase. (See Exhibit 3.)

In the programming area the control over schedules and programming time was handled somewhat differently. Here the lead programmer supervised the work of one to three programmers in the accomplishment of the required coding tasks. The lead programmer defined start and complete dates and the amount of man-days necessary to complete each activity. He met with each programmer informally during the week to discuss progress. Once a week he recorded the progress and made any schedule revisions that appeared necessary. The major difference between the method of control of the analysts' time and the programmer's time was the lack of detailed activity breakdown by the programmers. Hence, the various programs were viewed in their entirety and the record of progress was viewed from the start-date to complete-date of an entire activity. Exhibit 4 shows examples of the programmers' approach to controlling their time.

In addition, there was a weekly meeting at the Computation Center each Friday between the lead analysts from the Marketing Project, the Center's lead programmers, and the management of the two organizations, and a representative from Marketing Accounting. The meetings were on an informal basis so as to allow free discussion of "where we are and where we want to go." Each particular project was reviewed to determine status and possible schedule revisions. Exhibit 5 shows a summary of one of the meetings.

EXHIBIT 3

MP–22 Rev 1

WEEKLY STATUS REPORT-SYSTEMS PHASE

Activity		Expense Distribution						
Assigned to		A. Stevens						
	Phase 3	2/5/76 to 3/25/76						
	1-Date started	2/8	2/8	2/8	2/8	2/8	2/8	2/8
JOB PERFORMANCE	2- Original estimate of Man-days required	28	28	28	28	28	28	28
	3- Revised estimate of Man-days required	28	28	28	28	28	28	28
	4- Applied man-days	4	9	13	17.5	23	26	27
	5- Percent should be complete (4 ÷ 3)	14%	32%	46%	63%	82%	93%	96%
	6-Estimated man-days required to complete	24	19	15	11	4.5	1.5	.5
	7- Current estimate of man-days required	28	28	28	28.5	27.5	27.5	27.5
	8- Percent actually completed (4 ÷ 7)	14%	32%	46%	62%	84%	95%	98%
STATUS	9- Adjusted estimate of man-days required	28	28	28	28	28	28	28
	10- Man-days elapsed	7	12	16	21	24	27	28

TIME							
11- Percent time elapsed (10 ÷ 9)	25%	43%	57%	75%	86%	96%	100%
12- Percent ahead or	11%	−11%	−11%	−13%	−2%	−1%	−2%
13- Number of personnel assigned	1	1	1	1	1	1	1
14- Revised estimated completion date						3/22	3/28
15- Original estimated completion date	3/21	3/21	3/21	3/21	3/21	3/21	3/21
Today's date	2/11	2/18	2/25	3/4	3/11	3/18	3/25

Lost Time—Man/Days	Number	Comments (Include explanation of any impediments)
ACCUMULATED—LAST REPORT		
2/11	3	Phase II delays
2/18	3	
2/25	3	
3/4	3.5	Staff meeting
3/11	3.5	
3/18	3.5	
3/25	3.5	
3/25	3.5	
ACCUMULATED TO DATE		Note: Phase 4 to begin 4/1/76

EXHIBIT 4 □ Computation Center Progress Report on Marketing Project for Week 08/21/76 thru 08/27/76

					Applied man-days							
Prog. no.	Prog. name	Start date	Current completion date	REV	This week	To date	Required to complete	Start to finish	W.O. est.	REV	Percent complete	Calendar weeks left
	Trans	05/01/76	12/31/76	0	0.	6.2	63.8	70.0	70	0	8.8	18.0
	Dated	05/01/76	09/11/76	1	17.0	129.8	35.2	165.0	165	0	78.7	2.1
	Edit-1	05/01/76	09/11/76	2	10.3	75.1	16.2	91.3	23	0	82.3	2.1
	Edit-2	05/01/76	09/11/76	1	7.2	79.7	12.8	92.5	85	0	86.2	2.1
	Edit-3	05/01/76	08/22/76	2	4.1	59.2	0.9	60.1	68	0	98.5	−0.7
Stock control												
0401	Daily	03/15/76	09/01/76	1	8.4	190.5	0.6	191.2	168	1	99.7	0.7
0402	Month	03/15/76	11/08/76	1	0.	8.9	168.0	176.9	218	1	5.1	10.4
Tax accounting												
0501	Month	03/15/76	10/17/76	2	17.7	192.7	171.3	364.0	455	1	52.9	7.3
0502	Daily	07/05/76	09/11/76	1	4.2	26.9	5.1	32.0	20	0	84.1	2.1
Dealer accounting												
0601	Daily	12/29/75	10/01/76	1	20.1	412.9	111.4	524.3	393	0	78.8	5.0
0602	Month	01/13/76	10/30/76	3	1.4	23.1	64.9	88.0	45	0	26.3	9.1
0605	S Proc.	06/30/76	08/29/76	0	1.4	15.0	6.6	21.6	60	0	69.3	0.3
	S Cost	05/01/76	09/09/76	1	2.0	32.0	29.4	61.5	65	1	52.1	1.9
Sales statistics												
0801	Daily	04/25/76	09/06/76	3	4.4	75.2	21.8	97.0	55	0	77.5	1.4
0802	Weekly	04/25/76	09/12/76	2	1.9	50.8	9.2	59.9	55	0	84.7	2.3
0803	Update	05/15/75	10/01/76	0	6.4	77.2	87.8	165.0	165	0	46.8	5.0
0804	C Rep	05/15/75	09/19/76	1	9.9	113.3	44.8	158.0	145	0	71.7	3.3

REMAINING PROBLEMS

By late summer of 1976 Mr. Chutten, the head of the Computation Center, had doubts that the whole project would be fully ready for implementation in January 1977. Mr. Chairling also realized that the scheduled date was not very probable. During the latter months of 1976 more schedule slippage occurred to the point that expected dates for full project implementation now ranged from June 1977 to December 1977.

Briefly these problems contributed to the schedule slippage:

1. *IBM Systems 370 Model 168 software problems*—The first 370/168 computer arrived in July 1975. IBM turned it over to SAC on August 1. Operating under OS/MFT and lightly loaded at first, it performed with 97 percent availability for the first two months. Unfortunately, the testing of VS1 seriously reduced this reliability to the range of 80 percent availability during the next three months. Therefore, delivery of the second 370/168 was deferred until July 1976. Problems caused by VS1, and the additional testing of IMS and an online telecommunications monitor caused significant downtime until the delivery of the second 168. In March of 1976 the 7070, the 1130, and one 65 were sold. In August 1976 the second 65 and one of the 155s were sold. Net proceeds on all equipment came to $427,000. As of January 1977, SAC owned a 360/20, a 155, and two 370/168s with 2 million bytes of memory each. All machines were operating at approximately 95 percent availability.
2. *Growth in Computer Center*—The size of the Center was increasing rapidly to its present size. Hiring of enough systems experts in VS and IMS proved expensive and difficult. Retaining them proved more difficult. Six of the first eight hired left for higher pay. SAC also had many growing pains introducing and training new programmers.
3. *Communications between the Marketing Project Group and the Center*—Blame for delay in the schedule was shifted back and forth between the groups. For example, it was claimed that the test data prepared by the analysts wasn't satisfactory to the programmers because it didn't test all the parameters of the program. Programmers also contended that the analysts' specs weren't always adequate, and the analysts would counter complain that the programmers wanted to redesign their work.
4. *Documentation slipped*—For some months during the fall of 1976 the previously agreed-upon arrangement of documentation of the changes in procedures, additions, and corrections of programs, and the modifications of test data were relaxed. The relaxation of formal documentation was in the interest of gaining some time to meet the scheduled deadline of January 1. Both Mr. Chairling and Mr. Chutten now feel that

EXHIBIT 5 □ Excerpts from a Meeting on Programming Progress

MARKETING PROJECT JOINT STATUS
MEETING OF AUGUST 12, 1976

August 18, 1976
Chicago

J. R. Erickson
Computation Center

Mr. D. W. Della Roussa
Profit Improvement Projects (PIP)

Dear Sir:

The following notes summarize the joint status meeting of August 12 between PIP and Center personnel. The next meeting is Friday, August 26, at 1:30 P.M.

As of August 5, sixty-one of our programming personnel were working on the Marketing Project. This will increase slightly during August and drop in September when eleven summer programmers return to school.

Dealer Accounting

Daily .... Coding is 85 percent–90 percent completed, and the first acceptance test is currently being run on the existing part. (Completion date is still October 1.)

Monthly .... Completion has been rescheduled from October 1 to October 30. This program is not needed until the daily program has been run for a month.

Special Processing ...... No problems. We expect to be completed by the August 29 target.

Expense Distribution/Financial Reports

Subsystem 11-01 (4th day processing) of Expense Distribution has been completed and acceptance test output given to H. B. Dun on August 12 (due August 15). The rest of the work is on schedule.

Sales Statistics

Subsystem

1. Daily—currently testing.
2. Weekly—currently testing.

EXHIBIT 5 ***(concluded)***

3. Update—currently testing; coding is 90 percent complete.
4. Customer history—currently performing preliminary tests; coding is 80 percent complete.

Daily Stock Control

1. Program has been completely coded; except to start acceptance testing on August 15.
2. Daily Stock should be ready for integration test by September 1.

Monthly Stock Control

Work has been delayed on this activity due to revisions of Daily Stock. The earliest completion date anticipated is October 31, 1976.

Daily Tax Accounting

New specifications on control totals will cost the tax effort six man-days. Priority has been given to the daily at the expense of the monthly. Coding is about 90 percent complete, and testing should start with Control Edit-2 next week.

Monthly Tax Accounting

Additional test data was received. Coding is progressing satisfactorily on all seven programs. Testing should begin next week on three of the smaller programs.

Miscellaneous

D. W. Della Roussa requested that a five-word header to added to all records in the monthly files to simplify anticipated future requirements. The Center will consider the effect of this on meeting current deadlines.

Very truly yours,

J. R. Erickson

J. R. Erickson
Computation Center

JRE/pac

the relaxation of formal documentation during this period was a serious mistake, as it made the identification of real progress most difficult to isolate. Thus it was hard to state with certainty that the goal of a reliable working system was being accomplished.

5. *Turnaround poor*—Some schedules weren't realistic in the light of experience. For example, turnaround time for test and debug trials was planned at twice a day; experience proved it took two days to run, review, and correct each trial of a program segment.
6. *Field processing was inefficient*—Initial test indicated that with only 45 percent of the modules operating, the processing of representative daily field input was taking approximately 11 hours of 168 time. The systems design called for input of data from 56 locations starting at 5 P.M. daily with all output completely transmitted back by 8 A.M. the next day.

Bob Chairling pondered these problems with SAC's first big entrance into distributed computer utilization. Each month that went by cost SAC approximately $200,000 in forgone savings and benefits. Yet in January of 1977, Mr. Chairling was already busy assisting the production department executives in planning their own profit improvement project. This project, which was even greater in scope than the Marketing Project, also offered potentially substantial benefits through the successful implementation of a program that would stretch out over a three-year period or longer. As Mr. Chairling reflected on the past few years' experience, he hoped he could provide helpful guidance to production department management by communicating the knowledge gained from this first large-scale project.

APPENDIX A □ SYSTEMS SCOPE COMPUTER PROJECT

1. *Accounts Receivable.* This activity includes: *(a)* dealer accounts, including reconciliation of SAC checks-in-progress and credits to dealers with the verified credits by SAC regional officers, *(b)* fleet accounts, *(c)* attorney accounts. The system is expected to: *(a)* maintain records to account for all charges and credits made to a dealer's account, *(b)* maintain current records on dealers' names, addresses, and status, and *(c)* prepare accounting and credit reports as required. Aged receivables will be maintained for collection purposes. Open item statements will be prepared at regular intervals. Accounts receivable will be updated daily and exception reports will be available.

2. *Dealer Accounting.* This activity includes processing vehicle invoices, transportation charges, appropriate taxes, overhead allowances, rent where applicable, refunds, information now retained in Kardex files, and other dealer data. It is also expected to include an evaluation of customer, model, and location performance and to assist in developing statistical criteria for selecting future dealers and locations.

3. Expense Analysis. The expense analysis activity consists of several parts: *(a)* expense distribution, *(b)* selling expense reports, *(c)* transportation expenses, *(d)* financial statements, and *(e)* sales operations reports.

The expense distribution activity includes the distribution of marketing expenses by appropriate expense classifications and the preparation of appropriate reports. The selling expense report function consists of maintaining the selling expense subledger by district and region, maintaining expense controls for dealerships, and auditing, balancing, and distributing expense statements. Financial statement preparation concerns the periodic marketing responsibility reports showing sales, income, and selling expenses.

4. Sales Operations Reports. Currently this operation is primarily concerned with transport reports, but it is expected that other reports—showing detailed and summary costs of operating specified facilities or assets—will be required.

5. Marketing Statistics and Analysis. This activity consists of *(a)* sales costing, *(b)* sales forecasting, *(c)* sales income, and *(d)* sales statistics.

The sales costing operations would consist of identifying the net assembly and manufacturing costs on all vehicles and options and computing plant, model, and option revenues and gross profits for all product sales. The sales forecasting activity would allow for forecasts of sales and revisions of budgets, as well as the effect of pricing, advertising, and distribution upon the market. This area has not been completely defined at this time; it is expected that there will be management information needs in this area that will be identified in the coming months by the project team. The sales income activity will provide a statistical capability for profitability reports by product, model, option, dealer, and territory. The sales statistics operation consists of preparing periodic sales reports for the field (districts and regions) and the home office as required.

6. Stock Control. This activity is primarily concerned with maintaining stock control records for all finished vehicles. The system will *(a)* capture data as vehicles arrive at physical checkpoints such as end-of-assembly line, factory parking lot, transport, intermediate storage lots, regional lots, district lots, and dealer locations; *(b)* maintain records on inventory at each location; *(c)* compare book and physical inventories and compute differences; *(d)* generate inventory values for corporate records; *(e)* determine regional and district inventory mix reorder points; and *(f)* automatically restock intermediate storage locations. In addition to reduced accounting costs, more rapid processing, and more timely management information, the stock control system should allow for more consistent application of inventory policy, for maintenance of optimum stock levels, and should reduce the number of lost sales resulting from wrong dealer mix or poor delivery.

7. Product Tax Accounting. The purpose of this activity is to record, maintain, and provide information on product taxes required to make payments to appropriate tax authorities, and to prepare necessary reports. The taxes that will be processed in this manner are: *(a)* state and federal excise, *(b)* selected *ad valorem,* *(c)* state and local sales and use, and *(d)* others such as motor carrier and over-the-road taxes.

8. Nonmarketing Activities. At present there are several processing requirements in the accounting department that are not concerned with the marketing function. These activities, primarily in the spare parts area, are included because of their overlap with certain marketing functions.

9. Payroll. This activity would include the processing of pay records now done in Detroit, and (subject to further feasibility analyses) the work of existing processing centers in San Jose, Springfield, and Cleveland. It would include all aspects of the payroll function; distributing the marketing operation payroll, maintaining stock purchase plan information, processing pay records for casual employees, and preparing requisite statistics and reports. This activity is not scheduled for conversion until the beginning of the second quarter of 1978; 1977 requirements for payroll information will be met by using the output from the present systems.

10. Accounts Payable, Purchasing. This operation will process and pay marketing and nonmarketing vendor bills, including those now paid through the imprest fund and by the Accounts Payable Section of the corporate accounting department. It will include: *(a)* the preparation of checks and cash disbursement records, *(b)* check reconciliation, *(c)* forecasting cash demand on appropriate accounts for specified periods of time, and *(d)* providing information on items purchased by vendor and commodity categories to the purchasing department. The present schedule calls for converting this activity in the summer of 1977.

11. Company-Owned Dealership Accounting. Initial efforts in this area will include only the preparation of sales and financial reports. Simplified procedures in the field have substantially reduced the economic justification for processing daily transactions on a computer system.

Case 7-2 □ Dallas Tire Corporation—Project Planning and Management Control System*

In April 1978, Dave Swanson, General Manager of Corporate Data Processing (CDP) at Dallas Tire Corporation (DTC), listened attentively as Noel Abbott, CDP Manager of Planning and Control, summarized the feedback he received from users and plant data processing personnel on the Project Planning and Management Control System (PPMCS). PPMCS had been implemented for one year, during which 208 application development phases (approximately 52 projects) were completed. Swanson and Abbott thought one year was an appropriate time frame to formally assess organizational receptivity and effectiveness of the system. Informally they had received numerous comments, ranging from:

> . . . this methodology makes me feel like a robot. Creativity and personal initiative have been severely blunted by PPMCS. I'm certain it will be significantly revised in the near future, but, unfortunately it won't happen [the revision] before substantial turnover has occurred.

to

> . . . PPMCS provides an orderly approach to accomplish desired project results while producing more uniform and consistent results from an administrative viewpoint.

A questionnaire was designed and distributed which tried to identify the extent of use, advantages, disadvantages, and problems. After analyzing the returned questionnaires and generating summary lists of concerns and problems, Abbott scheduled the meeting to discuss responses to key issues and points. Among the things Swanson specifically wanted to review were responses to the new RISK ASSESSMENT procedure and how well it had interfaced with the new *system development methodology* and the old *profitability index*.

COMPANY BACKGROUND

Dallas Tire Corporation (DTC), the country's second largest tire producer, was established in 1910 when Albert K. Cotton acquired facilities of Dallas Rubber Company. DTC supplies approximately 25 percent of the country's man-made rubber; produces a comprehensive line of tires and related

* This case was prepared by Assistant Professor James I. Cash, as a basis for class discussion rather than to illustrate either effective or ineffective handling of an administrative situation.

products for autos, trucks, buses, trailers, aircraft, off-the-road equipment, farm and industrial vehicles; and has other operations in chemicals, mining, shipbuilding and repair, and plastics. The company employs approximately 95,000 people worldwide with facilities and operations that span three continents. Revenues for 1978 were approximately $6.2 billion, which attracted approximately 165,000 stockholders.

Corporate headquarters for DTC are located in Dallas, Texas, across Mockingbird Avenue from CDP. A corporate organization chart highlighting DTC's data processing organization is shown in Exhibit 1.

CORPORATE DATA PROCESSING

CDP was established in 1969. The current organization structure shown in Exhibit 1 was adopted in 1972. Prior to this structure, which has geographically dispersed plant data processing managers reporting directly to the CDP general manager, plant data processing managers reported to local plant general managers through plant controllers with "dotted line" responsibility to the CDP general manager.

Noteworthy is the existence of corporate and plant steering committees. These were formally titled the "Computers and Systems Development Planning Council" (hereafter referred to as Council) at the corporate level and the "Plant Computers and Systems Development Task Forces" (hereafter called Plant Task Forces) at the plant level. The Plant Task Forces meet monthly to monitor current ongoing development and to approve initiation or cancellation of systems/projects. The corporate-level Council has a "task force" subset which performs these tasks for "home office" (corporate) plans. The Council has nine official members—representing Planning, Tire Operations, Accounting (2), Sales (2), Engineering, Research, and Communications. The Corporate Data Processing general manager attends meetings while the CDP manager of Planning and Control serves as secretary of the group. The two highest ranking members of the group have assistant vice president titles (Planning, and one of the Accounting representatives). The assistant vice president of planning serves as chairman of the Council. Each Plant Task Force is chaired by the plant assistant general manager, and complemented with other first line plant managers chosen by the plant general manager.

These steering committees have been very active and effective. The Council was established in 1973 by DTC's president. Their charter was to assure that the company was getting the most efficient and effective use of data processing resources possible. Senior management commitment to, and support of, this group has been consistently strong. Some data processing personnel desired higher-level management representation on the committees, but felt there could be only minimal improvement in effectiveness.

EXHIBIT 1 □ Organization Chart

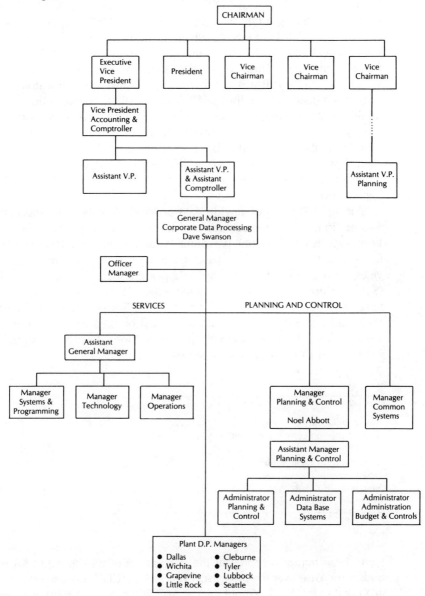

- CHAIRMAN
  - Executive Vice President
    - Vice President Accounting & Comptroller
      - Assistant V.P.
      - Assistant V.P. & Assistant Comptroller
        - General Manager Corporate Data Processing Dave Swanson
          - Officer Manager
          - SERVICES
            - Assistant General Manager
              - Manager Systems & Programming
              - Manager Technology
              - Manager Operations
          - PLANNING AND CONTROL
            - Manager Planning & Control Noel Abbott
              - Assistant Manager Planning & Control
                - Administrator Planning & Control
                - Administrator Data Base Systems
                - Administrator Administration Budget & Controls
            - Manager Common Systems
          - Plant D.P. Managers
            - Dallas
            - Wichita
            - Grapevine
            - Little Rock
            - Cleburne
            - Tyler
            - Lubbock
            - Seattle
  - President
  - Vice Chairman
  - Vice Chairman
  - Vice Chairman
    - Assistant V.P. Planning

CDP's data center, referred to as Corporate Data Center (CDC), is located in the same building with CDP staff. CDP has three IBM 370/158 Model 3 central processing units (4 MEG-MVS/SE, 5 MEG-Attached Processor-MVS/SE, and 3 MEG-MVS/SE) which serve as the primary node in DTC's communication network (companywide there are approximately 55 mainframe computers). These processors share a pool of peripheral devices which include: 44 IBM 3350 disk units, 22 IBM 3330 disk units, an IBM 2305 fixed head disk, an IBM 3540 diskette reader, 16 magnetic tape drives, an IBM 1403-NI printer, a laser printer (IBM 3800), and other miscellaneous unit record equipment. System development activities at corporate and remote plants are supported by a 60-terminal TSO network on one of the 158s. There are 244 IMS/VS-controlled terminals supporting various online applications on a different 158. The third 158 system supports RJE/batch applications.

During 1978, corporatewide data processing costs were approximately $40 million. The major components of this budget were hardware ($8 million), supplies ($4 million), personnel ($22 million), and other costs ($6 million—which includes DP-related communication costs and outside services). This cost level represented a 12 percent increase over the 1977 costs ($35.7 million) and 21 percent increase over 1976 ($33 million). In characterizing DP budget changes for recent years, Swanson indicated hardware costs had declined as a percentage of total budget, while personnel costs were making the most dramatic increase. More detailed explanations of incremental FY1980 budget increases were:

	Percent
New applications	25%
Maintenance on current applications	40
New DP sites	10
Conversions in existing sites	3
New hardware (1-year cost)	5
New staff	7
Inflation	10

Here these numbers represent the percentage of an estimated $6 million budget increase over the prior fiscal year, which CDP chose to classify in the given category. For example, .40 × $6 million = $2.4 million more than was allocated in the FY1979 budget will be allocated for maintenance. Two or more of the entries could be interrelated.

DTC employs approximately 600 data processing professionals worldwide (exclusive of order entry, etc. personnel).

As shown in Exhibit 1, CDP has the following major sections:

I. Services

Systems and Programming—This group is responsible for analysis, design, and implementation of information systems. Both new development and maintenance activities reside here. Most of the work performed is in support corporate activities and common systems development.

Technology—Provides technical software and hardware support, including communication. Primary responsibility is for the CDP environment; however they also consult and support plant data processing sites as required.

Operations—DP shop floor management and administration group which includes data entry, peripheral equipment control, operations analysts, tape and disk librarians, etc.

II. Planning and Control

Project Planning and Control—A staff service group receives, reviews, and verifies status documents on project development. In addition, they serve as the clearinghouse for assembly of the corporatewide data processing plan, as well as the primary facilitator of the planning process.

Data Base Systems—This group is assigned to maintain IMS standards and to oversee use and integrity of CDP's Synergetics data dictionary package.

Administration, Budget, Control—Responsible for general standards and procedures, audits, education, capital project administration, budgets, and controls.

Common Systems—This group surveys the corporatewide DP community on a regular basis to identify opportunities for consolidation and general distribution of systems.

Plant data processing installations typically had systems and programming, operations, and, where appropriate, technical support staff (Technology Group).

Dave Swanson, 55-year-old CDP General Manager, originally joined DTC in 1949, after acquiring an MBA from Lehigh University. He worked in numerous DTC positions, including Tire Plant DP manager and staff assistant to the plant controller before assuming his present position in 1969.

Noel Abbott, 59, had been with DTC for 38 years. Although his formal training was in accounting, Abbott amassed over 30 years of data processing experience, with the last 15 years in CDP. He had worked in DTC shipyards as a plant supervisor of analysts, administrative assistant to CDP general manager, and various other DP-related jobs.

HISTORY OF DTC'S PROJECT PLANNING AND MANAGEMENT CONTROL SYSTEM (PPMCS)

The first task pursued by the Council after its establishment in 1973 was a survey of how data processing was being used in the company. During this initial survey of current use and new projects that were planned for the ensuing five years, it was discovered that the planned work, given available work resources, would more realistically take 10 years.

"That finding," said Swanson, "dramatized our need to develop planning and strategy techniques that would give us selection criteria for doing the right things with our resources. We had to be able to answer the basic questions of what resources we should have and where we should allocate them. In addition, we needed to incorporate the answers into a realistic, manageable five-year plan.

"In October 1976 we got all the DP managers in a planning session to understand what our problems were, and how we could solve them. During those three days we discussed a lot of ideas andperspectives, and decided we were crazy for trying to control all projects from their inception to their completion as if they were single continuous processes. A user would say, 'I've got a problem,' and we would give them an estimate for solving their problems. Even before we understood the problem, we provided a benchmark for measuring our performance by giving them an estimate.

"We were experiencing continuing failure to get projects done on time and within budget. A typical system development experience was:

> We would make an initial estimate of $50,000 to do a job and get approval to start development from a corporate steering committee. Later, we would revise the initial estimate to $88,000 plus added facilities to do the job. By the time we received approval for the revised figure, new projected costs would be $120,000. Finally, upon completion of the system, our costs would be well over $150,000.

"It became obvious that this cost issue was the symptom of a much larger problem.

"Although externally it appeared we simply couldn't effectively manage or control system development-related costs, we were learning that systems development is an extremely complex process. Most important, the requirements of skill, knowledge, understanding, and cooperation from many individuals and groups was not fully appreciated or formally addressed. On top of that, the integration and interaction of the following constraints had to be formally addressed:

Organizational constraints.

Management requirements and constraints.

User functional requirements and constraints.

Technical considerations.

"Of course these problems are not unique to DTC," added Abbott. "Disorganized systems development has cost computer-using companies billions of dollars in budget overruns, lost productivity, and ill-devised systems. Here, at DTC, we had *no standard development* procedures, extemely *high redevelopment costs* because of a lack of common applications developed for all users, large overruns on budget and schedules, systems being patched to make them work, and high systems maintenance costs—all of which seriously inhibited our ability to do meaningful five-year planning and, more importantly, seriously impacted our credibility and image in the company. We had all the pieces, were using all the right phrases, and if someone asked if we were doing project planning and monitoring/control my response in 1975 would probably have been YES. However, there were no interfaces between these pieces and we *really* didn't know how to put the pieces together to make the total systems development process work.

"The October 1976 sessions forced the realization that effectively managing our five-year plan was impossible until we put all our pieces together. In addition, we probably also lacked *effective* procedures for generating, monitoring, and controlling any operational plans.

"At a conceptual level we decided we needed:

1. A definitive systems development life-cycle methodology.
2. The ability to control phases of systems development rather than the total project.
3. Better estimates for planning and executing.
4. Better resource planning to ensure systems development planning was consistent with resources available."

The Planning and Control group, under the leadership of Abbott, was given responsibility for developing the system. First they tried to define what the objectives for a *total* project management and control system were. This list included:

1. To assure you are *DOING THE RIGHT THINGS.* That is, the systems you are developing are effective, and consistent with corporate goals and programs.
2. To assure you are *DOING THINGS RIGHT.* This objective addresses increased productivity via making efficient use of resources.
3. To provide effective *MANAGEMENT CONTROL.* The system must facilitate intelligent reallocation of resources forced by dynamic replanning or taking corrective action. If achieved, this capability significantly improves accountability with management.
4. To provide better *USER SERVICE* which infers fewer missed due dates, fewer cost overruns and better communication. This objective has significant impact on profitability.

Next, they tried to define, in the most simplistic framework possible, what they did:

1. Plan.
2. Execute.
3. Monitor and control.
4. Adjust.
5. Recycle through 1–4.

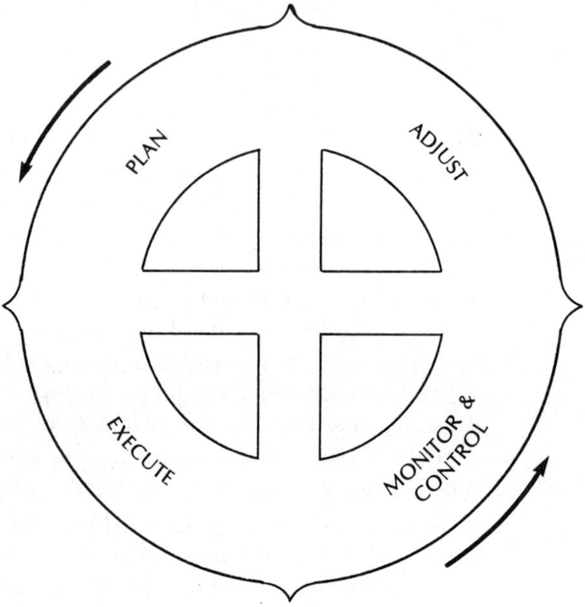

Finally, the mechanisms required to support this cycle and objectives were identified. Some of these mechanisms existed in an immediately usable form, some existed but had to be modified, others had to be designed and integrated. Exhibit 2 depicts PPMCS and lists the objectives and components (mechanisms) of each. Exhibit 3 presents the principal intent of the major mechanisms shown in Exhibit 2.

In late 1976, CDP issued a "white paper" describing the new system, received critiques of the system, and made revisions. Implementation of the system began early in 1977, with a target of 10 percent maximum variance from planned budget and time. (Abbott guessed they had experienced 90 percent variances in the past; and had experienced 40 percent variances on budget and 50 percent variances on time during the first year under PPMCS.)

PROJECT PLANNING AND MANAGEMENT CONTROL SYSTEM OVERVIEW

As depicted in Exhibit 2, DTC's PPMCS has four major process sections—PLANNING, EXECUTING, MONITORING & CONTROLLING, and ADJUSTING. This case will focus on the first two components.

Planning

(The information which follows is excerpted from the DTC Computer and Systems Development Planning Procedures Manual.)

EXHIBIT 2

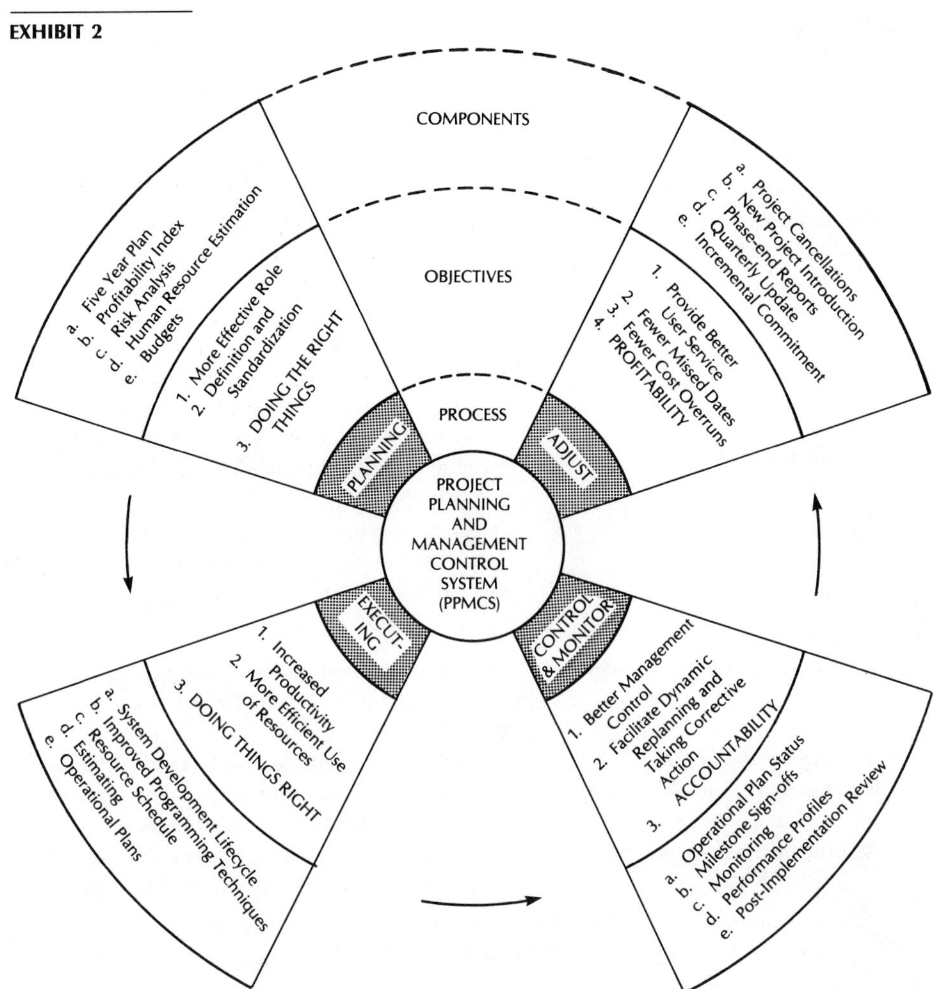

PPMCS's ongoing processes (Planning, Executing, Controlling & Monitoring, and Adjusting), the objectives each process tries to address, and the components or mechanisms used to achieve the given objectives.

Since the *primary objective* of computers and systems development activities is to implement systems consistent with corporate goals and strategies, *decisions* must be made which require careful analysis and evaluation of a wide variety of factors.

The process by which such decisions are made is a *planning process*. At DTC this process is defined by the following steps:

A. After analyzing key business activities, corporate objectives and strategies, the initial Systems Development *Five-Year Plan* is established by

EXHIBIT 3

Component	Principal intent
I. Plan	
Five-year plan	Display projects to be addressed over a five-year period and to show the allocation of resources necessary to accomplish them.
Profitability index	Provide a ranking technique to assist in prioritizing and scheduling system development according to corporate economic guidelines. Indicates relative economic impact of projects.
Risk analysis	Provide a procedure to determine inherent degree of system/project development risk. Weighed against system commitment and used to balance application development portfolio.
Estimating	Provide a standard technique and procedure for project estimating.
Budgets	Integrate development and maintenance of projected capital, human resource, and operating costs with planning.
II. EXECUTE	
Systems development life-cycle	Provide a standard but flexible framework within which application development work will take place.
Improved programming techniques	To increase programmer productivity, adherence to standards and documentation. This contributes to reduction of rework required.
Resource scheduler	Determine if needed human resources (including skills) will be available as required by a project.
Operational plans	Zero-in on near-term activities. Facilitates management and control of committed phases. Contains only currently active phases or those scheduled to begin in next 30 days.
III. CONTROL AND MONITOR	
Post-implementation review	Evaluate project development and performance—including efficiency and effectiveness, and to provide feedback.
Performance profiles	Measure department performance against predetermined goals. (Data collected by location.)
Monitoring	Check on progress of the operational plan. Enable the data processing department to determine if it is meeting performance standards. Upon completion of the project to determine if department functions as expected or desired.

EXHIBIT 3 (*concluded*)

Component	Principal intent
Operational plan status/variances	Provide "red flags" for variances in plan that need to be controlled and new developments which should be reported to management. Conveys whether project is on time and/or on budget.
IV. ADJUST	
Phase-end report	Essentially an updated PLANNING DOCUMENT A which facilitates making new project initiation and project cancellation decisions. Obtain incremental commitment.
Quarterly update	Revise the five year plan to reflect current situation (business conditions, plans, resources).

user department, systems development group, and local task force interaction. It is based upon current estimates of hours required for systems/projects within a Planning Reference Number.

B. Proposed systems must be defined and prioritized (explained later).
C. Capability to carry out the Five-Year Plan is determined by projecting a *Resource Plan*. Adjustments are made to the Five-Year Plan as necessary. Supporting plans (staffing, hardware, software, communications, facilities, education, etc.) are developed and appended.
D. Preliminary submission of the Five-Year Plan is presented for Council Task Force review. Any recommended changes are negotiated between the Council Task Force and local task forces. (Note that approval of a Five-Year Plan does not circumvent normal capital appropriation request procedures, nor other established approval mechanisms.)
E. An *Operational Plan* is established for control of committed system/project phases. Each phase is monitored and controlled at this level.
F. The Five-Year Plan is reviewed by all concerned each calendar quarter and updated as necessary.
G. Special updates to the Five-Year Plan are processed on an immediate basis if required.

A detailed description of the Five-Year Plan is given in Appendix A, which refers to the primary source document—Planning Document B (Exhibit 5).

Executing: System/Project Development Life Cycle

A very important component of DTC's system is the System/Project Development Life Cycle, which appears in the EXECUTING part of PPMCS.

EXHIBIT 4 □ Planning Document A

1. Location (Plant Name)
2. Area (User area, i.e., Accounting, Engineering, etc.)
3. Plan Ref. No. (Alphanumeric identifier assigned to the system)
4. Project No. (Project Identifying number used in Job Codes & Job Names, etc.)
5. Date Prepared (Date of this document)
6. Rev. No. (Sequential number used to track revisions, original submission is zero)
7. Descriptive Name of the System
8. Narrative Paragraphs
   A. Description of the problem or condition which exists and which the proposed system will "solve."
   B. Objectives of the proposed system.
   C. Basic assumptions which apply to the financial justification of the system, i.e., clerical hours saved, productivity increases, etc.
   D. Brief description of system being proposed.

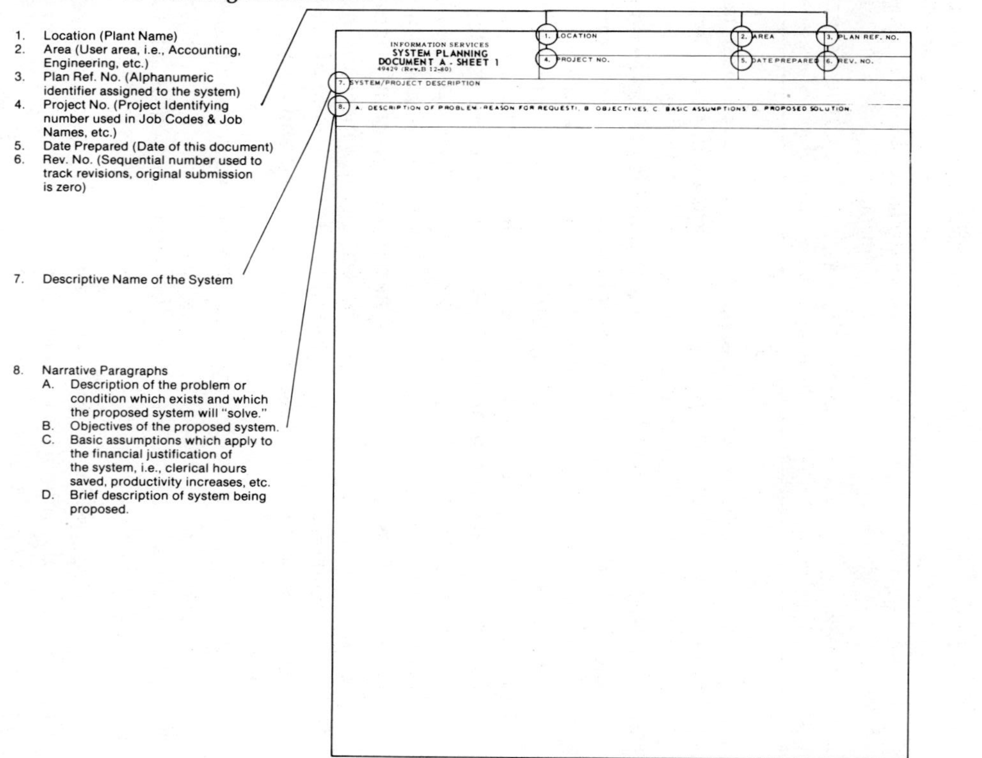

INFORMATION SERVICES
SYSTEM PLANNING
DOCUMENT A - SHEET 1
49429 (Rev.B 12-80)

INFORMATION SERVICES SYSTEM PLANNING DOCUMENT A - SHEET 1	1. LOCATION	2. AREA	3. PLAN REF. NO.
	4. PROJECT NO.	5. DATE PREPARED	6. REV. NO.

7. SYSTEM/PROJECT DESCRIPTION

8. A. DESCRIPTION OF PROBLEM (REASON FOR REQUEST), B. OBJECTIVES, C. BASIC ASSUMPTIONS, D. PROPOSED SOLUTION.

CONFIDENTIAL

Page ____ of ____

11. Relationship to other systems being developed

1.—6. Administrative information—Same as Sheet 1

DATA PROCESSING SERVICES
PLANNING DATA DETAIL
DOCUMENT A · SHEET 2

1. LOCATION | 2. AREA | 3. PLAN. REF. NO.
4. PROJECT NO. | 5. DATE PREPARED | 6. REV. NO.
9. CATEGORY | 10. REMARKS | 11. DEPENDENCY | 12. SYSTEM/PROJECT DESCRIPTION ABBREVIATION
13. ANNUAL BENEFITS | ONE-TIME BENEFITS: 14. CASH FLOW | 15. INVENTORY | 16. TOTAL | 17. ONE-TIME COST | 18. ANNUAL COST
DEVELOPMENT HOURS (TOTAL): 19. LAST APP'D. | 20. TO-DATE | 21. CUR. EST. TOT. | COST OF DEVELOPMENT HOURS: 22. COST TO-DATE | 23. CUR. RATE | 24. COST REMAIN. | 25. OTHER DEV. COSTS
EST./ACT. DATE: 26. START | 27. COMP. | CPU UTILIZATION: 28. TYPE | 29. RATE $/HR | 30. UTIL. MIN/MO | 31. RUN FREQ. | 32. TURN | 33. UTIL.
34. REASON FOR SUBMISSION: ☐ NEW ☐ PHASE END ☐ SCOPE CHANGE ☐ OTHER | 35. PHASE | 36. RISK | 37. PROF. INDEX
38. DESIGN CONSIDERATIONS: ☐ DATA BASE ☐ COMM. ☐ HIERARCHICAL ☐ INQUIRY/RESP. ☐ DATA COLL. ☐ OTHER
39. EXPLANATION OF COSTS & BENEFITS, DESCRIPTION OF HARDWARE/SOFTWARE, MANHOURS BY PROJECT/PHASE

40. DEVELOPMENT RECOMMENDATION: | 41. DESIGNATED AS MANDATORY BY: | DATE

APPROVAL SIGNATURES	DATE	APPROVAL SIGNATURES	DATE
42. PROJECT LEADER		43. DATA PROCESSING MANAGEMENT	
44. PROJECT MANAGER/USER REPRESENTATIVE		45. USER MANAGEMENT	
46. PLANT TASK FORCE		47. C & SD COUNCIL TASK FORCE	

CONFIDENTIAL

Page ----- of -----

10. Remarks Code
(i.e., related to capital projects, inter-plant activity, etc.)

9. Prioritization Category (i.e., Mandatory, Discretionary, etc.)

BENEFITS ($)

13. Gross Recurring Annual Benefits
14. Gross One-Time Savings which can be realized immediately upon system implementation
15. Gross One-Time Savings which will be realized gradually after system implementation
16. Sum of 14. & 15.

DEVELOPMENT HOURS

19. Total hours approved on previous submission
20. Hours already spent
21. Current Estimate of total hours required

DATES

Anticipated (Future) or Actual (Past) Dates
26. Start of development
27. Completion

34. Reason for submission

New—New system, first submission
Phase End—Normal resubmission at end of a life-cycle phase
Scope Change—Resubmission during a phase because of significant change of scope
Other—Unusual circumstances

38. Design Considerations—check all that apply

39. Further explanation of details or derivation of any items in preceding boxes.

40. Recommendation
(i.e., proceed, cancel, suspend)

12. Mnemonic name of system (abbreviated version of Item 7 on Sheet 1)

COSTS

17. One Time Costs other than development costs (i.e., purchased hardware and software).
18. Annual Recurring Costs
(i.e., Hardware and Software maintenance, charges for computer time, etc.)

25. Development costs other than development hours (i.e., computer test time)

DEVELOPMENT COSTS

22. Cost of hours spent to-date (Item 20)
23. Current Rate charged for development ($/hour)
24. Cost Remaining—hours remaining times current rate

37. Profitability Index—measure of economic value (discounted benefits/cost ratio)

COMPUTER UTILIZATION

28. Type (i.e., 370/158 Mod 3)
29. Current charge rate for CPU time
30. Anticipated utilization in minutes/month
31. Run frequency of batch jobs; in runs per day, week or month
32. Shift(s) during which work will be done (Midnite to 8:00 A.M. is turn 1, etc.)
33. Utilization expressed as percent of a machine (for long range planning purposes)

36. Risk-Index which defines relative risk based upon size, structure & technology

35. Last Phase Completed

41. If Category (Item 9) is Mandatory, this block must contain an authorized signature.

SIGNATURES

42. Data Processing Team Leader
43. Local Data Processing Manager
44. User Team Leader
45. User Manager
46. Local User Task Force Chairman
47. Corporate User Task Force Chairman

EXHIBIT 5 □ Planning Document B

LOCATION ______________ DATE PREPARED ______________

COMPUTERS AND SYSTEMS DEVELOPMENT PLANNING DATA SUMMARY

PLANNING DOCUMENT B—SHEET 1

	19	19	19	19	19
A. Force Size					
B. Total Available Hours (A × 2080)					
C1. Supervision					
C2. Support					
C3. All Other					
C4. Total Administration (C1 & C2 & C3)					
D. Technical Maintenance					
E. Requested Maintenance & Special Requests					
F. Request Evaluation					
G. Hours available for New Development* (B − C4 − D − E − F)					
H. Additional Hours from Other Sources†					
I. Hours Furnished to Other Locations†					
J. Total hours Available for New Development (G & H − I)					

Items C, D, E, F are to be completed according to the procedures set forth in Standards Manual K—Computers and Systems Development Planning Procedures.

* Item G—Hours Available for New Development is the difference between Total Available Hours and the sum of Total Administrative Hours, Technical Maintenance, Requested Maintenance & Special Requests, and Request Evaluation.

† Explain source or disposition of hours shown in Items H and I.

EXHIBIT 5 *(concluded)*

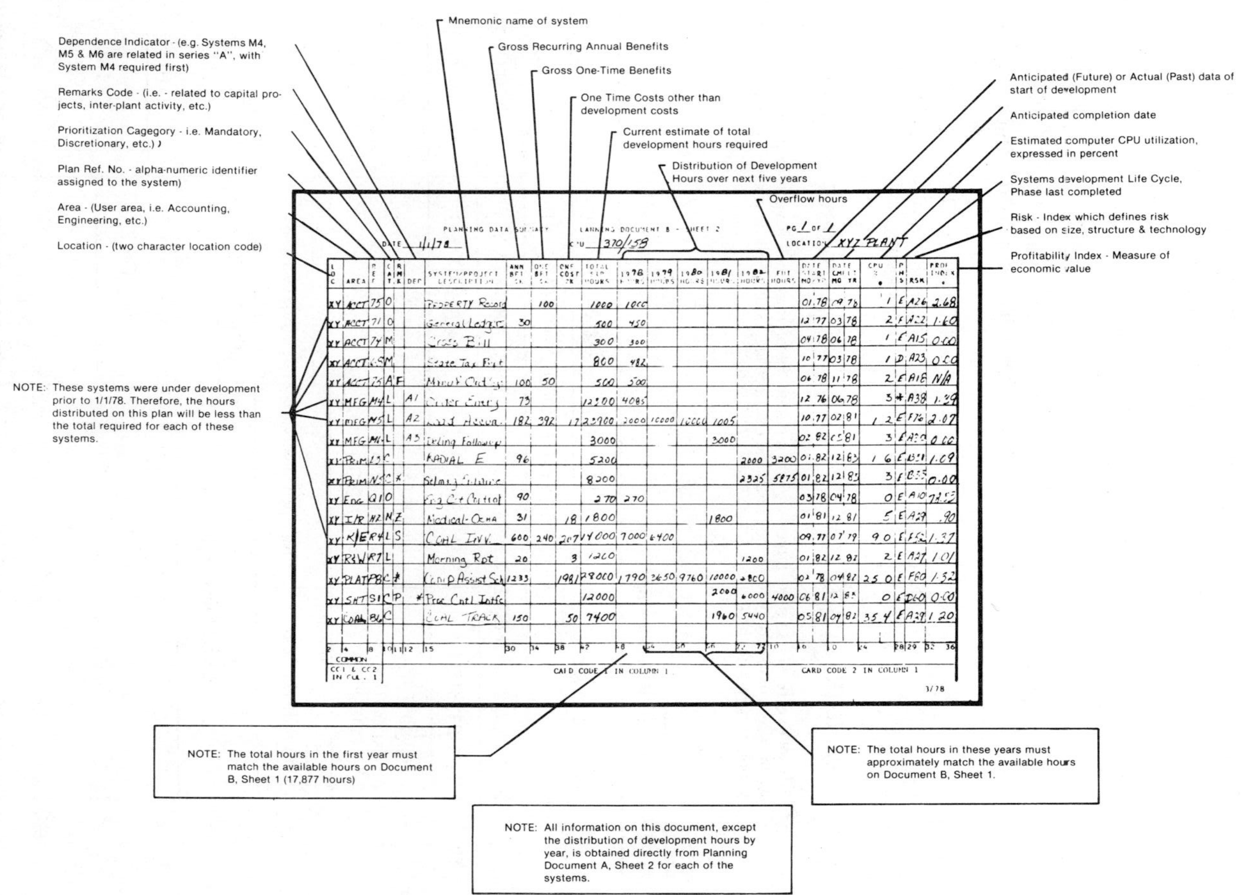

PLANNING DATA SUMMARY — PLANNING DOCUMENT B - SHEET 2 — PG 1 OF 1

DATE 1/1/78 — CPU 370/158 — LOCATION XYZ PLANT

LOC	AREA	REF	CAT	RMK	DEP	SYSTEM/PROJECT DESCRIPTION	ANN BFT $K	ONE BFT $K	ONE COST $K	TOTAL EST HOURS	1978 HOURS	1979 HOURS	1980 HOURS	1981 HOURS	1982 HOURS	FUT HOURS	DATE START MO YR	DATE CMPLT MO YR	CPU %	PHS	RSK	PROF INDEX
XY	ACCT	75	O			Property Record		100		1000	1000						01 78	09 78	1	E	A26	2.68
XY	ACCT	71	O			General Ledger	30			500	450						12 77	03 78	2	F	A22	1.60
XY	ACCT	74	M			Cross Bill				300	300						04 78	06 78	1	E	A15	0.00
XY	ACCT	65	M			State Tax Rpt				800	482						10 77	03 78	1	D	A23	0.00
XY	ACCT	73	A	F		Minut Cutting	100	50		500	500						06 78	11 78	2	E	A16	N/A
XY	MFG	M4	L		A1	Order Entry	73			12000	4085						12 76	06 78	3	*	A38	1.29
XY	MFG	M5	L		A2	Cost Accum.	182	392	17	23900	2000	10000	10000	1005			10 77	02 81	1 2	E	F76	2.07
XY	MFG	M6	L		A3	Ixling Followup				3000				3000			02 82	05 81	3	E	[illegible]	0.00
XY	PRIM	L3	C			RADIAL E	96			5200					2000	3200	01 82	12 83	1 6	E	[illegible]	1.09
XY	PRIM	N5	C	*		Salary Survey				8200					2325	5875	01 82	12 83	3	E	[illegible]	0.00
XY	ENG	Q1	O			Eng Cst Control	90			270	270						03 78	04 78	0	E	A10	72.52
XY	I/R	H2	N	Z		Medical-OSHA	31		18	1800				1800			01 81	12 81	5	E	A29	.90
XY	K/E	R4	L	S		COAL INV.	600	240	207	14000	7000	6400					09 77	07 79	9 0	E	F52	1.37
XY	R&W	R7	L			Morning Rpt	20		3	1200					1200		01 82	12 82	2	E	A27	1.01
XY	PLAT	P8	C	*		Comp Assist Sch	1233		1981	28000	1790	3650	9760	10000	2800		02 78	04 82	25 0	E	F60	1.32
XY	SHT	S1	C	P	*	Proc Cntl Intfc				12000				2000	6000	4000	06 81	12 85	0	E	D60	0.00
XY	COAL	B6	C			COAL TRACK	150		50	7400				1960	5440		05 81	04 82	35 4	E	A29	1.20

2 4 8 10 11 12 15 30 34 38 42 48 54 60 66 72 73 10 16 20 24 28 29 32 36

COMMON CC1 & CC2 IN COL. 1 — CARD CODE 1 IN COLUMN 1 — CARD CODE 2 IN COLUMN 1

3/78

DTC views systems development as a five-phase process—Feasibility, General Systems Design, Detail Systems Design, Programming, and Implementation:

INITIAL ADMINISTRATIVE PROCEDURES

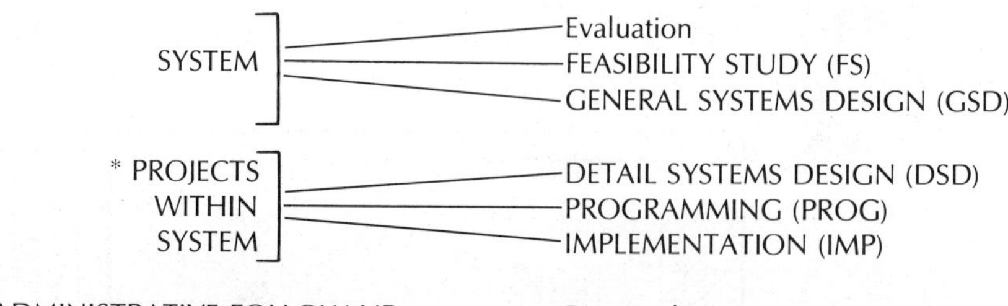

ADMINISTRATIVE FOLLOW-UP — Post-Implementation Review

* There may be one or more projects within a system. Each project will have its own three phases. Projects within a system may or may not be completed concurrently. Exhibit 6 illustrates this phase relationship for a sample system with three projects—X, Y, and Z.

EXHIBIT 6 □ Phase Relationship*

TIME

FEASIBILITY STUDY (TOTAL SYSTEM)

GENERAL SYSTEM DESIGN (TOTAL SYSTEM)

PROJECT X

PROJECT Y

PROJECT Z

SUBSYSTEM A

SUBSYSTEM B

SUBSYSTEM C

SUBSYSTEM D

DETAIL SYSTEM DESIGN

DETAIL SYSTEM DESIGN

PROGRAMMING

PROGRAMMING

REVIEW FEASIBILITY & GENERAL DESIGN

IMPLEMENTATION

DETAIL SYSTEM DESIGN

DETAIL SYSTEM DESIGN

PROGRAMMING

PROGRAMMING

IMPLEMENTATION

IMPLEMENTATION

* Relationship of phases, subsystems, and projects in the systems/project development cycle.

The five phases are listed in Exhibit 7 with their principal intent and major output.

The role of Planning Document A in this methodology is noteworthy. This

EXHIBIT 7 □ Systems/Project Development Life Cycle

Phase	Principal intent	Major outputs
Feasibility	Identify "real" problem or need.	Problem definition, objective, and scope. Conceptual solution. Technical, operational feasibility. Cost/benefit analysis. Feasibility study report. PLANNING DOCUMENT A.
General systems design	Determine external design characteristics of the solution.	Total system information flow and associated external specifications. Logical data base/file design. Hardware and software requirements. Risk assessment. Cost/benefit analysis. GSD proposal. PLANNING DOCUMENT A.
Detail systems design	Determine internal design characteristics of the solution.	Internal system structure chart. Programming specification. Physical data base design. Hardware and communication plan. Conversion specification. DSD report. PLANNING DOCUMENT A.
Programming	To transform specifications into machine code, verifying code conforms to specification and works without error.	Coded and tested modules/program. System, program, file and user documentation. Acceptance test specification. Training. Programming report. PLANNING DOCUMENT A.
Implementation	To install the system as maintenance-free as possible.	Completed site preparation and hardware installation. User-accepted production system. Post-implementation review schedule. Project termination report. PLANNING DOCUMENT A.

document and its attachments move with a project from inception to completion through every phase. As can be seen in Exhibit 7, this form is a required milestone document for each phase-end review and provides input for the associated go/no-go decision (mentioned in Exhibit 3). Any ad-hoc requests for projects status or project upgrades (incremental commitments of resources) begin with a reivew of this document.

Controlling, Monitoring, and Adjusting

At the conclusion of each calendar quarter, the following will be presented to the local task force for their review:

1. Operational Plan Quarterly Status Report and explanation of variances that exceed 10 percent.
2. A summary of budgeted hours and actual hours to date in each of the categories covered in Planning Document B, Sheet 1, with explanation of variances that exceed 10 percent.
3. A summary of progress against established goals for the current year.
4. Recommendations for five-year plan updates.

The local task force determines appropriate plan updates which become recommendations to the Computers and Systems Development Planning Council for plan revisions.

The Development Council task force will review recommendations of the local task force for plan revisions and negotiate with them on any recommendations with which they do not concur. Resulting recommendations for plan revisions will then be submitted to the Council for management approval.

Defining and Prioritizing Proposed Systems

Before entering the EXECUTE part of PPMCS, systems are prioritized (by sponsoring users and eventually approving task forces) based on three parameters—prioritizing category, profitability index, and risk assessment. All systems proposed for inclusion in the systems development five-year plan must be classified into one of two prioritization categories—MANDATORY or OTHER. MANDATORY systems are those which:

1. Are required to meet legal or contractual obligations.
2. Are defined as mandatory by a plant general manager or a corporate department vice president.
3. Are special studies directed by Council or Plant Task Forces with concurrence of the Council.
4. Are included as part of capital submissions for which specific justification cannot be separated from the capital project of which it is a part.

Resources available for new development are allocated *first* to *all* MANDATORY systems/projects. The remaining available resources for new development are allocated based on relative cost/benefit ranking—profitability index (PI)—and balancing the risk portfolio based on a risk assessment (RA) procedure.

The PI facilitates ranking systems/projects based on *relative economic benefit.* A "Profitability Index Calculation Form" (Exhibit 8) is used to generate a single number from the formula:

$$\frac{\text{Present value (BENEFITS)}}{\text{Present value (COSTS)}}$$

A system/project with a PI less than 1.0 is considered an undesirable investment of development resources. The discount factor used in the calculation is provided by a corporate accounting group. Generally, users designate "benefits" and data processing generates "costs" which are posted to this form. This index may be calculated at several points during the development cycle, and ignores "sunk costs" if they exist.

RA is an attempt to determine a probability that the system/project will not meet its original objectives in terms of:

1. Functional Specifications
   A. System objectives.
   B. Benefits.
2. Scope of Effort
   A. Man-hours.
   B. Calendar time.
   C. CPU test requirements.
   D. Hardware implementation requirement.

Both the profitability index and risk assessment value are posted to Planning Document A (Exhibit 4) and Planning Document B (Exhibit 5).

RISK ASSESSMENT

There are three dimensions or categories along which data processing projects may be classified. These determine the inherent degree of system risk.

Size. Size is determined by man-hours required to complete the system. Calendar time is a function of staffing. In general, systems are classified as follows:

Very large .... over 30,000 hours
Large ....15,000–30,000 hours
Medium .... 3,000–15,000 hours
Small ....100–3,000 hours

EXHIBIT 8

PROFITABILITY INDEX CALCULATION FORM 49471 (3-78)	PLANNING REF. NO. R4	REVISION 0	DATE PREPARED 9/15/77	LOCATION XYZ PLANT
	DESCRIPTION COAL INVENTORY ON-LINE SYSTEM			

DEVELOPMENT HOURS		COSTS		BENEFITS	
Current Estimate	14,000	Other Development	25K	One Time – Cash Flow	
Hours-To-Date	0	One Time	207K	One Time – Inventory	240K
Hours Remaining	14,000	Annual	250K	Annual	260K
Rate $/Hour	*$25.00				

Year	Pres. Val. Factor	Extended Costs: Dev. Hrs.	Dev. $	One-Time	Annual	Year's Total	Pres. Value	Extended Benefits: One-Time	Annual	Year's Total	Pres. Value
1	1.000	7000	175,000			175,000	175,000				
2	.735	7000	175,000	232,000		407,000	299,145				
3	.541				250,000	250,000	135,250	120,000	600,000	720,000	389,520
4	.398				250,000	250,000	99,500	120,000	600,000	720,000	286,560
5	.292				250,000	250,000	73,000		600,000	600,000	235,000
6	.215				250,000	250,000	53,750		600,000	600,000	129,000
7	.158				250,000	250,000	39,500		600,000	600,000	94,800
8	.116				250,000	250,000	29,000		600,000	600,000	69,600
9	.085				250,000	250,000	21,250		600,000	600,000	51,000
10	.063				250,000	250,000	15,750		600,000	600,000	37,800

COMMENTS:

TOTAL COSTS – PRESENT VALUE 941,145

TOTAL BENEFITS – PRESENT VALUE 1,293,480

P. I. = 1.37

* This rate is the ratio of total systems and programming cost (including space, fringe benefits, administration, telephone, etc.) to total billable hours (sum of Planning Document B—Page 1).

Structure. A system/project referred to as having *high* structure is one with little structural risk in which the processing routines and outputs are so determined by the systems environment in advance that there are few or no design options open to the system architect or the user. A system/project referred to as having *low* structure is one in which substantial structural risk exists when substantial judgment and flexibility exist in the system's design and/or implementation. The user's unfamiliarity with data processing and/or lack of management support can also contribute to a system with structural risk.

Technology. A *low* technology risk system is one which involves hardware/software features which are familiar to the given organization (even though few or no other organizations may have worked with them). Each data center is considered to be a separate organization. A *high* technology risk system is one which involves complex hardware-software features which have not been dealt with previously in the *organization* (although other organizations may use them routinely).

Exhibit 9 illustrates the *Risk Grid* used when assessing risk. Risk assessment will take two forms: Pre-feasibility and normal risk assessment. *Pre-feasibility risk assessment* is based on the project leader's or the initial estimator's experience and "gut" feel. It will have a value of A-H corre-

EXHIBIT 9 □ Risk Grid

SMALL (SIZE) LOW STRUCTURE RISK LOW TECHNOLOGY RISK A	LARGE (SIZE) LOW STRUCTURE RISK LOW TECHNOLOGY RISK B
SMALL (SIZE) LOW STRUCTURE RISK HIGH TECHNOLOGY RISK C	LARGE (SIZE) LOW STRUCTURE RISK HIGH TECHNOLOGY RISK D
SMALL (SIZE) HIGH STRUCTURE RISK LOW TECHNOLOGY RISK E	LARGE (SIZE) HIGH STRUCTURE RISK LOW TECHNOLOGY RISK F
SMALL (SIZE) HIGH STRUCTURE RISK HIGH TECHNOLOGY RISK G	LARGE (SIZE) HIGH STRUCTURE RISK HIGH TECHNOLOGY RISK H

sponding to the risk grid. *Normal risk assessment* is performed as recommended in the feasibility phase and general design phase of the system life cycle. It is performed by the project leader or comparable person associated with the system.

The *Risk Assessment Questionnaire* which operationalizes this concept, is divided into three sections: Size, Structure, and Technology. A category value for each of the three dimensions is generated by answering a set of questions and calculating risk values. Questions and weights were designed by two persons on Abbott's staff. They were instructed to list all the items which could affect system development in the three categories. Although this was a very subjective task, Abbott was comfortable that the two persons assigned had significant insight into the problem (12 and 10 years of development experience). Once the items or issues which impacted system development were listed, their relative importance within DTC was assessed, which led to the weights. The initial version of the questionnaire was tested with several project managers and revised. Finally, a version of the questionnaire was put into DTC's Computer and Systems Development Planning Procedures Manual.

HOW RISK ASSESSMENT IS USED

Risk assessment will normally be done at the SYSTEM level. System risk is the only way to evaluate risk through general systems design (GSD).

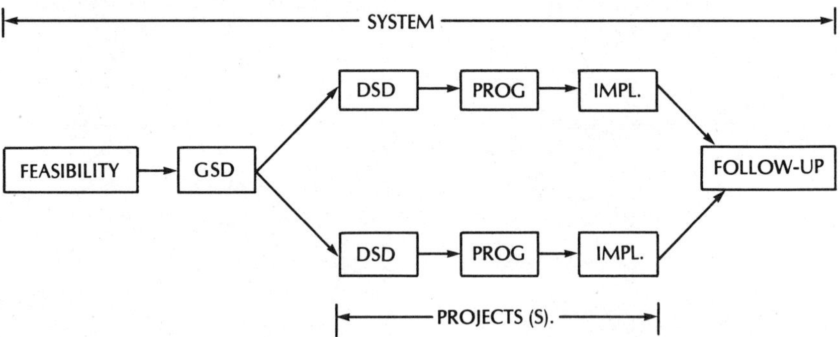

After GSD, we continue to look at system risk, but can also look at project risk. Even though the questionnaire is system oriented, it is filled out and evaluated for each project within a system. This exercise helps identify projects which have significantly higher risk than others. Management should be made aware of the presence of a high-risk project(s) so that appropriate judgment and/or control can be exercised. Examples of some of the questions which should be addressed under those circumstances are:

a. Is the system dependent upon the high-risk project?
b. Does the high-risk project have sufficient benefits to justify development?
c. Can the high-risk project be eliminated without unduly degrading the system?

In any case, *system risk* is the most important value. It is risk associated with the sum of the parts; plus it takes the number or project interactions into account. In addition, the Computer Systems Development Planning Council deals primarily at the system level. It should be noted that very high-risk systems require higher (level) visibility and approval than those of more limited risks.

In response to the question, "How is the risk information used?" Abbott replied, "Once the average risk percentile and risk grid position have been determined there are four ways in which this information can be used."

1. *System Risk versus System Commitment*
   As data processing becomes more committed to a system, the perception of risk should change. If risk decreases as a system goes forward, that system is progressing properly. If, however, risk increases as a system goes forward, that system should be brought to the attention of management as an exception condition.
2. *Risk versus Performance against Estimate*
   By tracking historical data relating to performance against estimate, we can identify trends which may indicate that high-risk systems are more prone to under/overruns, etc.
3. *System Risk As an Estimating Factor*
   Using the conclusions drawn from system/project risk assessments, system/project estimates should be correlated and managed accordingly. For high-risk systems, it may be advisable to lean toward the high end of the range offered by the estimating program. For systems having high structural risk, more hours may be required for meetings.
4. *Risk-Balanced Portfolio*
   In order to take advantage of new technologies, new environments, financial benefits of large systems, etc., high-risk systems generally have to be undertaken. On the other hand, in order to assure a high degree of systems implementation success (in terms of meeting budgets and functional specs), low-risk systems generally need to be undertaken. Obviously, no data processing organization can dedicate its total efforts to one or the other. The ideal situation is to have a balance between high- and low-risk systems. Having the ability to assign meaningful (although somewhat subjective) risk values to systems allows data processing to maintain a risk-balanced five-year portfolio.

According to Abbott, as he reflected on implementation of RA, "A company or data processing organization planning to implement RA and to exploit its various uses should keep in mind the following points:

1. RA and its various uses will be of little value unless a total system/project management scheme is also in place. This includes Application Development Definition (Life Cycle), Estimating, Effective Performance Tracking, Resource Management, etc.
2. Consistency in implementing the risk assessment procedures is very important. However, risk values and grid positions are relative to the given organization. Our definition of organization is a data processing site within DTC, not the entire corporate data processing organization. Within this definition different organizations may have different areas of technical and user expertise and, depending on the size of their staff, may have different opinions on what is a large or small project.
3. Determination of the risk value and grid position is based on an individual organization's status at that point in time (training level, experience with certain software, user involvement, etc.)."

REACTION TO PPMCS

As Swanson listened to Abbott's summary he jotted down the following comments:

A. *Advantages*

- The major advantage to using the methodology is the consistency with which we will develop new projects. It also provides a *comprehensive* list of tasks which must be completed.
- *Because of the methodology we have been able to:*
  1. Keep maintenance at a much lower level.
  2. Better inform the user.
  3. Control "window dressing"-type enhancements.
  4. Reduce "normal" start-up problems.
- The methodology provides an orderly approach to accomplish desired project results.
- Provides a well-defined guideline for development which produces more uniform and consistent results from an administrative viewpoint.
- The obvious advantage is an ordered and structured approach to the development of data processing projects and systems.
- Methodology should serve to provide guidance in developing systems correctly and completely.
- Provides for better project control because it makes the design more

visible, including system interfaces. I also think that it will produce better quality systems.

- Forces the function of planning in development.
- Encourages user involvement.
- Estimating procedure is a welcome improvement over previous methods.

B. *Disadvantages*

- Much clerical effort.
- Increased administrative paper work is not balanced with system benefits.
- Methodology is voluminous in content.
- Estimates and data are subject to go awry where heavier user involvement causes a project to progress at user pace.
- Causes initial delay in providing the user with tangible benefits.
- Additional time is required to follow procedures and issues documentation.
- It is more costly and disliked by employees because it requires a great deal of planning and documenting which doesn't appear productive. People would rather *"Get on with writing the code,"* because coding produces something tangible even though higher maintenance systems often result.
- The methodology is becoming a "checklist" of items to be accomplished to implement a project. It is not a complete substitute for experience, judgment, and creativity. It should be a "guide."
- It makes me feel like I'm a robot with no intellectual ability.

After discussing the general feedback on advantages and disadvantages, Abbott addressed specific problems and concerns which had been raised that needed widely disseminated responses. There were 21 total entries. After hearing the list Swanson felt the five which needed immediate attention were (1) problems associated with implementing PPMCS while systems development was ongoing, (2) inadequate user education before implementing PPMCS, (3) reducing PPMCS requirements for small staff and/or small projects, (4) comments concerning excessive paperwork and associated negative or marginal benefit from voluminous paperwork, and (5) the belief that general managers would not be receptive to discussing "risk" associated with DP development projects. Comments from users in the first four areas are listed in Exhibit 10.

Comments about the risk assessment technique focused on the negative inference a general manager would associate with such a discussion. As stated by one plant DP manager, "we have a hard enough time getting things approved without generating skepticism that a project will be suc-

EXHIBIT 10 □ Implementation Assessment Problems and Concerns*

1. *Getting on Board*
   - Specific problems encountered in implementing the methodology include:
     a. Attempts to get on board with the methodology where a large project was already well under way.
     b. Confusion coupled with conflicting responses regarding methodology interpretation.
   - Retrofitting sections of the manual has proven to be very difficult.
   - A serious disadvantage is moving systems already in progress, prior to methodology, to the new procedures which often require time-consuming paperwork and extra research.

     We recommend that projects not started under methodology not be required to provide detail tasks and documents.

     Some frustration has been felt in the short time allowed for a learning curve and transition from the previous procedures.
2. *Education*
   - There was no apparent effort to educate those in data processing services or the user community about the *purpose and scope* of the methodology.
   - Education—we have not been able to properly educate plant management or DP staff in the methodology due to manpower limitations.
   - Misinterpretation of some standards. Probably can only be corrected through more experience.
   - It is a very complex system of procedures. Education and interpretation of methodology guidelines should be developed to eliminate confusion and misunderstanding.
   - Provide the user with an orientation course.
   - Some frustration has been felt in the short time allowed for a learning curve and transition from the previous procedures. Additionally, a general lack of understanding still exists since there was no formal education or training provided.

3a. *Small Staff*

   a. *Technology–IMS data base administration*—No manpower (one half person) to properly administer data dictionary and other data base functions.
   b. *Project team, S&P*—We have been unable to staff the project with appropriate manpower and talent.

* This list had 21 total entries. Listed are those thought most important by CDP.

EXHIBIT 10 *(concluded)*

c. *Education*—We have not been able to properly educate plant management or DP staff in the methodology due to manpower limitations.

- Separation of DSD and PROG phases is impossible with our staff size and talent mix.
- Data base dictionary and data base administration functions in general are a specific burden on a staff our size.
- Personnel resources to accomplish formal documentation . . . is a major problem.
- At smaller plants the project team approach is not always possible.

3b. *Small Projects*

- Projects which are nominal in development size cannot be readily adapted to the life-cycle phases of the total methodology.
- Most of the resistance is coming from project leaders who are working on smaller systems. They know the system could be written and implemented both quicker and cheaper if the restrictions were reduced. More flexibility and freedom is needed for these systems.
- Provide a simpler version of methodology for development of small projects.
- We would like to see a condensed outline of those tasks and documentation that are absolutely necessary for each level of projects.

4. *Excessive Paperwork*

- We have some concerns about the amount of paperwork which appears to be needed.
- Too much tedious, time-consuming paperwork for very little benefit, primarily in the GSD area.
- Service analysis and its use in data base design at best is extremely time-consuming with questionable benefit.
- In some instances (e.g., data bases) experience has shown a simpler procedure would save time.
- Discretion in the use of recommended forms should be considered.
- A review of the required methodology reports and documents should be started to determine if some of the paperwork can be reduced.

cessfully completed *if* it is approved. In addition, the process is so subjective we shouldn't do it. If, for example, you examine the questionnaire, there is no way a project will ever be classified HIGH technology."

As Swanson began to organize his thoughts about the feedback he sensed the timing and forcefulness of his reply to these comments would surely provide informal feedback to the data processing community concerning his, and the corporation's, commitment to PPMCS.

APPENDIX A □ FIVE-YEAR PLAN OVERVIEW

The Five-Year Plan is a projection of development hours to Planning Reference Numbers, by year, over a five-year period, as of a particular date. It is a communication vehicle by which the local task forces and the Council Task Force establish priorities of projects and by which a systems development manager communicates back his ability to execute the plan with given resources.

Normally, all phases and/or projects associated with a system will carry the same Planning Reference Number. Each Planning Reference Number is supported by a Planning Document A form (Exhibit 4) which describes the system proposed for development along with its objectives and cost/benefit analysis.

Hours available for new development in each year of the plan are equal to total available hours (based upon force, approved additions to force, and approved contracting of outside services) less the sum of estimated administrative hours, hours for the maintenance/special request budget, and request evaluation.

The total hours allocated for new development in the current year and current year plus one of the plan may not exceed the hours available (as defined above), except when specific recommendations have been made for obtaining the additional hours required, or specific approval has been given by the Council Task Force for an overscheduling of hours. Hours for the remaining years of the plan need not balance exactly, but should reflect known requirements for new development. Such requirements should be scheduled to start and complete based upon system development guidelines, i.e., hours allocated to a plan reference number should not be arbitrarily spread over several years just to balance against available hours.

Once established, the Five-Year Plan is continuous and will not be resubmitted on an annual basis. It is updated on a calendar quarter basis and/or as directed by the Council Task Force. The plan update following the third calendar quarter includes extension of the plan another year such that each January 1 the plan includes a full five years into the future.

Five-Year Plan information is maintained by each systems development group and made available to all concerned in a formal approved by the Council Task Force.

Procedural Steps for Establishment of Five-Year Plan

1. Prepare (revise) Planning Document B, Sheet 1 (Exhibit 5). This establishes the hours expected to be available for new development during each of the five years in the planning period.
2. Prepare (review) Planning Document A forms for each system/project currently being developed and/or proposed for development during the planning period. For systems/projects with development durations in excess of one year, determine the maximum, minimum, and recommended number of hours to be expended in a one-year period. This information should be used when allocating hours for Planning Reference Number to a year or years.
3. Establish the priority of each Planning Reference Number item. The Profitability Index and Risk Assessment techniques (defined later) are used to determine profitability and ranking.
4. Prepare Planning Document B, Sheet 2 (Exhibit 5) which shows allocation of hours by Planning Reference Number to each of the five years in the planning period.
5. Determine capability to carry out the plan by projecting a manpower resource plan. Modify Five-Year Plan as necessary and/or determine what additional manpower resources are required.
6. Review documents with local task force and obtain approval of a recommended Five Year Plan.
7. Forward the Planning Document B, Sheet 1 and Sheet 2 forms, the new and/or revised Planning Document A forms, and supporting information as required to Manager, Planning and Control, Corporate Data Processing. One (1) copy of each document is required.
8. Planning and Control will review documents and contact the submitting location if any corrections or additional information are required. Information will be entered into the Five-Year Plan data base and be printed in a standard Five-Year Plan output report format. A copy will be returned to the submitting location for verification. The plan will be reviewed by the General Manager, Corporate Data Processing, and following his approval, will be presented to the Council Task Force. Any questions from the Council Task Force will be handled through Planning and Control back to the submitting location. Results of the review by the Council Task Force, that is, concurrence, recommendations for adjustments to the plan, etc., will be handled by a letter from the Council Chairman to the Plant Task Force Chairman for plant plans or the appropriate departmental vice president for the Home Office Plan.
9. The final Five-Year Plan will then be printed, distributed to all concerned, and become the basis for future quarterly updates.

Chapter 8 □ Operations Management

Manageable Trend / Chapter	Strategic Impact	DP/TP/OA	Organization Learning	Make/Buy	Life Cycle	GM/ User/ IS
IS Technology Organization Issues **Chapter 3**		●	●			●
Organizational Issues in IS Development **Chapter 4**	●		●	●		●
Information Systems Planning **Chapter 5**	●		●			●
IS Management Control **Chapter 6**	●		●	●		●
A Portfolio Approach to Information Systems Development **Chapter 7**	●				●	●
Operations Management **Chapter 8**	●			●	●	●
Multinational IS Issues **Chapter 9**		●				●
The IS Business **Chapter 10**	●		●	●		●

A major North American manufacturing company has a brand new $3.5 million underground operations center protected by four guards, nine TV cameras, and multiple levels of access security. The chief executive officer personally approved and supervised its construction. At the same time, the critical application being run in the center, an online order system, is 13 years old. Under tight head-count control, imposed by senior management, the systems and programming staff had decreased by nearly 35 percent over the previous four years and were barely able to implement necessary maintenance work, let alone major systems enhancements of new projects. Senior IS management was deeply concerned about the unbalanced allocation of resources between invisible required maintenance and visible facilities.

After years of debate, a major bank reluctantly built a second data center, 50 miles away from the primary data center. The source of debate had focused on whether a 7 percent increase in costs was a good trade-off vis-à-vis the extra security against disaster provided by the second data center. This bank currently has over 4,000 online terminals and is deeply dependent on the smooth, uninterrupted, 24-hour-a-day operation of IS services to meet its daily operating performance targets.

The chief executive officer of an industrial products concern discovered that the delay in year-end financial closing was not due to reduced emphasis on close control of financial accounting but to unexpected work and personnel problems in the computer systems department. Increased use of an online query system (and associated problems) to provide salesmen and customers detailed delivery and cost information had absorbed all available system support personnel to keep this vital system operational. No time had been left to revise the accounting system for changes in the new tax law before year-end closing.

The director of IS of a major engineering firm is pondering whether to break apart and totally reconfigure his operations center. At present, a single large computer supports the company's batch and online system. Workloads are quite erratic, and in the past year, long response-time delays on the online systems, combined with batch schedules, has put him under considerable user pressure to be more responsive.

Unusual problems? Hardly! Historically, the glamorous part of the IS function has been the technology orientation of systems development and technical support functions, with maintenance and operations occupying a distinctly backseat role. For the purposes of this chapter, we will define *operations* to include the running of IS hardware, data input, equipment scheduling, and work forces associated therewith. We have also chosen in this chapter to deal with the issues relating to the impact on the systems life cycle by the change in software make-or-buy decisions to outside sourcing. While this could have been covered in Chapter 7, the *operational* implication of this shift seemed so important that we choose to deal with it in its entirety here.

Both the type and amount of management resources devoted to operations activities and the sophistication of management practices within the operations center have often been inadequate for their growing and changing mission inside the company. The following aspects of changing technology are now triggering major changes in the way these activities are managed:

CHANGING OPERATIONS ENVIRONMENT

The explosion of online technology applications and increased sophistication in operating systems in the past decade has taken what originally was a batch, job-shop environment with heavy human control and turned it first into a process manufacturing shop and at present into a largely self-scheduled and monitored 24-hour-a-day utility. This change in manufacturing work flow has triggered a total rethinking of both what is appropriate scheduling and what is the definition of adequate service levels.

An increased recognition that there is no such thing as an ideal standard IS operations management control system, or set of performance metrics. The trade-off between quality of service, response time of online systems, handling of unexpected jobs, total cost, and ability to meet published schedules on batch systems appropriately varies from one organization to another.

Different IS operations environments must strike different balances between efficiency (low-cost producer) and effectiveness (flexibility) in responding to unplanned, uneven flow of requests. IS operations cannot be *all things* simultaneously to *all people* but must operate on a set of priorities and trade-offs that stem from corporate strategy. Implementation of this has sparked the reorganization of some large IS operations into a series of focused, single service-oriented groups, each of which can be managed to quite different user service objectives.

The types of staffing needed are changing. Many formerly appropriate employees are unsuited now for the new tasks. These problems have been complicated by the unionization of this function in many parts of the globe.

Continued change in the IS technology. This initiates the normal problems of change and new operating procedures, while offering potential benefits of lower cost and new capabilities.

The major shift toward more outside sourcing in IS processing and software sourcing decisions. This requires changes in the procedures of both the operations and development functions of IS if they are to be handled responsibly.

These issues are similar to those involved in running a manufacturing facility characterized by the words, *highly volatile technology, specialized labor, serving dynamic markets,* and *changing industry structure*. Consequently, much of the analysis in this chapter draws on work done in manufacturing management, particularly as it relates to balancing efficiency–effectiveness trade-offs.

A key question stemming from this manufacturing analogy is how focused should the department be. Should it subdivide itself into sets of stand-alone services or be organized as a general-purpose IS service. The example at the beginning of the chapter, of the late closing of the books versus providing online service for query, provided a stimulus within the company to review how operations were responding to the demands of new services. The company's review produced a conclusion similar to Skinner's plea for a focused factory.[1] They perceived it as being impossible for a single unit to adequately respond to such very different user needs; consequently, to address the problem, the IS development and maintenance group was reorganized into four independent systems groups, each of which operated independently of the others but reported to a common boss (the manager of IS).

One group was to support the online query systems with goals to provide 10-second response, one-day change implementation, and all data refreshed hourly. The second systems/customer group was devoted to the general ledger accounting system. Their goals were to keep the software up to date for month-end closing schedule work so as to not interfere with other systems, ensure the quality and reliability of accounting data, and operate to close the books five days after the end of the last working day of the month. The third group was to be responsible for all material management systems. Their objectives were to ensure all production control persons were well trained to use the system, to provide updated data overnight, and to maintain and operation of the system in a manner consistent with material policies on inventory and customer delivery. The fourth group was to work with the systems supporting new-product development. They were responsible for identifying system requirements of new products, maintaining the availability of the capacity simulator for planning new-product developments, establishing data standards and new data files in existing systems for approved new products, and developing and performing analyses on new products as directed by the vice president of product development. Each focused group included at least one user and two to three systems professionals. All worked full time on their respective services with the exception of the new-product group which had spurts of work as new products hit the market and lulls after the market settled down. This structure has produced happier customers and significantly better percentages of service as well as increased employee morale.

Historically, the evolution of IS systems has developed a series of services and products running out of an integrated IS operations unit. As noted above, some firms have reorganized IS development and construction to be more responsive to user needs. For example, several organizations shifted application programmers (e.g., construction) to users, allowing maintenance and operations to be decentralized around the local system. As IS's monopoly of system construction and make/buy decision erodes to more and greater user control, the result is fragmentation of the factory into a series of focused services (e.g., a word processing system for customer mailing). For some users and applications this may be very effective. For other users, however, their services may be dependent upon an integrated set of data, in which case severe coordination problems can be created. The chal-

[1] Wickham Skinner, "The Focused Factory," *Harvard Business Review* (May–June 1974).

lenge is to identify where focus in operations (either within the central unit or by distributing to the user) is appropriate and then execute it in a way which provides the necessary thrust. Implementation of this will be discussed further in the section on production planning and control.

To build on this manufacturing strategy theme, and develop an appropriate range of make-buy plans, our operations management discussion is organized around the following topics:

Development of an operations strategy.
Technology planning.
Measuring and managing capacity.
Managing the IS operations work force.
Production planning and control.
Security.

DEVELOPING AN OPERATIONS STRATEGY

As noted earlier, the management team of an IS operations activity is trying to stay on top of a utility that is radically changing its production system, customer base, and role within the company. Eight years ago, the manager and his staff were monopolists running a job shop where the key issues were scheduling (with substantial human inputs), ensuring telecommunications were adequate, managing a large blue-collar staff, and planning capacity and staffing levels for future workloads of similar characteristics. Today, they are operating an information utility providing a 24-hour/7-day-a-week service that must cope cost effectively with uncertain short-term and long-term user demand; manage a far higher skilled, more professional work force; and evaluate competing services, both internal and external, which in many cases offer the potential to solve problems cheaper and more comprehensively. Key issues for the IS operations manager are still staff, capacity, and telecommunications. Prominent additions to this list, however, are: appropriate assessment, assimilation and integration of software and services emanating from outside the corporation.

Senior management must assess both the quality of IS operations support and, depending on how critical it is to the overall strategic mission of the corporation, involve themselves appropriately. The central question both senior and IS management must address is whether IS operations as organized now effectively supports the firm.

In this context, we see the key issues an operations strategy must address as follows:

1. Ensuring that each phase of a system's life cycle appropriately address the critical long-term operating needs of the system.

2. Ensuring that the internal/external sourcing decisions are carefully thought through as to both their outcome and who should primarily influence the outcome with respect to operational characteristics.
3. Resolving the extent to which IS operations should be managed as a single entity or broken down into a series of perhaps more costly but more focused subunits which provide more customized user service than is possible from a monolithic facility.

The following paragraphs discuss these items in more detail.

System Design and Operations

A review of IS operations organization must start with an assessment of the first phase of the systems life cycle, the design phase, because the key operations decisions for a system are often made early in the design phase and, unless identified as such and handled appropriately at that phase, can cause great difficulty. Proper operations input to the systems design phase is complicated by the fact that the IS operations department is a victim of history. Past decisions have shaped today's operating environment, which influences the art of the possible in both today's operating environment, and in today's design decisions.

Both user operational personnel and IS operational personnel need to be involved in the early design phase to get their viewpoint of need across—as well as to be educated on the reality of the existing situation. This IS operations involvement not only ensures the operational integrity of the new system design but ensures that other existing systems are not adversely impacted operationally during the design and implementation stages of the new system and that the conversion plan from the old to the new is satisfactory. These issues are particularly important to review for externally sourced software, since interfacing issues are complex.

Externally Sourced Services—Pressures and Challenges

The recent shift in software construction, from a situation where the bulk of energy was devoted to in-house software construction managed by IS staff to today's position where there is a greater reliance on purchased software and service, is not surprising. The supply of cheap hardware is growing dramatically. However, the human resources to develop software for it have remained relatively constant and have thus shrunk significantly in relation to demand. Neither user-oriented programming languages nor programming efficiency aids have been able to fully address the problem of resource shortage. Consequently, significant increases in prices for skilled people have occurred. Appropriately, a large market has developed for software firms which can develop reliable products at significantly lower user cost by spreading these costs over multiple users. This industry started with software vendors developing complex technical software to support the operation of computers (operating systems, data base handlers, inquiry languages, etc.). This vendor software evolution has now evolved downstream to products such as standard user-oriented software services, including payroll and accounting packages, as well as report writers and procedural languages. This trend has caused the in-house system construction phase to be eliminated (or drastically shortened) in many office automation and data processing activities. The design phase continues to focus on careful definition of business operational needs (but often to guide a package selection). The system implementation phase's challenge is to understand the purchased service's key characteristics so as to train individuals to its operational use. Finally, systems maintenance involves ensuring that the vendor is prepared to be responsive to long-term needs.

These purchased systems generate special problems for IS operations management as noted below. These problems are particularly sticky where the user has full authority to purchase and operate the new service, while the IS operations department must maintain and operate other services and, at the same time, ensure that they are compatible where necessary with the new service. This loss of operations monopoly control poses three key challenges to IS operations management:

1. How to maintain existing services while building appropriate and necessary data bridges to the new ones.
2. How to evolve the IS operations organization from a primary integrated system of data processing to a series of services which are better focused on the specific needs of different users.
3. How to develop user understanding of both their real operational responsibility over the systems under their control and how to interface effectively with corporate IS.

Individual skill levels and perspectives of IS operations management further complicate resolving these problems. Many IS operations departments are run by individuals accustomed to exercising monopoly control over operations while sharing control with users over selection and implementation of maintenance changes. These individuals must now learn to adapt to new ways of operations. Evidence of failure to adapt is provided by the many organizations which, because of senior management frustration over IS's unresponsiveness, have delegated total authority for purchased services acquisition and operation to users.

IS operations must assume roles which include reviewing designs in the *design* phase to ensure that they are compatible with existing services; auditing documentation preparation in the *construction* phase to ensure long-term maintainability; ensuring essential services are still being provided during the *implementation* phase; appraising whether necessary skills are in the organization (IS and/or user) to assure effective operation in the *opera-*

tions phase, etc. The degree to which senior management needs to get involved in reviewing this depends on whether existing and planned services are critical for the organization to meet its day-to-day operating objectives (i.e., is the company at the bottom of the "factory" or "strategic" boxes?).

Service Sourcing—Decision Authority

Senior management must provide guidance as to where the company should be moving on the dimension of software/processing service sourcing decisions, and whether the user or IS should have a primary voice in these decisions.

This sourcing decision can occur in all phases of the information service life cycle, from design to maintenance, and for all three IS technologies of communications, data processing, and office automation. In practice, most of these decisions will involve at least some IS input and user involvement, particularly in the design and implementation phases; however, at the extremes, either group may be willing to take total responsibility.

Further, each phase of the project life cycle is in a state of transition in terms of options, both as to where in the organization the service sourcing decision should be made, whether the service should be sourced in-house or externally, and what internal work should be done by IS versus the user. For example, in the design phase in many organizations, the in-house users are developing more *make* capacity (decision support systems and user programming), therefore becoming less dependent on IS or an outside supplier (with the risk to the organization that it may lose operational control over key systems). Similarly, some office managers are personally purchasing and installing completely designed support systems.

What is being constructed is also changing—no one (outside the vendor) builds internal computer operating systems any more, and only a few construct data base systems software. A shrinking percentage of data processing applications are consequently being designed and constructed by IS staff, with an even smaller percentage of office automation systems software being designed and constructed inside the firm.

Implementation is changing from being almost the exclusive domain of IS to a situation where the user often has control over local department micro-based systems, and either IS or user may have the primary relationship with an outside software vendor. Operations has moved from an exclusive IS-controlled activity to one where service bureaus and user-controlled minis and micros have considerably altered the picture. Maintenance in some of the newer technologies can be done more by the users.

The nature of the application is important in selecting primary decision-making responsibility. On the one hand, implementation and operation of a customized new decision support system in a bank can be completely under the control of the portfolio manager fresh from school, because it requires neither two-way interaction with the organization's data files nor the controls implicit in day-to-day transaction processing. An office automation system implementation effort, on the other hand, may require significant IS professional support in user training to ensure that potential operating problems are avoided.

Different firms have chosen rationally to locate in quite different positions the sourcing decision for different phases of the systems life cycle for different IS technologies. Our concern here is twofold:

1. This is an important strategic decision and should be addressed explicitly rather than be left to chance.
2. The transitional nature of the information services industry makes it hard to be specific as to a long-term sourcing policy that a firm should implement for any phase of the system's life cycle or any IS technology. The dynamics of change defy either simplistic or long-term solutions.

Within these general caveats, however, we find that discussion on the location of decision-making power should flow primarily around the OA and DP technologies. Communications decisions have such a pervasive influence on the ability to distribute data and other information that they demand a strong central IS policy and decision-making role. In the two other technologies, however, although either the IS department or user may have the prime authority to decide, continuous consultation with each other is strongly encouraged.

Examples of Different Organization Approaches to Life-Cycle Control

Three comparative examples are presented of how six firms have allocated decision responsibility for each phase of the product life cycle, and how these vary by make-or-buy.

Exhibit 8–1 compares the IS sourcing decisions for two organizations where IS plays a role of *strategic significance.* The one which emphasizes central IS decision power is a bank, and the other which emphasized decentralized decision power is a multidivision consumer product firm. Both desire to maintain control over their integration of systems activity and develop expertise inside their firms while simultaneously gaining experience in purchasing services and reducing software costs. The bank, however, feels the integrated nature of its business and customer relationships are such that it must maintain central control of data and develop central standards compatible with its overall mode of operations. The consumer product firm, on the other hand, has traditionally decentralized profit responsibility along with all staff support to each division and felt that integrated data files were neither critical to its operation nor appropriate to its management philosophy and

EXHIBIT 8-1 □ Systems Are Strategic to Company—Two Organizational Strategies

Bank

	Technology	Life-cycle phases to be bought	Life-cycle phases to be made
User responsibility	Communications		I*
	Data processing		D* I* O*
	Office automation		D I* O*
IS responsibility	Communications	D C O M	D I*
	Data processing	D C M	D* I* O* M
	Office automation	D C M	I* O* M

Consumer product firm

	Technology	Life-cycle phases to be bought	Life-cycle phases to be made
User responsibility	Communications	C* O M	D* I*
	Data processing	C*	D I
	Office automation	D C I M	D I O
IS responsibility	Communications	C*	D* I*
	Data processing	C*	O M
	Office automation		

D - Design
C - Construct
I - Install
O - Operate
M - Maintain

Note: A letter appearing on same line twice means some aspects of phase are bought and others made.
*Indicates joint responsibility for phase by user and IS.

structure. Although the consumer product firm has a central DP department, all development is done by divisional staff. Each company reached its decision only after careful consideration of all elements, although obviously different structures emerged. Of particular interest is that the IS-dominated bank felt more need for joint efforts in implementation than the user-oriented consumer products divisions.

Exhibit 8–2 compares two organizations where IS, although large, was perceived to be relatively *strategically unimportant*. Both are choosing to buy more than make in order to reduce their professional work force (which they are understandably having trouble recruiting). One, a nationwide men's clothing chain with a strong inventory control and accounting system, decided to continue having IS control the development of systems although shifting their construction from primarily make to a strong buy orientation. In particular, they have been trying to buy more complete services. They were much concerned about how to avoid the danger of operational disruption. The other, an automobile parts distributor with four large warehouses in different states, decided to allow local general managers to purchase services.

The auto parts company assumed their small central staff would assist but wanted to develop local expertise in purchasing information services, as they did with purchasing for their main product lines. The IS department designed the communications system and spun off the former central DP and OA into one of the warehouse IS groups. A one-man corporate IS department now manages corporate communications and audits performance of the division's IS group. This company felt that each warehouse taking control of its operation was compatible with its managerial philosophy. Conversely, the men's clothing chain central IS department merged OA and DP into one vendor's system which included communications capability. They are now in the process of implementing this system in all stores.

A final example (Exhibit 8–3) compares two firms that *split equally responsibility* for acquiring services between the users and IS staff. The machine tool company felt that, because of the rapid developments in CAD/CAM, they should buy their software in light of their particularly good experience with a specific vendor's bill of material processor. The large chemical company, on the other hand, felt it must do most development inside, as they had several unique process control systems they wanted to link to their management systems. The exhibit shows the resulting structure where users are in control of OA and IS is in control of communications. Design and DP systems is split between the two. Both firms felt operational review required central coordination.

These examples emphasize the range of possible organization and control structures for each phase of the systems life cycle. Clearly, the final decision rests on the nature of the business, with each organization intending to have some user and IS involvement in design/construction/implemen-

EXHIBIT 8-2 □ **Systems Are Nonstrategic to Company—Two Organizational Strategies**

Clothing chain

	Technology	Life-cycle phases to be bought	Life-cycle phases to be made
User responsibility	Communications		I*
	Data processing		D* I*
	Office automation		D* I* O
IS responsibility	Communications	D C I O M	D I*
	Data processing	D C I O M	D* I*
	Office automation	D C I M	D* I*

Auto parts distributor

	Technology	Life-cycle phases to be bought	Life-cycle phases to be made
User responsibility	Communications	D C I O M	D* I*
	Data processing	D C I M	D I O
	Office automation	D C I M	D* I*
IS responsibility	Communications		D* I*
	Data processing		
	Office automation		

D - Design
C - Construct
I - Install
O - Operate
M - Maintain

Note: A letter appearing on same line twice means some aspects of phase are bought and others made.
*Indicates joint responsibility for phase by user and IS.

EXHIBIT 8-3 □ Systems Strategic to Company (shared user-IS control)—Two Organizational Strategies

Machine tool company

	Technology	Life-cycle phases to be bought	Life-cycle phases to be made
User responsibility	Communications	C	D* I*
	Data processing	D* C* M*	I* O*
	Office automation	D*	I O
IS responsibility	Communications	O M	D* I*
	Data processing	D* C* M*	I* O* M
	Office automation	D* C M	

Chemical company

	Technology	Life-cycle phases to be bought	Life-cycle phases to be made
User responsibility	Communications		D* C I
	Data processing	C* M*	D* I* O*
	Office automation	C M	D I O
IS responsibility	Communications	C O M	D*
	Data processing	C* M*	D* C I* O* M
	Office automation		

D - Design
C - Construct
I - Install
O - Operate
M - Maintain

Note: A letter appearing on same line twice means some aspects of phase are bought and others made.
*Indicates joint responsibility for phase by user and IS.

tation phases in both internally developed and purchased systems. The scope and balance of this decision, however, varies widely. The machine tool company felt that its large backlog of maintenance would preclude many inside developments, particularly since it believed its location would make recruitment of more programmers very difficult. The bank, conversely, was actively recruiting systems personnel because it felt their design needs were expanding rapidly and that even withdrawing from internal construction efforts would not free up adequate resources for maintaining key systems. In an urban market, they felt they had to, and could, compete for a substantial increase in staff resources.

TECHNOLOGY PLANNING

The technology planning for operations involves an ongoing audit for potential obsolescence and opportunities. The technology planning scope and effort associated with this audit depends upon the nature of the business and state of IS. For a bank, it should be across many technologies and be very extensive; a mail-order business may concentrate on OA technology, whereas a wholesale distributor may just focus on DP and TP technologies. The audit should compare the means of providing IS today with the potential available two or three years from now and, to be effective, must involve very high caliber, imaginative staff. (Outside technical consulting can be very effective here.) This potential must be based on technological forecasting. If a company is trying to differentiate itself from competition by application of these technologies, the resources focused on this technological planning should be quite extensive. If a firm is trying to just stay even, and the IS activity is seen primarily as support, comparison of their operations with their competitors or "leaders" in particular fields may be sufficient. A few firms periodically solicit bids from different vendors on the service they are providing to ensure their IS department is fully up-to-date. For example, a large insurance company, whose IS department is dominated by technology of one vendor, annually asks a competitor of the vendor to bid an alternative system, even though they do not perceive a need for change. As a result of these bids, in the recent past they switched to another vendor's minicomputers and on still another occasion installed a large machine purchased from a different vendor.

The objective of the audit is to determine, relative to available and announced systems, how cost effective and adequate for growth are the existing installed technologies. Such an audit should generate an updated priority list of technologies to be considered as replacements. This lead time is critical because technology replacement or additions planned two years in advance cause a small fraction of the disruption of those planned only six months in advance. This technological planning should sponsor external testing, field trips, education, and pilot studies as vehicles for obtaining an understanding of emerging technologies, in order to better define the architecture of the future information service.

A useful approach to this technology audit is to categorize the applications portfolio of operations systems by their age since development, or last total rewrite. Exhibit 8–4 identifies the four major eras of the information systems industry and the characteristics of applications and technology of each era. The hardware and software technology of each era was quite different and led to totally different systems design. If a significant percentage of IS systems running today was designed in an earlier era this is normally a strong tip-off to major opportunities for reduced maintenance and improved operational efficiency through a major redesign and rewrite.[2] A large financial service firm recently performed such an audit and discovered 40 percent of their systems and 75 percent of their systems effort were devoted to maintaining an accounting-like system constructed in the second era. The purchase of a general ledger package, four months of development, and a period of parallel runs permitted 28,000 lines of COBOL code to be scrapped and freed up almost half of their maintenance effort.

The identification and implementation of new technology can be transparent to the user when it involves hardware replacement or new systems which use existing hardware more effectively. Other replacement technology may impact users by providing different or improved service such as report writers for data bases or new terminals, but are basically supporting them rather than changing their basic operations style. Some are so integrated with user habits that it is important to obtain user leadership in the implementation. Each implementation situation requires a careful plan to ensure service is not interrupted and relevant individuals understand how to operate with the new service. Exhibit 8–5 illustrates the tensions and forces which must be managed.

When IS planning maintains an appraisal of user readiness and an inventory of use of existing technology, and an appropriate assessment of where technology is going, a program of new technology can be developed rather easily for each entity. For example, a large consumer products company has a very strong IS technology planning group. As part of their activity, they maintain for each division and function an updated log of services in use and an assessment of current problems. They are currently in the midst of a program of introducing OA which includes a large portfolio of different applications in a pilot division. Their detailed program for this division is scheduled over 24 months. This program includes benchmarks and reviews to evaluate both benefits and operating problems and progress. This pilot testing provides a useful vehicle to stimulate broader organizational aware-

---

[2] Martin Busch, "Penny-Wise—Pound Foolish," *Harvard Business Review* (July–August 1981).

EXHIBIT 8–4 □ Major Eras of Information Systems

	Industry	Technology	Hardware	Software	Portfolio
1955– Shake out era	Data processing firms Analog engineering firms	Vacuum tube to transistor Many memory types to core mag tape as secondary storage card-archival	Central logic memory Small peripheral in/out	Machine language to assembler language Start of operating system	Clerical replacements Computation improvements Accounting and engineering applications
1962– Data-processing-market formation era	IBM + several equal computer marketers	Transistor to integrated circuits Core dominates memory Disk emerges as secondary storage Tape archival	Growth of large central systems Huge tape files	Multiprogramming Multiprocessing Operating systems Start of time-sharing and virtual COBOL/FORTRAN/ BASIC	Operational control Reservation systems Completion of clerical automation Mathematical programming
1970– Computer market era	IBM + fewer equal competitors + Minicomputer manufacturers	Integrated circuit to LSI MOS memories Huge disks as secondary storage Tape archival Satellites	Linking systems Several remote terminals Mag card typewriters Stand-alone mini computer Store and forward communications	Growth of special-purpose systems (e.g., newspaper) Remote online data base Communication controller	Simulation to planning models Marketing systems Financial portfolios Personnel systems
1978– Information market era	IBM + ATT + DEC Xerox + several other	LSI to V^3SI Huge disk Laser Optical light pipes	Linked large systems Distributed systems	Large data base Report writer Fail soft systems Communication system	Decision support systems CAD/CAM Office automation Electronic mail

EXHIBIT 8-5 □

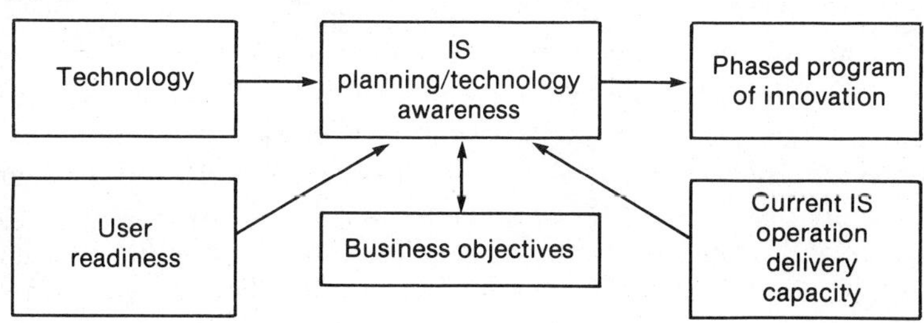

ness of the opportunities and operational issues associated with this technology and permits better planning for full-scale implementation in the other divisions. This approach has proven to be an effective means of marketing new IS technology to many organizational units. The art of technology planning is building a process to move from the raw technical idea to an informal awareness of its operational implications before widespread installations. The failure to build this bridge is a primary cause of implementation trouble.

MANAGING CAPACITY

The less one knows about computer hardware/software technology, the more certain one is as to what capacity is. In reality, the different hardware/software elements tend to interact in such a complex way that the diagnosis of bottlenecks and proper long-term planning of capacity is a very important task requiring a high order of skill to execute. Key elements of the changing capacity decision include the following items:

1. Capacity comes in much smaller, less expensive increments than a decade ago. This has created an asymmetric reward structure for capacity overages versus underages in many organizations. For these firms, a shortage of capacity in critical operating periods is very expensive, while conversely, the cost of extra capacity is very low. For these organizations, carrying excess capacity is a sound decision.

2. The approach of a capacity crunch comes with devastating suddenness. One large financial institution operated with few difficulties during a six-month period with a 77 percent load on the CPU during peak demand. Senior management refused to listen to IS management, which warned that they were on the edge of a crisis, and would not permit IS management to place an order for additional equipment. During the next six months, the introduction of two new minor systems and steady growth in transaction volumes brought CPU load during peak periods to 83 percent. This was accompanied by a dramatic increase in online systems response time, a

steady stream of missed schedules on the batch systems, and twice key delivery times of items to an industry clearinghouse were missed. The move from a satisfactory to a thoroughly unsatisfactory situation does not creep up on an organization but can arrive dramatically to the untutored eye.

3. There has been an explosion of diagnostic tools, such as hardware and software monitors, to assist in the identification of these problems. These tools are only analytical devices, and they are no better than the quality of the analyst using them and the detailed forecast of future demands to be placed on the systems. This has led to a significant growth in both the number and quality of technical analysts in a firm's operations group in situations where operations plays a vital role.

4. A dramatic increase has taken place in the number of suppliers of equipment to be hooked on to a computer configuration. This is reducing the number of firms totally committed to one vendor's gear. Additional features, coupled with attractive prices of specialist manufacturing, pushed many firms in the direction of proliferation. This phenomenon, when combined with the integration of telecommunications and office automation, has made the task of capacity planning more complex as well as increased the exposure to refereeing vendor disputes when their network goes down.

5. Complex trade-offs have to be made in innovation (with both its risks and economic opportunities) versus conservatism (with perhaps higher operating costs but more reliability). Companies where *significant* (in terms of overall company profitability) cost reductions are offered by this technology, or where significant strategic competitive advantage may stem from the operation of this technology, should appropriately be more adventuresome than other firms where this is not true. Similarly, firms which have great dependence on the smooth operation of existing systems must be more careful about the introduction of new technology into a network where unanticipated interaction with existing systems could cause great difficulty in ensuring reliable operation of key parts of the organization.

6. The cost and disruption caused by change often outweighs the advantages associated with a particular technology and it becomes attractive to skip a generation of change. This has to be looked at carefully on two grounds:

a. The system design practices of the 1960s and early 1970s were quite different from those being employed today. Some firms, anxious to postpone investment, have stayed too long with these systems and exposed themselves to great operational risk by trying to implement massive change in an impossibly short period of time, with disastrous results. Software is, in every sense, like a building—it depreciates. Unfortunately, industry accounting practices do not recognize this; consequently, it is very easy to get into difficulty through excessive, apparently innocent, postponement.

b. Some changes are critical if the firm is to be competitive, while others are nice but cannot legitimately be considered essential. Investments in this later category are clearly eligible for postponement.

7. As an increasing set of investments are made in the products of small software and hardware vendors, another cluster of important issues is brought to the surface. These issues relate to vendor viability and product maintainability over the past 15 years. There has been a high mortality rate among these suppliers. In evaluating hardware vendors, the issues are: If they go under, is there an acceptable alternative? Is it easy to keep existing systems going both short term and long term? What are the likely costs of these alternatives? In evaluating software vendors, the issue is: If the vendor goes out of business, has the contract provided for our having access to source programs and documentation? An additional area of complexity is their posture toward program maintenance, both as to the type of error correction and systems enhancement change which may be expected and as to the cost-charging policy for these items. As noted earlier, it is critical that experienced operations thinking be involved in these negotiations. All too often, very unhappy outcomes have ensued when either the user or the systems and programming department acquired software without understanding the long-term operating implications of the decision.

8. Finally, a hidden set of capacity decisions focus on the acquisition of appropriate backup infrastructure items, such as power, chilled water, and adequate building strength for the weight of the equipment. The importance of availability and reliability of these items are easily often underassessed. For example, recently the temperature in a large metropolitan data center suddenly went from 78 degrees to 90 degrees in a two-hour period, shutting down the entire operation. A frantic investigation finally uncovered the fact that, three floors down, a plumber had mistakenly cut off a valve essential to the provision of chilled water to the operations room.

These points suggest clearly that not only is capacity planning a very complex subject but it requires as much administrative thinking as technical thinking. In the 1980s, for most organizations, we are not talking about building a new factory but rather implementing a continuous program of renovation and modernization on the factory floor while keeping the assembly line in full production. This is a formidable and, unfortunately, often seriously underestimated task.

MANAGING THE WORK FORCE

The personnel issues in the operations function have changed significantly in the past few years. Most dramatic has been the major reduction in data input and preparation departments. The introduction of online data entry has not only changed the type of tasks to be done (keypunching, key verification, job-logging procedures, etc.) but has permitted much of this work to be transferred to the department which originated the transaction, often to the person who first initiates the transaction. A desirable trend in terms of locating control firmly with the person most interested, in many settings this has been exceptionally hard to implement with users turning out to be less enthusiastic than anticipated about taking over this accountability. In general, however, the large centralized data entry departments are fading and will continue to fade into history.

At the same time, the jobs in the computer operation section are being significantly altered:

1. Data base handling jobs are being steadily automated. The mounting of tapes and disks are being reduced in frequency. Some firms have even successfully automated the entire tape library function. Further, as CRTs have exploded in popularity, the amount of paper handling has been reduced.
2. Former manual expediting and scheduling functions have been built into the basic operating system, eliminating a class of jobs.
3. In the more sophisticated shops, many of the economies indicated in items 1 and 2, which are possible, have already been achieved. A point of diminishing returns has been reached in this area and the past economies gained are not a prologue to the future here.
4. The establishment of work performance standards in this environment has become a less feasible and useful task. As the data input function disappears and as the machine schedules itself rather than being paced by the operator's performance, the family of time-and-motion performance standards of the 1960s has become largely irrelevant for the 1980s. Inevitably, performance evaluation of individuals has become more subjective.

These factors clearly indicate that the composition of the operations work force has changed dramatically. The blue-collar component is significantly reduced, with a large number of new, highly educated technologists and production planners being needed instead. The issue is further complicated by the continuous change taking place in technology, which requires that both types of staff must upgrade their skills if they are to be relevant for future needs.

In this environment, career path planning is a particular challenge. At present, for the professionals, three major avenues are available. Those who have technical aptitude tend to move to positions either in technical support or in systems development. A very common exit point for a console operator is as a maintenance programmer. As a result of operations experience, he has developed a keen sensitivity to the thorough testing of systems changes. The second avenue is a position as a manager in operations, particularly in large shops where there are a multitude of management positions ranging from shift supervisors to operations managers, which are mostly filled through internal promotions. Finally, in banks and insurance companies in particular, there have been a number of promotions out of IS operations into other operations positions in the firm. This represents, particularly in the manufacturing sector, a neglected avenue of opportunity. All of these promotion paths, if given the proper attention, make the operations environment an attractive place to work and prevent it from becoming ossified and therefore unresponsive to change.

The introduction of the trade union movement in this department has been relatively infrequent in the U.S. environment. It has been quite frequent in Europe and in portions of western Canada. In many settings organizing this department gives the union great leverage because a strike by a small number of individuals can virtually paralyze an organization. In the past several years, strikes of small numbers of computer operations staff in the United Kingdom's Inland Revenue Service have caused enormous disruptions in its day-to-day operations. In thinking about the potential impact of being unionized, the following points are important:

1. The number of blue-collar jobs easily susceptible to being organized has been dropping. A convincing argument can be made that shops were more vulnerable to being organized in the technology of the past generation than the current generation. One reason some companies have embraced the new technology is to eliminate this unionization exposure through job elimination.
2. The creation of multiple data centers in diverse locations makes the firm less vulnerable to a strike in any one location. Reducing this vulnerability has been a factor (although generally not the dominating one) in some moves toward distributed processing.
3. The inflexibilities of work-to-rule in this type of manufacturing organization are enormous. The dynamics of technical change in necessary functions and jobs make this a particularly poor time from the firm's point of view to be organized. As technology stabilizes, the inefficiencies resulting from premature organization will be less a matter of concern.

Selection of Operations Manager and Staff. Another area of significance is the selection of the IS operations manager, and his or her key staff. There are several important factors which generate different skill needs for different environments.

1. *Size* is the most important dimension. As an IS activity grows in numbers of staff, the complexity of the management task significantly increases, requiring many more managerial skills at the top.
2. *Criticality of IS operations Unit.* Firms which are heavily dependent on IS operations ("factory" or "strategic") are forced to devote a higher

caliber professional resource to this area. The penalties to the company of uneven quality of support are clearly heavier and more effort must be made to avoid them.

3. *Technical sophistication of shop.* A shop heavily devoted to batch-type operations, with a relatively routine nondynamic hardware/software configuration, requires less investment in leading-edge management than a shop with a rapidly changing, leading-edge environment. The latter situation requires staff who can lead, effectively, efforts in upgrading operating systems, etc.

These factors suggest clearly the impossibility of defining a general-purpose operations manager. Not only do different environments require different skills, but over time the requirements in an individual unit shift. The overall trend, however, in the last decade is to demand an ever high quality of manager. Increasingly, the former tape handler or console operator of 15 years ago has proven inadequate for handling this job.

Human Issues in Managing the Work Force. Finally, there are a series of long-term human issues which must be dealt with in managing the work force effectively. These include:

1. Recognition that the problem of staff availability and quality is a long-term challenge for IS operations. Intensified efforts in an environment of decreasing entrants to the total work force are needed to attract quality individuals to the IS operations group. Career paths and salary levels require continuous reappraisal. For "factory" and "strategic" companies, IS operations can no longer be treated as a stepchild to the development group.

2. There is a critical need for IS operations to develop appropriate links to both the users and the development group. The linkage to development focuses on ensuring that appropriate standards are in place so that new systems and enhancements are both operable (without the development staff being present or on call) and that no unintended interaction take place with other programs and data files. The establishment of an IS operations quality assurance function is an increasingly common way to deal with this. The user linkage is critical to ensure that when operating problems occur, the user knows who in IS operations can solve them. Finally, it is important that development and operations have their respective roles vis-à-vis one another clearly defined and separate, so that a minimum of confusion exists in the user's mind when he or she has a problem as to where to go for the solution.

3. Not only does a long-term IS staff development plan need to be generated, but a specific training program must be prepared and executed for staff.

4. Quality-of-work-life issues need to be addressed continuously. This includes items such as flexible time, three-day (12 hours at a time) work-

weeks, and shift rotation. There is no clear right answer to these issues, but rather a continuous reassessment must occur.

PRODUCTION PLANNING AND CONTROL

Operations production planning is complicated by the fact that a multitude of goals are possible for an IS operations function. Among the most common ones are the following:

Ensure a high-quality, zero-defect operation. All transactions will be handled correctly, no reports lost or missent, etc.

All long-term job schedules will be met (or at least within some standard).

The system will be responsive to handling unanticipated, unscheduled jobs, processing them within x minutes or hours of receipt, providing they do not consume more than 1 percent of the resource.

Average reponse time on terminals for key applications during first shift will be x seconds. Only 1 percent of transactions will require more than y seconds.

"Day-to-day" operating costs will not exceed the given levels.

Capital expenditure for IS equipment will not exceed the budgeted levels.

Resolving Priorities. It is important to recognize that, by and large, these are mutually conflicting goals and all cannot be optimized simultaneously. For companies where IS operations support is critical to achievement of corporate missions ("factory" and "strategic"), resolution of these priorities requires senior management guidance. In environments where it is less critical, they can be sorted out at a lower level. In our judgment, failure to explicitly sort out the priorities in an appropriate manner (that is, widespread concurrence and understanding of the trade-offs to be made has been gained) has been a primary source of the poor regard in which some operations units have been held. Their task has been an impossible one.

The sorting out of these priorities immediately gives insight into how to address two other items.

1. Organization of capacity. The relative desirability of a *single integrated computer* configuration or a series of modular units either within a single data center or multiple data centers (assuming the nature of the workload is such that you have a choice) is an important strategic decision. Setting up modular units (plants within a plant at some cost) will allow specialized delivery service to be implemented for different types of applications and users. These multiple factories also allow for simpler operating systems in addition to allowing quite different types of performance measures and management styles be implemented for each. This focused factory concept has been too often neglected in IS operations.

2. *Ensuring consistent operating policies are in place.* Uncoordinated management specialists, each trying to optimize his or her own function, may create a thoroughly inconsistent and ineffective environment. In one large insurance company, the following policies were simultaneously operational:

a. An operator wage-and-incentive system, based on meeting all long-term schedules, and minimizing job setup time.

b. A production control system which gave priority to quick turnaround, small-batch jobs meeting certain technical characteristics.

c. A quality control system which focused on zero defects and ensuring that no reruns would have to take place.

d. A management control system which rewarded both low operating budgets and low variances from the operating budgets. Among other things, this control incentive had helped to push the company toward a very constrained facilities layout to minimize costs.

While individually each of the policies could have made sense, collectively they were totally inconsistent and had created both tension and friction within the IS operations group and a very uneven perception of service on the part of key users.

Job Shop versus Process Manufacturing. The conflicting needs posed by job shop operation versus process manufacturing operation causes significant tensions and confusion, because they each pose quite different production planning problems. The job shop (the predominant IS environment in 1970) involves the processing of multiple discrete jobs, each of which uses different amounts of computing capacity. Many of these jobs require different routing paths through the operation center (Inforex, check sorting, bursting, etc.), as well as within the computer.

Quality control in the job shop involves ensuring that key production deadlines are not missed, jobs and outputs are not lost, incorrect data is not processed, reports are not missent to the wrong locations, and so forth. Production scheduling is a complex task divided between a production control department and the computer's operating system. The production control department identifies desired target times for completing job processing, prepares schedules and establishes priorities for work stations outside the computer department control, prepares necessary job setup instructions, and determines relative job priority. The computer operating system then does the detailed allocation of the computer resource to each job (balancing its relative priority against efficient use of the system) and shepherds it through to completion. The production control department normally has both an expediting function, for squeezing short rush jobs through the system, and a tracing function, to allow them to answer user questions about the status of different jobs. Human expediting is an important part of ensuring that this happens.

In addition, since a job is moved from work station to work station, careful attention is paid to overall facilities layout to minimize congestion and confusion while ensuring staff resources are efficiently utilized. Within limits, machine downtime and rerun problems can be effectively hidden from the customer (assuming there is some excess capacity). In the job shop environment it is possible to identify precisely what jobs are to be run, assess closely the volume of transactions to be processed, predict the amount of time each job would take, and write a detailed production schedule. The week's production schedule can be formalized in some detail in advance and posted on a board in a GANTT chart or some similar type of format. Long-term production planning involves forecasting increases in business volume, hence transaction levels, and identifying major new applications and their potential requirements. Both of these turn out to be relatively cut-and-dried. Finally, throughout the day, tactical decisions as to how to juggle the schedule have to be made on items such as unexpected machine downtime, extra reruns, and the occurrence of more or fewer transactions than planned for in programs such as order entry. Other complicating items include submission of unplanned small jobs or programmer test shots. These changes are made by both production schedulers and machine operators. Production planning, in this environment is not only well structured but has a high amount of predictive power associated with it and can be fine-tuned with considerable human input.

Process manufacturing, or utility operation (most online systems), poses very different problems. It involves the continuous processing and flow of transactional work through a finite resource. The arrival of work in the IS environment takes place in an unscheduled intermittent fashion, with a variety of queues to hold it during periods of excess demand. Substantial control has been lost over the timing of the utilization of the computing configuration. It is difficult to forecast the number of transactions coming from dispersed users in half-hour periods. Forecasting becomes more probabilistic and the definition of service levels in terms of response time performance becomes more complex. A lot of terminal use turns out to be less transaction driven and more user-inquiry driven. In this regard, substantial organizational learning takes place and more individuals find it attractive to use terminals in ways they could not conceive of in advance. This significantly complicates the task of capacity planning.

Quality control in process manufacturing involves ensuring that an acceptable pattern of response time exists during the day, and ensuring that an acceptable level of systems downtime and machine downtime is maintained, etc. In general, much higher absolute levels of service are required than in the job shop, because failures are absolutely visible and cause great emotional problems. Day-to-day production scheduling outside the operating system priority-setting mechanism is not an important issue. Transaction-volume forecasting, capacity planning, and bottleneck analysis, however, are very important items. It takes only a very small increase in volume over planned levels when the IS computing resource is near capacity to go from satisfactory to intolerable response times. Human expediting is not necessary.

In 1982 the problem is complicated because, in most organizations, it is not an either/or situation but rather a mix of both types of processing occurring simultaneously. In general, the move from a heavily batch world to an extensive online environment that still handles batch work has resulted in the following changes:

There has been a pronounced shift in the number and type of staff working in IS operations. There has been a sharp decrease in the number of blue-collar workers (tape handlers, console operators, disk pack mounters, etc.), and an increase in the number of high-salary process engineers (i.e., tech support people). Not only has the maintenance and fine-tuning of the operating system become much more complex, but the payoff resulting from capacity fine-tuning has become more important and is having to take place on a more continuous basis than in the past.

There has been a move away from very detailed human production scheduling to a more macro approach, where analyzing and attempting to manage the patterns across the hours and work shifts of a week becomes the major role of a production control group. Individual production job expediters and schedulers have become much less numerous and important.

Hot-line troubleshooting advice on an instantaneous basis has become important. The immediate transparency of the operating systems glitches, and the frustration of one minute downtime to users doing operating tasks has increased the importance of this integration.

Much tighter quality control checks are needed, both on systems modifications and on the introduction of new systems, to protect against their unintentional impact on other systems running simultaneously. Similarly, the problems of introducing poorly tested new technology have become much more severe.

User priority rules built into the operating system have been established, so that in times of peak utilization the resource is allocated in accordance with some corporate priorities. Since many of the users are inputting data at locations physically remote from the operation center, these rules must be built into the operating system. The heavy loads posed by unexpected volumes of online transaction and inquiries make it difficult to meet batch-run schedules, unless their priorities are carefully built into the operating systems.

The combination of these factors means that the human scheduling on an hour-to-hour basis is much less important than in the past and that considerable attention must be devoted to the architecture of the priority system inside the basic operating system. Long-term scheduling and planning of IS is harder because of uneven and sometimes unpredictable organizational learning about the utilization of this technology. (In one bank the use of an online portfolio management system grew fourfold over a two-year period as, successively, individual trust officers became comfortable with working with this new management tool.) Even though new applications can be identified in advance, the growth in their use cannot be predicted in the same way as for transaction processing systems.

In many settings, this transition in management focus has not taken place smoothly but has been quite troubled, both because of resistance to change and lack of explicit definition as to how corporate goals have changed.

Strategic Impact of IS Operations. The type of management focus brought to the IS operation function depends on IS operation's role in the firm. IS operations in the "support" and "turnaround" categories can appropriately be dominated by cost-efficiency thinking. Deadlines, while attractive to meet, are not absolutely critical to the organization's success. Quality control, while important on the error dimension, can be dealt with in a slightly relaxed way. It is appropriate to take more risks on the capacity dimension for both job shop and process type IS operations in order to reduce the financial investment. Less formal and expensive backup arrangements are also appropriate. Finally, corners can safely be cut in user-complaint response mechanisms.

The "factory"-type operation poses very different challenges. Integrally woven into the ongoing fabric of the company's operations, quality in accuracy, response time, and schedule meeting is absolutely critical. Appropriate capacity to meet various contingencies is critical because severe competitive damage may occur otherwise. The issue of capacity not only needs to be managed more carefully, but usually more reserve capacity for contingencies needs to be acquired. New operating systems and hardware enhancements must be very carefully evaluated and managed to avoid the danger of downtime and the financial damage associated therewith. These factors in a budget crunch cause the company to make changes more carefully here than in organizations less dependent on the service.

The "strategic" operation, while facing all the issues of the "factory," has several other facets. Capacity planning is more complicated because it involves major new services instead of just extrapolation of old services with new volume forecasts. A stronger liaison needs to be maintained with the users to deal with the potential service discontinuities that will be associated with both new technology and new families of applications. These factors suggest that more slack needs to be left in both capacity and budget to protect vital corporate interests.

Implementing Production Control and Measurement. The above factors clearly suggest the need for an evolutionary and adaptive control and reporting structure. The same indexes, standards, and controls that fit one organization at a particular point in time will not meet other organizations' needs over an extended period of time as both the technology and the organization evolve toward an online system, and perhaps a "factory" organization.

Within the appropriate goals for the operations department, there is a critical need to identify both performance indexes and standards of performance. Actual data can then be compared against these standards. These indexes will normally include the following types of items:

Cost performance: aggregate performance versus standard for different types of IS services.

Staff turnover rates.

Average and worst 5 percent response times for different services.

Quality of service indicators such as amount of system downtime by services.

Number of user complaints by service.

Number of misrouted reports and incorrect outputs.

Growth in usage of services, for example, word processing, electronic mail, peak hours, computer utilization, etc.

Surveys focusing on user satisfaction with service.

While the underlying detail may be quite voluminous, this data, including trends, should be summarizable on a one- to two-page report each week or month. This quantitative data provides a framework within which qualitative assessments of performance can then take place.

SECURITY

One of the emotional topics surrounding IS operations is how much security is needed to protect the site and how much actually exists. We will not dwell at length on this as it is a complex subject that bears mentioning here only to call attention to the nature and importance of the problem. Exhaustively covered in other sources, we define the breadth of the issue by noting the following points.

1. Perfect security is unachievable at any price. The question for an organization is to understand, for its particular mission and geography, where the point of diminishing returns is located. Different units in the

organization or different systems may have distinctly different requirements in this regard.

2. Large organizations, where the activity is fundamental to the very functioning and existence of the firm, will appropriately think about this differently. The large firm where IS operations is fundamental to corporate success will be strongly motivated toward multiple remote centers. Duplicate data files, telecommunications expense, duplicate staff and office space, all make this an expensive (although necessary) way of organizing. These firms have come to the conclusion that if they do not back themselves up no one else will.
3. Smaller organizations, where this activity is critical, have found it attractive to go to something like the SUNGUARD solution, where a consortium of 80 users have funded the construction and equipping of an empty data center. If any one incurs a major disaster, this site is then available for them to use.
4. For organizations where the IS operation is less critical, appropriate steps may include arranging backup with another organization. (It always sounds better in theory than it is in reality.) Another alternative is to prepare a warehouse site with appropriate wiring, air conditioning, etc. (In a real emergency, locating and installing the computer is the easiest thing to do. It is the location and installation of all other items that consume the time.)
5. Within a single site, a number of steps can be taken to improve security. Listed below are some of the most common, each of which has a different cost associated with it.
    a. Limiting physical access procedures to the computer room. This can vary from simple buzzers to isolated diving-chamber entrances.
    b. Surrounding the data center with chain-link fences, automatic alarms, and dogs. Access to inner areas monitored by guards using remote TV cameras.
    c. Uninterrupted power supply, including banks of batteries and stand-alone generators.
    d. Complex access codes to deny file- and system-entry to all but the most qualified personnel.
    e. Significant number of files stored off-site and updated with a higher level of frequency.
    f. Installation of a Halon inert gas system to protect installation in case of fire.
    g. Systematic rotation of people through jobs, enforcement of mandatory vacations (no entry to building during the vacation), and physical separation of development and operations staff.

This is merely an illustrative list and in no sense is intended to be comprehensive.

SUMMARY

IS operations management is a very complex and evolutionary field. In part, this problem comes with changing technology obsolescing existing manufacturing processes and controls, in part from technology's impact on how best to implement the system life cycle, and in part from the changing profile of the work force. In thinking this area through, it appears the major insights come from applying the broad insights gained—in the fields of management of technological change and manufacturing—to this very special type of high technology factory. Most large firms now know how to schedule and control multiprocessing batch computer systems working on numerical data from decentralized input stations. Building upon this base to include word processing, electronic mail, and a host of more decentralized IS activities is a challenging growth opportunity. The critical resource for success in operations is the acquisition and retention of knowledgeable people to operate, maintain, and evolve IS services.

Case 8–1 □ New England Farmers Cooperative, Inc. (A)*

"I don't want to run out of capacity during the next two to three years, yet I don't want to spend any more on computers than we have to. Henry Webb [director of management information services] recommends getting the 148 just as soon as we move into the new building, while keeping our 145, and I understand that IBM also endorses this idea. I don't know whether it is right or not, but before we decide, I want to make sure that we've looked at every reasonable alternative. I personally don't think that IBM's newest is even the 'best buy,' particularly when you can get another 145 or a 155 or even a 158 on the used market at a good price. And I question Henry's recommendation that we triple our hardware capacity overnight." Thus began a conversation between Winston Smith, the financial vice president for Farmers Cooperative, and a consultant whom he'd hired to review the request for an IBM 370/148 submitted by Webb.

It was then mid-October 1977, and a firm decision was required by the end of November, or Farmers risked losing their delivery position from IBM on the 148. The planned delivery date was for the spring of 1978, concurrent with Farmers' move to their new corporate headquarters building in Springfield, Massachusetts.

FARMERS COOPERATIVE

Farmers was the principal corporation in a federated agricultural cooperative system comprising over a hundred local member cooperatives and 150,000 farmer-members spread over six northeastern states. Compared to other co-ops, Farmers was one of the largest and most successful in the United States. The company manufactured and purchased agricultural supplies for resale, principally to its members; marketed their products through retail outlets open to both farmer-members, nonmember farmers, and the public; and provided member cooperatives with management services. As a cooperative, Farmers was required to return all net savings (profit) to its patrons after provision for dividends on membership capital (limited to 8 percent per annum) and reasonable additions to operating capital. Patron

* This case is based on material prepared by Professor Brandt Allen of the Colgate Darden Graduate Business School and the University of Virginia. It is prepared for purposes of class discussion rather than to illustrate either effective or ineffective handling of an administrative situation.

dividends were paid to nonmembers in cash once a year and to member-farmers either in cash or non-interest-bearing certificates (membership capital) payable upon the death of the holder. Patronage was figured on net sales and was accounted for by issuing each patron a unique number which, if presented to the clerk at the time of sale, eventually resulted in an increase in the customer's patronage record for the year. For the year ending June 30, 1977, Farmers' sales had been $412 million, operating savings (earnings) $15 million, and of that $11.1 million was paid in cash or certificates to patrons.

The company's manufacturing and supply operations were divided into three divisions:

1. *Seed, Petroleum, and Supply* (SPS) Division, which bought and processed seed, stored it in warehouses, and distributed it through company-owned and -affiliated outlets, and had a small interest in oil prospecting, refining, and distribution.
2. *Feed Division,* which formulated livestock and poultry feed in eight mills and operated seven bulk feed stations and an egg marketing facility.
3. *Fertilizer Division,* which operated seven blending or granulating plants and had partial interest in several others.

The products of these divisions were sold through the distribution system of 80 retail branches, several hundred franchised agencies, and a hundred locally owned and controlled retail cooperatives managed for a fee by Farmers. Computer applications were found in each manufacturing division and in the retail system, all supported by the corporate data center.

PRESENT COMPUTER SYSTEM

In October 1977 the company operated a purchased IBM 370/145 with one half million bytes of memory running under DOS/VS, with an annual EDP budget of just over $2.1 million. Demand for computer services had been growing at a 30 percent average annual rate from 1969 to 1977. Exhibit 1 breaks out the 1977–78 budget by type of expense while Exhibit 2 illustrates the internal cost chargeout for the major applications running on the 145; these costs corresponded to anticipated machine utilization. Some systems analysis is decentralized while programming is centralized. The major applications were:

1. *Point-of-sale*—This application collected sales transactions by patron number for all company-owned and -managed retail outlets. Retail transactions (sales tickets) totaled over 4.5 million per year and were increasing at 15 percent per year. Each sales ticket averaged four item

EXHIBIT 1 □ Management Information Services Budget

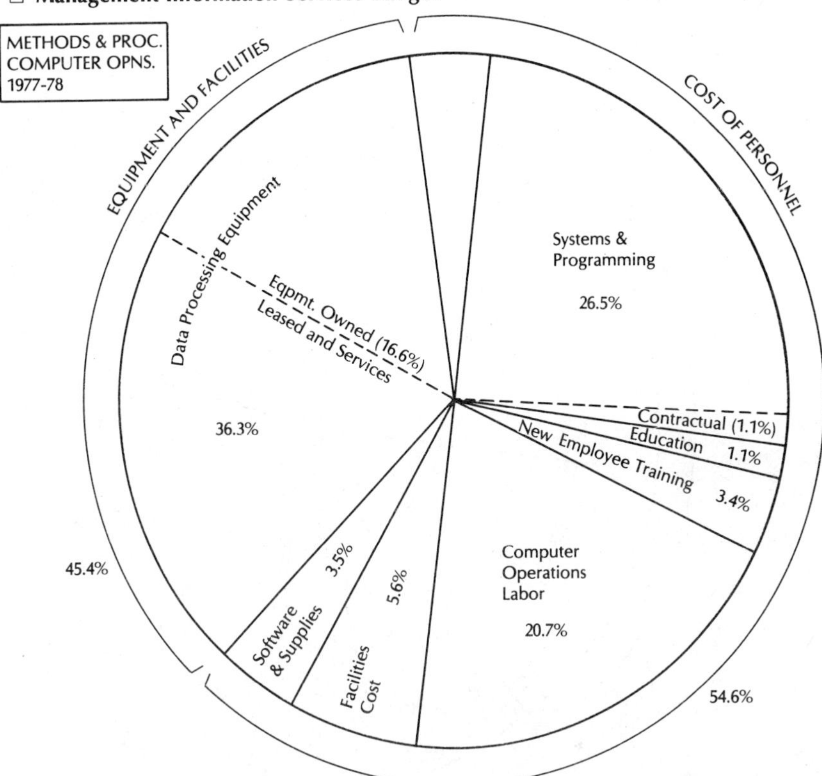

lines. (Dollar sales were growing 10 percent per year and the number of patrons at 20 percent per year.) In addition to satisfying the retail accounting needs, point-of-sale fed the stock record system with sales data by patron.

2. *Stock records*—This program collected sales or patronage records for about 1 million stockholders and patrons, handled the patronage cash refunds and certificates, and maintained stockholders' records on some 250,000 member stockholders.
3. *SPS batch*—Applications for the Seed, Petroleum, and Supply Division included order entry, inventory control, receivables, and payables. The volume of transactions handled by these programs was also growing rapidly due to greater physical volumes of product sold, more items or stock members, because of a broader product line, and the bigger warehouses being built by Farmers.
4. *SPS TP*, or the teleprocessing system for the SPS Division, was a start-up application which when completed would replace SPS batch except for accounts payable, purchasing, and the inventory management sub-

EXHIBIT 2 □ Budgeted 1977–1978 Computer Cost Proration

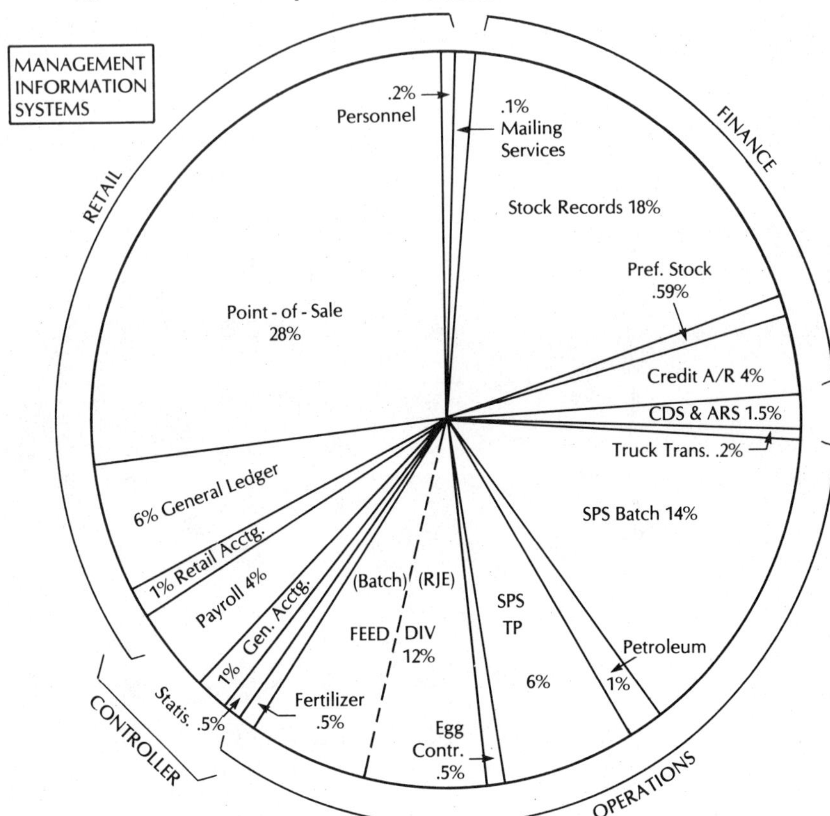

system. The transfer of these SPS programs from batch to TP would result in no immediate savings in computer time or resources, but it was expected to diminish somewhat the future growth rate of this area.

5. *Feed Division*—These applications were order entry, inventory record-keeping, receivables, payables, blending, and significant research applications. The Feed Division applications were being cut over from batch to remote job entry (RJE); eventually almost all the applications from this division would come to the computer over RJE terminals.

MR. WEBB'S REPORT

Henry Webb, who was just past 50, had been director of management information services at Farmers for 10 years, prior to that he had held a similar position with another company in Boston. Webb's department had prepared a comprehensive planning proposal in December of 1976 which projected computer volumes from 1978–84, evaluated four major hardware alternatives in terms of the projected workload, analyzed the cash flows for each alternative, and concluded with the recommendation to buy a 370/148 while keeping the existing 145. In his report, Mr. Webb analyzed computer volumes from 1968 to 1977, measured in terms of the number of jobs executed on a monthly basis. Each running of a single program was considered a job; jobs, of course, varied considerably in terms of their demand on CPU, memory, tapes, and disks, but the DOS operating system did not measure actual utilization of these system resources. Mr. Webb and his staff felt that the mix of jobs had been surprisingly stable over the years; furthermore, jobs executed was the only measure of volume that they had. In addition to projecting continuing increases in applications volume based on historical analysis, the projections of the future also included descriptions of five new major areas of growth:

1. Point-of-sale accounting for retail.
2. Teleprocessing for warehouse servicing.
3. Remote batch for feed service.
4. Grain marketing.
5. Internal time-sharing (to facilitate decision support systems).

Detailed estimates of jobs by application area were made for 1977 and 1978; beyond that, trends were used to predict volumes to 1984. The historical analysis and projection is shown below:

Historical and Projected Volume of Jobs Executed

Year	Average monthly jobs	Percentage increase over prior year
1968	2,000*	—
1969	2,400*	20%
1970	4,100*	71
1971	4,400*	7
1972	5,200*	18
1973	6,200*	19
1974	12,000*	94
1975	14,000*	17
1976	22,000*	57
1977	24,000	9
1978	36,000	50
1979	40,000	11
1980	44,000	10
1981	56,000	27
1982	66,000	18
1983	74,000	12
1984	88,000	19

* Actual count.

Webb's projection for 1977 had been made in December of 1976; by October, it appeared that the actual average monthly job count would, in fact, be in excess of 28,000. This volume of jobs just about saturated the three-shift capacity of the 145, and there were fears that the situation would be extremely tight by the June 1978 move date. Webb had remarked: "We're already overdue for a new machine, but till we move we simply have no more space." In an attempt to gauge just how much of the 145 was being used, Farmers had asked IBM to perform a special analysis of machine utilization in August of 1977, using their Performance Tool (PT), which was a software monitor program. PT generated voluminous outputs which required expert interpretation. The results, as read by IBM, indicated that CPU utilization was then about 55 percent of theoretical capacity; there seemed to be general agreement in the computer industry that a 145 under DOS/VS had a practical capacity of only 60–70 percent.

The December 1976 report from Management Information Services evaluated four alternatives: the first and second were upgrades to the existing 145 and the eventual purchase of a second used 145 in early 1980; the third was a replacement of the 145 with a 148 and the eventual purchase of a second 145; the last alternative was the purchase of a 148 at the time of the move while keeping the 145. As of January 1977, the tax book value of the total 145 configuration, including peripherals, was $487,000; for the CPU and memory alone, it was $275,000. Each alternative was costed over the 1977–84 period on an after-tax, cash flow basis using Farmers' combined federal and state tax rate of 50.6 percent. The net purchase cost (after sales taxes), monthly three-shift maintenance costs, warranty period (during which no maintenance is paid), tax life, estimated resale value, and total 8 percent after-tax net present value is shown in Exhibit 3. The present-value figures were backed by detailed exhibits (not shown in this case) produced by an IBM financial analysis program used by Webb.

It was generally agreed that no consideration should be given to the additional peripherals needed by a bigger 145 or 148 or any other configuration, since the incremental peripherals would be about the same no matter what the CPU configuration; for example, the number of printers needed was a function of the number of lines printed. That figure would be the same no matter what CPU configuration was chosen.

All four configurations were shown to be able to handle the projected workload through 1984 (see Exhibit 4). In fitting each machine configuration to the projected workload, Webb used the central processor capacity ratings shown below:

MIS Department's Central Processor Capacity Ratings

Machine	Capacity rating	Estimated jobs/month
1. 370/145 (384K) under DOS/VS	1.0	24,000
2. 370/145 (1 MEG) under DOS/VS	1.25	30,000
3. 370/148 or 370/145-3 (1 MEG) under VM	2.0	48,000
4. 370/148 or 370/145-3 (1 MEG) under VM *and* 370/145 under DOS/VS	3.0	72,000

EXHIBIT 3 □ Original Configuration Alternatives Considered—December 1976

Item	Ship date	Total cost ($000)	Monthly maintenance	Months of warranty	Tax life (months)	Residual value: Date	Residual value: Amount $000	Total present-value cost
			Alternative A					
Present 145	—	—	$1,820	0	48			
Upgrade to 1 Meg	2/77	$357	762	12	48			
Convert to 145-3	2/78	215	297	12	36	2/84	$228	
								$315,587
Purchase used 512K, 145	2/80	300	2,033	0	48	2/84	95	
			Alternative B					
Present 145	—	—	1,820	0	48			
Add 128K to 145	2/77	71	164	12	48			
Upgrade to 1 Meg, 145-3	2/78	501	896	12	36	2/84	228	
								$313,348
Purchase used 512K, 145	2/80	300	2,033	0	48	2/84	95	
			Alternative C					
Present 145	—	—	1,820	0	48			
Add 128K to 145	2/77	71	164	12	48	2/78	306	
								$294,647
Purchase 148	2/78	716	2,856	12	84	2/84	141	
Purchase used 512K, 145	2/80	300	2,033	0	48	2/84	95	
			Alternative D					
Present 145	—	—	1,820	0	48			
Add 128K to 145	2/77	71	164	12	48	2/84	105	
								$365,118
Purchase 148	2/78	735	2,856	12	84	2/84	141	

EXHIBIT 4 □ CPU Capacity Comparison

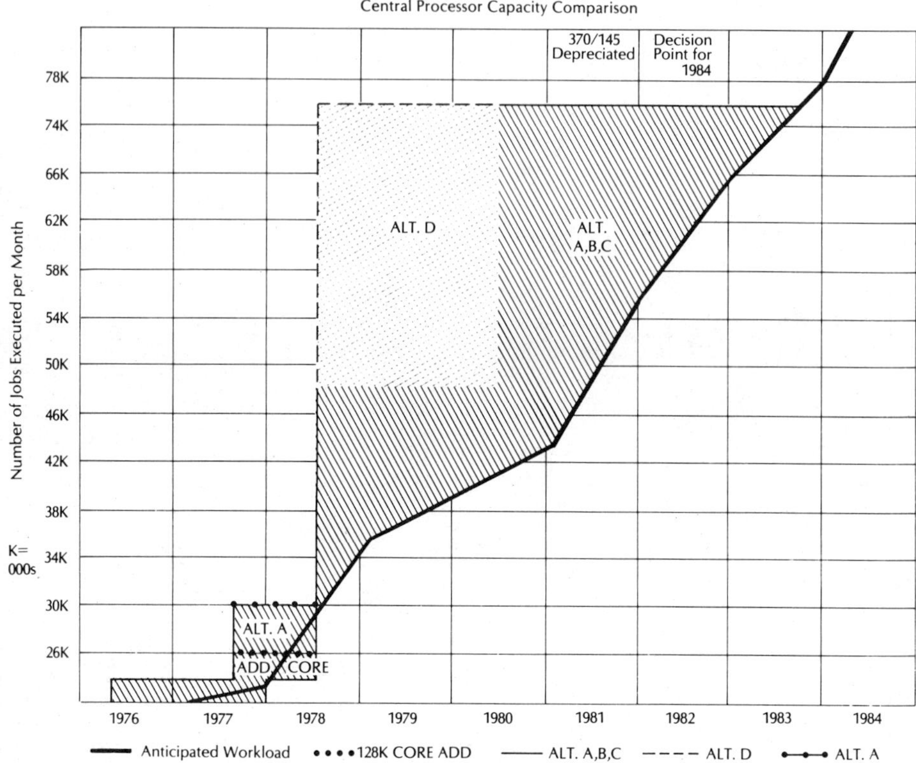

These estimates reflected Farmers' job mix, projected memory sizes, and the known internal speeds of the processors; they were felt to be the best estimates available. It was known, for example, that from a speed point of view the 370/145-3 and a 370/148 were equal. IBM claimed the 148 was 28–43 percent faster than a plain 145, and the 148 used a feature called expanded control program storage which upped the performance further.

The 148 came with a minimum memory of one megabyte (1 MEG or a million bytes) which could be doubled later; it could operate under either DOS/VS or OS/VS1 or by use of IBM's virtual machine facility (VM) could actually operate both operating systems simultaneously. Webb planned to develop most new applications under OS/VS1, including TP for the Seed, Petroleum, and Supply Division, RJE for Feed and new RJE and TP applications. Older jobs would be converted to OS or would remain under DOS. In a two-machine configuration (Alternatives A, B, D, and after 2/80 for C), one machine would support DOS/VS, the other VM running DOS/VS and OS/VS1. If only one machine were used, it would be necessary to use VM (with DOS and OS operating underneath it) to support both classes of jobs. VM would not be practical on the existing 145 configuration, but would be possible on the expanded 145-3 envisioned in Alternatives A and B. Another plus to the two-machine configuration was flexibility: the disk files could be easily switched between the machines if one machine were down.

JULY 1977 ADDENDUM

In July of 1977, an addendum was appended to the original planning proposal (no decision had been made on that proposal although an order had been placed for a 148). The addendum considered these topics: another approach to gauging expansion requirements (besides the number of jobs executed), operational plans in a two-machine configuration, and a comparison of the 370/155-II with a 370/148. The other approach to projecting workload was to forecast partition process hours daily for typical months and for peak periods. Under DOS/VS and OS/VS1, multiprogramming was accomplished by dividing memory into a fixed number of sections, or partitions (under DOS/VS it was 5, under OS/VS1 it was 7). Jobs were then scheduled into these partitions for typical days, as shown in Exhibit 5. Peak periods were analyzed separately. From this analysis, the monthly capacity utilization of a 148 was predicted, as shown below, along with predicted utilization under VM if additional memory, channels, and peripherals were added.

Percentages 1979 Monthly System Utilization—370/148

			Peak day	
	Normal day	Maximum possible utilization*	Normal day	Maximum possible utilization*
July	75%	49%	87%	57%
August	76	49	88	57
September	76	49	88	57
October	75	49	88	57
November	74	49	88	57
December	74	49	88	57
January	78	51	90	59
February	78	51	90	59
March	84	55	100	65
April	84	55	100	65
May	75	51	87	57

* Represents potential capacity under VM with appropriate core, channel, and I/O changes when needed.

EXHIBIT 5 □ 1979 Daily Partition Hours

Hour	F_1	F_2	F_3	F_4	F_5	F_6	BG
1	Power/ VS	CICS TP	Payroll	Feed RJE	MISC.	Software Test	Library
2							PEMG (Batch)
3			Feed Batch			TP Test	
4							
5							Library
6			Retail General Ledger		MO. Retail (6 days/month)	TP Test	PEMG (Batch)
7							
8				Fertilizer			
9				Stock Records			
10		TP INTERF					Library
11			CDS				PEMG (Batch)
12			DAY-DAV				
13		SPS Batch	SPS Batch				
14				T & Rental			
15				Retail Inventory			
16							
17				Point of Sale Daily			
18							
19							
20							
21		CR/AR	Statistical				PEMG (Batch)
22							
23			Mailing			TP Test	Library
24		CICS TP					

From this figure, it was decided "that the original conclusion of capacity support into 1981 appears correct."

The two-machine configuration was felt to obtain several advantages: The present 145 would be fully depreciated in January 1981; after that the only cost would be for maintenance; the 145 could always be sold if the 148 with VM proved satisfactory; and two machines would minimize the impact of outages and peak loading. Although there were a number of used 370/155 machines on the market, this option was not judged to be superior to the 148, as summarized in Exhibit 6.

EXHIBIT 6 □ Comparison of 370/148 and 370/155-2

	370/148	370/155-2
Memory size	1 Meg–2 Meg	¼ Meg–2 Meg
Std channels		
Byte multiplex	1 (256 SUB)	1 (256 SUB)
Block multiplexer	4 (512 shared)	2 (480 shared)
Block multiplexer speed	1.85 MB	1.5 MB
Optional block channels	None	3
CPU console	Video + optional printer	Required printer (3215) No video
3203 printer capability	Yes	No
Environmental		
(1 Meg.)	265 sq. ft. total	405 sq. ft. total
BTU and power	Even	Even
1 Meg. added	Unchanged	705 sq. ft. +5K VA +15,400 BTU
Reliability rating		
(Data-Pro survey)	+10 percent better	
Future I/O and software	Open	Frozen
Memory technology	Mosfet	Magnetic core
Control storage	128K	None
VM assist in control		
storage	Yes	No
ECPS assist	Yes	No
Maintenance cost measurement	$2,358.00/month	$4,242.00/month
(1 shift)	($22,608.00 less/year)	80 percent higher
Warranty	12 months	None
(Savings of $50,904 with 148)		

WINSTON SMITH

Winston Smith became vice president, finance in July 1977, one year after joining Farmers. Prior to that, he had worked for 10 years for a large oil company and then for a large regional securities firm.

Of the new applications scheduled for implementation, Smith was most interested in the decision support system (DSS) capability. Smith explained this concept as "the use of computers to assist managers in their decision processes in complex tasks. We hope to support rather than replace managerial judgment, therefore improving the effectiveness of decision making rather than its efficiency. We need a facility which enables us to gather many kinds of data, and store that data in a manner so that it can be used to answer questions, produce reports and graphs, and generally become an integral part of doing business. All aspects of this facility should be oriented toward ease, speed, and flexibility so that the nondata processor is able to handle many of his (her) own inquiries and reports. The need for formal programming using a procedural language should become so minimal, it should appear almost nonexistent."

Although not a computer expert, Smith had keen interest in both the new and used computer markets, since several of his business school classmates were active in the computer sales, brokerage, and leasing businesses. In October, Smith remarked that they had already added another 128K of memory to the 145 (going from 384K to 512K), which he hoped would be sufficient until the move to the new building was complete (then scheduled for June 1978). He saw several alternatives worthy of consideration:

1. A 148 and 145 as proposed by Webb.
2. A single 148.
3. A used 155.
4. A 145-3.
5. Two 145s.

Whatever the choice, he insisted that a five-year time frame be considered, with another hardware configuration decision not to be made within three years. "I don't mean we shouldn't decide now to make certain hardware changes in two or three years, but I don't want to have to do another of these planning studies for another three years."

"I'm particularly interested in the 155 since I understand that we might be able to pick one up now for $625,000 or so and realize at least half that on our current 145 CPU and memory. As I understand it, if we consider the present 145 to have a power factor of 1.0 then . . . [whereupon he drew the following table]:

Machine	Power factor
145	1.0
148	1.25
155	1.8
158	2.5

but I'd like your opinion."

3031 ANNOUNCEMENT

The consultant began his study in late September with a target completion date of mid-November (1977). Two weeks after their first meeting, the consultant received a letter from Smith which read, in part: "As you probably know by now, IBM announced last week a new piece of hardware called the 3031 which appears to directly replace the 370/158 and which should have some bearing on the 370/148 as well. My understanding is that even though deliveries are scheduled for March 1978, order positions won't be known under December 1977." On the day of the announcement, Mr. Webb placed a "just in case"order for an IBM, 2 Meg, 3031 with a CPU and memory purchase cost of $1,000,000. On October 10, *Computerworld,* "The Newsweekly for the Computer Community," announced the 3031 (and the bigger 3032 announced at the same time) with the table reproduced in Exhibit 7.

THE NOVEMBER MEETING

The consultant was the DP manager of a university in Massachusetts which used IBM machines for administrative data processing. His university had recently replaced their 145 with a used 155 which had a special AMS memory. This memory facilitated faster execution speed over a plain 155, thus the consultant was quite familiar with the operating performance of the machines under consideration. He busied himself studying the proposed hardware configuration (a list which seemed to grow weekly), Webb's proposal, and the impact of various alternatives on Farmers. Early in November, he met with Webb and Smith to urge that a commitment be made to a rapid conversion of all DOS jobs to OS/VS1 and to move eventually to a single mainframe, as opposed to the plan originally proposed by Webb. His reasoning was set out in a letter, excerpts of which are shown in Exhibit 8.

At that meeting, he produced a table of his estimates of the relative power of the various machines. For evaluation purposes, he decided to use a 370/145 running under OS/VS1 as a base, which was assigned a power factor of 1.0.

Relative CPU Power

System	Operating system	Performance	VM performance
370/145	DOS/VS	.7	.3–.4
	OS/VS1	1.0	.4
370/148 or 370/145-3	DOS/VS	.9	.5–.8
	OS/VS1	1.3	.8
370/155-II with standard memory	DOS/VS	1.2	.3–.5
	OS/VS1	1.8	.5
370/155-II with AMS PSU memory	DOS/VS	1.6	.4–.6
	OS/VS1	2.4	.6
370/158	DOS/VS	1.6	.7–1.0
	OS/VS1	2.5	1.0
3031 or 370/158-3	DOS/VS	1.8	1.2–1.8
	OS/VS1	2.8	1.8

EXHIBIT 7 □ Computerworld announcement of 3031 and 3032

No. 41 | October 10, 1977 | 75¢ a copy:$18/year

	370/148	3031	370/158	370/158-3	3032	370/168	370/168-3	3033
Purchase price[1]	689,000[5]	1,455,000[6]	1,916,200[6]	2,001,100[6]	2,368,000[6]	2,884,780[7]	3,103,210[7]	3,805,000[8]
Purchase price[2]	689,000[9]	1,455,000	1,966,965[10]	2,052,865[10]	2,728,000[11]	3,581,530[12] 4,105,030[13]	3,838,350[12] 4,388,460[13]	3,005,000
Price/month[3] (four-year lease)[4]	17,280	39,310	55,820	59,600	58,470[6] 67,470[11]	96,384[12] 110,874[13]	107,635[12] 122,629[13]	77,460
Maintenance/month	2,235	3,690	3,189	3,234	7,110[4] 7,675[11]	7,809[12] 9,305[13]	7,970[12] 9,466[13]	8,320
Relative CPU power[4]	23	52	46	52	135	100	109	170
Memory size in byte (minimum-maximum)	1M–2M	2M–6M	512K–6M	512K–6M	2M–6M	1M–8M	1M–8M	4M–8M
Memory cycle time (Nsec)	405–540	345–005	620–1,035	620–1,035	320	320	320	290–464
Machine cycle time — (Nsec)	180–270	115	115	115	80	80	60	58
Channels (minimum-maximum)	5 standard	6 standard	3 standard–6	3 standard–6	6 standard–12	0–12	0–12	12 standard–16
Price/channel	Built-in	Built-in	4th—14,970 5th—13,930 6th—7,005	4th—14,970 5th—13,930 6th—7,005	360,000/6 channels	(see note 14)	(see note 14)	320,000/4 channels[15]
Multiprocessor configurations	No	No	Yes	Yes	No	Yes	Yes	No
Buffer capacity	0	32K	16K	16K	32K	32K	32K	64K

[1] Includes CPU, power supply, operator's console, memory. [2] All of items in footnote 1 with channels added. [3] Lease rate based on purchase price in line 2. [4] 360/50 – 10. International Data Corp. estimates; CW estimates for 3031, 3032. [5] With 1M-byte memory and standard channels. [6] With 6M-byte memory and standard channels. [7] With 6M-byte memory, the extended channel feature (3855), but no channels. [8] With 6M-byte memory, 12 channels standard. [9] Five channels standard. [10] With six channels—three standard, three optional. [11] With 12 channels—six standard, six optional. [12] With six channels, all optional. [13] With 12 channels. [14] The 2870 byte multiplexer channel costs $117,900. The 2980 block multiplexer contains two channels for $174,500. [15] Users must add four channels; choice of four block multiplexers or three block multiplexers and one byte multiplexer.

EXHIBIT 8 □ Excerpts of November 1977 Letter to Farmers Cooperative

It is clear that OS/VS1 is the only reasonable operating system choice for Farmers. The question of how to get from DOS/VS to OS/VS1 does not have a clear and obvious answer. This conversion will require preparing new JCL for all of the thousands of in-place jobs, recompiling and relinking many of the jobs, and possibly some reorganization of the data bases. Conversion of the first 10 percent of the work will require-extraordinary management and technical involvement as people are trained and decisions made that will determine the future. Throughout this effort OS/VS1 will probably be required an average of less than an hour per day. The last 10 percent of the conversion will drag on for a long time, as "dead" jobs keep reappearing for "just one more run." This residual work can be handled with occasional DOS/VS periods such as "a couple hours of the weekend" or through DOS simulator programs. Software packages such as IBM's OS/DOS Emulator, DUO 360/370 (UCC TWO) and perhaps others should be considered for this residual work. The middle 80 percent of the conversion, involving most of the production programs, is the primary concern.

VM may be used indefinitely running DOS for old systems and OS for new. This will require extra machine cycles which probably will, at least at some time, require the purchase of substantial extra processing power.

A massive effort by the entire center may be scheduled for this conversion. Little extra machine resource will be required because *(a)* the part used by the development work for compile and test will be available, *(b)* no inefficient emulators or operating systems will be involved, and *(c)* the advantages of OS/VS1 will quickly start to be realized. The dedicated effort of the staff should be completed in two to four months. When a larger mainframe is required, it will be because of the production load rather than the conversion.

A more leisurely conversion could be planned (such as a 6–12 month effort for the central 80 percent of the work), or a separate conversion group constituted (that might take several years for conversion). Timely machine services in both OS and DOS must be available throughout the period, either through multiple computers or through the use of VM. Since program development will continue in spite of conversions, extra capacity will be required.

In summary, we question the first option of running the old work indefinitely under DOS. Allowing the conversion to drag out over an extended period has the effect of disrupting operations and morale throughout the period. A major conversion effort usually works best, mobilizing the entire staff to accomplish a single unified task.

In the long run a single mainframe will probably be preferable to multiple systems, as described below. However, there are two special considerations for the short term:

1. The teleprocessing load will need to be supported during the conversion, even though there will be requirements for both OS and DOS throughout the day.
2. The impending system move would be simplified by the availability of two systems.

We therefore expect that an interim, additional, "small" computer (such as a stripped

EXHIBIT 8 (*continued*)

down 370/145) could be installed to operate the "secondary" operating system (at first for OS, then for DOS, without a teleprocessing workload). Most of the conversion should be completed prior to the move, then the systems moved to the new building. In about one year, with most of the conversions done and established in a new location, it would be reasonable to install a larger single mainframe such as the 370/158 or 3031.

BACKGROUND: Multi-mainframe

Operation of a multiple mainframe system has substantial advantage in some situations:

In a critical teleprocessing environment a primary machine may support the essential load with an identical fully configured second system available for instant backup (thus not running any jobs that could not be immediately terminated, such as updates to disk files). The backup machine is often relegated to compile and test, listings, mailings, etc.

In a shop where roughly half of the work is large number-crunching jobs (many research organizations), a primary machine handling I/O and small jobs, and passing large jobs to a uniquely configured secondary machine, may be effective. This coupling is characterized by IBM's ASP (attached support processor) software.

If two distinct operating systems are required it may be more efficient to run separate machines than to try to use both systems on the same mainframe through scheduling or VM.

There are significant disadvantages to using multiple mainframes that must be considered. In a simple environment, such as a small DOS shop, a second operating system on a second machine may make additional scheduling partitions available, and thus allow higher thruput. The operating system overhead is small, and scheduling no more rigid than always. However, on a larger system the operating system constitutes a substantial overhead that should be duplicated on each mainframe. The system handles more of the job scheduling from an available pool of work (to more fully and effectively utilize the machine resources). This results in a corresponding loss of manual scheduling, and would complicate the protection and availability of

---

Presentation of this data generated significant concern about the service level of VM. He described the reasons for the degradation in performance introduced by VM and urged that Farmers only use it for as short a time as possible, or not at all. For example, he said if a 158 were to be used, it would be 2.5 times as fast as the 145 if both used OS/VS1; but if OS/VS1 operated under VM (which would be necessary in a single-machine configuration with many DOS jobs not yet converted to OS), the OS power factor would only be 1.0 and the DOS power factor only .7–1.0 "A 158 running OS/VS1 under VM can do no more work than a 145 running OS/VS1 in native mode!"

EXHIBIT 8 (*concluded*)

datasets required on both systems. (In a small shop, jobs may be manually scheduled sufficiently to prevent conflicts, while in a large shop the operating systems are "coupled" to control access to data by multiple jobs. Coupling requires similar operating systems that can communicate through a hardware link, and is not available between DOS/VS and OS/VS1). As the operating systems do more of the scheduling to better optimize the use of the system resources, the systems can be more effective with a larger pool of resources. (Simple queueing theory indicates grossly improved service when the servers are pooled rather than partitioned. This is directly applicable to computer memory, tape drives, disk space, and so forth.)

Backup is given as an argument for multiple mainframes. A power failure will affect two systems as well as one. A peripheral failure will have a larger effect if it is the only one on a small machine, or if it is part of a larger pool. An input, program, or operator error that stops one or several jobs while a job is restarted or the dataset reconstructed will have the same effect whether one or two machines is involved. If a program kills the operating system on one machine, it will probably do so again if it is moved to the other machine. The only real back up offered by a second central processor is against the hardware failure of the central processor. At Farmers this is only 3 percent of all failures, so a second processor would provide negligible improvements (0.1 percent) in reliability.

Farmers appears to have a large number of independent, distinct production computer applications. In the future there will undoubtedly be demands for much greater management information from a combination of several of these application areas. As the move into management information systems begins it is imperative that the ability exist to consolidate these data bases as required. Such consolidation will be immeasurably easier on a single system than where the resources are partitioned among two systems.

Recommendation

All long-range plans should include a single larger mainframe with a single pool of peripheral resources. As a short-term expedient, for the DOS to OS conversion, and perhaps to assist in the upcoming move, a second mainframe might be considered. The number of two-channel switches required in this mode of operation (as opposed to the previous backup mode of operation) should be considered.

To complete his analysis, the consultant next tried to assess prices for the processors under consideration by contacting brokers in used computers. He was told that the market was a fast-changing one and that the announcements of the 3031–3033 series had made the situation even more volatile. Farmers' 145 processor and memory (not counting peripherals) probably would bring $325,000, but that figure would drop to $200,000 in 18 months. A used 155-II, 2 Meg machine (without the AMS speed-up feature) was now available for $600,000–$625,000; it would bring about $350,000–$400,000 in 18 months. He also felt the 158 was a worthy machine. "Demand for it will continue strong for awhile, since IBM is having trouble delivering all of the 3032s and 3033s ordered by customers; but in 18 months it will be a good buy. You'll be able to get a 2 Meg, 158 in 18 months for $650,000–$750,000. A 384K can be rented with a three-month cancellation period for $7,700 per month, not including the maintenance contract, while a 148 from IBM is $21,000 per month on the same terms; because the 148 is a newly announced machine there are no used machines available in either the purchase or rental markets."

Case 8–2 □ Centralized Information Services*

On October 31, 1976, Mr. Brad T. Jackson, president of Centralized Information Services, an affiliate of the Serve-Master Corporation, was driving from the Catskills to his home in Stamford, Connecticut. Jackson had just concluded a productive off-site weekend meeting with 12 managers of CIS in which there had been agreement to implement Tier I of a major reorganization.

The Catskills meetings were the culmination of the first part of the reorganization work which had been initiated by Jackson three months earlier. He had asked Mr. Gus Simonides, his vice president of planning, to head up the study and Mr. David Lieberman, a CIS staff officer who normally was responsible for consulting work to other affiliate companies of the Serve-Master Corporation, to work with Simonides. Jackson had asked for an assessment of the current organization and for plans for reorganization if it proved necessary. The project arose because of Jackson's concern for the ability of CIS to meet long-term, strategic goals, his desire to improve internal efficiency, and because of some recent personnel problems in Operations that had come to his attention.

Jackson had been impressed with the speed and quality of the work of his staff in relating problems and needs to organizational issues and in planning the reorganization. Moreover, the Catskills meetings had resulted in a high degree of consensus among his managers on changes in organizational responsibility, authority, and personnel. The most visible change had been the matter of taking Operations out from Data Processing Services and having Pete Giliam report directly to him instead of through Wes Hicks (see Exhibit 1 and Exhibit 2).

* This case was prepared by Assistant Professor James I. Cash and Associate Professor Cyrus F. Gibson as a basis for class discussion rather than to illustrate either effective or ineffective handling of an administrative situation.

EXHIBIT 1 □ Organization Early in 1976*

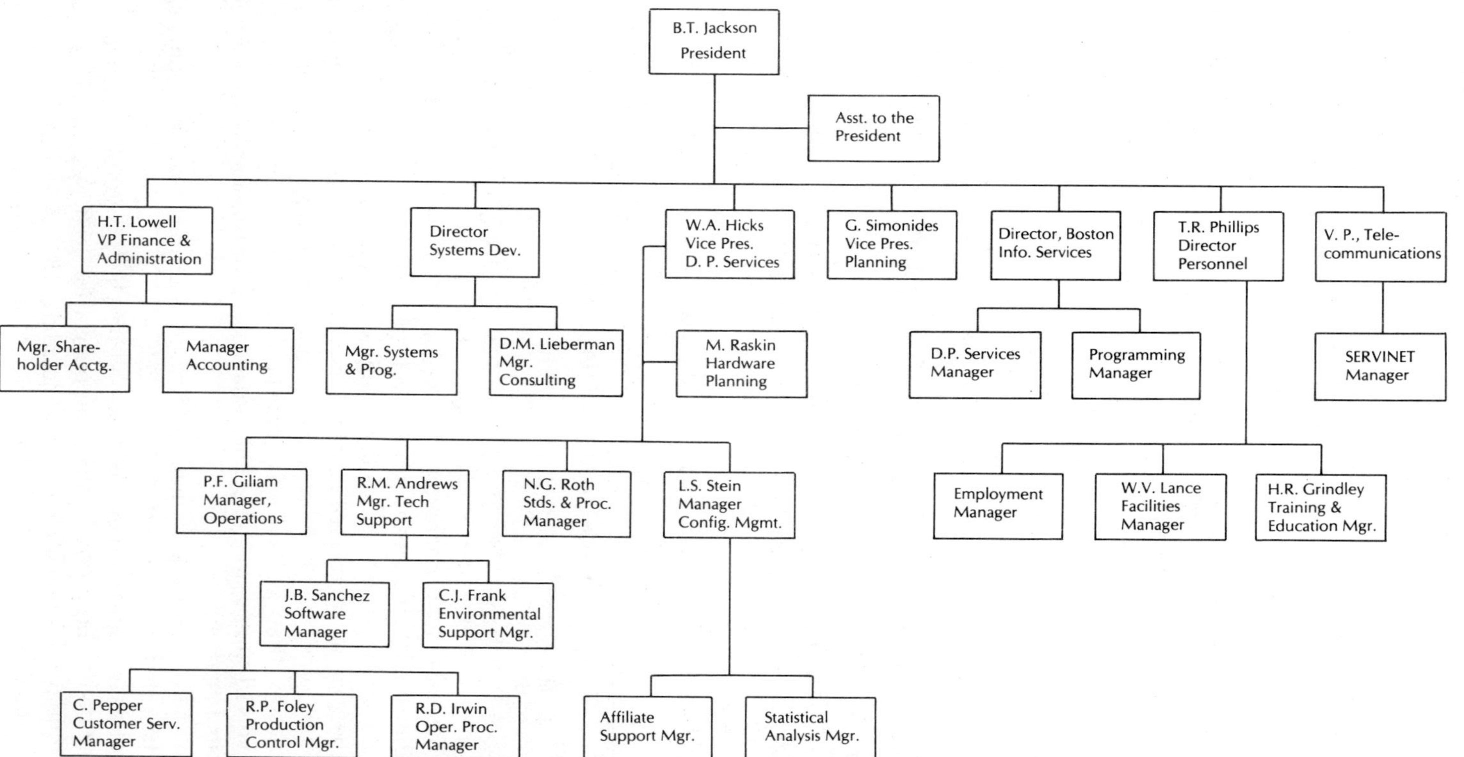

* Note: Names have been left on this chart for individuals mentioned in the case and for several whose titles or reporting relationships were changed by the 1976 reorganization.

EXHIBIT 2 □ Organization on November 1, 1976*

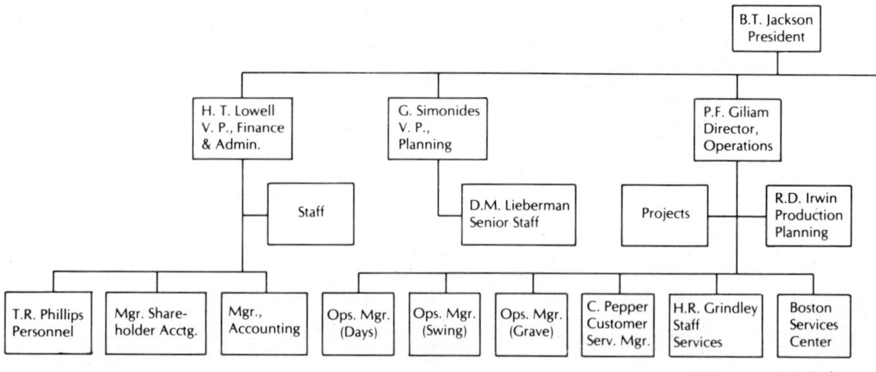

* Note: Names have been left on this chart for individuals mentioned in the case and for several whose titles or reporting relationships were changed by the 1976 reorganization.

Despite his satisfaction, however, Jackson was bothered by an uncertainty. "I wonder if it will work," he thought. "I wonder if by February of 1977 we can say to ourselves, 'We should have laid it out *this* way and gone about it *that* way rather than the way we did.' How does one predict that sort of thing? What other steps should I take now?"

BACKGROUND ON CENTRALIZED INFORMATION SERVICES

CIS was founded in 1968 as a result of a study by a consulting firm recommending the centralization of EDP hardware and service units of the Serve-Master Corporation. The mission of CIS was to provide a consolidated base of data processing support and technical advice in information processing and communications to the affiliate companies of Serve-Master, and to become an innovative center of information processing which would help the Corporation's affiliates gain a competitive edge in their respective businesses. Brad Jackson was hired from IBM, where his experiences had involved supervision of technical data processing functions, to head up CIS at its founding.

CIS was set up originally as a cost center and "division" of the Corporation and was located in New York City. It became an affiliate in 1973 although unlike other affiliates—all of which were profit centers—it continued to be a cost center. The budget for 1976 was at $12 million. CIS employed some 210 people, including 185 categorized as nonexempt. Virtually all employees were located in the company's headquarters or machine rooms in New York City.

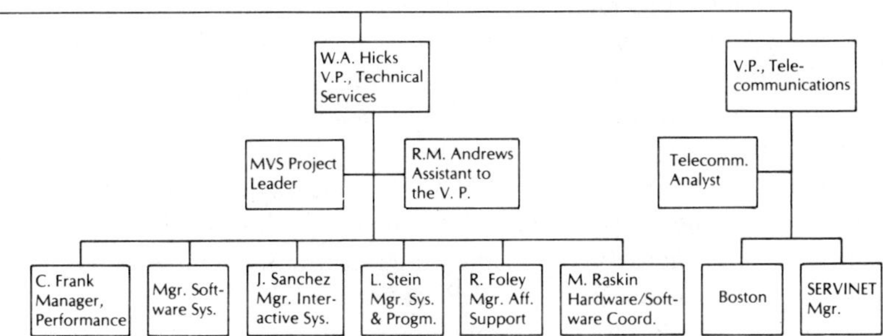

Serve-Master Corporation was a diversified service company of 20 highly autonomous companies. Corporate headquarters were in Boston. In 1976 Serve-Master was to report earnings of $115 million. The Corporation had reported increases in assets, revenues, and stock dividends for some 15 consecutive years. The businesses in which affiliates were engaged included: life insurance, property and casualty insurance, consumer finance, title insurance, and travel.

CIS had been created by the consolidation of parts of five previously separate computer organizations of affiliates in the New York area, the largest of which had come from the life insurance company. Brought together had been the hardware and software, operating personnel, and most of the technical specialists of each computer organization. Left with the affiliates had been applications analysts, applications programmers, and some technical specialists.

Day-to-day services of CIS to affiliate users occurred through transfers of input data and deliveries of output to and from the machine room, through interaction of an RJE (remote job entry) facility in Boston, and through interaction by time-sharing, particularly by the use of some 300-plus terminals. Aside from these contacts, relationships for other purposes were carried out by meetings of committees of officers at three distinct levels. These committees had been established over the years to discuss, recommend, and in some instances make decisions on matters of planning, policy, and hardware and software purchase. These committees were:

1. The Electronic Data Processing Technical committees, of which there were two, one with 12 members for New York and one with 9 members for Boston. Their purpose was "to coordinate the technical develop-

ment of consolidated EDP activities for major users." Members were individuals holding positions of vice president of line functions or very high staff positions in their respective organizations. CIS representation in 1976 included Wes Hicks, vice president of Data Processing Services, Gus Simonides, vice president of planning, and Harry Lowell, vice president of finance and administration.

2. The Council of Presidents, which included Brad Jackson and the presidents of four other Serve-Master affiliates, three of which had been among the organizations located in New York from which CIS had been formed in 1968. Its purpose was to "coordinate the development of consolidated EDP activities providing intercorporate data processing services for EDP operations in New York."
3. The Joint Planning Committee, a four-person group of vice presidents, including Harry Lowell of CIS. This committee served the Council of Presidents by developing recommendations "for equipment and operating systems changes, budgetary information, and other matters as assigned."
4. The Board of Directors of CIS was the highest level group. Its membership included the president and chief executive officer of Serve-Master Corporation, four other corporate-level officers, and the chairman and CEO of the largest affiliate and user of CIS services, Megalith Insurance Company.

In 1976 CIS was located in the Megalith insurance company complex. There was one building of 33 floors and two others approximately one third that size, all connected by enclosed corridors. The tallest building, very distinct on the New York skyline, had large neon letters spelling out MEGALITH on each side at the top. The offices of Jackson and his vice presidents of CIS were on the 24th floor of this building, and the machine rooms and other offices were on the 6th floor of the most distant of the two smaller buildings, a 5- to 10-minute trip on foot and by elevators. The computer facilities consisted of two IBM 370/168 machines and a number of second-generation computers and peripheral equipment. Both the 168 systems were supported by OS/RJE under VS2 release 1.7. The computers were linked by a shared HASP spooling technique and supported time-sharing (TSO).[1]

In 1976 some 70 percent of total computer utilization at CIS was devoted to batch processing of applications programs, many of which provided output critical to the day-to-day operations of affiliate users. Among these were the daily life insurance policy accounting for Megalith offices and

[1] OS/RJE refers to the particular IBM operating system that makes possible the use of remote job entry, or the submission of jobs from a distant location. VS2 further describes the operating system as supporting a virtual-storage capability, enabling a job to use more memory locations than are actually physically available on the computer and to make more efficient use of it.

agents throughout the country, and the daily loading and flight schedules for an airline affiliate.

ANTECEDENTS TO REORGANIZATION

By August of 1976 there were a number of indicators of satisfactory performance and accomplishment of mission by CIS. It was becoming clear that 1976 would become the fourth consecutive year in which CIS would meet or beat a flat budgeted cost target. Much of the improvement was attributed to the efforts of Harry Lowell, vice president of finance and administration, who had come in from Serve-Master Corporation in 1974 and had worked closely with his colleagues in CIS to bring about major changes in the chargeout system and better control over expenses.

An improved expense picture had also resulted from technical work and decisions. For example, at one time CIS had run an IBM 360/145, fully loaded, at its Boston facility. Through optimization efforts the utilization of the machine had been improved to the point where it was only half loaded, whereupon it had been sold at a profit and space rented on a 145 belonging to another company. This had resulted in a 40 percent savings in costs to users. Then in 1975 these applications were put into the 168 systems of CIS in New York and another 40 percent reduction in costs to users was achieved. Thus, for the same or better service, CIS had reduced those users' computing costs by some 64 percent in a two-year period.

While these improvements in control and efficiency, highly visible to affiliate users and the corporation, were taking place several affiliates who had retained or were developing their own EDP capabilities had experienced large overruns of anticipated costs.

In 1976 CIS began to be called upon by affiliates more often than had been the case before for consulting services relating to EDP and information systems decisions. CIS had won an important approval from the Council of Presidents committee and its board of directors for capital to continue a project for introducing MVS into its 168 operating system.

Yet, by the strategy and criteria for long-run performance for CIS which Jackson and his top managers believed in, there were problems which had not been solved. Management had believed 1976 would be a good year to attend to internal organizational matters, and discussions had been under way from time to time. Then, some unexpected events revealed the existence of other problems of which top management had not been fully aware.

One night in July an angry confrontation occurred between a black operator and the white lead man and the supervisor on the graveyard shift, resulting in the operator walking off the job. A few days later Jackson learned that CIS was threatened with a class action suit in which it was charged that there was discrimination against the individual by his immediate bosses, citing violations of rights specified in the Equal Employment Opportunity Act.

Jackson called a meeting to discuss the case with the company's lawyer and the supervisory and managerial personnel representing the layers of organization between him and the man in question. He noted that there were no less than seven supervisors and managers besides himself in the room, which struck him as symptomatic of there being too many organizational layers for effective communications to occur up and down the line. It seemed to Jackson that the supervisors had not been provided the training necessary to deal with their complex problems.

As an immediate follow-up to the incident CIS management commissioned an outside consulting firm to conduct a series of employee opinion surveys and follow-up group discussions among lower-level employees.

Steps were taken right away to alleviate some of the complaints revealed by the survey. The dress code for machine room employees was relaxed. Programs of training in communications and leadership were initiated for supervisors. Nevertheless, the tenor of the survey raised management concerns about the morale of the employees.

Jackson believed these current people problems might have something in common with a problem he had wrestled with for several years, or at least that both problems might be attacked at the same time. This was what he referred to as "organizational rigidity." As far back as 1972, Jackson had asked that line management take steps to increase the capability for more RJE, anticipating at that time an increasing environment of multiple products and services as opposed to strictly batch production for users in New York. There had been little in the way of response:

> We couldn't get change, couldn't get the systems which would represent flexibility in our operations and potentially provide us with new products. It seemed as though we had levels of people in the middle in operations who were emphasizing attention to day-to-day and traditional work and seemed to be unable to initiate or accept change.

In 1976 Jackson's concern over organizational rigidity was a reflection of his evolving strategic thinking with respect to future decisions that would have to be made on such matters as continued investment in large machines versus minicomputers:

> I think we will see some people, existing users and new ones, that will look to CIS for services before they buy the mini. Maybe we can't compete with the mini; we are watching that closely. But what we have decided is that small users cannot afford programming. We think the small users are going to have to go with packages, with time-sharing and with turnkey jobs. They just cannot afford the kind of applications development effort that a Megalith can.
>
> So we are trying to get ourselves in a position where we provide time-sharing, we provide RJE, and I think that is going to be a bigger part of our operations workload.

Discussions among CIS managers about the problems of rigidity at the middle levels often centered around the sense of incentive and loyalty of employees in Operations. Most of them were thought to "get their strokes" from users as opposed to their own line managers in CIS. A number of individuals, including some supervisors, had been in Operations since before the formation of CIS, and approximately 70 percent of nonexempt employees had been with CIS for more than five years.

CIS top management had also discussed that there was inefficiency in the way work was done on projects and in staff work, resulting in and related to inefficiency in the functioning of Operations itself. There were no reliable concrete measures of performance other than the usual ones of job reruns, on-time delivery, and the like. The problem was seen as stemming from a lack of division between line work and staff work. Virtually every manager in Data Processing Operations was believed to be working on several development projects. Indeed, some were on so many that most top managers doubted there was any way any particular project would get done.

Believing that "managers should manage," Jackson had wanted for some time to separate out staff and project work from line work. Such an approach, requiring lateral movement of individuals and an organizational change, was expected to make it possible to discover where and by whom projects were initiated, another difficulty experienced by top management. In one instance, for example, Jackson received a request for approval of a project which he asked some questions about. Looking into it, it was found that the project was already under way and that some 40 percent of the time budget he was being asked to approve had already been expended on it. At other times, management found there were no discretionary resources at their disposal to carry out high-priority tasks which had come to the attention of the top. It appeared that project initiation was occurring internally, or at the request of a user, without management of CIS having control and without the capability to initiate projects on their own.

With the immediate and longer-standing problems in mind, Jackson called a weekend off-site meeting at a resort on Long Island at the end of August. Present, besides Jackson, were all his immediate subordinates and staff and all the third-level managers who reported to Lowell and Hicks, some 16 individuals in all. The meetings resulted in an articulation of the symptoms and problems and a consensus that some form of consulting study of the organization was called for.

THE REORGANIZATION PROCESS

In the week following the Long Island meeting Jackson determined that the best approach would be to use his own management and staff to study, plan, and implement the reorganization. There was a need to do the job quickly—he hoped by the end of the year—and outside consultants would invest considerable time just learning the organization. Jackson asked Simonides and Lieberman to head up the work. They were chosen because, as Jackson put it:

> They knew the organization, had consulting skills and were thoroughly versed in the technology and operations of CIS. At the same time they were not line managers and therefore would bring an element of objectivity to evaluation of units and to any consideration of changes of responsibility or resources from one part of the organization to another

The three recognized at the outset that the process would be one of "learning as we go" and "pulling ourselves up by our bootstraps," as there were no universally appropriate ideal organizational structures for EDP and virtually no books or articles sufficiently specific to be of value to them. They agreed that a participative and team approach was best, one which would involve as many of the managers as possible in the study and planning consistent with the reality that everyone was busy.

Simonides and Lieberman conceived of their work as taking place in several distinct phases or tiers. Tier I would be an assessment of the current organization and if it proved necessary the design of a new one. Tier I would end with the announcement of any organizational changes. Tier II would be the implementation of change and was to be carried out by the line managers affected and who had been involved in the process. Tier II would end with an assessment of the extent to which objectives were being achieved.

Based on the discussions that had taken place over the recent months, a list of objectives for the study part of Tier I was drawn up. In the words of Simonides and Lieberman:

> The principal objectives of the CIS organization study . . . are to provide Mr. Brad T. Jackson, president, with an assessment of the current organization with regard to:
>
> 1. The degree of internal flexibility and creativity available to make the changes which are demanded by external and internal factors.
> 2. Adequacy of the current structure to maximize resources to meet changing environments.
> 3. The ability to communicate information throughout the organization reliably and validly.
> 4. The ability of individuals and work units to understand organizational goals and create and monitor plans to achieve same.
> 5. The ability to create, monitor, and react to performance measurements as well as provide necessary checks and balances to ensure effectiveness.

The two men devoted full time to the project, and at their request Jackson asked Lowell and Hicks to assist them on a part-time basis. A task force was thus formed consisting of these four.

As a starting point for their assessment of the current organization, it was decided by the task force to develop, on the one hand, a statement of existing and potential products and product strategies for CIS and, on the other hand, a set of job descriptions of all current supervisors and managers, including staff as well as line. Lieberman worked up the strategy and product statement in conjunction with other task force members. Getting the job descriptions proved to be more difficult.

At the Long Island meeting in August all managers with subordinates had been asked to write up job descriptions for their organizations. By October less than half had come in and those which did were judged by Simonides and Lieberman to be "inadequate and incomplete." In response to this Lieberman sent a memorandum to the 16 managers who attended the Long Island meeting, with a copy to Jackson. "Once again," the memo began, "you are going to be asked to prepare job descriptions." The memo stressed the utility of job descriptions to "both performance measurement as well as adequate appraisals," and mentioned that "turnaround time (for submitting the completed job descriptions) is of the utmost importance." Attached to the memo was a two-page guide of categories and topics to be written in for each position described, and two completed examples.

The results of the memo were still disappointing. Simonides and Lieberman saw that the only way they would get good job descriptions would be to fill them out themselves, but they recognized that this would be an advantage in giving them an opportunity to talk to middle- and lower-level management. During late September and October they interviewed individually each of the 30 or so managers in CIS. The question of duties and responsibilities became just the starting point for these interviews; they tried to learn as much as they could about the nature of organizational problems and potential as well. Additional work with senior managers, particularly Wes Hicks and Pete Giliam, who between them had nearly half the managers and well over half the total personnel in CIS, resulted in a complete set of job descriptions and a set of "task descriptions." The task descriptions were of the functions or missions which were being carried out and were written without particular reference to a division of labor into individual positions.

PLANNING FOR KEY STRUCTURAL CHANGES IN OPERATIONS

In mid-October Simonides and Lieberman, working closely with Jackson and the task force, drew up a new "functional" organizational chart. It showed boxes with task functions but no individual names. Two particularly important organizational changes from the existing organization were shown, both of which pertained to the Operations function.

The first change was that Operations was taken out from Data Processing and shown reporting directly to the president of CIS. The remaining function was renamed Technical Services. Wes Hicks, vice president of Data Processing Services and member of the task force, endorsed the change.

The other important change was that all employees in line operations functions under Pete Giliam would report to him directly through the shift supervisors rather than through the three managers of separate functions. As indicated in Exhibit 1, these functions were Customer Services, Production Control and Operations Processing.

Simonides and Lieberman were aware that these plans for changes had interesting precedents. Prior to 1972, for example, the operations function had been separated in the CIS organization. A manager hired from outside CIS in 1970 who had a strong technical background had been instrumental in achieving a combination of operations and technical functions under himself. When this man left CIS for another position in 1975, Wes Hicks inherited the job. Thus, this particular Tier I change was a return back to the original organization.

Beginning in 1974 and extending through 1976 a significant reorganization at the supervisory level had been carried out by Pete Giliam. Operations in 1974 had been structured in what Giliam described as "a fairly traditional way." The units reporting to him had been "operations" (preprocessing, data entry, output processing, and console operation), "data control" (staging of equipment and tape mounting on the input end), and "scheduling" (maintenance of a 24-hour process control schedule of jobs). The 1974 organization is shown in Figure 1. At that time there were some 45 people working in the three shifts under Operations. A particular feature of the work was the rotation among them, in conjunction with their shift supervisors, of job assignments, including console operation. Although only a few were trained and qualified for console operation, over time a large number came to earn the level of pay and rank associated with the highest skill job.

Giliam's reorganization in 1974 separated the people-intensive and relatively low-skill jobs away from the console operation function. A new unit known as operations processing took the functions of tape mounting, input processing, and output processing and organized the employees doing those jobs under the shift supervisors. Console operators went to a new unit known as production control. Another new unit, customer service, was created to handle user contact and some input preparation. The reorganization thus introduced by Giliam in Operations was as it appears in Exhibit 1.

INTRODUCTION OF THE TIER I REORGANIZATION

By the end of October, after two months of intensive work, Simonides and Lieberman had accumulated a large volume of findings, had developed the skeleton of the new organization, and had worked closely with Jackson and the members of the task force (Lowell and Hicks) so that there was full endorsement from them for the changes outlined in a new organization. The particular changes in Operations had also been discussed with Pete Giliam.

On Thursday and Friday, October 21 and 22, key managers met in the CIS headquarters offices with members of the task force to determine the

FIGURE 1 □ CIS Operations in 1974

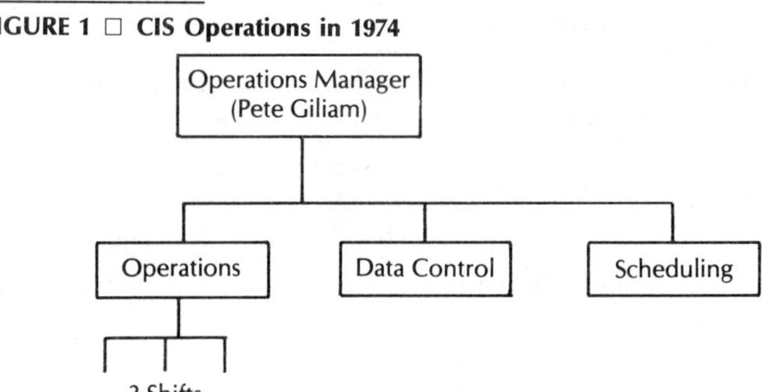

specific new organization of functions and of changes of people. In the meeting the names of every CIS manager who would potentially be changed were put on separate cards. An outline of the new functional organization was put up on a corkboard and as a group the managers discussed placement of people. The discussion centered on assessments of each individual's technical abilities and how those could best be fitted to the task and functional needs. Jackson played an active role in the decision making. This work came to be known as "the card game." There was lively discussion about placement of people. At the end of the meetings the new organization chart was completed (Exhibit 2).

The final steps in Tier I of the reorganization took place at the off-site meetings in the Catskills over the weekend at the end of October 1976. Present were all the members of the task force plus the line managers who would be affected by the reorganization, 12 people in all. In response to the presentations by Simonides and Lieberman, the consensus was that a number of benefits could be achieved by "taking out a layer" of the organization and moving Operations up. For one, it would *raise* the people below and provide them additional stature in the hierarchy. This was seen as a step in the direction of dealing positively with the morale issue.

The task force recommended that two middle-level people be "surplussed." Both these individuals had been involved heavily in staff project assignments. There was widespread support for the decision.

The managers present readily endorsed the summary of product strategies and products prepared earlier by Lieberman and the task force.

Most of the discussion at the Catskills' meetings centered on the recommendations of what was to be achieved and on the new organization chart itself. The complete list of recommendations as presented is given in Exhibit 3. The reorganization and assignments of individuals was accepted without major dissent by all the CIS managers present.

On Monday, October 25, a memorandum was distributed to all CIS supervisory and managerial personnel announcing the reorganization. It went into effect on Monday, November 1.

EXHIBIT 3 □ Recommendations for Tier I Reorganization

a. Separate Data Processing Operations from Technical Services and elevate the management level of operations to Director level.

b. Create staff functions within both Data Processing Operations and Technical Services to give cognizance to the separation of line and staff functions and responsibilities as well as establishing a mechanism for project control.

c. Reduce the reporting levels in Data Processing Operations and Technical Services to increase the span of control and shorten lines of communication. More specifically, provide for:

Shift managers to report directly to the director of operations.

Technical services managers to report directly to the vice president, technical services.

d. Increase the responsibility of shift managers, in order that they may assume more direct control of total operations. Incorporate within the shift managers' span of control those functions previously performed by the separate production control units.

e. Combine the staff functions of Training and Education, Systems and Procedures and Facilities into a Staff Services unit. Principal activities of this unit should provide direct support to the operational area and report to the director of operations.

f. Create a Boston Service Center unit whose construction reflects the planned environment of RJE and Interactive Services and support. This function should report to the director of operations.

g. Give cognizance to separation of measuree from measurer by the establishment of a performance unit within Technical Services.

h. Combine previous organizational units and staff activities associated with affiliate support, in order to maximize effective use of like skills and eliminate artificial boundaries. Achievement of this recommendation requires disbursement of previous Configuration Management components and Interactive Service functions.

i. Change reporting structure of Systems and Programming to Technical Services, in order to maximize use of like skills and project control.

j. Retain current structure and reporting relations of Telecommunications. However, coordination of plans and activities are required to achieve integration necessary to meet future goals.

k. Establish, within Finance and Administration, a staff function to provide business planning activities which encompass both traditional financial planning and budgeting as well as establishment and evaluation of measurements.

l. Transfer the Personnel function to Finance and Administration, in order to combine control and information sources.

m. Retain the senior staff function of Planning which is specifically devoted to evaluation of long-term technological trends and plans.

EXHIBIT 3 (*concluded*)

n. Retain the senior staff function associated with Affiliate Systems Consulting and augment this activity with internal CIS assignments.

o. Establish an "organizational development" function reporting directly to the president.

Case 8–3 □ Intercontrol Chemical Corporation*

Cyrus Meredith, assistant vice president of data processing for Intercontrol Chemical Corporation (ICC) was engaged in a heated discussion concerning the establishment and role of a data processing internal audit function. Other major participants in the discussion were Gary Waters, newly appointed internal auditor, and Jerome Hart, a data processing management consultant. It was mid-June 1980 and Meredith had spent the last two years implementing changes recommended by Hart to ICC senior management. Some of the recommendations were contradictory to proposals made by Meredith, but senior management had requested he follow the strategy outlined in the consulting report.

The meeting, scheduled to last one hour, was originally convened at 9 A.M. in the ICC board room on the top floor of ICC's plush 14-floor headquarters building overlooking the Wabash River in West Lafayette, Indiana. By 12:15, it had become apparent to Barry Loughton, chairman of the board (see Exhibit 1) that Waters and Meredith needed to resolve substantial philosophical differences before a presentation could be made to the ICC board of directors' audit subcommittee. Loughton instructed Waters, Meredith, and Hart to continue their discussions in the office of his vice president, finance, Doug Richards. Richards, who was in the board room during the meeting, had direct management responsibility for both Waters and Mere-

* This case was prepared as a basis for class discussion rather than to illustrate either effective or ineffective handling of an administrative situation.

EXHIBIT 1 □ Organization Chart

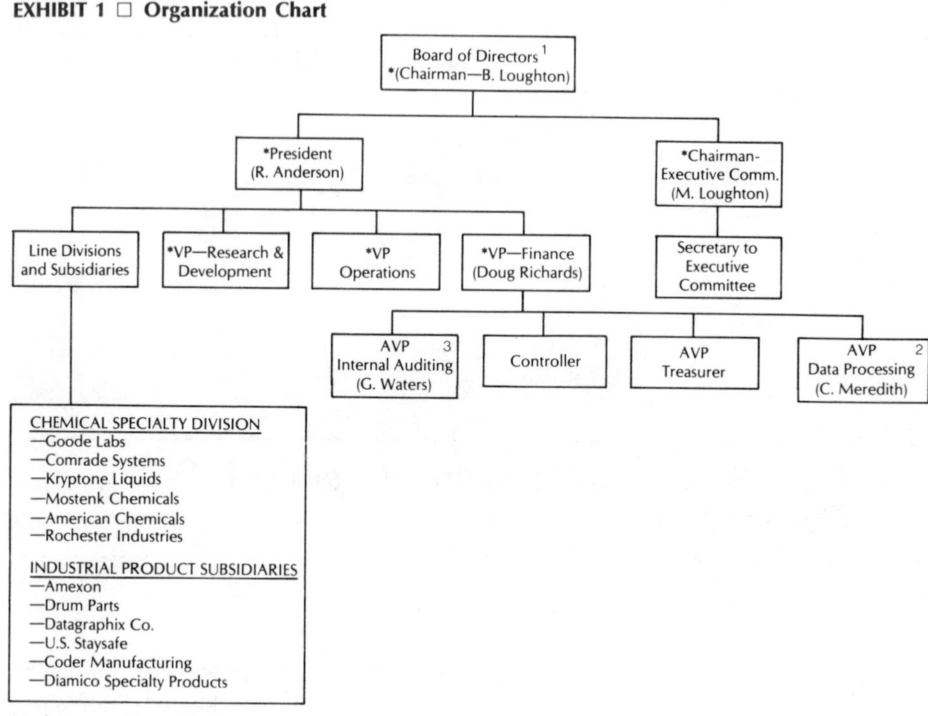

* Indicates member of Executive Committee.

[1] *Board of Directors:*

- ● Michael Goodman, EVP, Muncie National Bank
  Bob Anderson, President, ICC
  Barry Loughton, Chairman of the Board, ICC
  Michael Loughton, Chairman, Executive Comm., ICC
- ● Robert Poulet, President, Wabash Investors, Inc.
- ● Raymond Smith, Chairman Board, First Hoobles Securities
- ● Jerome Thomas, President, Ballinger Corporation
- ● Audit committee. (The two Loughtons are brothers while Anderson is a first cousin.)

[2] Although not reflected in his title, Meredith's organization is called Corporate Data Processing (CDP).

[3] Waters reported to Richards for administrative concerns; and to the board of directors' audit subcommittee for operational concerns.

dith. Loughton stated he would regard Richards' recommendations on these matters as a final decision. As the meeting ended, he made clear that not to establish the group was a viable alternative.

As Meredith walked to the second meeting location he reflected on the past two years. He felt that Hart's study had precipitated numerous unnecessary changes. Surely a small shop like his, in a very informal company, didn't need all the administrative systems of the larger companies with whom Hart spent most of his time. Cyrus had considered leaving ICC in the past but was never capable of matching the ICC compensation package. He dismissed any thoughts of pursuing that course of action and began preparing his arguments on issues related to the auditing group.

COMPANY BACKGROUND

Intercontrol Chemical Corporation was founded in 1948 by Barry Loughton, current chairman of the board, to manufacture and distribute chemical products used in the maintenance of industrial equipment. After a very successful period with chemical maintenance products, ICC added new nonchemical products to its product line. With an aggressive acquisitions program, ICC entered the business of replacement plumbing parts and maintenance tools. The most recent acquisition was made in August 1979, with two potential acquisitions being considered for 1980. Additional growth was achieved by expanding into international markets. Foreign sales are conducted through wholly owned subsidiaries throughout the world, including Latin America and the Far East. Currently, the company operates five domestic and approximately 70 foreign subsidiaries. Foreign subsidiaries provide approximately 50 percent of sales and profits.

At fiscal year end (May 31, 1980) ICC employed approximately 8,375 people worldwide. As shown in Exhibit 2, net sales grew 24 percent to $402,901,040. Net income was up 23 percent to $34,954,220, and earnings per share were $3.25 as compared with $2.50 reported for fiscal 1979 on approximately 13.4 million shares. ICC shares were sold on the New York Stock Exchange but the stock was closely held by top management.

Competition in the industry is primarily based on price, service, and product performance. No one company or group of companies dominates the market. ICC's emphasis is on service and product performance rather than price. Many ICC products are part of total maintenance systems that include equipment and tools to apply chemicals properly, or to install and repair equipment. ICC developed a successful marketing/advertising strategy which argued customers could extend the life of their facilities and equipment (thus delaying or avoiding costly purchases) if they used high-quality ICC products for scheduled (preventive) maintenance and repairs.

ICC sales are not dependent upon a limited number of customers, and no particular customer accounts for as much as 1 percent of total sales.

The company did not have a formal planning process, but all executive committee members agreed diversification and acquisition programs were expected to increase during the 80s. This posed major challenges to the corporate organization and specifically to the data processing group. Meredith suggested this business strategy ". . . would require greater flexibility, application effectiveness, and technical proficiency than had been required in the past."

THE DATA PROCESSING DEPARTMENT

Data processing activity in ICC had evolved as a highly centralized function. The Corporate Data Processing (CDP) Group (see Exhibit 3) sup-

EXHIBIT 2 □ Company Highlights (years ended May 31)

	1980	1979
Net sales	$402,901,040	$325,753,938
Net income	$ 34,954,220	$ 28,374,896
Earnings per share	$3.25	$2.50
Average number of shares outstanding	13,467,143	14,212,848
Treasury shares acquired		
Number of shares	294,000	808,000
Cost of shares	$ 5,584,534	$ 12,999,210
Working capital	$121,597,250	$107,425,740
Total assets	$269,692,561	$221,097,142
Net capital expenditures	$ 16,316,069	$ 7,412,564
Long-term indebtedness	$ 5,393,848	$ 2,648,299
Stockholders' equity	$173,541,384	$149,919,654
Number of employees	8,375	7,541

Historical Trend

NET SALES in millions of dollars

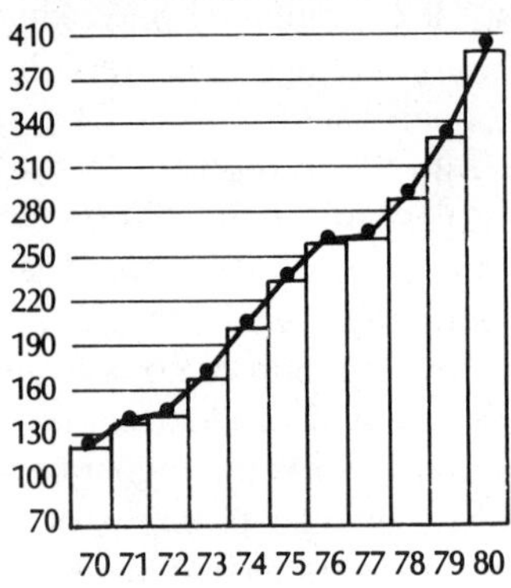

NET INCOME in millions of dollars

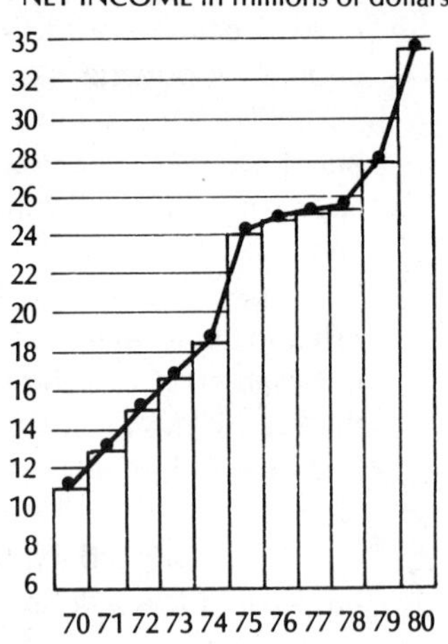

EARNINGS PER SHARE in dollars

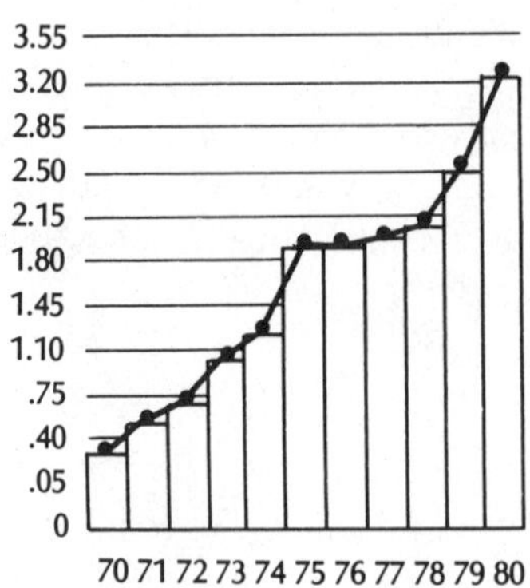

ANNUAL RATE PER SHARE DIVIDEND (at year end)

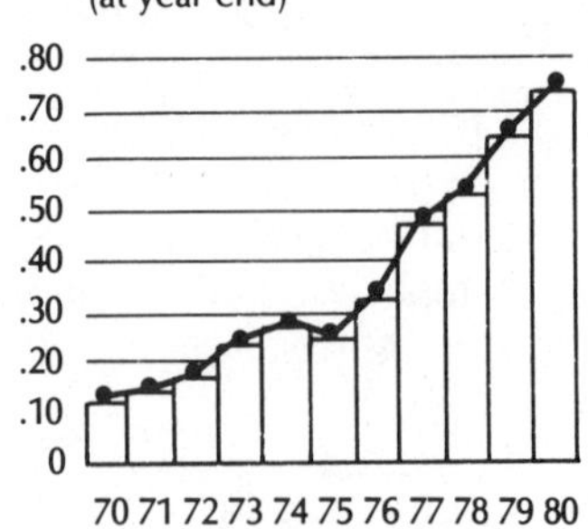

EXHIBIT 3 □ CDP Organization Chart

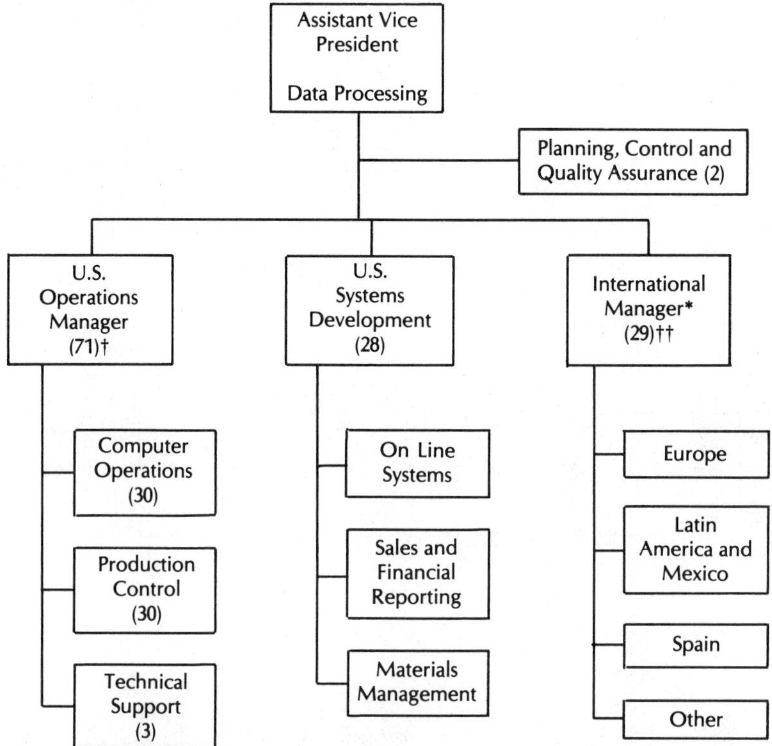

Note: Numbers in parentheses indicate size of work force.
* International manager resides in Washington, England.
† Includes 26 data entry personnel.
†† Includes operations staff in Europe (5), Latin America (3) and Spain (2).

ported both domestic and international operations. CDP, located in West Lafayette, maintains IBM 370/158 and 360/50 systems which support an extensive communication network. This facility supports remote Four Phase computers at seven branch facilites and at subsidiaries in Tucson, Arizona; Columbus, Ohio; and Austin, Texas. Exhibit 4 illustrates the equipment configuration and communications network. ICC corporatewide data processing costs totaled approximately $4.9 million and were distributed as shown below:

DP management staff and education	$ 171,364
Computer services	2,497,991
Domestic systems development	761,170
International data processing	
United States	526,680
Europe	627,625
Other	268,919

EXHIBIT 4 □ DP Equipment and Communications Network

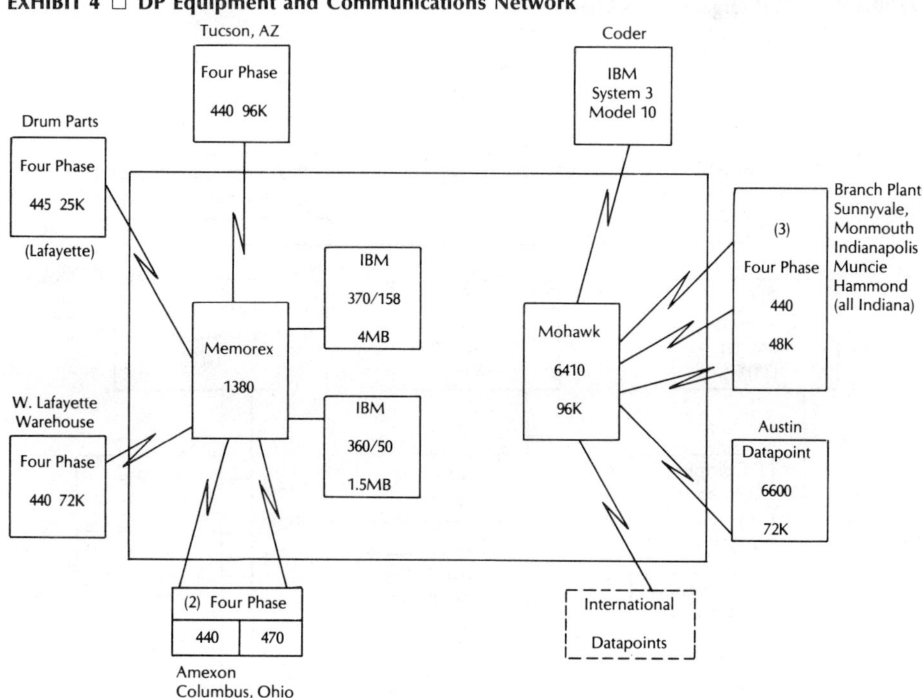

The CDP manager, Cyrus Meredith, was about 50 years of age and had never worked for another firm during his professional career. He joined ICC in 1951 after graduating from Purdue University with an engineering degree. During 1962 Meredith became the first and only director of data processing ever employed by ICC. During the early 60s he went to business school on a part-time basis and received a MBA degree from Ball State.

The Corporate Data Processing Group had developed various applications systems to support the functional requirements of ICC. These applications fall into four classes:

1. Order processing.
   Entry.
   Shipping.
   Credit.
   Collection.
   Invoices.
   Receivables.
2. Sales reporting.
   Sales management performance reports.

Statistical sales reports.
Weekly and monthly sales comparisons.

3. Financial.
   General ledger.
   Payroll.
   Sales commissions.
4. Manual control.
   Purchasing.
   Inventory.
   Work-order processing.

All of these systems were developed internally by corporate data processing to support the information processing requirements of the chemicals business. Subsequently, as the diversification strategy of the company was implemented, these systems were extended to support the nonchemical business.

CDP manages most computing activity required by ICC's international divisions and subsidiaries. An international application development group (29 persons) is located in Washington, England. This facility provides programming support for most of Europe. In some countries with small operations the subsidiaries used local service bureaus. The Washington-based group operates an IBM 360/30 computer which processed sales, commission, financial, and accounting information for the European offices. Finally, some of the subsidiaries operate their own Datapoint minicomputer for order processing. Computing activities in Mexico and Latin America are overseen by a system designer who resides in West Lafayette but reports administratively to the international data processing manager in England.

In early 1978, after the installation of a new operating system (OS) which replaced the disk operating system (DOS), users started experiencing a significant decline in the level of service. Many critical reports were received with delays of three or more days; and even worse, some of them were received with incorrect results. The amount and frequency of operational mistakes increased while the turnover in the data processing department reached an unprecedented level. Senior management began to receive strong complaints from the European users who criticized service levels and project priorities assigned by the Corporate Data Processing Group. For several months European managers had been requesting stronger support in their production and inventory control system. Instead of providing that service, data processing was planning and implementing the installation of datapoint minicomputers in some of the smaller countries of Europe and in several locations in Latin America.

Under a constant barrage of complaints, management decided to hire a data processing management consulting firm. The consultants were asked to perform both management and operational audits of the data processing function, and to provide guidance for solving the service level problem.

THE CONSULTING STUDY

The consultants confirmed the deteriorating level of service, and informed management that inadequate data processing policies and practices were the main cause of the ineffective delivery of computing support to users. The lack of a system development methodology and formal project management practices reduced responsiveness of programming services (i.e., increased the cost and time of system maintenance; significant rework costs). Operations management procedures were considered inadequate to support ongoing production needs. Other deficiencies mentioned were the lack of budget control, the limited use of cost-benefit analysis and the insufficient monitoring of companywide EDP costs.

The consultants' report recommended the development of an operational plan to improve the data processing service levels. The main components of this plan addressed establishment of the following:

1. Machine loading and job scheduling.
2. Operating errors and procedure controls.
3. Quality control/assurance.
4. Tape and disk management.
5. Backup and security.
6. Disaster planning.
7. User and internal coordination forums.
8. Senior management steering committee.
9. Formal acceptance testing and change control.
10. Documentation maintenance and procedures.
11. Resource management and performance monitoring.
12. Strategic planning.

The CDP management team was not pleased with the report. In addition to its very negative tone, the proposals set forth a totally different strategic direction than CDP had been pursuing (e.g., the installation of minicomputers in smaller countries). CDP management worried that credibility with top management had declined as a result of the report.

EVENTS LEADING TO THE MEETING

During 1978 and 1979 most of the recommendations were implemented. Jerome Hart or another member of the original consulting team, made follow-up reviews every six months during this two-year period. The reviews indicated CDP was making substantial progress in addressing concerns listed in the study. In early 1980, the consultants recommended that the establishment of an EDP audit function was imperative to monitor the performance of the data processing function on a continuing basis. Coincidentally, the current internal audit staff manager was retiring and Doug Richards thought this was an opportunity to hire a person capable of managing both financial and data processing auditors.

In explaining why he desired his lead internal auditor have the ability to manage data processing auditors, Richards replied:

> A number of forces have focused my attention to this skill mix. First, our management team has become increasingly dependent on data processing for controlling the activities in their functional areas. As we have geographically expanded our business the need to have data which has a high degree of integrity is critical to provide for consistent corporatewide planning, evaluation, and control decisions. I think EDP internal auditing is one mechanism to protect the integrity of our data. Second, there have been some spectacular losses reported in companies that didn't pay enough attention to adequate internal controls and Q/C (quality control) in their EDP systems. The one case that comes to mind immediately is the Equity Funding scandal. Finally, the most important to me, is the Foreign Corrupt Practices Act (FCPA). FCPA, as a matter of law, now mandates that companies subject to the securities laws maintain a system of internal accounting control sufficient to provide reasonable assurance that:
>
> Transactions are executed in accordance with management's authorization.
>
> Transactions are recorded so as to permit preparation of financial statements in accordance with GAAP (generally accepted accounting principles) or other criteria applicable to such statements and to maintain accountability for assets.
>
> Access to assets is permitted only in accordance with management's authorization.
>
> Recorded assets are compared with existing assets at reasonable intervals and appropriate action is taken with respect to any differences.
>
> Many attributes of our internal control system which address these requirements are buried in our EDP systems. Therefore we need a verification and compliance checking mechanism for that function (EDP), which most logically should reside in the internal audit department.

Recruiting such a person was more difficult than Richards initially anticipated, and salaries for persons with this skill mix seemed excessive. Finally, with help from the management consulting firm which employs Jerome Hart, he located and hired Gary Waters for the position.

Waters, 42 years of age, had extensive formal business education. He acquired both undergraduate and graduate business degrees in accounting. He was a CPA (certified public accountant) and worked as a financial auditor with three different public accounting firms during the first nine years of his career. In the next five-year period (age 33–37) he worked as controller and information systems director for a small ($110 million in sales) manufacturing company. During the last five years prior to joining ICC, Waters was director of operations for a medium-sized insurance company ($300 million annual premium income) where the lead data processing manager reported to him. Waters described his decisions for major career changes in the following passage:

> My decision to leave public accounting was because financial auditing became boring. I was one year from becoming a senior manager and five or six years from becoming a partner, but couldn't see myself doing that type of work for the remainder of my career. Because EDP was having a dramatic effect on my profession, and business in general, I decided a job involving EDP would be the most challenging and interesting. After a couple of jobs in which I had responsibility for the EDP organization, I began to miss some of the challenges and rewards obtainable when working in an auditing role. The ICC job presented me with an opportunity to bring these two worlds together.

Waters joined ICC May 1. During his first six weeks in the new job Waters spent most of his time trying to develop a plan for establishment of a data processing auditing capability in the internal auditing department. Waters' initial assessment of the financial/operational audit area of his department was very positive, and thus decided there was almost no need for work in that area. However, there was no prior activity or concentrated expertise for EDP auditing. Any need to review or verify data processing results were accomplished by "auditing around the computer" techniques.

Waters followed the outline shown in Exhibit 5 as he pulled together a proposal for establishing the new area in his department. His initial thoughts on an appropriate organization structure for the new area is shown in Exhibit 6. Waters used Jerome Hart to help refine his thinking on these matters and in early June arranged a meeting with Cyrus Meredith to share his current thoughts on role, scope, organization, and implementation of the new area. Forty-five minutes into the discussion, Meredith called Richards (Waters remained in Meredith's office) to convey his "total disagreement" with Waters on almost every key issue—especially the implementation time frame Waters planned to adopt.

> . . . although I think Gary developed an excellent framework for thinking about this area, I'm afraid he's been contaminated by Hart's big company perspective and his (Hart) insensitivity to the ICC culture. With all the changes implemented in the last two years, it would be devastating to hit CDP with internal auditors. As you know, we've lost a number of programmers as a result of formalizing system development and introducing formal project management which requires them to log their activity. Many of them interpret introduction of those administrative systems as an expression of senior management's lack of confidence in our organization. If Gary brings half-cocked auditors into our shops before the end of the year, as he currently plans, I may lose my entire programming team. . . .

EXHIBIT 5 □ Waters' Approach to Establishing the EDP Internal Audit Function

I. DEFINE OBJECTIVE (Done—May 6).

To work with other members of the internal audit department, and to assist all members of management who use computer facilities or provide computer services in the effective and efficient discharge of their responsibilities by furnishing them with analyses, appraisals, recommendations, and pertinent comments on all activities of the data processing department.

II. OBTAIN MANDATE FROM MANAGEMENT (Done—May 13).

Make formal presentation to management, addressing following issues: objective, need, projected cost, risks, and benefits.

III. IDENTIFY KEY ISSUES (Done—May 19).

- A. Establishing the area.
  1. Initial staffing, career management, and training.
  2. Internal organization.
  3. External organization.
  4. Development of policies, standards, and procedures.
  5. Salary base (auditing or data processing).
- B. Role and scope of activity.
  1. Systems Development.
  2. Operations.
  3. Existing applications systems.
  4. DP administration and control.
  5. Assist function (financial and external auditors).
- C. Process issues.
  1. Audit planning.
  2. Initial surveys.
  3. Communications.
  4. Developing findings.
  5. Reporting.
  6. Follow-up.

IV. DISCUSS KEY ISSUES WITH INTERESTED MANAGERS (In progress).

V. PRESENT PROPOSAL TO AUDIT SUBCOMMITTEE (Scheduled for July 2).

VI. HIRE/MOVE PERSONNEL (Following July 2 audit approval).

VII. IMPLEMENT (End of year).

EXHIBIT 6

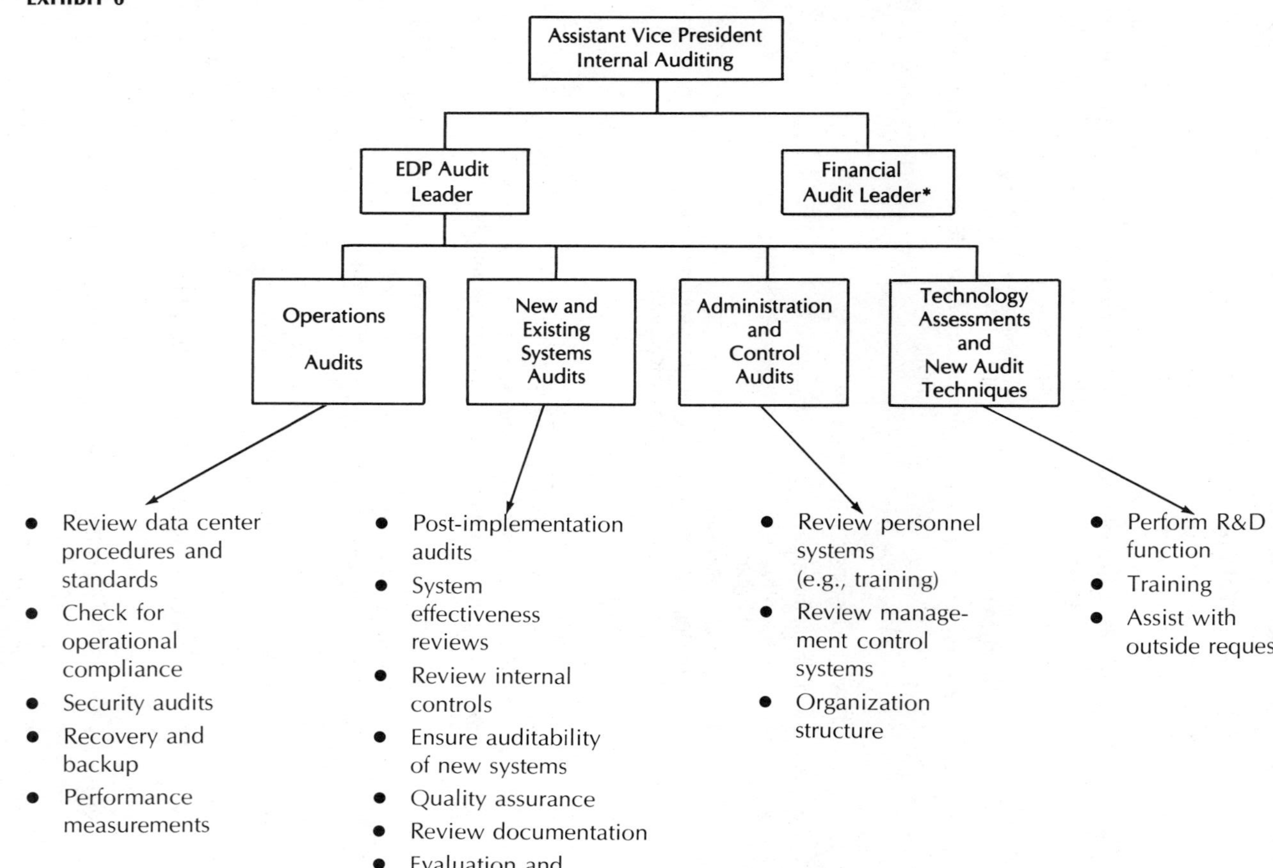

* There are currently six people in the Financial Audit Group (including the audit leader).

Unknown to Waters or Meredith, Richards took the call over his speaker phone. Larry Loughton, who was sitting in Richards' office during the conversation, overheard Meredith's concerns. Loughton had planned to have Waters present his proposal in the July 2 audit subcommittee meeting. The audit subcommittee was very eager to have an EDP auditing capability inside the company.

Loughton's first thought was to take Waters' proposal off the agenda for the subcommittee meeting. Richards suggested a brief meeting involving Loughton and other key persons (Waters, Meredith, Hart) and Richards might resolve the differences. The meeting was initially scheduled for June 17, and then rescheduled for June 20.

OTHER VIEWS

Stan Newlin, partner in charge of the account for ICC's public accounting firm, was supportive of the move to establish the data processing internal audit function:

> We [the CPA firm] have listed the lack of such a function as a glowing weakness of the overall ICC internal control system in our last three audits. I think everyone concerned would benefit. ICC's bill for our audit would be reduced; top management and the audit committee could attach greater credibility to their overall control mechanisms; data processing would get more frequent and less contentious reviews of their activities, we [CPA firm] would have a well-defined entry point for our review of data processing controls; and finally, we could use this group [DP internal audit] in some phases of our "processing results" review and gathering of evidential matter. . . . The issues of role and scope of the group must be decided within the company. There are no general guidelines. However, there is a significant trend to "operational auditing" inside and out of ICC which impacts this decision (ICC currently conducts operational audits).

John Conrad, financial audit leader, in ICC's internal audit department also supported establishing the new function.

> . . . to provide better service for the corporation. Our financial staff is moved to operational auditing. We define this approach as the "comprehensive review of administrative systems practice and procedures, in addition to traditional financial systems reviews. . . . The penetration of EDP into our operational systems requires we have the capability to review data processing functions. We have been totally inadequate in that (EDP) area and cannot profess to thoroughly examine our systems without such expertise.

When asked how receptive managers around the corporation had been to the new operational auditing role, Conrad replied:

> . . . there is inherent contention between auditee and auditor regardless of any specific context you may want to examine. ICC managers, in general, have not been receptive to our expanded role. They generally seem to think "bean counters" cannot and/or should not become general management consultants. However, we were commissioned in June 1979 by the audit subcommittee of our Board to pursue the expanded role and, I guess, ICC management will have to learn to live with us!

THE MEETING

Although most participants arrived about 8:45 for the scheduled 9 o'clock meeting it began about 9:05, when Loughton arrived. All the participants agreed that they were eager to resolve the differences and "get back to the desk." As each major issue was discussed, it became apparent to Loughton that Meredith's statement of total opposition to Waters' proposals was not understated. Comments during the meeting are organized by issue in Exhibit 7. The major themes presented were Meredith's concerns about the need for such formalism in ICC. He insisted that continued revamping of procedures and auditors would precipitate a mass exodus from ICC of CDP personnel. Waters and Hart also sounded convincing while conveying the risk of significant losses if their perspectives weren't adopted. After more than three hours of discussion and minimal progress towards significant agreement, Loughton suggested they move to Richards' office.

As the second meeting convened, Jerome Hart turned to Meredith, "Cyrus, I think you are missing a key issue here. If the EDP audit group is successfully established, you may never see me again! They will perform the services we've been providing."

Meredith replied: "Jerome, the prospect of getting you out of my hair provides almost enough incentive for me to agree with all of Gary's suggestions!"

EXHIBIT 7 □ Excerpts from the June 20th Meeting

Issue	Description	Gary Waters	Cyrus Meredith
Staffing, career management and training	What should be the skill mix of initial staff and what are their career path options?	"We should hire top data processing professionals and provide training in audit procedures and practice. They should have keen business acumen which will facilitate movement into line management. I expect that good people will have offers to leave IA (internal auditing) within the first two years of work on our staff. . . . I will strongly support an up-and-out process."	"Given the shortage of data processing professionals, your approach isn't viable. We're currently 10 percent under our allocated headcount. . . . Your plan to turn over employees on a two-year basis really worries me. This ensures we will have inexperienced people making redundant findings and reports. In addition, you will have significant incremental training costs, and I am willing to bet you will have low quality work being performed."
Internal organization	How will the IA group be organized?	(Waters' proposal for an organization structure is shown in Exhibit 6.)	"Your proposal isn't consistent with the skill and experience mix your auditors will have given the decisions on career path. There is no responsibility structure for training."
External organization	Where will IA report in overall corporate structure?	To promote independence this capability should report in the IA group.	". . . . these people should be part of my quality assurance function. This would permit their training and insight into the technology to remain current. I don't understand how you plan to evaluate these people without my input."

EXHIBIT 7 (*concluded*)

Issue	Description	Gary Waters	Cyrus Meredith
Developing policies, procedures, and standards	How are policies, procedures and standards for this function developed?	"We should borrow some procedures from financial IA. . . . the best option is to engage a consulting (or "advisory services' component of a public accounting firm) and piggyback their study."	"Hire an experienced individual from outside and establish a tailored (customized) version of his experience."
Salary basis	Should basis for salary be auditing or data processing schedules?	"Salary must be consistent with financial auditing staff since they reside in the same organization."	"This issue illustrates why your (external) organization decision is incorrect. You will not be able to recruit or retain qualified people using auditing salary ranges."
Role and scope	1. Should auditors be members of new system development team?	"Yes. . . . this would ensure systems will be available and adhere to appropriate internal control guidelines. Furthermore, it will serve as a training mechanism for the auditors."	"Absolutely not. They slow the development process and unconsciously inhibit the use of new technological approaches as they force traditional control techniques on a new environment. We already have a backlog of . . . activity without their help!"
	2. To what level of depth should IA review operations?	"We should focus primarily on security, procedure integrity (adherence to standards and controls), and performance measurement."	"My DP guys will enjoy blowing smoke at IAs . . . , but more seriously, your guys should focus primarily on hardware and physical reviews."
	3. Should IA review systems currently in production?	". . . check for compliance with designed controls; and to perform application effectiveness and sunset review."	"Those reviews are part of the planning process we implemented last year. Our quality assurance group should be monitoring this."

Issue	Description	Gary Waters	Cyrus Meredith
	4. Should IA review and critique DP management's administrative and control systems?	"Yes, IA should examine administrative processes (e.g., planning, personnel reviews, organization structure, charging system, etc.)."	"Absolutely not, that is the reason I report to Doug Richards."
Reporting	Who should receive findings and recommendations?	"Each report will contain an action plan detailed to quarterly milestones. They should go directly to the audit subcommittee in summarized form. In addition, Doug (Richards) and Larry (Loughton) should receive copies."	"I can't think of a better way to forve contention between the auditor and the auditee. In those companies where IA is working well, no one outside the organization being audited will receive a detailed copy of the final report. IA should present summaries to the audit subcommittee, and senior management should request copies from the auditee. . . ."
Follow-up	What process of checking progress against the audit recommendations should be implemented?	"IA will review progress against the action plans developed on a quarterly basis. If corrective action is still in progress, then we will revise the target completion data and refile an action plan. In those instances where I decide insufficient progress is being made to resolve a major problem, I will note this in a report to senior management."	"There isn't much you can do in data processing on a quarterly basis. I would prefer to have the resources you plan to use for follow-up allocated to my department to do productive work."

Chapter 9 □ Multinational IS Issues

Chapter \ Manageable Trend	Strategic Impact	DP/TP/OA	Organization Learning	Make/Buy	Life Cycle	GM/ User/ IS
IS Technology Organization Issues **Chapter 3**		●	●			●
Organizational Issues in IS Development **Chapter 4**	●		●	●		●
Information Systems Planning **Chapter 5**	●		●			●
IS Management Control **Chapter 6**	●		●	●		●
A Portfolio Approach to Information Systems Development **Chapter 7**	●				●	●
Operations Management **Chapter 8**	●			●	●	●
Multinational IS Issues **Chapter 9**		●				●
The IS Business **Chapter 10**	●		●	●		●

The head of multinational IS (MIS) of a major European research company's central IS activity suddenly discovered that subsidiaries in three of their largest countries had recently ordered medium-sized computers and were planning to move their work from the corporate IS department to installations in their countries (reducing the workload in corporate IS's data center by 45 percent). The reasons cited for this were better control over day-to-day operations, more responsive service, and lower costs. Located in a country with a high-cost, tight labor pool, the IS head was unsure how to assess the risks this posed to his operation and the company as a whole.

The head of corporate IS of a large pharmaceutical company recently held a three-day international meeting of the 15 IS heads of the company's major foreign subsidiaries. A major unresolved problem at the meeting was what should the relationship of corporate IS be to the more than 50 smaller foreign subsidiaries which also had computing equipment. Historically, the department had responded to requests for assistance (5 to 8 per year) but had not gone beyond that. The head of corporate IS was increasingly uncertain whether this was an appropriate level of involvement.

The chief financial officer of a major Singapore company in early 1981 ordered 13 APPLE II computers in his controller's department to stimulate awareness of how modern financial analysis could help the company. Five months later, with the experiment a great success, he found himself overwhelmed with requests for system support. The company not only lacked the staff to provide the support but even in the two- to three-year planning horizon were unlikely to be able to acquire it in the local market at any price.

These stories are the tip of a major, largely unreported, unstudied IS story; namely, that the management of multinational IS support for a company is very complex and its issues go well beyond legislation relating to transborder information flows. These issues have become more significant in the past decade as the post–World War II explosion of the numbers and scope of multinationals has continued. This growth has sparked the need for development and expansion of management systems to permit appropriate coordination of geographically distant business activities. In the past, investigation of this area has tended to fall between two schools. On the one hand, it has appeared to be so specialized and technical that the scholars of international business have tended to ignore it. On the other hand, those writing about management of information systems have tended to be highly national in their orientation and have tended to slide past the issues in this area of IS technology application.

We see this area as representing a major management challenge today, as well as one where the resolution of issues is likely to be even more significant in the coming years. Managing the forces driving transition in IS (described as six trends in Chapter 2) is confounded by the diversity of country infrastructure (for example, Germany vis-à-vis Sri Lanka), as well as prior discussed variations in corporate manufacturing and distribution technologies, current scope of IS activity, and relative sophistication in IS application. Building on our concepts of strategic relevance, culture, contingent planning, and managing diffusion of technology, we will focus on international aspects that impinge on IS.

This chapter is organized as follows: The first section deals with some important country characteristics which influence the type of IS support appropriate for a firm's operations in the country. The second section talks about specific IS environmental issues which influence how a firm can develop IS support in a specific country. The third section deals with company-specific issues which influence how it should think about IS development overseas. The final part suggests the types of policies that firms have adopted for dealing with these issues and discusses the factors which make them more or less appropriate in different settings.

COUNTRY DIVERSITY

There are a number of important factors inherent in a country's culture, government, and economy which influence what IS applications make sense, how they should be implemented, and what is the appropriate type of corporate guidance from an IS activity located in another country. The more important of these factors include the following:

Sociopolitical. The obvious factors of industrial maturity and the form of government are particularly important in considering the use of information services technology. Emerging countries with high birth rates have views and opportunities far different from those of mature industrial states with shrinking labor populations. Further, mature societies have stable bureaucracies which allow the necessary continuity for development of communications systems.

Language. Common languages of Western origin provide a sound means for technical communications and relevant documentation. However, this is lacking if the local language is not Latin-based. This is especially true for discussions of a technical nature, because, frequently, senior managers of the subsidiary are fluent in the parent company language, but lower-level managers and staff technicians lack this fluency. This tends to be true even in companies such as N. V. Philips (the large Dutch electronics company), which has made a major effort to develop English as a company-wide language.)

Local Constraints. A whole network of local cultural facets exist which make it difficult to develop coordinated systems and an orderly process of technology transfer. Union agreements, timing of holidays, government tax regulations, and customs procedures all force major modifications of software, for applications such as accounting, and personnel from one country to another. Further, different holidays, different working hours, etc. make coordination of reporting and data gathering an ongoing evolutionary process. Also important are issues relating to geography and demographics. For example, a large phonograph record company has found it attractive to have centralized order entry and warehouse management for Paris, which serves retailers around the country. It fit the structure of the French distribution system. In Germany, however, they were driven to establish multiple factories, distribution points, and a quite different order entry system to service the market. The German structure was a rational response to the realities of German geography and prevailing distribution patterns. Unfortunately, this also meant that the software and procedures appropriate for the French subsidiary were inappropriate for the German situation.

Economic. A mature industrial economy normally has a pool of well-trained, procedurally oriented individuals who typically get high wages relative to world standards. This incentive to replace clerical people is complemented by the limited availability of talent, and it is a sensible economic decision. In cultures with low-wage rates, often dependent on one or two main raw material exports for currency, there is typically a lack of both talent and economic incentive. The true need is to develop a reliable source of available information (a noneconomic decision). Implementing this, however, may move against both economic and cultural norms.

Currency Exchange. Organizing international data centers is complicated by both currency restrictions and volatility in exchange rates. The latter may mean that a location initially cost effective for providing service to neighboring countries may suddenly become quite cost ineffective. For example, several Swiss data centers which were very cost competitive in the early 1970s were very noncompetitive in the late 1970s as a result of the heavy appreciation of the Swiss franc, even against currencies like the German mark.

Autonomy. Another point of importance is the universal drive for autonomy and feelings of nationalism. The normal drive for autonomy in units within a single country is intensified by differences in language and culture as one deals with international subsidiaries. In general, a larger integration effort is needed to appropriately coordinate foreign subsidiaries than is needed with domestic ones (with not necessarily better results). The difficulties in this task increase not only with the distance of the subsidiary from corporate headquarters but also as the relative economic importance of the subsidiary drops.

National Infrastructure. The availability of utilities and a transportation system are often important constraints on feasible alternatives. On the other hand, their absence also serves as an opportunity for emerging technology. For example, to overcome the unpredictable transportation and communication systems, one South American distributor developed a private microwave tower network to link the records of a remote satellite depot with the central warehouses. This system enabled him to obtain a significant competitive edge which led to rapid growth.

All of the above factors make international coordination of IS activities, in general, more complicated than domestic coordination of domestic IS activities. Often development of special staff and organizational approaches are needed if these issues are to be effectively handled.

COUNTRY/IS ENVIRONMENT

In addition to the above more general issues, there are some very specific IS issues, which make the coordination and transfer of IS technology particularly challenging from one country to another. In part these are due to the long lead times to build effective systems and in part due to the changing nature of the technology. The more important of these include the following:

Availability of IS Professional Staff. While inadequate availability of systems and programming resources is a general worldwide problem it is much worse in some settings than others. For example, in 1981, Singapore had only 1,000 analysts and programmers vis-à-vis a need for over 6,500. Further, as fast as people develop these skills in English-speaking countries, they become targets for recruiters from the high-wage, highly industrialized countries. This has been a particular problem in the Philippines in the past several years.

When an attempt is made to supplement local staff with individuals from headquarters, the results are not always uniformly satisfactory. An initial outburst of productivity by the expatriates and effective transfer of technology at a later phase often leads to resentment by the local staff (whose salaries and benefits are usually much lower) and broken career paths on the part of the expatriates, who find they have become both technically and managerially obsolete when they return to corporate headquarters. Management of this reentry problem of IS expatriates, in general, has been quite inadequate.

Central Telecommunications. The price and quality of telecommunication support varies widely from one country to another. On both dimensions, the United States sets the standard. In many European countries, the tariffs will run an order of magnitude higher than those in the United States. In addition, in many countries, lead times to get extra land lines, terminals, and so forth from date of order can stretch to years instead of weeks. Variances in line capacity, costs, and up-time performance mean that profitable online applications are either cost ineffective or fail to meet adequate uptime or reliability standards in other countries. Also, communication quality, availability, and cost varies widely from one country to another.

Country/National IS Strategy. In some countries, development of a local computer manufacturing and software industry is a key national priority item (France, Germany, and the United Kingdom, for example). In these situations, subsidiaries of foreign companies often find it attractive to buy the products of the local manufacturer as part of being a good citizen and building credit for later dealing with the government. This may create a legitimate local need to deviate from corporate hardware/software standards. A related issue is that some countries (such as India and Nigeria) require that computer vendors sell a majority share of their local subsidiary to local shareholders if they are to do business in the country. Some vendors (such as IBM) have preferred to withdraw from a market rather than to enter into such an arrangement. Again, this may force a deviation in those countries from corporate-mandated IS standards. Finally, concern may exist about whether the country exporting the hardware will continue to be a reliable supplier in a world of turbulent national, and shifting foreign, policies. For example, a number of South African companies, uneasy about the ability to get a sustained flow of products from one country, have moved to hedge their bets on potential disruptions of equipment delivery by dealing with several countries.

General Level of IS Sophistication. The speed and ease with which one can either start or grow an IS activity is linked to the general level of IS activity in the country. A firm located in a country with a substantial base of installed information systems, and with a base of well-trained mobile labor, can grow more rapidly and effectively than where none of these preconditions exist. The countries with a limited base of installed information systems require substantially more expatriate labor to implement IS work. This is accompanied by greater effort and time to educate users concerning the idiosyncracies of IS and how best to interface with it. The staff mobility factor is particularly important to investigate carefully because both bonding arrangements and cultural norms add real rigidities into what on the surface appears to be a satisfactory labor supply situation.

Size of Local Market. The size of the local market influences the number of vendors who can compete for service in it. This means that, in smaller markets, a company's preferred international supplier may not have a presence. Further, the quality of service support often varies widely from one setting to another, with vendors who provide good support in one country turning out to be inadequate in another. Another important issue is the availability and quality of local software and consulting companies (or subsidiaries of large international ones). A thriving competent local information services industry can do much to offset other differences in local support and availability of staff.

Data Export Control. A topic which has received significant publicity in the past three to four years has been the specter of legislation to reduce dramatically the amount of information relating to people and finances which can be transmitted electronically across national boundaries. One factor is increased governmental prescription concerning the types of teleprocessing services that may be offered by suppliers. This involves both establishment of technical standards and type of nonlocally manufactured equipment which can be used. Another factor is growth of interest in regulation concerning the type of data (including quality and security standards) which should be permitted to be sent abroad. It is perceived that not only is privacy of individuals threatened but unacceptable security and quality controls exist over these data, raising the threat of substantial accidental danger to the individual. The potential scope of this legislation, and the procedures for effectively monitoring compliance with it, are very speculative at present. Our guess is that, when the dust settles, its practical impact on a firm's operations may be limited, although some modifications in procedures will have to be made to accommodate specific country problems.

Technological Awareness. One of the great management problems is that awareness of contemporary technology spreads very rapidly around the globe because key IS magazines and journals have international distribution. The authors have had as spirited discussions about the pros and cons of various data base management systems in Beijing (although none are there) as in New York. This awareness poses real problems in terms of orderly application development in less sophisticated countries, because subsidiaries often tend to push technologies which they neither really understand, need, nor are capable of managing.

Trade Union Environment. In the past five years, particularly in Europe and western Canada, there have been substantial successful efforts to organize IS departments. As mentioned in Chapter 8, in 1980 and 1981, for example, there were serious and successful strikes of the U.K.'s Inland Revenue Service's computer operations staff which substantially interrupted its operations. This has caused some companies to do a better job of distributing their IS activities, to minimize both the possibility of labor action and the disruption which flows from it. It has also become a factor in picking appropriate locations for regional data centers to support activities in several countries.

Border Opportunities. In periods of fluctuating exchange rates, significant discontinuities often appear in vendor prices for the same equipment in different countries. In 1980, for example, there was a period where a 15 to 20 percent savings could be achieved by buying equipment in Italy for use in Switzerland, as opposed to a direct purchase in Switzerland.

The practical implication of these factors is to restrain severely the degree to which standard policies and controls can be placed on diverse international activities. There are a large number of legitimate reasons for diversity.

The problem is complicated by the fact that considerable *local* know-how must be brought to the decisions. Rigid policy on many of these issues cannot be dictated from corporate headquarters, often located a vast distance from the operating management.

COMPANY AND IS REQUIREMENTS

Within the context of the different country cultures and current state of the IS profession in different countries, a number of factors exist inside a company which influence how far it must move to manage the transfer of IS technology, and how actively it should attempt to centrally control international IS activity. By definition, more control must be delegated locally because of the above-mentioned issues than are delegated in a domestic environment. However, important opportunities exist for technology transfer, and potentially important information service limitations will occur if these issues are not managed. The more important company-specific factors include the following:

Nature of Firm's Business. Some firms' businesses demand that key data files be managed centrally to be immediately accessible to all units of the firm around the globe or on a short delayed access basis. Airline reservation files for international air carriers require such access. A Pan American agent in Boston confirming a flight segment from Tokyo to Hong Kong needs up-to-the-minute access to the flight's loading to make a valid commitment, while other agents around the globe need to know that seat is no longer available for sale. Failure to have this information poses risks of significant loss of market share as customers perceive the firm to be both unreliable and uncompetitive. For example, a major shipping company has to maintain a file, updated every 24 hours, as to where its containers are around the globe, what their status is, and their availability for future commitment by regional officers in 20 countries. The absence of this data would lead to their making undoable commitments, subsequently presenting an unreliable image to present and potential customers. Other firms require integration and online updating of only some of their files. For example, a major European electronics firm attempts to provide for its European managers up-to-date online access to various key operational files on items such as production schedules, order status, and so forth. This is done for its network of 20 plus factories to manage an integrated logistics system. No such integration, however, is attempted for either their key marketing or accounting data, which are essentially processed on a batch basis and organized by country. While it is technically possible to develop such integration, they see at present no operational or marketing advantage in doing so.

Still other firms require essentially no integration of data and each country can be managed on a stand-alone basis. A major U.S. conglomerate, for example, manages each division on a stand-alone basis. Eight of its divisions have operations in the United Kingdom and, by corporate policy, they have no formal interaction with each other in IS or any other operational matters (a single tax specialist who files a joint tax return for them is the sole linking specialist). The general perception of the company's staff is that this is an appropriate way to operate and nothing of significance is being lost. These examples suggest the impossibility of general-purpose prescriptions as to organization of multinational IS activities.

Strategic Impact of IS. Firms where the IS activity is at the strategic heart of the company need tighter corporate overview of the area to ensure that new technology (and hence new ways of operating) is rapidly introduced to the outlying areas in an efficient way. One of the U.S.'s largest international banks, for example has a group of over 100 staff at corporate headquarters to both develop software for their international branches and to coordinate the orderly dissemination of this software—thus technology—to their key countries. The successful use of this technology is felt to be too critical to the firm's ultimate success for it to be managed without technical coordination and senior management perspective. At the other extreme is a reasonably large manufacturer of chemicals where the general perception is that IS technology is playing an important but distinctly support role. At least twice a year, the head of the European IS unit and the head of corporate IS exchange visits and share perceptions with each other. The general consensus is that there is not enough payoff to warrant further coordination.

Corporate Organization. As the firm grows in international activity, it adopts different structures, each of which requires quite different levels of international IS support and coordination. In the earliest phase of an export division, there are only limited numbers of staff overseas, who require little if any local IS processing and support. As the activity grows in size, it tends to be reorganized as an *international* division with an increasing number of marketing, accounting, and manufacturing staff located abroad. At this stage, there may be an increasing need of local IS support. At its full-blown level, this may involve regional headquarters in Europe, the Far East, and Latin America, for example, to coordinate the activities of the diverse countries. This structure can become very complex for a company to coordinate where there are not only vertical relationships of some form between corporate IS and the country IS activities, but where cross-border marketing and manufacturing integration requirements create the need for relationships between the country IS units. The best form of this coordination, of course, will vary widely from one organization to another. One multibillion dollar pharmaceutical firm, recently studied, was discovered to have very close links between corporate IS and its major country IS units (defined as those which had budgets in excess of $5 million). None of its major country IS unit managers, however, either know the names of their contemporaries or had visited any of the other locations. Since there was little cross-border product flow, and none planned in the near future, this did not appear to represent a significant problem.

At the most complex, we have firms organized in a matrix fashion, where there is a corporate IS activity, divisional IS activities (which may or may not be located at corporate headquarters), and country IS activities, where balancing of relationships is a major challenge. This may be further complicated by divisions having substantial vertical supplier relationships with each other and substantial integration of activities across national borders. Clearly, the policies that work for the international divisions are likely to be too simplistic for this latter situation.

Company Technical and Control Characteristics. An important input to the type of IS control that will work is the general level of functional control present in the company overall. Companies with a strong tradition of central functional control find it both appropriate and relatively easy to implement line IS control worldwide. For example, a major manufacturer of farm equipment for years has implemented very strong management and operational control over its worldwide manufacturing and marketing functions. Consequently, they found considerable acceptance by the organization of similar controls for the IS organization. Today, the majority of software which runs their overseas plants has been developed and is being maintained by the corporate IS headquarters group.

At the other extreme is a multibillion-dollar conglomerate of some 30 divisions whose corporate staff is approximately 100 people, who are involved mostly in financial and legal work associated with acquisitions and divestures. This company's philosophy has been total decentralization of operating decisions to the divisions, and corporate headcount is deliberately controlled to prevent meddling. At present there is a two-person corporate IS group who work on only very broad policy and consulting issues. In this organization environment, effective execution of even this role is very challenging and it would be very difficult to visualize its effective expansion.

Another element of significance is the technology base of the company. High technology companies which have a tradition of spearheading technical change from a central research and engineering laboratory and ensuring its dissemination around the globe have had success in processing a similar approach with IS. A receptivity to technical change exists, and a base of experience concerning the problems associated with technical change exists. Firms without this experience in their management teams not only have had more difficulty assimilating IS technology in general but have had more problems in transplanting IS technology developed in one location to another setting.

A final point of relevance here is the corporate size. Smaller organizations, because of the limited and specialized nature of their application, find transfer of IS packages and expertise to be particularly complex. As the scope of the operation increases, it appears to become easier to find common applications and to facilitate transfer of technology.

Effects of Geography and Size of Companies. Of potential benefit is the possibility of using the company's location in different time zones to creatively take advantage of excess capacity on the firm's large computers during the second and third shifts. The savings in hardware and staff in some cases have substantially exceeded the additional telecommunications expense. One manufacturing firm located on the East Coast of the United States uses the time between 1 A.M. and 9 A.M. to process much of the manufacturing load of its European subsidiaries. Daytime hours, 9 to 5 P.M., are primarily devoted to supporting its U.S. operations, and the early evening hours to handling the work of its Far Eastern subsidiaries. Obviously, because of data transmission costs, there are limits as to the extent that this can go on.

The number and relative size of foreign operations are important inputs to evolving appropriate policies. Large subsidiaries provide an opportunity for effective coordination on both technical issues and staff rotation. A large U.S. automotive company recently picked its new IS head from France. As the relative economic significance of the foreign unit drops, the intensity of the relationship between corporate IS and the local unit appropriately lessens. Less opportunity exists for both technical coordination and meaningful staff transfers. As will be discussed below, different policies and relationships need to be established for units of different sizes.

Economic Analysis. The relevant economies of hardware/software investment overruns need to be monitored carefully on two dimensions. First, vendors often adopt different pricing strategies within countries, and what may be an attractive or unattractive investment in the home country of the parent company may not be uniformly true in all parts of the globe. Related to this, and more serious, are the problems and discontinuities caused by fluctuating currency exchange rates, which can substantially change the economics of equipment/staff trade-offs inside a country. Fortunately for U.S. companies, recent changes in regulation FASB-8 have eliminated some of the artificial accounting considerations as to whether it is better to buy or lease computing equipment.

Other Considerations. Several other considerations in a firm's environment exist which also influence the resolution of IS coordination policy. Is there substantial rotation of staff between international locations? If this takes place, it is marginally more attractive to have common reporting systems and operating procedures in place in each subsidiary to ease the assimilation of the transfers? Does the firm's operating and financial requirement essentially demand up-to-the-week reporting of overseas financial results? Where this is not needed, consolidation of smaller overseas operations on a one-month delayed time basis is attractive.

MULTINATIONAL IS POLICY ISSUES

As the preceding sections identify, there appropriately exists great diversity in the policies used to coordinate and manage international IS activities between companies, and from one country to another. This section identifies the most common types of policies and relationships and briefly focuses on some of the key issues associated with their selection and implementation.

The scope of these policies and the size of the effort to be focused on their implementation are influenced by the nature of the business (central control needed or not needed), corporate culture relating to corporate-mandated policies, strategic impact of IS technologies, and so forth.

Communication and Data Management Standards. The opportunity to transmit data electronically between countries for file updating and processing purposes has created the need for some form of corporate international data dictionary. Too often this need is not addressed, leading to both clumsy systems designs and incorrect outputs. Where data should be stored, the form in which it should be stored, and how it should be updated are all items which require centrally managed policy (operating, of course, within the framework of what is legally permissible).

Similarly, centrally guided coordination on communication technology acquisition is needed. At present, communication flexibility and cost varies widely from country to country and is shifting rapidly. For example, in 1981 seven countries opened their communication systems to satellite inputs. Western Europe is in the process of developing a packet switched network which operates independently of "normal" communication. Effective anticipation of these changes requires a corporate view and broad design of telecommunications over a decade, to meet growth and changing business needs. It must be specific in terms of service levels needed and appropriate technologies. This plan requires both capable technical inputs and careful management review. An important by-product of the plan is to provide guidance for corporate negotiation and lobbying efforts on relevant items of national legislation and policies regarding the form, availability, and cost of telecommunication.

Central Hardware Concurrence or Approval. The objective of a central policy is to ensure that obvious mistakes in vendor viability are avoided and potential economies of scale in purchasing decisions are achieved. Other benefits are the additional support leverage which can be achieved by being perceived to be an important customer, the reduction of potential interface problems between national systems, and enhancement of portability of software between countries). Practical factors which require sensitive interpretation and execution of this policy include the following items:

Lack of awareness at corporate headquarters of the vendor's support and servicing problems in the local country.

Desire of the local subsidiary to exercise its autonomy and control of its operations in a *timely* way. The Korean subsidiary of a large bank recently wanted to buy a $25,000 word processing system. The gaining of concurrence took six months to pass through three locations and involved one senior vice president and two executive vice presidents before the process was completed. It was generally felt that, whatever benefits standardization might have achieved for the bank in this situation, they were more than offset by the cost and time of the approval process.

Need to maintain good government relationships locally. This may involve such items as patronizing the local vendors, not moving to eliminate certain types of staff, and using the government-controlled teleprocessing network.

Level and skill of people at corporate headquarters in setting appropriate policy in both technical and managerial dimensions. A technically weak corporate staff dealing with large well-managed foreign subsidiaries must operate quite differently from a large, technically gifted central staff dealing with many small, rather unsophisticated subsidiaries.

Central Software Standards and Feasibility Study Approval. This policy's objective is to ensure that software is written in both a maintainable and secure way so that the company's long-term operational position is not jeopardized. A second objective is to ensure that potential applications are evaluated in a consistent and professional fashion. The problems, if any, with this policy revolve around both the level of effort and potential erosion of corporate culture. Implementation of such standards can be expensive and time-consuming in relation to the potential benefits. The art is to be flexible in relation to small investments while sifting out for closer review the ones where there is real operational exposure. Implementation of this approach requires more sensitivity than many staffs are capable of.

A second problem with this policy is that in many decentralized companies it is directly counter to the prevailing management control system and the location of other operating decisions. The significance of this objection is partially offset by the size and relative strategic impact of the investment. Relatively small, distinctly support investments in these decentralized organizations clearly should be resolved in the local country. Large strategic investments, however, are often appropriate for central review in these organizations, even taking time delays and cost overruns into account.

Central Software Development. In the name of efficiency, reduced costs, and standard operating procedures worldwide, repeatedly firms have attempted to develop software centrally or at some designated country subsidiary for installation in other country subsidiaries. The success of this approach has been definitely mixed. Companies which have a well-established pattern of technology transfer, strong functional control over subsidiaries, substantial numbers of expatriates working in the overseas subsidiaries, and where some homogeneity exists in manufacturing, accounting, and distribution practices have had considerable success with this. The success has also been assisted by very intensive marketing and liaison activities of the IS unit assigned responsibility for the package's development and installation. Repeatedly, however, when these preconditions have not been present, installation has turned into a troubled situation. Most commonly cited reasons for the failure include:

"The developers of the system didn't understand local need well enough. Major functions were left out, and the package required extensive and expensive enhancements."

"The package was adequate, but the efforts needed to train people to put data in and properly handle outputs were significantly underestimated or mishandled. This was complicated by extensive language difficulties and insensitivity to existing local procedures."

"The system evolution and maintenance involved a dependence on central staff which was not sustainable in the long run. We needed more flexibility and timeliness of response than was possible."

"Costs were totally underestimated by more than an order of magnitude. The overrun on the basic package was bad enough but the fat was really in the fire when it came to estimating installation costs."

In our judgment, these statements emanate directly from the above structural factors. In reality, an outside software house, with its marketing orientation and existence outside of the family, often can do a better job of selling standard software than an in-house IS unit in a decentralized environment.

IS Communications. Investments in improving communications between the various national IS units, while expensive, have paid big benefits. Devices which have proven useful include the following:

An annual or biannual conference of the IS directors and their key staff in the major international subsidiaries. For organizations in the "turnaround" or "strategic" categories, these meetings ought to take place at least as frequently as meetings of international controllers. The smaller countries (IS budgets under $1 million) will probably not generate enough profitable opportunities to warrant inclusion in this conference or to have a separate one. The agenda of the conference needs to have a blend of formal planned activities such as technical briefing, application briefings, and company directives, together with substantial blocks of unplanned time. The informal exchanges of ideas, initiation of joint projects, and sharing of mutual problems are among the most important activities of a successful conference.

A regular program of visits of corporate IS personnel to the national organizations (as well as national IS personnel coming to corporate). These visits should take place at planned intervals rather than just around an operational crisis or technical problem. Obviously, on balance, less contact should take place with the smaller units than with the larger ones.

Preparation and circulation of a monthly or bimonthly newsletter to communicate staffing shifts, new technical insights, major projects completion, experience with software packages, vendors, and so forth.

Organization of joint education programs where possible. This may involve either the acquisition and/or creation of audiovisual-based materials to be distributed around the world. A large oil company recently supplemented communication of a radically different IS organization structure with the preparation of a special film, complete with soundtrack in five different languages.

The fundamental issue is to build a stronger sense of organizational identity between the national IS units by encouraging the development of better links between national IS units, rather than have the only links between a country's IS unit and the parent company's IS unit.

Staff Planning. A very important, if difficult to administer, way of addressing the issue of communications is through rotation of staff between the country IS units and corporate IS. Key advantages which stem from this include the following:

Better awareness in corporate IS of the problems and issues in the overseas IS units. The corollary of this is that the local IS units have a much better perspective on the goals and thinking at corporate headquarters as a result of one of their members having spent a tour of duty there.

More flexibility in managing career paths and matching positions with individual development needs. Particularly, in a crowded corporate IS department, an overseas assignment can provide an attractive opportunity.

Efficient dispersion of technical know-how throughout the organization.

Practical problems on the negative side of staff rotation include the following:

Career paths of individuals moving from corporate headquarters to less IS-developed portions of the globe have frequently been very unsatisfactory. The individuals bring leading-edge expertise to the overseas installation and have a major positive impact for several years. Upon returning to corporate headquarters, they find themselves totally obsolete in terms of the contemporary technologies being used, and also on occasion have been dropped out of the normal progression stream through oversight.

Assignment of individuals overseas is not only expensive in terms of moving allowances and cost-of-living differentials but it also raises a myriad of potential personal problems. These problems, normally of a family nature, make the success of an international transfer more speculative than a domestic one.

Transfers from corporate to smaller overseas locations may cause substantial resentment and feelings of incipient nationalism to arise. "Why aren't our people good enough?" Appropriate language skills and efforts on the part of the transferred executive, control over the number of transfers, and local promotions plus the clearly visible opportunity for local staff to be transferred to corporate does much to temper these problems.

On balance, appropriately managed within reasonable limits, the positives far outweigh the negatives.

Consulting Services. Major potential payoff exists from a central IS group providing consulting services on both technical and managerial matters to foreign subsidiaries. In many cases, corporate headquarters is not only located in a technically sophisticated country but its IS activities are bigger in scope than those of individual foreign installations. Among other things, this means:

Corporate IS is more aware of leading-edge hardware/software technology and has had firsthand experience with its potential strengths and weaknesses. Communication of this know-how can be of significance.

Corporate IS is more likely to have experience with large project management systems and other management methods. Communication of this expertise can be of value.

In both of these examples, the communication must be done with some sensitivity, as the art is to move the company forward at an appropriate pace. Movement through the stages of management practices or through the phases of technology assimilation can be speeded up and smoothed. It is very hard, however, to skip either a stage or a phase. All too often, the corporate group pushes too fast in a culturally insensitive fashion, creating substantial problems.

As an organization becomes more IS intensive, effective IS auditing becomes increasingly important to ensure that the organization is not exposed to excessive and unnecessary risks. As mentioned in Chapter 6 on management control, IS auditing is still a rapidly evolving profession which faces a real shortage of staff. The problem is far worse outside the U.S. and Europe. Accordingly, the corporate audit group of a multinational is frequently forced to undertake major responsibility both for conducting international IS audits and for helping to develop national IS audit staff and capabilities.

Central IS Processing Support. The extent to which it makes sense to push IS toward a central hub or linked international network is absolutely dependent on both a firm's type of industry and those particular dimensions along which it chooses to compete. At one extreme is the airline industry where significant competitive disadvantage comes from being unable to confirm seats on a global basis (hence most international airlines are driven to establish such a network—originally as an offensive weapon and now as a defensive one). At the other extreme is a company running a network of paper converting operations where transportation costs severely limit how far away from a plant orders can be profitably shipped. Consequently, it manages order entry and factory management on a strictly national basis with little interchange of data between countries.

Technology Appraisal Program. The development of an international appraisal plan can serve as a useful means to maintaining a perspective and coordination of the IS overseas effort. An example is a U.S.-based multinational company that had a long history of European operations and discovered that the Far East and South America were posing increasingly complicated information problems. A three-year program was initiated by general management to bring the overseas operation under control. The first step was to appraise the state of IS technology and its potential business in each country. This was done by corporate IS management. This appraisal was followed by a discussion, at the annual meeting of company executives, of a proposed set of policies, and where appropriate, action programs. The appraisal was conducted by a three-person IS technical team with multilingual abilities. Originally scheduled on a one-time basis in only 11 countries, the effort was considered so successful it was reorganized as an established audit function. The team learned to appraise locally available technology and to guide local managements' attention to judging its potential. This required a minimum of a week and often two weeks in the field, typically in two trips. The first visit appraised existing services, and generally raised a series of questions which could be effectively pursued by the on-site management as the audit expanded to include:

1. Government restriction.
2. Quality and quantity of available human skills.
3. Present and planned communications services.
4. Generation of alternatives to the present means of service.
5. Economic analysis of at least three standard alternatives, including:
   a. Expansion of present system.
   b. Transfer of all or portions of IS work to a neighboring country.
   c. Transfer of all or portions of IS work to regional headquarters.

The enthusiasm of local managers for this review was not consistent and in several countries long delays occurred between the first and second set of meetings. However, in 7 of the original 11, the appraisals succeeded in generating appropriate change through a better understanding of the potential impact of uncertainties, such as changing import duties, insight into planned market introduction of new technologies by U.S. suppliers, and a new satellite communications alternative. This organized appraisal significantly increased both awareness and comfort among senior management concerning IS. It resulted in the conversion of the activity into an ongoing effort and the addition of several more members to the team.

SUMMARY

International IS development must be actively managed if major long-term difficulties are not to emerge both within and between country IS activities. This is complicated, since as discussed earlier, foreign assimilation of IS technology must be more heavily influenced by local conditions than the current absolute state of the technology. Resolving these local situations is much more complex than simply keeping abreast of technology, thus a long view is required to succeed. For some firms, however, success offers the potential for a significant competitive edge.

Case 9–1 □ Northern Star Electronic AB (A)*

In late 1973, Mr. Schmidt, head of the systems and software department (SSD) at the Münster television factory of German Star Electronic faced a problem in preparing his annual EDP plan for 1974. German Star Electronic was a wholly owned subsidiary of Northern Star Electronic AB, a major Swedish concern. German Star's systems and software department in Frankfurt had been supporting Münster's data processing requirements through remote batch-job entry on IBM hardware; early in 1973, Münster was notified that this service would terminate in the middle of 1974. In return, Münster would receive an International Computer Industries, Ltd. (ICIL) 740 computer, but all programs would have to be converted—no small task.

Aware of the impending forced conversion, the product division for television at corporate headquarters had decided that Münster should install the product division's standard stores and supplies system (SASS) at the same time. Mr. Landfors, the Münster factory manager, wished to proceed carefully in development of in-house EDP capabilities. Therefore, he intended to review very thoroughly the 1974 EDP plan of his SSD manager.

COMPANY BACKGROUND

Northern Star Electronic AB had been founded before World War I to make generators and turbines. In 1973, with consolidated turnover of about Skr 5 billion, it was the fifth largest industrial company in Sweden and ranked about 100th in the world outside of the United States. It was best known for its industrial and consumer electrical equipment, including domestic appliances and electronic equipment. The company also had important interests in heavy machinery and engineering.

In 1972 the company had nearly 100 subsidiaries in more than 30 countries, and factories in 15 countries. Of Northern Star Electronic's 195,000 employees, 30 percent were in Sweden, 50 percent in Europe outside of Sweden, and the remainder in the Americas and the Far East. The Münster factory, with 1,500 employees, produced 750 color and black-and-white television sets each day and ranked second in output among the factories of the Television Division. It produced significant volume for export and for local markets.

* Case material prepared by the Harvard Business School is used as a basis for class discussion rather than to illustrate either effective or ineffective handling of an administrative situation.

In 1973, Northern Star's three-tier management structure related its broad range of products and its wide geographical representation by means of product divisions and national organizations (Exhibit 1). A seven-man board of management was the top policy and decision-making organ. Product divisions and national organizations at the next level shared responsibility for the functional units below them but differed in their areas of primacy. European economic unification required many functions to be of international scale; national considerations required sensitivity to local conditions. Hence, the product division was responsible for maximizing profit potential worldwide, within its product area; the national organization was responsible for maximizing profits of all product groups within its geographic area. Ultimate responsibility was often difficult to identify. As each had profit responsibility, differing judgments sometimes caused conflicts.

Staff services were provided at the corporate level. Among these was the systems and software department. The functions of the SSD were decentralized, with different responsibilities vested at the corporate level, in the product divisions, in the national organizations, and in the factories. Corporate SSD, with a staff of 300 analysts and programmers, was responsible for planning, research and development, and coordination of the data processing activities within the corporation. About one half of the staff worked on systems development; the other half was divided between advanced research and maintenance. Substantial company support of corpo-

EXHIBIT 1 □ Corporate Organization Chart

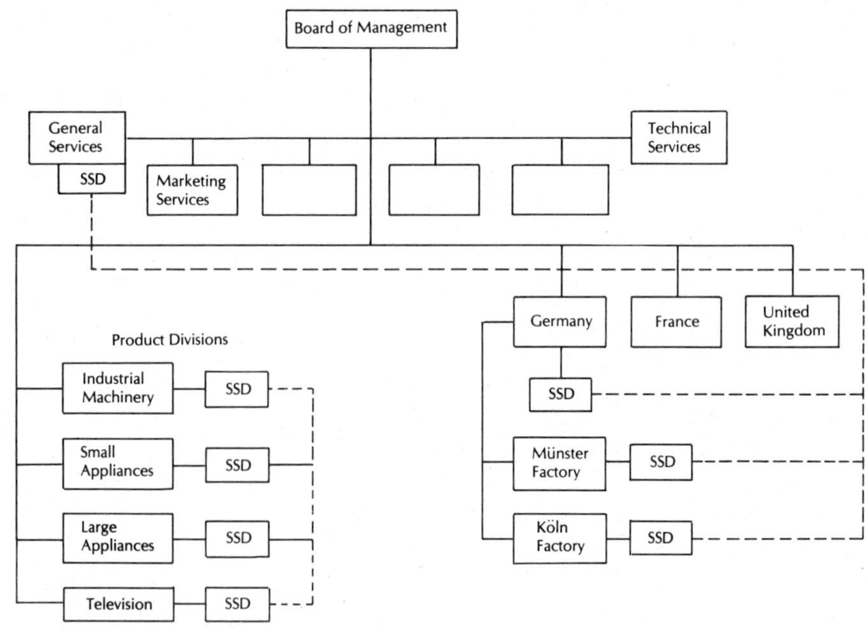

rate SSD permitted extensive development of standard systems and ensured a high level of support for automation within the corporation.

The product divisions and the national organizations both supported in-house SSDs, in accordance with the organizational philosophy of joint responsibility. In practice, not all of these SSDs were equivalent: Some were little more than computer bureaus, as in the case of some national organizations; others were full-fledged development centers nearly on a plane with corporate SSD.

Each factory supported an SSD which usually installed and maintained software packages for payroll, general administration, and various factory systems, although the staff frequently included analysts who designed small local systems. There were 22 computing centers associated with divisional, national, or local SSDs. Formal communication among SSDs went through their respective organizations. Informal relations between SSDs were in general weak, although strongest within national boundaries. There had been relatively few transfers of personnel from one SSD to another, for example.

Acting for the board of management, the corporate Policy Group on Computers evaluated broad policy decisions relating to automation. The Group comprised a member of the board of management, several managers of the product divisions and national organizations, and some staff members of the national organizations and product divisions. It coordinated and consulted with similar policy groups in the national organizations and the product divisions. Among its responsibilities were long-range plans for hardware policy and studies of the responsibilities and authority of the various SSDs.

DATA PROCESSING AT NORTHERN STAR

Northern Star had early recognized the utility of electronic data processing and had thoroughly integrated EDP into its operations. One source estimated that Northern Star spent annually as much as 3 percent of its turnover on computers and related projects. The level of in-house expertise was very high, and a number of factory systems had been developed or generalized by corporate SSD and by divisional and national SSDs. SASS, for instance, was being developed by corporate SSD for the ICIL computers while a similar system, the standard package of automation modules (SPAM), had been developed by a divisional SSD for the IBM line. An advanced version of SPAM was being developed by one of the national SSDs.

Northern Star was a two-vendor computer organization, using IBM because of its high technical standards and wide geographic availability and ICIL, one of the largest European computer manufacturers, because it was frequently less expensive and was occasionally suggested by certain national governments. A two-vendor policy had other advantages, as when one vendor's technical representative would point out a little-known deficiency in the other's product or offer a special discount to place a new piece of equipment in a competitor's shop. Offsetting such advantages, however, was the added expense and complexity of duplicate hardware. The architecture of the two computers differed somewhat and significant programming effort was necessary to adapt programs from one machine to the other.

German Star Electronic's SSD operated an IBM 360/50 with a staff of 150 programmers and support people. They performed routine system maintenance and provided computer time within German Star Electronic.

The corporate Policy Group on Computers had strongly recommended that the two-vendor policy for computer operations in Northern Star should undergo geographic rationalization; the goal was to reduce the range of major EDP equipment in each country to that of one manufacturer. Germany was assigned the ICIL line because ICIL was well established there and offered very good service. One consequence of this decision was that Frankfurt's IBM 360/50 would be replaced with an ICIL 760. The ICIL 760 was generally comparable to the IBM 360/50, though believed to be slightly faster overall.

Münster had entered the age of electronic data processing in 1967 when a proposal of its SSD to study replacement of the IBM 421 punched-card accounting equipment was approved. A configuration based on an IBM 360/25 was approved locally and sent to Frankfurt for review. Frankfurt's response proposed a remote terminal for batch-job entry on their IBM 360/50. This latter plan was implemented in late 1970 after some delay in 1968 with the installation of an IBM 2780 terminal, one of the first installed in Europe. A local estimate of the cost of this delay, in terms of lost efficiencies, amounted to more than 1 percent of German Star's annual turnover.

The data processing staff at Münster (four analysts, five programmers, four operators, and eight keypunchers and verifiers) has mostly been trained inhouse. Only one had prior experience in computers at another data processing center. This staff had adapted certain standard IBM software for use on the remote terminal. By the middle of 1973, this software included:

	Number of Programs and Modules	
Program type	COBOL	RPG
Wages and salaries	28	10
Administrative	23	39
Materials handling	83	—
	134	49

These programs run during two shifts per day in Münster, incurring direct computer and terminal charges of about Skr 1 million annually.

Because the ICIL 760 to be installed in Frankfurt would not support remote batch-job entry, Münster had been advised to acquire an ICIL 740 (roughly equivalent to an IBM 360/30) to continue its data processing activities. To be installed at the beginning of 1974, this was to be Münster's first computer under its own roof.

The staff of the Münster SSD had investigated the conversion from a remote IBM terminal to an in-house ICIL computer by direct translation of all necessary programs. With the help of ICIL computer-division staff, conversion costs were estimated and a conversion schedule was drawn up (Exhibits 2, 3, 4). The operating costs seemed comparable—the remote-terminal

EXHIBIT 2 □ ICIL 740 Anticipated Start-Up Costs (One-for-One Conversion)

	Skr (000s)
Personnel costs	
Instruction	
Programmers and operators: 300 man-days, 2,400 hours	75
Conversion	
Programmers—1 man-year, operators—1 man-year	100
Rent (hardware)	
Teleprocessing 6 months: IBM 2780 and related equipment	100
Processing costs—Computer Center, Frankfurt	
2 months at 60M Skr, 2 months at 30M Skr, 2 months at 15M Skr	210
Various conversion costs	
Travel, office supplies, telephone, etc.	15
Computer room	
Alteration costs	50
Total conversion costs	550
Capital expenditures	
3 Magnetic tape cabinets (1,050 each)	3,150
1 Disc cabinet (1,050)	1,050
2 Data transport wagons (525 each)	1,050
1 Record rack (750)	750
10 Disc packs (1,425 each)	14,250
150 Magnetic tapes (75 each)	11,250
Air conditioning	87,000
Total capital expenditures	118,500

(U.S. $1 = Skr 5.)

EXHIBIT 3 □ ICIL 740 Anticipated Annual Operating Costs (One-for-One Conversion)

		Skr (000s)
Personnel costs		695
Rent		950
ICIL hardware	885	
IBM hardware	65	
Office supplies		71
Punched cards, paper, magnetic tapes	60	
Postage, telephone, magazines	8	
Minor assets	3	
Travel		15
Repairs and maintenance		6
Depreciation of long-term assets		11
Air conditioning	5	
Discs (15 gross value)	5	
Other	1	
Capital costs for long-term assets		6
Air conditioning	4	
Other	2	
Subtotal, direct costs		1,754
Overhead		196
Social costs	45	
Building—280 m²	63	
Energy		
Electricity	70	
Water	18	
Total annual operating cost		1,950

(U.S. $1 = Skr 5.)

annual rental of Skr 200,000 and the annual computer charges of Skr 720,000 approximated the Skr 950,000 annual rental of the ICIL 740 and related hardware. The schedule allowed some parallel operation because the ICIL would be operational in the middle of 1974 but the 360 would not go offline until the end of 1974.

STANDARD SYSTEMS

Northern Star's experience with standard software packages had begun in 1967 with IBM and the bill of materials processor (BOMP) and the produc-

EXHIBIT 4 □ Schedule for One-for-One Conversion at the Münster Factory

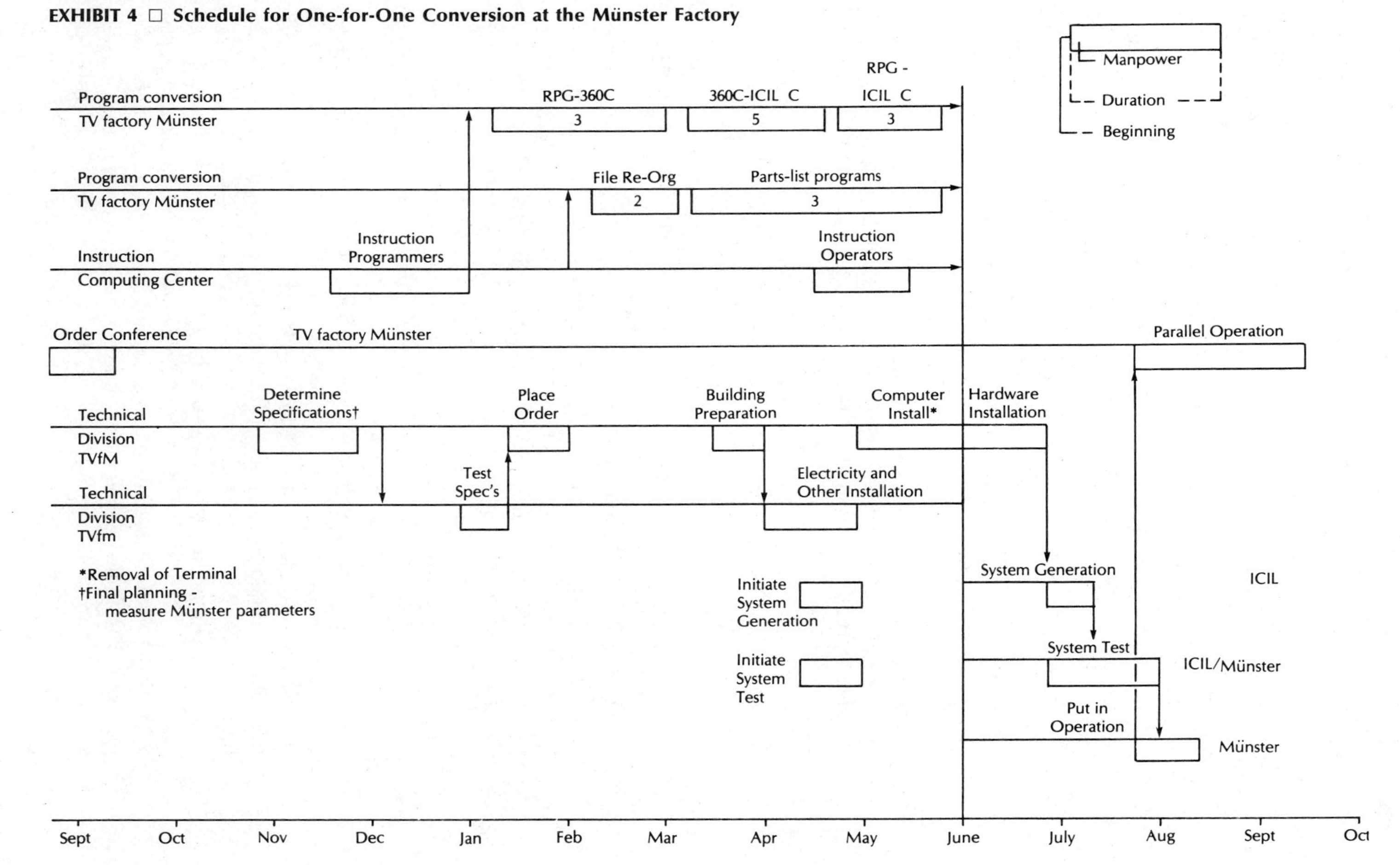

tion information control system (PICS). Their early development within the Northern Star group of companies resulted in a system widely used, primarily on IBM machines, SPAM. SPAM had been developed by users in each factory and national organization; as a result no two systems were identical, but all shared a common heritage of BOMP, PICS, and IBM. Since 1970 corporate SSD had played a significant role in the development of a similar system (SASS) for ICIL computers.

SASS was a package of standard software modules for ICIL computers. It included parts listing, stock inventory, purchasing, and materials-planning functions. Designed for the materials sector of industry, it reduced costs of materials ordering, purchasing, and storage, and reduced work in process-inventory and delivery times. The parts list file at the core of SASS used chaining techniques to relate finished goods to subassemblies to individual parts to potential suppliers. Around this core, the user could arrange standard or custom modules to perform any task relating to materials management. Corporate SSD estimated that the average SASS installation would be between 40 percent and 60 percent standard.

The development of SASS began in 1968 at German Star Electronic's Small Appliances factory in Köln. This factory had an IBM 360/30 with tapes and disks but had been scheduled to receive an ICIL 720 in late 1970. Consequently, the local SSD wanted a factory system suitable for the ICIL 700 series, one which would incorporate the most recent concepts in materials management. With the support of the ICIL Ruhrgebiet sales office in Düsseldorf, development began. In 1969, ICIL sent six programmer/analysts to Köln to assist Köln's own group of six. Their schedule called for project completion at the end of 1971.

Corporate SSD was interested in this project, the first factory system to be developed expressly for ICIL computers and took charge, promising to supply Köln with a standard system that would incorporate the necessary modifications. The Television Division Group, which used a large number of ICIL computers, also took an interest. Separately located in Stockholm, with its own divisional SSD, the Group was well situated to advise and observe system development by corporate SSD located only half a kilometer away. The Small Appliances Division, to which Köln reported, was less interested in automation. (It had not been happy with the results of an earlier joint effort with corporate SSD.) Thus it did not try to influence the development of SASS.

The development effort proceeded from late 1969 with 38 systems analysts and programmers from corporate SSD and 6 from Television Division SSD. These six furnished the only continuing user input to evolution of the package. The entire development costs were charged out to a suspense account in corporate overhead, and it was not clear that these costs would later be recovered by charges to users. By 1973, SASS had been brought online in the television factory in Stockholm. At factories in Malmö and

Copenhagen, it was running in parallel with former IBM systems. Estimates of system cost to that date were Skr 20 to 30 million; continuing development costs were budgeted at about Skr 5 million annually.

The Köln factory, which had been installing modules throughout 1973, was scheduled to complete Phase I of the introduction of SASS in the beginning of 1974. Köln was pleased to have achieved a usable system, as strong involvement of the Television Division Group had almost blocked development of the modules necessary for the "Small" Appliances Division. The factory manager at Köln felt that planning thus far had been deplorable and was uncertain of the direction that further development would follow.

VIEWPOINTS

Four groups were involved in the development and installation of SASS. Each saw the matter somewhat differently. Mr. Landfors, the 63-year-old manager of the Münster plant, had watched the situation develop without having been able to influence it:

> Look, we have people from Television, from ICIL, getting my people all stirred up. Okay, they're doing their job, but I'm doing my job, too, which is running a television factory, not a laboratory. I'd like to have a new materials system, a new scheduling system. But we ask, "Where are they? Are they running?" For the last two years, the answer has been, "No, but just wait a bit."
>
> We never had any visits from corporate SSD until they decided that we needed SASS. They don't understand a "small" factory like us. Frankfurt has not been very much help either. They give us advice, but they can't help us with SASS. ICIL has been helpful in the conversion, loaning us personnel and assisting us with retraining.
>
> Our EDP staff does not have much depth. Two programmers were advanced from the clerical staff, two had short courses before they came here, one came here from corporate SSD. We hope to finish program translation in June 1974 and have four months to test and run. SASS could not be installed until five months later, at the earliest.
>
> The real cost saving will be using a ICIL computer instead of an IBM; not in using SASS instead of our old system. By 1976 we expect to be saving over Skr 1 million.
>
> I am responsible for the livelihood of a lot of people. So we'll convert computers first, using our existing software concepts. Only later will we then move to standard software.

The German national SSD in Frankfurt, which advised and supported the Münster SSD, had conflicting feelings about SASS in Germany. Frankfurt's major responsibilities were computer operations and routine programming, but they had often commented to corporate SSD formally and informally about the design of SASS and its implementation in Germany. No formal response to these remarks had ever been received. A major disagreement concerned the practicality of a development effort which took place outside the country and with little communication with the ultimate user. Frankfurt was unhappy about the loss of authority to corporate headquarters and contributed reluctantly to the impending transition at Münster which would result from the German changeover in computers.

Corporate SSD strongly supported and promoted SASS for philosophical and for pragmatic reasons. Corporate policy encouraged software standardization wherever feasible; the intent was to provide better systems at lower cost by eliminating duplicate effort and by making better use of personnel. Installations following the first one might achieve 50 percent less expensive installations. A particular concern in this case was the knowledge that the current line of ICIL computers would be superseded by a new line in 1978–80 which might differ substantially from the old. If most factories at that time were using the same or similar software, conversion problems would be substantially lessened. The anticipated operational advantages such as a general trend to worldwide standards for nomenclature (in parts lists, for example) would facilitate intercompany transactions and personnel transfers. The long-range objective of coordination and consolidation of operations would be promoted.

More pragmatically, SSD's policy of system development from the top down without substantial user input, as in the case of SASS, had come under some criticism. Users especially believed that this approach lessened the usefulness of the system. Furthermore, the SASS project had gone over its budget and there was criticism on this account. As most of the design effort and much of the programming was completed, corporate SSD felt that SASS could be quickly put into wide use, which would abate much of the criticism.

Mr. Eriksson of the Television Division SSD was emphatic in stating his opinions about SASS:

> Landfors has a number of legitimate concerns about potential risks. I wish I could convince him that the payoffs are sufficiently high for him to take these risks. Sure, he'll have a few problems. But he has to convert his computer anyway. Why not convert the hardware and the system together. He'll save money on conversion and he'll have a better system sooner. I've got 10 more factories to convert after Münster. I can't afford to be stopped now. I have enough trouble already keeping corporate SSD working on my problems and keeping them away from the other product divisions, trying to sell it there. Imagine the confusion if the Small Appliances Division suddenly came into it and started making changes.
>
> Corporate SSD hasn't done a good job selling SASS so the national SSDs and the factories naturally resist. First, because they didn't invent it; then because they have to modify their normal operating procedures a little to use it.
>
> I would like to be the first product division to use it and get full support from SSD and ICIL. I haven't spent anything yet, except the salaries for a half dozen

of my people. I wouldn't want to be the second product division to convert though. Most of the same problems, but none of the support.

The market is getting more and more competitive. We need tight international control to survive in this business. Standard systems allow this, because we will soon be able to query the data base in any factory from Stockholm to see what they've got and what they're doing with it.

What is it worth to cut lead times one month, to speed up production and to cut inventory? I don't know. But certainly a lot more than it costs to install SASS.

SCHMIDT'S VIEWPOINT

In evaluating the various alternatives, Mr. Schmidt had summarized the advantages and disadvantages of SASS compared to the present system if translated one-for-one to ICIL hardware (Exhibit 5).

The biggest advantage appeared to be standardization. A single system supported by corporate staff would reduce the burden on his own small staff, a very heavy burden in light of their limited backgrounds. Going straight to SASS would also eliminate a double conversion. Furthermore, if another

EXHIBIT 5 □ Pros and Cons of Immediate Conversion to SASS

Advantages	Disadvantages
Uniform corporate program.	Not yet complete.
Avoid duplicate development effort.	Certain standard modules not yet available, must write temporary custom modules (estimated at 10 percent).
Savings on system maintenance.	
Standard portions updated by corporate SSD.	Conversion three times as expensive.
Easier conversion in the future.	Only 50 percent of eventual system standard.
Uniform software and hardware means new software will be supplied with new hardware.	Will need 50 percent permanent custom modules.
Newer conceptual basis.	Factory procedures must be modified.
Development started from zero in 1968.	Must institute closed stores.
	No firm completion date.
	No prior experience on in-house computer.
	Greater risk because of above factors.

conversion to new hardware were later required, the corporate staff would be able to handle the entire process. Finally, SASS was a more up-to-date system than the local system. Rumor had it that some of the local modules had run on IBM 650s.

The major disadvantage of SASS seemed to be that it was untested and only about half finished. Although Köln was converting to SASS with apparent equanimity, they had operated an in-house ICIL computer for over one year (and IBM machines for four years before that). Furthermore, they had participated in the early stages of planning SASS.

The schedule developed by corporate SSD for the direct conversion at Münster allowed minimal overlap for parallel operation of SASS and the IBM 2780—360/50. If the terminal were removed before SASS was operational, there would be serious difficulties. A different sort of disadvantage concerned the organization of SASS relative to the organization of the factory. SASS was designed, for instance, for factories with closed stocks (in which stocks are logged in on receipt and logged out on withdrawal—a common system in a large multiproduct factory); however, Münster had an open stock and kept no record of stock withdrawals. What dislocation would be required to adapt the factory to the system and whether it was worthwhile were unanswered questions.

On economic grounds, the situation was clearer. The Münster conversion plans for one-to-one conversion and those submitted by corporate SSD for direct conversion could be easily compared.

Münster's plans ran from September 1, 1973, to June 30, 1974; during an ensuing three-and-a-half-month test phase, output from both systems would be compared for consistency and accuracy. In-house analysts and programmers, assisted by four ICIL personnel, would perform the work in an estimated 500 man-days and 365 machine-hours.

The plan proposed by ICIL would start in November 1973 and conclude in November 1974. It would use one half the in-house staff assisted by two analysts from corporate SSD, 2 from Television SSD, and two from ICIL. This effort was estimated at 1,000 man-days. Concurrent running would be possible for only two thirds of the modules in SASS.

Approximately 200 man-days were required to convert either of the other programs. Thus it was clear that the SASS conversion was three times as expensive as the one-to-one conversion in terms of out-of-pocket charges to Münster unless many conversion costs were subsidized by ICIL. Nevertheless, the SASS conversion would eventually be required.

Case 9–2 □ Singapore Bus Service, Ltd.*

In late July 1981, Mr. Mah Bow Tan, general manager of the Singapore Bus Service, was concerned about the organizational placement and control of the company's data processing activity. Well satisfied with the progress which had been made in the past two years, he saw a series of new problems emerging which he felt required resolution if progress was to be continued in the data processing activity.

COMPANY BACKGROUND

The Singapore Bus Service (hereafter referred to as SBS) is probably the world's largest publicly held bus company. Sales for 1980 were $264,818,000,[1] with profits after tax of $6 million. Exhibits 1 and 2 contain copies of the company's income statement and balance sheet for 1979 and 1980. To further strengthen the company's capital position, and provide for future growth in early 1981, additional stock was sold which raised $74 million of equity. At present the company, with 11,800 employees, is the largest private employer in Singapore. (This includes 8,300 bus crew drivers and conductors, 2,100 workshop staff, and 1,400 others, including ticket inspectors, timekeepers, and administrative staff.) Carrying 815 million riders in 1980, the company has 3,000 buses. During the next five years, to

EXHIBIT 1

SINGAPORE BUS SERVICE, LTD.
Profit and Loss Account
For the Years Ended 31st December
($000)

	1979	1980
Turnover	229,433	264,818
Operating profit	19,084	10,065
Share of loss of associated company	(170)	(31)
Profit before taxation	18,914	10,034
Profit for taxation	(7,700)	(4,037)
Net profit	11,214	5,997

* This case was prepared as a basis for class discussion rather than to illustrate either effective or ineffective handling of an administrative situation.

[1] All numbers in the case are in Singapore dollars. In July 1981, one U.S. dollar equaled 2.15 Singapore dollars.

EXHIBIT 2

SINGAPORE BUS SERVICE, LTD.
Balance Sheet
($000)

	1979	1980
Assets		
Cash	14,546	34,429
Accounts receivable	7,801	10,486
Inventory	12,817	15,085
Investments	1,346	12,710
Fixed assets	108,759	132,300
Total assets	148,269	205,010
Liabilities and net worth		
Accounts payable	33,658	44,970
Short-term debt	—	13,940
Taxes payable	11,600	8,792
Miscellaneous accruals	1,395	3,032
Long-term debt	5,000	29,021
Deferred taxes	13,200	17,237
Capital stock	67,057	67,057
Retained earnings	16,359	
		20,961
Total liabilities and net worth	148,269	209,010

Note: These statements, based on historic accounting principles, are generally prepared in accordance with generally accepted U.S. accounting principles. The debt is payable in equal semiannual payments through 1987.

accelerate fleet modernization and provide for growth, it is expected that an additional 1,000 buses will be acquired. At present, *the company has a 95 percent market* share, with its only competition being two small companies who provide daytime service only on some of the densely populated routes. (Franchises to operate public bus services are under the control of government, who also control fares.)

In 1971, Singapore had 11 privately held bus companies. Through a series of mergers, by 1973 these private companies had been merged into SBS. In late 1974, to help the then struggling company, some 40 government officers were seconded to the company to help it out. By 1981, most of these employees had become permanent members of SBS. The executive director and general manager (see Exhibit 3 for organization chart), however, were still on secondment from government service. The company has had generally amiable union relations with no strikes since its 1974 formation. The stock of the company is widely held among some 26,000 shareholders. (To encourage widespread support in the community, it has been sold in 500-share lots. People were encouraged to buy shares with their funds in the

EXHIBIT 3 □ Corporate Structure

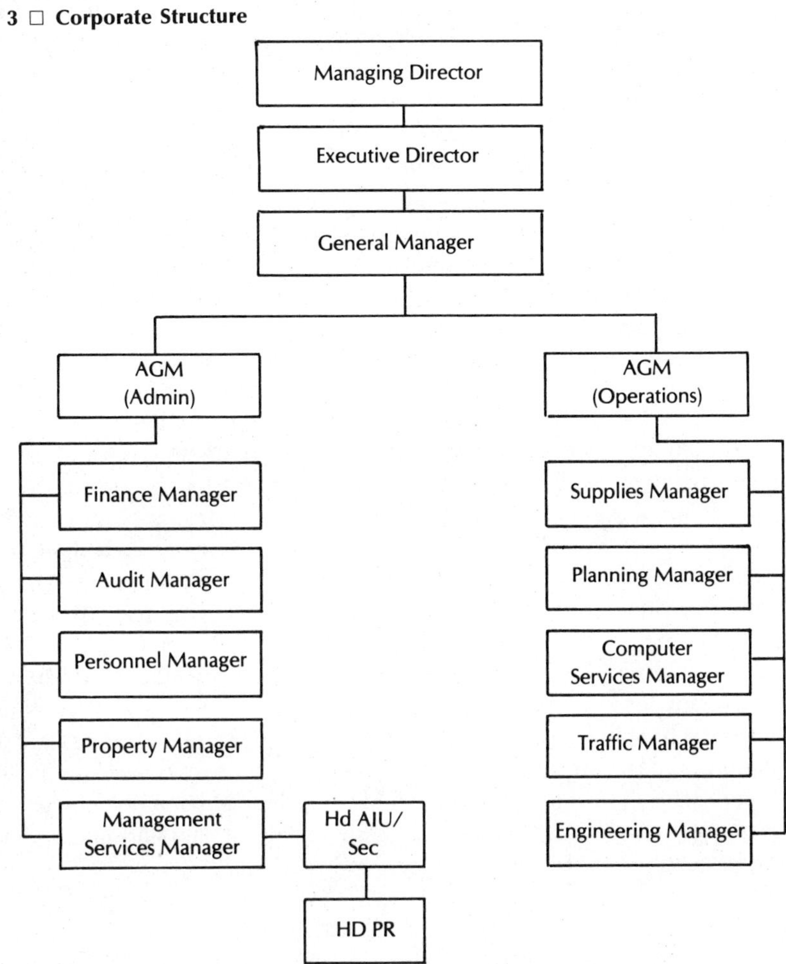

Central Provident Fund [roughly equivalent to U.S.A. Social Security]. Unlike the United States, however, money may be withdrawn from one's account before retirement for either a house purchase *or* for shares in SBS.) The board of directors, active in the supervision of the company, includes senior business and government leaders and a union leader, as well as the managing director and executive director.

SINGAPORE BACKGROUND

Located in southeast Asia, Singapore is an island of some 224 square miles located off the coast of Malaysia. It is densely populated, having a population of some 2.5 million people that is growing at a rate of 1.2 percent per year. Founded in 1965, when it split from Malaysia, the country has undergone steady and dramatic growth, with a per capita income of $9,282, and is one of the most dynamic business centers in the world. Key to this has been a stable government and very careful control over land use. Concerned about being overrun by cars (currently there is one car per 16 Singaporeans) the country has very heavy import duties on new cars (averaging 60 percent of purchase price), heavy annual taxes on a car (about $1,000/year), and there is a very attractive incentive when one buys a new car to either scrap the old car or sell it off Singapore. In addition, during morning rush hours, access to the core of the city is forbidden to cars carrying less than four people unless a special license is purchased and displayed on the vehicle. These factors have created a strong base demand for bus service. While the idea of mass transit subway service is being continually studied, no definitive actions have been taken to go forward on this. The view of SBS management on this is that whatever steps are taken, the role of SBS in providing the backbone of public transport in Singapore will continue.

As part of an effort to transform the economy away from manual labor-intensive industries, to more sophisticated higher-value-added industries, the National Wage Council has permitted wages to rise at a rate of 20 percent per year in each of 1979, 1980, and 1981 (putting labor-intensive companies similar to SBS under enormous cost pressures). The basic business language of Singapore is English, and the country has strong university and technical schools, which annually take in about 5 percent of the appropriate age groups (about 15 percent of Singaporeans graduate from high school). While greater emphasis is being given to Chinese in the schools, continued training and skill in English appears assured for the foreseeable future.

DATA PROCESSING IN SINGAPORE

In 1981, development of competence in data processing had become a matter of great national significance. Not only had the soaring wage rates, and external competitive conditions created a strong domestic need for far greater utilization of this technology, but the hope existed in some quarters that Singapore could grow to become a software hub of southeastern Asia. At present, some 450 installations of DP equipment exist in Singapore (most of them very small). Currently, about two thirds of the large computers are located in the government as well as a preponderance of the most highly trained analysts and programmers. This is because the most gifted students in Singapore who score A's on their A-level exams (given at age 17–18) are given the opportunity to study at full government expense either abroad or locally for their bachelor's and/or master's degrees. In return, they are bonded to work for their government for five to eight years upon return. (After completion of their bond, a significant percentage leave the government.) While the first computer was acquired in 1963, it was not until the mid-1970s that their use began to expand dramatically. A critical limitation is that, at present, there are only about 1,000 systems analysts and programmer professionals in Singapore. To respond to these shortages, four important initiatives have been undertaken.

1. IBM and the Singapore government have cooperated to set up an Institute of Systems Science, attached to the National University of Singapore, to train systems and programmer professionals. To be operational in September 1981, it hopes to train 150 professionals each year, in a year-long course. This project was initiated by the Singapore government.
2. The Japanese computer industry is cooperating with the Singapore government to develop a training institute for some 50 programmers per year beginning sometime in 1982. The initiative for this came from the Japanese government, and Nippon Electric Corporation is acting as their primary coordinator by providing staff, equipment, and training. At present, some 60 Japanese minicomputers are installed in various Singapore companies (mostly in the last 18 months). A prominent government official noted that Singapore, with its close proximity to Japan and its English competence, represented an ideal opportunity for the Japanese to develop software skills which could then be transferred to other English-speaking areas.
3. The Singapore government has allocated funds to ensure that all high schools can get their own computers and to encourage the universities to begin to offer professional courses in the area.
4. Establishment of the National Computer Board inside the government, under the leadership of Philip Yeo, permanent secretary of the ministry of defense (Harvard MBA 1976). Its functions are fourfold:
   a. Management of a pool of 400 systems and programming professionals by 1985 (120 in 1981) to work with the various ministries to automate their operations. (In addition, a wholly owned government software house, SCS, with about 100 employees, would continue to work on a variety of software projects.)
   b. Establishment of national accreditation systems for DP professionals, similar to those prepared by the British Computer Society.
   c. Encourage and shape the development of government incentives to spur the development of software firms.
   d. Stimulate professional training programs and establishment of career development institutions. These educational efforts will all take time.

Regarding hardware, the medium- and large-scale computer market is dominated by IBM. Outside of UNIVAC's installation at the telecommunication authority, and several Amdahl VS-5s, the major equipment base consists of 40 4331s and 3–5 3031s. At the same time, there has been dramatic proliferation in minis and micros, both through the explosion of small software houses springing up (local companies as well as branches of large international companies such as Informatics) and through vendors such as Apple, DEC, and Hewlett-Packard, who are setting up their own distribution networks. At present, some 10 mini-micro computer vendors are operating in Singapore. A further element of importance is the very strong, highly reliable telephone and telecommunications network present in Singapore which tremendously facilitates data communication. (It is not unknown, for example, for an Indonesian businessman, with a number of overseas calls to make, to find it cost effective to make the one-hour plane flight to Singapore to place the calls.) Data communication, however, still had to take place on leased lines and were not allowed on the public switched telephone network. Active investment was occurring in word processors in 1981 but other items, such as (facsimile transmission is widely available) electronic mail were a long way into the future.

A final element of importance was existence of the strong National Computer Society, with some 450 professional members. Under the leadership of Robert Iau (managing director of the Singapore Land Development Corporation, and former general manager of the Central Provident Fund) it conducted a number of professional training sessions and maintained close links with major overseas organizations such as IFIPS.

SBS CHALLENGES FOR THE 1980S

In talking about the key tasks facing SBS in the next five years, Mr. Mah Bow Tan noted the following items as being critical:

1. The need for heavy capital investment to modernize the fleet and gain economies in both fuel efficiency and maintenance as well as better uptime. The older buses which predate the formation of SBS pose significant problems of diversified maintenance.
2. Gain additional operating economies through the continued conversion of two-man buses (driver and conductor) to one-man buses. This was made necessary by a 20 percent increase in salaries authorized by the NWC in each of the past three years.
3. Intensified efforts on better cost control and economies. Better utilization of existing reserves, better maintenance of buses (less breakdowns, reduced smoke and noise pollution), and tighter management of inventories are all critical items to maintain profitability in a difficult environment and defer unpopular fare increases as long as possible.

4. Evolve even better service. While maintenance of perfect service and zero customer complaints is impossible, continued efforts in this area are critical to maintaining public support for the service. (A service such as SBS is forever vulnerable to attacks in the newspapers from a small number of dissatisfied users whose concerns can be magnified out of proportion.)
5. Continue the orderly transition from government involvement in SBS to a fully autonomous independent management team. Items 2, 3, and 4 were all items where Mr. Mah Bow Tan felt electronic data processing would be able to make a contribution.

COMPANY ORGANIZATION

Exhibit 3 shows the basic organization chart of SBS, while Exhibit 4 describes the general functions of each of the divisions. The managing

EXHIBIT 4 □ Brief Functional Descriptions

Finance	Development and operation of financial control system. Include normal functions of budgeting, treasury and controllership.
Audit	Manager internal audits (including DP audit) and links to external auditor.
Personnel	Responsible for overall personnel policies of the company. Functions include recruiting, establishment and management of compensation levels, and training.
Property	Responsible for building depots, maintenance work on the depots, and other construction-related work.
Management services	This includes the company secretary function, accident investigation, supervision of security guards, issuance of special fare reduction passes, printing and stationery, and public relations.
Supplies	This covers purchasing of supplies, management of supply rooms for all spare parts, and inventory control policies.
Planning	Long-term planning for route structures, broad architecture of schedules (including level of bus needs), and new depot construction.
Computer services	Responsible for operation of computer facility, data input operations, and all systems and programming activities.
Traffic manager	Controls all seven depots. Responsible for bus dispatching and road operations, employee time keeping, driving inspectors (check for ticket fraud and driving skills), and detailed schedule construction.
Engineering	Responsible for maintenance and repair of vehicles.

director, executive director, and general manager, not only acted as an executive committee headed by the nonexecutive chairman of the board to deal with important policy issues, but each took primary responsibility for supervising several of the functional units. Mr. Tan Kong Eng, the managing director (he was managing director of one of the bus companies prior to the 1974 merger), took primary responsibility for finance, audit, management services (including security guards and company secretary), and public relations. Mr. Lim Leong Geok, the Executive Director, who had been seconded from a government position in the public works department since February 1979, had primary responsibility for planning and property. In recent months, he was heavily involved in the government-initiated study as to what the role (if any) of mass transit should be. Mr. Mah Bow Tan, general manager, had been seconded to SBS since 1974. He had responsibility for supply, computer services, traffic, engineering, and personnel. In July 1981, although the two assistant general managers' jobs had been authorized, neither as yet had been filled. With the exception of the computer services manager, Mr. Wan Wee Jiun; property manager, Mr. Lim Yong Chua; and management services manager, Mr. Kelvin Kwok, the other managers indicated on the lower part of Exhibit 3 had been with the company since 1974.

DATA PROCESSING AT SBS

Data processing at SBS had begun in 1975 with the lease of a UNIVAC 90/30 computer and the automation of the waybill system on a turnkey basis by UNIVAC personnel. (The initial automation strategy was to start with the large data-intensive applications first.) At that time, the computer department reported to the planning manager. Exhibit 5 indicates key highlights in the subsequent six-year history of DP at SBS.

In early 1979, as progress continued on these transactions-oriented operational systems, senior management became concerned as to whether the data processing activity's development was on an appropriate trajectory to meet the needs of the company in the 1980s. Accordingly, Mr. Mah Bow Tan, then SBS's engineering manager, was asked to head a DP committee to review the current position of the company and establish future direction. The committee members included the DP managers, the special project manager (a recent MBA graduate) and the financial accountant. This committee, over a five-month period, working on a part-time basis, undertook the following activities:

1. Reviewed the efficiency and appropriateness of current applications. They also examined potential application areas for computerization, established priorities among them, and suggested an appropriate time frame for implementation (see Exhibit 6 for an overview of the plan).

EXHIBIT 5 □ Historical Highlights

Timing	Staffing	System	Progress
August 1975	1 systems analyst, 2 programmers	Waybills system	Turnkey job by UNIVAC. We did the parallel run.
January 1976	1 systems analyst, 2 programmers, 30 operations staff		Formalization of EDP department. Set up complete Operations Section with 3 subsections. Operations staff about 30. Installation of computer. Implemented WBS.
April 1976	1 systems analyst, 2 programmers, 30 operations staff	Fleet information system	A fleet register masterfile was maintained to keep track of buses in all depots and also the bus miles operated for monitoring of usage of the fleet.
January 1977	5 systems staff 40 operations staff	Payroll–personnel daily staff	Implemented daily-rated staff payroll (with partial personnel information).
January 1978	8 systems staff 50 operations staff	Payroll–personnel monthly staff	Implemented monthly-rated staff payroll (with partial personnel information).
January 1979	12 systems staff 60 operations staff	Payroll–personnel bus crew Fleet information system General ledger	Implemented bus crew payroll. Implemented fleet information/preventive maintenance module. Implemented general ledger.
July 1979	12 systems staff 60 operations staff	Inventory control system	Implemented inventory control/consumption and replenishment modules with implementation of SBS's own stock codes.
January 1980	12 systems staff 60 operations staff	Inventory control system	Computer Services upgraded to division level. Implemented inventory control/provisioning and purchasing modules.
January 1981	18 systems staff 70 operations staff	—	Completion of conversion to IBM. Installation of IBM machine Model 4331.
July 1981	18 systems staff 70 operations staff	Inventory control system	* Inventory control/Online inquiry.
September 1981	18 systems staff 70 operations staff	Inventory control system	* Inventory control/Online update.
December 1981	18 systems staff 70 operations staff	Personnel information system Accounts receivable system Scheduling system Fuel monitoring system	* Personnel information. * Accounts receivable. * Scheduling. * Fuel monitoring.

Note: Asterisks indicate targeted.

EXHIBIT 6 □ Work Plan

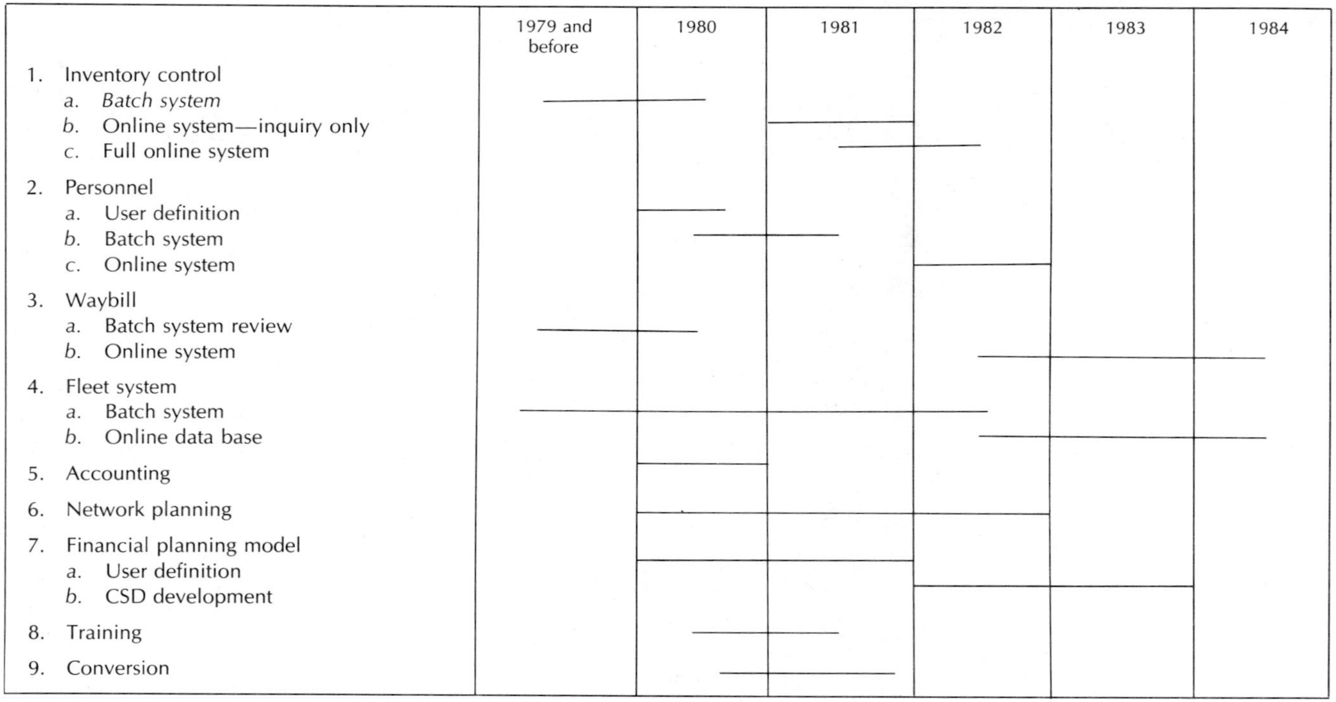

	1979 and before	1980	1981	1982	1983	1984
1. Inventory control						
a. *Batch system*						
b. Online system—inquiry only						
c. Full online system						
2. Personnel						
a. User definition						
b. Batch system						
c. Online system						
3. Waybill						
a. Batch system review						
b. Online system						
4. Fleet system						
a. Batch system						
b. Online data base						
5. Accounting						
6. Network planning						
7. Financial planning model						
a. User definition						
b. CSD development						
8. Training						
9. Conversion						

This included interviews with 30 current users. This plan, together with its estimated costs, was presented to both the executive committee and the board of directors, each of which, after appropriate discussion and some modification, endorsed both the direction and size of expenditures. These discussions were greatly facilitated by the presence of Mr. Robert Iau on the board. His vast experience in DP, combined with his position as the president of the National Computer Society, gave him a unique perspective on DP-related issues in Singapore.

2. Identified that achievement of these goals required a stronger, more experienced technically, and managerially oriented leadership. A job search was initiated which led to the hiring in early 1980 of Mr. Wan Wee Jiun as the new computer services manager. An experienced DP professional, Mr. Wan had started as a programmer on an IBM 1401 in 1968 in the Singapore Ministry of Defense. Moving from there to Keppel Shipyard and then to the Singapore Telecommunications Authority, he had served in a variety of management positions, including computer operations manager, computer systems manager, and data base manager. During the last seven years, he had been working in a UNIVAC 1100/12 installation.
3. Increased the reporting level of Mr. Wan to report directly to Mr. Mah who had become assistant general manager. Consequently, Mrs. Esther Yap's reporting level did not change.

DP 1980–1981

Under Mr. Wan's direction, a reappraisal of SBS's technical direction was undertaken, leading to a decision to replace the UNIVAC hardware with an IBM 4331. (This decision was heavily influenced by IBM's overwhelming market share in Singapore and UNIVAC's gap there in medium-sized computers.) The machine acquired was a 4331-Group 1, one megabyte internal memory, two 3262 printers (600 lines/minute), four 3310 disk drives, and two 8809 tape drives. The basic operating system is DOS/VS-E, and CICS is used for online systems.

At present, about 70 percent of the 4331 two-shift capacity was utilized. (This situation was expected to sharply change when the full online inventory system came up in January 1982.) Current capacity utilization is:[2]

Waybill system	25%
Payroll	15
Inventory (batch)	10
Accounting and fleet information system	10
Testing	10
Unused	30

[2] Estimates provided by Mr. Wan.

Mr. Wan noted that if DP became a service bureau operation, a much more sophisticated measurement system would have to be installed.

Orders were also placed for an upgrade to an IBM 4331 Group 2 and additional disk capacity to deal with future growth. Fortunately, because of the air conditioning in place, no investment was needed here. Mr. Wan elected not to invest in UPS (Uninterrupted Power Supply) because of the huge expense and the reliability of Singapore power supply. With the assistance of a local software company, all the UNIVAC source code programs (mostly COBOL) were converted to IBM code, and by early 1981 the new IBM gear had been installed and the umbilical cord severed to both UNIVAC hardware and software. All programming work was being done either in COBOL or RPG (RPG was limited only to general ledger—an acquired package). Total DP expenditures in 1981 were anticipated to be about $1,700,000, about equally divided between hardware and software.[3]

DP STAFF

Exhibit 7 shows the current organization chart of DP. With the development/programming staff of 20, in 1981 the company was enduring turnover rates of 30 percent/year. (While turnover rates had been stable in the period 1975–78, since then they had skyrocketed.) The tenure of 70 percent of the staff in mid-1981 was one and a half years or less. A major cause of the turnover in Mr. Wan's opinion was SBS's salary policy which kept DP in line with other staff salaries in SBS but which produced numbers about 30 percent below going market wages. (Staff salaries were heavily a function of years of work experience and level of academic training.) An appropriate market price for five-year programmers was $2,000–$2,500/month and for analysts, $2,500–$3,500/month. Personnel was very reluctant, however, to upset the company's existing salary structure. In the interim and as a partial solution in 1981, Mr. Wan had already hired five trainees and with a 70 percent subsidy for training expense from the Skills Development Fund[4] had put them through a three-month training course. In return for this training, each had signed a two-year bond (a common Singapore practice). If they left the company within two years of the completion of training, all salary and training expenses had to be refunded to the company. While equally severe turnover (40 percent/year) was taking place on the data entry side, Mr. Wan viewed this as unavoidable because of both the age of the employees and SBS's seven-day/week schedule which forced them to schedule operators on a five-days-on and one-day-off basis (normal work schedule in Singapore is

[3] This compares to $1,200,000 in 1980.

[4] The Skills Development Fund was set up by the government to encourage firms to upgrade the skills of their staff through more advanced training.

EXHIBIT 7 □ Computer Services Division—Organization Chart, 1981

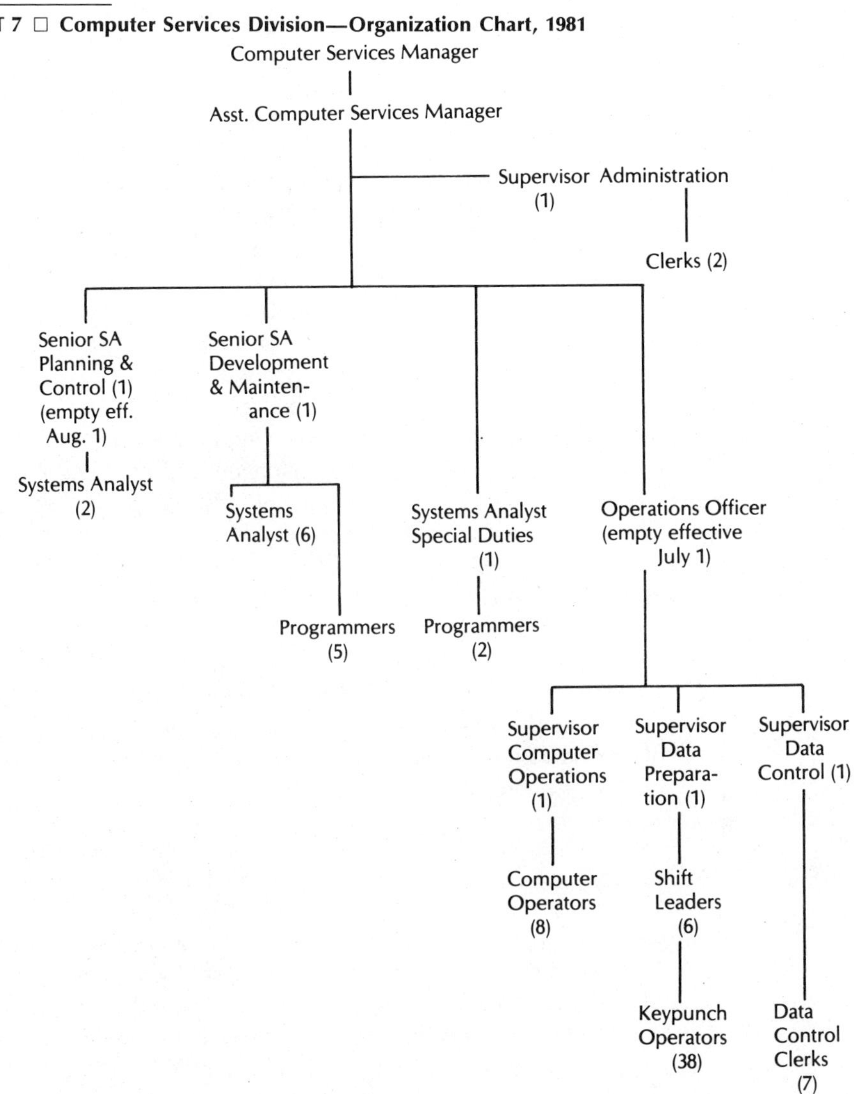

a 5 1/2-day week). Development of staff cohesion and good documentation practices was complicated by the fact that 50 percent of the development staff had relatively poor English (they came through the Chinese stream of the local schools). While this did not impact their coding work, it made them unenthusiastic about English documentation. While the company had recently adopted NCC standards, Mr. Wan saw practical problems in their implementation.

SENIOR MANAGEMENT INVOLVEMENT

As a divisional manager, Mr. Wan attended the monthly half-day staff meeting of all people listed on Exhibit 3, where status updates of key projects and operational difficulties of all units were reported and discussed. At this meeting, he gave approximately a 5- to 10-minute update on DP issues. In addition, he would meet formally twice a month for a half hour to an hour to brief Mr. Mah on progress of key projects. In addition, he frequently had lunch with him and other division managers. The conversation at these luncheons, however, was almost exclusively focused on personal issues. In addition, for key projects, a user steering committee was established which was chaired by the appropriate user manager as shown on Exhibit 3. In July 1981, three such steering committees were active. These were the inventory task force, chaired by the supplies manager, the personnel task force chaired by the personnel manager, and the fleet information task force chaired by the engineering manager. This support was critical, as understandably there was significant clerical resistance to change in general. There were as well the more specific items of better handwriting requirements needed by automation. This was in spite of a clearly articulated SBS policy that no jobs would be lost because of automation. In addition, Mr. Wan prepared two-page monthly status reports which were sent to Mr. Mah. In both Mr. Mah's and Mr. Wan's judgment this level of user relations was appropriate for the support role which DP was playing in SBS. No need was seen for the establishment of a corporate steering committee.

PROJECT MANAGEMENT

Project management relied heavily on informal manager supervision with no formal methodologies in place, although Mr. Wan planned to send several of his analysts to courses on project management later in 1981. Every week each project manager filled out a brief project progress summary for Mr. Wan so he would be updated on all important items. At present, there were five development (as opposed to maintenance) projects under way, the largest of which had three people working on it. All of them were scheduled to be completed within a year. No project controls were kept on maintenance jobs which occurred throughout the year.

MANAGEMENT CONTROL

At present, DP is managed as a cost center and no effort is made to charge out costs to key users. Basic control is exerted in the budgeting process through establishment of staff levels to meet anticipated development and maintenance needs and through approval of hardware purchase and leasing decisions. In addition, there are monthly cost versus budget reports which are reviewed by both Mr. Wan and Mr. Mah. Practically, within this framework basic development priority tradeoffs are made by DP. Similarly, because of the relative simplicity of the work stream, all scheduling decisions were handled daily by the computer operations supervisor.

PLANNING

At present, the basic guiding document is the plan prepared in 1979 which extended through the end of 1983. As experience in the time to develop projects has been gained, and as a clearer understanding of the implications of what the technology can do has developed, some applications (such as financial modeling) have been deferred. These changes, however, have been relatively modest. In Mr. Mah's view, 18 to 24 months from now, it will be appropriate to stop and go through a planning effort similar in scope and detail to that which was done in 1978–79. Exhibit 8 shows the January 1, 1981, plan for 1981. Exhibit 9 shows key priorities for 1980–84.

TECHNICAL INNOVATION

Although in July 1981 nearly all work on the 4331 was batch oriented, this was due for almost immediate change. In January 1981 four terminals had been acquired to support the programmers, a move which was not only popular with the programmers but was acknowledged to have improved productivity. On August 1 an online inventory status system was to be installed at headquarters (online access to files which would update daily on batch systems). By the end of the year, this system was to be extended to all seven depots. During 1982 the files were to be converted to an approach where they would also be updated online. At the same time the first steps to online systems were being made (integrated data base management was still considered to be three or more years in the future) SBS had just acquired its first microcomputer, an Apple with the VISICALC package. Mr. Wan felt both the package and hardware were sound and would clearly support finance's budgeting process. Mr. Mah noted that this was the only mini or micro present in SBS (he felt the budgeting and purchasing process was sufficiently tight that no other equipment of this sort could be acquired without management approval) and that Mr. Wan would be involved to provide a technical insight to all such future acquisitions. While no word processing equipment had yet been acquired, Mr. Wan was just finishing a

EXHIBIT 8 □ 1981 Plan

2 *Work Plan 1981*

2.1 *Installation of the New IBM 4331 Computer*

2.1.1 The new IBM 4331 computer system will be installed in January 81. Parallel running of the new and old computer systems will be carried out until the end of February 81 when the old Univac machine will be returned.

2.1.2 As the mode of operation of the new computer system is more advanced, featuring concurrent multiple batch, interactive, and online processing, new standards of operation will be formulated to optimize system performance in the following areas:

a. Job scheduling and production.
b. Program development and testing.
c. File storage, privacy, and security.
d. Usage of computer resources.

2.2 *Inventory Control System*

Following the completion of the batch system, design of the online system commenced in January 81. The system will be implemented in two phases:

a. Phase A in July 81. This will enable the online retrieval of information from computer terminals related to inventory management, such as stock balances in the various stores, status of outstanding purchase orders with suppliers, consumption history, etc.
b. Phase B in November 81. This will enable the immediate updating of the masterfiles via computer terminals with information related to the movement of stocks.

2.3 *Personnel Information System*

2.3.1 The task force has already determined the broad requirements of the system. Detailed system design is scheduled to start in March and the first phase is expected to be completed by December 81.

feasibility study recommending the acquisition of the first one for the Finance and Management Services divisions to allow them to more rapidly and efficiently prepare their numerous submissions to the board and government bodies. Mr. Wan hoped experience with this word processor would help plan how to move in the future and was awaiting approval from senior management.

EXHIBIT 8 *(concluded)*

2.3.2 Some of the areas to be covered by the system are:

a. Staff movement, job vacancies, and confirmation.
b. Staff performance—accident records, absenteeism, and disciplinary records.

2.4 *Scheduling System*

A study will be carried out in the first quarter of 1981 to determine the feasibility of computarizing the whole or parts of the system. Emphasis will be placed in areas where savings in manpower and speed in processing can be accomplished.

2.5 *Fleet Information System*

2.5.1 The updating of the fleet masterfile with more comprehensive data by Engineering Division is expected to be completed by mid-year.

2.5.2 Two modules of the system are scheduled for development during the year, subject to the recommendations of a feasibility study by the task force. The two modules are:

a. Fuel utilization.
b. Monitoring of the consumption of spares.

2.6 *Accounts Payable System*

Steps will be taken to integrate the procedures of the existing system with those of the Inventory Control System before the commencement of system development in the later half of the year.

2.7 *Waybill System*

The system will be modified to improve its operational efficiency especially with regard to its usage of computer resources.

AUDIT DEPARTMENT

The Audit Department was not only responsible for auditing the performance of DP to ensure the existence of appropriate controls but was involved in the design of new systems to ensure their auditability. Mr. Wan was concerned as to how this could be accomplished more effectively. DP was so relatively new to SBS that auditing was still struggling to come up with appropriate controls for batch systems. Online systems, of course, posed still different control problems. Development of appropriate procedures was clearly a very important task in Mr. Wan's view, who noted that this was not

EXHIBIT 9 □ Manpower Projection by Workload

	1980	1981	1982	1983	1984
1. Systems development and maintenance					
Inventory control	2	4	3	2	2
Personnel/payroll	4	3	3	2	2
Waybill	2	1	3	3	3
Fleet	2	2	3	5	4
Accounting	2	1	1	1	1
Network planning	1	2	2	2	2
Financial planning	0	0	2	2	2
2. Planning and control					
Review and control	3	3	3	3	3
Systems software	0	0	1	1	1
Data base administration	0	0	0	1	2
3. Conversion	0	4	0	0	0
	16	20	21	22	22

Notes: The approved strength for 1980 is 16.
The figures refer only to programmers, systems analysts, and senior systems analysts.

a unique SBS problem, but one of equal importance in other companies he was familiar with.

MR. WAN'S VIEW

In commenting on the management tasks in front of him, Mr. Wan noted his greatest challenge was in the area of manpower. High turnover, inadequate level of skills in the marketplace, and long lead times for training, he saw as the core set of issues he had to resolve. Project slippages, he felt, were inevitable in this environment. Fortunately, on the other hand, he felt that he had good support from the user management. Not only were they aware of his challenge but they were intimately involved in the overview of the management of key projects. Finally, he noted that the pressure on him was not intense because SBS's existing procedures were functioning smoothly and delays in installation of new procedures would not severely damage either the company's operations or profile.

MR. MAH BOW TAN'S VIEWS

Mr. Mah Bow Tan, while sharing many of Mr. Wan's concerns, was seriously considering whether spinning off the DP activity as a separate, wholly owned subsidiary might not be an appropriate way to move. Not only would it permit DP to solve its salary problems, but it would force it to come up with a way of charging its costs to the users, thus exposing it to the test of the marketplace and placing pressure on cost control. Such an approach, he felt, would encourage it to be both more efficient and effective. He further noted the possibility that this might become the nucleus of a service bureau operation for supporting other companies. He felt the rapid growth in interest in DP in Singapore offered a real market opportunity. Separated from the rest of the company, it would be easier to build an esprit de corps in the DP staff and thus help stabilize the situation even further. The ability to develop additional cash-generating capabilities through such a subsidiary would be of value to SBS as it faced a very competitive environment in the 1980s with consumer resistance to fare increases running directly into operational cost increases. He foresaw a market niche for them as a specialist in development of bus system software. He further noted that of necessity he had to rely heavily on Mr. Wan in developing IS (information services) strategy as the challenges posed by traffic and engineering consumed much of his time.

Chapter 10 □ The IS Business

Chapter \ Manageable Trend	Strategic Impact	DP/TP/OA	Organization Learning	Make/Buy	Life Cycle	GM/ User/ IS
IS Technology Organization Issues **Chapter 3**		●	●			●
Organizational Issues in IS Development **Chapter 4**	●		●	●		●
Information Systems Planning **Chapter 5**	●		●			●
IS Management Control **Chapter 6**	●		●	●		●
A Portfolio Approach to Information Systems Development **Chapter 7**	●				●	●
Operations Management **Chapter 8**	●			●	●	●
Multinational IS Issues **Chapter 9**		●				●
The IS Business **Chapter 10**	●		●	●		●

INTRODUCTION

The previous chapters laid out a series of frameworks for viewing the information systems activity and each function of IS management. In sum, the book specifies the concrete details as to how one should conduct an information system management audit for the organization. Our final chapter integrates these materials by highlighting the impact of our six major themes. We have chosen to view an organization's information systems activity as a stand-alone *business within a business* and, in particular, to apply the notions of the marketing mix analysis. This view, as will be described below, permits the development of a synthesis of the concepts of organization, planning, control, and strategy formulation for IS.

In this formulation, we will deal in depth with the issues of the marketing mix, strategy formulation, role of the steering committee as a board of directors, and the function of the IS director as the chief executive officer, because these items are particularly relevant in understanding the interface between the two businesses. We will not deal with the operational details of operating strategy, since many of the general elements of IS operations management have already been covered in Chapter 8. Similarly, issues of internal accounting and control within the IS organization will not be covered as they do not impact directly on the interface between the two businesses (IS business and host business). For similar reasons, only the portions of IS organization issues which deal with the IS business's external relations will be covered here.

The IS business is a high-technology and fast-changing business. Depending on the specific IS business one is dealing with, it may be a rapidly growing, more or less steady enterprise, or in a few cases, a declining business. The total territory of the IS business may be conceived as covering the development, maintenance, and operation of all IS technologies in a firm,[1] irrespective of where the various pieces are physically located or where they administratively report.

It is a business whose scope of technologies to be coordinated has expanded tremendously as computers, telecommunications, and office automation have all merged together, and whose product offerings are exploding into new consumer areas, such as electronic mail, editing, and computer-assisted design/computer-assisted manufacturing. The complexity of implementing projects, the magnitude of work to be done, and limited human resources have forced the IS business away from being a primarily production-oriented department to one where a significant percentage of its work is concerned with coordinating the acquisition of outside services for use by its customers (i.e., acting as a *distributor*). This shift has forced major changes in its approach to planning and controls in order to deal effectively with these new products and new sources of supply. Implicit in this formulation, as will be described below, is that, at least *at a policy level,* the overwhelming majority of firms require an integrated perspective and approach to IS activities. The IS activities include not just the corporate IS center and its directly linked networks but also the distributed islands of mini-micro-computers, distributed systems development activities, outside software company contracts, computer service bureaus, and so forth. *The various users of IS services may be considered to be its consumers,* who possess options in many cases to buy services other than directly from the central IS organization, as noted below.

We believe this formulation of the IS task permits the transfer of disciplines and ways of thinking in other aspects of managerial action to the IS function in a way which can generate new and useful insights. Similarly, as will be discussed below, for general management, we believe the analogy to

[1] Throughout this chapter, the term *firm* will refer to the parent holding company of the IS business.

the board of directors is a useful one in thinking through a realistic role for an executive steering committee and other aspects of how they should interface with the IS function. Like all analogies, this one can also be pushed too far and some caution must be taken. For example, the financing of the IS business has no analogy to the corporate capital markets, since its capital support comes directly from the parent firm (with no debt analogy), and its revenues, exclusively in many cases, also come directly from the parent. Similarly, the customer base in many respects is deeply interdependent on common files, etc., and so customers cannot be treated as being entirely independent. On the other hand the IS business is free from many of the legal and governmental constraints that the parent company has. Other legal and governmental constraints, such as the Equal Employment Opportunity Commission (EEOC), may be placed on it primarily in the context of the firm's total corporate posture, with little room or need for the IS business to strike an independent posture.

The rest of this chapter deals with three main topics relating to management of the IS business:

1. The IS marketing mix and its implications for managing the IS business.
2. The role of the IS board of directors and how it can best be managed.
3. The role of the IS chief executive officer.

THE IS MARKETING MIX

Product. The IS product line is a very rapidly changing and continuously evolving one. Exhibit 10–1 notes some of the key aspects of change.

EXHIBIT 10–1 □ IS Product-Line Changes

Past focus	Future
Developing new products	Heavy maintenance of old products meeting obsolescence challenges
Majority of manufacturing inside	Significant percent sourced from outside
Capital intensive (hardware economy of scale dominant need)	People intensive (economy of skill dominant need)
Product mix—mainly large, few medium, many small	Product mix—some large, many medium, thousands small
Strong return on investment	Many projects have intangible benefit justification
New technologies permit new products	New technologies and regroupings of old ones permit new products
Structured services, such as automated accounting and inventory control	Unstructured services, such as executive decision support systems and query systems

Part of the dynamism of the line stems from the enormous proliferation of opportunities afforded by the economics of new technology. The other element of dynamism stems both from changing customer needs as a result of ordinary shifts in business and from new insights (phase 2 learning) as to how this technology can be applied to their specific operations. The products range in size from very small to enormously large (in terms of both development time and complexity to operate on a day-in, day-out basis). The large products (usually a single, one-time customized effort) can have such a long lead time (four years, not dissimilar to rebuilding automobile manufacturing processes) that significant uncertainty exists whether it will really meet customers' needs (often evolving) at time of completion. While for some products, the possibility exists of delaying their introduction with limited damage, for other products, severe damage to consumers will occur if delays of any magnitude take place in development. In terms of day-to-day operations, wide variances exist in terms of the importance of cost, good response time, quality control, etc.

Product obsolescence is a major headache of the IS business. Changing consumer needs (made possible by new technologies) and new manufacturing technologies for existing products offer significant opportunities. The old products become so clumsy over time that it becomes more and more expensive to introduce the necessary enhancements (styling changes) to keep them relevant. In due course, a major factory retooling must be implemented.

The method of delivery of IS products is shifting as the IS customer changes sourcing decisions. As an increasing percentage of IS development expenditures goes to software houses and time-sharing vendors, and production expenditures go to stand-alone minis and micros, IS's role is shifting from one of being primarily a developer and *manufacturer,* to one where it is also a significant *distributor* of products manufactured by others. This distribution role involves identifying and evaluating alternate sources of supply (of both software and production) as well as professionally reviewing those identified by customers.

The products run the gamut from those where the need is clearly (and perhaps correctly) understood by customers and they are knocking down the door for the product (e.g., point-of-sales terminals) to those where there is no perceived need and where considerable and extended sales efforts must take place prior to a sale. They run the gamut from those which are absolutely essential and critical to the customers (inventory control systems) to those which are nice but whose purchase is essentially postponable. Projects at the two extremes require quite different sales approaches.

The situation is complicated by the difference in maturity in the competitive marketplaces for suppliers of different IS technologies. For example, a relatively stable competitive pattern has emerged for suppliers of large mainframe computers. Conversely, the supply side is very turbulent in the microcomputer and office automation markets, with considerable uncertainty as to who the winners will be and what the form of their product offerings will be five years in the future. A competitive pattern, however, is beginning to emerge here. In telecommunications, however, the recent AT&T divestiture has contributed to making the nature of competition very murky for the forseeable future.

Further in the past, monopoly control over product delivery gave IS businesses considerable discretion in timing the introduction of new products to their customers. The changed pattern of competition among suppliers means that in many organizations IS has lost control over the marketing of those products.

In terms of benefits, the products range from those where they can be crisply summarized in an ROI framework for the customer to those whose benefits are more qualitative and intangible in nature. Again, products at each end of the spectrum require a different marketing approach. Some products are absolutely cut-and-dried in focus (certain types of accounting data), while others must be tailored to influence individual tastes and preferences. Further, in many instances, the complexity of the product, and the inherent factors which influence quality, are not easily comprehended by many purchasers. (There are many parallels between the purchase of tires and IS systems.) Finally, some products require tailoring during field installation. These products need quite different field support and distribution staffs than the products without adaption requirements.

The above description of IS product characteristics captures the complexity of the IS marketing task. In terms of developing a marketing strategy, the IS business is one of distributing evolving products which are differentiated by a wide range of characteristics. In other businesses often a strong effort is made to rationalize the product line to permit economy of scale in manufacturing, plus focus and efficiency in distribution. It is the inability to accomplish this in many IS businesses that has contributed to the turbulence associated with their management. Too often they are trying to deliver many different types of products from their traditional monopoly-supplier position with weak promotion, surly sales, and a fixation of being a manufacturer (as opposed to a distributor, when appropriate). What works for one set of products often does not work for another. Recognizing the need for and implementing a differentiated marketing approach is very difficult, particularly for a medium-sized ($5–7 million budget) IS business.

IS Consumer. On many dimensions, the IS consumer is changing in terms of both needs and sophistication. Exhibit 10–2 captures a number of important aspects of these changes. The older consumers, after 20 years of working with the mature technologies, have some sensitivity to the problems of working within their constraints. They are often quite unaware of the newer technologies and the enormous behavioral modifications they must

EXHIBIT 10-2 □ IS Consumer Profile Changes

Older consumers	Younger consumers
Experienced with older technologies	Inexperienced in older technologies
Leery of newer technologies	Unsophisticated in newer technologies (but they do not know it)
Identifiable	Often unidentifiable; many more; are at all levels in organizations
Willing to accept IS as experts	Often hostile to IS; wants to develop their own solutions.
Low confidence in their own abilities (often cautious buyers because of cost)	High confidence in their abilities and judgment (often unwarranted)
High turnover rate	High turnover rate

make if they are to use them properly. They bring their old purchasing habits to the new environment, without understanding that it is new. The younger consumers, on the other hand, have close familiarity with personal computing and are more intolerant of the inability to get immediate access to it. They also are quite naive about the problems of designing and maintaining information service systems which must run on a regular basis. This generation gap suggests that both classes of consumer have major, but different personal educational needs if they are to be responsible consumers.

The new technologies have made the problem more complicated because many consumers see the opportunity to withdraw from reliance on the IS business and set up their own small business. They are often propelled in this direction by their own entrepreneurs or purchasing agents (i.e., decentralized systems analysts) who are long in hope and short in practical firsthand expertise and realistic risk assessment.

A real challenge to the IS marketing force, in this world of evolving technology, is to assess who the target new consumers are and reach them before they begin to make their own independent decisions. New application clusters and groups of consumers keep rushing to the surface.

Volatility in the consumer composition creates a sustained need for a field sales force. An effective sales job of educating some persons does no good if they move on to other assignments and their successors are both unaware of IS technology and the particular sequence of decisions which got their organization to its current status.

Firsthand personal computing experience and a barrage of advertising in the general press has substantially raised consumer expectations and general level of self-confidence in making IS decisions. Unfortunately, in many cases, this is an entirely misplaced confidence, with a total lack of appreciation for subtle but important nuances, and for the IS hygiene practices which must be installed if there is to be a significant probability of success. This again increases the need for sustained direct sales and follow-up of direct sales efforts.

As will be discussed below, apparently cheap external market prices are another source of confusion to the end consumers. Products essentially similar to those available in-house, appear to be available at much lower prices. It requires great consumer sophistication (often not present) to correctly identify what is a real IS bargain versus that which is really an inferior product. All this takes place in an environment where there is an explosion in the number of potential services from which customers can make a selection.

These facts, in composite, have substantially complicated the IS marketing effort. An unstable group of consumers with diversified, rapidly changing needs requires a far higher level of direct selling effort than do consumers in environments where this cluster of characteristics is not present. The need to spend promotion money on the difficult group has been intensified by the cultural heritage of IS in many settings. Consumers have been left hostile, about the quality of IS support and receptive to solutions which will carry them as far as possible away from reliance on the central IS business unit. These consumers, trained to respond in the correct way to many of yesterday's technologies, are inappropriately trained for today's technologies. Underinvestment in marketing to deal with these realities has been a major cause of dissatisfaction.

Cost. Significant changes from a marketing viewpoint are taking place in both the cost of the product and in delivery systems to get them to the users. Exhibit 10–3 identifies some of the major shifts. On the one hand, the cost of many elements of IS hardware has dropped dramatically and is likely to continue to drop significantly in the foreseeable future. On the other

EXHIBIT 10-3 □ Changes in IS Cost Profile—from Consumer Viewpoint

Past cost profile	Future cost profile
Hardware very expensive	Hardware very inexpensive
Major economies of scale in large systems; user stand-alones not feasible in most cases	Limited economy of scale in large systems; user stand-alones very attractive
Systems development expensive	Systems development expense down but not as much as hardware
Limited outside software acquisitions opportunities	Attractive outside software acquisition opportunities
Hard to estimate development and production costs accurately in advance	Still hard to estimate development and production costs accurately
Maintenance expense underestimated	Maintenance a soaring cost of keeping systems alive

hand, progress in reducing the cost of developing software, while positive, has been much slower and is likely to continue to be slow for the near future. On top of this, ability to accurately estimate both development and operating costs in advance for large, high-technology, low-structure systems continues to be both limited and disappointing.

A critical component of cost explosion has been the steady increase in the cost of maintaining already installed products (that is, software). As is true of an auto, these expenses are usually not carefully factored in at the time of purchase, and they tend to grow exponentially with the passage of years as the business grows and changes. The problem can be intensified in that in the short term these costs can be deferred with apparently little damage. In the long term, however, their neglect can cause a virtual collapse of the product.

This change in cost characteristics has accelerated the move of a significant portion of the IS business to the distribution of services. Specialized data bases accessible to many users can be put together in a cost-effective fashion that would be utterly uneconomic if done by single users for their own purposes. A proliferation of packages and software houses has exploded onto the marketplace, and shared software development has become very attractive. For example, a major consortium of 25 regional banks is funding a joint $13 million software development project (in areas such as demand deposit accounting and savings accounts) which will benefit them all. A final recent change has been the large numbers of users who have acquired their own computer capacity. (At a large eastern business school, nearly 40 percent of the faculty now own their own micros.)

As will be discussed in the section on pricing, it is difficult to identify what the total costs are or should be for any particular product or service. In part, this is because a piece of data or software development may be used to support multiple products and consumers, thus generating a concern as to whether they should be treated as joint costs or by-product costs. For any particular product, another complicating issue is the extent to which previously spent R&D costs (to get to today's skill levels) should be treated as part of product cost.

While management and control of costs is a critical component of the IS business strategy, the details of its execution will vary significantly between IS settings. High growth, very product-competitive environments appropriately take a softer line on IS inefficiency and cost control than environments where the IS products are more stable and where the customer mix is more concerned with cost than product quality.

In aggregate, the changing cost structure of IS *products* has forced the IS *business* to reconsider its sourcing decisions and has provided a distinct emphasis for the IS business to take on a much stronger distribution role. Internally, the relative emphasis placed on IS cost control at the expense of product-line growth, quality, and responsiveness of service to consumers depends on the IS business strategy; thus wide variances exist from one setting to another.

Channels of Distribution. As described in Chapters 2, 3, and 4, the number of channels for delivering to users and their relative importance have been shifting rapidly. Exhibit 10–4 shows some of the important changes in this domain. Historically, the major channel for both manufacturing and delivering the IS product has been the IS business itself. In most firms, it had a complete monopoly; changing cost factors and shifts in user preferences have put this channel under great pressure and have caused great pain inside the IS business as it has tried to adapt to the new challenges of a competitive market—which it cannot totally serve in a cost-effective fashion from its manufacturing facility. The IS business has had to adapt to a new mission and is now *not* the sole channel, but rather one of many sources of manufacturing, with a major new role being that of identification and assessment of cost, quality, etc. of products in other channels. Although for many IS businesses, adaptation to this new role has been very uncomfortable psychologically (involving incorrect notions of loss of power, etc.), successful and rapid adaptation by the IS business is critical for the health of its present and future consumers. This is because the new channels, while offering very attractive products and cost structures, in many cases also carry with them sizable risks. The most important of these risks include the following:

1. Misassessment of the real development and operations costs of the

EXHIBIT 10–4 □ Changes in the IS Channels of Distribution

Past profile	Future profile
Heavy development and production role; central IS	Significant development but lower percent of total
Limited direct purchase of hardware/software by user	Major direct purchases hardware/software by user
Individual user limited to service from large shared system	Individual user can obtain powerful independent system for use
Time-sharing service bureaus sell time	Time-sharing service bureaus sell products and time bundled together
Limited use of external data bases via time-sharing	Major use of external data bases via time-sharing
Only crude external software and processing services available	Large amount of external software and processing services available
Limited development of software by users	Major development of software by users (packages and user-friendly languages)
Retention of contract analysis/programmers	Less retention of contract analysts/programmers; more applications specialists

products in the channel. Important elements of short-term and (more important) long-term costs may be completely overlooked.

2. Consumer vulnerability to abuse of data by not controlling access, documenting procedures, and implementing data disciplines.
3. Financial vulnerability of the supplier. Is there a possibility of failure and, if so, what are the operational implications to the consumer? Is there an easy way to protect the consumer's fundamental interests if the worst occurs?
4. Obsolescence of products. Is the supplier likely to keep the products modernized (at a suitable cost, of course) for the consumer over the years? If not, what are the safety valves for the consumer and is it important that there be safety valves (obviously, a financial transaction processing system may be more vulnerable in the long-term in this regard than a decision support model)?

Considerable marketing and internal adjustment of perspectives are needed by the IS business unit if its consumers are to feel that they can rely on the IS staff to objectively evaluate alternate channels (instead of pushing their own manufacturing facility at every opportunity). It is probable that the long-run solution will develop knowledgeable consumers. Failure to execute this mission will ultimately cripple its effectiveness to service consumer needs. This will occur through fragmentation of data needed by many consumers, proliferation of redundant development efforts, and an increase of poorly conceived and managed local factories.

Competition. Of the elements in the marketing mix, the one where this analogy is weakest in describing administrative practice and *problems* is competition. In a generic sense, the IS business appears to have *two principal competitors*. These are:

1. The consumers going their own independent way to find solutions without engaging IS in either its manufacturing or its distribution capacity.
2. The potential consumers failing to recognize that they have problems or opportunities which can be addressed by IS technologies.

In the first case, competition has arisen by poor performance of the IS unit. Their inability to formulate and implement sensible, useful guidelines to assist the consumers in their purchasing decisions is a failure of IS to adapt its product line to meet the needs of the changing times. (It is worth noting that, for the broad purposes of the firm, it may be useful to run this aspect of the IS business as a loss leader.) It should be emphasized that loss of manufacturing business in a *planned* or managed way to other channels should not be seen as a competitive loss to the IS business, but simply as a restructuring of its product line to meet changing consumer needs. One of the most successful IS businesses the authors have seen in the past four years has halved its central IS manufacturing capacity. Under a rubric of general policies and controls, it has created a series of smaller manufacturing centers near major clusters of users (i.e., at divisional headquarters), including an explosion of stand-alone office automation systems under user control of all phases of the systems life cycle except the construction phase.

The second competitor, which is really cost-of-delayed-market opportunity, arises as a result of ineffective management of price, product, or distribution policies. These actions permit consumers in an imperfect market to allocate funds to projects which may have less payoff than IS products. However, the notion of aggressive external competition through pricing, product innovation, and creative distribution hurting the IS business is not appropriate in this setting. Defined the way we have done it, the IS business has a monopoly responsibility—sometimes producing a product, in other cases choosing the role of stimulating consumer awareness of appropriate external sources of supply.

Promotion. The rapid changes in IS technology, plus turnover in consumers, make promotion one of the most important elements to manage of the marketing mix because, unlike the previous items, it is largely within the control of IS management. Phase 2 learning by its consumers is at the core of a successful IS business. Even as today's mature technologies are being delivered to consumers, a strong need exists to cultivate tomorrow's consumers with tomorrow's products. Price discounts (introductory offers), branch offices (decentralized analysts), and a central IS sales force are key to making this happen. For example, one large multinational electronics company has a 400-person central IS manufacturing facility near corporate headquarters. Included in this staff are five international marketing representatives. Their job consists of preparation of brochure material to distribute to potential consumers, organization of educational seminars, and frequent trips to countries where they have a major presence to constantly promote new IS products and services. Their job is to develop a close professional relationship with the consumers. These relationships have permitted both effective dissemination of services and acquisition of insights as to performance of existing products and need for new products. This level of expenditure was regarded as being absolutely essential to the IS business in achieving its goals. In another firm, 7 APPLE 2s with VISICALC were distributed in the controller's department at no expense to the users by IS management, to help stimulate awareness of new financial analysis technology. Six months later, retroactively, the controller purchased the machines and ordered four more. This type of high profile *pilot project,* (or test market) to spark consumer interest, is another critical promotion tool.

In large part, this need to adapt is due to the recent shift in the industry. Most vendors who initially executed an overwhelming industrial marketing approach now have added a retail marketing one. From the beginning of the industry to the late 1970s, the large information systems suppliers sold primarily to the IS managers. Recently, in office automation and computers, the suppliers have not only opened a series of retail stores but also are attempting to sell directly to the end users. This has forced the IS business to promote the validity of its guidelines within the firm to protect the users from unintentional fiascoes.

A number of IS businesses have found it attractive to organize both their development and production control activities around market structure as opposed to manufacturing technology (that is, have designated development staffs dedicated to specific clusters of consumers rather than a traditional development group, a programming group, and a maintenance group). This structure permits the development of deep long-term relationships and better understanding and action on operating problems as they arise. Within these market units, it is appropriate to fund specific integrating and liaison positions as opposed to pure technical positions. This approach is critical since, as a result of past performance and poor marketing, the IS business is often in a worse position relatively than an outside software company with its large marketing staff. Money spent this way, although large, is often among the IS unit's most important expenditure, and should be the last to be cut back.

IS newsletters on new services and product announcements (that is, advertising or promotional material) should be sent to key present and potential consumers on a regular basis. Similarly, a program of IS-conducted consumer educational programs, as well as identification of appropriate external educational programs, can significantly assist the marketing effort. When complemented by an appropriate set of sales calls, this can accelerate phase 2 learning.

Consequently, the mix of these promotional tools will vary widely by organizational setting. Just as industrial and consumer companies have very different promotion programs, so also should different IS units. The strategic relevance of its products to its consumers, stability and mix of sophistication of consumers, consumer geographic location, are examples of items which all legitimately impact the structure of an appropriate promotion process.

Price. As noted in Chapter 6, the selection of IS prices is a very emotional and rapidly changing process. It is, however, a very important element in establishing a businesslike, professional relationship between the IS business and its consumers. Indeed, addressing pricing policies aggressively with a marketing view gives significant legitimacy to the notion of the stand-alone IS business. Issues which make pricing a very complicated topic include the following:

1. *Inefficient Market.* The establishment of rational and competitive criteria is very complicated for the following reasons:

a. Product quality is largely hidden and is very elusive to all but the most sophisticated and meticulous consumer. Prices that on the surface appear to be widely apart, if meticulously analyzed, often turn out to be quite comparable.

b. Different vendors have quite different goals, product mixes, and stability. A small vendor who is trying to buy into a market can come up with a very attractive price with which to defuse discussions concerning his financial viability.

c. Vendors may produce very attractive prices because they are pricing a service as a by-product of some other necessary business and thus produce very favorable numbers in relation to a system which attempts to make each user bear a proportionate share of the full cost of the manufacturing operation. This is particularly true for in-house operations which are trying to dispose of excess capacity for some "financial contribution." The long-term stability of this should be a matter of concern to the informed consumer. (What are the implications of his output becoming the main product and the other consumer's output the by-product?)

d. Excess capacity considerations may produce attractive *short-term* marginal prices which are not sustainable on a *long-term* basis as direct costing issues evolve into full costing ones. A variant of this is a bargain entry-level price to attract the consumer. Once captured, it is then easy to elevate prices significantly. This is particularly true for large, internally developed telecommunications systems.

2. *Introductory Offers.* To stimulate phase 2 learning, and stimulate long-term demand, it is often appropriate to offer deep discounts on early business to generate access to a stream of long-term profits at either quite different price structures or cost structures, once the initial learning is completed.

3. *Monopoly Issues.* Review and regulation of pricing decisions by senior management in many areas is needed because of IS's de facto monopoly position. Highly confidential data and data bases needed by multiple users in geographically remote locations are examples of IS products which cannot be supplied by manufacturers other than the IS business. It is important that the prices of these services be appropriately regulated to prevent possible abuses.

4. *Unbundling.* An effective pricing strategy involves two important elements not in widespread practice. The first is the unbundling of development, maintenance, operations, and special turnaround requirements into special packages, each having its own price. The establishment of these prices at an arm's-length basis in advance is a critical element in ensuring a professional relationship with the consumers. The prices need to be negotiated in as much depth and with as much care by the IS business as contracts between outside software companies and consumers. Often this negotiation can be a useful education program to alert users to the "true nature" of service cost. The second element is a need to produce understandable prices for the consumers. Prices established for reports, number of customer records, price per invoice, etc., are much easier for the consumer to relate to than prices in terms of utilization of IS resource units such as CPU cycles, MIPS, etc. The added risk undertaken (if any) by the IS business

in terms of a horror-struck consumer, who has just been educated in the facts of life, tends to be more than offset by much better communication with the ultimate consumer.

5. *Profit.* A final pricing issue, which again strains the independent business analogy, is how far notions of a profitable business should be pressed. It is not clear that, in the short term (in some cases, even in the long term), an IS business should make a profit, or even break even in some settings. Environments where consumers need a lot of education, and where a lot of phase 1 and 2 experimentation is needed, may appropriately run at a deficit for a long period of time. This issue must be resolved prior to the establishment of an appropriate pricing policy. (The answer to this may evolve over time.)

The establishment of an appropriate IS pricing policy is one of the most complex pricing decisions to be made in industry. An appropriate resolution is critical to establishing a healthy relationship with the consumer. This resolution, however, involves weaving a course between monopolistic and genuine competitive issues, dealing with imperfect markets, and resolving ambiguities concerning the role of profits.

ROLE OF THE BOARD OF DIRECTORS

A question of general interest, which first surfaced in Chapter 1, is: What should be the relationship of the firm's general management to the IS business? We find it useful to think of its participation as being similar to the role of a board of directors for any business. (In many situations, this is given de facto recognition through the creation of an executive steering committee.) Viewing its role in this way, we believe the key tasks of general management can be summarized as follows:

1. The appointment and continued assessment of the performance of the IS chief executive officer (a normal function of the nominating committee).
2. Assuring that appropriate standards are in place and are being adhered to. This includes the receipt of appropriate reports on the subject from the IS auditor and a more cursory review from the firm's external auditors (a normal function of the audit committee).
3. Ensuring that the board is constructed to provide overall guidance to the IS business from its various interested constituencies. Unlike a publicly held firm, the IS board does not need a representation of lawyers, bankers, investment bankers, etc. It does need senior user managers who can and are willing to provide user perspective. (As the strategic impact of the IS business on the business as a whole drops, the level of these managers will also appropriately drop.) At the same time, R&D (IS technology planning) and production (IS development and operations

backgrounds) need to be present to ensure that the art of the possible is represented in these sessions.

4. Providing broad guidance for the strategic direction of the IS business, ensuring detailed planning processes are present within the IS business, and satisfying themselves that the outputs of the planning processes fit the strategic direction. Practically, this surveillance will be executed through a combination of the following:
   a. General presentations to the board by IS management on market development and product planning, as well as financial plans.
   b. Review by the board of summary documentation of overall direction.
   c. Formal and informal briefings of board members by other members concerning current issues as to how the IS business is supporting (or not supporting) their legitimate business needs.
   d. Request for and receipt of internal and external reviews of these issues as they seem appropriate.

This definition of the role of the board is designed to deal with the realities of members' background and availability for this kind of work in relation to the other demands on their time. Wallowing in operational or technical detail is unlikely to be suitable or effective. In many settings, periodic (on a one- or two-year basis) education sessions for the board members have turned out to be useful both in making them more comfortable in executing their responsibilities and in bringing them up to date on broad trends within the IS business as well as in the IS industry in general.

ROLE OF IS CHIEF EXECUTIVE OFFICER

A historically high turnover job, the IS chief executive position has been a very difficult and demanding one, with a steadily shifting mix of skills required to be effective over time. Critical special responsibilities which must be managed by the CEO include the following:

1. Maintaining board relationships personally. This includes keeping the board appropriately informed about major policy issues and problems and being fully responsive to their needs and concerns. There is a strong link between the board and the customers that is not present in many settings.
2. Ensuring that the strategy-formulating processes are adequately evolved and that appropriate detailed action programs are developed. As in any high-technology business, high-quality technical scanning is absolutely essential. Its interpretation is crucial and may well lead to major changes in organization, product mix, and marketing strategy. Without

aggressive leadership from the top, the forces of cultural inertia may cause the IS business to delay far too long.

3. Paying close attention to salary, personnel practices, and thus to employee quality-of-life issues. The work force in the IS business is far more mobile and less easily replaceable in these businesses than an average employee.
4. Giving high priority to factory security. (It is more important for the IS business than for most manufacturing technologies; a single, disgruntled employee can do vast—and often undetected for long periods of time—amounts of damage.)
5. Making certain that there is an appropriate management balance between the marketing, manufacturing, and control parts of the business. Of the three, marketing in its broadest sense is the one most often neglected. The CEO, who often comes out of the factory and has been seared by operations fiascoes, has potentially more sensitivity to these issues. However, since this experience was at a particular time with a particular mix of technology assimilation problems, and a particular set of control responses, the CEO's perspectives in these areas may be too narrow, and inappropriate for the current challenges.
6. Developing an IS esprit. A key factor in the success of the IS business is its belief in the value and potential of information for the profit of the firm. Senior IS managers must develop team spirit and lead their organizations with enthusiasm into new ventures. At the same time, they must develop the confidence of the board by good judgment—not only taking risks but also making wise decisions on where to limit the market or when to knowingly forgo a useful technology. If they assess that the customer is not ready, they must balance keeping abreast versus the receptiveness of the market.

SUMMARY

The above discussion captures, we believe, several important complicating aspects of the IS business. Complex and shifting products, changing consumers, new major channels of distribution, and evolving cost structure have forced a major reanalysis and redirection of both its product offerings and its marketing efforts. This changed marketing environment is not only very complex to manage but has forced significant changes in the IS factory, organization and appropriate control systems, and most fundamentally, its perception of its strategic mission. Ted Levitt's great classic *Marketing Myopia*[2] best captured this as he noted the great growth business of the 19th century—the railroads—collapsed because the managers saw themselves in

[2] *Harvard Business Review*, (September–October), 1975.

the *railroad,* not the *transportation* business. The analogy to the information systems business is that it is not in the electronic-based *computer,* telecommunications, or office automation business. Rather, it is in the business of bringing a sustained stream of innovation in information services to change the company's internal operations and in many cases (banks, American Express, etc.) also its external products. Far too many directors of data processing centers myopically believe they are running a computer center. Failure to perceive and act on their broader role will lead to a collapse of their operations, probable loss of jobs, and great disservice to the customer base.

When IS is defined in this way, the dynamism in the elements of the successful marketing mix in the early 1980s suddenly snaps into focus. Reliance on existing product structure, more efficient ways of delivering the old technology, and old organization is a recipe for an uncontrolled dissolution of the IS business. This IS organization has been a group of change agents to their customers for 30 years. The change agent itself, however, must change to be relevant.

Case 10–1 □ Concordia Casting Company*

In late October 1979, Stuart McMillen, director of corporate information services (CIS) for the Concordia Casting Company, was attempting to sort out the factors underlying a major schedule slippage in his department's most important systems development project. The project involved the conversion of a basic online order entry and production scheduling system, known as CAPS (Concordia automated production scheduling), from Centronics to IBM equipment. McMillen had discovered that systems testing for CAPS was incomplete in late August, only three months before the scheduled conversion date. Now, after several weeks of intense investigation, some key management changes, and a major rescheduling effort, it was clear that CAPS could not be finally converted for almost another year. Although this was a significant slippage, it was only the latest in a long series of missed completion dates for CAPS. McMillen knew that Concordia's senior management was extremely frustrated about the conversion slippage, and yet he felt they did not fully understand the operating problems that his department was facing.

McMillen wanted to make several additional managerial and organizational changes within his department, but he believed that for the time being the department should concentrate on the CAPS project itself. Nevertheless, McMillen also knew that he had to think about CIS beyond CAPS; and he wanted his 1980 operating plan to contain his longer-term proposals as well. At the same time, McMillen thought it would be helpful to review how the CAPS project had developed such a major schedule slippage.

BACKGROUND ON CONCORDIA AND CIS

With corporate headquarters in Fort Wayne, Indiana, the Concordia Casting Company was a large, multidivisional manufacturing organization with 1978 revenues of more than $700 million. Though primarily an automobile parts supplier, Concordia had broadened its operations significantly during the 1970s. By 1979 the company had four well-defined business segments: Automotive (engine blocks and other automobile parts), Machine Tools (lathes, power presses, drills, etc.), Precision Parts (screws, nuts, bolts, and other machined parts), and Fluid Controls (valves and piping for com-

* This case was prepared as the basis for class discussion rather than to illustrate either effective or ineffective handling of an administrative situation. All names and figures have been disguised.

mercial applications). A major portion of Concordia's growth had come through acquisition, although the Automotive Division remained clearly the most profitable and best known of the operating divisions. Each division was treated as a separate profit center, and most divisions were actually composed of several independent companies.

Stu McMillen had been hired as director of corporate information services in March 1975. However, he had been intimately involved with the department for about two years prior to 1975 as an outside consultant, so stepping into the job had been a relatively simple process. McMillen had worked as a data processing/systems design consultant with Huntington and Wells (Concordia's auditors) for several years when he took over the CIS job. Prior to that, McMillen had spent six years in systems design and project management work with a major retailing chain. He held an MBA from the University of Virginia and an engineering degree from Purdue.

When McMillen took over CIS in 1975, he inherited a department in the midst of a major, long-term organizational transition. During the 1960s Concordia had embarked on an aggressive corporate diversification program, and had acquired a number of smaller specialty manufacturing companies in several related industries. Most of the acquired companies had data processing needs of their own; and there had been increasing, though ill-defined, demands for help from CIS (which had previously served only as the data processing operation for the Automotive Division). Jim Butler, the CIS director from the late 1960s to 1975, had been charged with building a corporatewide information systems function. Butler's response had been to begin developing CIS into a centralized corporate data utility. As a part of this effort Butler had recommended that the company select a single hardware vendor in order to facilitate the standardization and integration of the systems in the various Concordia divisions.

In 1974, senior management approved the selection of IBM as prime vendor. However, they were somewhat uncomfortable with Butler's concept of CIS as a centralized data utility. Concordia was widely recognized, both inside and outside the company, as a highly decentralized organization. Acquired companies retained their original names and identities, and were explicitly encouraged to operate independently. In the words of one senior executive:

> Concordia is not inclined to get into management's shoes. We bought these companies because it made financial sense, but we repeatedly tell our division presidents that they are autonomous. Our takeovers have clearly been friendly. In fact, in many cases they come to us and ask if they can become part of the Concordia family.

In this environment, Butler's attempts to achieve centralized control over all the data processing operations had not been well received. Butler's boss, Bradley Sherman (himself a former CIS director and in 1975 a corporate vice president and treasurer), had hired a team of consultants from Huntington and Wells to help develop a long-range plan for data processing at Concordia. In early 1975, while the consultant team (which included Stu McMillen) was conducting its study, Butler had apparently recognized his tenuous position and left Concordia for another job. After helping Sherman find the screen replacement candidates for six months, McMillen had finally applied for the job himself.

When McMillen took over CIS, the department was organized into five functional groups: Systems and Procedures; DP Operations; Process Control; Procedures, Administration, and Control; and Operations Research. There were a total of 52 people within the department, with 37 of them in the Operations and Systems areas (see Exhibit 1). The department had an operating budget of $1.2 million.

McMillen recognized that a fully centralized data utility serving all of the operating divisions would not be an appropriate solution at Concordia, and he continued working with the consultants to develop an alternative approach. Meanwhile, there was an immediate, substantial need to increase and upgrade the CIS professional staff, no matter what organizational structure finally emerged. McMillen knew that the required conversion projects would place severe strains on CIS. More importantly, none of the existing CIS staff had been trained on standard IBM systems, and only a few of them had a solid grasp of the existing CAPS system.

McMillen's operating plan for 1976 requested a budget allocation of $1.7 million. The plan recommended hiring 9 additional professionals during 1976, followed by 12 more in 1977 and 1978. With top management approval, McMillen began an aggressive recruiting program that in large measure succeeded in bringing to Concordia a number of qualified systems engineers and project managers who were well versed in IBM systems, equipment, and design methodologies.

McMillen also worked on strengthening and expanding his management team. Shortly after he took over CIS, he added a business systems manager and a voice/data communications manager to his staff. He also rearranged

EXHIBIT 1 □ CIS Organization Structure in Early 1975*

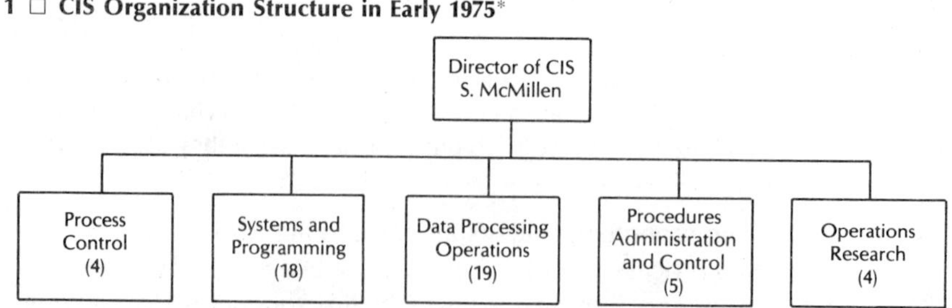

* Number in parentheses in each area indicates number of staff in that area.

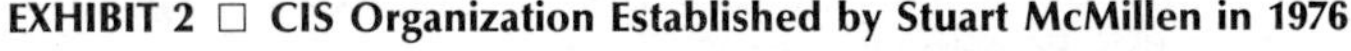

EXHIBIT 2 □ CIS Organization Established by Stuart McMillen in 1976

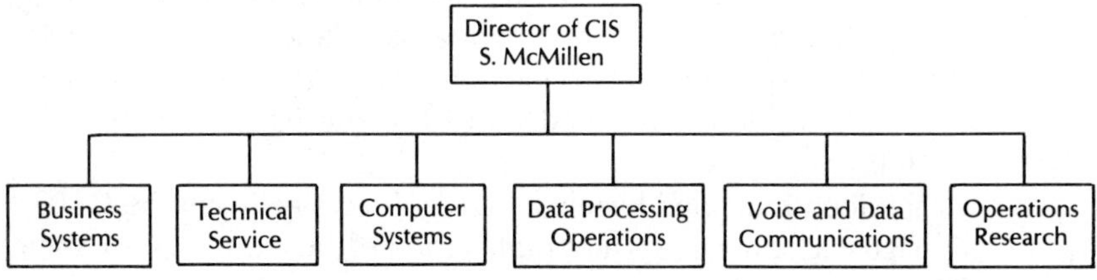

the existing CIS groups somewhat, so that by the end of 1976 he had seven managers reporting directly to him (see Exhibit 2).

In 1977 the Huntington and Wells consultants formally suggested a distributed organization for CIS that would more clearly separate the corporate data processing functions from the work done for the operating divisions. The key innovation in this proposal was the concept of several regional data centers. The data centers would service clusters of operating divisions, while the corporate staff would focus on corporate systems development, operations research, long-range planning, policy setting, voice and data communication capabilities, corporate DP standards, data base management, and business systems consulting throughout the company.

Exhibit 3 contains a simplified version of the organizational structure recommended by Huntington and Wells in 1977. Both McMillen and Concordia's senior management agreed with the basic objectives underlying the recommendations, and much of McMillen's time and effort over the next several years was devoted to moving CIS in that direction.

By late 1979, McMillen had constructed what he believed to be a strong,

EXHIBIT 3 □ CIS Organization Proposed by Huntington and Wells in 1977

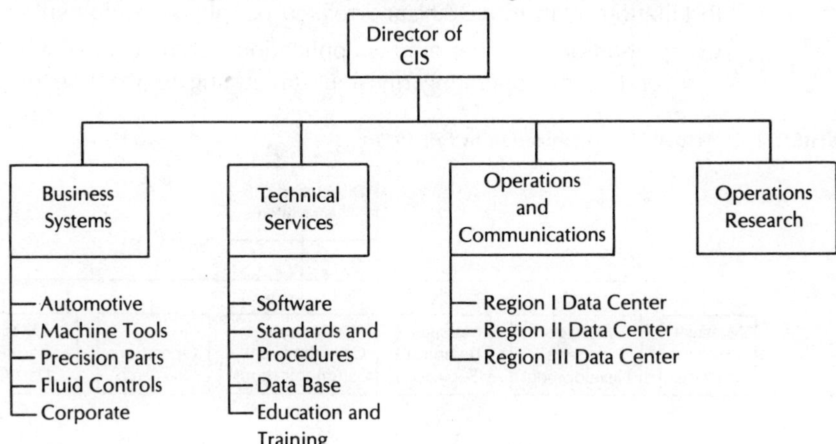

viable Corporate Information Services group. The staff numbered just over 100, including 22 in the Eastern Regional Data Center in Hagerstown, Maryland. The 1979 operating budget for CIS was in excess of $5 million; and the CIS organization was looking more and more like the one Huntington and Wells had recommended in 1977 (see Exhibit 4 for the fall 1979 CIS structure).

McMillen remained keenly aware of how significant the CAPS schedule slippage was. But he was also quite proud of the many positive things he and CIS had accomplished in the past five years. McMillen commented to the casewriter:

> In looking back over the past five years, it is important to remember the situation I inherited. The first thing I discovered was that Butler really hadn't done such a good job after all. CIS was operating without any basic design standards, without a formal systems development methodology, and with no chargeout system. What's more, there was a lot of unsatisfied user demand—almost a five-year backlog of projects—and nowhere near the staff to handle it.
>
> To make matters worse, in 1975 the CIS staff in Fort Wayne was spread out on eight different floors in three separate buildings, and we were in old, crowded offices to boot. On top of that, I found I had a staff of about 50 people and no personnel function to speak of. That meant no performance appraisal system, no way to measure individual development, and no formal training programs.

Reflecting on these problems, McMillen ticked off what he viewed as a major set of accomplishments:

Construction of a new, $1.5 million wing to the headquarters building that brought the entire CIS staff together for the first time (the first new construction at Concordia's corporate headquarters in over 10 years).

Significant increases in the CIS staff located in Fort Wayne (from 50 in 1975 to over 80 in 1979).

Installation of an IBM 3031 and related peripheral equipment.

Completion of a number of new applications, both at Fort Wayne and in several of the operating divisions (including two online purchasing

EXHIBIT 4 □ Actual CIS Organization in Fall 1979

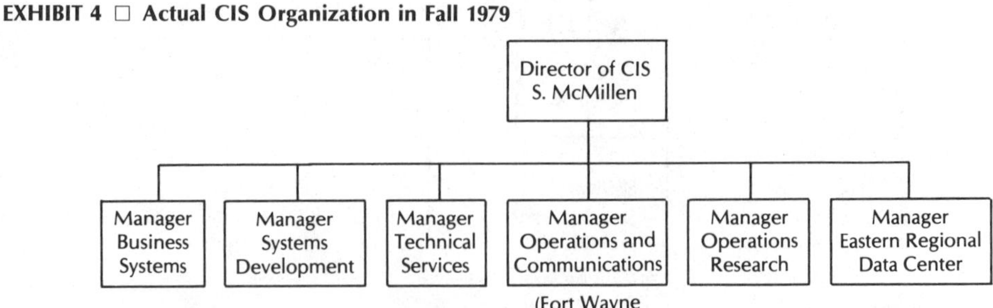

systems, a payroll-personnel system, and several period-end accounting systems); together these projects were as big as the CAPS effort).

The opening of an Eastern Regional Data Center in Hagerstown, Maryland, including the construction of a totally new facility for the data center.

The development of a formal college recruiting program to bring qualified systems designers into CIS.

Improvements in the operation of the corporate DP steering committee.

Brad Sherman also felt McMillen had been very successful in a number of critical areas. Sherman stressed McMillen's development of a structure for data processing within Concordia, and of a DP plan that provided a framework for future development:

> Stu's greatest strength is his conceptual ability, and his planning perspective. He's really a brilliant thinker, and he's had a very clear vision of where he wants CIS to go. Sometimes he's tenacious to the point of being more aggressive than people around here are used to—you know; damn the torpedoes, fullspeed ahead. But, actually, I don't see how he could have done as much as he has without being a little pushy.

As impressive as these accomplishments were, however, McMillen knew that they counted for little in senior management's eyes as long as CAPS was not yet completed. CAPS was the driving force in the department—it consumed the largest amount of resources; it was the most highly visible project; and it contained the highest potential for improved operations in the heart of the Automotive Division.

THE CAPS CONVERSION PROJECT

The original CAPS system had been developed at Concordia in the late 1960s. At the time it was clearly a state-of-the-art online system; it operated on a pair of Centronic 275s, and was composed of 12 interrelated, interactive subsystems:

1. Order entry.
2. Order maintenance.
3. Production scheduling.
4. Production maintenance.
5. Packed production.
6. Packing lists.
7. Shipping assembly.
8. Shipping maintenance.
9. File maintenance.
10. Inquiry.

11. Invoicing.
12. Accounts receivable.

In addition, there were 16 dependent batch systems that produced periodic and special status reports:

1. Order file reports.
2. Order analysis.
3. Customer allocation.
4. Delay notices.
5. Stock status.
6. Stock usage.
7. In-process report.
8. Shipment report.
9. File balance.
10. Accounts receivable.
11. Physical inventory.
12. Weekly inventory analysis.
13. Forecasting.
14. Product history.
15. Marketing inventory.
16. File maintenance.

The original Centronics programs had been written in machine language by Concordia systems staff; the operating systems was a unique, homegrown product as well. Although the system was still working adequately in the mid-1970s, it was increasingly apparent that a major overhaul was called for. Maintenance was difficult and time-consuming, the system was beginning to require more memory storage space than the Centronics equipment could provide, and the hardware itself was rapidly becoming obsolete and difficult to maintain.

These difficulties led the CIS staff and Concordia's senior management to conclude that it was time to replace the Centronics 275s with more powerful equipment. As they discussed their needs with the Centronics marketing representatives, they discovered that even an upgrade to newer Centronics hardware would necessitate a major rewriting of all of their existing software systems. This discovery led to a general concern with Centronics as a supplier; Concordia did not want to be faced with a major conversion project each time they changed central processors. In addition, they began to feel that the Centronics product line was not diverse enough to meet the varied data processing needs of the different operating divisions. All of these factors together had led to the management decision to convert to IBM as a prime vendor in 1974.

It was recognized from the beginning that converting all of Concordia's systems from Centronics to IBM would be a massive effort. McMillen recalled that IBM originally estimated the conversions would require 15 man-years and could run on a 370/135. By 1976, however, it became evident that the initial estimate was wholly inadequate. At that time McMillen asked IBM and Huntington and Wells together to review the conversion effort, and was told that it would take a minimum of 27 man-years, and should run on a half-meg 135. By 1979, it had become clear that by the time all of the conversions were completed they would actually consume well over 75 man-years (of which half would be dedicated to the CAPS system). Furthermore, the hardware actually being installed was a 2-meg 3031, which was roughly six times as powerful as the 370/135. In the words of a Huntington and Wells consultant who had been involved in the conversion almost from the beginning:

> The magnitude of the CAPS conversion project has been consistently underestimated ever since day one. Although the functions of the system have not been changed dramatically, both the software and the hardware requirements have turned out to be significantly greater than we realized. On the other hand, if we *had* predicted accurately what it would take, no one would have believed us.

Stu McMillen believed there were several factors that had contributed to the poor time estimates. In the first place, no one had fully appreciated the difficulties of building such a complex, interdependent system virtually from scratch. There were 366 online programs (with over 250,000 lines of code) and 117 batch programs involved, plus over 300 user procedures to be written. In addition, as the design effort proceeded a large number of enhancements had been added, so that by McMillen's estimate the new system had about 40 percent more functions than the old. Furthermore, the old system had, out of necessity, evolved on its own during the past four years. Consequently, the conversion design also had to be modified several times while the new system was being developed. Finally, in the midst of the design phase, the Automotive Division's management had revised its entire philosophy of how the plants were run, necessitating additional major changes in both the old and the new CAPS systems.

These changes in plant operations were described by Ronald Lawton, the controller of the Automotive Division, as follows:

> For a whole variety of reasons we improved our competitive position dramatically in the late 1970s. Our volume had been fairly stable for several years, but by mid-1977 we had obtained several long-term contracts that meant an upswing of almost 30 percent a year. Needless to say, when we landed those contracts, our shipping requirements increased substantially. We went to a seven-days-a-week schedule, and even had to allocate shipments to some of our customers. We found that by making some major changes in production schedules, by concentrating our product manufacturing in certain plants, and by working on other productivity improvements, we could substan-

> tially increase our shipments without any increases in plant capacity. In fact, in the first half of 1979 we took a strike in the plant and still shipped more than we did in the same period in 1978.
>
> The problem was that just as we were stepping up our business substantially, the CIS people were slacking off their attention to the old Centronics systems. They just weren't giving us the service we needed. We were bringing clerks in at 7 A.M. to enter orders through CAPS. At one point we had a 40-day backlog of orders, and yet CIS just didn't seem to be pushing to get anything done.
>
> What really scares me is how dependent we are on CAPS. If that system goes down for more than a day, we have to start thinking about closing the plant. We simply can't run without it.

Stu McMillen understood Lawton's frustration, but he did not believe that Lawton recognized how substantially the old system had been modified. It had been very time-consuming to handle the changes in production scheduling, shipment allocations, and price changes that were necessitated by the changes in production operations (and some of the old Centronics programs had pricing formulas embedded in the code itself). Furthermore, supporting changes in the old system had a double impact on CIS: the modifications consumed CIS resources directly, but they also meant substantial revisions in already completed portions of the new system as well.

STAFFING PROBLEMS

In retrospect, however, McMillen believed that none of the technical problems had been as severe or as frustrating as the personnel difficulties he had struggled with. The rapid growth in the CIS staff had not only been very difficult to achieve, but the addition of large numbers of new people had created a whole different set of management problems. While the new staff understood IBM systems and procedures, they were not familiar with the old CAPS system, with Concordia's basic business, or with the Concordia approach to solving problems. Furthermore, many of the experienced CIS staff resented the newcomers and were reluctant to share their knowledge of the existing systems. In the words of one long-time CIS manager:

> We do have capable, IBM-trained people, and we need them. But we don't have enough Concordia people. You just can't put everything about the system on paper; a programmer needs to know all the file structures, the program linkages, and so on. No one really knew if the system was doing what it was supposed to; no one knew the Centronics data base; and no one could just look at the programs and know if they were right.
>
> I offered to take them (the new staff people) along with me to meetings with the operating people, but they were always too busy. I guess they saw themselves as "professional" managers and thought that was enough. Around here it isn't. Most of the operations managers out in the plant have been here a long

> time. That's where I started; I fought my way up, but a lot of these college kids want to be managers overnight.
>
> A lot of old Concordia people have left because they were bypassed. I don't think management knew how good they were.

Managers outside of CIS were also concerned about the rapid influx of new technical specialists. Ronald Lawton commented:

> These new people have really affected the morale of the old-timers. They see new people coming in above them in the organization; and, what's worse, the old-timers worry about losing their jobs when the conversion is complete. After all, when we're 100 percent IBM, where does someone who knows nothing but Centronics fit in?
>
> Besides, I think the pressures for rapid expansion led CIS to be a little careless about whom they've hired. In a way, they've been adding bodies. I know they've had a lot of turnover in CIS—some deliberate terminations, and some voluntary resignations.
>
> To make matters worse, the newcomers have usually been pretty insensitive. I think it's better in 1979, but not too long ago it was like: "Hi, I'm from CIS. Here's the system you're going to use." It takes a long time for our people to forget being treated like that.

Brad Sherman told a similar story, stressing how radically different the newcomers were from Concordia's traditions. He commented to the casewriter:

> I heard about one instance where four people from CIS were visiting one of our divisions. When they arrived, each one of them rented a separate car, and the whole time they were there they were acting like "big shot" representatives of corporate headquarters—making pronouncements about company policies, and so on.
>
> Those people just don't understand Concordia. We're a low-key, very people-sensitive organization. We get things done by patient, gentle persuasion. Yet CIS, almost by definition, has to impose change on divisions who view themselves as highly autonomous. It's just too bad they have come across as so arrogant.

Stu McMillen was keenly aware of the difficulties he had had recruiting and retaining competent professional staff. Over the past five years, he believed, he had hired close to 90 people for the Fort Wayne operations, just to achieve a growth in staffing from 50 to 80. In 1979 alone, he had spent close to $200,000 in recruiting fees, travel expenses, and relocation costs to bring in 20 new people. Yet almost as many had resigned to take positions elsewhere, so he had just managed to stay even.

McMillen attributed the turnover problem to two primary factors: salary levels and location. The shortage of qualified programmers, analysts, and project managers was making it relatively easy for anyone with any experience to change jobs for significant pay increases. For example, a telecommunications analyst making $18,000 a year had recently left for a $26,000 salary at another company. The salary pressures were also creating massive internal equity problems. McMillen commented:

> We just hired a business systems analyst at $40,000—and my number two manager is making only $43,000. Besides, these salaries are getting way out of line with other Concordia departments as well, and we don't have a personnel capability within CIS to help us work out these kinds of issues.

McMillen actually felt that holding even in 1979 was a major accomplishment, though he pointed out that the replacements were younger and had less experience than those who had left, so that the "holding even" was really only in terms of headcount.

McMillen believed very strongly that Concordia's location in Fort Wayne had been a major drawback in his efforts to attract and retain quality DP personnel. He commented that Fort Wayne was a relatively small, rather provincial town, and it had proven very difficult to convince experienced people from outside the Fort Wayne area to relocate. McMillen recalled one prime candidate from Philadelphia who drove through town from the airport to Concordia's headquarters building, took a quick tour of the facilities, and announced he wanted to leave on the next plane.

McMillen commented:

> Most of those who leave have been here three years or less, and most are less than 30 years old. We train them, and then they go somewhere else.
>
> I think they also get very frustrated here. There are so many things to do, too many things changing at once, and a lot of shifting priorities. There is also an impression of a lack of consistent progress. Besides, we haven't done a very good job of training and career planning.

One short-term strategy that McMillen had relied on to overcome the turnover and personnel shortages had been to make extensive use of outside contract programming personnel. McMillen estimated that he would spend over $800,000 in 1979 on contract programmers. But he knew that many of them were disgruntled about living away from home for long periods of time, and therefore not very efficient. Furthermore, they usually traveled to Fort Wayne on Monday mornings and returned home on Friday afternoons. While they put in enough evening hours in mid-week to make up for the travel time, this work pattern irritated many of the internal programmers. In addition, it made the project management and coordination tasks all that much more complex.

RECENT HISTORY OF THE CAPS PROJECT

In retrospect, McMillen recognized that the CAPS project had always been understaffed. More significantly, it had suffered from inadequate project leadership and internal bickering among the newcomers and old-timers. The CAPS team had had four project managers in the last three years; one had been removed for incompetence and two had resigned. The most recent resignation had been in April 1979, just as the project was entering the testing phase. Frank Northrup, the man who had resigned, had left Concordia to work for a former boss (though in a different company). At the time he left, Northrup predicted the system would be up and running before the end of 1979; the Huntington and Wells consultants concurred in his assessment. Given that schedule, Northrup said that the new opportunity was just too good to pass up. Now, looking back, McMillen wondered whether Northrup actually had been uneasy about CAPS and had chosen to leave before the major problems surfaced.

The poor working relationships between experienced Concordia people and the newer, IBM-trained analysts also contributed to the CAPS schedule delays. McMillen had only recently learned that during the spring of 1979 the two key analysts on the project (one an old-timer, the other a newcomer) had literally not been speaking to each other. As a result, Northrup had been planning the testing of the IBM system without any involvement of the one man in the company who really knew the details of the old CAPS system, and thus what tests were really needed.

Testing of the individual programs also suffered from a succession of performance problems with the newly installed IBM 3031 central processor. During a two-month period in late spring the 3031 had over 200 hours of downtime—leading a senior IBM executive to label Concordia's machine "the worst-performing installation of a 3031 anywhere in the United States." IBM technicians, who arrived in Fort Wayne "by the planeload" literally rebuilt two thirds of the 3031 on site, and by early summer, it was finally performing more reliably.

As McMillen now understood it, the actual testing problems related primarily to the integration of CAPS' separate units. The project team had already tested the individual programs; they had thus assumed the system testing would proceed smoothly. Such had not been the case, however. During the summer of 1979, many unexpected modifications had to be made, and the project team continued to be short-handed. In addition, a test generator package had not worked as expected, and as a result the systems tests were taking much longer than expected.

The Huntington and Wells consultant who had been monitoring the project for the last three years told the casewriter:

> This is actually one of the most thoroughly tested systems I have ever seen. The problems have occurred in the planning phases, between major system development stages. In fact, they are paying the price of a hardware conversion in a tightly integrated software environment. This thing works in real time, and all the parts are linked very closely together. And it really isn't a conversion per se—it's a total rewrite.

The original CAPS plan had called for running the IBM system in parallel with the Centronics system for one day and then assessing the results critically before committing to the final cutover. It had finally become apparent to the CAPS project team in late August that the system was not ready to run in parallel. Ron Lawton (controller for the Automotive Division) recalled his frustration at learning of the delay:

> The stuff hit the fan at a review meeting on September 6. John Parnell [the project leader at the time] told me that the system wasn't ready, and wouldn't be until late in the fourth quarter. I got pretty excited, but I was told that they had announced the delay several weeks earlier. I said that's news to me, and they told me to go back and read my mail.
>
> Well, I finally found one sentence on page 3 of the monthly Executive Summary. Why hadn't they communicated it to me personally? Our manager of Production and manager of Scheduling hadn't known about it before September 6 either.
>
> When the word got to our division vice president, he started asking what was going on, and he got Brad Sherman to look into it pretty closely.

Actually, McMillen had initiated an intensive review of the CAPS project well before Lawton learned of the problems. John Parnell had come to McMillen in mid-August and told him the schedule could not be met because of the testing problems. As McMillen questioned Parnell he began to suspect that the problems were much deeper than just the testing schedule:

> I called the whole CAPS team into the office on Sunday, August 19. We met from 9 A.M. to 4 P.M., and by then I knew it couldn't be done until April or May 1980 at the earliest. I ordered a more exhaustive review of CAPS and of the other conversion projects as well, using a whole new set of assumptions about machine downtime, program modification, man-hour availability, and so on. By mid-September I realized the CAPS conversion couldn't be complete before September 1980.
>
> We purposely kept this information from the users until we could give them reasonable new estimates that we *knew* we could live with.

After some careful consideration, McMillen asked Len Creighton, his strongest technical manager, to take over the CAPS conversion project. Creighton, who had over 10 years' experience at Concordia, had originally developed the company's Operations Research effort and most recently had been in charge of the CIS Business Systems Analysis group.

When Creighton stepped into the CAPS project, he found:

> Chaos. The team was too small, the planning was almost nonexistent. The few Gantt charts they had weren't detailed enough. And unfortunately the guy who had been managing the project since Frank Northrup left wasn't strong enough. He's good technically, but his planning and control skills were weak.
>
> Stu and I sat down and talked with him and told him what he needed. He has taken this with a very positive attitude and is now helping out tremendously.

In addition to putting Len Creighton on CAPS on a full-time basis, McMillen had shuffled other assignments and added 10 new people to the project, bringing its staffing up to 18. Creighton made certain that the team included a project administrator who had extensive project planning and control experience. As Creighton put it:

> He's not only monitoring progress on a daily basis, but he's training others to do it as well. He's put up a huge magnetic board in his office, and now everyone can track their commitments, their progress, and their problems. That alone is helping the team watch interim deadlines, and rearrange their activities and schedules on their own.
>
> The other major change is that we're pushing authority and responsibility down, so the original project team members are all supervising other people who are doing the actual testing.
>
> The testing is already uncovering a can of worms, so there is a lot of need to constantly rearrange people and activities. But we are staying with the basic plan.

ORGANIZATIONAL IMPLICATIONS

McMillen was confident that Creighton's leadership would eventually get CAPS under control, but he was still concerned about the deeper organizational problems that the CAPS difficulties had revealed. McMillen picked up a memorandum that the Huntington and Wells consultant had written several months earlier (Exhibit 5). The consultant had essentially recommended a taller, narrower structure for CIS. The proposal called for an additional level of management, with only three people reporting directly to McMillen.

While McMillen was in basic agreement with the consultant's thinking, the two men had more recently developed a slightly different organizational plan that they believed fit CIS's current management capabilities more closely (see Exhibit 6). Like the consultant's original proposal, McMillen's current plan would create a sharper separation between CIS's two primary functions. The two data centers (in Hagerstown and Fort Wayne) were oriented toward meeting the ongoing data processing and systems development needs of the individual operating divisions. In contrast, the Field Support function was intended to provide corporatewide systems planning and coordination, as well as to serve the corporate headquarter's own data processing needs. The rationale for this division of responsibilities had grown out of extended conversations with Brad Sherman and the Huntington and Wells consultant. McMillen believed the planned organization was appropriate for Concordia, and he thought it would help to resolve many of the user relationship problems that had plagued CIS over the past several years.

EXHIBIT 5 □ Excerpts from Consultant Recommendations for Reorganization of the CIS Department, June 1979

The proposed three-tier structure (see accompanying chart) has been selected to replace the existing two-tier structure (after review of several alternatives) based on the following:

1. The director has too many people reporting to him at present, which limits severaly the time he is able to spend with corporate and divisional management.
2. The evaluation of the department and its increase in size has necessitated an increase in the number of functions performed and, therefore, an increase in the number of management personnel.
3. The conversion from the Centronics to IBM computers has revealed a number of problems in the existing organization which the revised organization should address.

The new organization calls for a greater division between "line" and "staff" activities within the department, which should enable the staff functions to concentrate on the longer-term issues affecting the company. This division will require a strong coordination effort between the two groups which should be accomplished by the general managers of corporate support and data center operations; an effective quality assurance function; and the establishment of a career path which requires employees to work in both major areas.

Below are brief descriptions of the nature of the revised positions:

1. *Director*—The principal role of the director will not change, but with three individuals reporting to him (instead of the five currently), he will have more time for liaison with senior management, both corporate and in the divisions.
2. *General manager–Communications*—A new position which separates communications from computer operations (these become the responsibility of the data center managers). Presently, 90 to 95 percent of communications work is associated with voice transmission although data communications requirements are expected to increase significantly in the next few years.
3. *General manager–Corporate Support*–A new position for the coordination of all "indirect" data processing support major functions, including:
   a. To coordinate activities within the "corporate" group for consistency.
   b. To ensure coordination between the two major groups by continued contact with the general manager.
   c. To screen information now going to the director and to assume some of the decision making.
   d. To respond to divisional planning needs.
4. *General manager–Data Center Operations*–A new position with initial responsibility for two data centers (each with their respective managers). Responsibilities may increase through the addition of data centers or separation from the existing regional data centers of the divisional support activities. Prime functions are:
   a. To control and coordinate activities of the regional data centers.

EXHIBIT 5 ***(concluded)***

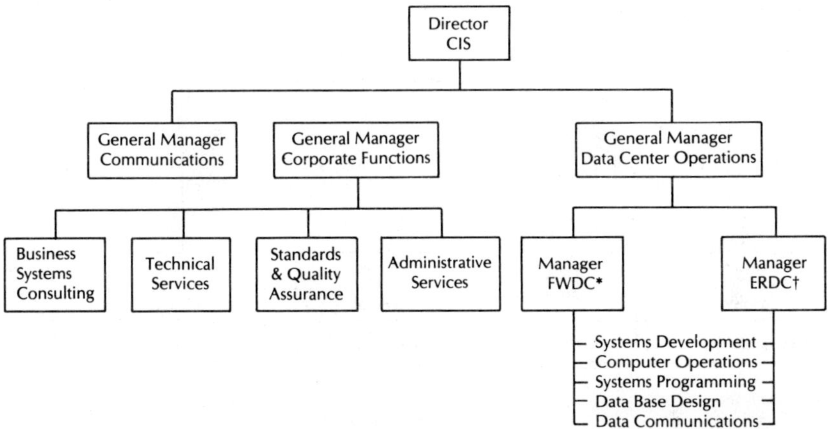

b. To ensure review by line personnel of proposed policies/procedures developed by corporate group, and to ensure adherence to them once they are adopted.

c. To report to the director on progress, problems, etc. on all aspects of data center operations and systems development.

5. *Manager–Business Systems and Operations Research*–Little change in functions from those currently performed by manager with responsibility in these areas.
6. *Manager–Technical Services*–A new position which would combine the current decision-making function of the existing technical services department with equipment requirements determination and selections. Selections would have to occur within the corporate guidelines as determined by the computer architecture study.
7. *Manager–Standards and Quality Assurance*–A new position which would combine the existing standards function with a new quality assurance function. The need for the latter exists in today's environment but this need will be heightened by the proposed division between line and staff positions. Quality assurance may ultimately grow to the point where a manager dedicated to the function becomes necessary.
8. *Manager–Administrative Services*–A new position with responsibility for user billings and associated follow-up, together, possibly, with training and other administrative functions.
9. *Manager–Regional Data Center*–A redefined position, following closely the role performed currently by the Eastern Regional Data Center Manager, but with provision for total unit responsibility for systems development (as indicated on the chart). Managers in this role would also have responsibility for ensuring adherence to corporate standards on a day-to-day basis.

EXHIBIT 6 □ Proposed Organization of CIS, October 1979

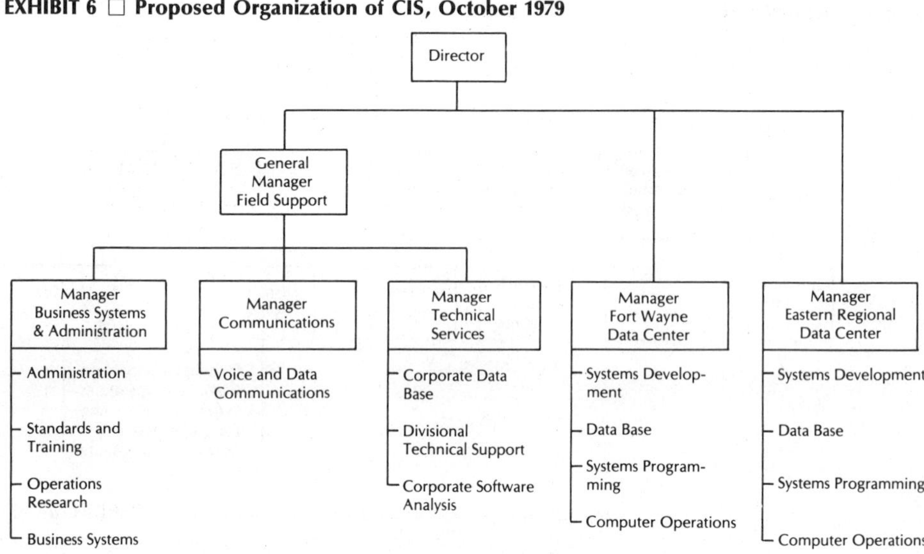

However, McMillen wondered realistically just how quickly he could implement the new structure. The Eastern Regional Data Center in Hagerstown was in place and operating. But the situation in Fort Wayne was more tenuous. The basic problem was a thin and adequate management team. CAPS and the other conversion projects were soaking up so many people that many other projects were being tabled or delayed, and there simply wasn't anyone available to work on fundamental problems such as recruiting, training, performance evaluation, career planning, project planning and control systems, and user relationships. Furthermore, McMillen knew that there was a tremendous backlog of user demand for new applications:

> The Automotive Division alone has requested 18 major new applications—for financial systems, planning, and so on. And I know that our other divisions have literally tens of man-years of work that they need done. In fact, most of the divisions' 1980 plans are being written with built-in assumptions that they will get new systems next year. They can't meet their business plans without those new systems.

As McMillen sorted through these operating problems and organizational alternatives, he wondered what sorts of goals and priorities he should set out for 1980. More importantly, he wondered how he could begin to implement those goals, and where he should be spending his time.

General Management Library for the IS Manager

Ackoff, Russell L. *Creating the Corporate Future: Plan or Be Planned For.* New York: John Wiley & Sons, 1981.

Anthony, Robert N. *Planning and Control Systems–A Framework for Analysis.* Boston: Division of Research, Harvard Graduate School of Business Administration, 1965.

[This book introduces the framework of operational control, management control, and strategic planning which has been a major contributor to thinking about the different areas of IS application and their different management problems.]

Anthony, Robert N., and James S. Reece. *Accounting Principles.* Homewood, Ill.: Richard D. Irwin, 1979.

[This is a comprehensive treatment of current accounting and management control thinking. It is very relevant to a broad consideration of IS management control problems.]

Beer, Michael. *Organizational Change and Development: A Systems View.* Santa Monica, Calif.: Goodyear Publishing, 1980.

[A thoughtful, useful discussion on managing organizational change by a leading practitioner/academician.]

Bower, Joseph L. *Managing the Resource Allocation Process–A Study of Corporate Planning and Investment.* Boston: Division of Research, Harvard Graduate School of Business Administration, 1970.

[This in-depth analysis of corporate planning and capital budgeting provides critical insights relevant to both the role of steering committees and how IS planning can be effectively done.]

Chandler, Alfred. *Strategy and Structure: Chapters in the History of the Industrial Enterprise.* Cambridge, Mass.: MIT Press, 1967.

[This classic by the preeminent business historian examines the inexorable relationship between corporate strategy and its organization structure. Its insights are relevant to many facets of IS organization and planning.]

Christensen, C. Roland; Kenneth R. Andrews; and Joseph L. Bower. *Business Policy: Text and Cases.* Homewood, Ill.: Richard D. Irwin, 1978.

Ennis, Ben M., and Keith Cox, eds. *Marketing Classics: A Selection of Influential Articles.* 4th ed. Boston: Allyn & Bacon, 1981.

[A collection of the best of current marketing literature, it provides a series of insights on how best to market the IS business.]

Lawrence, Paul R., and Jay W. Lorsch. *Organization and Environment: Managing Integration and Differentiation.* Boston: Division of Research, Harvard Graduate School of Business Administration, 1967.

[This classic presents the underlying thinking of the need for specialized departments and how they should interface to the rest of the organization. It is relevant for all IS organizational decisions.]

Kimberly Miles and Associates. *The Organizational Life Cycle.* San Francisco: Jossey-Bass, 1981.

[Reports, findings, and analyses of key issues concerning the creation, transformation, and decline of organizations.]

Porter, Michael E. *Competitive Strategy–Techniques for Analyzing Industries and Competition.* New York: Free Press, 1980.

[This book provides a new way of looking at corporate strategy and is invaluable in thinking about how to start IS planning.]

Schein, Edgar H. *Organizational Psychology.* 3d ed. Englewood Cliffs, N.J.: Prentice-Hall, 1980.

[The classic book on the field focusing on how to manage the tension between the individual and the organization.]

Simon, Herbert A. *Administrative Behavior: A Study of Decision-Making Processes in Administrative Organization.* New York: Free Press, 1976.

[This classic destroys many of the classic notions of administrative behavior and introduces more powerful and useful ones. Its generalizations are applicable to all aspects of the IS business.]

Skinner, Wickham. *Manufacturing in the Corporate Strategy.* New York: John Wiley & Sons, 1978.

[This very broad and powerful book on manufacturing strategy provides critical insights for how the IS operations function should be viewed and managed.]

Stonich, Paul. *Zero-Based Budgeting.* Homewood, Ill.: Dow Jones-Irwin, 1977.

[A workmanlike book on zero-based budgeting, it is must reading for the IS director who plans to do ZBB.]

Vancil, Richard F. *Decentralization: Managerial Ambiguity by Design.* Homewood, Ill.: Dow Jones-Irwin, 1979.

[A study of the managerial issues posed by decentralizing a firm's operations. It provides valuable context for IS organizational and management control decisions.]

Warren, E. Kirby. *Long-Range Planning: The Executive Viewpoint.* Englewood Cliffs, N.J.: Prentice-Hall, 1966.

[The classic in corporate planning, it provides valuable insights to how IS planning can be conducted.]

IS Library for the General Manager

Ackoff, R. L. "Management Misinformation System." *Management Science,* vol. 14, no. 4 (December 1967), pp. B140–B156.

[A classic, this article provides an early categorization of the real management issues in IS administration.]

Blumenthal S. *MIS—A Framework for Planning and Development.* Englewood Cliffs, N.J.: Prentice-Hall, 1969.

[This is the first book on IS planning which gave the subject a comprehensive and realistic treatment.]

Davis, Gordon B. *Management Information Systems: Conceptual Foundations,* Structure and Development. New York: McGraw-Hill, 1978.

[A good treatment of contemporary IS technology.]

Davis, William S., and McCormack, A. *The Information Age.* Reading, Mass.: Addison-Wesley Publishing, 1979.

[A well-written introduction to the jargon of computer-based systems and their important issues.]

Gorry, G. A., and M. S. Scott-Morton. "A Framework for Management Information Systems." *Sloan Management Review,* vol. 13, no. 1 (1971), pp. 55–70.

[A classic article which lays out the domain for IS technology application. It clearly identifies why the IS applications of the 1980s provide such different problems from the 1970s.]

Lucas, Henry C., Jr. *Information Systems Concepts for Management.* New York: McGraw-Hill, 1978.

[A useful guide on how to think about IS management issues.]

Hussain, Donna, and K. M. Hussain. *Information Processing Systems for Management.* Homewood, Ill.: Richard D. Irwin, 1981.

[A good conventional treatment of what the elements of IS technology are and how to approach their management.]

Maciariello, Joseph. *Program Management Control Systems.* New York: John Wiley & Sons, 1978.

[A contemporary analysis of how to manage the project life cycle to ensure good results in IS projects.]

"Managing and Using Computers" Harvard Business Review, no. 21340, reprint series, 1981.

[A compendium of recent *HBR* articles on IS management, it covers from a broad perspective many of the key IS management issues.]

Martin, James. *Introduction to Teleprocessing.* Englewood Cliffs, N.J.: Prentice-Hall, 1972.

[A primer on the basics of communication technology.]

McLean, Ephraim R., and John V. Soden, *Strategic Planning for MIS.* New York: John Wiley & Sons, 1977.

[A comprehensive and relevant treatment of IS planning issues and how it can be done more effectively.]

Nolan, Richard L. *Managing the Data Resource Function.* 2d ed. St. Paul, Minn.: West Publishing, 1982.

[A collection of classics which influenced current IS management thinking.]

Rodgers, William. *Think: A Biography of the Watsons and IBM.* New York: Mentor Books, 1974.

Sayles, Leonard, and Margaret Chandler. *Managing Large Systems—Organization for the Future.* New York: Harper & Row, 1971.

[A comprehensive treatment of the project management insights gained in the Apollo Moon Program. It is invaluable for the manager concerned with large complex IS projects.]

Scott-Morton, Michael, and Peter Keen. *Decision Support Systems.* Reading, Mass.: Addison-Wesley Publishing, 1978.

[This book identifies the type of systems which have followed the large transaction-oriented ones and their special managerial issues. This has been followed by a number of working papers by the authors and others under the auspices of MIT's Center for Information Systems Research (CISR).]

Synnott, William R., and William H. Gruber. *Information Resource Management—Opportunities and Strategies for the 1980s.* New York: John Wiley & Sons, 1981.

[A contemporary analysis of the tactical approaches to ensuring a successful MIS operation.]

Index

This book has been set VIP, in 10 and 9 point Optima, leaded 2 points. Chapter numbers and titles are 16 point Optima. The size of the type page is 30 by 47 picas.